Un-Willing

Un-Willing

An Inquiry into the Rise of Will's Power and an Attempt to Undo It

Eva Brann

PAUL DRY BOOKS

Philadelphia   2014

First Paul Dry Books Edition, 2014

Paul Dry Books, Inc.
Philadelphia, Pennsylvania
www.pauldrybooks.com

Cover: For the origin and meaning of the image of the clenched fist and open hand, see page xiii and page 265 note 5.

Cover: picture frames © iStockPhoto

Printed in the United States of America

Library of Congress Cataloging-in-Publication Data

Brann, Eva T. H.
  Un-willing : an inquiry into the rise of will's power and an attempt to undo it / Eva Brann.
     pages cm
  Includes bibliographical references and index.
  ISBN 978-1-58988-096-2 (alk. paper)
  1. Free will and determinism—History. I. Title.
  BJ1461.B686 2014
  128'.3—dc23
                                                      2014024356

To my colleagues
Peter Kalkavage and Eric Salem,
for years and years
of work and laughter
in amity unclouded by willfulness
but lit up by our common love
for the text and its meaning.

St. John's College, Annapolis
2013

Contents

List of Substantive Notes

In the extensive Notes section at the back of the book, a number of the notes are substantive enough to deserve a listing of their own. Here is a brief guide to them, arranged by chapter:

Preface

I should begin with the title of this book: UN-WILLING. Read it, please, as a *double entendre*. 1. To *unwill* (its participle being "unwilling") is a legitimate verb, meaning "to divest of volition." (I had considered "The Devolition of the Will," but that was too cute by half, though the volition's devolution, its retrograde evolution, is just what I wish for.) 2. "Unwilling" is also a participial adjective signifying "disinclination, aversion." Together these two terms exactly capture my intention: an aversion to the forcible meaning (defensibly the most characteristic one) of will, and a desire (not very hopefully held) to contribute to its diminishment, in others and certainly in myself: An early title of the book was "Against My Will."[1]

Then there is the name of the subject itself. In the literature you will find "freewill," "free-will," "free will," "will." These terms carry more baggage than you might think; precision would be out of place here, but a question will do: Is "will" just short for "freewill," meaning that will is *ipso facto*, inherently, free, so that "unfree will" would be a contradiction in terms? Is "free" a qualifying adjective applicable to will in gradations of intrisicality? Or does freedom belong only to choice, decision (*liberum arbitrium*), which is but a single moment in the long process of willing? To be up-front about it: I shall be finding some reasons for marginally preferring to assign the locus of free decision to the latter, choice, rather than to the former, an inherently more or less free will—but not enough reason to find either of these options satisfactory. Because even when put in terms of will, choice, or decision, human freedom remains unintelligible, even indefensible—for it becomes a problem not so much wonderfully perennial as peskily everlasting, of the sort Kant called "dialectical," hopelessly mired in logically assertible pros and cons. To me freedom seems a—highly conditioned—human fact, not attached to any one faculty, a notion that I shall try to delineate in the Conclusion.

Next, I shall pirate a saying of conservatives: "If it's not necessary to change, then it's necessary not to change." Here is my adapted version: "If it's not necessary to assume a will, then it's necessary not to assume a will." In this book (which I've tried, not very successfully, to keep brief—pregnant brevity being the one preservative of life-time that might really be in our power) I'll attempt, then, to show that even as the notion of willing was once devised, so it can be un-devised, probably for the better. This will began as a perverse potency for resistance to God, and God having been occluded, it morphed into an approved power of internal discipline, consequent self-assertion, and thus, finally, into externally asserted control. It also cast loose from souls and was reconstituted as an impersonal force to be—willy-nilly—acknowledged and obeyed.

My plan is to specify these sweeping claims by attaching authors to them. I go about my inquiry in this way to protect myself from any embarrassing imputation of innovation. In my reading around the subject at hand—admittedly not exhaustive, or writing never would have begun—I've learned that often the theory of the day derives its novel charm from a blissful ignorance of the tradition. Such salutary unknowing is just what we do indeed encourage in our students, so that their thought shall be their own—their *own* attempts at truth, not *novel* inventions for display; the former earns our respect, the latter only the world's kudos. In thinking things out we should, I think, not go for newness but adequacy.[2]

The specific good, however, of going first to old writings is to gain insight into life before the will. This condition is not a state of "having let go" (*Gelassenheit*) of self, Western-style, or the "blow-out" (Nirvana) of desire, Eastern-mode, but one of impassioned thoughtfulness—a way as open to human beings now as it was some two and a half millennia ago. Or so I believe and will attempt to make plausible. It is a mode—the Greeks called it *phronesis*, "mindfulness"—whose tenor is not dead serious, distantly academic, but live serious, engagedly human.[3]

I do not think that the will as it occurs in one strong strain of post-classical books is a very lovable subject. And since it seems to me that study should not too often be a willful engagement with what is repellent, I want to say how this book on the will came to be. There were three facets of our interiority that had previously fascinated me: First, the *imagination*, that interface between soul and world upon which are projected those annex- and counter-worlds that expand our mere existence. Second, *time*, that lamination of the soul through which the point-present loses its dominion over us by extending our being into layers of past and reaches of future—but which, conceived as an external force, becomes a tyrant. And third, *negation*, our power of distinction, definition, delimitation in thought, and of aversive denial and positive receptivity in sensibility—in short, our power of discrimination (a good word gone bad) and of resistance.[4]

The will was nowhere to be found in this trilogy, and I wondered why. My eventual answer was just the thesis of this book. Imagination, time, negation seem to me to be indefeasible aspects of our inner life: its scene, its treasure, its insight. The will, however, is not a *necessary* facet of our own interiority. Why not?

Why not *what*? What will is to be un-done? Some uses of the word seem perfectly fine to me. Language-rectification is, in any case, repugnant to me; I think of my adopted tongue as infinitely receptive to transgression—on the condition that the innovators know the tradition they are subverting: to trespass really felicitously, you have to know the territory pretty comprehensively. I will not ludicrously propose eradicating "I will" from our usage or avoiding edifying discourse—in any case somewhat out of style—that recommends the activation of will power. In fact, there seem to me to be contingencies when a dose of willfulness, of undeflectable bulling-through, is very salutary.

And yet—will power as a daily virtue is precisely what I don't have much faith in. So, to start with, that term will help me to a preliminary delineation of that more limited, concentrated notion of the will with which this book is—unfavorably—to deal. "Will power" I take to betoken a capacity for self-discipline, understood as an independent virtue, to be admired in itself, aside from, even especially divorced from, a particular application. Here is an example:

The imaginary German author who is the hero of Thomas Mann's *Death in Venice*, Gustav von Aschenbach, a writer become a classic in his own life and a man of lifelong self-control (whose will is to be devastated by a late-life passion) is depicted by a subtle observer as living life thus: here he shows a tightly clenched left fist; and never thus: and here he opens his hand and lets it hang comfortably over the arm of his chair. Forcibleness, resistance to opposing power as an end in itself, is the essence of will in the narrow sense; it may have a purpose beyond mere selfhood asserted, but that end is secondary. The laudatory name of this will gone passionate is pride—but recall that pride is also the evil name of Satan's vice.[5]

I cannot argue that such a will—the kind that Victorian pedagogues thought it their duty to break in children—is not a naturally developed propensity. Will is agreed to be to the fore in two-year-olds. Indeed, these demonic humans (my favorite age, as a one-time kindergarten volunteer) know what they are about. "I want not to want" is the most memorably revealing description of willfulness as reflexive intensity—the purest expression of will—that I know, uttered by a two-and-a-half-year-old whom I was trying to baby-sit ages ago and attempting to propitiate with offers of goodies. It is so illuminating because it expresses a not entirely sinless sense of the dual relation of the will, both to a *want*, to an external desired object, and to a *self*, a self-concerned reflexive being. However, like our appendix, some human attributes are natural without being necessary.[6]

In this book I intend to take up as well a notion of will, alluded to above, that is in no way natural but is a sheer artifact of misguided human inventiveness: the hyper-individual will, will cast loose from its moorings in the human constitution to become a world force. To me it is a simply pernicious notion, since this pre-human willfulness is, apparently inevitably, arrogated by very human individuals who claim to be this will's accredited agents.

So I am confessing to a prejudgment, precisely in the hope that it will not be thought to have prevented me from doing justice to the authors of whose work I shall be giving interpretative reports. For I have chosen them because they are, one by one, plain interesting to study and illuminating about a murky topic. Some of these writers of stature do mark an epoch or are marked by it. But far be it from me to imagine that they mold or express its spirit, for although epochs, times, are loosely spoken of as dominated by an idea, or having a spirit, they are not really a kind of substance such as can generate the one or sustain the other. If a problem becomes pervasive for a time, "its time," it is, I am persuaded, for the perfectly mundane reason that people take their opinions from those who aptly enunciate what circumstances have prepared them to hear—and they, in turn, propagate a sometimes deformed or diminished version. That's why it pays to go back to original texts. (This passing-about of opinions, and the associated notion of "influence" will be a continual concern in this book.) My sometimes a-chronically arranged chapters express my de-linking of "a time" and "its" ideas.

To distinguish my comments from the reports of texts, I have often enclosed the former in parentheses. Moreover, so as not to subject my reader to my—possibly not so welcome—*obiter dicta*, I have often relegated them to the Endnotes; nonetheless that's where some of the fun was, for me.

Furthermore, to avoid clutter, I have confined almost all external bibliographical references to the Endnotes and have foregone most internal, intra-textual references in favor of a fuller index. Every endnote appears at the end of a paragraph and usually refers to the black-letter items within it.

This book, as a readable object, owes a lot to the empathetic intelligence of one of our students at St. John's College, Laura Cleveland. Her enthusiastic participation in its great books program prepared her to be the manuscript's literal first reader as its typist. My warm thanks to her. My colleague Eric Salem read the manuscript with keenly critical sympathy; his marginal comments were like a really good conversation, and I have joyfully plagiarized many of his succinct formulations of my meanings. To him goes my very heartfelt gratitude.

E.B.

Un-Willing

chapter I

Before Will

It is notoriously difficult to prove a negative, to catch, as it were, non-being by the tail, but perhaps even harder just to get it in your sights:

> "Is there any point to which you would wish to draw my attention?"
> "To the curious incident of the dog in the night-time."
> "The dog did nothing in the night-time."
> "That was the curious incident," remarked Sherlock Holmes.[1]

With this, his most famous observation, the world's most famous detective teaches Inspector Gregory the importance of noticing negative facts.

I do not know that the toddlers of Hellas were not willful or her adults without will power. But the affect seems to have been without the formal accreditation of an articulated concept and thus inchoate and fugitive, as are motions of the soul untethered by uttered thought. There is, to be sure, *thymos*, a noun that expresses the proud, often angry, swelling of the soul that can appear as high spirits or as childlike sulking. There is *tolman*, a verb that signifies bold, even transgressing daring. There is the noun *hybris*, which betokens a heedlessly inflated sense of one's own fortunate being and forgetfulness of the gods' power. What we call "pride," in its range from proper dignity to preposterous arrogance, is involved in all three. But what is not present in these capabilities, characteristics, conditions of human conduct is—and this is crucial—a *sense of sin*. I will claim that sin is the first parent of will, and will is a progeny that then outgrows and squelches its instigator.

Even, or rather especially, *hamartia*, the word by which Aristotle in his *Poetics* designates the so-called "tragic flaw" of the heroes of tragedy, although it is sometimes rendered as "sin," is far more innocent than that; the tragic hero, and Aristotle cites Oedipus, becomes tragic "not because of badness or wickedness, but because of some mistake (*hamartia*)."

A mis-take is taking one thing for another; *hamartia* is a missing of the intended target, as when throwing a spear: "You missed (*embrotes*) and didn't hit." At least so it is in pagan times; in the Christian Bible *hamartia*

1

is indeed the word for sin, the very antithesis of innocence, a psychic state of depravity, secondarily expressed in deeds.[2]

So what is this sin, absent in the writings of the pagan observers of human nature, the sin I am here delineating in its densest sense, for the sake of clear distinctions? Truth to tell, Aristotle's *hamartia* is surely too narrow for its intended application to tragedy in general, since a tragedy may end as does Sophocles' *Antigone*:

> One must not be irreverent towards the gods.
> The grand words of the overproud pay them
> back in grand blows and teach them to be
> wise in old age—

which implies that something like sin, some guilt, is indeed responsible for the extermination of the Theban royals. But post-pagan sinfulness is something else.

Sin in the narrow sense is, it seems, that kind of depravity of soul that loads it with guilt, not in the objective sense of a fault imputed by others, but in the subjective sense of a flaw felt within. And why is this sense of sin, or sinfulness, not so explicitly established among pagans? Because, whatever is the catalyst-deed of sin, the action behind it is colored by rebellion against the deity, by a proud resistance to divinity; this perverse passion will be at the origin of the will in its originating essence.

Now the Greek gods are hard to spite, for they are immune to the soul's apostasy. The Olympians get offended if not given their material due, the pungent smoke of burnt offerings and the fragrant smells of vinous libations. But they are unanxious about being loved. If they want human love, they take it without much ado. Thus Zeus takes his mortal targets, such as Io or Leda, with bestial force, and Athena captivates her mortal parallel, Odysseus, with chaste fondling. They are even less concerned with being uniquely "believed in," since they do not suffer any inherent inhibition about being imaged: Athens, a plural in English as in Greek (*Athenai*), means "the Athenas." She is one of many deities, unproblematically all over the city, visible in her images to all her people among other gods—herself an unabashed polymorphous polytheist.[3]

At least, the above seems to be fairly true until the last of the great tragedians, Euripides, writes dramas such as the *Hippolytus* and the *Bacchai*, both of whose young heroes are savagely destroyed—the one for preferring Artemis's blood sports to Aphrodite's sexual love, the other for failing to recognize Dionysius's divinity. These Euripidean gods begin to be, balefully, more eager to be acknowledged than fed, but these divine resentments are individual and local.

The crux is that no Greek god has *made* mankind. The gods are themselves—mostly—*born*, sexually generated, and humans—not all, only the heroes—are, in turn, begotten from them by sexual congress; most of mankind originates in procreation, not creation. The creator god of the other root tradition of the West, single and (except in incarnation) sexless, is thus liable to an anxiety, to speak anachronistically, an insecurity, by which the Olympians are not burdened: the ingratitude and independence of the creature, original with the first couple and inherited by all conspecifics, since all humans descend from two parents who were created by God himself.

As a propensity, rebellious pride might be inherent in all creatureliness from its origin—in which case the Creator himself is co-responsible for sinfulness (if not for the sin). Or, as an act committed, it might be an impulse original with the human being, in which case the creature alone is guilty of sin (if not always responsible for its occasion). In any case, the actual deed, which hurts the Creator and devastates the creature, is an act of free will, an endowment that *is* given to created humanity by its Creator. And it is only a free will that can pervert itself, be perverse. With this tightly-clenched will to resist begins the will proper, I will claim. It is a sentiment that the Greeks of poetry and philosophy did not feel or choose to acknowledge—how would I, or anyone, know which?

A. Homer: The "Will" of Zeus

When you read these Greek texts in translation (as do we all), the word "will" does, of course, turn up. A prime example is in the fifth line of the West's first poem, the *Iliad*: *Dios d'eteleieto boule*, "And the Will of Zeus was being fulfilled." That is one way, frequent from early to recent time of rendering the line. Alternatives are "counsel" and "plan." "Plan" seems best to me. The Father of Gods and Men doesn't have a fixed, omni-temporal will; he has wants, desires, intentions, very budgeable by blandishments and barely enforced by threats. Indeed, he is not omnipotent but bound by Fate. This plan of his that is being realized, even as Achilles's anger sends the souls of many warriors—on his own side—to Hades, is a clever equivocation: Achilles will get what his pride requires: to be abjectly needed; and he will lose what he most loves: his dearest friend, who is among those Hades-bound fighters. Zeus's plan is a design to be sung—for our delectation and that of the watching gods. Consequently, then, there is a difference in tone. Homeric epic, the Pagan scripture, is *serious*, grand, while the Judeo-Christian Bible is *earnest*, intense.[4]

B. Socrates: Will-less Philosophy

I have titled this sub-section "Socrates" rather than "Plato" because it is Socrates—Plato's Socrates, to be sure, the most potently Socratic Socrates, as it seems to me—whose "way to be pursued" (which is the meaning of the word *methodos*) matters most to my story of the will. This is the Socrates of the Platonic dialogues, which their author attributes to Socrates, a Socrates "become beautiful and young." Said of the ugly, elderly man of most of the dialogues, this description sounds ludicrous, but it is true of his soul, particularly the youthfulness. His is the springtime of thought incarnate; his philosophizing is as a young green tracery of things to come, less ostensive and more malleable, more enticing and less determinate than the mature elaboration and stiffening to follow. This Socrates is inherently early, an embodiment of what in Greek is called an *arche*, a ruling beginning, one that disappears into but regulates the sequel. His conversations consist of questions that exceed his explicit answers in scope, and his questioning often leads to an im-passe (*a-poria*). Yet an answer to be developed lurks implicitly in every get-together; a pertinent example will be given below.[5]

I mean the above as an encomium, to be sure, but mostly as the backing of a claim: Socrates forestalls willfulness and will power well before their appearance in the going scheme of psychic faculties: a rebuttal before the charge.

For, to anticipate the outcome, if "virtue is knowledge"—a maxim attributed textbook-wise to Socrates but never so formulaically stated by him—then doing right is not a matter of purity and strength of will (not to be confused with strength of character, as in Aristotle's ethics). It is rather a matter of having learned and now recollecting knowledge at the moment of action—I almost said "of decision," but then there is no such moment. What we know passes straight into what we do, seamlessly.[6]

What is Socrates' supporting account, his *logos*? I think his way in is to begin from a vice in the soul. But first an adumbration of that key word "virtue" (*arete*): It means excellence, goodness, efficacy; vice is its opposite: lowness, badness, debility. In the second book of the *Republic*, Socrates distinguishes a deeply debilitating vice as the "lie for real," the true lie, the lie in the soul. It is being deceived about what there is and the ways things are. Even if this lack of truthfulness is below awareness, it is still imputable to us: Ignorance is never innocence. Thus Socrates firmly nails self-deception (a notion that seems to flip about so oddly between privity and nescience) to culpability. Ignorance about ultimates is a *choice*. In the last book of the *Republic*, Socrates puts a mythic frame around the guilt of ignorance as suppressed knowledge and ultimate responsibility: Souls released by death into a cosmic setting make a post-mortem and pre-natal choice of a "life," which will be their way of being, their pattern of conduct, when once they are reborn onto earth.[7]

I might point out here that Socrates tends to use "choice" with respect to whole lives, not for the single election that determines decision. This fact will soon be seen to have great significance, for the souls' choice of a life-pattern is to be based on what the souls have learned or ignored in their previous lives.[8]

At first, however, this myth seems off-puttingly confounding. Are we or are we not responsible for our excellence or lack of it when our choice was made before birth? But it can be brought back into daily life with this meaning: At every moment of this present life, our readiness to learn was, and is now, up to us, was and is our responsibility, and on every day our life breaks around the before and after of a life-changing choice, whatever our congenital predispositions may be—though all the past choices ease or obstruct the present one. Our cosmos, the place of ended and beginning lives, is here and now.[9]

Thus, unlike Aristotle, Socrates trusts in the possibility of conversion, in turning on a dime—not a religious or moral turn but an intellectual one. Past history is everything and nothing in a cosmically situated human life—this is Socrates' familiar mode of subtly sensible paradox. Once again, however: choice is of, and is, a way of life; I don't think that Socrates gets himself into quandaries requiring choice with respect to single acts of conduct.[10]

The lie in the soul can reasonably be thought blameworthy only if ignorance is thought to be eradicable. Socrates does not supply a cognitive theory (or any theory) but a working hypothesis for inquiry, one which removes the excuse for what might be called "ontological ignorance," ignoring the being behind appearances. On the face of it, such ignorance might be said to be "the last to know itself" and thus not really open to the charge of self-deception.[11]

Socrates, however, thinks that learning—not of facts or information but of thought-matters—is itself what might be called "activated ignorance"— acknowledged and knowledgeable ignorance. Learning becomes possible when we know *that* we don't know, and in such recognition there lies not only the positive readiness to engage in a search but also a negative knowledge of *what* is sought. We somehow know what we don't know, where "somehow" is not a handwaving evasion but an enabling qualification. It is an invitation to engage in "recollection," Socrates' descriptive term for, speaking archaically, "bethinking oneself."[12]

Thus prepared, it is possible to pass in time from ignorance as a vice to virtue as knowledge. For the converse of the former also holds: vice is ignorance, or so Socrates claims—as *apparently* disputable an assumption as can be for us who know how keenly knowing bad people can be, but it is at the heart of Socrates' way. No one, he says in the *Meno*, knowingly desires bad things, no one wishes for what's bad, understanding that it *is* bad, hurtful. Put positively: "This wish and love [is] common to all human beings": to have good things because they make them happy—and that humans want to be happy is an ultimate fact. Socrates' diction easily passes from "desire" (*epithymia*) or love (*eros*) to "wish" (*boule*); "wish" and "want" are the same to him here. It seems to me significant. *Boule* is the word often translated as "will," but that meaning does not work here. Who among us post-pagans could agree that no one *wills* evil, knowingly and vehemently? But it is not impossible to see how being bad or *wanting* bad things is always shrouded in a haze of unknowing, if all want happiness. In a word, Socrates asserts that wishing harm implies a condition of unawareness; we have learned that *willing* harm implies an acutely cognizant state. Wished harm may be ignorant badness; willed harm is knowledgeable evil.[13]

From that retrospective point of view, Socrates might be called a pre-lapsarian innocent: Evil and its conditions, knowledgeably intentional badness and its source, are not quite comprehensible and certainly not fascinating to him (not, of course, for lack of acquaintance with ineradicable corruption of soul—was he not off and on a companion of Alcibiades, Charmides, Critias, three attractive and promising youths who became repellently bad men?) Here he too stands as a beginning of philosophical tradition. He regards badness as non-being and sidelines evil as un-reality.[14]

As evidence of this ontological innocence and avoidance, I think of the famously puzzling inner voice of Socrates, that *daimonion*, the "divine something" that only tells him when to desist from an action. As I will try to show just below, Socrates' *acts* spring immediately from his *thinking*. But where the object of thought is, somehow, unpresent, incomprehensible, a thought-less alternative comes to his aid, something like an aversive instinct—the *daimonion*.[15]

Back to "vice is ignorance," which Socrates clearly wants us to think of as a convertible proposition: Vice and ignorance, as concepts, coincide in the universe of discourse in which Socrates is moving for the moment; they have as their logical complements—their exhaustive opposites or negations—their inverses, non-vice and non-ignorance respectively, any middle ground being excluded. Therefore we can think "virtue" and "knowledge" for these negative terms, and these positives too coincide: Virtue is knowledge, and the converse.[16]

I think there is more than one way through the different dialogues, explicit or implicit, in which Socrates reaches this conclusion. With respect to the dialectial logic of the dialogues, reasonable intuition is more profitable than inexorable logic, and a liberal use of the principle of charity is in order. We know what he's getting at and supply the missing steps, discovering, as we are intended to, the surely deliberate paralogisms and the environing assumptions on the way. What matters is to think out the moral meaning of the maxim "virtue is knowledge."[17]

Meno, that documented rogue, begins his conversation with Socrates about virtue by putting the cart before the horse. Instead of asking, as would Socrates, "What *is* virtue?" he wants to know how it's *acquired*. Being altogether set on acquisition and, here, on a free rhetorical lesson, he asks Socrates, "Do you have [something profitable] to tell me . . . (*echeis moi epein . . .*)," namely, is virtue teachable or does one come into our possession "in some other way"?[18]

Nonetheless this inverted start gives Socrates an opening, for if virtue is teachable it is, *ipso facto*, knowledge (one of those sly assumptions we might balk at, to be sure, but acceptable in the context). Much of the conversation is taken up with the crucial question of what teaching itself truly is (not delivering the goods for a fee), and whether there are any teachers of excellence (only one, Socrates himself, who practices a compelling sort of abstention). In a crucial episode, the dialogue, one of those that only *seem* to end with an impasse, delivers by demonstration a toned-down version of an answer to the true question "What is virtue?" A little boy, perhaps twelve or fourteen years old, a Greek-speaking slave, a possession of Meno, *shows* the inattentive Meno what it means to be good. He willingly, attentively, and out of himself, responds to Socrates' questions, admits to being mistaken and at an impasse, but bravely goes on to learn a piece of mathematics that is both practical and deep: how to double the area of a given square, and that the line which does it, the diagonal, has no articulable relation to its side, that it is irrational—inarticulable—when measured against the side. We can get hold of more than we can articulate.

What Socrates brings out in this boy is that excellence, effective goodness, virtue, is *learning* (*mathesis*), the acquisition of knowledge and also of *thoughtfulness* (*phronesis*), an effectively intent sort of mindfulness, a virtue-tinged quality of mind. Therefore one might say that virtue is finally knowledge, but the disposition to be attentively thoughtful is incipient wisdom, *sophia*; it is evinced in this lovable little boy as a young stage of philosophy, the love of wisdom.[19]

So what is the human effect of this identity of virtue with the inclination to learn, to admit confusion, to think responsively, so as perhaps finally to know? Excellence so understood is, I think, will-less in acquisition and in exercise—though not effortless. Although it is *not* a forcible exertion of some special power, innate to begin with, trained in time and exercised harshly, ascetically in self-denial, it *is* effortful. The meaning of "ascetic" tells the story: In Socrates' Greek, *askesis* means "regular practice, exercise" he certainly thinks that self-government and courageous exertion have a part in the life he loves. In our use—I surmise under the pressure of the Christian will—"ascetic" pertains to self-denying self-control, not self-fulfilling self-government. (Looking ahead, let me say this: Strange as it may sound, that precious Self of ours, *The* Self, hadn't even come on the scene yet. Its appearance will mark the final loss of that springtime innocence I've mentioned.)[20]

The knowledge coincident with virtue that Socrates means is—to use the spatial figures that speech about human non-somatic being requires—so deep in the self-knowledge of the soul and so high on the thought-scaled ladder of being that everything closer to the world falls in place immediately when the occasion arises.

There are various ways to put this effect. One is this: In acting well, there seem to be, as a first approximation, three elements: knowing what to do, deciding that it must be done, and launching into the doing. If virtue is knowledge *and* knowledge virtue, these stages are melded. To know is to do—smoothly, serenely bypassing difficult decidings and agonizing irresolutions. The choices that require decision and the reluctances that prevent action will have been forestalled ("prevented" in the original meaning of "being anticipated") by long thinkings-out of the way things are, not only here but also beyond, and of what is required to be in accord with that realm and its reflection here. Action then appears not as a spasm of the will, but as a work of love.Here is an example of what such virtue looks like, taken from Socrates' life, or rather his death. It is sometimes surmised that Socrates' defense of his activities before the Athenian jury is on his part a plain provocation, an invitation to assisted suicide because of failing old age. Xenophon, at the beginning of his version of Socrates' *Defense* (*Apologia*) says so outright. Aside from the fact that Socrates condemns suicide, this end seems to me to make cunningly ignoble nonsense of his life and of its public defense. If you want to die, why not just do it, without staging a public scene?[21]

What happens after he is condemned seems to me to give very different testimony. When his old friend Crito offers to arrange for his escape, Socrates is serenely ready with reasons (the basis, in our time, of civil disobedience) for not running away. On the day of his dying he engages his friends—one might almost say, entertains them, for though there is weeping in the background, there is banter in the foreground—in consolingly engrossing conversation, lasting to the moment of his death. In this conversation he sets out for these alert youngsters, under the guise of proving the immortality of the soul, all the main unresolved perplexities of his philosophizing, his legacy to them: questions concerning soul, sensation, learning, becoming, contrariety, causation, forms, numbers—no sign of failing in the old man here. When the last moment comes, it is blithe; Socrates has composed his own features in dying.[22]

This is not a portrait of strenuous self-control before the anxious youngsters but of genuine tranquility before an ultimate transition already fully thought-experienced. Nor is it a giving-up of self-will in resignation but a still-perplexed anticipation of a next possibility.

Now is the moment to admit that the above is much less than half the story. What is missing is the actual account of Socrates' reasons that virtue in its very being is knowable and that the knowledge which coincides with virtue is, I am tempted to say, a happy knowledge (for there can surely be an un-merry science)—one thought in which, we can be sure, Socrates and Plato were at one. Here is an indication, if not a proof: There are signature phrases that mark a human being's being; thus, closer to us, Bach ends his compositions with the dedication *Soli deo gloria*, "to God alone the glory," and thus Plato long ago begins his letters and Socrates ends his *Republic* with *eu prattein*, "Be—and do—well." The latter is a dual injunction both to prosper and to do right, and it is knowledge that supplies this *eupragia*, "right- and well-doing." Knowledge has this ability because it reaches for beings, divinities, which Socrates first, and Plato after him, calls "invisible looks," forms (*eide*). In this life these may remain just hypotheses all the way to the end, but since they are necessary to Socrates' philosophizing, they are, in their attractive perfection and power, the objects of Socrates' philosophic faith. (This may be logically circular, but what attempt to make things come together isn't?) These beings bestow at once such knowability and such goodness as the sensible world evinces.[23]

I have ended this subsection with so insufficient an account of what matters positively to Socrates because I am trying to track something, a designated human capacity, that is, so far, only negatively there—in hindsight, as an absence: the will.

For Socrates choices are of a life-pattern; they might occur any day by bootstrapping or under the care of a teacher who compels by abstaining: "I was never yet anyone's teacher," he says. Decisions, which are the deliberated choices that a particular occasion calls for, are not his mode, even at a crucial moment. Xenophon reports that Socrates told a friend that he tried twice to consider what to say at what was to be a capital trial, and that he was stopped when his negative sign intervened; he explains: "Don't I seem to you to have lived through my life preparing my defense?"[24]

Now however, just such choice, decision occasioned by the moment, will become the pivot of action, and one of the two roots of will, the pagan and the Christian, is about to begin to burrow its way up into conscious reflection.

C. Aristotle: Choice as Reasoned Desire

Aristotle's *Metaphysics*, the first and, arguably, the greatest of works of expository philosophy, begins with appetite (*orexis*): "All human beings by nature hunger (*oregontai*) to know." And there it culminates, in the appetite induced by the mover-god who remains himself unmoved but whose being explains all motion in the world as an affect, of which the most remote from the deity is the closest to us: our genus-specific desire to know.[25]

The affect by which this divinity moves everything is attraction; effortlessly, and unreciprocatingly, by reason of its blissful self-sufficiency, it attracts the love of the cosmos and its inhabitants, who are *not* its creatures. Therefore, these are its modes of moving—one might even say, its motivation:

> It moves thus: the objects of appetite (*orekton*) and of thought (*noeton*) move without being moved. As primary objects, these are the same—the beautiful. For while the desirable object (*epithymeton*) is the apparently beautiful, the prime wishable object (*bouleton*) is the genuinely beautiful (*to on kalon*). And we have an appetite for it because we deem it so, rather than deeming it so because we have an appetite for it. For thinking is the ruling source (*arche*).[26]

Almost every word in this high point of the *Metaphysics* could do with exegesis, but the subject here being the will, I shall focus on *kalon* and *bouleton*. *Kalon* also sometimes means "good" and will later be so understood—once it is not appetitive desire but moral will that is thought to move humans toward divinity. But that for Aristotle it is "the beautiful" which attracts us underwrites the effortlessness of this love. Accordingly, for *bouleton*, my "wishable" really is too weak and awkward, while "willed" would be too strong and anachronistic. The noun behind this verbal adjective is *boulesis*, a capacity—a faculty, again, is too strong—of the soul. For the exposition first of *boulesis*, and then of *prohairesis*, "choice," the two crucial terms, I go to the *Nicomachean Ethics* and *On the Soul*.[27]

But first two observations on the passage above: Note that the world is pervaded by appetite and, simultaneously, informed by thought. Both capacities have the same ultimate object, the true good in its beauty, though there is a sub-class of appetite, pleasure-drawn desire, which goes for the merely seeming good and another, that deliberating desire (the *boulesis* to be investigated) which pursues the genuine good. At the end of the passage, thinking is the ruler of appetite and, as it were, trumps it, but at the beginning, appetite and thought are drawn in the same way by the same god, who is Thought itself (*Nous*) and also the Unmoved Mover of Appetite. Thus Thought moves by affect, and Appetite responds to thinking. They are analytically separable, but up to the highest of the divine heavenly spheres and down into the human center of the cosmos, they are actually melded—Aristotle speaks of the human passions as "immattered reasons."[28]

Thus appetite and thought are mutually encompassing, a perplexity that Thomas Aquinas will wrestle with. Using Aristotelian terms, he engages in an extended and acute analysis of the will, in the course of which he, by making distinctions, converts the problem into the solution (which can be very good philosophy: clarify, qualify, and carry on). The pivotal notion here is *boulesis*, the (etymologically unrelated) avatar of Thomas's *voluntas*, our *will*.

Homer sings of the *boule dios*, "the *plan* of Zeus"—*not* his will. Perhaps "intention," meaning a plan backed by a purpose, is the best rendering. Behind this noun *boule*, which signifies an intentional product, together with the noun *boulesis*, which refers to a psychic capacity, stands the verb *boulesthai*, "to want or wish." From *boule* proceeds the verb *bouleuein*, "to deliberate." *Boulesis* is often glossed, that is, rendered by an explanatory phrase, as "rational desire." "Rational desire" is not in Aristotle, but it is plausibly cobbled together from several contexts in which *boulesis*, as wishful intention, is related to, or even set within, the reasoning part of the soul. Well, perhaps not so plausibly, if Aristotle was avoiding a formulation very close to a contradiction in terms, albeit one demanded by the nature of things.[29]

Anyhow, since "rational desire," which is attracted by the genuine good, belongs to that part of appetite opposed to the non-rational appetites bent on the merely apparent good, we might as well call it "rational appetite." That denomination places this compelling chimera of a notion, on the face of it composed of two incongruous terms, prospectively in a grand tradition of the will: *boulesis/voluntas* as intellectual appetite. Its pagan germ is intentional wishing.

Aristotle says that this wishing, though not the same as choice, is close to it. So here another piece of the will-to-be comes on the scene, since choice (Greek *prohairesis*, Latin *electio*) is going to be a close correlate of full-blown willing, the exercise of will as a faculty of choice.

There are two words relevant to choice, (both etymologically distinct from *boulesis*) which it is—in the one case unavoidable, in the other at least tempting—to render in terms of will. One is "willing or voluntary action" (*hekousion*)—a wider term than choice; the other is "self-controlled, having will-power" (*egkrates*), literally "being in power [over oneself]." But neither of these is a faculty, a distinct power or function of the soul; the former is an attribute of action, the latter, while distinguished by Aristotle from virtue, from temperance in particular, is still a way of coping with desire. Indeed, one might call it a "proto-will," because, while someone who is temperate, that is, in a settled ethical condition, simply feels no desires contrary to reason, someone who is merely self-controlled has to fight his base desires all the way. That, however, is what living with a will is like, except that—and this *is* crucial—there is no functional center instigating these struggles in Aristotle's psychology.[30]

Choice itself is, then, voluntary, but the acts of children and animals and people that lack self-control may also be willing, though not done by choice. Such willing actions will play a large role in a currently debated theory of the will called "compatibilism," though, or rather because, they are not really acts of choice. As so often, Aristotle delimits a notion by its negation: Unwilling action is done (with qualifications) by compulsion or from ignorance. So a willing act is freely and awarely done; choice is of this sort. Here is what choice is not: desire (the appetite for pleasure that drives acts in the absence of self-control), passion (which leads to undeliberated acts), opinion (which is true or false, while choice is good or bad), wishing (which though close to choice, is for ends, while choice is of *means*; moreover wishing can be of the impossible).[31]

It follows that choice is something willingly done, which is, literally, "*pre*-deliberated" (*proboulomenon*), that is, choice is accompanied by reason and thinking (*logos*, *dianoia*). Aristotle's name for choice itself, *prohairesis*, means something chosen *before* other things, as he himself points out. For plain *hairesis* means a seizing, picking, choosing, and *pro* means before. Well, he ought to know what his own word is mainly to mean, but another sense is plainly written into the text: "pre-deliberated" implies that choice happens before action, perhaps quite long before. This long-breathedness of what will later be an element of the faculty of will, seems to me to become very significant in thinking about current free-will research.[32]

Choice, then, taking in all of Aristotle's observations, seems to have these conditions and characteristics: Something, some wish-content, becomes our—weakish—purpose, by choiceless wish or want. Enter choice-and-deliberation, an inseparable pair. About here in the argument, Aristotle asserts what, from the aspect of the will-to-come is the most consequence-fraught claim of his ethics, for it is going to stand at the center of the free-will controversy that bedevils debates about the will: "The human being is the origin (*arche*) of his deeds." What springs from this origin, this ruling source, this beginning action, is shaped by our previous choices; this glancing reference to the powerful role Aristotle assigns to habituation in character development must do here. In any case, habits' claim to be effective should be qualified by "largely" and "eventually." For insofar as we are ultimate beginnings, we must be at some first time, and so ever after, unconditioned (certainly at our temporal beginnings as untrained children, though, then again, as children we can't be said fully to *be*).[33]

Still, this early choice is the true pre-choice, where by pre-deliberating, by an effort of thinking-through (*dia-noia*), we determine what will turn a weak-purposed wish into a choice—whether the wish can be practically attained and, more important, whether its object is in truth good or bad. Presumably a choice of bad is not a real, a thoughtful choice. Then deliberation really comes into its own, being mainly about means. Since most real-life actions are not deducible from a method, a set of rules, (whose formulation practically assures unintended consequences), an investigation and analysis of the possible options is the principal work of deliberation. Of course, the availability of discernible alternatives and some external freedom of action are the conditions for effective deliberation.

Here, then, is a second way to human action that does not call on a determinate faculty of assertive decision-making, though it is much closer to a fixed theory of action than were Socrates' limber inquiries. In particular, Aristotle locates the source of action in the originating human being and understands it as guided by ordinary, this-worldly thought-processes. Not so Socrates: The soul is drawn to and requires transcendent knowledge, which translates immediately into the deed.

(A short meditation on how to go about discovering the presence or absence of the will in texts appears in Note 34 to this chapter.)[34]

Now to some Stoics, who invent the will without saying so, and to Augustine, who overtly delineates its will for the West.

chapter II

Pivot Points

From Aristotle's dictum that the human being is the initiating source of deeds to the first appearance of the will in company with its most bedeviling attribute, "free," about two-hundred seventy years elapse.

A. Lucretius: Random Swerve

The phrase "free will"—later on it sometimes becomes a unit, "freewill"— first turns up for us in *On the Nature of Things*, by the poet Lucretius, the Roman expositor of Epicurus' philosophy. As the philosopher's Greek was, left to itself, unabashedly crabby, the poet's Latin seeks, under the patronage of Venus, is meant to have "eternal loveliness." It is indeed ravishingly artful, and we know why it must be so: to sweeten the rim of the cup holding the bitter draught of Epicurean philosophy, the harsh but healthful truths that are to trump the terrors of religion.

The lines of first occurrence are practically a compendium of the grim philosophy that became, falsely, known as a hedonism:

> Free—whence arises this for living things through the earth,
> Whence, I ask, is this thing wrested from the fates—will?
> Through which we progress—wherever leads, and
> whomsoever, pleasure . . . ?

> *Libera per terras unde haec animantibus exstat*
> *Unde est haec, inquam, fatis avulsa voluntas,*
> *Per quam progredimur quo ducit quemque voluptas . . . ?*

My contorted literal rendition aims to preserve the remarkable distance between "free" and "will," and the comparative closeness of "will" (*voluntas*) and vehement "pleasure" (*voluptas*) ending the plosively stuttering line: p-qua, p-quo, d-que. The harsh truth about to be enunciated is that this free will descends to human beings as a small version of that infamous swerve, uncaused and inexplicable, that occurs in the parallel downward rain, the fall, of the primordial elements, the atoms—which is also inexplicable, since the Epicurean universe has no inherent direction, thus no "down." This swerve first brings about the collisions that result in the atomic collocations and shapes. That dismal physics is repeated on a small scale within the material, atomic human mind, where these shifting conformations in their settling and unsettling appear as, indeed *are*, pleasure and pain. Driven by such impacts "we also swerve (*declinamus*) in our motions at neither a time certain / Nor a certain direction of place."[1]

No wonder Lucretius introduces a distancing hesitation in this first coming together of "free" and "will": free will is pure indeterminacy; our inclinations are declinations; our will is pleasure-driven randomness. No set of lines could be more future-fraught; more a compendium of modern physicalism, the freedom of the will as indeterminacy, the mind as a material complex whose inner motions constitute—not: subserve—our affects.

Nevertheless I shall here dwell more on the Stoics, precisely because they sidle sophisticatedly into the will, willy-nilly, so to speak.

B. Stoics: Implicit Will

The Stoics I shall appeal to are not the early ones, the boldest of cognitive "physicalists" (people who look on human knowledge as an activity of matter in motion). They are the ancient inventors of much of modernity. Their successors, the hugely influential later Stoics, are not quite up to them in intellect and are less invested in philosophy than in moral therapy, that is, in making life livable in the Roman world. Having displaced the earlier meaning of philosophy—the inquiry into Being—with a more popular one—the managing of Life—they preserved their precursors in snippets useful to them, a pity for us but better than nothing.[2]

Their writings are typically exhortatory, didactic "handbooks," pitiable and cantankerous, harsh and imperious, gentle and modest according to temperament. These are the three writers I shall put to use: Cicero, Epictetus, and Marcus Aurelius—minor Roman noble, Greek quondam slave, and Roman emperor, respectively, and respectively at work each in one of the three centuries from the first B.C.E. through the second to the third C.E. The two Romans were fairly orthodox Stoics, the Greek deviated. I shall cull from the three overlapping notions of an—as yet occulted—will.[3]

It seems to me that authors whose writings deserve, on the face of it, high respect are entitled to have us discount the circumstances of their lives: ancestral lineage, social situation, private affairs. The supposition should be that their self-knowledge is acute enough, their intellect independent enough, and their writings self-sufficient enough to neutralize their background—not to speak of the fact that nothing follows definitively from anyone's being a such-and-such socially or living in this-and-that environment.

These late Stoics, however, I take to be in a different case. They invite us, implicitly or explicitly, to think about their personal conditions. Cicero was a bereaved and grieving father when he wrote this therapy-seeking account of Stoicism, the third and fourth books of the *Tusculan Disputations*; Epictetus was a crippled freedman when he propagated the teachings collected in the *Diatribai*, "Discussions, or Life-Employments"; Marcus Aurelius was a very sick campaigner when he composed, encamped and at leisure between northern battles, his *Meditations*, actually entitled "Marcus Aurelius to Himself." All three texts are, more or less overtly, self-consolatory in a way for which "practical" is a euphemism; they are attempts to make life bearable. For all three it seems to be the case that the thinking through of the way out, and its formulation in writing, is itself the chief anodyne, a painkiller more effective (perhaps) than the human wisdom they drum into their readers, and first of all into themselves. Cicero reports Stoic prescriptions; but Epictetus talking to his school, and Marcus Aurelius to himself, issue commands. And, as eventually becomes explicit (most definitively so in Kant's practical reason), the faculty of imperatives, of laws that command, is the will.[4]

Behind this therapeutic morality lies a very advanced theory of nature and mind; it is, as I said, near-physicalist and cognitively-constructivist. I mean that, up to a certain last limit, psychic events are identified with organic ones and that external reality, although acknowledged, is highly processed by the mind. For example, the human psycho-physical constitution has within it a command-and-control center, the "ruler's seat" (*hegemonikon*), and a judgment-related representational structure. Taken together these seem to me to ground the kind of non-affective subjectivity given to self-forcing. This vigorously theoretical early Stoic philosophy fades increasingly, declining by way of derivative repetition to pervasive background-lurking.

1. Cicero: Distress-Avoidance

The gist of the Stoic argument with which Cicero arms himself is that the passions, distress and grief above all, are *voluntate*, "by intention." Latin *voluntas*, before it became the word for will, meant much the same as Greek *boule*, a premeditated plan. Cicero will also use *voluntas* for Stoic *boulesis*; as he glosses the term, it means appetite equably and prudently pursued—shades of Aristotle's "thoughtful desire." For there are indeed some passions—grievous distress is not among them—that have well-reasoned counter-passions, the so-called "well-passions." In fact, in time the stark Stoic teaching is embroidered with some affect-like notions. But these mitigations are intrusions on the radical, pure passion-theory of the original Stoics. Passions are *nothing but* judgments and opinions, namely of good and bad. They arise neither before nor upon but *as* opining thought.[5]

That is why our passions and, startlingly, even our grievously distressing ones, are voluntary—assented to willingly—though not willed. For judgments and opinions are in our control, "up to us, in our power" (*eph' hemin*)—practically *the* Greek Stoics' mantra. Cicero, as above, uses *voluntate* "by or with intention" or *voluntarius*, "voluntary."[6]

Yet more: passions are indeed judgments—but *mistaken* ones. The mistake is about the importance of the misfortunes and what is owed to its magnitude.

> But when this opinion, that the bad thing is big, is added to the opinion that it is proper, right, and that it is a matter of duty to carry this thing off as if in distress, then and only then is produced the mental perturbation of deep distress (*aegritudo*),[7]

the feeling that affected Cicero.

So the question presents itself, how to turn this teaching into therapy. It looks, on the face of it, like Socrates' "knowledge is virtue," especially since the Stoics think that the sage, who does not make the mistake of over-valuing circumstantial mishaps, is the most admirable of types. But Cicero's inherited Stoic doctrine is a world apart from Socrates' home-grown hypotheses. Socratic learning is charged with feeling, while Cicero will say that it is the "perfectly empty mind," the mind relieved, that is, of all perturbing passion, which makes people "absolutely happy." Again, for Socrates happiness emanates from the object of longing; Cicero says outright: Forget about the quality of the object; get rid of the desire itself. [8]

So, the feel of Cicero's Stoic enunciation is just totally different from Socrates' teaching. It is not a seamless transition from thought to deed but—and "voluntarily" for Greek "up to us" somewhat masks this fact—a hard road from rational persuasion to mental effect. It takes a lot of rhetoric, from me to myself or from impatient friends to me, to damp my "perturbation of the mind," *perturbatio animi*, the term Cicero proposes for Greek *pathos*, "passion." For all these "commotions" of the mind are unsound (*insania*). So he pays much attention to the devising of compelling arguments and the composing of consolatory speeches, all intended to impress the sufferer with this wisdom: the cause of distress is nothing but the distressed opinion that something seriously bad is present.[9]

I want to argue that, while the will is precisely not involved in the voluntariness of passions, particularly the harsh ones, it must be functioning—as yet inchoate and unacknowledged—when arguments and speeches by others to us or by us to ourselves force our feelings to give in. For the Stoic technique requires not what we call repression, when our feelings are down but not out, nor gentling, when feelings are informed by a tranquilizing wisdom, but simple abrogation—a mistake done with and gone when we learn better. Now *if* the Stoic theory that passions *are* false opinions is true, this should be smooth going. But if it isn't true, or too complexly true, then it does take some clenching of intention, some active functioning of a force that is alluded to when we say that something is "in our power"—something more than "being willing"; it takes willing, *tout court*. Thinking well, opining correctly, judging rightly have no executive force. Hume will much later, notoriously, say that reason can never be any motive to will, and this seems to me most certainly so when the reasoning is, as in the Stoic case, purely negating or critical, that is, intent on quashing the importance of the object of the affect.

Did Cicero himself derive relief from his distress, for him the most terrible sickness of the mind, by writing that his grief at the loss of his daughter was a mistake of his judgment? For he should have been prepared to lose her: "I knew my child was mortal"—and besides, it's a common event. The letters he wrote at the time show signs that the therapy didn't quite take, and not only because he expounded Stoicism as a scholar at arm's length more than he absorbed it as an engaged participant. However, that research itself, as I said, may have been the more effective cure. But at the very end of the fourth book of the Tusculan conversations, he reaffirms the value of Stoicism to his mostly silent conversational partner Brutus, and then concludes:

> . . . since nothing can be done right without reason and since philosophy consists in a collection of reasons, from it—*if* we wish (*volumus*) to be good and happy—let us seek all aid and help for living well and happily.

"*If*" (my italics) we wish or want it! Of course, we want a good and happy life. The thought below awareness is that wish-*voluntas* is not enough; it takes will—plain *voluntas*—for reason to transmogrify passion into reason; reason has to have a will of its own. At least that's how my three Stoic moralists all appear to me: as guided not by sweet reason but by harsh self-compulsion, however laid back, impassive, their philosophy requires them to seem to be.[10]

2. *Epictetus: "Up to Us"*

Epictetus's *Discourses* (*Diatribai*, "Occupations, Conversations," and other meanings) weren't written by him but by his pupil Arrian, who played Plato (or perhaps Xenophon) to his teacher. For unlike Plato, Arrian made Epictetus neither young nor beautiful. In fact he appears as somewhat curmudgeonly and peremptory; perhaps the honest Arrian tried for life-likeness; he must have had a phenomenal memory and an indefeasible affection for the crippled quondam slave. Since the language is Greek, this Stoicism, undamped by a stuffy Latin filter, comes over as both irascible and sprightly.[11]

Epictetus seems to have been well-read in earlier Stoics, but he was far from regarding book-learning with much enthusiasm. For him "philosophy" was what it is now for laymen: "a" philosophy, Stoicism of course, a consistent attitude to life, with conduct to suit—no metaphysics.[12]

The *Discourses* make a long—albeit readable—book with much acute human observation but also with a compact terminological gist. Here are the bullet points for my purpose, which is to present Stoicism as implying *and* subverting will: up to us, impression, judgment, choice, freedom. These were, of course, already in the background of Cicero's battle against grief.

I start with the Stoic signature phrase "up to us" (*eph' hemin*), which Arrian puts at the beginning of the *Discourses* and as the first of the maxims he culled from the *Discourses* for his compendius "Little Handbook" (*Encheiridion*): "Some things are up to us and some are not." "Up to us" is often translated as "in our power." Up to us are the mental motions, both cognitive and affective, such as opinion and desire—our interiority. Not up to us are our body's condition and what the world contains, things and contingencies—the world's externalities. What is up to us is—*ipso facto*—free, unimpeded; what is not, is servile and handicapped.[13]

"Up to us" thus assumes, first, a global division of all there is: internal and external. Second, it assumes that these cognitive locations are coextensive with opposite values: good and bad. And third—or probably really first—it assumes a value behind these valuations: control, because control determines good and bad. The implication is that the external world is actually *in itself* mostly indifferent or only distantly good.

This whole complex of assumptions has behind it that representational theory of the older Stoics, whose elements Epictetus uses as manipulable thought items, impressions most prominently. An impression—the Latinate word alludes, as I said, to an imprint, the Greek work *phantasia* to a "processed appearance"—is whatever is in or before the mind. Impressions are schematically classified by their descending relations to what we call reality, from those that have verisimilitude to something real to those that are imaginary representations of something unreal. In effect, then, there can be false, mistaken impressions, but either way, they are *our* impressions.[14]

To extirpate, expel, mistakes is the business of the judgment (*krisis*) issuing in correct opinions (*dogmata*). Logic, the application of reason to reasoning itself is indispensable for judging and opinion-forming, but the standard of a judgment, the *kriterion* of a *krisis*, is whether it is made "according to nature." Here the whole constitution of the cosmos and its god—nature and nature's god—is brought in, but that feature of Stoicism is not directly to the present point.[15]

As the root meaning of the word *krisis*, "dividing, distinguishing," implies, judgment is thus at once the recognition that a proposition may be true or false (logical quality); a decision for one of this pair as in accord with reality (truth value); and—this is what Epictetus cares about—the acceptance or rejection of the thing proposed as good for us by the criterion of its being in accord with nature: "Where is the good? In choice. Where bad? In choice. Where what is neither? In the choice-deprived (*a-prohairesis*)."[16]

In other words: Choice itself is what matters; choice bestows worth—one might say it is the good of goods. (Kant will one day go so far as to say that nothing unqualifiedly good in or beyond the world is to be conceived except a good will.) So all good things that come upon us or desert us unbidden—all the goods of the world—are to be rejected in the name, finally, of—freedom. For in choosing, we are free, we always have the final option of refusal.

Arrian makes Epictetus's chapter on freedom the longest of the work and puts it at the head of the last, the fourth book:

> That man is free who lives as he wishes, who can be neither compelled, nor hindered, nor forced, whose impulses are unimpeded, whose appetites achievable, whose disinclinations not disrespected. Who, then, would want to live mistakenly (*hamartanon*)? No one.

So Stoic freedom is very concrete; it is the absence of imposed restraint and the fulfillment of desire. Its definition sounds almost banal, yet its consequences are anything but. For since the world of natural occurrences, of human politics, and of material objects continually compels, hinders, thwarts and causes grief, it must simply be put beyond the pale. What is not up to us is *declared indifferent*: "for there is nothing either good or bad, but thinking makes it so."[17]

Freedom of this kind was not so central a concern to those predecessors of the Stoics who had the springiness of soul to suspect the world of being in itself unreal and to use it as an often beguiling base of departure for something beyond. Epictetus's morality is—he is candid about it—that of an unwell freedman. His Stoicism is a second, a self-emancipation.[18]

All that is not up to us is, considered in itself, indifferent, but as an option chosen it is bad, unvirtuous.

Where is that ruling center, the *hegemonikon* in all this? For Epictetus, this "miserable" command-center is ineffective as a force of discrimination; we accept every impression it offers, yawning. So where do right decisions come from? And why are they so hard to make, when we surely don't want "to live mistakenly"?[19]

Pragmatic philosophies have this frequent downside: they aren't practical. Does late Stoicism work?

Well, to be sure, there is testimony that it sometimes does, in exacerbated conditions. Its popularity in the Roman Empire must count as such an endorsement, but there are also (non-academic) contemporary Stoics, in fact and fiction. An example of the latter appears in Tom Wolfe's *A Man in Full*, a hyper-vivid account, written in breezy prison jargon, of an innocent prisoner unwilling to cop a plea, who receives the *Discourses* by a bookseller's mistake and feels, for once, *understood*. It's poignant, but it's not enough to induce belief.[20]

Epictetus's injunction assumes that we could if we would. But there are obstacles. Late Stoicism is, as it were, a rational religion, or better, a religious rationalism, and so it falls, I think, between two stools: The consequences are argued too logically for fervor and the premises are proposed too peremptorily for assent.

Yet could whole-hearted faith be perhaps more directly achievable in the soul than steadfast conviction is in the mind? For the latter has more conditions required for fulfillment: a far-reaching initiatory education and the right company close by.[21]

Epictetus certainly thinks that it takes training to become a Stoic— training (*askesis*), not education: continual self-admonishment and practice, for example, in restraining desire and restricting aversion until the pupil learns that these affects really pertain to the sphere of things up to us. In other words, Stoicism is a sort of stiffened Socratism. Rational activity is still the source of right doing, although it is judgment that correctly divides the world into outside and inside rather than inquiry that takes off from the world of Appearances to seek Being within and beyond, and it is disciplined tranquility that makes for happiness rather than ontological élan. But be it Socratic education or Stoic training, neither the thought-effort of the one nor the self-suppression of the other can be the barrier to efficacy, because they're both, once embarked upon, the very way to success—preparation readily entered on by those already predisposed.[22]

Nor do I think that the difficulty in becoming a serious moral Stoic lies not in accepting undefended, even indefensible premises (that absurdity often being a *cause* of belief) or in trying to live as a Stoic *before* being one (that being the very boot-strapping nature of habituation), but in the dog that didn't bark—the will. To be sure, no term in the *Discourse* begins to anticipate it; here *boulesis* clearly means "wish."[23]

And yet will is there as an unacknowledged sort of spook. The required attribution of indifference to the world's pleasure- and pain-giving contents and the forcible discipline of tranquilizing the mind's responses give, willy-nilly, the impression of being *very* effortful. Why is it such a struggle not to struggle? Because it is not the case that, with respect to being at peace, we could if we would, but rather, exchanging consequent and antecedent, that we would if we could—but we can't. We can't because the soul is larger than the mind, it harbors affects not readily convertible into products of—even true—reason.[24]

The sense of laborious effort comes, I think, from a vestige in the Stoic's consciousness that the rational conversion can't work unless some unacknowledged faculty comes to its aid. And that is going to be the will, a needful new faculty that can alter affects not by cooption or persuasion but by coercive subjugation.[25]

I can't resist observing here that once this faculty has come on the scene, the conventional attacks on Western *rationality* as (successfully!) stifling the emotions may be faulted for forgetting to blame this imperious power, *volition*.

Now to an emperor who moves gently but no longer just implicitly towards a will.

3. Marcus Aurelius: The Comfort of Facts

The Roman emperor (who writes in Greek) wins my sympathy because of his own universal sympathy—he thinks of himself as a social being in an interconnected universe—and his human decency. He was given Epictetus's *Discourses* as a boy. But that book presents, if anything, a theory of anti-action, of quiescence, not so helpful to a warrior-emperor who wrote his *Meditations* during a weary campaign against the northern tribes threatening Italy, a pacifist by temperament driven to be a pacifier by duty; the early parts of his book are poignantly subscribed: "Among the Quadi at Granua, etc."

The *Meditations*, once again, are full of injunctions, but they are, appealingly, not addressed to followers but to himself. In them Marcus works out a Stoicism for himself, not philosophically (going up or down to beginnings) but thoughtfully (considering life meditatively). In particular there is a somewhat inexplicit theory of action, telling how a Stoic, who does not let things touch the soul, could act at all. It is because as a part of a universe governed by reason and by our own ruling rationality we are all fellow citizens and also members of a particular community. Human beings are, by reason of their reason, social beings: "The prime principle, then, in men's constitutions is the social." Therefore they hold a position in the scheme of things and should stick to their post.[26]

But as Marcus situates himself cosmically, he concentrates himself psychically. There are two fairly startling insistences: First, whatever is not the work of the understanding is indifferent, though whatever is, is in its power—so far this is orthodox. But now Marcus says: Of these latter things only those which are done with reference to the *present* are in our power; past and future activities are indifferent to this moment, here and now. In short, concentrate on the present; the present alone matters. That Stoic concentration on the present prevents Marcus from having a full-blown notion of the will, I think. For the will is a capacity for futurity. (See Ch. VI, herein).

Second, and in accord with this pointillistic temporality, Marcus mounts an uncharacteristically fierce repetitive attack on the imagination: "Wipe out your imagination," he says to himself. This command is evidently nearly identical with this one: Always abide by first appearances. He means, I think, stick with sensible fact now at hand. He explains: say your child is ill; that's a simple fact; you now see it. But that the child is in danger, that's an interpretation; you don't see it. So don't be perturbed by an imagined future.[27]

The two commands are thus closely connected, though perhaps only implicitly in Marcus's mind. The imagination is the faculty for internal time—for previews of the future and for memories of the past. Neither of these are live impressions of sensory facts. So if we are to remain "real," the imagination is an excessive faculty. Worse, it is, in Stoic theory, the faculty of imaginary, false appearances, "phantasms," and thus removed from what is now and really there, from the fact. And conversely as the imagination is doubly counter-factual because of being both essentially un-present and inventive, so the present, properly lived, precludes imagining. You can't face the real and dream at the same time or live tranquilly at a moment while envisioning contingencies. I am bringing together these scattered elements of Marcus's meditations so that I can ask finally: at what price?[28]

Throughout the book, the ruling principle, the *hegemonikon*—the authority for receiving facts and issuing commands—pops in and out, as a familiar notion recovered from Epictetus's side-lining. This interior ruler uses as material the very matter that opposes it, it makes both itself and all that appears before it to be such as it wills; it makes its own wants. Is it, thus unimpeded, invincible, self-collected? "It does nothing which it does not choose to do, even if it resists from mere obstinacy." Marcus makes scattered references to the freedom of something like the will; do they not describe the ruling principle?[29]

If so, then freedom is now connected with a potent and self-empowered principle of choice. "Consider that everything is opinion, and opinion is in your power." Here is self-directed will directing thought; this is incipient psychic omnipotence. And why, if the mind was exercising such power, was so much self-admonishment necessary? Why, once again, was tranquillity so effortful to achieve? I think the Stoics displaced something necessary to their own notion of autonomy. Augustine brings it front and center.[30]

C. Augustine: The Discovery of the Will

Here is the true, the *crucial* pivot point, though not, I want to think, a point of no return. There is, I must stop to confess, a danger to my enterprise, one that reveals itself at this juncture. Some part of polemical thinkery, including both critical scholarship and philosophic reflection, is quixotic. That is to say, its proponents fight windmills; indeed, they construct them so as the more knowingly to demolish them, like the Knight of the Sad Countenance, always lugubrious in demeanor but sometimes joyful at heart. That approach holds particularly for overviews of our West, for example the notion that we've gone comprehensively rational and have stifled feeling. There is this jeopardy to my present attempt to undo the will, the will about to be established in this section. A doubter might argue that any argument is redundant, that willing is already fading, that the neuroscientific establishment is resolutely deterministic, the therapeutic professionals are unanimously opposed to repression, and the "folk" (as academic departments denominate their lay-fellow-citizens) want to relax. If that is so, I should be mindful of Achilles' case: Be careful what you pray for. Well, the reply is triple: First, our present condition seems to be one of coming and going in all directions at once, and every way of being is alive and awaiting its day. Second, it is almost an obligation to clarify the way that led up to our present, which is indeed continuously superseding itself, so that quick and chaotic change dominates the public realm, while many of our private, daily lives remain, with luck, blessedly humdrum. And, third, there might be some readers whose views and ways are, encouragingly, confirmed here, since the gist of my line of thought is somehow familiar to many people.

So now to Augustine, who has envisioned our soul's layout as a landscape (while Thomas will know its design as an organization) and has done so more engagingly than any writer I've read—and very recognizably, I would think, by anyone at all given to self-observation. His book on memory in his *Confessions* will seem to be describing home territory to all with an imaginative life. The book on time will seem to be delineating the sense of time for anyone who has puzzled over *being* now, while having a past that is no more and a future that is not yet, and will moreover anticipate Husserl's deep work on time. Yet under the aspect of the agony of knowing the truth and not believing in it, of seeking faith and refusing it, but first and above all, of transgressing, not for the sake of a pleasure gained but for the sake of the wrong perpetrated, of *being evil*, sinful—from this perspective a faculty, a function of the soul comes to view that has not been fully present, activated, observed, acknowledged, before: the Will.[31]

Here is a prime perplexity: Even amateur readers of anthropology—their appetite grows with feeding—come to know the multitudinous and material differences that divide us from non-Western human communities. Some tribes see the future as coming up behind them, when most of us expect it from out ahead. Some eat their conspecifics (the left-overs from feeding of the gods), which we do only symbolically; some even eat their deceased parents and others bring them to their feasts, while we inter them. Some see a global pattern connecting rainfall and plant and human fertility with circumcision, an association alien to us. Some use hallucinogens routinely and daily, which we decry. These examples come from reports of Andeans, Aztecs, Indians, Incas, Cameroonians, and Amazonians respectively.[32]

But eventually the anthropologists learn to live with their particular *anthropoi*. Analogies with Western ways are found, reasons discovered, schemata worked out, and on some level a common human nature reappears. Sometimes even equal love comes about to corroborate the common humanity.

But what of a shared development within the souls of one civilization? Does it make sense to say that the human beings of the West *acquired a novel psychic function* like the will? I merely pose the perplexity here and will grapple with it as I go; it may be, as they say, "just semantic," meaning, just a matter of formulation, or it may be more drastic.

So the question is: Was the will invented or discovered? I think my reading of the three Stoics shows that there comes a time when a situation meets a propensity. Thence a bent of the soul finds its enunciation by someone who is original in both senses—who goes to universally comprehensible roots and does it in an inimitably particular way. That is Augustine.

The works I will be looking to are *On Free Choice, Confessions, On the Trinity,* and the *City of God.* The first, *De Librium Arbitrium,* is usually elaborated as "On Free Choice of the Will," but that redundant addition of "will" in fact smudges a distinctive point: This will, the one which is certainly being established here, is *itself* the faculty of decision, of judging. The will is an arbiter, in the original sense of one who intervenes between two parties. *On Free Choice* discovers the ways and works of the will, the will as cause.[33]

The *Confessions* describes the feel and failure of willing, the will as experience. *On the Trinity* locates the will as an activity in the mental part of the soul by means of an image of the Trinity, will as one of Three that are One. The *City of God* touches on the—defective—cause of evil in the economy of Creation, will in the divine community. So, in brief: will in action, will in life, will in the mind, will in history. The first two of these are more like inquiries and most to my point.

On Free Choice is a conversation of Augustine with his friend Evodius— he would become a bishop—moved by these questions: Who causes evil? Is it God? The implication is, from the first question, that evil is intentional, caused, not contingent; thus it is to be imputed to a "who," not a "what." The two friends fix on lust, *libido,* as the exemplary, perhaps the root evil, inherent in us. It sets us up for a psychic affect Socrates thought was impossible: a desire for positive badness, a natural propensity for *evil* choice.[34]

And so the will appears. Nothing superior or inferior in power to the mind can enslave the mind to lust—"only its own will and free choice." Do we have such a will? Evodius is curiously resistant to finding out, but he agrees that he has a will, a good will, a will to virtue and wisdom. And it is—proto-shades of Kant—more valuable than anything else on earth (though not, as Kant will say, also beyond it).

This will is radically, ultimately, *self*-will: "What is so much in the power of the will as the will itself?" Why, I ask myself, does the reflexivity of thinking, thinking about thinking, perplexing though it is, seem less bizarre than willing one's willing? It might be, speaking descriptively, because, while thinking is expansive and self-transcending, willing feels clenched and contractile. More of this later. In any case, this arduous self-gripping of the will turns out to be an essential aspect of this new will. (I might say here prospectively that thinkers about the will who reject "second-order" willing seem to me to have prematurely hobbled their insight.)

Then comes, very precisely, Augustine's moving in on the Stoic vacancy: Won't people be miserable, he says, if they cleave to things they can lose, things they do not love except in virtue of willing them, while they lack a good will which is incomparably better than those things and which can be theirs if only they will to have it.The Stoics ought to have acknowledged outright (this is my exegesis) that what they were after was a will, a power exercised primarily on itself and only secondarily on exterior objects— the power to be in power as the very condition for peaceable tranquility.[35]

Evodius has agreed to having a *good* will, one by which we live upright lives and will to be wise. And again, it is a set-up: If there is a good will, an incomparable source of happiness, then there must also be an *evil* will. How can that be?[36]

Augustine begins with a will-version of the Socratic teaching that everyone wants to be happy: Everyone wills a happy life; no one wills to be unhappy. But as wanting wasn't enough, for knowing was needed, so willing happiness directly is insufficient, for willing to live rightly is required. You can't will happiness directly. It is not a deed but a consequence.

As virtue came with apprehension, so now willing rightly comes with obedience. Law enters, God's eternal law that constrains us to forego the false freedom of the unrestrained indulgence of libido, of cupidity, of incarnate excess. Yet we have a God-given ability to choose temporal goods over the eternal law. And that is evil-doing or sin.

One might read the above as a succinct account of the move from ethics, a shaping or misshaping of the soul, to morality, a will to obey or disobey the better law, or a choice between eternal and temporal law. More of the relation of will to law below.

The second book of *On Free Choice* begins with an advanced version of Evodius's first preoccupation: Is God the cause of evil? Now: Why did God give us free choice which made us capable of sin? It ends with the claim that God is not responsible for sin, since the movement to sin, a turning from God, is not caused by him. And then comes a high point:

> But then where does it come from? If I told you that I don't know, you might be disappointed; but that would be the truth. For one cannot know that which is nothing.[37]

So begins the first exposition of this new power, a true *arche*. Augustine (or his formulation) implies that this power (or perhaps affect) comes on the scene in three aspects: one, as essentially a *pervertible power*, meaning that if it could not go wrong it would have no point; two, as essentially fixed on an ungraspable object, namely a *negative being*; and three, as essentially semi-imputable, because it is *at once* directed altogether by itself—a *self-caused cause* (*causa sui*) and undirectedly random—*reasonless, causeless, contingency.*

To prepare for this climactic non-conclusion is the work of the second book. Augustine reaches deep and high, for "unless you believe you will not understand," so we must first know what we believe: Do we ourselves exist? Does God exist? Do only good things come from Him? And finally, is free will among these? There follows an inquiry into the hierarchy of psychic capacities, and the conclusion that whatever understands must also exist and be alive; this is our human case. (Here Augustine anticipates Descartes' "I think, therefore I am.") Our sensations and our consumption of sensory material are individual—each of us has his own take or share. But aside from this "private property," there are features of Creation perceived and taken hold of in such a way that they remain common and untransformed. Augustine's introductory example is number, but it is wisdom that he cares about; every material object has its numbers, but rational souls have wisdom, which gets hold of unchangeable Truth—truth that is not yours or mine but reveals itself in common: a right ordering of inferior to superior things, comparing like with like, giving everyone his due in justice and with prudence. Moreover we judge this unchangeable, common truth (which is beginning to appear to the reader as God, a God who reveals himself as a craftsman working with the forms of reason that constitute the being of his works) in accordance with "inner rules of truth." These rules that direct our thinking, we simply discover; we do not in turn judge them. (Again, this is proto-Descartes: think of his "Rules" for the mind and of innate knowledge).[38]

Now the will. There is no security in goods that can be lost against our will. But Truth and wisdom, God and human virtue—those cannot be lost against our will. That event requires "a perverse will that loves inferior things," and, Augustine adds, "no one wills something unwillingly."

This, however, is the great feature of Truth, of God: "It is always wholly present to everyone"—"No one tears off a piece as his own food." Truth is *essentially* not parceled out but held in common. And so the will's perversity is in fact its *privacy*. That accounts for the intractability of its nature, for privacy, privation, lack, and nothingness are only somehow, skewedly, apprehensible.

So why is free will nonetheless a good from God? Because only with it can we act rightly by choice, be willingly good. Evodius sees that this evades the perplexity, because it assumes a good will, and so tacitly subverts choice. The implication is that perversity has to be a realizable possibility for the will to be free: *Possible perversity is the very condition of free will.*

Augustine replies: The powers of the soul, among which the will belongs, are intermediate goods, located between the virtues that are necessary for living rightly and are never misused, and material possessions that are dispensable and often misused. The will uses things rightly *or* wrongly. Evodius, alert as ever, wants to know how this will that uses things rightly or wrongly can use itself. Augustine points out that reason is similarly turned on itself.

And so Augustine brings in a second deep feature of the will, one which seems to me to be the condition of possibility for the first feature, pervertibilty—its aforementioned strange capability for using *itself* wrongly: reflexivity (not Augustine's term). Just as reason knows itself and memory recalls itself, so will uses itself, misdirects itself. Will, when it ceases to cleave to the common and unchangeable good, turns away toward *its own* private good, toward inherently inferior things. This is *sin*: will wanting to be under its own control, will willing itself. This self-involvement shows itself as lust; the expression of self-will is cupidity for otherness, material lust—a dark implication. Augustine's formulation is that the will turns from unchangeable (common) things to changeable (material) possession and consumption. And this turn is, to begin with, inapprehensible. In any case, it does not issue from God; it is our own: "If you do not will it, it will not exist."[39]

In the third book, Evodius, the persistent, wants nevertheless to know the source of the perversion of the will. How can it not be God? If we agree that God has complete foreknowledge, how can it be that we do not sin by necessity? Sin appears to be predetermined, if it is foreknown.[40]

It is Augustine's ungrateful task to take on the relation of determinism implied in omniscience to the freedom implied in willing. The argument teeters on the brink of a sophism: What God foreknows is precisely the willing of a will, that is, the will in its freedom, the will in our power. It follows that foreknowledge does not abrogate this power; in fact it confirms it. For this argument to be effective, it must mean that God has knowledge radically divorced from causation; He does not foreknow the determinations of our psychology (for then free choice would be forestalled). He knows events simply, causelessly. In any case, God's knowledge forces nothing, and Evodius has to put up with that. What is more, a sinner is still better than a stone, a soul is better than a material object, an unhappy life better than no life. Most of the book is devoted to showing that a flawed something is better than nothing.[41]

There are, it turns out, two sources of sin. One source was our own spontaneous thinking concerned with the things before it: the mind itself, the body it governs, and material objects present to the sense. The second source is the will of another, particularly the persuasions of the devil. And even these redound to the goodness of the whole, because they place the human sinner, as the devil's focus of desire, a rung above him in his pride. Here *pride*, the third deep feature of willing, comes on the scene.

Perhaps a third source of sin is what we now call "original" sin, the sinfulness with which humanity is infected by the first couple; the long discussion of this inborn sin is somewhat aporetic. Its climax is the assertion that in temporal affairs it is not the past but the future that matters. And this turn from our given genesis to our chosen intentions underwrites, it seems to me, the nature of will as a power of futurity.[42]

Augustine, who is by now in a monologue, has not done with the cause of sin. He distinguishes reason, by which we understand a commandment, from wise will, by which we obey it. Sin is evil because it involves neglect—neglecting to receive the commandment in the first place and, if received, neglecting to obey it.

And now at the very end of the work, another high moment: This neglect, in appearance a fault of omission, is really a fault of commission. The fourth source of the turning away is a dark folly:

[S]omeone whose good is God wants to be his own good, as if he were his own God.

That is pride, embodied self-will, so to speak. It happens when

Someone takes pleasure in himself and wills to enjoy his own power in a perverse imitation of God . . . This is "pride, the beginning of all sin," and "the beginning of Pride is apostasy from God."[43]

So concludes the founding charter of the West's will: a distinct power given by God to thinking creatures so that there may be freedom in his law-ruled creation. Thus it is a power for receiving and obeying commands; hence it has an—implicitly—defining propensity for disobedience, because the exercise of free choice requires the ever-ready capacity to reject a command. When sound, the will cleaves to the unchangeable, eternal common law that rationally informs God's creation, but in defection, it is perverse, turned wrongly inward as self-will, self-subjected to a private law, a deprived, privative privacy, expressed as the law of lust, of libido and cupidity, excitation and possession, which by its very turning inward, becomes enslaved to external things. The ultimate expression of this lust is dominion for its own sake—pride and self-deification being grounded in unintelligible nothingness.

Another way to place the mystery/problem of the will into a grand theological setting is this: Free choice, the defining operation of the will, has application only in a world ever-distinguishable into good and bad. But that diremption, that scission, that schism, is itself the consequence of an original act of insurgent willing, of which the devil is the paradigmatic perpetrator, the true original sinner, and as the originator, the creator, of evil in the creation, God's rival.

In his *Confessions* Augustine speaks of the will that is embodied in a human being as a source of suffering. When he was sixteen, he had a searing experience of pure self-will. He and a band of bad boys stole great loads of pears off a local tree, undesirable as fruit, only good for pigs. Whatever the other adolescents felt about the deed, Augustine was shamed because "I willed (*volui*) to do the theft, driven by no need," but for the sake of the sin itself: "I loved my own fault." Here is a confession of an acute attack of the will's reflexivity, of willing for willing's sake. For will is, to begin with, desire, and in this episode will has no object it really wants, except to do its will. This experience, I am convinced, planted the notion of a pervertible will in the adolescent's mind. How interesting, incidentally, that the occasion of his sin was nasty pears, not tasty apples. The fruit that caused the first fall was at least luscious. Lesser falls are also less lusty.[44]

As a young man of thirty-one, he began to be preoccupied seriously by the problem of evil, under the certainty that he had a will as sure as he was alive and that "I alone was he who willed and refused to will." He finds that iniquity is not a substance but a "perversity of the will" (*voluntatis perversitatem*), a twisting away from God, the highest substance, toward lower things, as he casts away his "innermost parts and becomes outwardly swollen (*tumescentis*)." Again self-will is at once a contortion of the will onto oneself and a loss of inwardness.[45]

Now out of his sense of having put his will in the control of Satan—by serving lust, which having become a habit, turns into bondage—arises a new, a second will, a spiritual will against the carnal one: spirit, "the law of the mind" against flesh, "the law of the members." In accordance with his teaching in *Free Choice*, Augustine was not unwilling to excuse the first will's sin as long as he himself was uncertain of the Truth, "but by now, fully mature, he knows it for certain." Yet the will is still—now culpably—recalcitrant. This struggle between "those two wills of mine" lays waste his soul.[46]

Two wills—thus they can't be called a power, a faculty of the soul. And so scholars say: The will is for Augustine not a faculty but an act. Yet that cannot be quite right; he *calls* it a power, a *facultas*:

> For in that state that power (*facultas*) is the will (*voluntas*), and to will is now to do it.

In what state? When I assuredly will it, will it "strongly and wholly" (*fortiter et integre*), I have, or my integral will has, the power directly to do it.[47]

This discovery of the two wills comes to an agonized climax in the eighth book of the *Confessions*, just before Augustine's moment in the garden, when "all the shadows of doubt fled away." The plethora of terms—power (*facultas*), desire (*affectus*), and doing (*facere*)—which indeed makes one's head spin, is, I think, the consequence of Augustine's acute experience of willing—for it seems, will is a power; we call it "will power." This power is moved by desire; we call it "wanting." And it sometimes brings its power to bear on effecting its wishes; we call it "doing."[48]

The dual will is, Augustine says, a sickness of the mind. A man of cruder intellect might simply note that "what I would, that do I not"—it is just the fact of the sin that dwells within me. But Augustine gets caught up in the complexities of the novel faculty; above all the ever-collapsing complexity of mind commanding mind: "For the will commands that there be a will and that this be itself . . ." So the mind would not give this command unless it willed it, and yet it does not do what it wills.[49]

The solution is that the will does *not* command itself so "strongly and wholly" as to be a will in its entirety. This is the one, an incomplete will. The other will is the complete will. Are we to understand that there are two natures within us, one bad, one good? That would be sheer Manicheanism, the belief that evil is a substantial world-principle on par with good and this duality is expressed in us—a belief that Augustine abhors: "It was myself who willed it and myself who did not will it."

Whence, then, comes the maimed will? It is a monstrous vestige of Adam's first sin, an indwelling inheritance, a punishment for the first ancestor's "freer sin" (*liberioris peccati*). So the will's handicap is essentially indecisiveness, a hindered freedom of choice; it can affect both good and bad desires in their multitude. What and where, then, is the other, the complete will?[50]

It seems to me that Augustine has derailed himself a little. Earlier in the eighth book, there was an old, carnal will, and a new, a spiritual will, two desires in devastating contention. But a few chapters later these have modulated into an incomplete and complete will, the former lacking will-power because of insufficient commitment, the other perfect in that respect.[51]

The perfect will is, however, no longer a will: "For were it full, it would not command that it might be, because it would already be." Just as in the Socratic case there was no daylight between thinking and living, so in the Augustinian case it is no sooner said than done, except that now it is a command that is obeyed rather than a thought that is appropriated. I think, then, that the full, the complete will is an image of God's will; in the human being it appears as the sudden decision to give up and give in, to give in to an already known Truth and to give up carnal lust. And that is what the confessional climax of the *Confessions* concludes.

On the Trinity treats the will not as embodied in an agonizing human being living through time, nor even as a part of a whole soul that includes the senses and their appetites, but as an activity of the innermost man, the mind, which is the seat of spiritual life.

The device of *On the Trinity*—if one may call so grand a scheme a device—is to illuminate the Trinity that is God by finding its images in the human mind, an undertaking legitimized by *Genesis*: "So God created man in his own image, in the image of God created he him." I might say right away that the mental structure suggested by Augustine's understanding of the Trinity—a unity of three equal yet mutually subordinate persons, each marked by a function at once distinct and exercised by all—yields a theory of mind of terrific complexity and much contemporary resonance. This sort of re-entrant thinking is particularly congenial to Augustine, I think, and one reason why those of us who know him even a little want to know him more.[52]

Augustine gives a preview of the way mental trinities image the divine Trinity in the fourth book:

> Father and Son and Holy Spirit, God the Creator, of one and the same substance, the almighty three, act inseparably . . . In their own proper substance by which they are, the three are one . . . one and the same all over Creation . . . But in my words . . . [they] are separated and cannot be said together . . . Here is an example: When I name my memory, understanding, and will, each name refers to a single thing, and yet each of the single names is the product of all three; there is not one of these three names which my memory and understanding and will have not produced together.

Memory, understanding, and will are the major triad of the mind, and the later books of *On the Trinity* will explicate their functioning. One more early mention will also set the scene:

[N]o one willingly does anything which he has not spoken previously in his heart.

Nothing we do through "the members of our body," at least such acts as others approve or disapprove, happens without a preceding word within. Augustine thinks that inner speech, be it cordial or mental, lies behind all willed conduct. That is, I think, how a language-expressed inquiry into the inner man, particularly into the seat of the rational soul (*anima rationalis*), the mind, becomes both possible and needful, and why Augustine might supplement scripture with accounts, might wish to express meanings explicitly.[53]

Thus he begins with introspection. The (Socratic-Apollonian) command is: "Know Thyself." Where to look?—that is the "remarkable question." Augustine's remarkable answer is: Let the mind discern itself as present, not as absent. He means that, though the mind is drawn outside itself by its love for sensible things, these corporeal things "leave their footprints," so to speak, on the memory, so that even when they are absent they are present to thought. Let the mind, then, "fix the alienation of its will" by which it wandered outside "upon itself, and think of itself." So introspection begins with an act of the will, an inward turn that repairs the self-alienation of self-will. There follows the famous chapter of the tenth book in which Augustine anticipates, as I mentioned above, Descartes' "proof" of his own existence, *cogito ergo sum*, "I think therefore I am." Augustine needs an assurance of human existence not to establish the perfect certainty that Descartes craves, but to express what everyone believes is certain to begin with. "No one doubts that no one understands who does not live, and that no one lives who does not exist." So Augustine starts earlier than Descartes. The latter employs doubt as a willed device for clearing the stage of his mind so that thought may uniquely appear, while Augustine uses doubt as a direct testimony to existence—indeed not only doubt but even error: "If I err, I am" (*si fallor, sum*).[54]

He anticipates Descartes' term *cogitatio* for thought and gives it its full force: the verbe *cogere* (*co-agere*) means "to drive together, to collect." For Augustine thought is not a collecting but a collection, the trinity of "memory, inner vision, and the will, which unites both." This is a unity of functions; for Descartes, as I said, it will be an identity. In this respect too Augustine is the anticipating forerunner.[55]

He also surpasses Descartes in the future direction, being in tune with a very current view, our anti-representationalism. Descartes acknowledges no problem in principle with self-knowledge, difficult though it may seem for the "I" to concentrate on the I: ". . . I know plainly that I can achieve an easier perception of my own mind than of anything else." So this I, a self, which *is* the thinking thing, can also set itself apart, set itself to perceiving

that "thing," the thinking—although the mind is also "utterly indivisible."
Now as I see it, Descartes' usual understanding of perceiving is indeed rep-
resentationalist, meaning that the mind puts between itself and its object
an internal representation, be it an image, impression, or even some other
conceivable analogue. It is, however, hard to see how the I would perceive
its own thinking in that indirect way, what a representation of the pure I as
the source of representations would be.[56]

Augustine does not, it seems, admit such intervening images, at least
for mental objects. The mind knows itself directly since it is immediately present to itself, and so cannot *not* know itself. What, then, does that
injunction "Know Thyself" mean? As one might expect, the command
is applicable because the mind has deformed its desires and diverted its
attention, forgotten itself. It is the old story: The mind wants to be its own
God and so becomes intent on itself in a bad way; it feeds itself with dis-
turbing pleasures and external knowledge; the mind thus replete loses its
self-transparence. This original mental defect—one might call it self-dis-
placement—the graver forerunner of Pascal's mundane "diversion," is the
consequence of the Fall.[57]

Then comes the great mental trinity. There are many others; Trinitiar-
ian triplicity is a mind-constituting principle. These lesser, more somatic
triples do seem to be cognitive *acts*; in fact Augustine speaks of their
"wills," and the plural makes more sense for acts than for one faculty, that
is, a separable, distinct mental power. But Augustine insists on the simply
undivided unity of the mind, and that superior mental trinity about to be
established seems to me to be not a single act but an ongoing activity, that
is, a persistent capacity being exercised—call it a faculty-less function, a
function of the whole mind.[58]

In this mental trinity of "memory, inner vision, and the will which
unites them," the body has receded, everything has been drawn inward.
The will's general function is what we call "attending," the "bringing-
to-bear-on" activity. To my mind, the subtlety of Augustine's analysis of
mental functions really lies in the gradations that the second member of
the trinity undergoes as the trinities penetrate deeper into the soul: from
sensory seeing, through imaginative vision, to the mind's sight. For the
analysis implies an appealing global theory of "eidetic" cognition, meaning a sight-like knowing (though not of "representations"). However, the
will is my focus here, and it functions on all levels as mediator, director,
coupler, applier; it brings cognition to bear on its object. For the sensory
trinity, Augustine uses the figure of a quasi-parent (the object) and quasi-
offspring (the cognition) —"quasi" because the object alone can beget no
vision, while the sense perception begotten is a cognition only to a low
degree. The will is neither object nor cognition in the lower trinities but
the enabler of their relation.

The sacred analogy, that to the Holy Trinity, is beginning to take shape: The will as intercessor is like the Spirit, and like the Spirit, it is more allied to the cognitive offspring than to the object-parent. Augustine has another figure for this soul-trinity: The will is like a weight. For measure is in memory (where bodies are kept in image form and each image has its limiting extent), and numbers are in inner vision (since there are numerous incidents of vision, ready for counting), but weight is in will (because it chooses to rest its desire by bearing down on measure and number to bring them together). Thus will completes, by bringing gravity to bear on it, the intelligible aspect of the physical Creation spoken of in *On the Free Will*, where, however, the concern was with numerability alone.[59]

In preparation for the ascent to the mental trinity that most perfectly mirrors the divine Trinity, Augustine distinguishes wisdom, the atemporal cognition of eternal things, from knowledge, the rational cognition of temporal things. By attending, the will brings about knowledge, but for wisdom something new must enter: *love*. Will is that very "love or cherishing" (*amor seu dilectatio*) which unites parent with offspring. As far as I can tell, Augustine does not spell out how will becomes love. But I imagine that, to begin with, the thought of love was actually what suggested the will's binding function to him; and second, that there is a reminiscence here of the Aristotelian tradition of *boulesis* as rational desire; and finally, that the Spirit of the Holy Trinity is the conduit of God's love to human hearts. It is this last that makes the will/love analogy work. The human will-image in the upper soul, in the mind, thus yields a kinder, gentler will of greater gravity than the all-human will of *On Free Choice* and the *Confessions*. It is this latter, fiercer faculty that will spook modernity and us.[60]

We should not forget that the mind is one, so that with its loving will it loves itself as a whole, as it remembers and understands itself. Thus it is now finally an image of God, who is both "Will of Will," and Love—Love in himself, in "his own greatness," and Love for his creatures, as being their ultimate cause.[61]

On the Trinity ends with the observation that the trinitarian image of the human mind is *only* an image, in this way: both the panel and the picture upon it are called "image." In the case of the Holy Trinity, there is no panel, no material, only the figure, so to speak. Therefore its oneness incomparably surpasses that of the human image, in which the mutuality of activities is not perfect. For God *is* the Trinity, but we are not our trinities. In us their activities remain distinct, because even the mental acts are bound to the body's nature and so independently moved by passion. Nevertheless, the human will of *On the Trinity*, despite its incapacities compared to God's will, is, though imperfectly, *all* of cognition, as are the other functions, memory and understanding; each is the whole. Yet, as the enabling bonder of objects to powers, *will preeminently suffuses the*

soul, transmuted into Love only in its upper reaches—a tremendous, consequence-fraught revisioning of human being.[62]

The City of God, a huge book I have not completely read, is a parallel history of sacred, heavenly and secular, earthly polities, interpreted in
terms of the theme of the work, the defense of God the Founder's sacred
city against those who prefer their own pagan politics. Concerning the will,
Augustine argues in order, as follows: that with respect to our actions we
are not under necessity but can will freely, God's foreknowledge not withstanding; that God's enemies are so not by nature but by willful vice; that
the apostate angels sinned by reason of a bad will, but that nothing is the
efficient cause of the bad will itself, because it is not an effect but a defect;
that the will comprehends all the motions of the soul, so that desire, joy,
fear, and sadness are all volitions of consent or aversion; that a man, so as
to live according to God, ought to love good and hate evil; that a right will
is thus well-directed love; finally that God's Will is eternal, timeless, not
ceasing to be a will, although he has already performed all he willed, just
as human beings for whom sin has no delight have not, therefore, their free
will withdrawn from them, but keep it still as a will, though a will at peace:
"They take unfailing delight in not sinning."
   To me the most significant of these points is the utter explicitness with
which Augustine announces the absolute primacy of the will. If the will is
wrong, so will be the motions of the soul; if right, they too will be praise-
worthy. For

> the will is in them all; yea, none of them is anything else but will. For what
> are desire and joy but a volition of consent to the things we wish? And
> what are fear and sadness but a volition of aversion from the things we do
> not wish?

For Aristotle all the motions of the soul were comprehended under
appetition, as desires. For Augustine all fall under will, as volitions. Consider that desires may be meretricious—but volitions tend to be sinful. We
are in a new moral world.[63]
   This is, then, a compendium of the chief features of Augustine's will.
Above all it confirms that the proper arena of its operation is sin, evil-
doing. The proof is that *the free choice made by a good will dissolves it*
(Augustine's denial notwithstanding) by turning it into one more affect:
the enjoyment of the freedom from choice, of being settled in goodness.
But original will is recalcitrant.

Lest the passage to Descartes seem abrupt, here is a reminder of the two
all-important notions that make him the direct heir of Augustine: doubt as
the way to certainty about one's own existence with the consequent *cogito*

ergo sum, and more pertinently, the mutual encompassing of all the activities of the mind. Descartes will turn that unity into an identity. He is, in addition also deeply indebted to the Stoics, so my leap into dawning modernity is doubly legitimized.

D. Descartes: Will's Power

Descartes too allows the will to take over. That becomes most manifest in his last book, *The Passions of the Soul.*[64]

A chief intention of the *Passions* is to bridge the notorious Cartesian dualism of soul and body. The solution is here given with almost ludicrous brevity: shrink the problem to a pinpoint, as if a point-like interface made mind-body contact intelligible. Thus the tiny pineal gland in the brain is the locus where the soul most immediately exercises its active control over the body and receives in return somatic passions. These interactions are the subject of the work.[65]

Its first notion is the relativity of the terms action and passion; what is a passion in the subject is an action in the agent. The event itself is a single thing: The soul's actions, as we find by experience, depend only on itself, but many of its perceptions and some of its knowledge come to it as passions, as representations received from the body; action and passion coalesce in the psychic representation.

These psychic actions of knowing or perceiving are *volitions*, and they are of two sorts, those that work on the soul itself and those that issue in the body and govern its motions. Perceptions—what defines a perception is that it has an object, that it *represents* something to itself—are themselves dual, some caused by the body, others by the soul; the ones within the soul are obviously volitional.

The point of this somewhat confusing exposition is made explicit in this sentence: "For it is certain that we could not will anything unless we perceived that we willed it," and then: "And though with respect to our soul it is an action to will something, it can be said that it is also a passion within it to perceive that it wills." That is to say, volition, willing, is self-affection, action and passion in one; it might be said that it is the most thoroughly self-sufficient, deeply interior of our capacities.[66]

Volition remembers, imagines, attends, and it even controls the passions. It retrieves memories by moving the gland to drive the bodily "spirits" toward the brain's traces of the object—Descartes is the aboriginal modern neuropsychologist: then the spirits reciprocally move the gland to represent the recalled object to the soul. Volition performs the other functions similarly. And though it cannot excite or displace the passions directly, it can control them indirectly by arousing reasoning representations opposed to the passion it wants to reject. Thus no soul, no matter how weak, need fail to gain complete control of its own and the body's passions. What the ancients identified as a struggle between the lower and the higher parts of the soul is really only the opposition of movement in "the little gland" excited respectively by the natural appetites and the will. The weakness of the soul in this struggle (what we call lack of will power) is a lack of firm, resolved judgment of good and evil. Here Descartes says something proto-Kantian that Spinoza and Hume will deny: To do battle with the passions by other passions is using improper weapons; passions are properly fought by reasons based on truth. However, it will turn out that the domain of pure given truths is small; most thought is willed.[67]

"Free will/choice" (*libre arbitre*) enters in the latter part of the treatise. I will be brief about it, since now Descartes reveals himself as a neo-Stoic moralist, and his arguments are modifications of Stoicism straight up. Though he obviously cannot say that passions are mistaken thoughts—in fact, he accords them a use—he does enjoin avoiding desire for things not "up to us," and he does think that the soul—here read "mind" (*esprit*)—can regulate the passions by correcting errors of judgment about them.[68]

Here is what is new: Free Will is now clearly the controlling agent. The ancient Stoics' reliance on a reason with dubious enforcement powers is gone. Free choice, free will, is filling the gap, and even if cogitation is present, that too is will-involved: put the Stoics together with Augustine and Descartes emerges.

Much of the latter part of the *Passions* is given over to the order, definition, and assessment of the primitive and derivative passions—not to my point here, except for this revealing sentence under "What reasons we may have to esteem ourselves." Descartes sees only one:

> namely the exercise of our free will and the control we have over our volitions. For we can reasonably be praised or blamed only for actions that depend upon this free will. It renders us in a certain way *like God* [my italics] by making us masters of ourselves, provided we do not lose the rights it gives us through timidity.[69]

The Stoics' god governed a world that made "living according to nature" right, "appropriate." Augustine's God is the creator whose image we are and see within. Descartes' God is a master whom we are like, which suggests that he is like us, something akin to a competitor. It is significant that the *Meditations on First Philosophy*, which aim to found a new world starting from a radical beginning, are six in number, and for all we know, take place over six days, for each "meditation," each radically destructive and willfully constructive pondering, with all the modes that belong to cogitation, seems to be taking place on a different day. There is no Sabbath.[70]

As a bridge in going backward to the *Meditations*, where the will is given its place at the very foundations of human nature and cognition, I shall quote or paraphrase passages from the *Principles of Philosophy*, because of their hard-hitting succinctness.

One. We have only two modes of thinking: the perceptions of the intellect and the operations of the will. Sensory perception, imagination, pure understanding, are modes of perception; desire, aversion, assertion, denial, and doubt are modes of willing (shades of Augustine, above).

Two. Judgments require both intellect and will, intellect because we must perceive something to make a judgment about, will to assent.

Three. Will has a wider scope than the pure intellect, which has only very few objects presented to it. Will, however, can, in a way, be called infinite, for:

> we observe without exception that its scope extends to anything that can possibly be an object of any other will—even the immeasurable will of God.

Four. We never err when we give our assent only to what we clearly and distinctly perceive. ("Clear" means strongly present and accessible to the attentive mind; "distinct" means so sharply separated from all other perception that it contains within itself only what is clear.) Although we do not wish to err, we go wrong by our own free will, because we give our assent when we lack clear and distinct perception.

Five. The freedom of the will is self-evident; it is equally certain that everything is preordained by God. This is a particularly bold early modern theological expression of compatibilism, the issue concerning free will that is the principal current preoccupation; nowadays the question is whether free will is compatible with the determinism of natural science; those who offer a way to believe this are called compatibilists.[71]

The *Meditations* are an inquiry not into Being, Nature, or God (except as ancillary), but into the Self (not to be confused with human being), that is the "I," and its mental activities. Thus ontology, the account of being, yields to epistemology, the account of knowledge—but in a particularly acute way: how to know with *certainty*. Socratic hypotheses, Aristotelian *theoria*, Stoic logic, Augustinian analogy—all are set aside to make a new beginning in which the Will is no longer an as—yet—unborn nonentity unneeded for action, nor an intellectual appetite for the inquiry into being, nor a hidden executive power for giving force to reason, nor a mediating activity for joining a cognitive power to its object. It is now a full-blown mode of the very substance of self-hood—thinking:

But what then am I? A thing that thinks [*res cogitans* in the original Latin]. What is that? A thing that doubts, understands, affirms, denies, wills, wills not, and also imagines and has sensory perceptions.[72]

Here Descartes has not yet distinguished the willing-thinking from the perceiving-thinking as he does in the *Principia*. And he immediately goes on to say that all these cogitative modes belong to one and the same I—or sometimes, *mind*; they belong to it even if none of their objects are real. It is the functioning of the I that counts. Thus Descartes says that when I will, an object of thought, that is, a perception, must be present, but the willing of this and that object is something more than the perception. That something more is, I think, precisely the willing, the more or less vehement for-ness or against-ness attending the perception of object—be it thing, event, or plan.[73]

The most extended meditation of the will occurs on the fourth day, entitled "Truth and Falsity." (Neatly, it is the day of the Creation on which the command "Let there be light" went forth so as "to divide the light from the darkness.") The will comes in with the darkness, it being, as we already know, the source, if not the cause, of error. The intellect only enables Des-cartes (all the meditations are reported in the first person) to perceive ideas for possible judgment, so it is, properly speaking, pre-lapsarian, incapa-ble of error. This mode of thought is finite; it lacks many ideas of exist-ing objects; that, however, is not positive error. But the will, the freedom of choice that he received from God, is infinite. Nothing else in him is so perfect; the very idea of a greater faculty is beyond his grasp. And again: Although God's will is incomparably greater in scope and efficacy, in its essential, strict sense God's will *as* will seems no greater than his.[74]

What is the will, then, essentially? In the *Passions*, the will was that genus-function of the soul which consists of actions; perceptions belong to the class of passions. In the *Meditations*, where passions are not in play, Descartes says the same thing in other words:

The will simply consists in the ability to do or not do something (that is, to affirm or deny, to pursue or avoid).

"Or rather," he goes on, amplifying definition with description,

it consists simply in the fact that when the intellect puts something for-ward for affirmation or denial, or for pursuit or avoidance, our inclina-tions are such that we do not feel we are determined by any external force.

So far, then, will is an ability to act backed by a feeling of non-con-straint from alien sources in following our bent. But what makes it actually operate? Descartes says that it is not "indifference"—lack of an inclination or a reason is the lowest grade of freedom. (That is, then, one more reason why will cannot fully come out for the Stoics: they regard too many possible objects of inclination as indifferent.) On the contrary, the stronger his inclination, be it by reason of truth and goodness or by a divinely produced innermost disposition, the freer his choice. (This is precisely one of the compatibilists' chief arguments: a feeling of being free to follow a strong inclination, however either feeling or bent is produced, is all that free will is, and it can live in peaceful parallel with any predetermination.)[75]

So now to error. The will being ample and perfect, it cannot be the *cause* of error, but its very amplitude is error's *source*. Its scope exceeds that of the intellect, and in that excess territory, indifference *ought* to reign, by reason of *objectlessness*. But this isn't what Descartes says. He says that the *will itself* is indifferent, and so it easily turns aside from the true and the good to error and sin. He gives as an example his recent deliberate doubt about his own and the world's existence, as contrasted with his continuous irresolution concerning the identity of his mind and his body. The resolution of the former problem, "I doubt therefore I exist," is entirely internal to him; there was no external force, and thus a great light of the intellect resulted in a great inclination of the will. But concerning the latter problem, whether he, as a thinking nature, is identical with his corporeal nature (a question answered with a firm yes *and* no in the *Passions*), he is as yet unresolved, so his will is indifferent, having not yet found a persuasive reason either way; he must refrain from making a judgment. The trouble is, he doesn't always refrain, and that alone leads to error. The will has an inclination to do an end run around its proper indifference. If without sufficient perceptions of the intellect, without reasons, I go on mere conjecture, "then am I not using my will correctly." Who, we may ask, is in charge here? The will is the faculty of decision; should the I supervene? What is coming out here is the confusion consequent on selfhood, on the ego-ism of pitting me against my faculties—in Descartes' case, a "myself" against its thinghood. Descartes, to be sure, has covering language. The essence of error, he says, is proceeding on insufficient grounds—which is a privation, a lack, rather than a reality, on which to proceed would be a positive evil. Descartes wants to maintain the perfection of his will by differentiating the self's willing from the faculty of will:

> The privation, I say, lies in the operation of the will insofar as it proceeds from me but not in the faculty of will which I received from God . . .

This is saving the perfection of the will by making it a *penultimate power*. If its operation originates in him, then there is a more ultimate willer than the will, the I, and if its excesses are mere privations, then they aren't sins—though this is arguable; indeed it is a form of the old question: whether evil is non-being, compounded with a new question: how the I and the will are related. (Occam's razor has become very dull here.)[76]

Descartes' *Meditations*, which might have seemed an exercise in rationality, turn out to be an assertion of volitionality. This meditation ends in a list of complaints against God that he regards himself as not entitled to have, among them, the excesses of will over intellect and the fact that God did not endow him with his two root powers equal in scope. (Articulated complaints that one mustn't have leave one wondering.)

One element is so far rightly missing: How are the decisions of the will exerted in the world? For that to happen, the whole soul, the one attached to its body, needs to be brought in, and that is what *The Passions of the Soul* will do.

It remains to be said that this mode of magnifying the will raised objections. I mention two by Pierre Gassendi that express problems any reader of the *Meditations* might have. First, how can, or why would, the will have larger scope than the intellect, since the will can't address itself to anything not perceived by the intellect? Second, isn't the cause of error actually in the intellect, namely when its perceptions don't correspond to the way its object really is?[77]

Descartes responds to the first of these two objections (Gassendi has others) by amplifying how the will comes to exceed the intellect by a margin filled with our error. It is because we do have some understanding of any object perceived, but "there may be many things about it that we desire but very few things of which we have knowledge." Moreover, we never "exercise our will in a bad fashion," but it is the object of our willing that is bad. So it turns out that desire, wanting, fills out the gap between understanding and willing. (And whose desire could that be? Mine, I suppose. Furthermore, if our will is always in the clear, what then could judge the object to be bad? I do, I suppose. In other words, this wonderful will is to be held harmless on all accounts, while the self is loaded with hidden liabilities.)

Gassendi, infelicitously I think, agrees with Descartes that it is will which assents or dissents, that is, judges, so his second question, a deep one, loses its force. For who decides whether the intellect has formed a perception corresponding to reality? If it is the will, what exactly is left to perceiving, to clarity and distinctness? Descartes replies to Gassendi that, if the intellect decides, then what determines the will to guard against error? This reply seems right, but it's right because it's circular: Descartes had already decided that the will can be the final arbiter of true and false. He does what he, responding to acerbity with insult, accuses Gassendi of doing: Gassendi's a materialist, so Descartes addresses him as "O Flesh," and says that he, Gassendi himself, is an example of the will's outstripping knowledge. An example of that is Gassendi's believing, Lucretian-wise and wrongly, that the mind is a rarified body. He believes it beyond his understanding because he wants to. One might say to Descartes: *tu quoque*, you too.

What does Descartes want? To collect all mentation under *cogitatio*, thinking, as its modes, and yet ultimately to empower one of them, will, to do the work of the understanding. I see this difficulty: Assertion and assent (or their opposites) may be a psychological background to a declarative sentence, a so-called "propositional attitude": "I know/think/believe that . . ." It may even have a willingness to it: "I am willing to assent to . . ." Yet all in all, knowing, thinking, believing seem to be more truth-receptive than choice-activated; moreover, willingness is not willing; recall *hekousion*, "voluntary" in Aristotle.[78]

Why does Descartes so spectacularly enlarge the scope and enhance the competence of the will? Some conjectures: To enforce the certainty obtained by the intellect's clear and distinct perceptions, to give them, as it were, the Stoic imprimatur of "up to me." Why certainty? Because the most certain thing, his stripped-down Self, that is, stripped of all perceptions by the will to doubt, is an indivisible, "intensive" *self*, pitted against a wholly *other*, alien "extended" natural world, the other substance: *res extensa*. The sixth meditation reconceives, prepares, this world for human apprehension through the mediation of the mathematical imagination. This imaging faculty "is not a necessary constituent of my own essence," but a kind of extra, serendipitously outward-turned faculty. It differs from pure understanding in that the latter is mind turning within, while the former enables it to engage with corporeal things "which are the subject matter of pure mathematics"—cleaned up corporeality, so to speak. Recall that on the sixth day of Creation man enters the world—man created "to have dominion over all." And unless his knowledge has certainty, his dominion over his domain lacks perfection.[79]

So, then, why control, why executed will? Surely everything has led up to it, from the strangely fierce need to "prove"—or should it be "create anew"?—both one's own existence and that of a world. Descartes, so he says in the sixth part of his *Discourse*, seeks tranquility and "uninterrupted leisure"—not, for pure contemplation, but rather for devising mental techniques, such as rules and methods that can solve problems, and for discovering mathematical truths that can be applied to technology—all for the relief of the human condition. Instead, he is oppressed by lack of resources and time; his potential godlikeness is, ironically, curtailed by mundane restrictions on the infinite possibilities that might be exploited in this reconstructed creation.[80]

Am I psychologizing—a grave sin against greatness? Perhaps. But then, where the power of the will is invoked, the question of motives *will* arise.

chapter III

Mainliners and Extremists

The proponents of the will are dividing themselves in my mind between those who, following Aristotle, think of the human will (now an established term) as rational desire and those who think of it, with Augustine, as pervertible self-assertion. The former, the mainliners by reason of their rooted tradition, will have their culmination in the magisterial Thomas Aquinas. The latter, the extremists by reason of their deliberate radicalism, will find their purest expression in the heretical William of Ockham. The mainliners will fade, not so the extremists.[1]

A. Thomas Aquinas: Intellectual Appetite

The Greeks have a term, the *epigonoi*, the "late-born." By and large it's not a great blessing to be among them, at least in philosophy: matter accumulates but doesn't coalesce and books grow more sophisticated but no wiser.[2]

Thomas's writings seem to me a grand exception. In them he casts genuine sums, in which the cumulative tradition comes together so that the whole is more than its parts, and he is both subtle and decisive, observant and definitive, but above all very detailed and very comprehensive. I shall consider the questions on will in two of his writings: the *Summa Theologiae* and *On Truth*.[3]

Thomas situates the treatment of the will in the *Summa*'s "Treatise on Man" that follows the account of the Six Days' Work of Creation, on the last of which days man was made. Actually that's not quite right. The will appears earlier in the *Summa*, for Thomas treats of God and the angels, both of whom have will, before treating of Creation in general and Man in particular.

What is said both of the divine and the angelic will, particularly of the will belonging to fallen angels or demons, yields some fundamental understandings that reach the human realm. Thus we learn that "the appetible," meaning the proper (general) object of appetite or desire, is the good, an Aristotelian notion of great consequence to Thomas's analysis of willing: good, the object of will, and true, the object of intellect, mutually include each other, as do their powers, for intellect understands will and will wills the intellect to understand. Furthermore, there are here established five overt signs that willing is going on: operation, when a person manifests will in deed, and prohibition, permission, precept, and persuasion, when a person works his will on another.[4]

In the superhuman realm, we learn that God, too, has a will; he does not act as cause by the necessity of his nature but by his will. Moreover, since he has no predetermined nature to constrain his action, he himself determines his will. We learn further that angels too have wills differing from their intellect, for the will tends to the appetible, the good, which is outside it, while the intellect extends itself to knowledge, which is both without and within. In God alone intellect and will coincide, for he has both all good and all knowledge within. Angels thus have free choice, for they have the intellect to make free judgments. The angel that fell, the devil, could be affected by one sin only, pride, since being a spiritual, non-bodily being, he could not lust. He desired to be God-like by turning his appetite away from the bliss bestowed by God and attempting to gain it by the power of his own nature. The demonic will is obstinate and irredeemable precisely because, unlike the human reason, the angelic intellect is non-discursive, immovable; since, then, the will is always proportionate to the intellect (Descartes notwithstanding), the demonic will is, once determined, fixed.[5]

Aside from the fascination of viewing so sure-handed a portrait, much more detailed than my review, of the supernal and infernal psychic economies, these delineations will all have a bearing on the human case about to be set out. Here Thomas begins with the largest divisions of the soul's power: the "apprehensive" and the "appetitive."

The higher of the *apprehensive* powers, the intellect, *receives within* the forms of all things that it apprehends, and so it, as it were, becomes them (this is pure Aristotle), but the higher of the *appetitive* powers, the will, *goes out* in desire to the things without. By "higher" is meant attending to nonsensual objects; there is also knowledge through the senses and sensual or "natural" appetite. The higher appetitive power is, as I said, the human *will*. Human souls have this special power because they are receptive to the forms of things, and with this receptivity goes an inclination that is above natural appetite. In other words, we have a will above mere sensual desire *because* we have an intellect above mere sensory experience; by will we desire in fact what we know in its form. The will is not coercible by violence and desires nothing by forcible necessity, but only by its own inclination, which is "voluntary." It does, however, stand under the natural necessities of the means to the desired end and, in another way, of the end itself, which is *happiness*. But the will is not bound by necessity to this one great end only; there are some particular goods that have no necessary connection with happiness and toward these the will may or may not incline.[6]

The intellect moves the will, because a good has to be apprehended to be willed. But, then again, as an agent that impels to action, the will moves all the powers of the soul (except the natural bodily needs); it determines them. That is to say, in individual cases of understanding, when the intellect focuses on particulars, the will, which wants the general good, is more comprehensive. So the intellect moves the will by presenting it with truth, and the will moves intellect by providing direction toward the good. Each reciprocally moves the other—but finally, the intellect precedes in scope, for some intellectual insight is un-willed: that of God. Yet, again, the love of God is higher than and exceeds the knowledge of him. But this love is not a passion; the affections of the intellectual appetite are not like those of the sensory passions, which are either fierce (irascible) or lustful (concupiscent). Our will is neither angry nor libidinal, and in that we are like God and the angels—who have dispassionate affections. (Understand that who may; perhaps it is like the minimally libidinal love felt in old age.)

Having will, man has free choice; if he didn't, there would be no point in advising, exhorting, commanding, prohibiting. Here "judgment" enters, a rational act for particular cases. In contingent cases, "matters of judgment," as we say, the judgment is not predetermined. Free choice, the power of election, is an ability of the will; as the intellect has reason to reach the conclusion implied in its principles, so will has free choice to elect the means to its end. (Note that for Thomas free choice is only a phase of willing; their later identification is, I think, the most consequential diminution the will is to undergo.) [7]

On the basis of this placement of the will as a power in the human soul, together with an account of the fundamental features that distinguish it from other powers in Part I of the *Summa*, the will is treated in the second part of Part II as it appears in human acts. We are to bear in mind that acts are "properly said to be human when they are willed," since "will is the rational appetite (*appetitus rationalis*), which is proper to men." In other words, Thomas offers a human psychology of acts of willing (*actus voluntarii*). And what an analysis it is! Twelve long questions cover the field from the specific humanity of the will to its non-human objects, from the willing within the soul to the execution without. As is only sensible, I shall condense this vivid account—vivid by reason of its detailed observation of psychic activity—with an eye to confirming the mainline view of the will as intellectual or (somewhat lower) rational appetite. It is the kinder, gentler view of a will, a will seated in a soul receptive to given being with its truth and aware of its finitude as a creature dependent on its Creator for its good.[8]

This might be a good moment for an, always appreciative, disclaimer. It seems to me, as I said, to be impossible not to marvel at Thomas's detailed comprehensiveness, but it is by no means impossible to disbelieve its informing framework, its Catholic Christianity. Yet there is an, I had almost said, saving grace: Thomas's Aristotelianism, which he evolves so ingeniously into a Christian system. In matters of thought, what has been evolved can be devolved; the analysis of the will in the *Summa* can be appropriated by non-believers as a more highly specified *Nicomachean Ethics*—though it may grieve us thus to turn his noblest trait, his receptivity to truth-telling anywhere, against him.

But back to the text. What qualifies willing, volitional voluntariness, as maximally human is that it is a self-movement toward an end well understood, an inner principle of action moving a knowledgeable agent. Can lust or fear then make action involuntary? No, lust is desire and is *ipso facto* voluntary. Even when this desire swamps judgment, it is still ultimately voluntary, because the will was responsible for a man's not concentrating and thinking. Lust is about a good, but fear is about an evil. Thus the latter is more apt to make for a non-voluntary action, an action in which the will in itself remains unwilling. An unrestrainedly lustful man is, whatever else he may have willed before, quite "willing" to do as he wants at the moment; a frightened man remains unwilling but is overcome by an urgent situation. When the urgency becomes too dire, will cuts out in either case; but for future reference, Thomas adds a caveat to this realistic view: All in all, the will *can* resist passion.[9]

The circumstances of human action are next enumerated: setting, motive, agent, mode, and then the objects of willing. As we already know, the good is the prime object of the will: "There is no appetition except for the good." The reason is deep, metaphysical: Wanting is for something; any something is a being and a substance (*ens, substantia*), and that means something good. Aristotle has already said that the good is that for which all hunger, and Thomas cites him.[10]

That *to be* is *to be good* is really the guiding thought for delineating a will that is desire rather than power, going *to* rather than *at* the object, wanting the object rather than the assertion of self, affirming another existence rather than seeking domination—the palatable version of will. For if being, insofar as it is, is good, then there is a reason for desirous reaching.[11]

As for the rationality of that appetite (where rationality covers both direct intellect and discursive reason), it means that desire occurs with a backing of knowledge such as distinguishes it from physical desire, which may be for an apparent rather than a real good. As the will seeks good, just so it shrinks from evil; hence the opposites, volition and nolition (*noluntas*) are a pair. The willing of ends and means is distinguishable, for an end can be willed without the means, but not the converse. This distinction is crucial to Thomas's theory of choice (*electio*). Choice is as specifically human as will. Animals and children choose voluntarily, but in the sense of "willingly" and by natural, sensory appetite, not by deliberation. Deliberation is the function of discursive reason, the procedural aspect of the practical intellect. Deliberation is never about ends but means, and though we may deliberate together, deliberation is, first, about our acting not jointly but severally, about things we can each do, and their possibility. Choice, then, is a melding of reason and desire; "election," preferential choice, involves both an understanding of desire and the converse, desire directing reason. Choice is not necessitated but free, in a double way: Humans can will to act or to abstain, and they can choose which option to take; they can decide whether or not to act and which possibility to prefer. The prime end is indeed necessary: happiness. Humans cannot will to be happy or unhappy; they *must* desire the former. Choosing is both more free and less significant than willing. Here willing, a participle, means "using the will," whereas willing, the adjective, means "being ready." The distinction is significant.[12]

(As I observed before, this, Thomas's—and Aristotle's—fundamental principle of human being and human action, that choice is of good, is, to me, very shaky. It is evolutionarily implausible that in the blip of species-time that has elapsed between Aristotle, Thomas, and us, human nature should have changed. But assuredly there are people now—and so, I suppose, there always were—who choose misery. It confounds speech utterly to say they enjoy their despair; it is not adolescent drama but a self-cocooning in unhappiness that I have in mind. Thomas himself knows such a character, the arch-demon himself, the devil, whose will is fixed on evil, loss of good. The motive for the insistence on happiness as the human end simply, starting with Socrates (for whom, however, it is not a will-choice), is not obscure: It provides the human complement to the ontological optimism inherent in classical philosophy; this affirmative ontology proscribes human unhappiness as a mistake or a perversion rather than admitting it as an intelligible way of being in the world. However, it may be that the invention/discovery of the will is exactly what made chosen despair, if not into a really new possibility, at least into a new soul-type.[13])

The clear distinction Thomas makes between means-directed choice and end-governed will seems to me a crucially missing element particularly in certain contemporary will-experiments, in which decision-making is taken for willing. The result, or rather the (perhaps unconscious) intention, is that the scope and dignity of the will is cut down to a quantifiable remnant. More of this later (Chs. X and XI, herein). For the moment, choice is, in summary, the employment of reason by the faculty of will to obtain a judgment about the best means (or intermediate ends) through which a willed end can be achieved. The choice is, narrowly speaking, the consequence of a reasoned conclusion. In modern terms: Choice is the end of a decision-making process.

What moves the will, what is its motivation (*motivum*), how does its motion originate? To begin with, its power is only potential, in two ways:

Its baseline is not to act at all, and it doesn't act in a specific way. Yet as a general power of willing the final end, the will is self-motivating, and it sets the other powers in motion.[14]

But as a specific desire, it is motivated by the intellect, which presents its object to it in its (mental) form. This latter is the will's "objective" (rational, internal) motivation; the former is its "subjective" (desirous, external) origination. But the human will can also be enticed by sensory desire. Thus in a human being mastered by a passion, the will can be overruled, which means that a sensory external object can move the will. In fact, however, though the will is self-moving "proximately" in its narrower setting, in a wider frame it needs a first mover, namely God. And though this may be as obscure as the Aristotelian physics that it follows, it seems to do justice to the phenomenon of willing: self-started yet also under other influences.[15]

Next, once in motion, what are its ways of going on to its end? Its first mode is simple volition; we want something like health or wealth. Second, the will has "intention," literally its "tending toward" something; this is willing on its way, passing through the immediate stages to its final terminus according to its plan of reason. The terminus is "fruition" (*fruitio*), enjoyment of the completed intention, the gaining of the aim. It is delight, the culmination of appetition; here the will is at rest. Full enjoyment is only in the ultimate end; there are subsidiary stations of delight where the will is not yet utterly at peace. Hence, there can be enjoyment along the way, when the end is possessed only in intention. For example, one may love what is yet absent, and that too is enjoyment.[16]

What seems to me especially worth noting in Thomas's view of the fulfillment of desire is that it is both rest for the will and enjoyment of its end. For us Americans, living under the auspices of our Declaration of Independence, happiness is a pursuit, both an occupation and a chase, rarely a fruition or enjoyment. ("Having fun," one might say, is the nation's active evasion of restful enjoyment.) There is an ancient tradition regarding pleasure-seeking as inherently incompletable and unfulfilling: The soul is, in that respect, a "leaky jar." Nothing I can think of more vividly describes the different between pleasure as a sensory excitation and happiness as a resting place of intellectual desire than Thomas's treatise on the will.[17]

There are three more topics left in this treatise: consent, use, command. "Consent" throws light on willing as an organized process, since the question arises just when it kicks in. The view of willing as a complex time-taking sequence seems to be a significantly missing element in contemporary will research, so it's worth dwelling on.

But first, what does Thomas mean by "consent"? Here he works on his own without Aristotle's guidance, for Aristotle's appetitive *boulesis* isn't quite will, a faculty; it's still close to wishing, an inclination.[18]

Thomas considers the literal meanings of assent and consent. Both mean "to sense," as in "having a feeling"—the first "towards" (*ad*) something, implying distance, the second "with" (*con*), implying union. He had earlier distinguished will, as going out to be with its object, from intellect, which draws it into itself. So consent is of the will as reaching out to be with the object; assent is of the intellect as bringing it in from a distance. Recall that Descartes will re-assign "affirming" to the will, which as it were, captures its object and brings it within—a motion more of rapacity than love. And yet even for Aristotle-Thomas, the intellect is ultimately moved to assent by the consenting will—but will as love rather than as captor.[19]

Consent then, is the setting of the appetite on one object, its definite application, its cleaving to a thing. The sensation involved, this being the higher appetite, is only *analogous* to the sense-arousal in the body or even in the imagination; it is nonetheless a certain inclination, a "bending toward" the object, an intellectual feeling-analogue. Consent is the application of appetite to something that lies in one's power. Then this is how consent fits into the "order of things transactable" (*ordo agibilium*): When the intellect apprehends the one primary end, happiness, the will's simple, inborn volition, its appetite for the good follows (no consent yet needed); secondary objects are recognized and desired; reason deliberates on the means; a choice is made; it arouses a more specific desire; here consent, a determination to do it, comes in—the last application of appetitive motion to the specific choice of means. The process may, however, go on because several choices may seem viable until a last choice is preferred and elected; the final act of the will is its use. In this process, intellect and will are tightly interwoven, each one acting on the other in turn.[20]

The question arises whether this impulse to consent belongs only to the higher appetite, the will, or also to sensual desire. It is of interest because it touches on the psychic location of the origin of sin in human beings, generally thought to be in sensory desire. Thomas, however, thinks that the *ultimate* responsibility for consent is in the higher reason or intellect of which, to be sure, the will is a part. He reinforces that later, by arguing that the voluntariness that attaches to sin indeed places it in the higher appetite. For while many actions pass into the material world, sin, like all moral actions, is an action that remains in the agent, that is in the non-sensory will. Here is presaged what will bloom into a truly terrific Protestant notion, perfected by Kant: that morality is a matter merely of will, wholly *internal* to the subject seeking self-justification. Speaking theologically: Only sin counts. Consequently the action in the world may be absurdly pure and *therefore* condemned to ineffectiveness, to wit Lutheran hesitations in the face of tyranny and Kantian extremism in pursuit of self-consistency. But for Thomas, while the sin and its morality stay within, the will in use goes determinedly without and turns toward human goods.[21]

Of course, the source of sin in the lower, the sensual temporal powers has to be dealt with, and Thomas has regard for these. The lower reason takes its own pleasure in its "cogitation" (recall that Descartes will borrow this term for all undifferentiated mentation), but will-inclusive intellect with its consenting pleasure is the final arbiter. Yet a passion of the lower appetite *can* influence the will, though only indirectly. One way is that, since the soul is one and all the faculties are rooted in its essence, when one part is too engaged, the others suffer from a depletion of their agency; there is a sum total of energy which is lessened when distributed (Freud's quantitative libidinal theory *in nuce*!). Another way is that the imagination, which leads the passions on, overwhelms the judgment of reason and makes people intractable.[22]

The last stage in willing is its "use" (*usus*), its application, its real operation, its execution. Use comes directly after choice, the determinism of means (where there are several), the last stage. Now the will operates as prime mover, reason as director of the operation, the bodily organs as instruments. Use is primarily and properly an act of the will, which extends through the lower bodily functions to the outside. And that use only goes outwards into the world, not backwards, up: God cannot be a theater of operations, and enjoyment in him is truly the will at rest.[23]

Where does the will fail? It appears to be vulnerable all along the process, and Thomas does not stress the last movement of execution; failure is possible anywhere in the chain. The importance of this long-term view of willing can be estimated by a comparison with Hobbes's dictum, "*Will therefore is the last appetite in deliberating*." In thus docking the process, willing becomes a link in a deterministic chain. Intelligibly free will is gone, for it appears—and this is to me the chief insight to be gained from studying the *Summa*—to be inherent in the *procedural complexity and temporal lengthiness* of human willing.[24]

This hypothesis is confirmed by the fact that "free will," a big topic in *On Truth*, is not given a question in the *Summa*'s "Treatise on the Will." To forestall confusion: "Free will" or "free choice" is the usual translation of *liberum arbitrium*; perhaps "free judgment" would be best, since that is how Thomas defines it elsewhere. "Choice" in the "Treatise" is *electio*, now a narrower notion fitted into the willing process as a choice of means. That pretty well explains the absence of *liberum arbitrium*: in thinking through the completed act of willing, the decision-judgment has shrunk to a stage and its freedom has expanded to a process. I repeat: The freedom of the will is developed in willing, and that is a long, complex action—a perplexing thought, for while it divorces psychic freedom from impulse, it also diffuses its manifestation.[25]

The last question of the "Treatise" deals with commands, and Thomas provides a surprise. Command is an act of reason rather than of will—or rather, an act of reason based on will. (He now speaks of "reason," presumably discursive reason rather than intellect.) Acts of reason and will bear on each other in turn. Still, command is essentially an act of reason, for a commander gives orders to a subordinate by means of a sentence articulating the thing to be done and then adds "Do it!" (In the old British navy a description of a maneuver was issued, followed in a moment by the order of execution: "Make it so!") Thomas regards both elements, the direction and the "bidding motion" (*intimativa motio*), as being an act of reason. The paragraphs setting out the interrelation, the "turn and turn about" (*invicem*), of the two powers, reach heights of convertibility: The will is the root of freedom (*radix libertatis*) . . . but the cause (*causa*) is the reason." The acts of these powers "are mutually reflexive" (*invicem reflectuntur*). Even though Thomas has already put reason in command over the will, he raises the tricky questions whether acts of the will *can* be commanded, or for that matter, acts of reason, and by which power. The answers are equally tricky: All that is in our power, that is voluntary, is subject to "our" command. "Our" (*nostra*) and later "man" (*homo*) is significant here. Thomas is appealing to the whole soul, in which all the powers work on behalf of all the others, not just for themselves. So a man commands the act of his own will because he is *both* an intelligent and a willing being, and the will is receptive to reason. (There is, however, a limit, for will cannot be commanded to turn from truth even by rationalizing reason.) Reason is free in focusing its attention and in exercising its various capacities as it will; whatever we do of thinking, we do by our command, for acts of reasoning *are* initiated freely. So not only will, but also reason, is free, namely in directing its attention; it has, so to speak, a will of its own—a directedness.

By the same token, our sensory appetite is under our control, and so it can be commanded, though here too there are limitations. They stem from the fact that the desire of the senses is the capacity of a bodily organ, unlike the "intellective" will that has no bodily seat. (Such a non-physical capacity is, of course, precisely what neuroscience will deny.) It is that physical underpinning which makes the lower desires partly intractable by the higher powers. Command fails completely for our "vegetative" soul (approximately like the bodily system we call "autonomic"). Control reappears in the external members, like the hands, yet fails again in the genitalia: the sin of the first parents has left those wholly to nature.[26]

Where in the chain of willing is the command link? It precedes use, the executive application of the will, for command is issued to the agency that is to do what has been chosen before the executive order has been given.

So here is the complete sequence of the stages that make up willing:

1. The intellect apprehends the primary end: happiness.
2. The will's simple inborn volition desires it, and if its object is God, it rests in complete enjoyment.

3. But the will also intends diverse objects of less consequence.
4. Reason deliberates about their preferability and the means for attaining each option.
5. Will makes a choice, an election, of options and means, perhaps in several rounds.
6. And consents, that is, applies an appetitive motion to the choice.
7. Reason commands the execution, articulating the plan and adding impetus.
8. Will executes.

The whole act of the Will is thus a continual interchange of intellect and will, apprehension and appetite.

(I submit that the above is a more complete a phenomenology, a more exhaustive account of the internal experience of willing, than any now in general circulation. Moreover it is, I think, verifiable by introspection, at least in the sense that an attentive observer may recognize some of the elements and concatenations. It makes one wonder how Thomas himself came by it—and how could that have been except by looking within? And that, in turn, raises the question how scientific, that is, laboratory research could ever proceed to capture the will except by means of an acutely detailed description of experienced inner processes. In any case it is remarkable to me that with a derivative philosophy, a scholastic vocabulary, and a theological agenda, Thomas should have been so able to make himself so plausible to a—willing—present-day reader.)

The Thomasion tale is not quite finished. Three underlying or overarching topics remain to be made explicit: Why do we have wills? Where lies the will's freedom? When does love come in?

This is Thomas's ontological account of the reason why the human being has a will—meaning what it is in human *being* that requires it. Substances—and human beings are the very exemplars of substantial, that is, individually real beings, namely rational animals—must have wills *since* they have intellect. For everything desires, hungers for good; the reason for that appetite must be (though I am not sure that Thomas says this explicitly) that God's creation being apprehensibly good, its creatures should be endowed with an affective inclination, a love towards it.[27]

So, once more, desire (*appetitus*) is universally directed to the good. Human desire, which belongs only to animals who are rational beings, has, as was said, a lower aspect, seated in the body. It in turn has two capabilities, a "lusting" part (*concupiscibilis*), which is very liable to corruption, and a "fierce" part (*irascibilis*, from *ira*, "anger"), which is nobler and more controllable by the higher will.[28]

This lower appetite is moved largely by external objects, as indeed are the propensities of natural things like stones which must seek the cosmic center and the lusts of brute animals, which must eat. But the thinking soul is in a large degree self-moved. For its movements issue from its own conceptions, thought up by itself, be it its self-understanding or in its planned actions. These latter arise analogously to the way a craftsman operates on matter according to the form he has conceived. So intellectual substances moving themselves to activity must have wills, for these are the motivation of movement; thus substances are masters of their own actions in plan and execution.

To the goodness of creation and the self-movement of rational creatures is added a third factor, the will's mode of desiring in accordance with its being seated in an intellectual being: Its desire proceeds from the good itself, a universal, for the will is incited, moved, by the forms presented to it by the intellect. And it is "proportionate," in adequate accord with what moves it, namely with the intellect's universality. Therefore it is not fixed on this or that good and is hindered by no natural prohibition opposing its proper freedom—its freedom to decide on this or that good.[29]

So here is the narrow crux of this freedom: it lies in the *liberum arbitrium*, in the freedom of decision among many *permissible* goods. I cannot keep from quoting here a saying of Bach (a faintly Catholic and very apt Protestant source): It is a musician's task "to make a well-sounding harmony to the honor of God and the *permissible delectation* of the soul"— my italics.[30]

This condensation of the sphere of freedom into one locus, namely choice in the sense of deciding judgment, arises as a consequence of Thomas's theological framework and has the effect of concentrating the inquiry. Both elements, cause and effect, taken together pose a danger to thinking about human freedom, one amply realized subsequently. The theology makes sense of will as *intellectual desire* for a good of goods, namely God. This will is not coerced but compelled, meaning that it is not *violated* by external force but that it is *voluntarily*, by self-compulsion, drawn to its one proper end, its true desire in which "true" and "good" coincide. It is an immensely influential notion—the basis of so-called compatibilism— that there can be voluntariness *within* determinism, will acceding willingly where there is no alternative, under compulsion.

But if the theology drops away, the higher will becomes unemployed, and freedom is pinpointed as decision making; the will becomes vacuous, no longer accepted as giving the soul a general direction, while freedom becomes abbreviated, concerned with essentially indifferent objects without reference to goodness; this is, indeed, the "will" that is most amenable to non-introspective research. It seems to me that Thomas's distinction between the compelling universal good and the indifferent particular goods—those that nature does not oppose—carries that outcome as a possibility within itself. But that is in the remote future.

As I observed, Thomas, who has been so copious on free decision in *Truth*, hardly gives it notice in his "Treatise on the Will" in the *Summa*. The reason is, I think, that there, in working out the psychic process of willing, he does indeed pinpoint a meaning of that choice called "election" as *one* moment in willing, that of a choice of means for achieving a selected end. However, from another, more fundamental perspective, freedom stands behind all willing, because God wanted man to be ultimately free—free to accept or reject good and also to have a secular sphere of ends contributing to, but not necessary for, happiness. Therefore the intellectual will has one compelling object, happiness in God, yet even with respect to that, it does have a sort of freedom, that of negation, a negative freedom: to reject it, and to turn itself away, to pervert itself.This is the larger sense Augustine writes of in his originating book, *De Libero Arbitrio*. From that aspect, the fact that the will also has the freedom to make decisions concerning less binding ends, of which there are many, is of much smaller consequence to our soul.[31]

What Thomas says about this topic of decision, that will most preoccupy later writers—and us, can be put under two headings: One is the narrower matter of choice, *free decision*, among different but somehow *indifferent* options that is a moment, already discussed, in the process of willing. The second is the larger issue of willing itself, of its *freedom* in the most ample sense, to become active toward a single, engaging goal that governs its activity as a whole—and in so governing willing, infects its every moment with freedom.[32]

First, free decision: How do we know we have it? We reason that God alone acts freely out of nothing, without condition and therefore without necessity. Nature, unfree, is all conditioned and so necessitated. Where there are extremes, there are means; therefore, man in the middle is the free agent who is also conditioned—and that describes choice. Moreover, there are commands, which would be mere instructions if man could not freely choose obedience and disobedience. Also, human actions are so unpredictably various that they must have multiple causation, namely choices. Finally, no sin can be identified or blame assigned if there has not been willful choice; anarchy would ensue.

How then does choice, decision, function? Intellect is bound by truth and will by good, but under the latter there are many indifferently good goods, which require selection from options as their accomplishment requires a choice of means. Moreover, although human beings are constrained both by impulsive passions and by ingrained habits, passions can be damped and habits can be broken, after proper pondering, by a decision of the intellect-informed will. Thus the root of freedom is in reason (which man alone in nature has), for reason freely judges not only the situation but its own judgment, and that is the sort of reflection that issues in free choice, free decision, *free judgment* (*liberum arbitrium*). Free choice is thus a subordinate power of the will that draws on judging reason to make the will capable of deciding, of *determining itself* to action.

Second, freedom itself: What is it? For this quest, a phenomenology of willing, occupied with its appearances, no longer suffices. A deeper inquiry is needed, concerned with the will's ontology, the account of the very being of the will. The basic assumption for this inquiry is all that went before: Human beings in fact originate action, and the process can be described. Thus freedom is an observed internal phenomenon, a fact; moreover if it were not a fact, there would be either total moral anarchy or complete natural determinism.

This is the will's constitution that makes it an agency of freedom. First, as *intellectual* desire, it shares in the intellect's capacities: Just as the universals of the intellect cover many particulars, so the universal object of the will is open to many particularizations. Hence the will as an intellectual power is free to specify itself. Second, the intellect's receptivity to the form of things acts, so to speak, *without*, going toward the object to pull in its form, and that yields being and truth; the intellect thus apprehends and therefore can place a good before the will. But the will as intellectual but staying *within*, simultaneously affects the intellect and puts the goal of its truth as a good before it; hence intellect feels: "I think because I *want* to." So as intellectual *desire*, will has bestowed affect on the intellect. Note that the motions of intellect and will described above are thus reversed—each shares in the other's.[33]

Thus the will puts all the soul's other abilities to work, and just so it moves *itself* through the whole reason-infused process of willing. This is not self-coercion, because as an *intellectual* will, it willingly moves in tandem with reason. But the will doesn't always will; to make a first movement, Thomas says, it needs an outside stimulus. That can't be a physical mover, but it must be something above it: God as the ultimate Good. Yet even this first mover does not coerce; he impels a motion but not the decision.

The goals that move the will by attracting it are both good and appropriate to the circumstances; in a particular setting a good can attract by its greater gravity (as health may be preferred to pleasure), by happenstance (because a person happens to think of it), or by disposition (since goals depend on who you are). These particular goods can in fact compel the will—but not to the exercise of the willing activity itself. Just as the intellect is compelled by necessary truths, the will is compelled by an object that can overpower the will itself, namely, the complete good, which belongs to happiness—but even here the will can escape by not thinking of it. Its ultimate power is that of self-renunciation, willful withdrawal.

It has, however, a complementary positive power. It can move itself—because it is a co-power of the intellect and mirrors its capacities, one of which is self-knowledge, reflexivity; thus, sympathetically, as it were, *the will can even will itself.*

The above may seem more like a description than an analysis, but in fact it contains enough to attempt a sketch of what enables the will to be free and where its freedom lies and, hence, what it is.

As encompassed by the reasoning power, again as *intellectual* will, it can conceive positives and negatives, affirmation and denial: consent and dissent. As intellect, once more, it can distinguish a multitude of particulars under universals; its universal is the Good, and under it, it can conceive the many goods that the world offers. These two capabilities together ground the possibility of choice.

As in turn embracing the intellect, as intellectual *will*, will that suffuses reason, it has the structure of desire, which is the affect of affects. This structure delineates and delimits the freedom of the will quite precisely—that is what makes Thomas's treatment so determinative.

Desire is the affect that is both passively excited by a good and incited actively to go for it. It is said that the overarching object of desire is the good of goods, as if that were a synthetic judgment, one where the predicate "good" says something new and interesting about desire. In fact, it's just an analysis of the meaning of desire: this affect, when sound, is constitutionally positive about its object. To want *is* to want good; variety, error, harm come later as degradations of will. For Thomas, the supreme good inherent in desire is God; so it is for Aristotle. To possess this good is happiness, and that implies the other feature of desire: an acquisitive, go-getting element. It might help to recall here that Thomas's will *is* desire for a good; it is *not* an impulse to be active in the world, be it by re-constructing or wrecking it—sometimes to identical effect.[34]

The good, as inherent to desire, is as compelling to the will as truth is to the intellect, and as God, it stands behind the whole willing process: In this aspect will is love, the last topic.

Thus will is, as was said, thoroughgoingly compelled, though not coerced. Coercion, once again, is violent; compulsion finds the will willing. Compulsion effects the will's voluntary reception of what it inherently desires. But it is not freedom (and this confusion between voluntariness and freedom bedevils contemporary compatibilism). Indeed, at the lower end, when intellectual will turns into sensual desire, coercion is sometimes present. The body-bound desires don't allow much freedom of escape—except perhaps that of taking a therapeutic trip, the age-old prescription against love gone wrong.

Where then is the freedom? Well, it would be largely defensive freedom: the freedom not to will, for even God does not require *that* human beings will, only *what* they must will—happiness. The will can, as was said, refuse to will. This is the will's freedom, not to exercise its power—*not to will*, to omit to go out to its good, as distinct from the will *to not-will* (*nolere*), to decline, to say no.

But it also has a second freedom, the one people focus on most because they experience it daily. This is the freedom of choice made possible by the will's intellect, by its ability to conceive particular goods and to say yes or no to them. In this respect the will sets an end, determining itself in the three ways set out above: gravity, chance, and predilection, since the goods before it all are all passably good. Since the process is getting close to execution, means have to be decided on, and this is the notorious free decision—a very curtailed but also a very concrete freedom, perhaps scarcely worth the fuss made over it. In any case, "free choice" seems a redundant locution; to have choice, options, is to be free to prefer and pick one over the others, and there is a mode of the intellect that does the job. This is deliberation, an ability not of establishing ends but of finding and choosing means. Strictly speaking then, it isn't even the will as will but as intellect that decides, but then again, since judgment here does not look to the true but to the better, it is judging as will after all. Wherein lies the freedom here? It is in the non-necessity, the contingency, the variety of possibilities of the outcome. This sort of rationality is free from strong pushes and raises a liberating sense of non-coercion. Moreover, the decision is close to execution, and so it has the feel of a powerfully free practical act, especially when it co-opts the body.

There is a third, the most intimate freedom of the will, its self-movement. We can will to will and at each stage rev up the will to act. It is, as I said, a capacity analogous to self-knowledge in the intellect, but it is also a familiar feature of desire: the desire of desire, the longing to be full of affect. So the will willingly moves itself, assents to itself as willing.

Freedom, then, as explicitly delineated by Thomas, is a thoroughly delimited, intermediate property of the will. From above we are—normally willingly—compelled by the good inherently sought by the intellectual will; from the bottom we are—frequently unwillingly—coerced by the pleasures similarly sought by physical desire. In between, the will as a whole can *not* will, be supine, just as the human intellect can not think. That is freedom because it is in our power, but it is negative. At one of its stages, it has the opportunity to decide because it has begun to intend (which is a kind of pre-choice) a particular end and is now, almost at one with the intention, presented with a choice of means. That is freedom simply as the lack of necessity inherent in a plethora of options. (For more on the issue of choice as the locus of freedom, its bearing on contemporary views, and on "indifference" of the will, see Note 35 to this chapter.)[35]

Finally, and fourth is the *real* freedom: The will is self-moving and is free to move the other powers. This self-motivation is compatible with the compulsion exercised over it by the thought-objects presented to it by the intellect, because the will as intellectual is, after all, itself that intellect. It is also compatible with the will's attraction to the real object, for as the intellect deals with things as they are known in the soul, the will meets them as they are in themselves—good. It goes out to them and sometimes acts on them in reality. The compulsion of their attraction is thus received voluntarily; it is the compulsion of the object of desire, which is willingly undergone. This intimate freedom is essentially being at one with one's own; it is the interiority Thomas values. The ground of this ultimate and genuine freedom is, I think, the mutual embrace of intellect and will, though Thomas does not say so. This oscillating figure—analysis of the soul being inevitably ambiguously figurative—displays the reciprocal involvement that is tantamount to a mutual self-reflection of the chief powers of the soul; this facing-mirror language is unavoidable.[36]

Why exactly should that be freedom? Because under the non-violent compulsion of God's will (which *is* his own goodness), human will is its own mover; it is moved not through an object but as a subject, as a self-starter of its own activity. And that is Thomas's (and Aristotle's) understanding of freedom for a human being: to be *causa sui ipsius*, "cause of oneself," and free from another's coercion; for the intellectual soul, it is precisely to have as another self a will that can move it to activity. As far as I can tell, Thomas himself never puts the adjective "free" with "will" (that would be *libera voluntas*). I think, however, that the narrow "free decision" is only that most concrete willing where a choice of object is implied. The real freedom of the will is what distinguishes it from its Siamese twin, the intellect: its self-control. This characteristic is—somewhat opaquely to the understanding but very plausibly as an experience—connected to one of the features that distinguishes will from intellect: its tending out towards the thing itself in its reality so as to attain it. Hence, without self-control, the will could become grievously aggressive.

Will and intellect are, then, interpenetrating complements, economies of activity and receptivity, rendering the soul inwardly alive as continually motivated to think and the human being outwardly active in gathering forms as the intellect requires and achieving possession as the will directs—a will that is only as lovingly aggressive as is in keeping with intellectual desire—the desire for a perfectly common good.

Love, like freedom, is not an explicit topic of the "Treatise on Will," though enjoyment, the will's attainment of its end, either in present reality or prospective intention, is. Love is locally absent, I think, because it is ever-present, behind all willing. The unique and universal good, God, is known as the supreme Good only indirectly, for in this embodied life we cannot behold him immediately. But once known in the intellect, the thing itself that moved the intellect intermediately now moves the *passive* affections immediately. This direct love is, I suppose, outside the frame

of the "Treatise on Will," which is part of "Human *Acts*." Moreover both
at the upper and the lower end of desire, the "appetible" object needs to
enter, and this Treatise is not about objects but about the human subject
(in our terms).[37]

The "Treatise on the Passions," however, does speak of love and its objects. Love is seated in both sensory (passionate) and intellectual (quasi-
passionate) appetite, since the object of both is the good. In fact, as tending
to some good, it is a pervasive presence in the soul and the initiating impulse of every desirous passion—passion, because there is a sense in which
intellectual appetite is a passion, an affect as much as a faculty. This duality is figured in the circular motion of love: First, the object of love moves
desire by working itself into its purposive conception (*in eius intentione*)—
that is the passive mental reception of the object, the affect. Then desire
reaches out to the object to obtain it in reality—and that is the active reciprocal work of will. Love proper forms the receptive part of the circle, the
willed completion of which produces union. So objects of love move the
will as affect, as desire, in the first part of the cycle, and as faculty, as actor,
in the second part.[38]

The will here delineated is, then, as I've said, a kinder, gentler one than
the dominating power of Augustine, Descartes, and the two theologians
still to come in this chapter—or of later moralistic will-breakers. It is not
a mental clenched fist, nor an expansionist invader of cognitive territory.
It lives in mutual embrace with reason. It is an "imperative" power but not
imperiously so, for it does not command but functions simply as a moving
power, motivatingly. In attempting to reach down into the body not as a
totalitarian ascetic but as a wise director, it is sometimes defeated, depleted
by physical passion, be it lust or anger. It sometimes turns away from its
proper good above, but being a human and not a devilish will, it does so
more in truly sorrowful obstinacy than in perverse delight; contra Augustine, Thomas thinks that "evil cannot be intended by anyone for its own
sake." In accordance with its title, "rational *desire*," it is, as intellectual love,
probably as much a quasi-passionate affect as a power.[39]

B. Duns Scotus: Rational Will

In terming Duns Scotus, an extremist I could not possibly mean that he
is an irrationalist of the will. He is much more attached to strictly logical
argument than Thomas (which is why I am more attached to Thomas than
to Scotus). What I mean is that he raises the will above the intellect and—
ipso facto—diminishes its scope to decision.[40]

Scotus goes into his treatment of the will by way of this primary truth:
"Some being is contingent." First principles are not deducible, because they
themselves have no adequate ground: Those who deny this one "should be

subjected to torments until they concede that it is possible for them not to be tortured."[41]

Contingency is a member of the logical disjunction "necessary : contingent," which cannot be shown to belong to being by any prior understanding; nor is "contingent" in any way demonstrable from "necessary." Hence instead of going back behind the disjunction (here meaning a pair of terms which are opposed), one must look to consequences. Without contingency the future would be fixed and deliberation idle. That shows what contingency is: In its effect, for us, it's unforeseeableness. In its own nature, in itself, it's causelessness. In God, as understood by us, it can only be a "perfect causality," that is, the operation of a first cause that acts immediately, without a chain of humanly apprehensible, lawfully acting, general intermediate causes.

Scotus argues that this first-and-immediate causation must reside either in God's Intellect or in his Will. (These two attributes are known to us as creatures in their imperfect form and attributed to God with their imperfections removed.) But there cannot be contingency in the Intellect, for as in humans, so in God it is a "natural power" that must obey the truth: It apprehends by a "natural necessity"; it is not a "free power." That free power, then, must be the Will.[42]

To see how the divine will acts, Scotus looks at the human will, though it works less perfectly. Now the human will is *free*, free to choose to do this or its opposite, about this or its opposite object, to this or the opposite effect; moreover it has the power of opposites in willing and not willing at two successive moments (though not at the same moment, for that thought "is nothing," unthinkable). And even if one imagined a will so created as to act only once, in one single moment, it would still be free, for its contingency is not bound to a prior moment.

God's Will differs from human will in that, instead of needing diverse acts of volition for diverse objects, it can reach them all at once; it has the perfect freedom of a simple, unlimited volition. Furthermore, while the divine Will has a relation of necessity toward the divine essence, it is disposed to everything else contingently, so that prior to the act of willing it can elicit from itself either of two opposite acts—as we do, but more extensively. It has this power both logically and really. And so contingency is not some privation or defect but "a positive mode of being."[43]

The will is totally the moving cause of its own willing and is most specifically free, for the argument that mover and moved must be distinct holds only for bodies, not for immaterial things. And the argument that will is an appetite and thus receptive rather than effective forgets that "free" is its most intimate property, more defining than any other because it is a highly specifying attribute. In sum then, if what happens contingently is the avoidable—without which, once again, deliberation would be pointless—then willing itself is contingent. For willing is precisely decid-ing for one of two opposites from a cause undetermined to one or the other, that is to say, by a *free* will. Thus indeterminacy, contingency, and freedom come together in our agency for deciding between two opposites.[44]

I'll take this moment to contrast Scotus on the will with Thomas. Sco-tus has, so to speak, broken the mutual embrace of intellect and will, got-ten them out of each other's hair. Thus disentangled, the will is truly on its own. The downside is that it then becomes unclear how the preservation of deliberation as the antecedent of thoughtful decision can now be used as an argument for free will. For with the decoupling so complete and the will undetermined through to the last moment, practical judgment really has no way to get into the act: The more willful our willing is, the less thoughtful it is—and the more god-like. Furthermore, Scotus condenses willing, which for Thomas was a time-extended, articulated process, into the very moment of decision. But freedom is contingency—avoidability— and that turns into necessity once the will acts, which means that it has determined itself. Moreover that action is not a sort of choice among mul-tiple good ends plus a real choice of the best means, but a constricted choice between opposites: that or not that. This has an odd consequence: pre-cisely by reason of dividing the universe of discourse into a position and its negation, its logical complement, any choice is apt to turn into a global dilemma—"to be or not to be." There is then no room for voluntariness, for the will's willing submission to a command in accord with its desire. And in fact, for Scotus it is only the will that commands, whereas, recall, Thomas regards thought as commanding; for the latter the will decides on intellect's command.[45]

What is the will's basic nature, then? First, the will has a twofold "incli-nation," a double bias that might be thought of as what is left of will as a higher desire. In its duality it is inward-turned, toward its own self-per-fection and self-actualization—self-will, which is less noble than its com-plement, the bent toward justice, an "inborn liberty" (*ingenita libertas*) for willing some good beyond itself. It is not clear to me how a truly undeter-mined will can coincide with congenital biases; I suppose that by belonging to a free will they are *ipso facto* compatible with its freedom.

There is also consideration of a "natural will" (*voluntas naturalis*) and its willing. Under this heading, Scotus all but admits that will is no longer immediately appetite; he speaks of will as "properly understood" as, or as "under the general mark" of appetite. So also, "natural will" is "not a will nor its natural willing," because "natural" cancels "will." "Natural" is just the relation a power has to its perfection as free, and "free" is what the will is intrinsically and specifically. Natural will is, then, not a power, but just the will's tendency, its inclination to receive passively (*passive recipiendum*) what perfects it. This passivity raises just the perplexity noted above, how it is compatible with freedom.

Happiness now becomes a problem. If the will is free, it should be able to reject happiness, which was, recall, non-coercively but voluntarily compelling for Thomas. But Scotus too recognizes that the (natural) tendency of will is to happiness. His solution seems to me, at first, a lame compromise and, on consideration, actually according to experience: To begin with, misery is just not a suitable object for willing or happiness for nilling. Will can, however, by its perfectly proper, "elicited" act, *will* without reference to happiness at all, by ignoring, evading it, so to speak, or by having other things in mind. But the natural tendency underneath is always really toward happiness. What Scotus has gained here is in accord with an observably human possibility: There are people who don't have happiness in their sight, who are miserable by a kind of negative volition (as distinct from those who are out of luck in life) but who sometimes manage to keep alive a desire for happiness and consequentially earn the moments of its achievement.[46]

That is Scotus on the will as an appetite for ends. Now more toward its free center, its ontology: Scotus references two "potencies" (*potentiae*) or rather one, with two different modes of action. In the first mode, it is called "nature." Nature cannot fail to act in its determined way, unless externally impeded. In the second, it remains undetermined and can either act or not, or act in this way or the opposite—and this potency or power is will and its willing. That the will wills thus is not a conclusion, for as was said, its contingency is not deduced necessarily from a necessity. The "cause" is simply, immediately, that the will is will. If there is a proof of freedom it is *a posteriori*, from what follows, namely, our experience. (As we come up to modernity, this experiential proof, this reliance on "that's the way it feels," becomes more and more, if not questionable, yet questioned. Among neuroscientists it is apt to be devalued under "folk psychology." It is the question of questions for our future, who will win this battle to make internal experience count, the folk or the experts.)

The indeterminacy of the will is not, then, an imperfection, a lack, but rather a "superabundant sufficiency," that of not being bound to a predetermined act. And so is solved an Aristotelian quandary: that all want happiness in general but often don't choose it in particular. Scotus thinks the will contingently wills both in general and in particular and mostly for happiness—but that is by its natural inclination. In other words, general happiness does not compel as an object. But, as I said, Scotus stops short of leaving the will positively free to will misery. The argument seems to me lame. It is interesting that in the pursuit of the essence of will's freedom, the appetitive relation to happiness always butts in.

What, finally, is this will's relation to intellect from the aspect of its own being? The will, being pleased (*voluntate complacente*) with one or the other of the intellect's notions, turns to it, and so intensifies it, while directing the intellect to focus on it: It joins parent (intellect) to offspring (knowledge) and concentrates intellect on (or averts it completely from) an object. As far as intellect's activation is concerned, will is fully in command.

Scotus, then, establishes a will that is really neither given to voluntariness, meaning a willing passivity in the face of a comprehensive good, nor to cooperation with, and in its turn, submission to the intellect, nor to an extended process of willing. Instead, it is self-activated in absolute freedom understood as contingent "causation" (albeit mitigated by certain natural tendencies), situated in a position of command toward the intellect (with respect to its selection of object), and concentrated in the single act of decision (in which deliberation has a dubious part).

I have ranged Scotus among the extremists. Perhaps it would be fairer to call him an enabling forerunner of extremists.

C. Ockham: Absolute Will

First among whom is William of Ockham. In my early life as an archaeologist, I observed, and myself obeyed, the custom that the more fragmentary the find, the more extended the publication—a pot got a page, but a sherd got two. That ought to be the case for Ockham, for though he says comparatively little about the will, that little is part of a true revolution—which to explicate here goes beyond my plan and indeed my powers.[47]

Nonetheless, because his way of thinking, called "nominalism" from its central feature, is so boldly new and so prolongedly "influential," but also so coherent, my account of the human will must be thoroughly enmeshed in it, and I shall draw on its features as I go. (Note 48 to this chapter treats "influence" a little more extendedly.)[48]

The Will of God is the all-determining beginning of nominalism, which is, for all its novelty, first and last, a theology. Ockham was indeed later thought of as a *modernus*, and the founder of Ockhamism and its *via moderna*, the "modern way," was characterized as opposing the *via antiqua* of the ontological realists. To be sure, he presented himself as living in the tradition, but he ended up being excommunicated. How could so independent a thinker not know his place in the scheme of things?[49]

In beginning with God's Will, I am following Aristotle's distinction between what is more knowable for us and what is more knowable in itself and am supposing that a theologian might well begin with the latter. Though for all I know, Ockham may, on the contrary, have arrived at his understanding of the divine Will by analogizing the higher to the lower, God's Will to the created will; they are indeed each other's image. It is an undeterminable private, psychological question. I am speaking loosely here to express my sense that a great logician will not, professionally, reveal the groping motivations behind his thinking. In fact, this one decries the use of analogy as a cognitive method in general (because of the ultimate individuality of things) and for the knowledge of God in particular (because God is even more radically diverse from us then we are from each other). The question arose for me because I asked myself how Ockham can know that God *has* a will. More of that below.[50]

God is absolutely powerful, or put in terms of powers attributed to him, he has a will unconstrained by anything but one logical impossibility, self-contradiction. But, since in a universe that has no natural laws (laws obedience to which is inherent in created beings), whatever is not impossible may become actual. That is to say, this dictum may be *at once* a formulation of total contingency and an acknowledgment of God's absolute power—really *absolute*: absolved from every obligation or dependency. For the absence of natural law normally intervening between God and his operations means that he can and might do anything at any time, and that every intuited fact is radically individual, not threaded on a chain of cause and effect (although human logic does relate thoughts to each other by a rational causality). Recall that for Scotus, God has an essence and ideas that his will is bound to; not so for Ockham. Essences and ideas are gone; that is what "nominalism" means: the doctrine that universals such as species, once regarded as ideal beings (be they mental or extra-mental), now exist as nothing but names—as we say, "nominally." What is so named is the abstractive act by which the understanding collects similar objects and settles them together in the mind under a name.[51]

The nominalistic God is not directly knowable. There is no intuitive, evidential, distinct knowledge of him. So we are largely left to speak of him in negative or connotative (oblique, indirect) terms. The identity of God's Will and Intellect must be so spoken of, among other reasons, because there is no divine essence, such as was for Scotus the ground on which the divine Intellect produced ideal natures, marked to distinguish its work from that of the Will for us. Instead, for Ockham, God's Will-Intellect acts in two direct ways: It wills and knows itself necessarily—that is God's one logically necessary act, that he will and know himself to be a will—and everything else contingently, all at once.[52]

The implications are tremendous, perhaps, more precisely, terrific. They prefigure the Reformation. For the whole burden of the human relation to God is now in simple, image-less non-intellectualized faith—none of Thomas's "faith seeking understanding" with its implication that knowledge strengthens faith. So now, if the nominalist's bare faith fails, everything fails—unless the human being can be made to stand in for God as an exemplar of thinking and willing being identical. So this nominalist-trained human being will in turn be willfully creative—exhilaratingly emancipated and anxiously thrown on himself, self-willed and atomic. For in his freedom, the post-theological God-less nominalist is also alone—there is no fellowship in suffering. As Ockham has said of creatures: They have no common essence, and God can annihilate any man without destroying another, so a poet will say of the world: "The world does not hear the cry of leaves that do not transcend themselves."[53]

But to backtrack: First, why does Ockham so simplify God's nature? The answer is deep in Ockham's future-fraught way of going about things. A predecessor might meditate on God first and worry about the knowing later, if at all, but Ockham establishes a rule for attending to understanding first. It is the antecedent of the modern way: first epistemology, and only then, knowledge-theory permitting, ontology, an account of being. To be sure, once again, it seems that there is no way to tell whether he had the sort of vision that sees a world of starkly lit, hard-edged individual beings and wanted to devise a universal knowledge that would both preserve and order those atomic beings, or whether he was tired of the scholastic paralogisms and equivocations accreted around ideal beings and intelligible species. In either case, the result was that he moved front and center an old guide for giving accounts of things: Reduce entities, "for it is vain to do through many what can be done by fewer"—it being finally unclear whether this principle of parsimony is dictated by taste or truth. (One might, after all, side with conceptual plentitude.) In any case, species are a first casualty, but so is God's duality of will-intellect, as well as his Trinity—both safe beyond cognition, as matters of faith.[54]

Second, how can God's own radically free will, which is expressed in the total contingency of his creation, be reconciled with 1.) his own foreknowledge and 2.) with real human freedom? The answers, though surrounded with logical subtlety, are: 1.) It is without doubt, it is a matter of faith, that God's Will remains completely free and contingent and also that he foreknows human actions completely. However, a conjectural explanation of these apparent incompatibilities lies in his kind of intuitive knowledge, all-at-once knowledge. 2.) One might be tempted to say that human beings depend on God's contingent Will for the freedom of their own will because, as soon as God determines his will, they cannot help but "coact," in accord with his omnipotence. But that cannot be, because then "all merit and demerit are done away with," which is absurd; humans must be free. When all is said and done, "to explain this evidently . . . is impossible for any intellect in this life."[55]

So, finally, where does that leave human will, under God? Ockham regards a human being as plural: rational soul, sensing soul, body. Or rather, Ockham is willing to accede to such common and orthodox opinions as—sometimes questionable—hypotheses. For example, by natural reason and intuitive, direct, self-knowledge, we would never come to the notion of an incorruptible soul separable from the body; there is no experience of a soul-substance, but we may talk that way. Nor is it evident that, in the rational soul, intellect and will are distinct. We are each one person who thinks and wills, and to this one being both sorts of acts are to be referred. That is the duality we do experience, so we name the items.[56]

Our free will too is evident from our experience—and *entirely undemonstrable*. Psychic freedom (*libertas*) is just what theological freedom was: the power to do different things indifferently and contingently, so that conditions being the same, we can cause opposite effects. Human free will is felt to be as causeless as God's was thought to be uncaused. Our human experience is that, though reason may dictate an action, the will can will it or not.[57]

(It would take great courage to question Ockham's logic, but it takes mere alterity to doubt his experience. The introspective "we" he appeals to is, in any case, a dubious court. Inner life, aside from intellect, is not where our commonality mainly lies, and to infer from the first person singular to the first person plural is what scholastics called the fallacy of composition: arguing from parts (one human being) to the whole (humanity). Is it really everyone's experience that the soul is *not* separable from the body? I, for one, have been miserable with a splitting headache but joyful over a letter received—or what is worse, felt myself luxuriating in the flesh and anxious in the spirit. Is it really the case that, when the time comes to act, the power of decision—call it "making up one's mind," and it is the project of this book to figure out what that is—is to the last instant contingent? Or is it rather that the progressive, time-extensive diminution of contingency by the compulsion of passion and thought down to a moment of necessitating conviction is just what freedom is?)

Ockham on psychology in general and the will as a psychic power is curiously spare—though copious on the will's involvement in morality. It makes me wonder whether my earlier conjecture, that he gets to God's Will by analogy to the human will, isn't plain wrong—as he himself argues (albeit he sometimes forgets it). Perhaps for a human being like Ockham, indefeasibly his own man, his soul now disporting itself in logical subtleties and now reposing in absolute faith, God's nature *is* more present than his own natural affects. The more devastating for those conscious or unconscious Ockhamists, in whom faith has failed![58]

Finally, what of the ethical consequences? The will here is everything (as, I have pointed out, it will again be so for Kant in a most vigorous but very different way). There are human actions that are natural to us (though not as proceeding, lawlike, from our nature but as—contingent—facts of our existence), and others we perform by God's direct causation in us. The latter are not done freely and are therefore not imputable to us. Indeed, all conceivable actions can be performed in this mode, and they are all morally neutral. No action, then, is *in itself* virtuous or vicious—only an act done with good or bad intention, that is, one done by the power of the will, can be given a moral mark.

Now to some detail. Ockham, in fact, does not believe the will to be quite as free as Scotus does. For one thing it is, after all, under God's power to determine—if the human being adheres to God. Second, "right reason," prudence, the application of intelligence to action, can determine the will to some degree, as can habit. Moreover, the will's action is not completely undifferentiated. It sometimes experiences a first movement, an unsuppressible impulse (such as the Stoics observed). Yet ultimately the will is free; it can always reverse itself. The principle of parsimony, *the* nominalistic motive, requires, however, that this freedom should not be accorded an independent reality. Freedom is a term that names just the will's power to "elicit," to bring about its own acts; it *is* the will. Willing *expresses* itself as freedom.

Where Ockham goes to greater extremes than his predecessors is, as I intimated, in making the virtue or vice of a human act, whatever the circumstances, ultimately a matter of the quality of the will: "No act is virtuous or vicious unless it is voluntary and in the power of the will." So no act has merit in itself; it is the "intention" of the will that makes it so. (This is surely proto-Protestantism.) The will must knowingly act, and that means "according to right reason," which dictates the manner of practice, and prudence, which provides the good end. Will needs these intellectual powers just because its freedom needs direction—but it is nonetheless not determined by the intellect. For prudence itself is an object of the will, which thus retains its near-perfect freedom.[59]

On the other hand, though the goodness or badness, that is, the meritoriousness or blameworthiness, of human beings comes entirely from the will, no deeds being intrinsically meritorious, God's Will is total in this too: that only God's acceptance or rejection makes them so. This evident paradox is resolved by a complex understanding of God's grace, which is beyond my interest here. In any case, although the ultimate attribution of virtue or vice rests in the will's quality, this is not complete moral subjectivity, because ends, objects, do matter. (Yet it *can* flip into the dissolution of morality, into ultimate self-will, if the objects lose their standing or God is thought to be morally antic.) Again, Ockham has very subtle theological distinctions to resolve this paradox, but it lingers.[60]

What then is the good object and what is sin? The object is clearly God and the love of him. And sin, again, is a term denoting nothing, no real or mental thing; it is simply the will's act of commission, or rather of omission—namely omitting, refusing, to love God. The created will is indeed perfect in its freedom to do that.[61]

A notorious example: *Deus potest praecipere quod voluntas creata odiat eum*, "God has the power to bring it about that the created will hate him." This is pure paradoxical willfulness on the part of God's absolutely free will. But the very love of God determines the human will to obey, and this obedient "hatred is then not in itself a sin."[62]

This daringly extreme case, censured by the authorities, encapsulates everything: the primacy of the will's one determinative end, love of, expressed as obedience or disobedience to, God; the total authority of God; the non-intrinsic goodness or badness of an actual deed; the dependence of that valuation on the will's intention, whether it determines itself to obey God—and finally, not expressed but perhaps intimated, the creature's ultimate ability to say no even to God and, who knows, even to win God's acceptance by this display of freedom. But this last is my fantasy.[63]

What, finally, is it about Ockham that makes him, for all the patient subtlety of his logic—requiring an answering patience which a modern *moderna* finds it hard to summon—so impressive, so "impending"—I think that is the right word—so future-fraught? It is, I imagine, his extremism, by which I mean something very particular: a position that, if one element fails (here, God) the whole falls into a desperate opposite: individualism into atomic aloneness, contingency into terminal insecurity, divine authority into human tyranny, obedience into slavery, and free will into bottomless willfulness. But as I've said, "influence" being so protean a notion (see note 48), these consequences are not listed by way of imputing guilt to Ockham but from a certain sense of awe. Being a great believer in specific examples, I shall end by offering the uncanny case of an ostensible relation which it would, I imagine, take a lot of research to verify. Romantic extremism is fairly described in terms of "two elements—the free untrammeled will and denial of the fact that there is a nature of things . . ." Now how did these Romantics come to echo Ockham?[64]

So, next, the Catholic, the universal, faith has fallen apart in the world, and two representative contenders about the consequences for the freedom of the will, Erasmus and Luther, will join battle—though "join" is too connective a word for their differences; what is gone is the remarkably respectful detailed attentions that the scholastics, Ockham above all, accorded to their opponents. Wherefore these two antagonists will go into a Note.[65]

chapter **I V**

Will Reduced

A. Hobbes: Last Moment

Hobbes writes with the brusque beauty befitting his reductive philosophy. By "reductive" I mean "nothing but" philosophizing: "For seeing life is but a motion of limbs . . . , why may we not say that all *automata* have an artificial life? For what is the *heart*, but a spring; and the *nerves*, but so many *strings* . . . ?" That is an abbreviation of the second and third sentences of the *Leviathan*, from a "nothing but" introduction if ever there was one.[1]

Accordingly, this is Hobbes's view of the will:

> [T]he whole sum of desires, aversions, hopes, and fears continued until the thing be either done, or thought impossible, is what we call DELIBERA-TION . . . In *deliberation*, the last appetite, or aversion, immediately adhering to the action, or to the omission thereof, is what we call the WILL, the act, not the faculty of *willing* . . . [t]he definition of the Schools, that it is *rational appetite* is not good. For if it were, then could there be no voluntary act against reason . . .

Thus, will is understood just as "the last appetite in deliberation," and so it is nothing but the last in a series of affections just before action or inaction.

As the chain of alternate appetites "in the question of good and evil" (these never being in an object but only in human opinion) is called "deliberation," so the chain of alternating opinions "in the question of true and false" is called "doubt." Thus one might say, drawing on Hobbes's analogy, that will puts a stop to waffling appetites and aversions, whose common name is "passion." His theory of motion says that these begin as small *non-*figurative motions (for the metaphorical psychic motions of the Scholastics are "absurd"). They issue from the imagination's "decaying sense," remnants of sensation. Internal motions are, in other words, bodily, though beneath our awareness. An endeavor, when it is toward something which causes it, is called an "appetite." In Hobbes's materialistic psychology, the will must therefore be a kind of counter-impulse, a resultant of the preceding back-and-forth—as Hobbes says, a sum of passions and counter-passions, as if each passion-moment had a sort of reactive elasticity. (I say "resultant," but I cannot tell whether the stop-motion will is in fact the *outcome* of a developing conclusion or a mere *term* in an undirected succession of moments—probably the latter, since, *if anything*, mere force is being transmitted.) As the sequence ends, it "undoes liberty"—his etymology of the word "de-liberation" (a false one—the origin is in *libra*, "scales" for weighing). It needs saying that "the last appetite" differs from "the most desirable" theory of choice, with which it has been lumped. Hobbes' "last appetite" has the virtue peculiar to brutely mechanical arguments—it is utterly unequivocal. "The most desirable" as determining choice, on the other hand, leads to question-begging. Whatever deciding motive is offered, from self-aggrandizement to self-sacrifice, can equally be claimed to have been "the most desirable," because *in a way* it must have been; after all, that's where it ended up. But everything lies in that: In *what way*, with *what sort* of desiring? One might forego what one desired most fervently for what seemed right. And then the "greatest desire" theorist would just claim that *that* was what one desired. Well, it was and it wasn't.[2]

I might point out here that there are enough extreme Ockhamist elements in Hobbes reductive philosophy to justify letting him follow right on that Scholastic, whom he must have, if he read him, despised least of the lot: There is the aversion to superfluous terms, for example, metaphysical universals as "insignificant," that is, meaningless; there is a God who is introduced in the first sentence of the book as creating by fiat a world that is an artifact, employing nature as "the art whereby [he] hath made and governs the world . . . ," that is to say, as a willful, self-ordained procedure—a mode of creativity well-suited to a God of contingency, himself free to the last but pleased to make a mechanical artifact of a world; there is Hobbes's belief in the radical atomism of human beings who, in the absence of an overarching power, are always, each with each, at war; there is his theory that "accidents" of bodies are that abstract name by which the mind conceives a system of causes connecting bodies.[3]

So far Hobbes's treatment of will has the brisk, positive style I have ascribed to him, and that because it is how he conceives the thing itself. But there is another, lengthier writing, in the negative mood. Hobbes was invited by a patron to join a debate on human freedom, which turned into an extended controversy. Hobbes was against free will, enunciating what is now called a determinist and compatibilist position, and I shall consider only his side, which has more force—as distinct from greater truth.[4]

His antagonist, the Bishop Bramhall, had written: "If I be free to write this discourse, I have obtained my cause." This is the standard appeal to the *fact* of free action. Hobbes answers that, to be sure, he is free to do a thing who can do it if he so wills. But the question is not whether a man is a free agent, can act or here write, according to his will, but whether he is free to will, whether "the will to write or the will to forbear can come upon him according to his will." He has the liberty to do as he will, but whence comes the will? "[T]o say that I can will if I will, I take to be an absurd speech."[5]

This absurdity is exactly what the Scholastics accept: the reflexivity of the will, its power over its own action. This is where Hobbes, after all, parts decisively from Ockham. For the latter, the will remains undetermined to the last moment and then acts truly contingently; for the former, the last act is determined (somehow) by the preceding sequence of alternating passions and is a will at the moment of the stopping impulse only insofar as it is the ultimate desire. (Once more, I cannot tell whether the will is "determined" here at all, whether there is a mechanistic or an organic causal line or development leading up to it, or whether the antecedent moments are just strung out continuously, like beads on a chain, connected, but not causally.)

The Hobbesian position seems like compatibilism pure and simple (acting as one wills but predeterminately), but, of course, it rests on the opponents talking past each other: By "will," one means a faculty of making a choice and coming to a decision; the other means a last passion going over into action. It's an equivocation that begs the question: the outcome was assumed in the use of the term.

A next argument concerns a question with which present-day neuroscientists, who tend to be advocates of determinism, are much concerned: how to answer the "folk opinion" that determinism of the will makes the legal criminalization of socially undesirable behavior irrational. Hobbes gives what is still the best determinist answer going: Although all human action is necessitated, the prohibiting law is just. For "the intention of the law is not to grieve the delinquent for what is done and not to be undone," but the punishing law is conducive "to the preservation of the rest, inasmuch as to punish those that do voluntary hurt, [the law] frames and makes men's will such as men would have them." By "voluntary," Hobbes means actions proceeding from the will, and by will, recall, the last appetite before action—and the sum of (somehow) necessitating antecedent passions—or just the last appetite—might indeed well be changed by seeing others punished for their actions. Praise and blame, he goes on to say, are not in vain under such necessity, for they do not depend on its absence. Praise is nothing but saying that something is good, and that can be said, for example, of someone who can't help being good, who is necessarily good, being so by nature. As for sin, it is not taken away by necessity either, because—it is always the same compatibilist argument—what is done by necessity yet proceeds from the will.[6]

Hobbes turns to compulsion, which only occurs when terror makes a man do something. Thus, it appears, compulsion is only a specially urgent case of universal necessity, and therefore yielding to it is unlike, say, lust, a preference. Bramhall responds that terror is not compelling; some men choose freely even in the face of ultimate terror. As ever, they are talking across each other. By terror, Hobbes means an irresistible aversion, Bramhall a resistible one, as resistible as is lust. So the real issue is not the existence of free will but the power of the grip of passion.[7]

A question arises about Hobbesian will as "the last feather [that] necessitates the breaking of the horse's back." Bramhall had argued that even if "the will did necessarily follow the last dictate of the understanding, in that is no extrinsical determination from without," but a man's own resolution. And once again, they cross each other. Hobbes does not believe 1. that understanding—I take Bramhall to mean reasoning—is indeed involved, and 2. if it were, it wouldn't matter because it itself is not unnecessitated, being nothing but a mechanical reckoning, a "mental" motion of casting up of the consequences of conventional general names.[8]

Hobbes's tract ends with a summary of his opinions on liberty and necessity. To summarize a summary: Some actions follow no deliberation but are done simply and suddenly; these are the acts the Bishop calls "spontaneous," and Hobbes calls "voluntary." When a man deliberates, he "does nothing else but consider whether it be better for himself to do it or not to do it," that is, he imagines whether the consequences are good or evil. Deliberation is simply the name for "all alternate successions of contrary appetites," the last of which we call the will. The consequent actions are said to be voluntary and done "upon choice and election;" to say an agent is free is to say he is still in doubt, has not finished deliberating. Liberty is the absence of impediments to a thing's acting out its nature or natural propensity, as a river's water is said to descend freely, but is impeded from running crosswise by its banks. Nothing begins on its own, including the will, which is itself caused by things out of its control. Necessary and sufficient cause are the same; for if a sufficient cause cannot produce the effect, then something necessary was lacking, and so it was not sufficient, while if it is impossible for it not to produce an effect, then it is necessary. He concludes that all effects are necessary. (This identification of "sufficient" and "necessary" is less inconsequential than it might seem. While Hobbes is right that these terms don't name different kinds of causes, they could, taken as distinct, be informally understood so as to mark out some wiggle room for free will: All the conditions that are *needed* to bring about an effect may, in an actual case, be present in the sum that would be *sufficient* to make it happen of necessity—except for that margin by which sufficiency exceeds necessity. That is where free will might find its space:

Everything is set to go; all that is materially necessary is at hand; but it is not quite enough. In Thomas's term, the will must consent and execute— and in executing it completes the sufficient conditions). Finally, Hobbes says that all things needful being present to produce an effect, it is nonsense to say that the cause "may be sufficient, that is necessary, and yet no effect will follow." (This is the exact consequence pointed to in my argument above; Hobbes is simply presupposing the coincidence of necessary and sufficient conditions.)[9]

The treatise ends with "my reasons": Having explicated (to his own advantage) spontaneity, deliberation, will, natural propensity, free agency, and liberty, Hobbes finally lets the cat out of the bag—which is not a different creature from Ockham's: "There can be no proof offered but every man's own experience, by reflection on himself and remembering what he used to have in his mind . . ." Thus for Hobbes what determines belief is experience recalled in introspection—asking oneself, it seems, what a term brought to mind and what one imagined by it. Imagination comes in because "consideration, understanding, reason, and all the passions of the mind are imaginations." Recall, however, that imagination is, in turn, "nothing but *decaying sense*," weakened internal sensory appearance. (But, however internality be constituted, for Hobbes belief comes from individual self-consultation, not from persuasion by objective truth.) Finally, Hobbes points out to his lordship, the Bishop, that the doctrine denying necessity has the inconvenience of destroying the prescience of God. (Should we suspect a smirk?) Yet the argument might fail: Why shouldn't God foreknow contingencies?[10]

Bramhall's denial of Hobbes's most vigorous reason, common experience, seems to me quite persuasive, for it is not directed against experience *per se* but against Hobbes's idiosyncratic account of common experience. He is simply wrong that "rational men . . . understand as he [Hobbes] conceives," or for that matter, imagines. But, for all that, Bramhall's argument is not determinative, but rather a promise of endless disputation.[11]

(I doubt that appeals to anyone's own experience—certainly not to mine, even if they are what really settles my mind—can tip the scales in *formal* debate or scientific argument—though perhaps so much the worse for such debates. In fact, in the terms of present-day scientific will-research, "rational men" are demoted to the "folk," who persist in giving trouble by having experiences of freedom—although with proper science-based instruction, they might be broken of the habit. So as the "common experience" debate goes on between latter-day Hobbeses and Bramhalls, there has entered a third set of antagonists, who devalue experience systematically. Meanwhile here's mine: I find Hobbes seductive by reason of the forceful simplicity and beautiful succinctness of his thinking on the will, but all my mental life rebels against it.)

B. Locke (and Leibniz): Mitigated Reduction

Locke was not directly influenced by Hobbes, but he continues the line of undoing the will, without, however, giving up free agency: "I think *the question is not proper, whether the will be free, but whether a man be free*," for "*Liberty belongs not to the will . . . But the agent or man*." The question for me is whether it makes any difference to say so. My answer will be yes, insofar as it shifts the mind to a new perspective, and no, insofar as it does not resolve the question of freedom. (And since for me philosophizing is an activity that achieves—occasional—stability by way of a sequence of destabilizations, the review of Locke's moderated reductionism is profitable.) I should say here that like Hobbes, Locke had a serious contemporary critic in the matter, though of greater originality than Bramhall, namely Leibniz, whose carefully appreciative paragraph-by-paragraph annotations I'll partly absorb into my text (and partly put into Note 12 to this chapter).[12]

As the title of Locke's treatise "Concerning Human Understanding" shows, the philosophers' attention, led by Descartes, had turned on a grand scale toward what is called epistemology, "the account of human 'knowledge'" or rather "cognition" (as being activity rather than object). Kant will term this enterprise "critique," that is, the knowledge of the cognizing subject that must precede knowledge itself so as to guarantee that it meets the criteria of "science." People had always thought about thinking, but usually by beginning with the external object and going inward, rather than by starting from the cognitive constitution and reaching outwards. The primacy of epistemology is a consequence-laden turn, which will, in its most deep-reaching form, appear to Kant as a veritable second Copernican Revolution.[13]

One great perplexity that had already been all but pushed into obsolescence by the new preoccupation was that of human free will under God's foreknowledge. Locke himself has given up on the question—a hundred years after it had been newly approached in epistemological terms by a theologian, Molina, in an argument from God's cognitive powers so subtle, however, as to spell the end. (I make an attempt to set it out in Note 14 to this chapter.)[14]

The emphasis now is not on what God can do but on what man can do. The long chapter on the will is entitled "Of Power." Leibniz, who is much more versed in the ancients than Locke, comments that "power" corresponds to Latin *potentia* (a term current in the Scholastics), which is used for mental powers, for their receptivity in the passive, for their function in the active sense. Leibniz himself, however, takes "power" back to Aristotle's *dynamis*, the capability of mere material, its potential to become an actual being under the right conditions. He reinterprets *dynamis* to give it "a more complete sense," one whose area of application is what we call, following him, "dynamics," the science of motion under force: "The word *force* might be appropriated to it [*dynamis*]." In other words, Leibniz relates Locke's chapter title to the new physics. Active power has become change in physical motion; "passive power" is associated with impenetrability and inertia.[15]

Locke is a step behind him in this (if you want to be ahead, look to the ancients), for he says: "*The clearest idea of active power [is] had from spirit.*" We get this idea, to be sure, from an analogy to sensible qualities, because they, and even their underlying substances, are in continual flux. But bodies, simply observed, afford us no clear and distinct idea of active power. They are moved passively, while we must infer the active power to move. Here Locke anticipates Hume (though, as Leibniz points out, he gets his physics wrong): "1. Of thinking, bodies afford us no ideas at all; it is only from reflection we have that. 2. Neither have we from body an idea of the beginning of motion"—in other words, we never observe any active causality (exactly what Hume will claim). So any power to begin or to refrain, whether of or from mental or physical motion, Locke says we will have to find in ourselves.[16]

(I must observe here that it seems to be a logically unnecessary but psychologically understandable consequence of the epistemological approach that power wanders into our spirit or mind and, as will turn out just below, makes us uneasy—potently and anxiously endeavoring. Here is an epoch in a bi-millennial journey that has reached, in early modernity, a point of simultaneous turning inward to the mind's power and outward to nature's dynamics; with it comes a search for certainty about the self that finds very spare satisfactions. Its complement is a novel repose in, and a sense of power from, the search itself. These termini are expressed in two juxtaposed quotations:

> Ancient: "It is reasonable to suppose that the way of life of those who have knowledge is pleasanter than of those who are searching for it."

> Modern: "Not the truth in the possession of which some man is or imagines he is makes the worth of a human being, but the honest pains he took to get behind the truth. For not through possession but through the search after truth are widened his powers in which alone his ever-growing perfection consists. Possession makes serene, languid, proud . . ."[17]

This is a perpetual perplexity: Is this sequence of thoughtful ways, from valuing the atemporal fulfillment of possession to preferring the time-driven excitement of pursuit, brought about by chance, choice, or fate? Is it analogous to biological evolution, driven by natural determinants combined with happenstance environment, or is it more like a spiritual development drawn by intellectual finalities? Does it add up on its own or does it fit into a conceptual scheme only by some intellectual shoehorning?

The will does seem, approximately, to fall into some such schema: In classical antiquity this uneasy, striving power was unnecessary; it comes to, sometimes overwhelming, prominence in early Christianity and modernity. This was the moment—it could have been earlier, with Hobbes or even Ockham—to raise these questions because my object of study, the will, can now be seen progressively to fall into two opposite philosophical conditions, as might a power that so well fits the radically dialectic modes of modernity. Will is now subject to: 1. deliberate diminution, ending in our day with its total neutralization in neuroscience, and 2. ardent augmentation, be it as world-principle or human omnipotence. Between these two, the will is nothing much and everything whatsoever.[18])

Locke begins with the idea of power itself. It comes from the mind, which, noticing that its ideas continually change, some by the impression of outward objects on the senses, some by its own choice, concludes that there are agents and patients that affect and accept change. That dual ability is power. Locke accepts the two traditional powers of the mind, will and understanding—in his terms, powers of preferring and of perceiving. People call these powers "faculties" and mislead themselves into thinking that there are so many distinct agents in us. Thus they say of the will that it is the commanding and superior faculty, or that it obeys and follows the dictates of understanding, or that it is or is not free. Locke thinks that this way of thinking leads to wrangling and obscurity.

The idea of liberty comes to us from our observation that often we can act or refrain, and the idea of necessity comes from the experience that often we can't. An example of the former are the times when we feel free to "remove [our] contemplation from one idea to another," of the latter, the necessity of "having some idea constantly in our mind," that is, of our inability to stop ideating. (Practitioners of yoga would dispute that necessity.) But this idea, this *"Liberty belongs not to the will."* Consequently the question of whether a man's will be free or not becomes "unintelligible; it is as insignificant to ask whether a man's will be free or no as to ask whether his virtue is square." Locke, tolerantly, permits the word "faculty" to stay in common speech, as long as its users understand that it denotes not an agent in the mind but an ability belonging to a human being. The proper question is not *"whether the will be free, but whether a man be free."*[19]

Is he? Yes, insofar as a man can "by the direction of choice of his mind preferring the existence of any action to the non-existence of that action, and vice versa, make it to exist or not exist, so far he is free." But people require more: They want to be free to will or not to will—and this is what Locke imagines people mean by the will being free.

And *that* Locke denies to be possible. Once a man proposes to himself in his thoughts an action within his power, volition has to follow: It must be done or not. He cannot avoid preferring one to the other, that is, willing it. So the will is not free but is under the necessity of willing; a man is, in most cases, not at liberty to will to will. The question whether a man is free to will which of two alternatives he pleases is also absurd; it is as if to ask if he can be pleased with what he is pleased with.

In sum, freedom consists in being able to act or not, as we choose. Since "volition," or willing, is an act of the mind "directing its thought to the production of any action and thereby exciting its power to produce it," and the will is therefore "nothing but a power in the mind to direct the operative faculties of man to motion or rest," the answer to the question "what determines the will?" is: "the mind." And if one should ask what moves the mind to determine the will to direct faculties to rest or move, the answer is: its present state of satisfaction or uneasiness. "This is the great motive" that works on the mind to put it into action, the motive called "determining of the will."

By the way, Locke explains that will, a power, must not be confused with desire, an affection, as self-observation shows: Willing is only about our own actions and terminates there. Moreover it can go quite contrary to desire; for example to oblige someone I may choose to act toward an end I have no desire to obtain. So if the will has now been deprived of its traditional relation to desire, what does determine it?[20]

"*Uneasiness determines the will*," as has been intimated. It is not the greatest positive good that fixes the will, but uneasiness; we may call this—"as it is"—*desire*, "an uneasiness of mind for want of an absent good." I think Locke's apparently self-contradictory presentation—displacing and admitting desire—intends to accomplish this: to divorce desire from its intention, an absent good, so as to focus attention on the state of mind rather than on the direction of longing, and so to present the will as being determined not by the object of desire but by an internal state. No man moves until made uncomfortable by a lack. No one will bring himself out of penury to attain desirable plenty unless he is uneasy in his poverty. Explicitly put: Not the object of desire moves us primarily, but our own restlessness under absence. The will is reduced to being the mind's—read, I think, the man's—executive power that calls on faculties of action to move or stay as they are, much as in a naval ship the executive officer commands the crew in accordance with the captain's intentions. This will is indeed neither free nor unfree, since the mind's preference determines it, and that preference does not come into play until the mind gets unsettled, feels unease, is, as we say, "motivated" by discomfort. Therefore the most pressing dis-ease that is judged to be curable determines the will.

What moves this uneasiness, this *quondam* desire? "Happiness and that alone." What is apt to produce pleasure in us is what we call good and what produces pain, evil. And therein consists our happiness and misery, our good and evil—in pleasure and pain. (The reader should notice the casual but consequence-fraught identification of happiness and pleasure, in the distinction of which some ancients showed so much acuity.)[21]

But we have a power to suspend "the prosecution of desire" and to consider and then to be determined by our judgment. Far from being a restraint on liberty's proper use, it is "the hinge on which turns the liberty of intellectual beings, in their constant endeavors after, and steady prosecution of true felicity"—an early version of our Declaration's "pursuit of happiness," with the same indeterminacy concerning the content of felicity. For just now, recall, happiness had been defined as consisting in pleasure, but at the end of Locke's chapter on the will, it seems to be some greater good and finer end—but left undefined.

Here Locke opens a space for free will: There is an interval of time for suspension of "the prosecution of desire," a time before the will is determined but when a judgment can be formed after due examination. Actually, however, Locke is consistent: Since it is the mind that suspends the "pursuit of happiness," it is, in fact, the mind that is the locus of liberty, not the will—but it is a small locus.[22]

Leibniz, wrapping his critique in words of appreciation, shows this demoted Lockean will to be unviable. So gracefully are the cavils framed that I, for one, cannot tell whether or not he meant to be in fact devastating.

Leibniz begins by drawing attention to the insufficiency of Locke's definition of power merely as a relation, a description that goes for practically anything. This definition ought, however, to be precise since it is of consequence in distinguishing between a power belonging to a faculty of the soul or to a man. He recalls that this distinction was already in contention between the scholastic Realists, such as Thomas, who regard faculties as really distinct in the soul, and Nominalists, such as Ockham, who regard them as abstractions, as merely aspectual capacities of one mind. Leibniz himself thinks of volition as yet something else, as *conatus*, a quasi-physical term, meaning a tendency, endeavor, effort, *impulse*—a potent impulse toward what is considered good or away from bad; it is "a celebrated axiom" that this impulse, will-plus-power, issues in voluntary internal, mental action and in voluntary external, bodily movements. Besides these conscious actions there are also efforts resulting from insensible perception, which Leibniz calls "appetitions" rather than "volitions"—subconscious desires.[23]

Freedom of the will is understood in two senses, Leibniz says. The first is opposed to the slavery of the spirit arising from passion because of deficient understanding; this is the Stoic sense. The second is freedom of the spirit apart from understanding; this is the "naked will"—free will proper. It is true contingency, opposed to necessity. In this way, "I am accustomed to say," the understanding can determine the will by a *prevalence* of reasons, which even when infallible inclines without compelling. This view—tacitly—just about overthrows Locke's will, which is not to be inclined by reasons nor ultimately free to resist the uneasiness of mind or man, not being the kind of being that *can* be independent, but a mere power-relation.

Locke had claimed that the will is not a power able to interfere with mental representations—ideas—by suspending them; Leibniz thinks some men have enough control to do that and even, by *vigor of will*, to change thoughts; thus he implies that there is something faculty-like in their will. Moreover, general usage attributes freedom, which Locke thinks can belong only to agents but not powers, to this very will. Locke's novel view was that not the will but the man was free. To be sure, he recedes from "man" to "mind," since man includes body, and as Leibniz points out, what we are really asking about is not the freedom of our limbs but of our spirit: Is there enough independence in our will itself? And are we free to choose between alternatives? So what people generally are really concerned with is their radical freedom of the spirit—whether they can ultimately will *against* all considerations. Although Leibniz thinks (contrary to the Scholastics) that we do not will to will, and thus do not will to will against our reason, he understands that these convolutions are just what cause people to engage in inquiries about the will as a separate ability.

So Locke's claim that we are not at liberty to will or not to will is rejected by Leibniz, as also is his notion that it is absurd to ask whether a man is at liberty to will which of two he pleases, for example, motion or rest. For the will is not just the executor of the more pleasing alternative—it makes a choice and does so as follows.[24]

Preliminary to grappling with the mind's "uneasiness" (which is Locke's motive power commanding the will) Leibniz points out that the case Locke uses to divide will from desire is not dispositive: When desire goes one way and will goes another, it is actually because will is in a mode of incomplete volition, called "velleity," that is, a kind of inclination, a desire only half desired for fear of an undesirable consequence, and so not determinative.[25]

Now to Locke's "uneasiness" as the will's motive rather than the traditional "greater good": The sum total of his argument is the psychological observation that the discomfort of present deprivation is always stronger than the desire for a prospective good. Leibniz comments that "there is something beautiful and solid in these considerations" and then proceeds to contradict the psychology with his own, which preserves "those ancient axioms" which say, in sum, that the will follows the greatest good. The reason it appears otherwise is that, though our thoughts are indeed often made "surd," mute, enfeebled by our feelings, Locke's account of these is wrong. Though he agrees that happiness is the universal aim, he thinks that uneasiness is incompatible with it, so its removal is what we primarily attend to. Leibniz answers that uneasiness is in fact essential for happiness. We are full of little "unconscious" physics-like impulses, those "appetitions," which need to be apprehended and regulated by means of not-so-feeble images of the greater good. If the uneasiness were truly unpleasant, the way to happiness would be continual pain. So while for Locke the relief of pain is the uneasy way to a happiness defined as pleasure, for Leibniz the very recognition and regulation of unconscious enlivening impulses achieves a happiness based on good. The imagination, the presentation of what is not yet as if it were now, is a real source of persuasion for Leibniz, while Locke regards absence as enfeebling and still-absent good as "the object of bare, unactive speculation." I would say that Locke's *lack of a faculty for absence* is what really distinguishes his dour description of the will's motivation from Leibniz's. Note that Locke has managed to write a book on the human mind in which the *imagination* is not a topic.[26]

The sum of Leibniz's critique of Locke is that the will must be in some sense an independent faculty, in some sense a desire, in some sense determined by the good. It is a traditional view, to be sure, but better defended than is Locke's denial of these features—though as a novel denial, *ipso facto* more future-fraught. The next Englishman will go much farther along this new path.

C. Hume: Will Disconnected

I want to think next about the will in the subsequent great English treatment, Hume's *Treatise of Human Nature*, a much larger, more comprehensive book than Locke's, which, although beginning, as it does, with "ideas," adds a treatment of human passion and morality, including a part specifically devoted to the will; the notion, moreover, turns up all over the work.[27]

The way into the will, as understood by this young epistemological radical and later political conservative, is to say what traditional features it hasn't. It's not a faculty, nor has it any inherent causal connection with its effect; it is not moved by reason and has no liberty. That is the anticipatory summary; now to Hume's arguments.

But before I begin, I want to confess a certain resistance I feel toward skeptical skeptics like Hume, who as a "true skeptic will be diffident of his philosophical doubts as well of his philosophic convictions," and who is inclined to yield to the propensity "to be positive and certain on *particular points.*" In fact, Hume is quite peremptory, even forcible—a closet dogmatist masquerading as a skeptic. If Hobbes's "nothing but" philosophy had a certain curt beauty in its unabashed positivity, the elegant clarity of

Hume's nothing-but-ism becomes more complex as it goes, despite his dis-
claimers of philosophical subtlety. I think he is a far more difficult writer
than Kant (our students' Exhibit No. 2—Hegel taking the prize—in supposed obscurity). It is a feature of this semi-skepticism to tell people what
they might stop thinking about (which galvanizes the usually very slug-
gish rebel in me), and that is exactly how Hume begins his treatment of
the will.[28]

    "[B]y the will," he says, "I mean nothing but the internal impression
we feel and are conscious of, when we knowingly give rise to a new motion
of the body, or a new perception of the mind." He had given the condition
for this effect earlier: "When a person is possess'd of any power, there is no
more required to convert it into action but the exertion of the will; . . ." He
goes on to say that it is impossible to define this impression and needless
to describe it further; "for which reason we shall cut off those definitions
and distinctions, with which philosophers are wont to perplex rather than
clear up this question; . . ." Disembarrassed, then, of all previous thought
on these disputed matters, Hume now examines the "question of liberty
and necessity which occur so naturally in treating of the will."

    He now considers the operations of external bodies, in which there is
not a trace of liberty. All the actions of matter are absolutely determined;
all are necessary. That's to begin with, but also (and here Hume is spectacularly and influentially original) in spite of this necessity, "in no single instance [is] the ultimate connection of any objects discoverable, either
by our senses or reason." We simply cannot penetrate into the essence of
bodies to discern a principle of mutual influence. All we know is their regular union, their constant conjunction, with each other, and from this
union we learn to make an inference of cause and effect and of a necessity which is associated with them. Bodies have no inherent causal connection we can know of; it is only this constant conjunction, this union in
experience together with the inference of the mind, that gives us necessity.
Luckily (we might say) but inexplicably, the external world shows us regularities and so do human affairs, and what is most to the point, so does
the mind. It is a principle provable from experience: (This is a prime case
of the differences of experience I intimated above; in my experience, the
constant conjunction of any two human phenomena has a probability of
about 0.5—fifty-fifty. For people and their conjoining relations just aren't,
couple by couple, all that constant.) Hume gives several examples among
which is this wonderfully inept one: As certainly as two flat pieces of marble will unite together, two young savages of different sexes will copulate.
Plausible or not, however, his point is that external objects display regularities which we acknowledge as necessities, and that human actions are
analogously conjoined. No, more: The consistency of the union between
motives and actions is the *same* as that of any natural operation. Should

anyone object (as I have just done) that human conduct is irregular and uncertain, the answer is that there are always "concealed causes," which, were they known, would prove the uniformity. In other words, the constant conjunction of known human actions is, in fact, an unfalsifiable principle, not really a result of induction. On it the argument proceeds, and very tersely: We all reason that way, that is, on "moral evidence," which allows us to conclude what actions to expect, considering people's motives, temper, and situation: "A man, who gives orders for his dinner, doubts not the obedience of his servants." (But one long generation on—which takes us to 1776—and that effect wasn't so reliable either.) And whoever reasons that way "does *ipso facto* believe the actions of the will to arise from necessity. From this constant union [the mind] *forms* the idea of cause and effect and by its influence *feels* the necessity." Hume is positive that no one will refute this argument except by changing his definitions of cause, effect, necessity, liberty, and chance. Necessity has just been defined as the *feeling* that the constant conjunction of cause and effect gives us. Liberty is now defined, negatively, as removing necessity and, positively, as chance. Chance, however, is contrary to experience—which obeys the principle of constant conjunction. So, in fact, chance must be only concealed cause.[29]

Liberty, and with it free will, seems to have evaporated, squeezed out between necessity and chance, between known and unknown conjunctions. Why then is there a "prevalence of the doctrine of Liberty," absurd though it be? Few people can distinguish between what the Scholastics call "liberty of *spontaneity*," which they understand in contrast to imposed violence, and "liberty of *indifference*," which means the nullification of causal necessity in the face of a perfect equilibrium of the conditions attending choice. People wish to think that they could have acted otherwise, so they assert their liberty of indifference when they are only entitled to maintain freedom from violence; in that sense they can have liberty by redefinition: It now means absence of coercion, of unwelcome, presumably external, restraints. A second reason people have for adhering to this indifference-doctrine of liberty is a *false sensation* of looseness in performing an action; they feel that they are subject to the will and the will is subject to nothing. They produce an image of the will as moving faintly toward the side on which it did not settle and are persuaded that it could have gone over. But all that reasoning is in vain, since it has its determining motive in the *desire* to preserve our free will, and *ipso facto* proves no escape from the bonds of necessity. A third reason for belief in liberty of the will is *religion*; in philosophy we should refrain from such appeals. So faith is as vain as was reason. Nonetheless Hume now defends his doctrine of necessity. First, he is not arguing that he places human actions on a footing with *senseless* matter; he is, much rather, ascribing to matter an intelligible quality. (How much comfort will that be to religiously inclined persons?) Moreover, he

will now argue that his kind of necessity is essential to religion and morality: Divine and human law operates through rewards and punishments
intended to be an effective motive in the mind, a cause that is, in fact, an
instance of Hume's kind of necessity. (This sophism has a whiff of the derisory about it.)

Hume says he "cannot doubt of an entire victory" for his proofs that liberty is chance, that moral evidence shows the regularity of human actions,
and that only the doctrine of necessity can preserve the causal efficacy of
rewards and punishments; this necessity, recall, derives neither from logic
nor physics, but from habit. He then goes on to particularize the causes
operating on the will.[30]

The section on "the influencing motives of the will" contains what
is, it seems, the most quoted sentence of this huge book: "Reason is, and
ought only to be, the slave of the passions, and can never pretend to any
other office than to serve and obey them." Hume adds that this opinion,
which we "ought" to hold and live by, may "appear somewhat extraordinary" and is in need of confirmation. Indeed, it turns the main tradition,
even Thomas's moderated version that makes will and intellect mutually
superior, upside down.

Note the significant absence of the traditional term "intellect." Hume
does not merely demote the office of thought; he first changes, curtails, its
nature. His reason is not intellect, thought-vision that is reached by rational stepping-stones. Reason is one of those "nothing but" terms: It is merely
passage from idea to idea; an idea in turn is merely a copy of an impression
that has weakened in "force or vivacity;" an impression, in turn, is—somehow—directly derived from sensation. These impressions, taken in themselves, present a world of disparate, atomic—almost Lucretian—beings,
whose connection is entirely derived empirically, from the regularities of
experience. As for the originating sensations, "their ultimate cause is, in
my opinion, perfectly inexplicable by human reason"—that is to say, we
cannot get behind the sense-impressions to their connection to an instigating real-world object (if any). This ultimate disconnection descends to
reason, which "can never satisfy us that the existence of any one object does
ever imply that of another." Thus reason has no dignity to speak of—no
substantial integrating, and certainly no originating or grounding function; the "principle of association," the generalization of the "constant conjunction" that was so prominent above, turns into a custom, a habit, for us,
and so we comfortably pass from idea to idea.

To return to the will: Hume shows the fallacy of all this "[traditional]
philosophy" by insisting on the limitation of that reason which expends
itself in logical demonstrations or probabilities. Reason's realm is the
abstract relation of ideas; the will places us among realities. So demonstration and volition are totally separate. Even reason-structures such as math-

ematics, arithmetic, and mechanics only become potent in application. "Reason itself can never produce any action," since, when objects themselves don't affect us, their connection cannot give them any influence, and "reason is nothing but the discovery of this connection." Nor can it give rise to volition or prevent it or "dispute the preference with any passion or emotion." In sum, reason has no impulsive power, and only a contrary impulse can direct a passion. Being without such original influence on the will, a quasi-passion, reason has simply no power over volition.

And it is volition, our—internally arising—impression of starting something new, that initiates the performance of the actions which our passions call for. The will is not, however, properly speaking, "comprehended among the passions;" thus it too is "only secondary," as we hear late in the exposition: The will is an epiphenomenon upon an action.

There *is* a role for reason in willing, but it too is only secondary. Reason attends to passions, but not as correcting them, for passion "can never, in any sense, be call'd unreasonable." When we think so it is only because we falsely suppose that a proper object exists for the passion—though it doesn't, or that there are means to reach it—though they are insufficient. Then it is not the passion but the reason that is, properly speaking, being unreasonable: "'Tis not contrary to reason to prefer the destruction of the whole world to the scratching of my finger." But, Hume thinks, being convinced of my mistake concerning a valid object, the longing ceases, and I cease to will any action in its behalf. (This piece of "moral evidence" makes me wonder, once again, whether I may not simply be differently constituted from a writer such as Hobbes before, and now Hume, since my longings rarely or only lingeringly cease because reason tells me they are falsely or ineffectively directed—though my actions may be inhibited. In any case, it seems to me that to make reason impotent, Hume has needed to admit that passions are rational, that is, capable of hearing reason. Hume's position seems to me a sort of inverse Stoicism: The Stoics consider the passions themselves to be mistakes of reason; Hume considers reason itself to be unreasonable about the passions.)[31]

Now to morality itself: Since "reason is wholly inactive" in the making of moral distinctions and is not the source of a sense of morals, actions may be laudable or blamable, but never reasonable or unreasonable. And that extends back to volition; reason deals with true and false, not so volition. But neither is good and bad imputable to the will: An oak drops an acorn that then grows by degrees to overlap its parent and at last kills it; a child grows and finally kills its father. The relation, so far as it is discoverable by reason, is identical: parricide. But it has no moral connotation. For the will is only a cause—an a-causal cause—analogous to the last growth of the acorn (I suppose). It cannot introduce any new quality into the effects it brings about. Promises, for example, moral obligations, are the pure effect of the will that engages itself, and for that reason have no *natural*, objective force—for will brings no change into the world, being only a power of starting, not of shaping any objective effect.[32]

Morality thus stems neither from reason, not being a matter of true-or-false, nor from the will, which is merely the feeling of being a cause. So it remains for it to be a sentiment, a very gentle passion that the philosophers have confused with reason, because it also is associated with emotional calm. Moral qualities, virtues or vices, are therefore not very different from natural abilities, and are indeed often similarly praised and blamed—for, Hume thinks, being feelings, they are not necessarily any more voluntary than natural gifts. Moreover, we make moral distinctions on the basis of the pain or pleasure that another's qualities give us—and he thinks that this effect on us does not depend on whether that quality is voluntary (meaning unconstrained) or not. "Voluntary" and "free" are not the same: "Our actions are more voluntary than our judgments; but we have not more liberty in one than in the other."[33]

In summary: "The will being here considered as a cause, has no more a discoverable connection with its effect, than any material cause has with its proper effect . . . Nor is the empire of will over our mind more intelligible . . . We have command over our mind to a certain degree but beyond that lose all empire over it."

To what degree? Do we know, after all, what Hume thinks the will is and does? Well, insofar as one *can* know something that isn't much—"by will I mean nothing but . . ."—and whose scope is so contracted, yet so indefinite—"to a certain degree"—Hume seems right not to brood over the nature of an item whose powers he must be at pains to disconnect if it is to fit into his scheme.

The result is curiously like the Cheshire cat's grin: finally there is the grin without the cat, for this will is only the ghost of a passion. Yet though not properly a passion, it is treated among the "direct" passions, those that arise immediately from good, evil, pleasure, pain. That is because will too arises as an immediate effect of these, as a fairly vivid impression rather than a faded idea that comes about by "reflection"—meaning one that originates within the soul. It does not, however, have the emotional bulk of an immediate passion, such as love or hate. It is rather a doppelgänger of an action, a companion-feeling of inceptiveness, when we are conscious of making a *new* beginning. Though a feeling, it seems to be a judge of the novelty of the act it witnesses; thus it seems to have a sort of memory. But is will an impression and/or a trigger? "When a person is posses'd of any power, there is no more required to convert it into action than an exertion of the will." So is it a special catalyst-impression, and thus a faculty of some sort after all? Is it an explanation to say that it is a Humean cause, constantly (or often) conjoined but never connected to its effect, an a-causal cause, one that acts, as it were, consciously in the dark: "*an internal impression we feel and are conscious of when we knowingly give rise to any new motion of our body, or new perception of our mind*"? Who is "we"—the fading cat behind the willing grin or the grinning will surviving the atomized personal identity? (Some clarification from Hume's *Enquiry* is provided in Note 34 to this chapter.)[34]

I am expressing my fascination with Hume's treatment of the will by laying out these perplexities as an end result. By drawing the will into a system of systematic disconnection, by reducing it terminally without letting it fade out entirely, he becomes a minimalist of volition, and the last vestige of volitional effectiveness thus discovered is *newness*. Hume himself makes nothing of this innovative function of the will, but it will be front and center for his great beneficiary and subverter Kant, who, though far from accepting Hume's conclusions, declares:

> I confess freely: It was the memory of David Hume that many years ago interrupted my dogmatic slumber and gave my researches in the field of speculative philosophy a totally new direction.

One result will be that new beginnings are precisely the first mark of freedom. We think of freedom when we see the world not as an uninterrupted chain of events physically determined but as a sequence of states occasionally redirected by an initiating cause, which intervenes in nature with that opaque freedom which Kant will term "practical." That "practical" cause is, of course, the will.[35]

chapter **V**

The Will as Ego-Founder

In the beginning of philosophy, which may be said to have lasted over two millennia—beings, human, non-human, and supra-human—were the center of interest, and inquiry took its departure from them. Then, from motives too complex to consider here (but all constellated about the discovery of human potency), intense attention was given to what Kant, the first philosopher of this chapter, calls "critique," the "special science that has to do not with the nature of *things*, but with the nature of *cognition*," that is, with epistemology.

A. Kant: Subject-Will

Thus attention migrates from man, nature, and God to the "I," now called by Kant the *subject*—what underlies understanding. But it is not only the philosopher's attention that moves inward; the world itself will come to be within, at least insofar as it is knowable. Thus the critique that grounds the science of physical nature—our knowledge of the world—turns out to ground nature itself—our very world. This line of thinking is continued by two followers, Fichte and Schelling. For all three, the will is a factor in the "I," as ground or founder of personal and public freedom, variously understood.

Meanwhile, Kant is himself an heir in a very particular way, to which the quotation at the end of Chapter IV attests. Kant's inheritance was, as he insisted, Hume's single most potent idea, and it is the essence of empiricism—if we mean by empiricism something like what the Greeks meant by *empeiria*, that is, experience derived from sense-based observation and practice and more or less innocent of universal principles. Hume's idea was that no one has ever observed a necessary connection between a supposed cause of a so-called effect. Hume was confident that constant conjunction, never known to have failed consequence, was sufficient to make us regard nature as not ruled by mere chance. But anyone can see that, in fact, since this non-necessary connection makes all "causal" connection inductive, makes it, that is, a confidently expectant generalization from a limited number of instances, an exception (a miracle, if you like) *could* occur at any moment, and so, oddly enough, all nature becomes ultimately chancy—or miraculous.

One way to read Kant's *Critique of Pure Reason*, then, is as a global attempt to save the science of nature, that is, physics, from chanciness, to make it, in Descartes's spirit, reliably certain, and to do that without denying Hume's undeniable observation.

In the course of awakening from his "dogmatic slumber," the ungrounded belief that cause and effect do have an inherent connection (*Verknüpfung*), Kant works the greatest revolution ever produced in philosophy—a dizzying turning inside out, or better, outside in, of the world, which he himself regarded as a complement to the Copernican Revolution, which had moved the human observer from his fixed position at the center of the cosmos and had enormously enlarged his scope by making him a traveler through the universe on a huge orbital trajectory. In the course of this first *Critique*, cause and effect are recaptured for science by means of an inquiry into the "causality" of a cause, in German *Ursache*, literally, an originating event. (More on such revolutions in Note 1 to this chapter.)[1]

I need to follow this stupendous—yes, that's the right word—exposition (and its difficult implications) only as far as it concerns the will. The connective causality of a cause and its effect, which Hume had denied, is established by the following principle of any temporal sequence in accordance with the law of causality: "All changes occur according to the law of the *connection* [my italics] of cause and effect." What makes the principle more than mere peremptory law-giving is that its enforcement is attributed to a constitutional faculty of the human subject, the imagination. This capacity, here not a psychological but a logical function, is "a hidden power in the depth of the human soul." Its absolutely central responsibility is to supply internally precisely a relation that is not available through sense-perception, namely to *connect* two such perceptions of change in one and the same substance following each other in time. This "product," a synthetic, that is, a constructively unified result, is the contribution of the aforesaid "logical" or transcendental imagination—where "transcendental" means practically the same as "critical," namely, belonging to the knowledge-grounds of our experience. But this newly discovered function of the imagination is *not*—and this makes it novel—only an epistemologically defined, a cognitive, operation. It is antecedently the work of world-construction. Once again, what makes nature reliably—that is, both empirically and more than empirically—knowable, is this condition: Our faculty of understanding is, even *before* it acts as a faculty that gives *us* knowledge, the power that gives *nature* its constitution. This faculty requires nothing from beyond the subject except a fulfilling material to which the senses are receptive; Kant calls it the "*a priori* manifold," a received primal multifariousness.[2]

This is a tiny excerpt from a large foundational edifice, but it is the most crucial element in the main structure of the first *Critique*. Later, in an annex, as it were, Kant draws the consequence for human freedom and its agent, the will: Nature has been shown to be ruled by a strictly deterministic causality, not by the chancy custom of our empirical thinking but by the necessary constitution contributed by its grounding subject, ourselves. Nature's very internality has made it unassailably non-contingent. The sharp definition of a deterministic Nature, however, has opened a clear space for freedom, for new departures that are not jigged by laws of succession. This realm must be beyond the nature investigated by the *Critique of Pure Reason*. Then Kant says something astounding: "The greatest and perhaps the only use of all philosophy of pure reason is therefore really only negative"—namely to discover the *limits* of speculative reason. In other words, not the grounding of physics but an opening for the moral will was Kant's deepest purpose.[3]

Freedom, in its cosmological sense, appears in the world—though "appears" is precisely the wrong word; it doesn't appear any more than does real causality—as "the faculty for beginning a state of affairs spontaneously," one whose causality escapes the laws of nature. Since it doesn't appear and is thus empirically uncorroborable, it *is* an "idea of reason," though not any mere idea, but rather a thinkable, coherent concept. However, there is a freedom in the human sense, the freedom known from inner experience, which is not the capacity for new beginnings but for being unconditionally independent of sensual drives, of passions. Kant calls the conditioning, the compulsion, of the will by affects "pathological," meaning "affect-ridden," passion-driven (from Greek *pathos*, "passive suffering, passion"), well aware, I imagine, of the association of "pathological" with disease that goes back to ancient times.

Here, in the latter part of the first *Critique*, other terms relevant to the will are also introduced: "*Freedom in the practical sense* is the independence of "choice-will" (*Willkür*) from the *necessitation* by the impulsions (or "drives," *Antriebe*) of sensuality."[4]

Some attention to terms is needful here. (In grappling with Kant's works, if the terms are understood the struggle is half over.) I've already spoken of "pathological." "Practical" seems to be opposed to "theoretical"; this is the Aristotelian sense, in which practical thinking is distinguished from theoretical thinking as involving choice. Political action is a—no, is *the*—highest and most immediate function of practical thinking and its life. But not quite so for Kant. The practical use of reason is a matter of moral law only, and its function is to know and accept what *ought* to happen—the realized doing of it is at a remove. The longest exposition of practicality is in the second *Critique* called *Critique of Practical* [as opposed to *Pure*] *Reason*; reason (*Vernunft*) is Kant's comprehensive term for all fundamental cognition. But in a narrow use it is a superior faculty for dealing with ideal principles, as opposed to a more restricted understanding (*Verstand*); the latter operates with logical functions and dominates the theoretical first *Critique*.[5]

Note what a revelation this title exhibits! Up till now the mainstream notion of the will, the line that did not consign it to a last impulse or the resolution of an uneasiness, oscillated between "rational desire" and "desirous reason." The old non-problem—because thinkers could live with a mutual embrace that was a fact from every experiential aspect—became precise and problematic for Kant: Can the use of "practical" (free and moral) reason be unified with "pure" (theoretical and speculative) reason and in what sense might there be primacy and subordination? The question has shifted into a proper, that is, soluble, problem because rational desire has lost its desire. To be sure, Kant will allow an attenuated compensatory sentiment to survive—un-immediate and non-passionate, called "pure reason-interest." But practical reason is *all* rational, fiercely and unyieldingly: In fact, it will be, as I am about to set out, the primal incarnation of the Law of (non-)Contradiction. Thus the question of whether we have one or two psychic roots—reason and desire or reason alone—becomes precise and approachable.[6]

Note a term I have translated literally: *Willkür* from *Wille* and *Kur*, a word with the same ancestry as "choice," so "choice-will," the will that chooses. Kant himself glosses it as the familiar *arbitrium liberum* when it is not enslaved to sensuality; it is to be called *arbitrium sensitivum* when the senses affect it, and then it becomes pathological, suffering a loss of freedom, because impelled from the outside—so to speak.[7]

How the outside? Even without having actually read it, a caring student could infer that Kant's subject has an inner part that ought to be kept inviolably free of compulsion, and a part turned toward the outside and subject to natural laws. This latter is receptive to and partly conditioned by the senses; here the subject inhabits, or rather, encompasses, a Kantian sensorium of time and space. I make only bare mention of it because to bring it into the text would lead too far afield. (More on time and space in Note 8 to this chapter.)[8]

In the transcendental arena of this pure (pre-empirical) sensibility appear the pure phenomena that are structured and connected by our understanding to yield, when immattered, objects of cognitive experience. This part of our soul (*Gemüth*) would be studied by a proper natural science of psychology parallel to the physics grounded in the first *Critique*, but Kant has no hope for it; there is no rich, pure psychology of inner nature parallel to the pure physics of outer nature grounded in the first *Critique*. (See Note 9 to this chapter; I surmise in passing that the absence of a structure-rich psychology lies behind the rather harshly repressive role Kant assigns to human freedom.)[9]

Human sensuality, the affection of the soul by the senses, has usually been regarded as inimical to virtue when excessive (pagan), or to morality even when within normal bounds (Christian), at least in the mainstream. But when, as for Kant, the will is an agency of a freedom far deeper than mere free choice, the will's radical independence from the senses and their desirousness becomes central to morality. The willing faculty contains an inherent demand for independence from necessitation, that is, from external compulsion; the senses evince an inherent tendency to exercise impulsions, that is, to have pathological effects. Therefore the will and the—always desirous—senses are mutually exclusive: *no rational desire is possible.*

Those are Kant's terms defining practical freedom as a will unaffected by necessitation from the sensibility. Compare it to his definition of cosmological freedom as spontaneity, the faculty for starting a new state of affairs on one's own. These two faculties might be called the inner and the outer will, free will of the subject within, in the soul, and free agency of the subject without, in the world. One might even go so far as to term the first negative, as a capability for resistance to internal nature (the sensual soul), and the second positive, as a power to intervene in external nature (the law-governed world). To work out the character of the free will a little more, I shall turn to the *Groundwork of the Metaphysics of Morals.*[10]

It begins, famously, thus: "There is nowhere at all in the world, nor indeed outside of it, anything that can be thought good without limitation except only a GOOD WILL." All the virtues are undoubtedly good, but they can become bad when the will that makes use of these gifts of nature and those of good fortune is not good. Kant thus begins by announcing a tremendous upgrading of the human will: Although it is unlike God in being neither omniscient nor omnipotent, it *is*, to coin a term, omnivalent; its value lies in its limitless capacity for imparting value. This new will is thus not to be esteemed for its capacity to obtain intended ends—which mere natural inclinations might effect more expeditiously—but simply for the quality of its willing. A human being might be deprived of natural means by "stepmotherly" nature, but if his will be good and he tries hard, the uselessness of his endeavors cannot detract from his value: "He would yet shine like a jewel for himself."[11]

This migration of value from works to intentions, from object to subject, appears like a human-centered and humane view of human endeavor. I shall claim that it nonetheless harbors—foreseeably—dangerous consequences. Were one in the name-calling mode, this raising of an interior condition over worldly action might be denominated, in its uncompromising righteousness, an ultimate *protestantism*, or in its terminal subjectivity, a formalized *romanticism*. I shall return to these opinions off and on. Meanwhile it is necessary to add that there will be nothing vague or emotive about Kant's treatment of "morals." Under the heading of *Metaphysics of Morals*, Kant presents a doctrine of "right," the application of the will's moral law as it applies in the external world to dealings among persons, and of "virtue," the establishment of a personal ethics, that rectifies internal consciousness. This much more concrete work fleshes out the *Groundwork*, but, being its realization, it is not spectacularly novel, and indeed not alien to ordinary decency—except in one notorious, because exemplary, case. Kant says "The greatest violation of a human being's duty to himself [that is, to the humanity in his own person] is . . . *lying*." A liar "violates the dignity of humanity in his own person." He renounces his personality and is thus "a mere deceptive appearance of a human being." Thus the harm that can come to others from lying is not what distinguishes this vice and is therefore "not taken into account here."[12]

This extreme view of lying, which will be seen indeed to follow very consistently from Kant's explication of the will, is noble in conception but can be dreadful in application. Kant himself gives the infamous example: Let a man bent on murder come to your house and ask you whether the intended victim is within. If you lie to protect the person you are harboring, you are legally responsible for all the possible ensuing consequences; if you speak the truth, public justice can find nothing against you. But legal consequences aside, "Be truthful" is a sacred, unconditional command of reason, which trumps the harm to the victim. To those of us who have lived in a modern police state, this logical purity looks like moral insanity (see Note 31 to this chapter).

With those scruples stated, I now turn to what is the most *intellectually potent* version of the will with which I am acquainted. Kant explicates the will that is good apart from any further purpose in three propositions which accomplish the transition from "the common rational to the philosophical moral cognition" of a good will. The first of these sets out a concept of duty—doing as one *ought*—that separates will severely from inclination. People often act in conformity with duty from expedience mixed with ordinary decency. For example, a merchant refrains from overcharging a child—*as* he ought to. But he doesn't refrain *because* he ought to; his inclination to keep his clientele tells him that it is unwise to cheat his customers' children, and he may like being nice. Thus in common morality, you can hardly ever tell whether an action was dutiful or self-seeking. Kant thinks that this distinction does dwell within natural sound understanding but needs to be developed.[13]

The second proposition is that moral action is valuable not for its particular purpose but for the *maxim*, a subjective rule of action that the subject adopts as its own—how it will act. As has been said, what matters is not the object of an action but the subjective *principle* of volition, and that is the maxim. A third proposition is a consequence of the previous two, really a tighter definition of duty: It is the necessity that an action be done from *respect for law*. The object or effect is to be put aside precisely because I can feel inclination for it and approval, even love—but not respect. For it *is* merely an effect and not an activity of the will itself. Objectively the law itself and subjectively pure respect for the law: that alone should determine the will.[14]

What is this law that is to determine (*bestimmen*), that is, to give a definite direction to, the will? The maxim was a subjective rule adopted by each subject and valid for it; the objective law tells not what I decide to do but what I ought to do. In the foregoing chapter, I have raised the question whether the will issues commands itself or executes those given by the intellect or the passions. Kantian will constitutes a third case: The will itself conceives the law that commands it; it is *self-commanding*. For recall that will is reason, is practical, and is pure. Thus, as *reason*, it conceives universal propositions—laws. As *practical*, the law it conceives issues commands—imperatives. And as *pure*, it is non-pathological, unaffected—prior to all experience. "I have," Kant says, "deprived it of every [external] impulse . . ." Therefore, "nothing is left but the conformity of its actions with general lawfulness"—it is self-conforming. In other words, my will does not obey this or that law or impulse but enacts law-like universality itself:

> I ought never to act except in such a way that I could also will that my maxim become a universal law.

This is the first formulation of that famous *categorical imperative*. It is an "imperative" because it expresses a moral command, an Ought, an "I should." It is "categorical" in the sense in which we might say: "I categorically deny . . . ," meaning no ifs or buts, unconditionally and absolutely. This single law of the will does not, once more, say: Do this or that! It commands rather that whatever rule you should choose to act on, let it be such that it is *universalizable*. (I am not the only one to use this non-dictionary word.) Shape your personal maxim in the image of universal law! Alternately: Whatever you do, do it as a subject whose cognitive constitution culminates in reason, a faculty for thinking universals, laws, even in its practical aspect. Or more concisely: Above all maintain the integrity of your reason, even in action! This is the moment to recall that Kant is convinced, even before having completed the argument, that "there can, in the end, be only one and the same reason," albeit with two different applications, theoretical and practical. Thus the practical reason, the *will*, is ever and always *reason*. (More on the Categorical Imperative in Note 15 to this chapter.)[15]

In this section on common rational morality, Kant avers that in fact this moral law of the will is, if not yet explicit, implicitly before everyone's mind. We know that we shouldn't make exceptions for ourselves and do what we would not want others to do. Innocence, however, Kant says, is splendid, but it is easily seduced by "inclination" (Kant's prissily careful term for sensual desire, passion), so that a proper science of morals is needed to supply a counterweight.[16]

Therefore he starts again, this time beginning with popular morality as experienced and taking it through to its metaphysics, that is to say, to the particular *a priori* principles that in fact underlie it. The long and short of ordinary morality is that "it is absolutely impossible by means of experience to make out a single case" of true morality, one in which a person is actually acting *from* duty, *because* he ought to and not from convenience and self-love—certainly not by us with respect to ourselves. Morality is simply, like Hume's cause, below observation. So no moral teaching drawn from, or pointing to, experience can do anything but subject morality to ridicule, and nothing is to be learned here. That is why another ascent to principles of pure reason must be undertaken. It will show them as grounding the sense of duty implicit in ordinary morality. It proceeds as follows.[17]

In the *Critique of Pure Reason*, we learned that nature is constituted by laws, concepts imposed by the understanding. Rational beings, however (and Kant means any imaginable such beings), are not simply and directly compelled by laws, as are natural bodies, but are capable of "representing" the law to themselves and then acting in accordance with it. That is just what the will is: a capacity we have for not being pushed around by the laws of nature, as are bodies which are *under* laws, but for putting the law *before* ourselves and consciously embracing it for its lawfulness. Its necessity is *only* its own rationality.

This law is, of course, the categorical imperative, a law devoid of any specificity and commanding only that the rule of action should be lawlike. The categorical imperative has three versions, each introducing a different aspect of one and the same law, which in its first, fundamental form demands, to say the same thing twice (as Kant does), that the rules of individual action should be universalizable in scope. A second version requires that the maxim of action be one that could be willed into a law of nature. One of Kant's examples is suicide: If shortening one's own life from self-love were willed into a law of nature, then nature would become unthinkably self-contradictory, for the same feeling that is intended to further life, self-love, would now be destroying it. So, like the first version, this one prevents self-contradiction, though now not in the realm of freedom but of nature, in which human beings exist as physical and biological bodies. A third version reaches into the realm of human community as a venue for freedom. It says that humanity must always be treated—in one's own or in another's person—as an end and not as a means. This imperative, which unifies all rational beings into a "kingdom of ends," establishes a systematic union of completely independent, free beings who are subject not to each other, but only to laws arising from their own wills. Each will legislates with the above-mentioned universality; hence all legislate for all. Each member of the kingdom is thus a moral being, one whose will is determined by the categorical imperative—and morality is what gives him and all fellow-subjects dignity. Again, this version of the imperative prevents a self-contradiction—that a human being, the unconditional law-giver, constituted as a self-ruler, might in society undergo the indignity of serving as a means for another's purpose. Thus the categorical imperative commands in order how persons ought to act individually, as fitting into nature, and as participating in society. (For the relation of the kingdom of ends to Rousseau's general will, see Note 18 to this chapter.)[18]

There are several other ways to think of this imperative that brings the subject out of its selfhood into a community. One very revealing way is this: Rational beings differ from merely natural beings (bodies animate or inanimate) by setting an end for themselves—setting an end being "the matter of every good will." But for this end not to be just some *particular* purpose that might be *positively* effected (which would make the will good only relative to our own being), it must be thought of in *abstraction* from all such particularity, hence only *negatively*—as "that which must never be acted against." Such a negative end can only be that subject of all possible ends, a human being. No volition can consider such a subject only as a means, for it too has a will, such as can never without contradiction be considered as a mere means, that is to say, subordinated to another's will. Since every will not only gives laws that are universally valid for all other rational beings, who are thus in a systematic union of mutual law-giving, but also regards all others as ends rather than means, there is founded a community of ends, or rather a communion of mutually end-respecting rational beings.[19]

What is particularly revealing here, though it was clear enough before, is the abstractness or formalism of this formulation of human practicality, even in a community. It never says: Do this or do that to achieve this or that particular good you desire. For all the imperatives contain an "Ought," which is the ought of duty. Thus duty pertains to a good will that labors under hindrances; a "holy" or perfect will knows no duty. Duty, the Ought, being the "objective necessity of an action from obligation," that is, moral necessity, is a mark of a will, such as, on its own, might be swayed by the world of sense, by desires and inclinations—the mark of a less-than-holy will. People know this implicitly and not from any external experience: They should do as they ought, and being human, that is apt to hurt.

For the passions are in the way; they ever were what ethics or morality has to contend with—to rationalize or to suppress. In this, at least, Kant is traditional. But for him the faculty of "lower" desire is, as one would expect, quite disconnected from the will, from pure practical reason, indeed mostly antagonistic to it. (There is, however, as I mentioned above, a ghost of a desire attaching to the will, called "interest," to be explained in a moment.) Here is Kant's definition of the faculty of desire (*Begehrungsvermögen*: given in a footnote!): "*Life* is the faculty of a being by which it acts according to the laws of the faculty of desire." And: "The *faculty of desire* is the faculty such a [rational] being has of causing, through its ideas, the reality of the objects of these ideas." This latter is a curious, apparently far too sanguine, definition. (It is rarely Kant's intention to make us laugh, but on a few occasions, his effect.) However, elsewhere he moderates the definition, albeit not of the faculty but of the desire itself: "Desire is the self-determining of a subject's power by means of a representation of something futural as an affect"; in other words, we imagine an object of desire and are activated by it [*to try*] to bring it about—a much more likely but reduced effect. What is truly remarkable is that by these definitions of life and desire taken to together, the will is, properly speaking, excluded from life; it is a supra-animate faculty—a dessicated latter-day example, one might say, of Socrates' assertion that to practice thoughtfulness is to practice dying, to live now, as it were, in Hades, in the Afterlife. The will is, accordingly, moved by a ghost of a passion.[20]

This attenuated feeling, this unfelt feeling, is the "interest" mentioned above. Interest, in the pure sense, is not, as in ordinary life, a motive we act *from* (as "I have an interest in the success of my efforts"); rather, it is an attachment truly without motives, either up-front or submerged. (Thus not even "I take an interest in my students" qualifies, for it is a claim which inevitably is burdened by all sorts of pathological baggage—as honest teachers know, but find humanly natural). Since the human will, vulnerable as it is to the affects, needs an incentive or reward in accord with its purity, its formalism, Kant has devised the notion of "interest"—desire purified of the influence of an external object. It is a sort of complement to the earlier demand that we should act not in conformity with, but from, duty: We should act *not from interest*, but *take an interest in* our actions. How such a non-pathological attachment is possible, how, by means of pure ideas, interest can be aroused is, Kant thinks, inexplicable. And this is really the same question as why *pure* reason is moved to become *practical.* So while we cannot grasp the "why" of willing, we can partly explain its "how."[21]

So far, metaphysics has yielded a "supreme principle of morality": The will, practical reason, is "autonomous"—literally "self-law-giving." All "heteronomous"—other-law-receiving—moralities are therefore spurious. But what is yet lacking is the condition on which such autonomy becomes possible. The key to this condition is freedom, and so in its last part, the *Groundwork* reaches into a critique of practical reason, for now we touch on the human cognitive constitution itself.

The positive meaning of the will's freedom is not so difficult to state and is given in the *Groundwork*. We already know its name: this very autonomy. Indeed, if we presuppose the will to be free, which in fact we did, a mere analysis of the concept of a free will does tell us this much (which accounts for the formalism of autonomy): To have a free will *means* to give one's own law to oneself. Moreover, that law can't be determined by anything beyond or alien to its own lawfulness; therefore it can have no content except the imperative to universalize.

The negative meaning of the will's freedom, or better, an explanation of negative freedom, is now in order. All rational beings must, *ipso facto*, be free, since reason "cannot consciously receive direction" for its judgments from outside impulses. And if a rational being has a practical side, a will, so much the more must it be thus negatively free. To will is to choose, and to choose is to think of oneself not as driven but as deciding. So the will must have a property by which it can be effectively causal without being determined by a natural impulse (occasioned by an alien object) such as an object of desire. This negative freedom needs a pre-metaphysical, a "critical," consideration.[22]

Now, as I said, if we want to know how we come to have an interest in morality—which is really the same question as why pure reason does become practical, that is, why, it does not merely represent to itself what *ought* to be, but also cares to assent—then we are in trouble. For this "is impossible for us to explain . . . and all the pains and labor of seeking an explanation of it are lost." Moreover, it is similarly beyond the limits of our reason to know how freedom as volitional causality is possible, for as a cognition such a causality is a mere content-deprived idea, a left-over "something" after every sense-motivation has been excluded from determining the will. To repeat: "But reason would overstep all its bounds [that is, become dialectical] if it took upon itself to *explain how* pure reason can be practical, which would be exactly the same task as to explain how *freedom is possible*." I suspect that the inexplicability of Kantian freedom lies largely in its negativity, its impenetrability to affect, to desire.[23]

It *is*, however, possible here and now to explain how the practical proposition conditioned on freedom, the law of morality, the categorical imperative, is possible, though for a subtler and deeper treatment we must go to the *Critique of Practical Reason*. In neither of the foundational works must we expect to come down to earth to learn how the will becomes executive, goes actually to work. Indeed, it is a question whether it ever needs to or does. There are, however, a number of books in which Kant deals with issues closer to the psychology of willing.[24]

Freedom taken simply as a *fact*, a fact of pure reason, is known *for a fact* to that strangely indefinite class of "rational beings," and so to every *human* being. We all, as ordinary folks, know that we *can* act contrary to impulse, and Kant thinks we all *despise* ourselves when we have transgressed the moral law. We know it even when we don't know its metaphysics, namely *how* a categorical imperative falls out from freedom, *how* it is possible. This last *is*, however, permissibly explicable, and the explanation reaches back to the *Critique of Pure Reason*. It runs this way: We belong to two worlds. One is the deterministic, totally unfree, world of nature, that system of appearances shaped from its own sensation for its own experience by the law-imposing subject (myself)—behind its own back, as it were. The other world we inhabit as beings of reason. We count ourselves as belonging to a super-sensible world of reason in which we are conscious of ourselves as giving law to ourselves, and of becoming efficient causes. This causality we call *will*, and we know that it is not apprehensible to the senses, because if it were it would have to conform to the determinations of the natural world of appearances.[25]

Having thus dual citizenship, the idea of freedom makes me a member of a world in which I know that my actions *would* be autonomous, true to a (free) will, were I wholly of it—but since I also sense myself as a part of nature, as a being of sensibility, I know rather that I *ought* to will freely, undetermined by natural impulses. That exactly explains the categorical imperative, which connects the freedom of an autonomous Will, which always *would* act lawfully, to the weakness of a natural will, which *should* act freely. It does so by framing its commands so as to insure that my actions shall conform to the very character of a rational, a law-giving will: It enjoins me to make the specific maxims on which I intend to act universalizable, that is, law-like.

In what follows, I shall write Will (*Wille*) for the pure, supersensible Will, and will (*Willkür*) for the will intending to become efficient in the world, since Kant himself seems finally to have settled on this clear duality: *Wille* as autonomy and *Willkür* as "will-choice," the one pure, the other sensorily engaged.[26]

Here, then, is an accumulation of four questions that I want to address to the second *Critique*, imagining that a reader might have the same:

1. What is this rational sentiment, this pure interest, which is to activate the will, and what does it do?
2. How does pure reason help itself in its practical mode, that is, as Will, to form maxims?
3. How are the two wills, the will (*Willkür*) of spontaneity, of new beginnings, and the Will (*Wille*) of autonomy, of self-containment, related?

And finally, the question of questions:

> 4. Does pure Will actually descend to doing work in the real world, that is, does will actually start, that is, execute, anything?

1. Within the first *Critique*, laws kept nature strictly in her pre-determined courses; in the second *Critique*, law is in fact the first expression of freedom. How could law, apparently an instrument of compulsion, be an agent of freedom? Not, we learned, by its content, but by its form, its universality. Law is imperial; it betokens the internal imperium of the subject as a free being that is its own last resort and absolute ruler in its empire, the arena of independence from external determination. This "I," however, rules over a realm of ideas that has been shown in the first *Critique* to have no real, that is, no experiential cognitive content. So it cannot help but engage with the other, the realm of experience, nature. (This is my way of putting it to myself, as if the realm of reason had the initiative, being closer to the underlying I.) Thus, on an essentially non-affective subject must supervene some sort of responsive affect to relate it to a natural world that is full of affects. This natural world has an inner aspect, our soul (*Gemüt*), whose very thin science is psychology, and an outer one, nature, whose very full science is physics. In the inner side are seated the *lower* faculties, as well as the affects, all the sources of heteronomy and intrusions on the Will's self-sufficiency: first, desire, which is a faculty for representing an object so as to cause its future reality; next, pleasure, which is a consciousness that the object has been attained and that the ensuing state should continue; and finally, the resultant happiness, which is pleasure indeed continuously maintained. These all pertain to inclination (*Neigung*) and thus to being affected; they are dependencies, and so to them attaches a lower acquisitive interest. The higher, pure interest to be explained is the opposite of such sensuous impulsions. Yet it is "that by which reason becomes practical, that is, a cause determining the will," meaning that it is an incentive, impulse, or motive (*Triebfeder*: "mainspring") arousing the will—but *not* one arising from an alien object. Hence, will does not act *from* interest, pathologically, but *out of* interest, as, so to speak, a disinterestedly interested bystander of itself. This interest is identical to respect for the moral law, which is a similarly unsentimental sentiment. To put us out of our misery: Interest, like freedom, cannot be explained. How a mere thought with no sensory element can generate a feeling of pleasure—for there is a corresponding *higher* pleasure as well—is simply beyond conceiving, but it is certain that we have this interest—an *ex post facto* interest, to be sure. For the moral law is not valid for us because we are interested in its being so, but our interest arises from its validity, which springs "from our most authentic self." So the answer concerning this sentiment of reason is: It is another fact about ourselves, that we all know by an "experi-

ence" that is different in kind from the cognitively informed experience we have of psychological or physical nature. I ask myself: Do I have such a "feeling?" *My* answer is yes—at critical moments; explanation to follow a little below.[27]

2. In the second *Critique*, Kant gives operating instructions, so to speak, for the formation of maxims, the more immediate rules governing particular action. Recall the second version of the imperative: Choose your maxims as if they were to become laws of nature—which are, in fact, universal in their realm. Kant here solves a problem of practical reason that he sees as analogous to a problem of theoretical reason in the first *Critique*. There it was: On what common ground can the logical conceptual understanding engage sympathetically with our affective sensibility? The difficult answer was in the schematism of the imagination. Its practical analogue is: How can pure practical reason engage knowledgeably with the sensory realm of human action? Kant's even more difficult answer here is that a meeting ground of pure and applied will is implied in the second version of the imperative: Use the laws of nature as a model or type by which to test the universality of your maxim. Ask yourself if you would live with or in a nature governed by this, your maxim-become-law. The self-abridgment of one's life was an example given above. (It is, in fact, fun of a sort to try this second imperative on the old ten commandments or, contrariwise, on the latest piece of permissiveness. However, I ask myself: *Ought* we not to develop enough mindfulness, the ancient "practical wisdom," *phronesis*, to allow prudent, readily remediable exceptions—such as apt, benign lying—to the general law? Does the totalitarianism of legality not place a taboo on the development of moral ingenuity, the lubricant of real life?)[28]

3. The problem of the relation that the Will of autonomy, of self-rule (which might find its satisfaction in itself) bears to the will of spontaneity, of starts (which must intend to reach into the world) comes closer to the final question about really efficacious willing in the real world, but it is not quite there. Kant does not explicitly resolve this problem of the dual will, the Will and the will in tandem, though the mere idea of a will at once "obligation-creating and obligation-executing is one of the most dramatic theses in Kant's philosophy," analogous to the Copernican Revolution of the first *Critique*. A resolution can, however, be extracted as follows, and it uses, once again, the "two worlds" argument. Our one Will finds itself as free, and because free, as universal. But as facing the world in its action-focused aspect, as lower-case will, it has to be involved in the world. As I've said, I don't think Kant tells why—why the Will could not will to remain uninvolved, to retreat from the world into "holiness." Perhaps it is simply another great fact that our sensory self can move our pure Self. (I marvel, by the way, at how many facts of life the *Critiques* assume and respect.) If so, the solution is simple: We have a pure Self and know freedom; we have

a worldly self and act. Yet I ask myself: Has the subject's interaction with, really its initiating intervention in, nature been grounded? Surely all the subjective conditions for a moral imperative have been given. Is there then implied an objective command: "Execute." I don't think so.[29]

4. And that raises the question of questions. Can the Kantian subject, the "I," interfere with the world, whose strictly necessary rules it has produced behind its own back from the depth of its transcendent ground? Can it belatedly mount better or worse initiatives? Begin with the evidence. Kant has already said that there can never be any certainty that a particular human action was indeed done freely, and not from the lower, the sensual sort of interest. But worse: Kant remains a Humean with respect to the system of appearances constituting Nature—*never* does causality *appear*, and *ipso facto*, so much the less would moral causality, change for better or worse, be sensibly evident. Above all, there is no way to breach the causal necessity, the determinism of nature; even our deepest characteristic of reason, freedom, cannot be the ground of a break in the constitutive laws issuing from our understanding; if freedom became causal within nature—that would be the chaos-death of Kantian philosophy.

There is, it seems, one resolution: Let the Kantian subject live in one world in two different respects, so that the distinction between freedom and nature is perspectival, a matter of dual description: moral and natural. Then Will and will, autonomy and spontaneity, are just the names of our dual sense of freedom. We feel *as if* we were self-determined internally and *as if* we could re-determine the world externally. "As if" makes for a deflated system; how could it be re-animated? Fichte will mount such an attempt.[30]

I think, in conclusion, that the great question (the practical one, in the ordinary sense) concerning Kantian morality is double: Should *everyone* and could *anyone* live by it? By "should" I mean: Would the imaginable consequences, not of everyone trying and failing, but of all of us trying and *succeeding* in regarding our Wills as Kant bids, and determining them as Kant prescribes, seem good to me? By "could" I mean: Would human beings, as they live and breathe, endure the censorious, never completely satisfiable oversight by their own imperiously pure will? Kant considers it of great importance that all human beings implicitly acknowledge the Ought of duty and the unconditional imperatives of the will, and for better or worse carry on. The question is whether the moral law made explicit, as it is in his two great works, has the same livability as it does in its submerged "common" or "popular" mode, or whether it might, as an explicit philosophy, become life-curdling and rigidifying. The present-day receptivity for a duty-bound life is, however, so low that the "could" question may no longer be worth worrying about.

The first, the "should" question, although it becomes practically moot when personal Kantianism has gone out of style, remains worth thinking through. The reason is that the pure, desire-free Will, is so awe-inspiringly original that one must wish to know what kind of an ethical life it would project into the world phenomenally. After all, with a little imagination, Socratic-, Aristotelian-, Stoic-, Scholastic-, Lutheran-, Hobbesian-, Humean-type volitions are all projectable onto the living scene: why not the Kantian?

And there, imagined into the living world, it doesn't look as good as it does in theory, for in the live world incorruptible rationality should, I think, trump workable reasonableness only rarely, and we should know when a maxim should tacitly be amended with a limiting clause (a modification Kant must categorically reject, even if it is done with a silent promise not to make a habit of it). For example, to know when to lie, seems to me more rather than less free. (For additional thoughts on Kant's ethical effect, see Note 31 to this chapter.)[31]

(Yet on the other hand, in moments of moral crisis, what is more indispensable than a Will that is ready to accept permanent harm to soul and body, ready to forego the incentive of a full-bodied joy to act from a bone-hard moral interest alone, and thus to do simply as it ought, or feel forever ashamed? To my mind, the ever-viable use of the dutiful Will, be it for salvation or subversion is *this*: Put it in the stand-by mode and activate it just for that exceptionally critical instant when one thing is urgently desired, and the other is simply right. For the rest of life, the grand tradition—Plato, Aristotle, Thomas—seems to prescribe a better way: Let the object of love lead the will, provided that it is a good object eliciting a genuine love—or perhaps even do without Will, that assertive volitional intermediary, since it is not really needed when duty is in service to love.)

B. Fichte: Primeval Will

One might say that Fichte means to be to Kant what Plotinus is to Plato. Plotinus collects lines of thought scattered through Plato's dialogues and works them into an onto-cosmological framework, which is thus at once derivative and original. Above all, he develops Plato's grandest intimations into an explicit first principle, the One. Similarly, Fichte accepts the terms of Kant's, albeit already systematic, exposition but finds insufficient grounds below and fissures within it. The chief case of the latter Kantian failure is the unbridgeable chasm between pure reason's theoretical and practical products, nature and morality. The chief case of the former is the absence of a primary principle, one approachable source of what there is. For Kant, as for Fichte, the candidate is the "I," the subject underlying all thinking and all sensing. One might say that what the One is to antiquity, the I is to modernity, the "Being" beyond all things. But for Kant, knowledge of this I is illusory. It is a "transcendent" idea, going beyond our cognitive capacities. Fichte's *Doctrine of Science* (*Wissenschaftslehre*), however, begins: "The I posits itself, simply" (*Das Ich setzt sich selbst schlechthin*), and from this absolute, abrupt beginning develop in serial order the realms of intellect and nature. Thus the irreconcilable rift, the Kantian parallelism of the moral realm of pure practical reason and the natural world of theoretical understanding, is obviated, not perspectivally but originally. For nature, as *derived from intellect*, is now an ensouled secondary being. What makes Fichte a figure in this book is this: "Willing is something immediate and original, which cannot be derived from anything higher." Willing is assigned a primeval function by Fichte.[32]

How primeval? Is the "I" a personal pronoun and the will my will, or something beyond? In Chapter VII, I shall be giving an account of the supra-human will. It seems pretty clear that the will that is truly primeval for Fichte is *not* individual, but that a personal will does fall out of it. So his "I" differs radically from Kant's, which is, for all its ultimately untouchable, impersonal-seeming character as a mere "subject," an underlying something, certainly individual, a *person* or, at least, a proto-person, distinct from other I's—though it be a distinction without a difference. I am including Fichte in my chapter on Kant because he writes in a mode so characteristic of our philosophic tradition: dialectically derivative, reactively original—in other words as a Kantian! (The same goes for Schelling, who is treated in Note 33 to this chapter.)[33]

The Fichtean work in which a supra-human will appears very clearly is *The Vocation of Man*. The small book extols faith: "All my conviction is only faith." It is not to be foisted on others by argument; all education is of "the will, not the intellect." I must do as I ought, follow conscience, promote earthly good, "but whether this lawful willing *really* promotes it is not my concern." This is Kantian inconsequentialism boldly stated, but now it is grounded in a law of the supersensible world, which it must conceive and express. This Law is self-active reason, which *is* will. "Self-active" means something like "revving itself up, self-inciting," a characteristic of reason explained below. This Infinite Will operates purely as will, without working on any sensible material, yet it is not withdrawn from finite beings; it is, unlike the Aristotelian Intellect, moved by human willing. A human being can, by obedience, raise itself to this One, and it in turn bows down to humanity by intoning within us as a voice of conscience. Is this eternal Will God? It is "surely the creator of the world," but it is not the God of the Bible who *has* a Will; it *is* a Will, a philosophic notion raised from grounding principle to faith-inspiring godhead.[34]

The above breathes the fumes of philosophical intoxication, but there is hard-working ontology behind it, as well as clear-eyed observation. To come down from infinite Will to finite, humanly personal will: Fichte has a lot to say about this will, though nothing at all in his young, tone-setting *Doctrine of Science*. His revision of this work, *The Doctrine of Science by a New Method*, contains everything necessary to the system, is much clearer, but above all, brings in the will extensively. So that is my main source.

The beginning is a postulate, one proscribed by Kant: "Construct the concept of the I and observe how you accomplish this." For Kant, mere "thoughts without content are empty, intuitions without concepts are blind." Since intuitions, which deliver experiential givens, can only be sensible, the concept of an I that transcends experience can only be empty, for there is no purely intellectual intuition. Fichte's postulate explicitly overrides Kant's prohibition, for the concept so found is to be called the *"original intuition of the I"* and is presupposed in the explanation of all other consciousness. In observing oneself observing oneself (presumably by an ultimate kind of introspection), one comes—of course—on oneself as active and as acting on oneself; thus the concept of the self as derived from self-observation is, *"one posits oneself as self-positing."* Note that this discovery of the I (or self) as a sort of iterated positing is the consequence of the demand that its concept be constructed. I mean that it appears the way it does to the self looking for itself—as something looked at, as answering the demand to "come to grips" with itself, to become a concept, a *Begriff*: "The concept of the I comes into being only by means of an activity that can go back into itself (*in sich selbst zurückgehen*, "self-revert")." But what is this "positing"? The German word is *setzen*, the verb from which is derived the noun *Satz*, which means (among many other things) an "affirmative proposition," a statement. Behind this declaration of the self as affirming itself as self-affirming is the idea of a primordial action: Fichte invents the word *Tathandlung* ("Deed-doing-action") as a variation on the German word *Tatsache* ("Done deal, fact") to describe this primordial self-activation upon which the I then exerts its observational activity. It is a coming-apart, as it were, of an identity into itself and its expression. An immediate further discovery is that one cannot posit oneself as acting without positing oneself as *in repose*.[35]

Thus begins a second, of course an atemporal, phase. The I discovers that it must be *determinable*. "In repose" is just what the I is as determinable, since self-activation must have been the transition from indeterminate repose to definite action, a transformation from an indeterminate passivity to self-determined activity. For determinability is the capability of being determined, and determination (*Bestimmong*) is the delimitation of an indefinite underlying subject by the addition of specifying features, while self-determination takes place when the determination is done by the subject to itself—and in these contexts that is a general description of the will. We are approaching the point here.

What the I thus discovers as a negation of its activity is Being. Being, perfect repose, is therefore by no means an original concept; it arises as the "concept of canceled activity"—a negative concept, a Not-I—for the I is activity. (Here Fichte states in so many words the deepest difference between classical and modern philosophy: the primacy of the subjective Self over objective Being. And since the inquiry is about Knowledge, this ranking is simply the consequence of the demand, the postulate, to conceptualize. It is *epistemology as ontology*. For Being is secondary just because it is a derived concept—which is at the same time the very warrant for its reality.)[36]

A third phase then introduces the notions of "real" and "ideal." The transition from "determinable" to "determinate" was utterly internal. Now it turns out that this is the *real* activity, opposed to one which merely copies it, the *ideal*, conscious, conceptualizing activity. Nonetheless, those two condition and comprehend each other. What is posited in concept has real power behind it; what is intuited as a fact (*Tatsache*), empirically, needs a concept to make sense of it. For Fichte thinks that the primordial deed-action (*Tathandlung*) is found by abstracting from the facts of experienced consciousness. By setting an object before itself, the I achieves actual consciousness. This utterly self-sufficient internality of the development of consciousness is *freedom*, self-determination; the "ultimate ground and the first condition of all being and all consciousness."[37]

Immediately, another feature emerges, overturning Kant's separation of theory and practice: "*Free self-determination* is intuitable only as a determination to become 'something.'" Therefore practical, real power needs a concept of finality, the concept of the good. It follows that the intuiting subject that possesses practical power must also be the intellectual, comprehending subject that forms concepts. The true character of the I lies in this identity.[38]

I hope it is clear why the way to the will must go through and up from these delvings, although a reader may have doubts, as do I, that a personal self-reverting, "going back into oneself" (*in sich selbst zurückgehen*) would recover the same results for everyone. We are now only two proto-wills, so to speak, removed from the Will itself: First, Fichte constructs a "drive" (*Trieb*), a manifold of feelings. The I must posit such a drive, a direction-giving limitation, an action, that accords the free intellect a horizon of possibilities. He goes on to show, in order, how things come to be present to us both as independent *from* us and as re-presentations *to* us, and how space, and the matter within it, arise.[39]

Second, he shows how "a rational being posits itself in space as a practically striving being." By now, the absolute I, if it ever was meant as a supra-personal Self, has surely become individualized. Here we are right next to willing, for Fichte understands striving (*Streben*) as a relation to the external, spatial world. When I place an object in space, its place is determined by my action, although *and* because the thing has been posited by me as independent of me, as an object. In other words, the object is posited not as having its being but as having its position from me. The first inference is that I must be myself in space, immattered. The second is that I must have a means of determining the object's distance from me. I do this by appraising the amount of energy, the striving, I would have to expend to reach the object. This appraisal of my striving toward the object is known to everyone, immediately, though it can be improved by practice. Fichte concludes that this is the first notable point where a necessary relationship between our representations (of objects) and our practical powers (of striving) presents itself. Moreover, it has been shown that I can posit other things in space only if I posit myself as matter in space.[40]

So the I has gone into space, not in the mode of a mere appearance (as Kant claims it must) but as that very primordial self that is doing all the positing.

Energy or force figured in determining the relation of spatial objects to me, but our concept of force "can be derived only from our consciousness of willing and of the causal power (*Causalität*) that is united with willing." Once again, however: "Willing is something immediate and original which cannot be derived from anything higher." In other words, will is as primordial as the I.[41]

Fichte describes the phenomenon of willing and its necessary antecedent deliberation: In deliberation, striving is dispersed, goes in all directions. In willing, striving is focused, determined. Willing makes a demand that something become real, something that in deliberation had been an ideal possibility. Again ideal, conceptualizing activity and real, practical power work together. But how can I become conscious of that conclusive act of my own will? It is because to will and to be conscious of willing are identical. In representing an object to myself, I distinguish between the represented object and myself. In willing, however, there is no such distinction. To will is to think that I am willing; the will is aboriginally reflexive. Willing is like feeling, absolutely immediate. "Nothing exists if I do not think of myself as willing." Here is a line of descent into the depths that bridges Kant's abyss between the intelligible and the experiential world: The possibility of the world of appearances is conditioned on an intelligible world—the very realm Kant proscribes as one of inaccessible *noumena*, "things [merely] of thought." The Fichtean world in turn "rests upon its own proper center, namely the I itself, which is a whole only in the act of thinking of [of = issuing from] willing: All its representations originate in the I's act of thinking its willing."[42]

Why is willing the conception on which everything rests? Because only in willing is the I as ideal subject and as real object united with itself, and only in willing can the I originate, produce something new, bring forth novel representations. As will, the I is *both* at one with itself and productive of objects. Nothing can tell us this but intellectual vision.

Another way to think of this volition-mode is as reasons's self-affection. Kant had introduced an enigmatic rational feeling, the sentiment of satisfaction arising from having respected moral law. For Fichte, an "intelligible feeling" arises when the will has compelled the imagination to contain itself so as to focus on an outcome. As it appears in consciousness, it "hovers between feeling and thinking." This feeling of genuine efficaciousness is a way in which the intellect as will has effected itself: The concentration of the intellect generates a feeling of force; it is the sense of the intelligible world's connection with the world of appearance. What was for Kant a puzzle is for Fichte the will-intellect's transition into the world of space and time.[43]

This is, for present purposes, the crux of Fichte on the will: Kant could not explain—so it seemed to me—how the will could go to work in the world by way of "spontaneity"—*originating* a natural course of events. Fichte now attempts this explanation. Here, to begin with, is a definition: "The object of willing is a determinate series of acting and sensing. 'I will something'—this means that the present state of my feelings or an object that is presently in a certain condition, ought to become other than it is."[44]

Fichte begins by *assuming* that the will has this causal power. Then he traces out what ideal and real factors must be involved: an ideal activity that is being realized—"*temporal succession.*" "The first, undivided act of willing is repeated and is, as it were, extended over the manifold [of sense], and from this there arises a temporal succession." In this sense the will achieves its worldly object.[45]

It works this way, first experientially: I determine my self to move from A to B—that is, I *will* to go from here to there. This act of self-determination, of willing, does not originally occur *in* time, but is posited over and over in the heterogeneous, alien externality of the sense-manifold. Iterated acts of willing make for a unified stretch, not (as it seems) so much of a continuous as of a continual experience. And so it appears in the form of time, that form of sensibility (as Kant would say), within which occurs a movement of transition. Each of its links is dependent on the foregoing one, but all are caused by the spontaneous and ongoing will, which is exerted over and over, extendedly but "*in fits and starts.*" It operates through interdependent intermediary states. That intermittence is why I experience it—my own force—as limited, as subject to laws other than my own, "as a *natural force, as a sensible or physical force.*" "I, so to speak, 'carry myself over into nature' for nature always resists me," and my efficacy extends itself through time only insofar as it encounters natural resistance. So my energy appears to me as an object, but not a mere object: "a *subject object.*"[46]

Fichte has *assumed* the causal power of the will to change the natural world and *described* the real fact of our experience of being the agents of natural change. What is there in the ideal, the intelligible world to make this willing in the world possible? It is simply said: It all begins with an ideal activity. The subjective, intellectual feeling of efficacy is posited objectively, "realized"—not the feeling, to be sure, but its content, the object of my willing, *both* as object and as dependent on my will. What is being realized is *myself* as conscious of self and as concentrated on an object, as intellect and will, both. In relation to my thinking, the sensible energy of the will focused on an object is conceptual (ideal), but the form in which it occurs, time, is sensible (real). This will-force is thus "neither purely sensible nor purely intelligible but partially both." It mediates between the two worlds. The promise of the New Method was to bring together the worlds of theory and practice, and that is what Fichte has done—though we readers may well find ourselves somewhat past the limit of our dialectical abilities.[47]

Fichte is by no means finished; there are about two hundred pages dealing with Freedom and Desire, the Ought and Doing, the I among other rational beings and in opposition to things outside, the personal Body and organized Nature. But enough said for the present purpose—to delineate the concept of the will when the absolute origin of the world is the I.

Here is the place to mention that Fichte, as well as Schelling, found a receptive following in a circle of young Romantics. What primarily attracted these moderns of their day to the former was his positing of a primordial I that repels a natural world out of and from itself, and to the latter, the presupposition of an ideal Nature that expresses itself progressively as the self-unfolding of Spirit made visible. An absolute I that is world-creating and an objective Nature that is spiritual together satisfy Romantic longings for a subjectively conditioned world. The same two notions can also wreak havoc in weakly romantic souls. Ludwig Tieck, an opponent of Fichte, albeit himself among the Romantics, depicts a fictional hero who, infected by Fichtean idealism, uses it as a pretext for letting his passions run wild, and comes to an ignominious end. This is how he thinks:

> Thus my outer sense dominates the physical, my inner sense the moral world. Everything subjects itself to my choosing will (*Willkür*); every appearance, every action I can call whatever pleases me; the animate and the inanimate world hangs on the chain ruled by my spirit; my whole life is but a dream, whose various shapes form themselves according to my will. I myself am the sole law in the whole of nature; everything obeys this law.

This impotent dream of omnipotence is a corruption, but not an unrecognizable one, of Fichte's occasionally abstrusely abstract thinking. But even healthier dreamers, and, moreover, actual people, transmogrified the system—for example, Novalis, who turned Fichte's metaphysical idealism into his own magical idealism. Here are four of his notes:

What I will, I can.

To the interior goes the mysterious way.

The greatest magician would be he who could magic himself at the same time, such that his magic came before him as alien, self-empowered appearances. Might that not be the actual case with us?

The art: to realize our will totally.[48]

And again, the perplexity is: Once a system is given to the public, how to assign the degree of responsibility the author has for what followers (including those whose, often ardent, engagement is in the mode of detraction) make of it—which is not to say that the transformations are *necessarily* deleterious.

To complicate things further, Fichte and the younger Schelling lived right among those young Romantics, and that invites some interpreters to look at their philosophies themselves as Romantic, or better, as the desiccated emanations of Romanticism. There is—rightly—no end to worrying these bones of contention, when serious works have dubious effects: Who is the follower and who is the followed, who is to be held harmless (thus leaving their philosophies a toothless tiger), and who is to be held responsible (thus assigning blame where no live control was possible)? I think the least worst solution is to honor the capabilities of these texts by believing that something in them called forth skewed or perilous readings, to protect them, as it were, from ascriptions of harmlessness. (For a neat presentation of Romanticism as a crux of modernity, see Note 49 to this chapter.)[49]

I am put in mind of these problems because I am about to take up a group of philosophies that do seem to have pernicious possibilities. Both Fichte and Schelling present the will as a supra-human actor in some works, but in their systems, whatever it may be primordially, it develops individuality along the way. In the next chapter but one, in Chapter VII, the will casts loose from persons, and this faceless force has indeed captured souls, to their detriment.

But first an interlude on the *will* as a *word*.

chapter **VI**

A Linguistic Interlude

Since I am coming into modern territory, a brief consideration of *will* as a word with a past and of *willing* as used in sentences seems in order.

A. Etymology and Syntax

The etymology of *etymology*, the term used for the study of word origins, is an "account of what is true (*etymon*)." Yet it is surely not obvious that the earliest meaning of a word that we can discern, the one we are then apt to consider as the originating sense, is indeed *the* "true" meaning. Nonetheless, there is no getting around the sense that origins set things off. Thus, to go back to them often tells us what lies most deeply in a word's significance, sometimes hidden under the "sediment" of traditionalization—the forgetfulness that comes with constant use. Sometimes, this significance actually seems to manifest itself over time, in the development of a word's use—as when it acquires a harder edge as it goes. The will is, I think, of the latter sort. In any case, word-archaeology is as much fun as artifact-archaeology, my first love. (More on etymology in Note 1 to this chapter.)[1]

Syntax (a part of grammar) is to sentences (meaning-conveying expressions of thoughts or feelings) something like logic (a part of reasoning) is to propositions (units of logical thinking, such as for Descartes were the object of the will's affirmation or denial). Much as logic has modes—possibility, contingency, necessity—so syntax has moods—indicative, subjunctive, optative, imperative. And the modal use of the verb "to will" is simply fascinating.[2]

The word "will" has the same root in the three languages in which the texts I am appealing to are written: French, German, and English. *Volonté*, *Wille*, and *will* all go back to the Indo-European root (the last stop before a reconstructed proto-language): *wel*. From it are derived, Latin: *velle*, "to wish," and the noun *voluntas* with a connection to *voluptas*, "pleasure" (which Lucretius plays on in the lines quoted in Ch. II, Sec. A, herein); French: *volonté*; German: *Wahl*, "choice"; English: *wellfare*, *weal*, *wealth*, and the like. And so to *will*, "strong wish, intention," and from it, the verb *to will*; "the will to . . ." is a locution adopted from German, as in *der Wille zur Macht*, "the will to power"; *willful* has degenerated into "obstinate."[3]

This etymological accumulation tells a story pertinent to my point. Will begins in a sense of something good, desirable, pleasurable, takes on a meaning of choice—which is why free choice and free will run side by side—is ratcheted up into an intense intention, sharpened into a will to power, and when exposed, is denigrated as willfulness, obstinate self-will.

The syntactical function of the verb *to will* is even more illuminating, particularly its moods. The verb gives a sentence its modality, whether it asserts (indicative) or wishes (optative) or commands (imperative), or even expresses the mixed moods of the speaker. The gist of the following exposition is: Grammar serves to focus us on the deeply enigmatic relation between the will and the future, a relation that involves tense (time) and mood (intention).

English is not alone in having *no pure future tense* for its verbs. (By "pure" I mean built into the verb and non-modal.) There was, linguists have determined, no such future tense in Proto-Indo-European, our reconstructed aboriginal language. Then some languages, in a secondary development, acquired built-in marks of futurity. Among them were Greek and Latin, though their future tense was used not only for prediction but also for command. Moreover, these future forms were derived from modal forms (meaning here the non-indicative moods) that express non-facticity: wishes, intentions, requirements, commands.[4]

The outcome is a wonderful perplexity. I have several times spoken—as most people will—of the will as being a faculty for futurity. In talking that way in my head (and then writing it down), I was obviously thinking that wishing is for a hoped-for future and willing for a firmly intended future. Not so obvious was the echo in my head of such English sentences as "He will come tomorrow." But—is it a prediction or an expression of hope, command, or attribution of intention I am hearing? What echoes is the oscillating sense of the future-bestowing auxiliary. This use, almost a double entendre, is particularly to the fore where self-repression and assertion are locked in battle, and people take to confidently predicting the actions of, or boldly imputing desires to, other people whom they wish to order around. The books of that example of Victorianism incarnate, the most popular author of her day, Charlotte Yonge, abound in phrases like "you will feel it to be for his true welfare."[5]

Yet on the face of it, "*will*" is the way to turn a verb's tense to the future. Unfortunately, there is also "shall."[6]

Shall has a different etymology from *will*, but a similar modal meaning—a debt or duty owed; *should*, the past of *shall*, is akin to *Schuld*, in German. The English auxiliary verb for expressing futurity is inflected in a curious pattern: the first person singular and plural, I and we, takes *shall* for the declarative future tense of expectancy, *will* for the modal, the will-imbued meaning. Here they are in a Yeats poem:

> I *will* arise now, and go to Innisfree, [willed intention]
>
> .   .   .   .
>
> And I *shall* have some peace there . . . [simple expectancy]

For the second and third persons, you (singular and plural), as well as he, she, it, and they (people in groups forego their gender), it's just the reverse. That is what makes Miss Yonge's phrases so pregnant with meaning. The auxiliary *will* is correctly futural, but surreptitiously imperial. But by the first part of the twentieth century the distinction was getting lost, particularly among us transatlantic boors. Nowadays the inclination to contract—*I'll, he'll*—is so great that the uncontractable *shall* is naturally forgotten.[7]

The modal auxiliary, indicating the whole modal works—desire, intention, willingess, inclination up to determination—seems very strange, once it comes under observation. In the first person, I declare my will to myself in all the modes just listed: "*I* will do it." But when speaking *to* you (or *about* him or them), were I to use "will," my auxiliary would become an imperative of a very peculiar sort—not an ordinary order issued by an I to a *thou*, "Thou *shalt not* . . . ," but a command issued to your *will*, and an order not to *do* but to *intend*! As one might think, grammar often tracks human ways, and so it does here.[8]

For I own and tell my wishing and my willing; I may also predict and announce your and his desires and deeds. Moreover, I can say "you shall . . ." and mean "I command you to . . ." or "he shall" and mean "he is commanded to . . ." Here I am brought up against the original meaning of *shall*, namely *ought*. That may well be why *shall* really makes sense for the second and third persons, while the modal *will* really ought, old-country snobbery aside, not be used with them; I *can* say: "you ought," but I *cannot* say "you will . . . ," unless I use the verb *either* in its auxiliary function (w_2) to make a prediction *or* in its primary sense (w_1) to make the straightforward but unlikely observation that you are applying your will to a proposed object. I *cannot*, however, thinkingly say "you will" in any modal, here imperative, sense, as I might predict "You *will* go to Innisfree, and take a picnic!" That is because I am not you and do not own your will, except insofar as you have willingly given it up to me and are will-lessly obeying my commands. But then there's no will left in you for me to enjoin. Of course, one might argue that we make attempts on other people's wills all the time, though we generally do it surreptitiously. As Miss Yonge's imperious Victorians infected expectation with command, so we civil Americans mitigate command by expectation: "You'll do it, won't you?"

To condense this disquisition to its point: The modal use of the verb *will* is inalienably first-personal—I cannot use it to or of someone else. This is largely true of all mental functions. "I feel your pain," doesn't happen for real pain—except perhaps as some attenuated twinge. "I think your thought"—a rarer claim because it wins fewer kudos—is possible, since we do have a simulacrum of thought made publicly available to us for appropriation: that unthought-out, unowned thought-package, which the ancients called "opinion." But "I will your will" is an in-principle impossibility. A directed will is a will-less will, for the will *is* selfhood in its intensity, and if it has a virtue, that is it. So our language was after all admirable both in evading *to will*, that oscillating modal-future verb, for not-myself persons in the imperative mood, and in using the deontic *shall* for myself, telling in the indicative mood what my future should be. "Deontic" means "morally obligating"; thus futural "I shall" intimates that I'm assuming responsibility for my future—Will has snuck into prediction.[9]

A brief return to etymology: The profit from this interlude is, then, to bring out the fraught relation between will and futurity, and so the word *future* itself needs looking at, for its capacities will turn out to bear on the will. (Incidentally, no verb has, I think, more different roots—or variations on them—than *to be*: I *am*, you *are*, he *is*, I *was*, you *were*, he *was*.) Again, the verb uses an auxiliary to form the future: I *shall* be, you *will* be. What is so interesting is that the word *future* itself is cognate with *be*, Greek *phynai*, "to bring forth, to grow," and Latin *futurum esse*, "to be about to be." Both have the same root as *to be*, *bhu*, and so does Latin *fuisse*, "to have been." *So all express being, and none real futurity.* The English noun *future* itself is listed in the O.E.D. as appearing as late as 1400. So as with English verbs, which need *will* to speak of things to come, being *might* be said to need time to develop a future. I mean something concrete by that oracular saying—the claim, not made until modern times, that Being itself has both a past and a future.[10]

B. Will's Futurity

Then to the question: Is it right to call the will a faculty of futurity? Not if we allow our language some revelatory capacity and not if we follow its lead. It tells us that there *is* no simple future. The past, though passed away, was once in being. The present, somehow, manages to be, though it is difficult to say when, *now* being too vanishingly short for existence. (People get around that by introducing a "specious present," a short duration experienced as one in awareness—a necessary fudge.) But the future neither was nor is—and here, whatever futurity syntax may have cobbled together, it is "pragmatics" that decides, since it considers speech in living use. For when we say that "it *will* be or *is* about to be," we are speaking *now* and it is now that willing expectation and being *are* happening; the future is purely notional, a construct of language and imagination. I think it was John Maynard Keynes who said "Prediction is difficult, especially about the future." That is so true because the future has no empirical handle to grasp it by. Whatever projective experience we might have of it, whatever lawful determinacy we may bestow on it, whatever predictability it may thus acquire for us, is *ipso facto* at odds with the free will that is to fashion it.[11]

For while determinism, the notion that events follow causal laws undeflectable by human will, fixes a future world as a real commonality, it is the radical idea of the will as a boundless faculty free of external constraint, that introduces creative acts decided in ideating privacy. I use "creative acts" advisedly, meaning the attempting of radical novelty, a self-aware usurpation of divine functions, born as an idea in an individual mind.

Here futurity and willing do come together. If the will is capable of radical novelty, really new beginnings, then it is indeed a faculty for the future. "Novelty" is probably the wrong word here, because I am not thinking of a blip in time, a spurious innovation conceived in a specious present, but of a story that has, as the journalists say, legs, that takes off, contrary to first appearance. For, one might argue, what is predictable is not really futural. Be it deterministically cyclical, such as the re-entrant planetary orbits, or probalistically arrow-like, such as the tendency toward increasing disorder in molecular motions, time—the band over which moves that "now-present" around which past and future break—serves merely to locate the observer in a past- and future-indifferent continuum. The future is only *his* future and predictions only foretell a future relative to him; in itself, the passage of time may be reversible or forward-directed, but absent an observer, it has no now, no past, no future. And if nature on her own "has" no future, neither does, strictly speaking, a human being, not even a dreaming, wishing, planning one. For dreams, wishes, schemes for the future are, once again, *now*, in the present, as Augustine, above all, knew, and their contents are derived from that keeper of the past, memory—mother of the Muses and projector of plans. We *think* of the future, but we don't "have" it, can't pre-live it as we can, sometimes, re-live the past.

Except under one circumstance: if we have a power of radical innovation, of real newness, unformed by memory, unshaped by imagination, indeed unbeholden to any mental capacity whose material is experience accumulated and transformed over time—if we have a faculty of purely spontaneous action, a true *will*. Then we might, for a moment, experience true futurity, the "never-yet." What kind of a faculty that will might be, the theologians do think about and name: Creation. It must, it would seem, be a faculty more allied to thinking than to the more overtly representational powers—those that bring before themselves pictures necessarily cobbled together from now available snippets of present and past. However, I have no experience of that capacity—certainly not in its executive effects.[12]

In any case, the modal syntax of our linguistic future, which mixes prediction with intention, would become literally apt if there were a human will that was indeed the faculty of the new, a creative will. For prediction would then be self-confirming: "shall be" would be the same as "will be," "Let there be light . . ." would coincide with "and it was so." However, if a human will attempted that operation, it would not necessarily follow that "it was good."[13]

chapter **VII**

Un-possessed Will

Communal and Cosmic

Once again, candor compels me to admit, not indeed, I hope, to a simple prejudice, but to a settled opinion, albeit stated here before its premises. Up till now, I have reviewed theories of will as a human faculty or non-faculty. But there are also views of the will as trans-personal. They can be classified, roughly, as cosmic and communal. (And I am not thinking here of the Divine Will, which although supra-human is not impersonal, since the Judeo-Christian God is a person.) I think, and will try to confirm the claim, that both kinds are simply pernicious. The cosmic will subjects nature to an anonymous agent-analogue that is merciless with impunity. The communal will abstracts society from individual variety in the interest of an inexorably homogenous whole. The authors of these notions are not always inconsiderate; sometimes they are self-intoxicated. In thinking out, then, which philosophers belong under this chapter heading, I must try to determine whether the world-will is a feature belonging to a divinity or has cast loose from any subject and functions on its own. Spinoza, a writer of importance to the Romantics of the last chapter, is a terminally undecidable case. Is he atheist or pantheist? He says "God" and adds "or Nature" (*Deus sive Natura*). Although the lines and attendant perplexities of influence are one preoccupation of this book, and although Spinoza is a deep writer on the will who assigns it the deepest function, I just can't tell where to place him—perhaps the best testament to his originality. (I shall therefore put the treatment of Spinoza's will in Note 1 to this chapter.)[1]

A. Rousseau: General Will

The first writer, then, is the one who first introduces a communal, a social will—Rousseau. I shall argue that his presentation is a masterpiece of an "iron fist in a velvet glove" insinuation. I imagine that others besides myself to whom the American Founding is a lodestar of political soundminded-

117

ness wonder why its well-read fathers took so little notice of Rousseau, their older, famous contemporary. Jefferson, indeed, moved in circles close to Rousseau when he was in France and when at home was on occasion called a "Rousseauist doctrinaire," an insult meaning something like "radical intellectual." However, Rousseau seems not to turn up—at least not prominently—in his writings. Madison's case is clearer, since he really wasn't an intellectual radical and certainly no Rousseauian. There is one writing of his, on "Universal Peace," a response to Rousseau's "Perpetual Peace," in which he refers to Rousseau's project as one of those doing "the greatest honor to the hearts, though they seem to have done very little to the heads of their authors"; he thinks Rousseau's judgment might have been less woolly if he'd lived to study the Constitution. (In my opinion, nothing much can be done for the heart of a sentimentalist.)[2]

Our Constitution, it turns out, may be interpreted as the practical antidote to Rousseau's most consequence-fraught political idea: *the general will*. This idea is set out most extensively in *The Social Contract*.[3]

Toward the middle of this work, we learn that there are three wills—actually, there turn out to be four—and since these rise in order of generality to the general will, it makes sense to begin here. The first is a *particular* or private will, which attaches to the individual interest of each human being; this will is directed to what one might call a peculiar human commonality—that we are each most interested in ourselves; it is the will of self-interest. The second will is somewhat larger in scope; one translator calls it "the group will," the will of partial associations of the kind we call "interest groups" and Madison calls "factions." Third is "the will of all." It is not mentioned here by Rousseau, for he seems to have identified it (or at least let it overlap) with the "group will," perhaps as that limit case of the latter in which the whole body politic turns into one "great dictating dissentient." This "will of all" is, however, actually quite different from the group will in conception; it is a nose-counting sum of individual wills, which might, as in democratic voting, be a majority of one or, as I intimated, a unanimity of all. In any case, Rousseau thinks, fourth, that the pluses and minuses of private wills can cancel each other, "and then the general will remains as the sum of the differences."[4]

This remainder-will is, again, quite differently understood from the sum-will of all; it is frequently diverse in its object and fundamentally different in concept. In fact, it might be no one's will in particular. For as the will of all is but "a sum of particular wills," so the general will "regards only the common interest"—and it is quite imaginable to Rousseau that no private will understands the common good. That is because, though the people are never corrupted, they are often deceived; only then do they will what is bad. Thus: "Some must have their wills made conformable to their reason, and others must be taught what it is they will."[5]

Now comes the crux: If people were kept from communicating with each other, so that no "partial associations" could be formed, the trifling individual differences would always be sunk in the common good. So it is essential that no interest groups be formed in the state and that "every citizen should speak his opinion entirely from himself." Where partial societies do form "it is politic to multiply their number that they may be all kept on an equality."[6]

Here is the Social Compact itself:

> Each of us places in common his person and all his power under the Supreme direction of the general will; and as one body we all receive each member as an indivisible part of the whole.

To prevent this compact from being an empty formula, whoever refuses to obey the general will is to be compelled by the whole body: *"this in fact forces him to be free"* (my italics).[7]

This compact produces, instead of separate persons, a "moral and collective body" on which the compact bestows a—conceptual—will. This body, when active, is called "Sovereign"; state, citizens, people, power—these are all merely its modes. This Sovereign cannot conceivably injure any and certainly not all of its subjects, having no interest contrary to theirs; in particular it needs to give no guarantee to them: "The Sovereign, by its nature, is always everything it ought to be." Moreover, it is indivisible, and therefore Rousseau proscribes that Montesquieuian division of powers which organizes our Constitution.[8]

Rousseau now inverts the determining direction of individual to body politic. The general will is the common good, but how would it be always right if "each" did not appropriate that term to himself and think of himself as voting for all? Thus the general will is so not only in its essence, which is that it applies to all, but also in its object, which is that it satisfies self-regarding human nature—insofar as its self-regard has been altruistically re-formed—generalized.[9]

The enacted general will is law. How can an unenlightened multitude formulate such acts? "The general will is always right, but the judgment that guides it is not always enlightened." I repeat a remarkable sentence, this time italicized by me: *"Some must have their wills made conformable to their reason, and others must be taught what it is they will."* Consequently there is a legitimate role for censorship in preserving morality, preventing corruption of opinions, and fixing opinions when they waver.[10]

How do I know if my private will has become consonant with the general will? Only by a free vote of the—dis-associated—people. A majority of votes binds all the others; the social compact implies this. The general will is found *in fact* by counting votes. So when a motion I oppose carries, "it only proves to me that I was mistaken, and that what I believed to be the general will was not so." Moreover, if my minority opinion had happened to prevail, I would have done "what I was not willing to do, and consequently, I should not have been in a state of freedom," at least on the supposition that all the characteristics of the general will are still found in the majority. Where they cease to be so, there liberty no longer exists.[11]

To conclude: "If there were a nation of gods they might be governed by a democracy. So perfect a government will not agree with men."[12]

There is something—to me unintelligibly—seductive in Rousseau's politics. One of the texts in my library, a half-century old and much used in its day, is introduced by the words "The *Social Contract* is a bible of contemporary politics . . . an adventure in the discovery of our political selves." Since to me it seems more like a devil's dictionary of totalitarianism—albeit one that has the aspect of courageous critique, the brilliance of real originality, and a dose of humane sentiment—I had better particularize my repulsion.[13]

Let me begin with an—admittedly Madisonian—criticism of the institutional aspects of the *Social Contract*, brief but not strictly on point: The persecution of the group-will, the partial-association-will, which constitutes those middle-tier combinations, Madisonian factions, where ordinary initiative finds its scope—that atomizing of citizens into individuals (Latin for "atoms") to reconstitute them into a unified *collective* rather than a diversified *community*—is, to Madison's mind, "worse than the disease." It means that constructed *unanimity* rather than pragmatic *compromise* will be the civil mode. The proscription of governmental division of powers and of institutionalized checks and balances intended to protect citizens from their rulers, the denigration of representation, which permits disinclined citizens to withdraw from the personal exposure and the time-burdens of public life, and the absence of Constitutional protections against majoritarian tyranny and of a Bill of Rights to guard against ideological persecution—all these lacks seem to me dangerous, especially in a new-founded state without traditions of civil life.[14]

A second set of objections deals with the manipulativeness of Rousseau's politics; in real life it would issue in outright propaganda, secret thought-police, and diffuse conformist pressure. Rousseau, of course, allows censorship backed by public opinion, exactly what Madison's First Amendment, understood by him as above all the guardian of our spiritual life, but also of our intellectual discourse, intends to prevent. Did Rousseau ever ask himself how his own book, the *Social Contract*, would fare in his state? In any case, he speaks of citizens being forced to be free, of having their wills made conformable to reason, of being unfree because their opinion prevailed. These sayings have the sophisticated charm of paradoxicality; is there civic safety in them?[15]

And finally, most to my point, the wills themselves: The first three are all tethered to actual souls—one, some, all, the extensional quantities of working logic. It is the general will that escapes all such approaches. Whose is it? Everybody's? No, there is a chance that it might be missed by every private will. Some people's? The same chance, if reduced. One person's? Possibly, but how would that one know, since corroboration lies in the generality?

In the *Discourse on Political Economy*, Rousseau says something that seems to offer a solution: "Do you want the general will to be carried out? Make certain that all particular wills are in accord with it, and *since virtue is only the conformity of the particular will with the general* [my italics], to say the same thing in a word, make virtue reign." That throws a more favorable light on the meaning of the general will and, moreover, makes it immediately clear why Kant felt indebted to Rousseau: The passage seems, if not to say, at least to intimate, that a citizen's morality—Rousseau actually uses the term "duty"—is the ability to universalize his one particular will, to make it jibe with a general good. Thus it permits Kant to take the further step, here put in Rousseau's language: The general will is the public good exactly because it is *general*, that is, law-like and universal, quite aside from any objective content, and the moral individual must will in this generalizing mode. The general will is, so understood, the civic appearance of Kant's practical reason, the self-law-giving will.[16]

But as I observed, in the *Social Contract* the citizen discovers whether his will in fact does conform to the general will only upon a vote being taken—if his opinion carries it was indeed the general will. But it was not so because it was *in principle* general but because it was *in fact* so. The general will is an iridescent enough being to escape being *a* human will—though it is certain, indeed is expected by Rousseau, to be highjacked by some human being who has the self-confidence to claim to discern its drift. It will be, in the words of the *Social Contract*, someone like this, a self-elected re-former of humanity:

> Anyone who dares to undertake the founding of a people should feel himself capable of *changing human nature*, so to speak, *of transforming each individual*, who by himself is a perfect and solitary whole, *into part of a greater whole from which this individual receives, in a way, his life and being; of altering the human constitution* in order to strengthen it; and of *substituting a partial and artificial existence* for the physical and independent existence we have all received from nature. He must, in a word, take away man's own forces in order to give him new ones which are *alien* to him (my italics).[17]

In this book, called *Un-willing*, I intend to un-do—perhaps even a little too late—the emphasis on human will that it has accrued over the millennia. But better any day human beings with their natural, private wills, one by one or in "partial" aggregates, than this artifact-creature, this robot, and its general will!

B. Schopenhauer: Ill Will

Rousseau's general will was a supra-individual political construction; Schopenhauer's noumenal Will is a suprahuman metaphysical insight. The former is meant to unite a civic body, the latter to ground Nature. Thus they concern community and cosmos, respectively.

But Schopenhauer's will, beyond being a non-human will (though also expressed in humans), has a character that I have not come across in any writer I know of before him: It is *unfriendly* to human happiness. Sometimes it helps to get a full sense of the distance that notions of the same name may have from each other by contrasting quotations.

Here is Thomas:

> [N]atural reason should minister to faith as the natural inclination of the will ministers to charity.

Here is Schopenhauer:

> We have observed the great multiplicity and difference of the appearances in which will objectifies itself, and indeed we have seen their endless and unforgiving battle against each other.

The theologian's human will by its nature inclines to the love of God, to charity, which is "the motor of other virtues" (*motor finis aliarum virtutum*); the philosopher's grounding Will expresses itself in Nature as implacable strife, the necessary law of life. To understand such tremendous clefts is part of the ambition of my book.[18]

This harsh philosophy is *first* felt and *then* delivered—in an elegantly forceful, hugely learned style. The book is usually called *The World as Will and Idea*. "Idea" renders *Vorstellung*, literally "pro-position," or "pre-sentation," something that is "put before" us. I shall use "representation," which although redundant by reason of the "re," sounds least strange. Thus the exposition begins: "The world is *my* representation" (my italics). The world is to be regarded as something *we* put before ourselves. We will see that Schopenhauer means this very radically: *esse est percipi*, "to be is to be perceived," in Berkeley's famous phrase. I shall contract the account of the "idea" part severely; it is a large and unfailingly interesting one, but my point here is to bring on the scene a new kind of will (except, perhaps, for Spinoza's), and as always with real philosophy, that will is conceived within a large setting, of which I will supply the bare outlines.[19]

Schopenhauer had two early attachments, both of which shaped the one masterpiece that occupied him most of his life—Kant and "ground." By ground, that is, "sufficient ground" (*zureichender Grund*), is meant the reason why something is at all and why it is the way it is. By the "principle (*Satz*) of ground" is meant the claim that everything is in fact grounded, that it has articulable reasons. From Kant comes the notion that "that which cognizes everything and is cognized by no one is the *subject*. It is thus the bearer of the world, the thoroughgoing, ever presupposed, condition of all appearance, all objects: since it is only for the subject that whatever exists is." Hence, Schopenhauer gives to the first book of his work the subtitle "The World as Representation Subjected to the Principle of Ground."[20]

I think one can see right away that Kantian critique and grounding are on a collision course, for one of Kant's meanings for "critique" is precisely the enunciation of the limits on real knowledge of what transcends experience. Hence, for him the subject itself is a *noumenon*, a mere "thing of the intellect," of which experiential, that is, real, knowledge is illusory. But that is to say that the principle of sufficient ground is *implicitly denied*. Kant's *Critiques* are full of ways that things just, inexplicably, are; this was the very motive for his successors, the idealist school of my Chapter V, in looking for an absolute, all-round, ground; for them it is found in the fact of an I that is incidentally a *will*.[21]

That word, *will*, names, Schopenhauer says, "the enigma." Already in his pre-*World as Will* writing on the principle of sufficient ground, he says, "will, or rather the subject of willing, had been posited as a special class of representations or objects; even there, we saw this object coincide with the subject, that is, ceasing to be object."[22]

To make this crucial pre-*World as Will* sentence reveal its sense, we must backtrack to say something more about ground and object. "Ground," in general, causes every object to be enmeshed in necessary relations to other objects as determining and determined. Thus, it is a principle of the universal reciprocal relativity of all existence. It takes four forms: It reveals itself first as "intuitive," a Kantian term that applies to what comes to us directly, under the form of a shaping sensibility, as that which has been organized as cause and effect—in other words, actual things, such as science deals with. A second kind of ground is the opposite of intuitive, namely "abstract"; this is the relation found between conceptual items, judgments. A third kind of ground consists of the "*a priori*" intuitions of space and time, the very shaping sensibility itself, the succession of time as expressed in counting and the positions of space as exhibited in geometry. This third ground particularly shows that the subject really underlies every object, for these forms of sensibility can become pure objects to the knowing subject even in the absence of sense-objects. (Schopenhauer relies here on very debatable passages in the first *Critique* intimating that the sensibility not only functions as a *form* but also supplies a pure, intuitable *content*, a mathematical material shaped into virtual objects, so to speak.) The fourth ground makes one unique connection, that of the volitional subject as itself an object to the knowing subject, of which more below.[23]

The term "object" enters on the very first page of the first book, the one on representation. It is the correlate of "subject," being what presents itself to this subject: an "object [is] for the subject." "Representation" is, however, really the prior term; within it are contained subject and object, and their "falling apart" is its most general, essential form. That event invokes yet another term, "objectification" (here used both for the result, *Objektität*, "object-being," and the activity, *Objectivation*, "object-making"), which names the way the subject becomes, or repels itself into, an object. (Here Schopenhauer shows himself as heir to the Idealists of Ch. V, Sec. B.) What objectifies itself is the thing-in-itself, the transcendental subject that is identified as will. But what the character of that transmutation might be is not, as far as I can tell, specified. —By what atemporal act of timeless instantaneity so blind a force as the will turns out to be reveals itself in so essentially visible a mode as is appearance, is not enunciated. It is, apparently, just a given metaphysical event. For Kant, the subject could never know itself in itself but only as an appearance, as an empirical I that appears to itself as a body in space and as a consciousness in time. So Schopenhauer's problem must be: How can the subject as transcendent ground, not merely as an appearing representation, ever become known to us?[24]

This is the answer, a complex one, since it must consider both how and what we know: Only one object is known to us not only as *Vor-stellung*, something standing before me, but *also* from another, deeper aspect, from the inside. We are conscious of our body in this second, totally different mode (one not found in Kant's subject). We know it in itself, in its activity, motions, and motives. That inner mode has the denotation *will*. Schopenhauer adds something startling: That insight is also the key to all the beings, animate and inanimate, found in nature; their internality, too, is, by analogy, revealed to us as will-like. This formulation follows: As bodies in the world, we are not only natural objects grounded in causality, but we *are*, and *know* ourselves as, "the appearance of the will, the will become visible, *the objectification of the will*." Our body is the visible will. That is how we learn of the ground of our being. It is that fourth, unique grounding relation mentioned above. Everyone knows this concretely, immediately, as a feeling—not quite clearly, nor as a whole, but through single, individual actions.[25]

(This is a daring teaching, for it appeals by fiat to an inner experience all properly human beings are said to have; there is behind it no theory of cognition beyond this claim. That would be no problem at all—for not all truths are arguable—did all our experience in fact converge on it. But far from it. This book is working its way toward urging a directly opposite claim, that willful willing, as a vehement mode, though indeed a human capability, is a mostly relinquishable one, of which we see traces within ourselves mostly in our stuck, arid moments.)

Having given the briefest sketch of the "how" of our noumenal self-knowledge, it remains to tell the "what." What is this will, which appears as so intensely individualizing a thing as our organic body? That explication will be my main business, since this chapter is devoted to grand versions of the supra- or sub-human will. But for now I will skip briefly to the last two books of Schopenhauer's work, since I have just raised the question of opposition to Will. Schopenhauer will paint so terrifying a picture of the ground of human being—that is why he is rightly called a philosophical pessimist—that he himself looks for ways out, for escape from the way things are in their depths.

He finds two ways, one transient—esthetic contemplation, which "lifts us suddenly out of the endless stream of willing," and the other final—renunciation of the Will by its very own objectification, that being ourselves. I will pass over the latter, which finally reaches for its elucidation into Eastern wisdom and a nihilism I am not constituted to grasp.[26]

As for the former, let me begin by completing the famous passage on esthetic contemplation just quoted:

> But when an external occasion or an internal mood suddenly lifts us out of the endless stream of willing, when cognition tears us away from the slave-service of the will, when attention is now no longer directed to the motive of willing but grasps things as freed from their reference to the will, that is, without interest [self-interest], without subjectivity, contemplated purely objectively, completely devoted to them insofar as they are only representations, not insofar as they are motives—then the repose, ever sought along that first way of willing but ever fugitive, has all of a sudden come about by itself, and we feel wholly well. It is the painless condition that Epicurus praised as the highest good and the condition of the gods—for we are, for that moment, rid of the ignominious oppression of the will; we celebrate the sabbath of the penitentiary's labor of willing; the wheel of Ixion [an endlessly revolving instrument of torture] stands still. [My brackets][27]

This is the effect that absorption in a work of art may have, although rarely: The subject experiences a sudden transition from the cognition of single objects to the Idea, and tears itself from the service of the will. The I ceases to be an individual and become will-less; it no longer pursues relations in accordance with the principle of ground, but loses itself in the object offered, which it contemplates serenely. The artist achieves such a work by looking to the will's most "adequate specification of the thing in itself,"

namely, the Platonic Ideas. To me, this objectification is the most unintelligible (and the most captivating) of all: If before, the question was how
the most shapeless of powers is to be transfigured, or better, how it is to
begin to assume a figure, an appearance, at all, the question is now inten-
sified: How can the essentially horrid will, that wheel of torture, reveal
itself in the very models of intellectual shapeliness, the Platonic forms?
An answer would tell us what will is "like." But there is none; there can be
none. However, it helps that the notion of the Ideas as the Will's adequate
objectification is separable from the insight that artists look to ideal beings,
to imitate; thus, their works at once embody beauty and reveal truth—an
insight that seems to match the reported experience of a certain kind of
artist. (For more on art see Note 28 to this chapter.)[28]

One last comment on the remarkable supplement to this third book in
which the will is divorced from its dependence on representation for coming forth: This supplement, about the metaphysics of music, gives music
a special position among the arts: "The fact that music does not exhibit
(*darstellt*), as do the other arts, the Ideas or stages of objectification of the
will, but immediately *the will itself*, also explains why music acts immediately on the will, that is, the feelings, passions, and affects of the lis-
tener . . ." As *mediately* represented, will had, so to speak, shape, visibility.
As *immediately* presented, will has—but how to finish that sentence? Schopenhauer uses the neutral term *darstellen* ("set forth, exhibit, present")
several times, perhaps because the auditory appearance of the will that is
effected by "the mightiest" of all arts, is hard, probably impossible, to articulate verbally. For the will is formless and music is form *par excellence*.
Similarly, it both does and doesn't make sense that Schopenhauer says,
"Words are and remain for music an alien accretion, of inferior worth . . ."
The wordless music he is thinking of is, *ipso facto*, inarticulate, yet he himself refers to the strict form, expressible in numerical rules, without which
music ceases to be music—a wordless logic.[29]

In any case, because music is the image not of Ideas but "the *image of
the will itself*, whose objectification the Ideas are too—for that reason is the
effect of music so much more mighty and forceful than that of the other
arts: for those speak only of the shadow, but music speaks of the essence."
If one then asks how this essence, this horrid will, can be pleasing, even
ravishing, the answer is precisely in the numerical formalism: "The connexion of the metaphysical significance of music with this its physical and
arithmetical basis now depends on this, that what resists our apprehension,
the irrational or dissonance, becomes the natural picture of what resists
our will and, reversely, consonance or the rational, in easily yielding to our
comprehension, becomes the picture of the gratification of the will." The
secret then seems to be 1.) in providing an—acoustic—simulacrum of the
will's affects (for they themselves must not be excited) in terms of numeri-

cally irrational dissonances; and 2.) in offering a gratification of the will in terms of consonances and resolutions.

But now we seem to have returned to the shadow that masked the essence, to an artful representation rather than an immediate expression. These are some unresolved difficulties with the immediacy-theory of music, but they are not what is crucial.[30]

(I have stopped over music because it is the most telling example of what Schopenhauer requires of his reader: empathy, sameness of experience. What if one's experience is the opposite—that the most passionate music is text-based, composed as a commentary mostly on sacred texts that are to be treated not as secondary add-ons but as the very meaning of the sound-affect? And what if this verbal-acoustic whole is not an ameliorating emanation from the hell below but an intimating image of the heavens above?)

And now back to the "what" of the will—in the human individual and in the grounding subject. The second book of the *World as Will and Representation* sets out the inquiry, under the heading "The Objectification of the Will": "We want to know the significance of those representations; we ask if the world is nothing more than representation, in which case it would pass by us as an inactual dream or a ghostly phantom, not worth our attention." The search is, then, for the essence behind the representing appearance, and it is not to be captured from the outside. (Now is the moment to comment on this novel introspective undertaking. It seems to me novel because most philosophies seek comfort or splendor from beyond—few find enough of it right here. Schopenhauer knows that he is advancing into nothing good. It takes a kind of tooth-gritting pleasure in awfulness, which deserves the name of courage, to go within looking for such truth—a real break in the tradition that thinks of truth as salvific rather than excruciating. But of course, it also raises a question which, from respect for the text, one ought to be chary of letting in—the influence personal life-mood might have on a great conception. Insofar as such an arrière-pensée is hard to eject from one's mind, there will be something almost voyeuristic in studying such a book as Schopenhauer's.[31])

The embodied human individual (and in their different gradations every body) is the expression of the Will, or better, it *is* will individuated. So, to begin with what is on the surface, the will is human. The human body in all its parts is objectified will, which manifests itself as desire— teeth and guts are hunger objectified, genitalia, the sexual drive, and so on—but so is the force that attracts the magnet to the north pole; it differs only in the grade of appearance. The thing-in-itself that enters appearance thus borrows its name, once it has become object, from what was most perfect, clearest, most developed in all appearance. "But just that is the human will"—not, however, the traditional will, which is guided by rational motives. This traditional will is usually subsumed under "power"; Schopenhauer inverts that. Every power of nature is will, and all of nature as a system of powers is will. Insofar as it is merely "understood," its grounds are those *a priori* forms of appearance listed above: time, space, causality. And here the relations of nature in its manifoldness, its individuation, are unproblematic; they are, however, also contentless form without internality. They are low-grade expressions of the will.[32]

But they *are* will. "Thus we see everywhere in Nature strife, battle and victory; each stage of objectification contends with others over space and time." (Schopenhauer illustrates with lots of bloody nature-episodes.) The rising gradations of objectification represent greater specification and individuation, each manifest in a physical organ until at one blow, *the world as representation* itself comes into being with all its forms: object, subject, time, space, multiplicity, and causality." It is the human being, "complicated, many-sided, adaptive, highly needy and exposed to countless wounds." At this stage, "Will has lit a light for itself." But the deliberations of man interfere with the sureness of willing; errors happen, the adequate objectification of the Will through deeds is hampered. Be it rational or intuitive knowledge, it is only a "device" (Schopenhauer uses the Greek word *mechane*), a means for the preservation of the individual, intended for the service of the Will. It goes without saying that Schopenhauer accords the will absolute primacy over the intellect. Nonetheless this human will is not free. All our actions follow with strictest necessity from the interaction of our motives and our individual character. This character unfolds no differently from the way the nature of a physical body is manifested in the interaction of its constitution with its environment. For an individual is not Will itself but only its appearance, and thus it is strictly determined by the grounding principle.[33]

The Will in the world is chase, fear, and suffering, for it is a hungry will, and, since there is nothing but itself, it must consume itself. The human will is correspondingly aimless. Each act has rhyme and reason, but if you ask anyone why he wills at all, he can have no general answer—for "he himself is nothing but will," and only individual acts at individual points of time need a particular motive.[34]

To describe what this world as will—adequately objectified in humankind—is like for us, Schopenhauer avails himself of every term in the dictionary of suffering; it is a hell in which we are savaged as we savage each other. "From where else then did Dante take the material for his hell, but from this, our actual world?"[35]

So finally, *the* Will. Schopenhauer is forced to take the *via negativa*, the "way of negation" of the theologians. For all we know of it is by an analogical leap into the dark, and that knowledge has got to be misleading, since the Will as subject is far less like the will as object than any divinity was ever like humanity. To begin with, the Will is a thing-in-itself—itself a ground and so itself groundless, hence without explanation. As opposed to the absolutely pre-determined human will, the Will is said to be free, since it is outside of time, space, and causality, but this freedom is strictly by negation, because being ungrounded is a wild sort of liberty. Nor can the Will's nature—actually it hasn't got a specific one—be expressively objectified, since to be an object (I am repeating myself) is to be 1. related to a subject, 2. individuated, 3. in a system of relations with other appearing objects, and 4. under the conditions of time, space and causality—the last being responsible for the first three. What I mean is that, be it from our ineradicable ignorance or from such glimmers as we have struck from the darkness, we must think or feel that the Will is and has *nothing* to connect it to its object-appearance.[36]

So is there anything positive to be said of the Will? There might be a way of thinking, neither completely negative nor effectively stymied, to reach the notion. Mere Kantian understanding gives knowledge only of experienced nature, but there is a cognition, Schopenhauer thinks, that goes to the things-in-themselves behind nature:

> The first step in the basic cognition of my metaphysics is this: The Will, which we find in our interior, does not, as philosophy had assumed until now, first of all arise out of cognition, in fact as its mere modification, thus as something secondary, derivative, and like cognition, itself conditioned by the brain; rather it is its *prius* [first], the nucleus of our knowledge and that primordial power itself which creates and maintains the animal body insofar as it executes its unconscious as well as its conscious functions

—though it may seem a paradox that "the Will in itself is non-cognitive," when it is the principle, the "first" of cognition. This unabashed positing of what is at least interpretable as pre- or un-conscious knowledge is, one might say, stupendously prescient. (And I might also say that everything depends on readers' ability to follow Schopenhauer, so to speak, into their own inner being—where I, for one, come only on the most occasional up-welling of will—and that only until the better angels of my nature reassert themselves.)[37]

To conclude, here is what the Will looks like not as thought *about* but as entered *into*: It is, in its metaphysical property, both a creative power (*Schöpferkraft*) and "the omnipresent substrate of the whole of nature," hidden below but somehow inferrable. It is the "Will to Life" (*Wille zum Leben*) but not, it seems, itself alive, alive only in its objectification, just as it was cognitive only in its human expression. "I understand by objectification (*Objectivation*) the [Will's] self-presentation (or "self-exhibiting," *Sichdarstellen*) in the real world of bodies." However, "Cognition of the external world is *consciousness of other things*, as opposed to *self-consciousness*."

It is, however, in the latter that, subjectively, we have "found Will as its true object"—found it *as its object*, but a peculiar object, an *internal* object, more an intimating than an objectifying representation. In sum, we somehow know it, unconsciously, intimatingly, *negatively*. (I find that notion attractive insofar as "somehow knowing" is how everything begins. Should it end there? And if it doesn't, can I welcome this unalive (dead, it seems), non-cognitive (dumb, it seems), dark (human-unfriendly, it seems) non-being as it emerges into articulate thought?)[38]

The force one learns about in school is formulaically presented in terms of accelerating masses, or geometrically in terms of an action-producing field; when summed over time, force becomes impulse, over space, work. A body that can do work is said to possess energy, and energy is equivalent to mass. This is "science" in general insofar as all the events are observable, and it is "physics" in particular because all the relations, transformations, and conversions are mathematically formulable. It is certainly mysterious, because no one knows why nature happens to be mathematically forthcoming, but it is not mystifying, because the concepts and their dimension can be, in a normal way, understood.

I don't think the Will, as Schopehauer sets it out, can be so understood. It is un-illuminating, in fact, injurious, to exonerate it as a metaphysical, not a physical notion, both because metaphysics should be doubly intelligible and because Schopenhauer means to ground natural science in the Will. It seems to me a deeply felt and deeply pondered piece of irrationalism; this Will is unintelligible as being no one's will and (I think) misconceived as being a life-burdening life-principle. Oddly enough, what saves it is its very unflinching pessimism and so its utter want of triumphalism. That raises a fascinating question. Must one, driven by love of truth, contrive a notion one cannot live with? Schopenhauer's apostate disciple asked himself this very question. His answer, here phrased with deliberate indelicacy, will be: If you must philosophize, make it life-enhancing.

C. Nietzsche: Will Triumphant

There is and there isn't a book by Friedrich Nietzsche called *The Will to Power* (*Der Wille zur Macht*). The "book" is notional, meaning a mental project. Nietzsche clearly intended to write it and at one time produced drafts of a title page and over time notebooks full of preliminary aphorisms. Since philosophy is largely notional anyhow, there is every reason to work with the published text that we have.[39]

It might make sense to begin with Nietzsche's frequently expressed views of his honored but rejected predecessor, Schopenhauer. Their writings are, so to speak, temperamentally opposite. Schopenhauer is, as I said, expansively (though not long-windedly) expository; Nietzsche prefers to be concisely (though never opaquely) aphoristic (or briefly essayistic), at least in his later works. There is no doing English justice to what it takes to make German dance. That must be said, to avert seduction. This way of composing (and, one imagines, of thinking) is a kind of doctrine-prevention, and if it seems undecidable whether there is a Nietzschean "system"—probably not—it is only partly because, even when he had ceased writing, his vision was still *in statu nascendi*.Edifice-building was simply unsuitable to his project, which was to play at once undertaker and midwife to a dying world being reborn. Indeed "being reborn" is the wrong term—it is a novel future more willed into being than prognosticated. As Kant entitles the summation of his critical philosophy "Prolegomena to any Future Metaphysics Whatsoever" (*Prolegomena zu einer jeden künftigen Metaphysik*), meaning to delimit and stop such a metaphysics in its track, so Nietzsche called his *Beyond Good and Evil* a "Prelude to a Philosophy of the Future," meaning to invoke the birth of a possible world.[40]

So now I turn to Nietzsche's critique of Schopenhauer. The name of the chief of "my precursors" appears all over Nietzsche's books, fascinatedly and critically. Nietzsche objects on these many counts: Schopenhauer's pessimism; his over-all conclusion of "better *not* to be than to be"; his labor to escape from affects, that is, from will; "his scandalous" employment of art as a bridge to the denial of life and as soporific rather than a stimulus; his claim to have cognitive access to the thing-in-itself; and his "old wives'" morality of mutual aid and pity. But perhaps most revealing for the Nietzschean will is this: "Schopenhauer's interpretation of the 'thing-in-itself' as will was an essential step; but he did not understand how to *deify* this will"; he did not know that the will is one of "an infinite variety of ways . . . of being god."[41]

And there I'll begin, with a pregnant perplexity raised by the will as a god. It leaps to the eye focused on the title "The Will to Power," which is announced projectively in the *Genealogy of Morals*. The puzzle centers on the little preposition "to"—"*zur* Macht," and also "*zum* Leben." Does "to" signify that will *shows* itself in power and life or that it *is* power and life? Does "to" mean "*strives towards*," or does it mean "*belongs to*"? In Schopenhauer's case, a—perhaps unwelcome—logical construal showed that the will itself can't be life or power—hence its ineradicable unlovableness. How is it with Nietzsche?[42]

And behold, that question has no definitive answer. In most passages "to" means just what it ordinarily would, striving *toward*: Dominance is the will's aim. Thus we find this phrase, "a will and way to greater power," or more expansively, "Life is specifically a will to the accumulation of force . . . [It] strives after a *maximal feeling of power*; it is essentially a striving for a plus of power; striving is nothing other than striving for power; this will remains the most basic and the innermost thing."[43]

But then we find the alternative in yet one more critique: "*Schopenhauer's* basic misunderstanding of the will (as if desire, instinct, drive were the *essence* of the will) is typical." And, "I value a human being according to the *quantum of power and plenitude of its will* . . . I assess the *power* of a *will* by how much resistance, pain, torture it can endure and knows how to transform to its advantage; I do not make its evil and painful character a reproach to existence, but cherish the hope that it will one day be more evil and more painful than it has been up till now."[44] Here power and vitality are not what the will *strives for* but what it *is*.

This question, whether the human will *seeks* or *is* power, is, it turns out, acknowledged by Nietzsche: "[L]et us be unphilosophical—let us say: in every willing there is, first of all, a multiplicity of feelings, namely the feeling of the condition from which *away*, the condition *towards* which, the feeling itself of this 'away' and 'towards'," and an accompanying feeling of the muscles. Second there is also thinking; "in every act of will there is a commanding thought," and one must not attempt to cut this thought off from willing. So Nietzsche's answer is one of meaning-fraught duplicity.[45]

For above all, will is not a mere complex of feelings and thoughts. It *is* an *affect*, but, most significantly, it is a *specific* affect, and that is an affect of a command. "What is called 'freedom of the will' is essentially the affect of superiority" in respect to him who must obey: "I am free, 'he' must obey." Nietzsche goes on to describe the straight, fixated, unconditionally evaluating vision of someone who expects to be obeyed not, in the first instance, by another but by himself. That is what we call "will power" (a word used by Nietzsche himself); it is not the will *to* power that I want but the power *of* the will I have—the willing to will and the striving to strive: the primal exemplification of a second derivative in the calculus.[46]

Nietzsche has a dramatic way of putting this indeterminacy of meaning: "Willing is not [just] 'desiring,' striving, demanding; it is distinguished from these by the affect of commanding." "There is no such thing as 'willing' but only willing *something*; one must not remove the aim from the total condition—as the epistemologists do." Nietzsche repeats this often in succinct form: *There is no will*. He means that there is no faculty (which is what the epistemologists of my last two chapters kept finding) such as practical reason, with now this, now that determining aim—abstractable from its direction and effect.[47]

Willing, then, is not a faculty but, once again, an *affect*, a root-affect. As an affect and a feeling, its being, its tending, its object are one: It is vital in itself, assertive by its vitality, goal-informed in its assertiveness—and basic by bestowing their *value* on all the other feelings. "Attempt at a Revaluation (*Umwertung*) of All Values (*Werte*)" was the intended subtitle of the *Will to Power*—*nota bene*, "value" is unquestionably the right translation of *Wert*; it seems to me fateful that German, unlike English, does not distinguish between worth (high quality) and value (the assessment of worth), for this masks the fact that "re-valuation" is the insidious business of *assigning* worth, not of discerning it: Value is a human doing. What Nietzsche intends is precisely the re-assignment of worth under the aegis of the will, and therewith the rescue of the will to power from millennial suppression to recovered glory. And since a powerful will as an ultimate value—for "life just *is* will to power"—is not "good" but is, as the term says, *potent*, its possessor will often appear evil to the weak-willed seekers of protection and pity. (Question: Why is personal potency—similar in this, oddly enough, to historical inevitability—thought to be in aid of a philosophical path-breaker? Wouldn't a *true* believer in their vitality leave these longed-for masters of the future strictly and silently to their own potent devices?)[48]

One of the consequences of making will the "ground-affect" is that pleasure becomes an *epiphenomenon* (as it was for Aristotle—but in how different a tonality!—the *bloom* on excellent activity); it is the sense of an increase of power. Pain, however, is not the opposite of pleasure, not a negative affect, a diminution of that sense of power, but it is different *in kind*. It is the *judgment* of harm (as it was for the Stoics: a—false—belief of badness), an intellectual fear of the consequence of trauma. That is to say, at some moment in his ponderings, Nietzsche denied the affective reality of pain; perhaps that was because, if pain is the negative of pleasure and thus an increasing sense of powerlessness, then he must give up the exhilaratingly excruciating intensity he ascribes to suffering, its salvific function (though, of course, converting it into an opinion scarcely preserves its searing quality). But Nietzsche's exposition of human will is so subtle and various that I will leave off my own account with the above chief features, to come to the great last question: Is the will ultimately an individual will or a single, trans-human principle?[49]

Here is the answer, one hypothetical, the second categorical:

> Supposing (*Gesetzt*), finally, that one succeeded in declaring our total instinctual life as the elaboration and ramification of *one* basic form (*Grundform*) of the will—namely the will to power, as is *my* principle (*Satz*)—supposing that it were possible to refer all organic functions back to this will to power and to find in it also the solution of the problems of procreation and nutrition—it is *one* problem—then, having done this, one would have gained the right to determine *all* effective force unequivocally as: *Will to Power*. The world seen from the inside, the world determined and denominated with a view to its "intelligible character"—it would be just "Will to Power" and nothing besides.

In the previous sentence, Nietzsche had already opined that every mechanical event, insofar as a force becomes active in it, is in fact "will-force, will-effect."

The second quotation is the final published notebook entry for *The Will to Power*; it speaks of "this my *Dionysian* world of Eternal-itself-creating, of Eternal-itself-destroying, this mystery-world of the double voluptuousness [pain and pleasure], this my 'Beyond Good and Evil,' . . . do you want a *name* for this world?"

> This world is the *Will to Power—and nothing besides*. And yourself too are this Will to Power—and nothing besides![50]

Question upon question: Assuming that *this* Will to Power is, as a principle, trans-human, though it shows itself in humans, what is its positive character? Here is a collection of features as it appears in human beings. The sum is put together from Heidegger's *Nietzsche*: Will is, above all, the affect, passion, feeling of potency; it is creator and destroyer; it is self-assertion and self-transcendence, self-augmentation and self-command, self-obedience and commanding domination. But first and last, it is *affect*. And here is what it is not: a separable faculty, a unitary function or its effect, a blind drive or a mere wish; it is not an impulsive affect (like anger) but a persistent passion (like hatred); it is not cut off from thought but melded with it; it is always intelligent, though not conspicuously so. The summary statement Heidegger then formulates exposes the phrase "will to power" as a crucial redundancy: Power (*Macht*) itself is will (as distinct from force, *Kraft*). So the will to power is *essentially the will to will*, self-iterating self-assertion. (For Heidegger on the Will to Power in more detail see Note 51 to this chapter.)[51]

This portrait seems to me most recognizable. Will is not a constituting faculty of the soul (for there is no soul structure) but rather a potency awaiting its occasion, a capability for self-ratcheting-up. That is will appearing in man. But it is not *the* Will. Again Heidegger formulates: "The Will to Power is never the willing of an individual." And so arises the ultimate question: What is this non-individual Will, this ultimate Will that makes Life alive? What is an affect that is not *someone's* affect, an affect antecedent to a subject?[52]

There might be a semi-answer, namely, when Nietzsche speaks of this Will of wills not as an affect but as an *affect-form*: "My theory would be: that the *Will to Power* is the primitive affect form—that all other affects are only its elaborations." Is an affect-form then perhaps not itself a basic affect but rather an affect-generator? If so, is it essentially different from a phenomenal affect such as the feeling of voluptuousness, which is only a symptom of the striving for power? It must be, since voluptuousness *happens* on the occasion when a living being achieves what it strives after. It accompanies but does not move. Where could we go to tell whether the originating "affect-form" is or is not itself an affect? "Affect-form" is a half-answer, an intimation.[53]

The question reaches as far as Nietzsche's last thought. If, as Heidegger convincingly argues, the Will to Power is realized in the Eternal Return, then we must ask whether this will to persistence in change, to timeless-ness in time, is the bearer of a grand affect or is the affect itself, a passion-wind without substrate, sweeping the world around.[54]

The answer seems to have to be: Whether we have in mind the Will before or after it was reconceived as the Eternal Return—it cannot be an ultimate subject-bearer of affects, for that would make it meta-physical, unconditioned. Now here is Nietzsche on metaphysics: "Nonsense of all metaphysics as a derivation of what is conditioned from the uncondi-tioned" So there remains what seems to me a zone of unintelligibility in Nietzsche's conception of the Will as subjectless affect.[55]

There is a poem by the surrealist Christian Morgenstern:

A knee walks lonely through the world,
It's nothing but a knee.
It's not a tree, it's not a tent
It's nothing but a knee

An affect without a subject, a feeling on its own, seems to me like that knee—a dissociated phantasm. But a potent notion so untethered is soon misappropriated: The Will to Power seems to me—to pile up figures—to be a philosophical loose cannon.[56]

So far in this chapter on the supra- or super-human will, I have expressed revulsion for its political expression and non-conviction of its metaphysical being. This is the moment to turn what is perhaps a prejudice into a problem—to me the most preoccupying in philosophy. The three wills of this chapter, the wills of anti-individual generality, of sub-personal sadism, and of trans-human potentiation, are so suspect *because* they are "non-human" and that seems immediately to go over into "inhuman." "Inhuman" in turns means "affectless"—at least without those affects that collect us within ourselves, bond us to other living beings, connect us with the external world. These wills are, so to speak, innocently vicious—innocent from soullessness, vicious from sheer potency. It is, I think, this thought—no, this immediate sense of things—that underlies the fact that the deity of faiths is always personal. But here is the question from the side of thought (I don't say from reason, because rationality can be pure thoughtlessness): Is personhood, such as we understand it from analogy to the individually ensouled human being, a requirement for being an object of our affirming affectivity? Can we be genuinely moved by, alertly receptive to, a Being that has no *subjectivity*, no inwardness responsive to objects? Beauty being to objects what lovability is to subjects, our affec-tivity, our capability of being moved, probably resonates in both modes:

affected by others' affection and moved by beauty. If that is so, then what is wrong with these a-human wills is not that they are *not* human, but precisely that they *are* human-all-too-human—ambitiously conceived in the image of one of our sorrier propensities, which is to think that power itself augments existence. (In Note 57 to this chapter I return to that bedeviled yet inescapable issue, Nietzsche's responsibility for the—illicit—appropriation of his Will to Power by the Nazis.)[57]

chapter **VIII**

Will's Last Ontologies

Between 1830, the date of Hegel's *Encyclopedia of the Philosophical Sciences*, and Heidegger's *Essence of Human Freedom* of 1930 lies the last century of grand systems, the last time—perhaps for a while, perhaps forever, who knows?—that the will is understood as defined and operating within a large ontological framework, a doctrine (be it affirmative or destructive) of Being that is explicitly worked out.[1]

A. Hegel: Dialectical Will

I know of no understanding of the will that is so firmly seated in a system as Hegel's, though perhaps that is because there is no system so systematic as his. By "systematic" I mean, following Hegel, a self-developing (=dialectically unfolding) thought-whole, all of whose parts are intrinsically connected, not externally aggregated. Only a system, *the* system, guarantees that its notions come together to form a genuine philosophical science. Each particular science of the system forms a circle—"it unfolds within itself, and gathers and holds itself together in unity," and the science of the sciences itself, the Whole, Truth itself, the Absolute, is "a circle of circles." Thus its exposition is called an en*cyclo*pedia, an instructive cycle whose end was in its beginning, self-completing and all-inclusive. Some of these descriptive gestures will be made concrete below. The system, as a triad of triads, has three major "moments." The first moment is Logic, in which pure Being develops all that is "concretely," meaning determinately, within it. Logic is the thinking of thinking, of concept-positing and -overcoming, which, through its progressive unfolding attains the Idea, the ultimate, fully determined, completely conceptualized Notion (*Begriff*). Once fulfilled, the Idea closes its circle and goes over into its Other—pure internality into pure externality, Nature, the second major moment.

The will is treated preliminarily in the *Logic* and not at all under *Nature*, that is, in the first but not in the second parts of the *Encyclopedia*. It reappears, full-blown and presented in all its aspects, in the third part, *Spirit* (*Geist*) or *Mind*. Spirit, the third moment, issues from mindless

Nature as a return to the Idea, as a transition back into itself, now enriched by its Other, Nature. It emerges as the genus of a rational animal—Man. I will therefore begin with volition as a humanly mental, a "subjective" idea.[2]

Volition, willing (*Wollen*) as Hegel says, first comes up in the third part of the very end of the *Science of Logic*, just before the culmination, the whole Idea itself. Here is the will as it appears in pure thought, as a mere concept (these un-embodied manifestations are not easy to take in; whoever has no taste for what we—not Hegel—call "abstractions" may just skip the next four paragraphs). By a dialectical route, logic has come to see itself as cognition, as knowing, as possessing—somehow—the categories of, as being adequate to, a *given* content. Cognition meets the world and finds that it fits this Other, receptively but inactively. This cognition is finite, for it is confronted by various stark facts of external nature or by its own categorical constitution, which compels and so delimits it.

However, cognition produces Demonstrations. It is dialectical and so reverses its beginning, which was in the merely given or found; necessity can never be just given or found. (Recall Hume's argument against observable necessary causal connection.) Therefore, it must be immanent in the cognizing subjective "idea" and contributed by it, that is to say, demonstrated. This subjective idea (the concept-name of mankind, which will, as was said, appear embodied when Nature has been absorbed by Logic) now has evinced something original and active beyond its passive receptivity; from this moment on, it must be apprehended as subjectivity, as a notion self-moving, active, and form-imposing: "It has passed over into the idea of the will."[3]

"While Intelligence merely proposes to take the world as it is, Will takes steps to make the world what it ought to be." The "simple uniform content" of Will is the Good. Its impulse toward self-realization is ". . . the reverse of the idea of truth," for it is intent on molding the world it finds and on making it conform to its purposed End. But here it finds itself in a quandary, for while it tries to denigrate the world as merely its object, as in itself nothing, it must also regard its own End, the Good, as merely a subjective idea and thus the objective world as being, after all, independent. In consequence, the Will can never regard the Good as completely achieved. For in acting, it seeks to make the objective world coincide with its subjective idea, but here it learns of its inadequacy in the face of stubborn existence. And so it comes to imagine its Good as an endlessly progressive project, a mere "Ought," a receding goal of perfection. Moreover the Will, in its finitude, in its conceptual short-coming, actually *requires* that its Good must ever fall short of perfection, for were it attained, willing should cease.[4]

But the will is not meant to be thus limited and self-contradictory. Its self-reconciliation is achieved when will recollects the presupposition of cognition, which is that the world is actual. With this return of the will to knowing, the practical and theoretical ideas are unified: Theoretical cognition took the world as an idea and so as already having all the being and actuality that Hegel ascribes to ideas. Practical Will took the world as a becoming, to be rectified by its own prescribed Good. When objective cognition and subjective will come together, the Good is *known* as already really, currently, achieved in an objectively existent world, as well as *pursued* as the final end of this same world, "which has being only while it constantly produces itself." "All unsatisfied endeavor ceases when we recognize that the final purpose of the world is accomplished no less than ever accomplishing itself."[5]

Thus, when Will is willing to become cognitive, it recognizes that "the Good is radically and really [already] achieved" in a world that is *at once real and rational*, "just as it at the same time lays itself down as End, and by action brings about its actuality." That is the truth which the unity of the subjective and objective, the practical and theoretical, the volitional and cognitive idea tells: The world is "always already" implicitly what it strives to become actually.[6]

This union, this identity-in-difference, is the culmination of Part One of the *Encyclopedia*, the *Logic*. Its title is "The Absolute Idea," for it leaves no logical concept outside itself and has no dialectical motion left within itself. It is, in Hegel's term, "concrete," determinate, through and through. Thus, instead of developing from within, it passes without, into otherbeing, into Nature, Part Two, wherein Will, as I said, plays no role.[7]

So it is in Part Three of the *Encyclopedia*, "The Philosophy of Mind [or Spirit]," that the Will comes fully into its own. Since we are now in the human realm, this treatment is much less abstract and so more readily intelligible. Again there are triads of triads, and they are roughly parallel to those in the *Logic*. The major triad, more to my point here than it was in the *Logic*, is first, Subjective Mind, constituted of Soul, Consciousness, and Psychology; Will comes on the scene in the last. Second, there is Objective Mind, constituted of Law, Morality of Consciousness, and Social Ethics; here Mind, including Will, appears in its external manifestation. Third is, once again, Absolute Mind, the union of Subjective and Objective Mind.[8]

"Psychology," then, is the triad of Subjective Mind relevant to the will. The preceding, middle moment of the subjective mind was called "Phenomenology," an "account of the appearances" of mind *to itself*, of consciousness and of self-consciousness, in which Mind now begins to have internal objects, a mental content. (I say "mind" here rather than spirit because all topics are now what we would usually call "mental," such as sense-perception, intellect, imagination, and finally, will.) Next, "Psychology . . . studies the . . . modes of mental activity *as* mental . . . apart from their content . . ."[9]

The *Logic* was abstracted from all animality; it was the Thinking of an unembodied mind—God's plan for the dialectical, the rational development of the world. With Mind we are among Mankind; human beings do the willing here set out. Consequently, the psychological development of Will is parallel to the logical one, but lacks the transitioning logical factor of *necessity*, which cognition recognized as its very own contribution. Now Will is conceived (one might say) more dialectically, more concretely, as arising from a "last negation of immediacy." For the concreteness of a concept (the Hegelian opposite of abstractness) comes from its being shot through with internal determinations, rich in thought-distinctions, and such riches are acquired when the negation of immediacy (meaning the abolition, by the mediation of thinking, of the undifferentiated simplicity—call it the un-thought-outness—of the given) is absorbed back into the concept.[10]

The case in point (and also a good example) is the Will. What was in the *Logic* cognition, is now Theoretical Mind, a dialectically developed result of Consciousness and Self-consciousness and its inner appearances. This Theoretical Mind has Representations, thoroughly appropriated modes of having internal objects—as already intimated. There are three representative modes or mental ideas.[11]

The first Hegel calls "inwardizing," the literal translation of *Erinnerung*, which ordinarily means Recollection. This is the mode in which a sensory object passes from external time and space into internal time and space as an image. Forgetting is the first fate of Recollecting. The inwardized images fall into the black hole of the unconscious. But Imagination (*Einbildungskraft*, "the power of forming a picture within") is a second, contrary ability of the theoretical mind, by which it disperses "the night-like darkness" of the abstractly indeterminate wealth of forgotten images and reproduces them in a connected, lucid way, ready to be named, to become verbal; so language arises. The third supervening mode is Memory (*Gedächtnis*, cognate with *Denken*, thinking—no doubt Hegel's intention), by which he means the capacity for recalling and ordering images by words alone. Memory thus easily transits into Thinking. (It is not clear to me whether these verbalizations refer to "mental language" or utterance.)[12]

Thinking, then, the last mode of the Theoretical Mind, is determinate Intelligence, our general cognitive ability to appropriate the being before it. In thinking, intelligence—which *recognized* objects that confronted it immediately (but only because they were already its own)—now in addition knows itself to be explicitly, determinately cognitive. It knows the identity of its subjective and objective side; it knows that "its product (the thought) is the thing . . . The thinking of intelligence is to *have thoughts*: these are its content and object." Here, in thinking, intelligence reaches its consummation.[13]

"But when intelligence is aware that its determinations of the content . . . [are] *its* mode[its own doing] . . . *it is Will*" (my italics). In thinking, intelligence has "completed *taking possession*" of its own property. The last negation of immediacy, its consciousness of itself, made it *free* to determine its own content. Thus Mind becomes *practical*; it is now the author and the origin of its self-fulfillment. Here starts a new development, that of the Will's very own moments, the resting places of its dialectical movements.[14]

This path will lead from a selfish will, bent on its mere "abstract ownness," to a truly free will, a thinking will. For "true liberty, in the shape of moral life, consists in the will finding its purpose in a universal content, not in a subjective or selfish interest." Thus by its very genetic path, will is intended for morality, and its freedom is in the universality of thinking. (The goal as Goodness and the way as Thought—these are the marks of will in the great tradition, and in preserving them in his developmental system, Hegel proves himself to be the receptively absorbing, the conservative thinker he means to be.)[15]

Practical Mind, Will, is, first, as are all firsts, immediate, that is, it is without rational mediation—unthought-out, un-universal, un-objective, inexplicit. Thus it is "merely formal," by which Hegel means that mind here just finds in itself an individual, insubstantial, "practical feeling." Such a feeling, an instinct for action, is "natural, contingent, and subjective." Hegel warns against two excesses: discounting this instinct in favor of rationalism and, conversely, trying to do with mere feeling what requires thought—the second being the worse, though a good intention is preferable to a bad reason. The truth is in the implicit thoughtfulness of the practical feeling, whose various determinations may well abide into fully thoughtful willing. Dozens of feelings, non-moral ones from joy through fear and ethical ones like shame and remorse, are modifications of practical feeling since they are positive or negative reactions to our sense of control, to what we think *ought* to be. It is for logical intelligence to refrain from imposing the false concept of various separate mental faculties on the mind; Mind is all one, developing its implicit potentialities into explicit actualities. (Here Hegel implicitly corrects Kant, for whom genuine willing means the denial of feeling.)[16]

To practical *feeling* belongs the above-mentioned Ought (which was for Kant the very quintessence of practical *reason*, the call of duty). This practically felt Ought is now the claim to control some—any—existing fact, without any particular objective content. This "ought-to-be" requirement in fact is a merely immediate (un-thought-out) subjective one, whose attendant general feeling is the superficial duo of mere "pleasant or unpleasant." The above-mentioned feelings are its slightly more determinate versions, which give the Ought its feeling tone.[17]

Now arise Impulses (*Triebe*, "drives") and Choice (*Willkür*, "will-choice," the term familiar from Kant). They come about dialectically, namely as the consequence of a contradiction within practical feeling. On the one hand, willing is by its nature in control—it does not *find* but *forms* the world. On the other, it is "a matter of mere contingency" whether the way the external objective world affects the willing subject is in harmony with it, feels agreeable or not. So "volitional intelligence" resolves this contradiction by *positing* what it has found objectively as a moment of self-determination: an objective determination of the will becomes—by the fact of the will's nature—a subjective one.[18]

The impulses so generated are distinguished from appetite, which seeks a single, momentary satisfaction, by embracing a whole series, a whole universe of possible satisfactions; this impulsivity has the universality accruing to an intelligence, and yet it is also still a collection of particulars. Sometimes the impulsive drive concentrates and floods an individual's whole subjectivity. This is passion, without which, Hegel says (again tacitly chiding Kant), nothing great or good gets done: "It is only dead . . . moralizing which inveighs against the passions as such." But passion itself is purely "formal," has no content; it simply signifies that a human being "has thrown his whole soul . . . onto one aim and object." The question thus immediately raised by impulses (drives), passions, propensities, inclinations (Hegel now uses all these terms) is: Which are good and rational and how are they connected? The answer is postponed to the moment when Mind becomes objective and the *content* of autonomous (self-determining) action loses all contingency and divides into concrete legal, moral, and social duties.[19]

(The foregoing psychological exposition of aspects of willing strikes me as very acute. Unlike Thomas's setting out of the internal progression of willing, which consists at least in part of temporal sequences, Hegel's account of the internal/external dialectic of the will is not necessarily temporal—after all, the three major parts of the *Encyclopedia*, Logic, Nature, Spirit, are selectively simultaneous—since the dialectical moments render the genealogy of the concepts in terms of their inner connection, not of their chronological descent. Thus the background feeling, the practical feeling of just wanting to act, to mark the world as my own, attended by the sense that it *ought* to be agreeable to my control, and the foreground propensity, the impulse, the unconscious judgment that it is not the world that is piercing me with a multitude of affects but that it is I who am driving into it—these proto-willings seem to me to be lifelong experiences.)

Hegel adds a final impulse-term: *Interest*, the subject's "moment of individuality," the agent's conscious involvement in his aim. For since, *pace* Kant, impulse and passion are "the very life-blood of all action," the aim must engross the agent's "whole efficient subjectivity." Even in a completely thought-out, fully willed, absolutely free action, a particular natural individual actor can be separated off; it is *his* interest, *his* immanent aim, *his* indefeasible selfless selfishness, as one might call it—"selfish" insofar as "I do not wish, nor ought I, to perish in pursuit of this aim" and "selfless" insofar as the aim is not particular to me but has universality. (It is an obscurely put but commonly experienced fact of psychology—this element of ineradicable individuality in even the most unselfishly conceived actions.)[20]

"The will as thinking and as implicitly free distinguishes itself from the particularity of its impulses" and as simple subjectivity from their diversity. In this reflecting on itself, it achieves its specific individuality beyond the multiplicity of its impulses. From this standpoint it can *choose* among inclinations. Hegel here departs seriously from the Aristotelian tradition, in which choice is only of means to an end already given; for Hegel, choice, which is not between this or that branch of a forked path of action but among various impulses of the mind, is in fact the moment when will claims to be free. Not quite yet, though.[21]

For thought now holds itself as above and beyond its various impulses. To be sure, these, or rather their aims, are still its content in spite of their acknowledged individual nullity, which is evidenced by the fact that each can be set aside, each desire suspended by another. The will "finds a satisfaction in what it has at the same time emerged from." It experiences an apprehension of what it needs, that is, a true, no longer self-contradictory satisfaction, a universal one. Thus *happiness* becomes its aim.

This happiness is therefore the idea of a *universal* satisfaction. This is Kant's understanding too, and it is a most significant lowering of Aristotle's, who does not regard happiness as a supersatisfaction but as an activity, a "being at work of the soul in accordance with [human] excellence." It will, however, be shown right below, that the satisfaction of all desires is not for Hegel, as it is for Kant, a finality, but rather a moment on the will's way to freedom. For such satisfaction-happiness is a mere "abstraction and merely imagined universality of things desired." It is a mere "Ought," the ought surviving from practical feeling, the aim of the instinctual springs of action. But while happiness is thus self-contradictory—a desired particularity of satisfaction on the one hand, which is, on the other, abolished in the push to universality—the will is the more confirmed in its universality, pure and concrete at once. For its very content is now *choice*; it is the *will to will*, "infinite" because unlimited by any external object. It has come into its own truth in which its concept as "impulse toward" and its object as "content aimed at" coincide. Hegel calls this self-contented will an "*actually free will*."[22]

(Here is the moment to stop and ask, with the tradition in mind: Why doesn't Hegel ever speak of will as rational desire? His terms are "inclination," *Neigung*, and "volitional intelligence"; it is almost as if he were avoiding "desire" as well as "reason," *Vernunft*, which is certainly already on the dialectical scene.[23]

I think the—significant—answer, showing him to be, after all, not only the *traduttore* but also the *traditore* of the tradition is this: In both languages, "inclination" signifies a "bending toward" and is somewhat pushful, while "desire" is felt in English as a more passive longing—not so, however, for Hegel who, consonant with its fierce German name, *Begierde*, cognate with "greed," understands desire as destructive of its object, which it consumes. Therefore, because the will as practical mind is now the pushy principle that remakes the world, passivity should not suit it, but even less would the negativity of the consumption, greed. Furthermore, for Hegel, will is not impulse rationally controlled but thinking gone active. That is a way of saying that—whereas for the originator of the tradition, Aristotle, appetite, the never quite fulfillable longing for the divine Intellect, is ultimate, and for its great transmittor, Thomas, Intellect and Will are in mutual embrace, one might even say, in an unresolvable static dialectic— for Hegel, Mind, feeling-absorbent and humanly comprehensible, is absolutely final. Thus Will is not rational desire but fully developed Mind. And in the course of its progressive motion, its dialectical fulfillment, it must actively, practically, reconstitute the human world in its own image. That moment in its movement will be termed "objectifying" itself.)[24]

Back to the tracing of the Will in its system—where it is about to go out to form its own world, now as "the Free Mind" (*der Freie Geist*—the translation "free spirit," with its Nietzschean resonances, is best avoided here). The actuality of free will is the "unity of theoretical and practical mind." It is now purged of all contingency and limitation. It is at once a self-posited *singularity*, an individual will, and purified into a *general* determination, that of freedom. Moreover, it has this generality as its object and aim, because it *thinks* itself, knows its own concept, is free *for* itself. This will is free intelligence, where "free" means not externally limited but having its object within, fully appropriated; self-thinking is freedom, inner freedom, no longer impulse-driven—self-chosen choice.[25]

But this will is so far notional, an idea, though a very "concrete," a highly determinate one. It must now release its content, itself, into existence (*Dasein*). It must unfold itself in action, become actual: Objective Mind. Here a translation—not Hegel—might wisely shift from freedom to liberty, which tends to signify external, *civil* freedoms (and who can estimate what disasters lay hidden in the absence of this Anglosaxon-Latinate distinction in German).

Objective Mind is Will at work in the world. This event occupies the second section of the third part of the system, the last before Spirit becomes Absolute, having run through its dialectical movement by completing the expulsions and resorptions of all its contradictions. It is beyond my scope here, as is indeed Mind's Objective phase, where Will becomes embodied. Its stations are Law (Right and Wrong), Morality (Good and Evil), and Ethics (social institutions). This order follows from the understanding of Law as formal and abstract, of Morality as more concrete and determinate, of Ethics as fully actual and substantial. The reason why Law or Right (*Recht* means both—another word-collapse of consequence; *Unrecht* is both injustice and wrong) is said to be abstract will be given below. The reason why Morality is more concrete is that here the Will is not purely external but internal as well; morality is then located at once in action and in the acknowledgment of the deed, hence in a knowledge of the good and evil intention of doing or not doing one's duty. Therefore moral will has *conscience*, but it is as yet non-objective—it makes purely subjective decisions. The reason why Ethics (*Sittlichkeit*), which covers social institutions from the family through civic society to the state, is last should then be clear: In Ethics the will is actualized in its subjective and objective conceptual facets. It includes the human world; the subject's will progressively identifies itself with the rationality embodied in these institutions. It becomes a self-conscious substance, as developed into an organic actuality.[26]

Just where the system is about to culminate, and where Hegel is most invested—he wrote a whole book about Right (of which more in Note 28, no. 2)—I will leave off, since my topic is, in Hegel's terms, the subjective will, and morality only incidentally. But to give an example of the objective will, let me reach for its first movement, to Law or Right as expressed in *Property*. Property, startlingly—could it be that Hegel here, for once, had an "English" thought?—is Objective Mind's first accomplishment. Mind now knows its individuality as "an absolutely free will; it is a *person . . .*" But this inward sense of freedom is still abstract and empty, hence the abstractness of Right. Not being fulfilled by and for itself, it depends on an external *thing*. A thing has no volition, hence no rights against the "subjectivity of intelligence and volition," and so it is by this subject made "a property" of the subject (in the logical sense: *Akzidenz*, something that falls to it)—a *possession*.[27]

This "practical predicate of *mineness*" belonging to a possession gives me not only external power over it but also the ability to inject my own will into it. Thus it becomes as possession, a *means*, as a part of my personal existence, that is, a *purpose*. This union of the person with himself in property brings him into another external relation, that with other persons, to whom he can alienate his already arbitrary interest in a thing. The thing passes with his will under another's will: a *contract* arises. Here I end, having given a sample of how the Objective Mind is free and is will.

In Note 28 to this chapter, I consider briefly 1. Hegel's horrendous example of Will in the world and 2. Hegel's alternative development of the Will that also readies it to rule the world.[28]

A concluding summary: Hegel's system-sited Will seems to me, in spite of the often obscure and unconvincing dialectical transitions between moments, very plausibly set forth in the moments themselves: its beginning in our subjectivity as an indeterminate *feeling*, a mere instinct toward a re-forming *action*; an accompanying sense that the facts *ought* to conform to our control and the attendant *pleasure* or *displeasure*, which are modified into a *variety of feelings* by circumstance; the articulation of this basic feeling-complex in a multiplicity of *impulses* and inclinations with their aims, sometimes coagulating into one *passion*, sometimes requiring supervening *choices*; the recognition that choice, which suspends one desire for another, *nullifies* them all; the realization that one universal satisfaction, *happiness*, must become *the* aim; and finally the *union* of the theoretical and objective sides of the mind in which the will becomes *free*, having its objective content, itself, within and so ending up altogether self-determined—all these phases of willing we may find in our experience. And surely the last, the externalizing moment, is a common experience: as human beings fully involved in our volitional individuality, with an acute awareness of our freedom, we are now compelled to invest our inner freedom with *existence* and to let the subjective mind actually unfold itself outside as Objective Mind—to let our individual freedom become social liberty. It is, after all, the familiar call to go forth and act.

One bonus of this dialectic of the will is that it disposes of the problem of free will by *obviating* it. The problem is nowadays usually located, post-positively, at the first moment after choice has issued in execution: *Were* we free to do otherwise? Hegel regards neither the choice nor its execution as such a juncture, for choice, though it first appears as merely the pick of a preferred inclination, is revealed as a will's way of *being* a will, as independence from externality and *self*-determination. Freedom is located, negatively, in *independence* from what is other and external, and positively, in *self-determination*, involving self-knowledge. So free will is not a way of deciding but of being—"freedom *is* the will," and that implies a task but not a problem. (This thought will be worked out by Sartre, in this chapter, Sec. E.)

Finally, the will's systematic siting has one really global effect on its essence. In this system of ever more concrete concepts, it stands high up, and so it absorbs the universality belonging to its mental setting just as it is about to issue into the world as Objective Mind. Hence it goes forth imperially. This empire of the will is embodied in the spiritual history of the *Phenomenology of Spirit* as the Terror (see Note 28). I ask myself: Would a reader of Hegel's rational history not ardently wish that humanity could get out from under the empire, eventually the tyranny, of the will?

It is now half a century later. I cannot even argue that Nietzsche (whom I ranged, out of chronological order, with his kindred in proposing a supra-human will) fills the gap, since *Beyond Good and Evil* is exactly contemporary with Bergson's *Time and Free Will*, to be considered next. I simply do not know—others may—of really interesting theories of will around the mid-nineteenth century. In fact, nothing says these need to appear with decennial regularity. Bergson's theory *is* really interesting and comfortingly benign to boot, since it is intensely individual, yet acutely cognizant of natural science—indeed worked up in terms of a still potent critique of certain misapplications to mankind of concepts perfectly legitimate in the world of nature.

B. Bergson: Time-intensive Will

In his *Time and Free Will*, Bergson offers a refutation before the fact of a phrase that will, because of its brusque succinctness, become the most bruited about contemporary definition of free will: "could have done otherwise." That's what makes him most relevant to the final chapters of this book, but it is by no means the essence of his original view and defense of free will.[29]

Like all deep theories of the will, Bergson's is set within an interpretation of the way things are; as the English title of his book indicates, here it is time that is reinterpreted. The key terms of this revisioning are "extensive" and "intensive," roughly classifiable respectively as quantitative and qualitative, as physical and psychic, as observable and experiential, but above all as mistakenly spatial and truly temporal.[30]

In the modern science Bergson is considering, time is taken as a dimension and is symbolized as *extension*, either as a one-dimensional spatial continuum, a line, or as a numbered succession of discontinuous digits, a sequence. In either case, the parts of the whole are contiguously and intactly outside one another. Similarly, each sub-part is preserved when comprehended in the whole. Thus, in the extensional time-line representing, say, hourly units, every minute is an internal part of each hour. The point is that the parts of such time do not meld with or leach into each other so as to affect their quality, and that is the reason why idealized laws of mechanics (those discounting friction) are time-reversible: This physical time is qualitatively homogeneous; it has no discernible internal alteration that might give it direction. The same goes for digitally counted ticks marking moments of times—the third tick, say, is qualitatively homogeneous with the ninth.[31]

Bergson claims that the extensional symbolization of intensities, which is perfectly common, is also completely destructive of the very nature of intensities. To be sure, you can represent the descent of desire into deep passion by numerable degrees along a time-line (as shown in Note 30). But then the growth of desire is effected by addible parts, each moment being quantified by a new desire-sum which is homogeneous with the earlier stages.

But this is not the real time of the soul, whose successive moments are qualified rather than quantified, for intensities are qualities rather than quantities. Psychic time is not mechanical but dynamic, and it is as inhomogeneous as anything can be. Indeed, nothing but the soul's time is truly intensive, though perhaps the sensations connected with muscular effect have a sort of intensity. Here is what all this description signifies.

Successive psychic states, sensations of more or less intensity, are not, as they might seem to be, just quantitatively different. Their molecular underpinnings may be so, but not the feelings they accompany. Whereas extensive quantities do not affect each other going forward or backward, as is characteristic of the parts of space and spatialized, extensive time, the soul's intensities are absorbent. Each successive moment has sucked into itself the previous one, which qualifies it irreversibly. Thus no moment of sensed life is qualitatively the same, homogeneous with any other. By reason of memory it is qualified, by reason of expectation it is modified. Emotions of joy and sorrow, sentiments of pity and morality in general, but perhaps most poignantly, feelings of beauty and other aesthetic sensations, are explicable only in these terms.

For example, we experience flowing curved lines (presumably either given and successively observed or being generated while we watch) as graceful because 1. at every instant, every direction is contained in the previous position-movement (this makes sense if you regard each line-infinitesimal of a curve as sprouting its own tangent, the line of its direction); 2. we also "master the flow of time" toward the future in intuiting the next position; and 3. when the graceful movements are incarnate in a dancer accompanied by music, we identify with the dance and feel as if we shared in its control, participating from both behind and before in its positions. But as intensive time passes, we also experience a nascent "mobile sympathy . . . the essence of a higher grace." It is the resultant of a cumulative interpenetration of many different feelings, each moment of which eclipses the antecedent ones. (In asking myself whether this account matches my experience, it occurs to me that it elucidates one aesthetic desire—that for repetition, for that "again-and-again, time-without-end" iteration, which, with restorative pauses, can gain in acuteness over a lifetime. Not only is any moment in a beautiful event *both* the fruition of all its predecessors *and* incomparably itself, but also each repetition of a reading, a listening, a viewing, surpasses the previous one, *just because* it comes thereafter. Might one say that people who revel in repetition have time-intensive souls?)[32]

Before the application of this theory to will and free will in particular is set out, another time term, already foreshadowed, must be introduced—

time as concrete *duration* as opposed to that homogeneous time, that dena-
tured time so to speak, which is representable symbolically *in* space and
of space, *as* spatialized time. This durational time is now more concretely
characterized: "Pure duration is the form which the succession of our conscious states assumes when our ego lets itself *live*, when it refrains from
separating its present state from its former state." To *endure* means neither to forget, nor to set the past states alongside the present ones, but to
form them into an organic whole, letting them "melt" into one another—
"a mutual penetration, an interconnection and organization of elements."
In counting moments of time or watching its progress on a dial, on the
other hand, we are always at the forefront, the present. The past has completely disappeared, left behind in the digital summary count that tells *the*
time or left blank on the analogue dial whose hands show *the* now. We may,
however, also "extract mobility" from movement and then, if we know the
applicable law of motion, draw a fixed spatial trajectory of the past or an
orbit of the future. We get either a locus of points or a homogeneous line,
but no duration, no coexistence of past with present—mere simultanei-
ties, discretely external multiplicity, but not mutually penetrating internal
organization.[33]

Yet it is this internal, dynamic, durational organization that can account
for free will. "Dynamism" (nothing to do with the causal aspect of physics
called dynamics), as opposed to completely law-governed mechanism, is
for Bergson the notion that the higher human facts escape the grasp of natural law and evince ever more spontaneity. Such self-movement he regards
as richer, more self-sufficient, and thus as more basic than the first law
of mechanics, that of inertia. This law-released psychic spontaneity is, in
turn, the opposite of determinism, the necessitation of our conscious states
by previous conscious states or by the properties of the underlying matter,
particularly insofar as deterministic action obeys the law of the conservation of energy. For this law is interpreted as having the consequence that
every material particle's position is determined by the sum of mechanical actions of all the others and is thus calculable for every moment with
unfailing certainty, if all previous positions are known; hence every person's physical organism is completely predictable, *un*spontaneous.[34]

Bergson objects that the nervous system, by compounding rather than
merely accreting influences, may not be thus predictable. But even if it
were, it would not follow that conscious states correspond exactly to cerebral states. Thus he asks (and that is *still* the great unresolved question in
the era of neuroscience): "[Is] consciousness an *epiphenomenon* . . . which
may supervene on certain molecular movements?" Bergson, of course, opts
against mere dependent "after-appearance" (which is what "epiphenomen"
means) and for the originality of inner life—and its deepest distinguishing mark, temporal unreliability. "In short, while the material point, as

mechanics understands it, remains in an eternal present [that is, it is qualitatively isolated from its past—the very crux, recall, of Nietzsche's Eternal Return] the past is a reality, perhaps for living bodies, and certainly for conscious beings." Thereon is built his theory of free will, which avoids the scientific confusion of concrete duration and abstract time, of lived and symbolized time. Positions geometrically, externally, depicted as identical are entirely different as felt actualities on the inside. The former are, to be sure, explanatory, being verbal and rational, but they also invite said confusion between philosophical construction and lived fact.[35]

This is the line drawing that sows confusion:

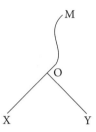

Here MO is consciousness up to the decision point O, where it faces alternative possibilities—this or something other (possibly several others; OX just happens to be drawn by Bergson as if it were the branch of least resistance with one alternative). Here is the trouble: We suppose that the symbolical diagram depicts the action *while progressing* when, in fact, it symbolizes it *as complete.*

Thus it looks geometrically as if one moment of consciousness linearly and homogeneously followed another up to a branching of courses (that "garden of the forked paths" of later chapters), all apparently equally available to conscious choice. The "impartially active" ego will choose the one, and the other will remain as a depictable possibility, and "it is in this sense that we say, when speaking of a free act, that the contrary action was equally possible." By this way of talking, by referring to hesitation and choice, we are "hiding the geometrical symbolism under a kind of verbal crystallization."[36]

For that isn't what happened; "this figure represents a *thing* and not a *progress*." Its inertness represents a "stereotypical memory" of the dynamic process of deliberation and decision (a linear view of what, in our vocabulary, would be called a wholistic event). Since every successive moment is fraught with all its predecessors, there never is a dryly rational forking of the paths, a diagram of choice representing a linear aggregate of psychic moments suddenly coming to a pivot point of decision. Consciousness is not determined by some one last emotion, some prevailing desire pushing or pulling it into the branch finally taken. (Here is the antithesis of Hobbesian will-as-last-impulse.)[37]

Instead, there is a free act—if only it issues from deep, mutually pervasive, reciprocally reflecting feelings, giving their particular coloration to every moment. For that is precisely what *self*-determination means: acting from and out of one's own psychic states; "the self alone will have been the author of the act which will express the whole of the self." Bergson's great point here is that free will is to be understood as the deep and integrated, past-fraught and present-ready state of the whole soul. We are free when it is *our* past that shapes our future.[38]

It follows that the question of predictability drops away as devoid of meaning. To be sure, if we view a person's decision from the outside, we may, after the fact and falsely, see it as issuing from a linear series and therefore foretellable. But if we put ourselves in his place, become him, then foretelling is no longer in it. We are one with him and arrive, by his lived process of self-determination at this moment of free action. "As far as deep-seated psychic states are concerned, there is no perceptible difference between foreseeing, seeing, and acting."Here willing has lost its willful aspect; it is essentially readiness.[39]

My chief complaint against the main approaches to the will that are to be set out in the final three chapters will be that they reduce willing to decision-making, a process to an instant, where "can do otherwise"—or rather, retrospectively, "could have done otherwise"—becomes the definitive criterion of free will, a criterion leaving human freedom logically and experimentally vulnerable—and partly chosen for just that very effect.

Looking backward to the great medieval tradition, we might see in Bergson's book a return to the notion of willing as a life-span activity, though where Thomas Aquinas unrolls its stages analytically, Bergson spools them in intuitively—gaining in experiential immediacy what he pays for in intellectual articulation. Looking ahead to specialized modern studies, we might see his book as forestalling, that is, as indicting before the fact, the highly operational idea of will as bare decision-making and more generally as a type of psychic determinism.

I turn now to a transatlantic trio, one of whom, a philosopher, Peirce, will be in the text, the other two, psychologists and Peirce's heirs, James and Dewey, in a note (Note 47). Whereas a certain animus against natural science—when this science is misapplied, to be sure—is undeniable in Bergson's defense of freedom, the three Americans have the greatest expectations of the science to come; nonetheless, the first two at least, both offer fresh understandings of will that do not prejudice its freedom. Then I shall recross the Atlantic to a darkening Europe and a really ugly view of the will: Heidegger—and his humanely responsible apostate follower, Sartre. So first, then, to the American Pragmatistic will.

C. Peirce: Two-faced Will

Peirce writes of the will with ever-scintillating and sometimes less-than-lucid originality—and in the grand style that places experience in a comprehensive intellectual framework.[40]

This is the framework: In his charming outline, Peirce says that for his part he is "a determined foe of no innocent number," but leans toward the number three in philosophy. This tradition, albeit here non-Trinitarian, is reminiscent of Augustine's *On the Trinity* (discussed in Ch. II, Sec. C, herein), the more so since, as for Augustine, it descends into the soul, into psychology. And here, just as in *On the Trinity*, it takes in the will.[41]

Here is Peirce's philosophical "trichotomy." This latter-day Pythagorean opts not so much for the cardinal three as for the ordinal First, Second, and Third, "ideas so broad that they may be looked upon rather as moods or tones of thought, than a definite notion, but which have a great significance for all that . . . they are intended to go down to the very essence of things."

"The First is that whose being is simply in itself . . ." It refers to nothing beyond itself; it is present and immediate, fresh, new, vivid, conscious. Nothing, such as a representation or a determining cause, is second to it, because then it would be reciprocally second to that. It is (I would use the word "absolutely," here however eschewed by Peirce) original, spontaneous, initial. It has no unity and no parts. It is what Adam was when he first opened his eyes: vivid, conscious—and evanescent. Its every description must falsify it. It is pure, unadulterated firstness, basic but delicate. It has the place that Being has in Hegel's *Logic*, the first of the first of all dialectical triads, but instead of flipping, on being thought out, *precisely* into Nothing, it has more than logical life; it is the first moment of living experience before distinctions set it. As such, it is also like Aristotelian potentiality, a primal, indeterminate material, *hyle* (which is *not* a solid matter), not homogeneous but full of undeveloped possible variety—but then again also unlike Aristotelian *hyle*: pristinely fresh and easily tainted by form, not the abstracted murk beneath formed beings but the first morning of the world.[42]

The Second is second by force of (Peirce doesn't say by "reason of") something to which it is second. To think the second rightly we must think of it as the absolute last, banishing a third. It is simply and only what cannot be without the First. "It meets us in such facts as Another, Relation, Compulsion, Effect, Dependence, Independence, Negation, Occurrence, Reality, Result." There is a shallow secondness, evidenced in a *mere* relation to the first, the kind that would leave the second unchanged if the first were destroyed. Nor, on the other extreme, must the Second degenerate into a mere accident or incident of the First. The deep, genuine secondness "suffers and resists, like dead matter, whose existence consists in its inertia." It is what we knock up against, hard fact, something which is indefeasibly there. One might say that it is the form of Other in Plato's *Sophist*—Otherness with attitude.

The Idea of Second, says Peirce, is easy to comprehend, while "that of the first is so tender that you cannot touch it without spoiling it." The two together are as agent and patient, Yes and No, categories that have long satisfactorily described the facts of *experience*. But eventually a Third is called for, something to bridge the chasm between "absolute" First and Last (here Peirce uses the word). The third arises when yes and no is too rough a distinction, when mediation is needed. Yes and no are qualitative (as affirmation-and-negation is called a "quality" of propositions in logic). What mediates between them is a quantity, represented by extension, by a *spectrum* (it seems to me; these are not Peirce's words), by "a possible half-way" between any polar dualities. Peirce himself specifies this interposing thirdness in various ways: It is a mediating representation, an action by which the first as agent influences the second as patient, a process leading from first to last, from God the Creator as First to God completely revealed as Last, all the points of time of creation—these are the thirds. Peirce thinks that One, Two, Three turn up in all our reflections of any kind—"vast though vague." Notice, incidentally, that the ordinality of thinking is inverted in the cardinality of things thought: Here Three comes between One and Two. (His prime example, somewhat technical, is reported in Note 43 to this chapter.)[43]

The (here abbreviated) metaphysical, psychological, and physiological triads should, then, partake of this tonal thought-ordering. Will occurs in the second of these, in the pyschological triad of Feeling, Knowing, Willing. These mirror a Kantian triad (which was not new even with Kant) and is accepted by Peirce as corresponding to "congenital tendencies of the mind." Its three members are indeed connected by him to the ideas of One, Two, Three. However, in working out that assignment, Peirce revises the old trinity quite radically. First, feelings are indeed what we have in immediate and instantaneous consciousness: "Of nothing but the fleeting instant can we have absolute immediate consciousness, or feeling . . ." In the instant there can be no change, no influence, no process. We can only feel. So far, so good. In Peirce's triad, however, cognition is not second but third. In it are mixed feelings; even pleasure and pain are the "warp and woof of cognition," and will, as attention, enters as well. But cognition pure and simple is process—the sense of learning, of mental growth over time. "It differs from immediate consciousness as a melody does from a prolonged note." (Immediate consciousness should actually be, were Peirce consistent, a short, plangent note, I think.) Cognition is consciousness of synthesis, and thus thirdness—listed in the triadic order where thirdness conceptually speaking belongs, namely second, since it is the mediating element. (The confused reader is getting it.)[44]

Although there is willing—as attention—mixed into cognition, Peirce also advances a new notion of will that is not cognitive. He is reluctant to assign a whole third of the mind to it as the tradition does. Nor does he agree with a "great psychologist" that will is simply the strongest desire. For, he says, that overlooks quite the "most obtrusive" fact of experience, that between dreaming and doing: "Surely he who can confound desiring with willing must be a day-dreamer." (An objection: In my experience, *nothing* is a more potent precursor of sure action than day- or night-dreaming. "In dreams begin responsibilities.")[45]

Consciousness of willing "does not differ, at least not very much" from a sensation." Such consciousness has an "intense reality . . . a sense of saltus," of a leap. It feels as if I were sitting in the dark and suddenly a light were turned on. It is not a process of change, yet something more than an instant, as if that instant had two sides. Will, then, as one of the three great types of consciousness, is "*the polar sense*," and that is what it should be called.

I think one might describe the psychological triad this way: Feeling is a first, being of the moment; cognition is a third, being in time; willing, then, is a second, a two-faced instant, temporally between instantaneous feeling and extended cognition—but metaphysically a last. (Recall that secondness is Compulsion, Reality, Occurrence, Result, *Finality*.) The "polar sense," formerly "will," is the turn to fact, the revolving of the subject toward an object—the subject's focusing and the object's recoil.[46]

Pythagoreanism, ancient and modern, is always captivating, and its trinitarian form above all. Sometimes it works, at least in its own terms. Here, I think, it is meant to solve the problem of what is going to be termed in the next chapters the executive will or "agency." For in the physiological triad that follows the psychological one, will as action and reaction, as polar sense, reappears as "external volition." Peirce does not doubt that the activity of nerve-cells routed through the brain is requisite for consciousness, and in particular that the polarity of willing, the sense of action and reaction, is underlain by a sudden discharge of nervous energy into the muscle cells. Similar nerve activity, except of an inhibitory sort, is involved in "internal volition, or self-control." In other words, the physiology of will is analogous to its psychology. That at least broaches, if it does not solve, the problem which will dominate the latest will-studies: the relation of mind to matter.

Peirce stands behind James and Dewey (addressed in Notes 47 and 48). For James, Peirce establishes that "volition, as distinguished from desire, is nothing but the power of concentrating the attention, of abstracting." However, this is said by Peirce in aid of denying a power of introspection: "[T]he knowledge of the power of abstracting may be inferred from abstract objects, just as the knowledge of the power of seeing is inferred from colored objects." Therefore, we need not presuppose a power of introspection and must investigate psychological questions "by inference from external facts." To this Peircean prohibition, James, a very vivid reporter of inner events, is not amenable (and indeed Peirce himself was an acute observer of inner experience), but the abstraction of the will from all but the focusing of interest—that will be James's theme. Hence he doesn't pick up on Peirce's polarity theory.[47]

Dewey, too, is Peirce's heir in respect to the will. Peirce says, elegantly, of belief: "It is the demi-cadence which closes a musical phrase in the symphony of our intellectual life." It is an awareness that appeases irritation, but most to the point for Dewey, it establishes "a rule of action, or say for short, a *habit* . . . The *final* upshot of thinking is the exercise of volition." The exercise of volition is no longer thought but a mental action based on habit established by belief, the—temporary—coming to rest of thought. In other words, willing is thought settled into a rule of action, which is (it seems) an inductive rule and so sensation-congruent, *not* an intuited principle, for that would be thought-derived. Thus habit, the precipitation of such thinking, mediates between active thinking and exercised will. (I would denominate this will-rule a demi-principle.)[48]

So much for the Americans who, whether or not they produce complete conviction in matters of philosophical adequacy, do leave me entirely persuaded of their depth *and* decency.

D. Heidegger: Waffling Will

To report on Heidegger's thinking on will is a devilishly difficult task, one that would take decades of study to do on my own. Therefore, I will rely almost completely on a meticulously thought-out book by Bret Davis titled *Heidegger and the Will.*[49]

I can discern three distinct reasons for the difficulty. I list first, because it casts its shadow over the others and is so touchy a subject, the fact that Heidegger's notion of the will is deeply implicated in his—never candidly repudiated—Nazi episode. In support of this assertion I quote:

> Our will to ethnic self-responsibility [*völkische Selbsverantwortung*— "national responsibility" would not render the racial, self-centered tone] wills that every people [*Volk*] find and preserve the greatness and truth of its destiny [*Bestimmung*: "determination"]. This will is the highest voucher for the peace of people, for it binds itself to the fundamental law of manly respect [*manhafte Achtung*] and unconditional honor. This will the Führer has brought to full awakening in the whole people and has fused together

into *one* single decision. No one can distance himself on the day of the manifesto of this will. Heil Hitler![50]

Davis refers to this involvement as a "political misadventure" and a "blunder." Belonging as I do to an older generation, that description of such dictatorial gabble seems to me morally inadequate. This, however, I can say for Davis's judgment: I imagine it would have displeased Heidegger. For I have yet to hear of a philosopher who would not rather be thought bad than inept, and Davis's implication is that a great thinker's political obtuseness must be rooted in intellectual slippage.[51]

The second reason is that from book to book Heidegger underwent at least two self-abrogating changes of mind, announced to the public in his hieratic tone as "turns" and "turnings" (singulars: *Kehre*, preferably used of the turn-abouts in Being itself, and *Wende*, used of the corresponding revolution in Heidegger's thinking). Thus it takes much labor to discern and weigh breaks, bends, and continuities. The third reason why studying Heidegger on the will is so tricky is similar, but internal to the texts—built-in contradictions, which require careful clueing-out as ambivalences or ambiguities, that is, as intentional double-mindedness or mere indeterminacy.[52]

That the will, either as an individual mode or an epochal determinant, plays a central role in Heidegger's thinking—of that there can be no doubt. To be sure it is news to nobody that resolve of will is a crucial trait of human character and that modernity is almost synonymous with the will to control, but *how* these traits and effects are rooted in human beings— that is presented with great originality by Heidegger.[53]

The difficulty begins with his great, early *Being and Time* (1926). It is the philosophical founding work of "existentialism," the claim that there is a kind of being—human being, *Dasein*—that is cast into the world and must there deploy its mode of existence, its possibilities, in "projects," whence, post-existentially, so to speak, it derives its nature. Since this existent being is thus prior to all fixed, natural whatness (essence), and since its possibilities (potentiality) come before its fulfillments (actuality), therefore all philosophical interpretation must begin with this *Dasein*, this "Therebeing." One would imagine that a being so described would elicit a treatment of the will, (unless one thought that will specifically belongs to *the self* here replaced by *Dasein*). The difficulty is precisely that *Being and Time* has next to nothing to say about willing; what it does say is meant to subvert its ontological significance. Davis cites Heidegger's frequent suggestions that it is a philosopher's "Unsaid" that is most decisive. In this work, which is most people's portal to Heidegger, this Unsaid is taken to the tenth power, and its manifestation, complexity, is so great that I wonder what it means to take it as other than—possibly deliberate—confusion. What is overt is, as I said, that the will is "treated as second-order phenomenon, more of an ontic than an ontological concern." ("Ontic" pertains to worldly effect, "ontological," to prior ground, somewhat as physics is to metaphysics in the older tradition here intended to be overcome.)[54]

The ontological grounding of the phenomenology of the will depends on these factors: a "prior disclosedness of the for-the-sake-of-which in general," and also of "something [in the world] with which one can take care (*besorgbaren*)," and third, "the understanding self-projection of *Dasein* [human existence] upon a potentiality-for-being towards a possibility of the entity 'willed.'" "Care" (*Sorge*) is Heidegger's term for the meaning of human existence in the world, as having a care, and being concerned for its own existence and "taking care" (*besorgen*) of things. As concerned, care depends on "disclosedness," which is the basic character of the *Dasein*, the "There-being"—what allows it to be *there*, to be "in its truth," where truth is a primordial-ontological phenomenon. In ordinary language, disclosedness allows us to be that being to which the world has disclosed and laid itself open, has become interpretable by us and an object of our care. We may recognize in these factors familiar elements of mundane willing ratcheted up into a primary level: a general disposition toward purposeful action, a world that invites action, and the conscious pursuit of self-realization in an object that is apt to fulfill one's purpose. (This paraphrase is mine, not Davis's.)[55]

Two main elements of *Being and Time* serve as a heads-up about the undeterminable standing of will therein, whether it appears as deep or mundane. One is the way the environment (*Umwelt*) of mere beings (things) rather than existences (humans) is described. These things are *for* existences, *for human* beings who are cast into their world. They are primarily "equipment," "ready-to-hand" for its projects; their very being is to be "for-a-purpose" (*Wozu*)—and that not derivatively, but primordially—ontologically. Thus they only reflect *Dasein*'s proper and unique being, which is consonant with the way it is in the world, namely, as caring, as being "for-the-sake-of." The willful sort of purposefulness may be lurking behind projects of existential caring after all, for its world is full of—*horribile dictu*—utilities.[56]

My next suspicion of what Davis terms "existential voluntarism" results from the equivocality of a word similar to the aforementioned "disclosedness" (*Erschlossenheit*), namely "resoluteness" (*Entschlossenheit*). These words are formed on the verb *schliessen*—itself multi-denoting: from closing to concluding—and can with different prefixes have a dozen meanings. For example, with *er-* the verb means "to disclose, to unlock," but with *ent-* it has to do, in ordinary usage, with closure. *Sich entschliessen* means to make up one's mind, to decide and thus "to be resolved," but in the etymological sense, which Heidegger intimates, *ent-* signifies opposition and thus is similar to *er-schliessen*, "to un-close, to open." That ambivalence in the noun *Entschlossenheit* itself spells confusion, fatal confusion because it is the word "resoluteness" on which is centered such ethics as *Being and Time* develops. Davis in fact discerns four interpretations of *Entschlossenheit* in *Being and Time*.[57]

Heidegger means: first, willful resolve or decision-making; second, its opposite, as above, amounting to an "un-willing" of the term; third, an irresolvable ambiguity in which earlier "unofficial . . . resonances" of a will that exerts mastery beyond the self, a will that is for the sake of its own power, survive side by side with intimations of a later thought, that of *Gelassenheit* (say, for the moment, "serenity"); and fourth, a "dynamic ambivalence" in which "*Dasein* not only wills to resolutely choose" its possibilities but also (I will put this in my own words) recoils from choice in view of the intimate experience of its own finitude, its mortality—for that limitation continually invades and disrupts *Dasein's* willful projects, which thus require continual reconstruction. (These are three too many meanings for the determinacy I value when delivery is magisterial; moreover, this plethora is the set-up for the confounding turns and turnings to come.)[58]

After his clear exposition of the hopeless unclarities of the 1920's in *Being and Time*, Davis faces the disruptive turning of the 1930's; the latter is not, as far as I can tell, claimed by Heidegger to be a philosophical necessity. Now the problematization of the will achieved (as Davis puts it) in *Being and Time* is forgotten, and the will is embraced as human freedom—not, however, "my will is free," but "our will is freedom"—surely here, as it was not in Hegel, a word-miasma and mystification (though rescued by Sarte; see this chapter, Sec. E). I abstain from entering upon this episode and refer the reader to the first quotation of this section for judging my reasons. Davis calls this sacrificial notion of the will, its communal relinquishment to the Führer, "deferred-willing," the deferential yielding up of the individual's will to another. (For its ontological phenomenology, I imagine one would go to Homer's Hades of anemic shades, who reacquire their reality only after being given blood to drink.)[59]

In the later thirties, after the failed venture into politics which had involved a sharp reverse of the radical individualism (perhaps better called "singularism") of *Being and Time*, Heidegger began to rethink this wewill, this relinquished will that produces a depersonalized freedom. This "twisting free" had many sub-inflections. It becomes positively pivotal in Heidegger's critique of Schelling's metaphysics of the will (see Ch. V, Note 33). I begin with the gist of his opposition to Schelling's notion of freedom as spontaneity, as a "capability-[of originating]-out-of-oneself" (*Aussichselbstvermögen*), which for Heidegger constitutes just one more system of subjectivity, a system that declares will to be "the essence of all the Being of all beings." He considers this willful subjectivity to be the core of Western metaphysics in general and of modernity in particular. This will-defined subject is both a groundless ground (being ultimate) and self-affirming being (one that presents itself to itself and strives for itself). This will-subject or subject-will therefore has a double character: It strives at once to *be* and to *know*, to affirm itself and to represent itself to itself—and, since it *is* all the world, it will strive to know the world in its totality. Consequently, Heidegger issues a call for a leap from Schelling's spectral apex of idealist metaphysics into the real finitude of existent being.[60]

Now evil enters. The root of evil, as Heidegger interprets Schelling, and the high-point (so to speak) of the fallen modern metaphysics is, as Davis points out, that "nothing less than the *actuality* of evil is needed so that God's love may realize and reveal its superior power." As Heidegger puts it, "Only by letting the ground operate does love have that in which and on which it reveals its omnipotence—in something in opposition." Schelling has laid down that "the ground must operate [in such a way] that love may be . . . There must be a particular will . . . turned away from love . . . so that love may appear in its omnipotence." Love requires "something resistant in which it can realize itself." In other words, God, who is beyond the individual willing subject-ground, requires an independent being of this sort, one capable of turning away from love to evil, in order to let his love operate. To treat of freedom is thus to treat of the faculty of good *and* evil, whose concern is *not* a mundane freedom of choice but a prior freedom, one that binds the subject to a God who needs to actualize his love through the conquest of evil. (To me this construct reads like a wildly exacerbated version of one reason cited in traditional theology for the Creator's giving his creatures freedom even unto resisting the divine will and perverting their own—namely to give scope to his grace.)[61]

Thus Schelling's attempt to think out a system of freedom as a metaphysics of evil is in the end a justification of an omnipotent divine Will to love. However, Schelling—this is the properly theological aspect of Heidegger's critique—cannot bring together in one system humanity, the unruly, self-willed subject-ground, capable of rebelling against reason, with God, an absolute, understanding Truth and its bonding love. The *Ungrund* (Abyss, literally "Un-ground") from which the two principles are said to arise is a failed subterfuge. Moreover, Schelling says, God is at the end "not a system but a life." He does not see what this means—that if the Absolute is not Truth, but itself just a Life, then "the essence of all beings is finite, and only what exists finitely has the privilege and pain of standing in being as such and experiencing what is true of beings." Schelling has missed the essential step of overturning the "rigidified tradition of Western thought" by acknowledging that all there is living, finite existence. So again, Schelling serves to precipitate Heidegger into the realm of human finitude.[62]

This not altogether lucid exposition of his critique of Schelling was necessary to set the scene for Heidegger's abandonment of a failed metaphysics of the will altogether. What comes next is a suspicion—perhaps a residue of Schelling's metaphysical theology of the creaturely will—that, "perhaps it is in general the will itself that is evil." (That thought in itself is not news. Davis himself quotes Blake: "Will is always evil." Indeed, in the tradition, Satan's evil *is* his willfulness—though the very notion of perverse will, a self-will, might imply the possibility of a good, a receptive will. Anyhow, Heidegger's application of the tradition of the wicked will to modernity sports a pregnancy of diction that has captured the imagination of modernity-resisters, for example, environmentalists. The underlying insight has become a commonplace of contemporary sentiment: The re-configuration of nature by human control—willfulness perverting givenness—is the modern sin of choice.)[63]

The piece of vocabulary at the center of Heidegger's critique of modernity is *Gestell*. To understand it, one must take in Heidegger's inimical attitude toward mental "representation" (*Vor-stellung*, intentionally hyphenated). It is that notion of cognition in which the mind sets "before" itself an object (*Gegen-stand*) that stands over against it (somewhat like a schoolboy on the carpet) and is required to give an account to the mental self of its adequacy to the mind's requirements of certainty. Thus thinking *is* willfulness. It is a mastering *Vergegenständlichung*, a monster word, fairly rendered (I think) as "perversion-into-what-stands-against," meaning controlled objectification. Representational cognition is, in its very nature, a striving, a willing. It is the mind-set of technology, in which will-representation allows being to appear only as usable, as useful for human projects, so that all nature becomes a "resource" (*Bestand*). Compared to *Gegenstand*, *Bestand*, what we usually call stock or supply, is no longer a thing in its own right, but something "standing at the ready," put aside for use.[64]

Gestell is a made-up word from the verb *stellen*, "to set up, make to stand up." It alludes to a cascade of verbal meanings: *vor-stellen*, "to imagine"; *her-stellen*, "to produce"; *be-stellen*, "to set in order" or "to place an order"; *ver-stellen* "to misplace" (literally) or *sichverstellen*, "to dissemble, to misrepresent oneself." There are more. The whole connotative complex comes along with this meaning of *Gestell*: a re-framing or composing of the world for technological manipulation. It is not just an incarnation of will but of will to the second degree, the will to will—sheerest willfulness; the idealists' subject-will has become selfhood invested in control. *Gestell* thus represents the world as made to order for the will—and that most particularly includes nature-reservations, like national parks. It does not need saying that *Gestell* is a word of deep aversion, though it is the mode of this phenomenological analyst to disclaim the derogatory meanings of his deprecating terms. Yet that is not quite fair. Heidegger overtly fears for the future of mankind, as did his predecessor Nietzsche. It seems to be an anxiety peculiar to philosophical historians, who believe that Being itself, including human being, has a destiny. (Those who think that no future is coming at us and no Fate is lying in wait for us allow that a man may well go to hell, but not mankind with him, and therein is comfort.)

Heidegger, to be sure, sees both the danger *and* the salvation. Salvation is neither in being coopted into the *Gestell* nor in indulging in romantic archaism. It is in *Gelassenheit*, Heidegger's final "twisting free" from the will. The next few pages will more or less follow Davis's meticulous unpacking of this word, which Heidegger has appropriated from the German mystics, particularly from Meister Eckhart. *Gelassenheit* is a kind of non-willing.[65]

Gelassen is an adjective ordinarily meaning "coolly relaxed, serenely self-possessed." But the old noun *Gelassenheit* has a much more august meaning—non-willing, as I said. Thus its explication has the intertwined features of positing a negation, non-willing, and of specifying that negation, for there is more than one way to say no to willing.

Indeed the first task is to say what the non-willing of *Gelassenheit* is not. But before that, a translation: *lassen* means "to let, let go, let be." *Ge-* betokens continuity and *-heit*, a quality. So the whole signifies "the attribute of having let be" in the double-faceted sense of having left off doing or being something so as to allow something else to be. Davis uses "releasement" or "letting be."[66]

For Meister Eckhart that "something else" is of course God; thus *Gelassenheit* is interpretable as *deferred-willing*, a transference of our will to God, which is not an entirely will-less condition. Nor is an *assertion* of anti-willing, or of a will to nothingness, or of refusing to will, proper nonwilling; they too are still willings. Nor is *renunciation* really beyond the domain of willing. These negations are themselves still willings, behind which will stands undisrupted.[67]

What then is *Gelassenheit*, letting go of the will, non-willing, positively? Heidegger presents the answer conversationally, though there is a guiding teacher and an argument-outline is established. There seems to me to be no way around it: Non-willing begins in a rejection, a rejection of the kind of thinking, the representational thinking, set up above, that Heidegger regards as willing, the thinking of Western modernity, which posits a "horizon," a "circle of vision" to which our outward view limits itself. Looking to it, we step over appearances to encounter objects only within our preconceiving stance; our vision is limited by our subjective construal. For example, a tree is seen not as a thing in full but as a reduced frontal surface ready to be marked as a resource. (That is not how the people I know see the world, nor American outdoor poets like Robert Frost; not all who live "in" modern times are moderns.) This approach is to be left behind in favor of thinking that which lets things show themselves out of themselves. The question for Heidegger is not *how* we think in this new way but *where*—in other words, it is not through a once more subjective control of our thinking but through looking now in the right quarter. The German word is *Gegend*, usually translated as "region." Heidegger wants to avoid the etymological suggestion that *Gegend* comes to meet us or accommodate us (as in the adjective *entgegenkommend*, which means both "coming to meet from the opposite direction" and "ready to be of service"). Nonetheless he assigns to it a motion, for he invents the verb *gegnen*, to mean "to region" (the normal verb is *begegnen*, "to encounter"). In any case, the quarter, region, place meant, is described as "an abiding expanse, which, gathering all, opens itself in letting each thing emerge in its own resting." It is the place of "beying" (*Seyn*, see Note 71), which is here treated as a quarter, topologically. (Thus Aristotle speaks of *Mind*, *Nous*, as "somehow the place [*topos*] of forms.")[68]

The question then is how human beings relate to this region, and so we return to *Gelassenheit*. It is the letting-be pertaining to humans that corresponds to the letting-be that enables being. This sentence is salvaged from double-talk by calling on Heidegger's ontological humanism: Human beings are needed, "used," to assist in letting beings be. But *how* can humans participate in the letting-be of beings? For as it is outside the will, *Gelassenheit* is neither a sort of activity nor of passivity. It is rather a *waiting*—a sort of complementary counter-openness to the open region of being. Initially a trace of willing would be required to "release oneself to belonging to the open-region," but this trace vanishes as *Gelassenheit* becomes complete. At that moment *Gelassenheit* is genuine non-willing, the complete extinction of will.[69]

Nevertheless, the attainment of non-willing remains paradoxical, doubly so. First, it requires an "ascetic abnegation" of the will—which is surely willed and so is a paradox in its own right. Second and ultimately, it needs a positive "twisting away" from willing altogether by a "paradoxical willing non-willing."[70]

(I have misgivings. First, does the specific paradox of willed non-willing not have a wider, even more obstructive setting, namely what I might call Heidegger's didactic propheticism? Is a teaching thus manifested not from beginning to end suffused with intention, purpose, will? And to express a less *ad hominem* doubt: There is the perfectly sensible Socratic inquiry into the one being, the *eidos*, intended by words in common use that have multifarious instantiations in the world—even in our world—for example the virtues and vices. But what does it mean to search arduously for the meaning of word-conceit used in now-archaic language and then in different significations, words like *Gelassenheit* and *Seyn*, entirely without use-context, without living exemplars? It seems to me that one may say, "I originated this word, thought out its meaning, and now I intend to project it into the world that it may be efficacious there, for good or evil." But is that an open inquiry? It seems to me part of the *Gestell*, its counter-will, a resolve. I might observe here that the title-term of this book, "Un-willing," is intended to preserve the thought-provoking aspects of resolving to undo a kind of resolve.)

When the will is in question, decision must come on the scene. As ever, Heidegger's treatment involves a ratcheting up of realms, namely the "ontic" (worldly appearance) to the ontological (the account of the appearing of being). "Decision can and should at first be meant as a human 'act' . . . until it suddenly means the essential occurrence of being."

De-cision is (creatively) etymologized as "non-scission from being"; it brings man and being *together* in mutual appropriation. It happens in stillness, not as a "resolve" (*Beschluss*; recall the multitude of meanings of *schliessen* above), but as a "resolute openness" (the above *Entschlossenheit*). Thus there is still a proto-decision in the face of "being able to do otherwise," but with the destiny of being and the dawn of a new non-metaphysical existence, human subjectivity at its deepest has been pulled out of deciding.[71]

(The question of ordinary, individually imputable responsibility has, once again, been "deferred," pulled up onto a higher plane. The first way was to build willful evil into being itself and in the face of that aboriginal fact to call for the relinquishing of will for a new non-willing. Now even decision, the motion of the will traditionally preceding particular actions, has been pushed back into an ontological, non-individual event. I will try to say in my Conclusion why will is an emergency mode that requires acknowledgment even, or especially, if better ways are recommended for daily use, and why this ontologizing of the will seems no better to me than the human willfulness it eclipses.[72])

Before long I shall end with three chapters giving an account of will in terms that are the polar opposite of Heidegger's phenomenology—will as a logical problem and willing as a research project: facts of mind and nature. There is, however, one more ontology of the will that tackles very originally the ever-live question of the relation between will and freedom.

E. Sartre: Freedom First

In the chapters to come, the question is rarely "What is Will?" and even more rarely "What is Freedom?"—in fact it never really is either—but rather "Do we or don't we have Free Will?" That is to say, will is mostly reduced to decision-making and freedom is shrunk down to having options, understood *ex post facto*. "Could I have decided to do (or could it have happened) otherwise than I (or it) did?" Thus freedom is a property that could belong to any subject at all—free fall, free world, free country, free verse . . . And these are the questions then (somewhat scandalously) submerged: "How did 'free' and 'will' get together in the first place? Is the intractableness of the question of free will perhaps to be found in the very notion of adjectival freedom, in treating it as a qualifying adjective of a will-faculty? It is hard to imagine that to people setting themselves to think about will, there would not come a glimmer of suspicion along these lines: "Freedom seems to go with "will" more intrinsically, less metaphorically than it does with "world" or "verse"; why is that?"

Sartre answers this question directly in *Being and Nothingness*. It is not hard to see that such an answer will have to be located within a fundamental view of human and non-human being. I will try to set out that frame with a minimum of special language—only as much of it as is specific to the will. But before I get to the much more intrinsically interesting locating of volition in Sartre's work, the question of derivation obtrudes itself. Sartre belongs to a movement which is a fusion of Phenomenology, whose originator is Husserl, and of Existentialism, whose great modern exponent is Heidegger (a movement whose chief characteristics, painted in bold strokes, I won't scruple to lay out once again below). It is therefore a condition to be expected by the reader that Sartre's thinking will move in the originators' terms, as it is a challenge to be faced by the critic whether he is confirming, subverting, or just tweaking his predecessors. For my part, I am easily seduced by a clear answer to a long-lurking question, such as Sartre attempts, and will therefore make an end-run around these puzzles to attend to his meaning.[73]

The question is: Does will come first and then acquire or fail to acquire a general attribute called freedom? Put bluntly and briefly, Sartre answers: *Freedom is first*, for freedom *is* human being. Since the standing of the will is so vexed a problem in Heidegger's writings, and since the Frenchman Sartre is not averse to denying his own originality in favor of faithfulness to his German predecessor (a fact in itself remarkable, considering that *Being and Nothingness* was conceived under German occupation), while Heidegger rejected Sartre's interpretation, the question of indebtedness is—once again, at least to me—convoluted beyond profitable disentanglement. There is, however, a work by Heidegger clearly pertinent to the issue that does anticipate the priority of freedom, *The Essence of Human Freedom: An Introduction to Philosophy*.[74]

The work is actually an exposition of Kant's theory of Practical Reason insofar as it arises from an aboriginal freedom. The pretext for the denomination of this interpretation as "an introduction to philosophy" is a teaching to the effect that philosophy cannot be approached in general, but must be understood "*in a positive way from itself*" and that means "*from the content of a chosen problem*." Here Heidegger chooses freedom. (I call this dogma a pretext because it is by no means clear that the love of wisdom has benefited from falling apart into codified problems, a fact to which Heidegger himself is acutely alert—witness his continual attacks on philosophy as an industry. And what underwrites this institutionalized business but a highly particularized problematic, the stuff of articles? In fact, *me quoque*.)[75]

In the paragraphs of his work headed "First Breakthrough," Heidegger presents an illuminating diagram:

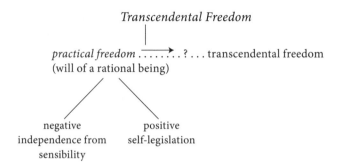

Transcendental Freedom

practical freedom . . . . ? . . . transcendental freedom
(will of a rational being)

negative   positive
independence from   self-legislation
sensibility

An explanation of this figure will serve as a preparation for Sartre's theory.[76]

"Transcendental" means "beyond the laws of nature." Transcendental freedom is identical with "spontaneity" (which Heidegger traces back to Greek *spendein*, "to give or offer freely"). It means to originate oneself, to be self-originating, *sua sponte*, "by one's own 'spending'" (*sua sponte* ordinarily means "willingly"). Transcendental freedom is, then, "*the power of the self-origination of a* [conscious] *state*." From it descends "practical freedom," a narrower notion, namely that of the human rational will, the one treated in chapter V, section A. There it was presented as Kant takes it, in its "practical" sense, meaning as dependent on freedom and as we experience it, as a negative, harsh, self-imposition; free will involved the self-denial of our whole sensory, desirous nature. But it also had a positive aspect as evidenced in our moral feeling, our satisfaction in our power of self-rule, self-legislation. Heidegger, however, notes something else in the concept of will, deeper even than its practical autonomy, namely its power of self-determination. This power is interpretable as an even more fundamental feature than *self-law-giving*; it is *self-origination*. Thus the will is, albeit somewhat implicitly, yet more positive, namely, as said self-determination, self-causation. As such, is it not *equivalent* to spontaneity? Heidegger signifies that this equivalence is problematic by a question mark. It is problematic because it construes Kant's freedom as a logical antecedent to will, a superior will-category, a proto-will. Is Heidegger not saying that Kant's concept of the will exceeds Kant's own understanding of it? Fair enough, but it does leave the reader with a "hermeneutic," an interpretational, unease. So perhaps (I am not sure) *this* priority of transcendental freedom over autonomous will, *this* absolute spontaneity of practical free-dom that Heidegger reads into Kant, is after all not quite the precursor of Sartre's theory. First because it may be a misconstrual, and second, because for Sartre freedom is *not* the proto-will, and will is *neither* convertible with spontaneity *nor* constitutive of human being.[77]

After these lengthy though, I hope, pertinent preliminaries, I finally come to the framing philosophy of *Being and Nothingness*. It consists of the merging of a "-logy," Phenomenology, a method of inquiry, and of an "-ism," Existentialism, a theory of Being. The well-known formula of the latter is, *Existence is prior to essence*. First we *find* ourselves existing here and now, and then we *construct* our nature; *that* we are (existence) precedes *what* we are (essence); our possibilities are antecedent to our actuality.

Phenomenology engages in the most acute possible observation and description of the structures of our consciousness. Its method is to attend to these as pure "appearances" (*phainomena*), and therefore it "brackets," it excludes, existence. Thus it gives its account (*logos*) unburdened by ques-tions of reality. The hypothesis behind this method is that what appears in our consciousness is unaffected by real existence; the what of things is unaffected by their—mere—reality. Phenomenalism might be said to be, in its Husserlian beginnings, essentialist. Moreover, for consciousness to be describable, to yield an account of inner appearances, it must have con-tents, objects. Observation shows that it has contents, to be sure; it *intends* its objects, its phenomena—meaning that it "tends toward" and lays itself about them. But not as we wrap candies in foil, where the wrapping enfolds a dissimilar object. Rather the contents of consciousness are of the same sort as consciousness itself: thinking gets hold of thoughts. Further, in order that the different appearances, the multitudinous perspectival views that arise for consciousness as it moves around, lays itself about its phe-nomena, may come together into unified objects, a unifying agent is called on by Husserl. He names it the "transcendental ego"—an "I" that belongs to, but also goes beyond, consciousness. Thus, if a set of phenomena under observation display now a circle and now an ellipse, now luminosity and now dullness, now flatness and now solidity, this ego unifies these into, say, a lampshade.[78]

On the face of it, this Phenomenological method and an Existential-ist ontology are at odds. Phenomenology regards appearances as intuit-able (directly viewable) essences and regards the ego as the same in all human individuals. Existentialism rejects such intuitable essences and identically constituted egos. Therefore Sartre works a huge modification so as to devise an existentialist phenomenology: While retaining the notion of philosophy as descriptive, he excises all essence, all pre-existent com-mon human structure. The transcendental agent-ego is translated into a "transcendent" ego. While "transcendental" (as Kant uses it) refers to a "behind-beyond," meaning a beyond connected as ground to dependency, "transcendent" refers to "simply-beyond," meaning absolutely, disconnectedly beyond. What is simply beyond consciousness is an *object* brutely confronting it. The ego, on the other hand, what we mean when we say "I," does, to be sure, come on the scene but only reflectively, secondarily, as itself an object of conscious intention. Consciousness is *absolutely* first, prior to any ego, that might have been said to "have" consciousness. The ego is not, in any ordinary sense, its property, mode, or effect. This counter-intuitive relational order will loom large in Sartre's account of the will, for it makes aboriginal freedom possible.[79]

To backtrack: Why must the Cartesian-Kantian-Husserlian, the old ego be removed from *behind* to *beyond* consciousness? Because consciousness, if it is *ego-structured*, is not perfectly translucent, absolutely, untaintedly clear, terminally *open*. But so it must be, if it is to allow an object to show itself *as* itself. Thus consciousness is *nothingness*, the nothingness of Sartre's title; it can have no being, no properties. We are ultimately an open nothingness; human consciousness is nothing to itself and only *of* another—purest featureless intentionality. Into it can come the *only* being there is, non-human matter. "Being" is in this extreme existentialism very nearly a term of degradation.

Between this introductory exposition and the treatment of the will lies three quarters of *Being and Nothingness*, in which all the problems that such a radical view of humanity must raise are ingeniously resolved: what, concretely, it means to speak of human nothingness and to assign being to brute matter *only*. Whatever else is set out in the almost six hundred intervening pages, we may guess this much: If we begin as nothingness, we make ourselves out of nothing, and if the only being is matter, there is no God. Both of these intimations are to be confirmed in the section on the will, to which I now finally return.[80]

Sartre begins by undermining the endless philosophical arguments "about determinism and free will," by going behind them to "make explicit the structures contained in the very idea of action." He finds that "all action is on principle *intentional*." Thus the careless smoker who unintentionally causes an explosion "has not *acted*." This is a curtailed example of Phenomenology at work very precisely on cases; note that the use of "intentional" here has shaded from mere "aboutness" to the common use of "motivated"—of which more below. (Incidentally, it seems problematic to me, whether careless behavior is not in fact imputable as negative action, like negligence is in law.)[81]

This sort of intentionality, the purposive kind, implies that something is desired, hence absent. Sartre interprets this lack-structure as follows: Consciousness, so far immersed in being, that is, in material circumstances, withdraws itself from the world (of being). It goes negative in pursuing its want. Now a want, in being something wanting, that is, lacking, is a positive absentness; Sartre terms it a *negatité*, an objective lack. But it is not being that has lacks, it is consciousness that creatively apprehends lacks as such. Immersed in being and habituated to it, consciousness knows no lack, at least not such as to cause action. No factual state can of itself motivate action, for no factual state can determine consciousness to apprehend a lack. Consciousness must wrench *itself* away from being, from the objective world; it has a "nihilating power," not of *mere* withdrawal but of a rupture with its past. In this nihilating rupture, a meaning is conferred on the world—not *its* meaning but that of consciousness. It follows that, although the world of beings may well be the cause (*motif*) of action, meaning its external moving occasion, it can never be its motive (*mobile*), meaning the subjective origin of action. *This, then, is freedom*; the fundamental condition of action: our nothingness asserting itself by injecting lack into what is impervious to lack, being.[82]

In the ever-indecisive free will debate, the free-willers look for a causeless action. That is an absurdity, because every act is intentional, which means it has a purposed end, and every end has an occasion, a cause. The determinists, on the other hand, fix on the decision phase of willing and its causes, ignoring the truth that everything that matters has preceded deciding, for freedom lies beyond the "cause-intention-act-end" complex.

A related way to understand action is in terms of the transcendent ego, the Me-object. My motives are ideal existences, "not-yets" (one might say). "Cause and motives have meaning only inside a projected ensemble . . . of non-existents." But that ensemble *is* "ultimately myself as transcendence; it is Me insofar as I have to be myself outside of myself." I think Sartre means that in facing the outside, the world of beings, in transcending consciousness, there open up future *possibilities* of action, of modifying the world. The meaning-bestowing withdrawal from the world that reveals want is a move that is close to, perhaps identical with, the movement of the self-consciousness that yielded the object-ego.[83]

Yet these are superficialities; the fundamental, ultimate condition of action is freedom. But freedom, just because it is primary, is *not* an essence. Recall that we are in an existentialist book. Sartre simply quotes what Heidegger says of *Dasein*, human being: "In it existence precedes and commands essence." I have not gone into the why's and wherefore's of the priority of existence for Sartre. There seem to be in play two root-values—not arguments but deep preferences—the second of which is, in fact, very pertinent to the will. The first is a keen experience of the "facticity," the brute and also bewitching thereness of things. That second value is deep human freedom and ultimate self-responsibility, to which Sartre is now coming.[84]

"How then are we to describe an existence [here freedom] which perpetually makes itself and which refuses to be confined by a definition?" Happily what has no essence may indefinable, but it is not indescribable. Here the aptness to Existentialism of Phenomenology as a descriptive method shines out. To be sure, the description is not intended to be common to Sartre's and to anyone else's freedom; he means *his* freedom only. (A difficulty: I, who am not Sartre, am reading and, to some extent, apprehending the description reported. I am doing my best to honor, to accede to, his urgent forfending of commonality, but I succeed only by reverting to an old notion, that the locution of "communicating" an experience is indeed a solecism: You *can't* make your experience common with me, make me have it. But no sooner is that conceded than I recall that I *can* describe a general structure, fit it out with slightly more specified particulars, and then begin to imagine, and though that's all I can accomplish, experience being terminally individual and words indefeasibly common, that's a lot. I think that Sartre will in fact accomplish just that in the following description of "his" freedom—*his* by a tacked-on fiat, but *mine* as well—provided I comprehend his description—as I may by the *communicating* function of language.)[85]

Here then is his description of the freedom of an existent: Actually freedom does not "belong" to an existent being, it *is* its way of existing—"not a quality added on." It turns out that my reference to experience above was inept. "I cannot *experience* my freedom, since I *am* it." I am indeed an existent who *learns* of his freedom through his act . . . ," that is to say, I do come to possess "a certain comprehension of freedom." *That* is what Sartre thinks he can make explicit; what he paradoxically succeeds in communicating is the fundamental unsayableness of *this* freedom.[86]

For freedom is "nihilation" (*néantisation*). The human existent "nihilates" being, which means that it disrupts the totality of being to discriminate one thing from another. (Sartre advisedly speaks in the singular so as not to sound as if he were describing a common essence.) It can thus nihilate because it is itself nothingness, translucent awareness—its discriminations and its receptivity are one. Nihilation is the escape from fixed essence and the release from fixed definition; it is always other than what was said of it—its essence is always past (from Hegel: "*Wesen* [essence] *ist was gewesen ist* [what was])," and its existence is always beyond the property assigned to it; "all this is to say . . . that man is free."[87]

We are coming up to the will and its freedom, for Sartre is now ready to delineate determinism. It occurs "when the 'for-itself' [the human existent] has the urge to incorporate the 'in-itself' [unconscious, non-human being] as its true mode of being." (This definition, here expressed in terms of the existentialist framework, says just what one would ordinarily say:

Determinism arises from a human propensity to regard human beings as simply and entirely natural, as of a piece with nature; to be sure, as a *general* inclination this belief is a fairly latter-day development.) Deterministic belief, Sartre thinks, results from my choice to hide from my freedom by giving myself over to "causes," that is, to causation, to fixed linkages, as my essence. But causes and ends serve as essences precisely because they are always has-beens. (The reference is to Hegel's—correct—etymology, just quoted, of *Wesen*, essence, as from the past of "to be.") Sartre is here giving a temporal (Heideggerian) interpretation of causes and ends as *Dasein*'s presuppositions, as pre-given, pre-human, encountered as pre-ordained by God or society; in other words, causes are "always already" *in* the world, preceding acts, while ends are projected *onto* the world, also before action. To give ourselves over to them is to "stifle freedom under the weight of being." Why exactly?[88]

Because the freedom of human existents, their very being, *is non-fulfillment*. (Recall that a watchword of existentialism is that possibility stands higher than actuality.) An existent's freedom consists in its being "perpetually wrenched away from itself." It has no essence but is "precisely the nothingness which *is made-to-be* at the heart of man and which forces the human existent *to make itself* instead of *to be*." Being so absolutely aboriginal, it has but one necessity. We existents cannot escape it; we are compelled to be free if we are to be human. And now comes the crucial declaration: "[F]or the human existent, to be is to *choose oneself*; nothing comes to it either from the outside or from within which it can *receive or accept*." Humans are radically on their stripped-down own. Here now is the opportunity for a discovery: ". . . to bring to light the relations between freedom and what we call the 'will.'" Recall that that relation *was* the original question. The beginning of an answer perhaps looks inconsequential, but it is spectacularly potent: Choosing, deciding are commonly considered the specific work of the will; Sartre has just intimated that choosing, the choice that makes us what we are, *precedes* the will.[89]

First, two negative observations: Free will is commonly thought of as besieged by our passionate nature. Not only does Sartre find such an inimical duality at the heart of our being inconceivable, but the will's spontaneity, its original freedom, has no way to come to grips with natural passionate being—the given is simply beyond freedom's reach, which has no tool that works in the opposing natural realm. (Recall that this is a problem that Kant leaves as an unacknowledged enigma—how practical reason can *alter* the natural course of things as theoretical reason *knows* them.)[90]

Now the positive delineation: Given that if freedom is to be attached to the will, it cannot be a psychic fact (facticity, mere givenness, being opposed to freedom), it must be a *nihilation*, the generator of nothingness—of distance (in people-speak). But then how does it, in that respect, differ from the passions? Don't they nihilate, that is, "posit a state of affairs as intolerable"? And does desire not also imply a project?[91]

In short, the will is not a unique nor a "privileged manifestation of freedom." Rather, as we have just seen, it presupposes an "original freedom in order to be able to constitute itself as will" to begin with. Moreover it doesn't create its ends; it is instead just a mode of being in relation to them. (In a very different register, this claim is to be found in Thomas: The will is *given* both its overarching end and the subsidiary ones tied to it; it *chooses* only its means; see Ch. III, Sec. A.)

Sartre considers causes (my apprehension of the external situation), motives (my subjective ensemble of passions urging me to act), and ends (the projected outcome), in their relation to each other, which was opaque in the standard free will debate but has now become intelligible. They are henceforth three indissolubly conjoined terms. Cause and motive are correlatives in the light of the end. This is how it works: The human existent (here revealed as a relative of Heideggerian *Dasein*) experiences itself as a project—"it projects itself towards its possibilities"; it has ends. In the light of these, it apprehends causes. Sartre means this literally. Our projects, our futurity, casts what was until now mere being into a causal mode—first come subjective ends, then follow objective situations, suitably construed. (This inversion of the ordinary view makes great psychological sense to me. We do, on occasion, *find* our cause to suit our self-realization.) And the "motive," my passionate engagement, "surges up" together with end and cause.[92]

Then why does the naturalistic psychologist sees the motive as a fact, a "made past" of consciousness? Because the motive has become fixed in memory as past consciousness. It is now like an outside thing; it is at once mind and beyond me—transcendent. To be sure, the motive has motivated the construal of an objective structure in the world. I have *given myself an essence*—the *what* that I *have been*. By an act of recovery, an "upsurge" of the freedom that is beyond causes, motives, ends, beyond the whole willing complex, I can regain my futurity, my possibilities, my freedom.[93]

Thus "voluntary deliberation is always a deception." (It is surpassing strange that Sartre's existentialist reduction of willing to self-delusion will have a successor in Wegener's naturalistic reduction of will to illusion [Ch. XI, Sec. A, herein]; thus sophisticated analyses sometimes flip into their abhorred opposites.) Why is deliberation self-deception? Because I can't evaluate causes and motives when they themselves were my own choice. I can't weigh them as permanent properties and as contents of consciousness at once. (This is the moment to enter a cavil: Sartre's Heideggerian inheritance of thought-out and recollectable thoughts as dead presences may not be such a windfall; perhaps there is Being with clean contours that precisely preserves its life, even a life of vibrant possibilities—for instance,

Platonic eidetic forms, which, pervaded by Nonbeing in the form of Otherness emanate instances, or Aristotelian divine *energeia*, whose vibrating
stasis attracts moving life.)[94]

Free spontaneity thus makes the choice behind the choice made by
the will; the will is just the loud-speaker. What then distinguishes voluntary from involuntary acts? The involuntary act is unreflective; the voluntary act, on the other hand, has put Husserlian brackets around the cause
insofar as it already contains the choice. Thus it has achieved for itself the
semblance of a preceding "appreciative deliberation"; it has become, albeit
illusionistically, reflective.

Here Sartre injects an apparently extraneous comment that proves to
be climactic. He says that although the result of reflection, which is nihilation *par excellence*, appears to widen the split between "for-itself" and
"in-itself" (human existents and mere beings), that is not its goal. Its goal
is rather the reverse, to institute that unrealizable totality of "in-itself-for-
itself," which is human existence's fundamental value. For the moment,
I hold in suspension the significance of introducing this new notion—a
goal—in order to complete Sartre's exposition of the will.[95]

In sum, when the will comes in, it is already the case that "the chips are
down . . . [so that] voluntary deliberation is always a deception." What is
the project behind the will that brings the latter into play? It is a profound
intention, which makes the human being turn to willing, when a passion
might have achieved the same end. Sartre does not further specify. He says,
in conclusion, that a full phenomenology of the will is yet wanting. (I propose that we do have it in Thomas on the will.)[96]

What he hopes to have shown is that the will is not a "privileged manifestation of freedom" but is on the same plane as other psychic events, all
supported "by an original, ontological freedom."

To prevent the idea that this freedom is, although unanalyzable, a series
of capricious jerks, Sartre collects such results as his analysis has so far
obtained: Freedom is one with human existence which is free to the extent
that it "has to be its own nothingness," and that it is so in multiple dimen-
sions. These are: its distance from its own determining past, its projection
of itself into futurity, its presence to itself as consciousness *of* itself and *of*
other being (that is, its intentional structure, which insures that nothing is
external to consciousness), and its transcendence (that is, its outstripping
all fixed being and forever going beyond itself as its own project).

Sartre then faces directly the "could have done otherwise" version of
free will. Actually, he doesn't very directly, but rather by way of an evasive account of an apparently personal experience, namely giving up from
exhaustion during a mountain hike. His point is that one's ontological life-
choice may sometimes call for giving in, when one could, on the will-level,
have gone on, though with dire consequences—well, OK. (I append, in

Note 97 to this chapter, an early non-continental consideration of this version of free will, done in the very different spirit of language analysis, by G. E. Moore.) In any case, "could have done otherwise" has been obviated by ontological choice: Our very "being is precisely our original choice." The rest is consequence. But since "choice and consciousness are one and the same thing," this original choice is not lost in the mists of primordial time; it is ever and always being made. (I am torn here. On the one hand, when a very sophisticatedly original, counter-intuitive re-founding yields ordinarily recognized results—that is confidence-inspiring, especially if one thinks, as I do, that philosophy is best employed in grounding common beliefs, not in overturning them. On the other hand, when I reach as far back into myself as I think I can, I find not a choice but a nature, not a project but a place, not something made but something given. It raises a tremendous question: Are there several kinds of ultimate human experience and so of humanity?)[97]

To end, I return to the "goal" that appeared *in medias res* above, the hopeless goal of a human existent to constitute itself into an actually unrealizable totality, an "in-itself-for-itself," a "being-existence," so to speak.

In the penultimate chapter of *Being and Nothingness*, this goal is explicitly named—named so as to fit into the existential complex that, between brute contingent being and aboriginally free existence, has no room for God. "[T]he best way to conceive of the fundamental project of human existence is to say that man is the being whose project is to be God." To become God is here understood as the free existent's, the for-itself's desire to achieve "the impermeability and infinite density of the in-itself." This goal comes close to the desire for an essence; it is unachievable, for existence's freedom is incompatible with fixed being. Sartre seems to be saying that, existence and being now having been shown to occupy the whole of conceptual space, the existents (the nothings) fall to desiring to come literally into being (the something)—to appropriate it so as to become replete and thus both to *exist* freely and to *be* substantially—and that is what it means to be God, a conceptual contradiction. Sartre's explanation of how man lives with this hopeless desire is beyond my brief except to note that this passion is conceived as negating Christ's: "[M]an loses himself in order that God may be born. But the idea of God is contradictory, and we lose ourselves in vain. Man is a useless passion." So ends this last full chapter, on a not-so-exhilarating note.[98]

I have given room to this existentialist desire to be God, the desire to become essential, because it is at once parallel to and at odds with an episode in Dostoevsky's most potent work, *The Demons*. Kirillov is a purely good man (there are only two such permitted to be strong characters in this book full of powerful people, Shatov and Kirillov), though he is in the grip of a theological insanity. He believes that once men recognize that there is no God, they become Gods—and *live* in glory. But there must be a first man who must *die* in fear to prove this, one—Kirillov ordains himself—"who is still God against my will." He is the one whose "*duty* it is to proclaim self-will, . . . to believe that I do not believe." This sacrifice will save all men, for it will prove "my insubordination and my new fearsome freedom," for "the attribute of my divinity is self-will!"[99]

The project fails: Kirillov does not die as a free man whose will is absolute but as a petrified beast cornered between terror and shame. Sartre's analysis is exactly inverted by Kirillov's terms: Mankind is destined to *achieve* divinity, and freedom *follows* from ultimate willfulness. And Sartre's judgment is similarly countermanded by Dostoevsky: Kirillov fails, not because God is a contradictory idea, but because Kirillov cannot will unbelief. (I ask myself: Does this Russian proto-existentialist insanity not have a greater gravity than the European analysis?)

I conclude this chapter with a brief note (Note 100) on two philosophers, Wittgenstein and Ryle, who by their reinterpretation of philosophy as analysis, applied by the former to language usage, by the latter to conceptual mistakes, countermand these continental will-agonies and undo volition well before the neuroscientists go to work. These two might, therefore, be taken to mark the demise of the great will-ontologies—the end, at least for the time being.[100]

chapter **IX**

Compatibilism

An Academic Question

As a prelude to a new phase in the study of the will, here is a chapter on its most preoccupying issue. The new phase is the dismemberment of the inquiry concerning the will into special studies done in an academic format, either because grandly comprehensive attempts have run themselves into the ground or because the human capacity for them is, for the moment, running on empty. Who knows? The complaint that the philosophical life receives the kiss of death in the arms of the academy is as old as the hills and is pretty implacably pursued by the very philosophers who were themselves professors, *exempli gratia*, Nietzsche and Heidegger. Yet it's hard to be much exercised by the fact that matriculated students of philosophy hope to make money and reputation by being "productive"—what else are they supposed to do?—and that they are trained to academic standards of knowledgeableness and acknowledgement—how could there be an academic community without such constraints? On the other hand, something has gotten lost in this assimilative process in which the passions are studied dispassionately, that is, disengagedly, and the will is researched objectively, that is, without deference to its ferocious possibilities.

The problem of compatibilism *is* characteristically academic. For one thing, it was somewhat shopworn before it entered its present phase. For another, there is a way to take it as what used to be called a "semantic" problem, one that can be evaporated by attending to terms—here by distinguishing between will and willingness, of which more below.[1]

What, then, is compatibilism, and why does it get so much attention in our day? *"Compatibilism is the thesis that an act may be both free and determined by previous events and the laws of nature."* This is as brisk a description as I've come across. Incompatibilism, then, is the denial of this thesis, or the thesis that previous events and the laws of nature determine human behavior so as to leave no room for free choice. In the vocabulary of the debate, the latter is usually expressed as "being able to do otherwise," or more restrictedly, as "being able to refrain from performing certain acts." The issue then explodes into main and modified positions, such as "libertarianism," "compatibilism," "semi-compatibilism," "incompatibilism," "hard incompatibilism," and more particularized or diffuse notions. Libertarianism is the thesis that we have the free will which the common sense of ordinary folks attributes to us and that determinism, the belief that we are completely governed by conditions and laws, must therefore be false. "Semi-compatibilism" is a theory constructed to make compatibilism more plausible by devising distinctions in the kind of control we exercise. Hard determinism is an uncompromising insistence on such determinism as makes free will impossible.[2]

Although compatibilism is the non-intuitive and so the most attention-arousing position, it makes sense to zero in on it from the most hardline—minority—view. These frank hardliners claim that we are items of nature, driven by laws operating on conditions set from way back. Actually, as Hobbes, the original hardliner, said, only the most proximate condition comes through to, actually effects, the last consequence, that last moment of completely jigged human conduct, or rather of behavior (if conduct denominates morally focused action and behavior merely directed motion). The past only comes in as known to have progressively, that is, causal-chainwise, determined the current ultimate, present. For strictly speaking, just as the moment proximate to "action" (it's not agency-action, of course) is all that counts in determining the motion made, so the initial condition (that is, the beginning of the world) is all that matters in giving the laws of nature something to work on; once they kick in, the "in between" has no particular explanatory value. In other words, history tells nothing, being devoid of instructive choices, since at any moment at any locale the story is, as it were, at its beginning; thus all presents are *indifferently* beginning or transitions—or ends. Imaginatively put: If the world had begun a day ago with yesterday's conditions and identical laws, today's decisions would be the same as if it had developed over billions of years.[3]

There is a next step that the *hard determinist* needs to take, which will be discussed in Chapter X: Human behavior must be governed by brain functions, a fact that shows itself as "psychological causalism," consciousness-determinism in our decisions. With this hypothesis, the study of the will transits into experimental science.

At first sight, the beauty of *hard determinism* is that it is candidly, even brutally, decisive. One might say of it (as also of its extreme opposite, libertarianism) that it has a certain manliness—were such terms not proscribed nowadays. We are bits of nature and must recognize that free choice (made here and now) and free will (exercised over a span of thinking time) are illusions, and we must live with that hard fact. But on taking a second look, the welcome clarity of this thought-parcel morphs into a can of worms.

Here are the perplexities, first from the point of view of the assumptions made, then of the human consequences.

There seems to be (as far as a lay person can tell from secondary reading) no agreement about the actual hard determinism of the real world. Nature might obey deterministic laws only in gross situations and become probabilistic in the small. The laws of nature might turn out to be ultimately unifiable or ultimately disparate, even incoherent. In the language of academic philosophy, determinism might not "be true," meaning not in accordance with experimentally verified fact, or better, verifiable by means available to human beings.

Probabilistic nature might seem to give free will a chance, so to speak, an opening in which to assert itself. (This view might be called "soft determinism," though it is more like indeterminism.) On the other hand, basing human freedom on probabilism might make things worse, because whatever free choice is, we do not want to say that it is a chance event—a consequence we face whether we regard a probabilistic law as leaving loose loopholes of possibility or as prescribing the limits of possibility with rigorous precision. But even if the laws were rigidly deterministic and the past altogether under their control, *we* could never know *all* that goes into "the present condition." That would be, even were it in principle achievable, in practice impossible (as set out in Note 1 of this chapter). Yet in the practical incompleteness of our knowledge, the hypothesis of complete determinism remains in practice unprovable. It might even transit into in-principle undecidability, namely, if nature herself was incapable of "processing" the complete condition; I mean that one bit of nature, the brain, might not be able to deal with all the "past" and so might in some sense, cast loose from it and respond randomly (on the assumption that its absorption of conditioning couldn't be in the least choosy if it is to be vestigially deterministic). Or, horror of horrors, the brain might not even on its own level of matter and force, quite apart from its ability to process information, produce the significant conditions underlying moments of choice and passages of willing. Recall here, however, that nature is not the first preemptor of human freedom—that was God's omniscience, way back.

Now the human consequences, which disturb laymen and professionals alike: The problem is usually phrased as that of abrogated alternatives. "Could *not* have done otherwise" seems to preclude moral responsibility and consequently the community's right to assign blame. Most people think this condition will lead to individual implosion and social chaos, and consider that result intolerable. Hard determinists therefore feel obligated to show how, while on the one hand retributive punishment makes no sense, preventive restraint is discriminatory, and demonstrative (scaring-off) punishment is unfair, some individual training and social control is still possible. This attempt runs into trouble at its source, because a reader of such prescriptions who is a convinced determinist will say, "*He* says that only because that's how his past and his brain drive him, and *I* will do what I must"—and mean by this, "I'll do as I do and thus find out what it was I was destined to do." The non-determinist, on the other hand, will say, "He says that because he has a false opinion, so what's it to me?" Or a reader of suspicious mind might say, "He says that because he wants me to think of myself as a mere machine, which he, who is in secret a master of control, operates; what's more I recognize his agenda." For the social prescriptions of determinists tend to have what in America is called liberal, that is, permissive and victim-concerned, agendas, where offenders quite logically rank among the victims, namely of psychological or social deprivation. (This fact, incidentally, displays a rather appealing, typically American, paradox: the philosophical hardliners tend to have soft hearts. I will critique one, particularly lucid, determinist proposal in Note 4 to this chapter.)[4]

On the other end of this opinion-spectrum are the libertarians, who defend a real, robust free will as our very ability to be agents, that is, to *act*. This ability is understood, first, as being able to initiate events in the world (for good or bad) and second, as the actor having been, for each action, capable of doing otherwise. (This ability to do otherwise is what the Stoics took for granted and called "being up to us;" however, since they assumed very little ability to change the world, all their initiative was in changing our aims.) The reason libertarians need to speak *both* of originating agency and of alternative choice is that the first is (though barely) conceivable without the second; an agent might be able to intervene in the course of worldly events without "being able to do otherwise." (The reverse case, of having options but no efficacy, is, of course, moot.) I pause here to mention the sophism, named after its inventor, "the Frankfurt-example," which constructs the case of an ostensibly free subject that has no actual alternatives.[5]

Its essentials are, first, a descendant of Descartes' evil demon, an intervener to foul things up, here a neuroscientist, and second, a clueless victim, the person who credits himself with free will. The victim-subject does what he likes, that is, does it "willingly" or voluntarily as long as the (all-but-divine) intervener approves. As soon as the scientist detects a mental motion on the subject's part toward deviation from his intention, he intervenes via an electrode implanted in the brain (or some unspecified device), so that the subject must "willingly" do something else. The occasion for this intervention may never actually arise. It doesn't matter; in fact that's the most telling case: The subject is in effect "free" to do as he likes all his life without having the ghost of a chance of doing otherwise; it is of the essence to remember that this "doing as he likes" is itself deterministically rigged.

I said before that being the initiator of non-determined, hence unfore-seeable, events is "barely conceivable" without the ability to do other-wise. That, however, is so as a *crude* thought, namely if "to do otherwise" means just the vacant possibility of doing something-or-other, or to follow a whim, a personal preference, or a moment's choice—as it is taken in the above sophism so as to enhance its shock value. But I think that there is a serious and more subtle sense of "*not* being able to do otherwise," which, far from abrogating free will, *is* human freedom, understood as *acting responsibly.* (The consideration of the connection between moral responsi-bility and free will—*not* understood just as "being able to do otherwise"—will begin at the end of this chapter and continue in Ch. XI, Secs. C–E).

First let me give a famous example. In 1521, Luther, who had been excommunicated, was summoned before the Diet of Worms to defend himself. He is said to have ended his rousing speech with these words, pro-claiming his freedom as a Christian:

Here I stand, I can [do] no other.

In other words, freedom—for Luther, to be sure, not broadly human, but Christian freedom—does not mean doing what you want, but doing what your conscience commands as being right. That, however, need not be true, I think, just of a Christian conscience or, for that matter, of a conscience at all, at least not just of that "remorse of conscience," that "being eaten up by self-knowledge of sinfulness," which is rendered in the medieval phrase "the Agenbite of Inwit," aptly cited by James Joyce. For that is not the only way we have of being tied to one best decision. There is, for instance, the less mordant knowledge of wanting to be in psychic balance within and in compliance with communal bounds without.[6]

So, while the ability to do otherwise seems to me too to be an unnec-essary mark of freedom (of which more in Ch. XI, Sec. E), the Frankfurt-example seems to be a bad defense of a good position, for it takes freedom as a feeling of doing as you *like*, when it is more defensibly the sense of doing as you *must*. The example that has been subjected to many other close critiques, among which this simple one (but my own) seems to me very persuasive: When can the intervener begin to ensure that the sub-ject will not contravene the former's intention? Since the subject is by the hypothesis originally "free," that is, capable of doing otherwise and so as yet undetermined, if the intervener waits *until* a decision has been made, it's too late; the subject has decided between genuine alternatives. If he intervenes as soon as he has evidence of things going wrong, *before* the final decision, the subject is not free (in the has-an-alternative sense) at the moment of decision. Ergo, the example is, in principle, an impossible case—not to speak of the fact that it assumes one unequivocally free will, that of the neuroscientist.[7]

In-principle impossible experiments (as opposed to in-practice types) are often imaginatively satisfying. But I can think of three kinds of other, more down to earth objections: from the type of example, from the perpetrator's part, and from the victim's side.[8]

The example is what I call the call the "clever-constructionist" type. It depends on several so far unlikely assumptions. One is that it will in fact turn out that, by brain-manipulation, it is possible to achieve not only general but highly targeted behavior in the absence of the victim's cooperation, that is, to induce *this* particular alternative, rather than wildly irrelevant choices, and that if a victim did make the latter he would not realize that he "wasn't himself" and disown the choice. In general, we might question that completely constructed, unnatural cases prove anything. Reasonable Aristotle says that nature is "what happens always or for the most part." Can what is going to happen rarely if ever, even were it logically possible, prove anything about the way things are? It is a perennial question, to be sure. But as unanswered, it weakens my readiness to be convinced by such cases.[9]

Second, there is the perpetrator, clearly of the type of evil scientist, the power-hungry soul-manipulator who appears in the prescient pre-Nazi movies of the 1920s. Conscienceless implanters of mind-devices are imaginable, but their protocols would not be accepted by the scientific community any more than were Dr. Mengele's. That is a circumstantial objection, but this isn't: At the moment the subject comes under this scientist's control, it could be said to have been effectively de-humanized. Thereafter, nothing that this victim-subject does, either way, can be morally imputed to it, for it is beyond morality. The experiment is void. Third, there is this victim himself. If he permitted the implantation, or willingly let the criminal near him, *he* is morally culpable. (Unfortunately, this case is not quite science-fiction anymore, since technology watchers forecast the commercial availability of *apparently* benign implants, receivers that, with the subject's cooperation, transmit messages to the brain directly and project text images to the palm of the hand without the need of a hand-held screen.) My point is that, if one imagines the example as real, it seems impossible that the victim is not either colluding or aware of being (somehow) possessed, and therefore (also somehow) responsible—at least for not decisively withdrawing.[10]

Now to the more plausible middle positions between hard determinism and libertarianism: various kinds of compatibilism—the claim, recall, that the determinism of nature is compatible with the freedom of human beings. While these theories seem to me worthy of study as the products of sophisticated mentation, I will put forward right now my sense that they rest on three conflations, fusions, as it were. They are, in ascending order of gravity: First, these theories tend to meld will with willingness, that is, they conflate our active ability to work ourselves to a point where we choose with our passive capacity for voluntarily going along with what suits us. Second, they tend to confuse willing with decision-making, that is, the long thoughtful process of determining a serious choice with the final moment of decision. And third, they tend, without further ado, to identify self-determination with the exercise of will, be it as a faculty, power, or affect. (Of course, these are broad strokes; my guess is that there is no exception, no limitation, in short, no cavil with all the versions of compatibilism that hasn't been developed somewhere.) I will question all three fusions—that being part of my purpose in this book.[11]

First, I must say that compatibilism is exceedingly perspectival; a brief look at the summaries in the Chapter Bibliography heading the endnotes will confirm this—there are simultaneously current views from each of which it's a different concept. The best example is Kant's theory of Practical Reason. It's sometimes referred to as libertarian because I alone determine my will. Those, however, who regard reason as necessitated might call it doubly determined, once by the laws of nature *(Willkür,* directed by desire) and again by the impositions of rationality *(Wille,* defined as practical reason). To me Kant seems the most extreme compatibilist: action-originating human freedom in the realm of noumena and complete natural necessitation in the world of appearance—without any need for intermediating explanations. Alternatively, one might think of compatibilism longitudinally, watching it develop in time, beginning with Aristotle, the inventor of the distinction that is the predominant enabling notion of compatibilism. It is the distinction (speaking anachronistically) between the *willed choice* of alternatives (being able to do otherwise), which compatibilists must reject since they believe that human action is constrained by the laws of nature plus given determining conditions, and *voluntariness* (being able to do as one desires even in the absence of the ability to do otherwise), which they seize on, since they regard being willing as equivalent to willing (the free choice element). Succinctly, compatibilism is defined by substituting passive willingness, the sense of being unhindered, for active will, the *actual* exercise of choice. Hobbes (followed by Locke) is Aristotle's most powerful successor—that is, where Aristotle merely distinguishes, Hobbes chooses: Free will is just the ability to fix one's final wish in a "de-liberating" (freedom-terminating) settling of desire. There follow all the elaborations culminating in the new compatibilism of contemporary theories. Perhaps the ultimate one, in the sense of being close to giving in, is semicompatibilism, the somewhat elusive theory intended to preserve the control needed to ascribe moral responsibility to ourselves while keeping determinism unequivocally intact: Our control can be prized apart into a "regulative" control, an ability actually to make initiating interventions in the world—which must be given up—and a "guidance" control—which is sufficient to render us responsible. This second control is so described as to be expressive voluntariness, now revisioned as a soft type of control, namely, the ability to express ourselves: "it is not that we make a difference but we make a statement"—that we make a meaningful narrative of our lives. This seems to be control as myth-making.[12]

(I think a lay reader, among whom I mean to be counted, will find her mind set oscillating by compatibilist theory. Baldly stated, it seems now wildly counterintuitive, now quite unavoidable. The notion that all the natural systems, up to my brain, subserving my personal self should be completely causally jigged by nature while I am nonetheless free to start the world on a new course or, which is something similar on a narrower scale, to choose between two options, sometimes seems wildly implausible. (I should recall here that the hope that refuge from the deterministic laws, those that are strictly causal, is to be had in the subatomic world of probabilistic laws, those that leave room for random or chance events, is generally discounted because 1. randomness is not what free-willers should want, and more important, 2. in the macro-world of human life, particularly in "systems as hot, wet, and massive as the neurons of the brain," quantum mechanical indeterminacies are said quickly to cancel out so that, practically, classical "determinacy rules the brain." Thus, physics itself cannot save us from determinism.[13])

On the other hand, compatibilism sometimes seems not so much plausible as simply the case, *de facto*. We exercise our will, make choices, accept responsibility all day long, but reject responsibility when we are convinced that an action of ours was not "up to us"—and so we *feel free*. And yet we are not disposed to deny that all the stuff around us is obedient to rules than can be mathematically expressed, or at least will be, eventually. In other words, most modern Americans don't believe (I think, I don't know) in a lawless nature or in one of incessant irregularities or continual miracle-like interventions from beyond the physical realm. Yet would they—were they ever to read an article on compatibilism (there's a miracle!)—agree with writers who have adopted the phrase "obscure and panicky metaphysics" for libertarians who defend such non-physical interferences? More of this below. Meanwhile, my point is that I imagine most of us are *practical* compatibilists, who believe in lawful nature and human freedom together, undeterred by the fact that the bridging theory is implausible. We live the fact and haven't heard of the theory—as I once hadn't.[14]

I suggested that one more sense of compatibilism is that it just substitutes willingness (which is easily shown to be compatible with determinism) for will (which is an eviscerated power when under strict, external causality); on second thought that might be a legitimate maneuver if candidly offered as the "free will worth wanting." Give up prior free choice and settle for posterior fulfillment of desire. But then, again, what about 1. your own and others' responsibility and 2. your self-respect?[15]

Obviously, if libertarianism were acceptable ("were true" is the standard locution of the industry—but no "ism" is true for me), the compatibilism debate would evaporate. Truly originating, initiating free will has, however, few open followers (though perhaps just a few more closet-adherents) among scientists. They are committed to determinism as the enabling theory of their enterprise. Thus: "If you want to be a scientist, you had better be a determinist . . . It is the proper job of a scientist to find and document (via experimental studies) the cause-effect relations that form and guide human actions." That is almost too candid, for it exposes determinism as a working *faith*—and in that vein a libertarian might say, "If you want to be a free agent, you had better be a non-determinist." This libertarian wouldn't say "indeterminist," because indeterminism is not real freedom. It denominates a certain undecidability in the processes of nature, such as the firing of neurons in the brain, which, while not the only alternative to determinism (of which more below), is the least offensive to the scientific establishment. A scientist *might* accept *in*determinism, for it does not introduce non-natural "extra factors." Instead, chance plays the role of the friction, as I understand it, that gains traction for the will; it is an "*ingredient*" in a complex, goal-directed process, in which, if there were complete, chanceless control, there would be no "doing otherwise," and thus no free will. So freedom and its responsibility is the "consequence of an *information-responsive complex dynamical system*" into which indeterminism introduces conflicts of motivation needed for realizing a possible (non-libertarian) conception of free will. Hence indeterminism is at best a suitable basis for yet another kind of compatibilism in which free will is an element in a formalizable psychological process.[16]

In all fairness, I imagine many scientists would agree to the proposition of determinism as a practical faith quoted above—not in the sense that "it's my metaphysics *because I need it*" but rather in the sense "I'm engaged in the work I love and just haven't got the time to think it out, but everything I observe makes me *prone to believe it to be true.*"

It seems to me, however, that there is something more immediately questionable in this manifesto. If determinism is the enabling principle, then, *ipso facto*, the scientist is in principle disabled from discovering non-determinate events. That's not to imply that a scientist might make such a discovery if only he had a more inclusive hypothesis, but is rather a restatement of an old claim: Science is competent to discover and formulate natural processes, but not to pronounce on the possibility of transnatural, not to say supernatural, ones.

This, then, is what libertarianism might look like to a conforming scientist: If you believe that free will springs from an immaterial soul (as some libertarians do), then you must think of it as "hovering happily in your brain, shooting arrows of decision into your motor cortex." (This ascription assumes that believers in a soul place it *in* the body, that is, in the brain; it is a common locution, but not what they in fact always do or could believe, not if the soul is non-spatial.)[17]

Here, on the other hand, is what libertarians look like to themselves. Besides the non-determinist libertarianism described above, they hold two bold doctrines, possibly but not necessarily collapsible into one: "unmoved mover" and "*causa sui*." The first says that "[I]f we are responsible ... then we have a prerogative which some of us would attribute only to God: each of us, when we act, is a prime mover unmoved ..." Alternatively, we are causes of ourselves, of our acts—alternatively, because it is not necessarily the case that an unmoved mover is a self-causer, a self-originator, he might be causeless, un-originated. But an unmoved mover might be the more scandalizing to hard-headed devotees of naturalistic accounts (in which a cause and its specific effect must be distinct in time and/or in space), since it is not only an *uncaused* cause, which has neither source nor motivation, but also an *uncausing* cause, which has no effective relation to the objects it attracts. For it is not just an unmoved but an *unmovable* mover, being outside of place and time. Such is Aristotle's Intellect, *Nous*, who is eternal and unmotivated, and so, without budging, induces motion only by attraction.[18]

There has been a lot of reference in this chapter to two naturalistic theories, causal determinism and probabilistic indeterminism. Our whole bodies, whether seen as anorganic or organic, are investigable as falling under these theories. But what matters for the study of the will, a faculty of governance, is concentrated in one part—the central organ of incoming information and outgoing control, of receptivity and response, the brain. Thus neuroscientists investigating the brain as the organ of consciousness and cognition have taken up the study of the will, and in the next chapter I shall report, as far as I understand them, their chief experiments and attendant problems.

But before leaving the compatibilism/incompatibilism debate, I should perhaps say whether I "endorse" one or the other (the academic complement to "cashing in" a theory). If compatibilism simply takes cognizance of the fact that we are sometimes receptively willing to live with what's available, without attempting to initiate action by the will, it is surely justified, for that does seems to happen—but not always. So the fact that willingness, voluntariness, is tranquil under, indeed mostly unaware of, deterministic necessity may meet with an abrupt check when we become unwilling. Moreover for beings who think beyond mere present fact, the willingness solution is an evasion—not good enough, it seems to me. They—we—*want* responsibility.[19]

Nor is the indeterminist alternative, which shifts from willingness/ determinism compatibility to a free will/indeterminism compatibility, devoid of difficulties arising from the fact that indeterminacies are either defined within natural processes or as mere randomness. If indeterminacy is of the probabilistic type that makes subatomic instances undecidable for us, it is yet a rigorous scientific theory assigning with exactitude the limits of expected outcomes. And if it were—as it isn't—a cleft in nature by which to enter a law-free zone of chance and randomness, that would not save freedom, which is surely not a form of antic lawlessness. Moreover, as was said, the indeterminacies of the micro-world evidently cancel out in the macro-regions where we function.

The belief in "hard determinism" sometimes induces in its faithful, especially in neuroscientists, a very confident assertion, termed the "Consequence Argument," which says that as a consequence of the truth of determinism *nothing we do is up to us*. It seems to me a sort of idol worship. An idol is an object of adoration, natural or artificial, which was selected or made by the worshippers themselves—"They that make them are like unto them." It is, moreover, regarded not as a representation of a deity but as the deity itself. When physicists (or neuroscientists) are physicalists (more of them lately than in bygone centuries), they display some analogous practices and dogmas: They overlook the fact that science is a human artifact, that they themselves wrote the book of nature, the scripture which they believe in, forgetting that it is a representation of nature, not nature itself. And as idolaters, being self-worshippers, miss out on the mysteries of divinity, so they deprive themselves of the real wonder—that nature actually accepts mathematical formulation and submits to stringent discipline of verification; that nature opens herself as a book that humans may read and copy out in human symbols; but that the reader *of* a book cannot be altogether *in* and *of* the book.[20]

On the other hand, the faith of libertarianism seems to me to be too often compromised, namely, when its proponents allow themselves to be drawn into the normal academic mode of arguing *to* free will as a *theory*, whereas their best hope is to argue *from* human freedom as a *fact*. Of course, everything depends on stating well what that fact is. I will try to say what it appears to me to be—and appeal to what seem to be truly exemplary examples. Here, to begin with, is one: In 1965, Sandy Koufax, a pitcher for the Dodgers acknowledged as an incomparable left-hander, did not accept the opening game assignment in the World Series, because it fell on Yom Kippur, the highest of Jewish holy days. He came from an observant Jewish family, and though he had played on Yom Kippur before, he now *decided* to honor this High Holiday. It was understood that he *wanted* to pitch, very much. To me it seems a great question whether this was an exercise of free *will*, but no question at all that it was an exercise of human *freedom*—not because "he could have done otherwise," but because he said to himself (so I imagine) some Jewish version of "I can do no other."

After a brief report on neuroscience, I shall return in Chapter XI, my last, to the more broad-gauged volition theories of the twentieth century in order to think about the relation of will to human freedom and of freedom to right action. The compatibilist/incompatibilist debate, albeit a cul-de-sac, had to be a station in my inquiry, since it was such a current preoccupation of students of free will. However, it did nothing to settle the mind, and its terms left unregarded the question I care about in this book: Is willing a good way of being human?

I conclude the present chapter by returning in Note 21 to a rather early and very compelling argument for *theological* compatibilism by Boethius and by presenting a very acute and amazingly apposite dystopic fiction of a compatibilist society by L. P. Hartley.[21]

chapter **X**

The Science of Will

Neuroscience and Psychiatry

The unresolved—probably unresolvable—debate concerning the fate of will in the face of nature, which I set out in the preceding chapters, was carried on by writers who regard themselves as working in philosophy. On looking back over these not uninteresting yet unsatisfying efforts, what seemed to be amiss? I think it was a deficiency in the *phenomenology* of will being brought to bear on the issue. Put another way: The debate about the relation of the possible freedom of human beings to the accepted law-boundness of natural events was too far removed from the inquiry into the experience of willing.

By phenomenology I mean the attempt to describe, to give a precise account of, what is to be found in our consciousness when we engage in willing; Thomas Aquinas's extended sequence, whose main elements are will, choice, decision, and execution (Ch. III, Sec. A, herein), might be a model.[1]

The occasion for such a phenomenology in the contemporary mode is the fairly novel neuroscience of the will, backed up by cognitive science. The latter was an interdisciplinary effort (begun in the 1970s) to ana- lyze—not only human—activities exhibiting intelligence. Whatever the approaches used—computer models, linguistic theories, psychological pro- cesses—it was assumed that visible brain activities subserved the processes that were thus discerned. A decade later, the techniques now available to neuroscientists seemed to make it possible to turn conceptual hypotheses into observational results. It is significant that cognition and emotion fig- ure far more in this research than willing—for the latter is more elusive as a definable phenomenon.[2]

Yet the possibility not only of applying neuroscientific but also of sta- tistical methods to the study of the will did spur on more modest analy- ses of willing—modest in acknowledging the far-and-wide origins of any act of will and the consequent difficulty in pin-pointing relevant brain activity. This approach, while it helped to mitigate the over-emphasis on the moment of decision, also gave more weight to the actual "executive moment," to enacting the decision.[3]

A. Libet: Readiness Potential

Nonetheless, the most famous set of neuroscientific experiments, carried out in the 1980s (and so actually quite old as neuroscience goes), by Benjamin Libet, concentrated on just such a narrow aspect of willing—small-scale decisions such as flexing a wrist—because a laboratory setting demanded a manageable time frame. In other words, the protocols of science defined the object, nugatory decision-making.[4]

Before I give as minimal an account as possible of Libet's method, results, and interpretation of his research, let me state my conceptual and in-principle doubts up front: One, just mentioned, concerns the behavior taken as displaying will, for example, wrist-flexings or finger-bendings. Flexing or failing to flex in a hooked-up laboratory situation seems to me to have as much to do with human will as a twinge of lust when glued to a television screen has to do with *eros*; it comes from the same psychic region as willing but is too miniscule a phenomenon to represent a grand volitional complex.

A second doubt arises from the very fact that there *is* will involved, namely the willingness to cooperate in an experiment. This receptiveness seems to me to cast the experimental subject into a mental mode, a readiness condition, that cannot help but affect reactions in some way—though an amateur is in no position to imagine a way of discounting the neuronal consequences of a longer term co-operative disposition. Consequent question: Would the brain pattern of an *unwilling* or non-willing subject somehow tricked or stimulated into responding be the same or different? Is conscious willing neurologically distinct from a general readiness to respond anyhow, just to respond?

A third doubt comes from the immediate identification (general to will-studies) of "unconscious" with "in the brain." I mean something different from the all-but-universal assumption that all mentation is brain-based, under which consciousness is at the least distinguished from the effective brain activity as an "epiphenomenon," a mere accompanying appearance. I am pointing to the assumption that what is unconscious, not at present in my awareness, is *not* a kind of occluded consciousness, that all the memories not now before me but retrievable, or all the knowledge not now present to me but recollectable, all the intentions not now active in me but re-thinkable, are *ipso facto* nothing but neuronal conditions, active or inactive. To put it another way, I have doubts about the assumed association:

(brain = unconscious) ↔ potentially conscious, as opposed to this, implicitly rejected one: brain ↔ (unconscious + epiphenomenal conscious).[5]

The Libet experiments assume all three problematic elements. Much more fine-grained critiques will be reviewed below.[6]

Now to the experiment itself. Libet himself gives a very clear summary:

> I have taken an experimental approach to the question of whether we have free will. Freely voluntary acts are preceded by a specific electrical charge in the brain (the "readiness potential," RP) that begins 550 msec. before the act. Human subjects became aware of intention to act 350–400 msec. *after* RP starts, but 200 msec. before the motor act. The volitional process is therefore *initiated* unconsciously. But the conscious function could still control the outcome; it can veto the act. Free will is therefore not excluded. These findings put constraints on views of how free will may operate; it would not initiate a voluntary act but it could *control* performance of the act. The findings also affect views of guilt and responsibility.[7]

Note the claims: 1. An "electrical charge in the brain" is interpreted as "the volitional charge is initiated unconsciously." 2. Consciousness has a window of opportunity for control, for a veto. 3. These findings have (huge) human moral consequences.

There had been earlier experiments showing that voluntary acts, here moving a finger, were preceded by electrical activity in the brain, measured as electrical potentials (at the scalp) surrounding the action. The electrical activity, which occurred widely in the brain and started increasing at 0.8 seconds before the voluntary finger movement, was named RP or "readiness potential." But in these experiments, *consciousness* had not figured, so what they showed was only that brain activity preceded action, not intention. Libet himself had done "a very tricky" experiment on the connection between the beginning of a stimulus (the pricking of the right hand) induced in the brain directly and awareness thereof; the latter lagged 0.5 seconds behind cortical stimulation, although the subjective experience was that of simultaneity. Libet interpreted this in terms of "subjective backward referral," that is to say, an illusion of (contemporaneous) consciousness.[8]

The Libet experiment on free will then brought together the need to introduce consciousness and the suspicion that it is *not* related temporally to a physical action in the way we, subjectively, experience it. Thus he undertook to research how the "time of conscious intention is related to the onset of cerebral activity (readiness potential)." The subject was instructed to bend his finger whenever he wanted, as an urge, intention, decision—as "wanting" directed. Repeated instances showed that on average brain activity began from 0.5 to just under 1 second before movement—a startling fact, because in ordinary experience such a free motion follows our decision to execute immediately, without delay. A fast rotating clock was provided for subjects to note and report the onset of their intention. These reports placed such awareness at 0.2 second before the movement. Hence between the commencement of readiness potential and of awareness there was a lag lasting from 0.3 to 0.7 seconds.

Libet attached importance also to the 0.2 second *before* action: Here was a window of opportunity for conscious intervention—not to *do*, that having been decided—but to *veto* doing, to stop the action: "Our conscious minds may not have free will but rather 'free won't.'"[9]

"The existence of a veto possibility is in no doubt." (There are some urges, like those to shout obscenities in Tourette's syndrome, that lack an RP altogether—no readiness, no final veto zone.) The veto itself, the aborted act, was in fact observed in the experiments. Libet himself thinks that free will might be confined to the control of acts, and he points to the negative form which ethics so often takes, such as the nine prohibitions of the Ten Commandments.[10]

This concentration of our freedom on negation, on being free to be *unwilling*, to resist tempting opportunities seems to me very suggestive. Recall that for Kant, the presence of a good will is *proved* only by resistance to inclination. Oddly, the test works, *mutatis mutandis*, for monkeys.[11]

There is an experiment in which those "behaving animals" were trained to make directed reaching movements (or to inhibit them) upon the appearance of a stimulus. There was found to be a time (a fraction of a second) between the stimulus and the initiation of the movement, and this reaction time can be interpreted as a time when the movement is *intended*. The monkey can be *instructed to delay* the motion both when the stimulus is still present and when it is turned off; in the latter case, when the "go" signal is given the animal is working from memory. There is a technique for monitoring the activity of neuronal populations for reaching-movements. In this experiment it was possible to read these neurons as indicating that during the "instructed delay," whether memory was involved or not, there is readiness for, but no execution of, movement. This gating of neural activity, "so that it remains a 'motor speculation,' so to speak, without being translated into an overt movement, is the essence of what makes a movement 'voluntary.'"

In this animal analogue to intentional action, the intention is countermanded without being deleted, or at least the neuronal activity looks that way. This does have features of that human criterion for free choice, here a pre-executive "being able to do otherwise." For here to do otherwise means to negate some original intention which must be somehow present before it can be abrogated. "Strangely," say the authors, "the best definition of voluntary movement seems to be 'the opposite of involuntary movement—that is, a movement that can be suppressed at will," since involuntary movements, such as result from brain damage, *cannot* be thus suppressed. Again, I find the "window of opportunity" for countermanding the action that Libet discovered and the readiness to make a reaching movement nonetheless not executed in the monkey experiment suggestive: Whether the brain subserves or directs intention, it seems to track the will's inherent relation to nay-saying—here a vaguely expressed notion, more of which in my Chapter XI.

Meanwhile, I return to the Libet experiment. It has undergone close critical scrutiny without so far diminishing its influence. I began with putting forth some very general in-principle doubts of Libet-like experiments; I will end by reporting some of the more fine-grained critiques of their design and interpretation; all my misgivings appear in these, though in a more technical, experiment-specific version.[12]

B. Mele: Critique

Alfred Mele, the most acute critic, begins by distinguishing, as Libet does not, between an urge and an intention, in particular a "proximal intention," one close up to the decision to act and evidently most often connected to trifling acts. (Its complement, a distal intention, is one formed long before action; it cannot figure in these laboratory experiments, but it comes closer to the process of willing. Intentions are said by Mele to be "acquired," that is, formed; the "how" of this formation—it has a whole life and its purpose behind it when regarded as part of willing—is not itself under investigation. Moreover, as I said, the very willingness to become a laboratory subject must involve a parallel sort of distal and persistent intention, stemming from one's view of oneself.)[13]

Then one fundamental criticism is that Libet is throwing together decision, intention, urge, wanting, will. These must be picked apart. Mere urges or wants are *not* intentions or volitions, since the latter are focused on executions. Quite aside from difficulties about the accuracy of awareness-onset, reports in particular and in general about "cross-modal synchronizations" (here at the same time becoming conscious and reading the fast-moving clock), it is not clear what Libet's readiness potential indicates. Mele thinks it could well be an *unconscious want or urge,* that would be indicated by this pre-conscious brain activity *rather than an unconscious intention.* So Libet has not shown that the brain decides to initiate actions at a time before any reportable awareness of such a decision has taken place; Mele makes no claim to have shown the opposite, either. (One might go on to wonder whether one of Libet's "ethical implications," that unexecuted urges, such as lustful longings, are not blameworthy, are not to be condemned as innate evil, because they are out of our control, also becomes problematic—as an *experimental implication*, not necessarily as a moral truth—unless one wants to interpret the priority of brain action as a physiological basis for original sin!)[14]

Mele's reinterpretation of the pre-conscious brain activity from a somewhat paradoxical "unconscious" intention to a more acceptable unconscious urge seems to be an—incidental—example of the collapse of "unconscious" into "neural" mentioned above. (It is, at any rate, a convenient postulate of brain study: "Unconscious mental causation seems to be in the domain of normal science"—meaning, usually, that a psychological hypothesis is legitimately tested in the terms of neurophysiological and other sciences. The convenience is in not getting into the problematic of unconscious mentality; "folk psychology" tends, I think, toward claiming psychic rather than neural ownership of "subconscious" activity, as I have suggested—but that is no recommendation to scientists.[15]

Finally, Libet's window of opportunity for consciously prohibiting will, the "veto": The critique of this element, so startling in Libet's interpretation, reveals the scientifically unacceptable philosophical basis of his experiment. For one thing, consciousness might be such that there is no clockable instant of time when it "begins." Next, perhaps merely being conscious is not a guarantee of free will, certainly not if the states of consciousness are in themselves "mechanistically" determined. Moreover, Libet appears to assume a Cartesian, that is, a dual theory of mind and body, one in which mind *can* affect nature, namely reciprocally: Neural processes produce consciousness and as soon as it is present it, in turn, affects brain processes causally. A more precise critique considers intention. For Libet, the intention to bend the finger, or rather to veto bending, is directly causal for abstaining—but "intentions are not direct cerebral causes," says the critic (and I must wonder: then what is?). Above all, the intention to act *or* to veto the act was preconceived, as it were, when the subject committed himself to the test. (Here enters the very kind of actual willing, a longer-range commitment, that seemed to me to stand in the way of regarding such tests as having to do with will to begin with—wrist-flickings and finger-bendings are not *bona fide* willings. To my mind such nugatory immediacies are perfectly random, purely antic: I have no idea which of these indifferents I'll execute *now*.)[16]

To read the hopeful experiment and the critical analysis is to grow skeptical of the will-watching enterprise. Thus the Libet experiments induce the question, *Can an experiment be devised that displays conscious intentions as doing any causal work?* So Mele asks, Does an agent's *conscious* proximal decision—one close to the intended action—ever have a determining place in a causal explanation of that action? (Note that his assumption here is the very one I doubt—that proximal, close-up decisions on matters of human indifference really bear on freely willed action as distinct from mere behavior.) Mele, however, devised such an imaginary experiment (one excluding physical correlates). The subject is instructed to make a then-and-there conscious decision to act, say, to press a button, that is, to be actively forming an intention and then to execute it. It is not, the thought experiment assumes, as plausible a claim that a subject good at following instructions would, at a certain time, have pressed the button on the basis of an *unconscious* decision, although he hadn't formed a conscious decision, as it is that at that time he didn't press the button because he *hadn't made* the decision. That plausible preference in turn supports the claim that the fact that he did make such a decision at that time helps account for the fact that a little afterwards he did press the button. Mele himself points out that you can't ever tell whether the subject did as told—make a conscious decision. (As I said, to my mind, you can't make a *decision* to do or refrain when you couldn't care less. Moreover, it seems to me that this thought experiment is, for all its formalisms, to be ranged under the category of what used to be called a rhetorical proof, the kind dealing in the probable and the plausible. Perhaps proof—or disproof—of causal consciousness is in principle not possible.)[17]

Besides neuroscientific experiments, there are, of course, many psychological and psychiatric studies of the will, particularly of the failures of will power. A well-known precursor-treatise, by Ribot, has survived from the nineteenth century; an account is given in Note 18 to this chapter.[18]

Next I report on a particularly striking example of an empirical study concerned with long-range willing by a working psychiatrist. The results make sense on reflection without being of that "everyone-knows-that-anyhow" type, which make "studies show that . . ." reports so underwhelming.

C. Ainslie: Intertemporal Bargaining

George Ainslie formulates his research results in ethical terms. The problem informing his book *Breakdown of the Will* is the "puzzle of *akrasia*." *Akrasia* is Aristotle's term for weakness of the will, lack of self-control (literally "impotence," powerlessness). The first problem is to find an empirical account of the self-defeating behavior that is attributed to the weakness of will.

Ainslie makes it clear that his approach is "reductionistic," or deterministic, that is, it assumes naturalistically determined causes. (It should be clear by now that for scientists "cause" means physical cause, and in this context, temporally prior cause. But Ainslie admits that these causes may be too hidden, complex, or "internally fed back" to become available for prediction. This candid reservation seems to be equivalent to saying that the reductionist approach is a program, belief in which exceeds the practically obtainable evidence.)[19]

What Ainslie means to show is that the *experience* of free choice is explicable in terms completely consistent with determinism. This differs from the conceptual compatibilism of my last chapter in this way: the philosophical compatibilism was essentially based on voluntariness (doing what you want), which gave a *justifiable* sense of freedom as long as desire was promoted by necessity. Ainslie aims to show that the psychological mechanisms of preference and choice themselves occasion that feeling of freedom of choice or its failure. In other words, what was missing in the old debate was a plausible explanation, given in naturalistic terms, of the intuitive experience of choosing—where psychological processes are understood as causally, thus, once more, naturalistically, determined.[20]

Ainslie's empirical research in preference and choice-making led him to the following discovery, one with practical therapeutic consequences.[21]

The starting point is that the realm in which to look for certain revealing characteristics of choosing is not behind but ahead of the choice; research must delve not into the accomplished past of "could have done" but into the projected future, of "intend to do." What he finds is perhaps after all not so surprising to lay people, but quite contrary to standard utility theory, whose protagonist is an artifact, "Economic Man." For this creature, options compete for a motivational, quantifiable quality called "reward"; he simply tries to maximize his satisfaction. Looking into the future—whence rewards come to us, so to speak—this satisfaction, or value, decreases, "is discounted," more the further off the reward is temporally and increases the closer it is to its realization. The "discount rate" of value as it is further off in the future is a constant proportion of the value for every additional delay (which is how banks discount). If I value a drink at 10 "utiles" and my discount rate is 20%, then tomorrow its value will have dropped to 8 "utiles" and the day after to 6.4 of those value-units. This discount function is called "exponential" because such a steady, proportional discount (or increase) is expressed by raising the variable, here time, to an exponent, a power, to get the value. Its shape, here a parabola, is steady and relaxed; the closer the reward comes, the higher the value, but at a relatively moderate, consistent, rational pace. Thus, moving *backwards* into future time, away from the prospective immediacy of the moment of reward, "utility" becomes less, though it never becomes zero. Or, looking at the reward, say a drink, from a now going *forward*, it becomes steadily more desirable as its moment, say "happy hour," comes closer.[22]

But human beings aren't always instances of Economic Man. They yield to temptation, and temptation happens in the here and now. Utility theory cannot explain this behavior. The empirically verified curve that depicts this immediate, sometimes irresistible avidity is *more sharply* bent upwards, more bowed toward the moment of reward. The shorter its prospect the more irresistible becomes indulgence; the drink is at hand, and *the will breaks down.* The curve that displays this uneconomic but human propensity is a hyperbola, for which the time variable is in inverse ratio to the value—the less time to the moment of satisfaction, the more greatly it is valued (just as before), but at a steeper increase than for the previous exponential curve; the hyperbola shows temporal closeness overcoming rational pacing of valuation; it's almost as if a shortening span of time made for the increasing visibility and thus attraction of the object of desire. Come within sight of your desire and its desirability shoots way up, or reversely, "out of sight, out of mind."[23]

This observationally documented result, that people's rationality is hostage to time, that a close reward shifts long-term favorable choices, is a novel finding and is made significant by the fact that the rational utility curve is actually more adaptive, more in line with what believers in evolution (the whole scientific establishment) would expect. For any rationally exponential trader, say, gets the better of a hyperbolic temperament, since the latter is short-sighted; this improvident, Uneconomic Man might sell his winter coat right now in spring, for a drink, having discounted the next winter because of the temporal distance.

In summary, people make choices based on their temporal vantage point. There are helpful, even therapeutic consequences to understanding choice as conditioned by time. Well-instructed people can engage in "intertemporal bargaining" with themselves to mitigate the tyranny of close-time impulse. All they need to actually recruit the knowledge concerning such bargaining is this fact: "[T]he extra motivation that forms will-power is a practical awareness that current decisions predict the patterns of future decisions." This empirically based observation will help in negotiating more long-term satisfactions with oneself. Ainslie also extracts from his discoveries some unexpected consequences for will power, which he regards as not always beneficial. I shall return to such reasons in my Conclusion. (More of will power in Note 24 to this chapter.)[24]

Nietzsche treated this so elusive ability to take yourself in hand, the opposite of *akrasia*—the Greeks called it *egkrateia*, "being in power (over yourself)," the Romans, *continentia* "holding (yourself) together," containing yourself—as the grand virtue that bestows domination. For most of us will power is at once a daily problem and a useful virtue (at least on the—to me dubious—hypothesis that right action originates in or with the will). Under the heading introduced above, "intertemporal bargaining," Ainslie proposes persuasive strategems for keeping the will in control, for helping will power to power; *egkrateia* has now become a therapeutic virtue. He begins with a list of candidates known to most of us advice-giving teachers. In general they involve helping a sound interest win out over temporally close-up temptations by making commitments favorable to future choice. Some are extrapsychic: make it physically impossible to give in to temptation (as did Odysseus when he had himself bound to the mast of his ship so as not to succumb to the sirens' song). Others are internal: avoid thinking about temptation; cultivate impulse-controlling techniques such as imaginatively pitting desirable affects against the one to be avoided. But one stratagem, which stands above all the others, is intellectual: make a resolution that takes account of Aristotle's analysis of *akrasia* as the failure to form universal opinions and instead to focus on particulars. For there is much evidence that choosing "categorically" can *partly* undo hyperbolic, that is, impulsive, discounting. Intellect wins over will—sometimes.[25]

The "intertemporal bargaining" possibility is based on an interesting understanding of willing. "Intertemporal cooperation" is Ainslie's definition of the sound will, a will in which your *interests* are not held hostage by your *temptations*. So a first element of willing is that its control is strongly directed to the future for the long haul—not in terms of a single event but as an extended phase understood to be afflicted by the fact that motivational force declines differentially toward the farther future. Since futurity is built into the very name of "will" (as shown in Ch. VI), such an approach is bound to be arresting. It means attempting to make the future, the "not-yet," *presently* real. Ainslie does not enunciate the agency that makes the absent future present. It is the imagination.[26]

Three chief alternative views of the will are contrasted with the intertemporal one: The null theory, that will is a superfluous concept (paradoxically adopted by Nietzsche and in its truly reductionist form discussed in my next and final chapter, Ch. XI, Sec. A); the "organ" theory, that the will is a strong or weak faculty, directing or guided by the intellect (Thomas's and the traditional theory); the "rational choice" theory (the standard rational Economic Man theory—incidentally again under attack in the post-economic-collapse period after 2008).

Ainslie also offers a fourth view. He regards the will as *a brokering activity*. The experimental evidence for this theory of choosing is persuasive, though difficult to obtain, largely because the theory involves extended times. Here is how sound choices made by an *unbroken* will work both according to evidence and theory: Universal rules, principles, are not, as Kant thought, primarily cognitively derived, that is, in the form of universalized cases accepted as commands on *a priori* grounds. Rather, the universality lies in a "recursive" self-bargaining, a sequence of psychological brokerings of interests in which every decision is influenced by its precursor and in turn impinges by the same rule on its successor; here the bargain is understood as being made in view of a time *behind* a nearer pleasure in terms of futurity—further away from the actor; in other words, the recursion works from the far future inward, toward the present. In particular, if you consider (here meaning "consider letting yourself be motivated by") a number of brief and immediate proposed pleasures, say binges, which form a slippery slope into bad days of regret and hangover, and dwell, as against these temptations, on the extended pleasure of a long healthy future, a kind of psychological calculus will allow the far-in-the-future pleasure, multiplying its projected strength by its expected length, to outweigh the motivation to indulge now or soon but all-too-briefly. Learning about this calculus will itself have a therapeutic value; it will aid in developing will power. This self-bargaining on the basis of our psychology, taking the temporality of temptation into account, is not a cognitive but a practical theory because, like Kant's, it does not take *knowledge* of objective good as determining its aim but rather *motivation*, though it differs from Kant's in looking to motives of satisfaction rather than to incentives of morality. Moreover, though framed in terms of temptation, it is, after all, not a moral but a medical theory. Its advantage is that it closes a gap in the compatibilist notion of the will, which cannot account for the *experience* of something beyond just getting to do what I want, namely, the experience of really deciding, of self-determination, of free will: We have, the bargaining theory holds, a psychological mechanism, involving both motivation and calculation applied to choice as a *future-directed* activity.[27]

As a pure empirical-theoretical psychology, Ainslie's theory "sits well," to my mind. But it too has a gap, to me a crucial lack: *the* object of will, Good, is left in outer space, while a calculus of future satisfaction rules. Succinctly though inchoately put: "Good" is associated with solid happiness, passing pleasure produces satisfactions; a theory of volition ought to deal with the most desirable of human conditions—or so I think.

D. Tse: Criterial Causation

Of all the books dealing with the will physicalistically that I have read and cited, Peter Tse's *The Neural Basis of Free Will: Criterial Causation* is the most philosophically mindful, carefully reasoned, and intellectually inclusive. It appeared too late for integration into the text, so I have appended an account, in layperson's terms.

I must note that this book, like others on this topic—books that should engross everyone's attention since they bear in the deepest possible way on the conduct of human life—is exceedingly difficult for the lay reader. In ordinary language, highly specific neologisms, those for example denoting nuances of internal states, function as private language and are partly intended to be exclusionary (as, for example, the private languages observed between Siamese twins). In science, highly technical terminology is intended to serve accurate brevity of communication, but there are occasional hints of satisfaction in inaccessibility to non-professionals. Tse is obviously not at all beguiled by a desire for exclusiveness. So in his next book on the will (announced in Chapter 8.26) he will perhaps find user-friendly ways to integrate research and reflection—as he already does in his logical presentations (where he supplies the verbal reading of his symbolizations). The stylistic trick would be to find that middle ground between large-gestured vagueness and fine-grained myopia—a ground which is, in fact, his intellectual demesne.

The book is an attempt at a non-compatibilist (that is to say, an non-equivocating) salvation of a "strong will." Such a will is defined as one that makes non-random, real decisions among actually possible choices with a real post-decision sense of "could have done otherwise" (7.1). [One might argue that a "strong" will, in both a common and a philosophical sense, is just the opposite: Luther's "Here I stand, I can no other" is regarded as a model of (Christian) freedom. The reason is, recall, that in the tradition, will is "rational desire," and reason having approved the desire, there is no "could have done otherwise"—any more than truth having been apprehended, there is any "could have thought otherwise." The freedom of the will is not post-positive. (This is not altogether what I myself think, but what needs to be dealt with.)]

The matter-of-course presupposition of Tse's book is physicalism; indeed, this commitment seems to be simply defining for scientists and philosophers of mind. Physicalism is the doctrine that there is only one fundamental substrate, energy, which changes according to natural laws in space and time or in space-time (A[ppendix] 1.1). [If this doctrine is adopted by a human being *as researcher*, it is a necessary *presupposition* for work to proceed; it gives his field of inquiry the necessary delimiting definition. But this same scientist *as human being* might also, in a reflective mood, bracket his scientific commitment as a useful *conjecture*, and reflect on alternatives—even on possibly unresolvable enigmas. That would be philosophy not as conclusive position-taking but as ever-at-the-beginning thinking. Tse hints in this book that he is open to this mode, though his introductory claim is that neuroscience *will* solve the mind-body problem (p. 1).]

Tse rules out the hard determinism (or eliminative reductionism) which permits no mental causation (2.1), because no one doubts that we have some voluntary control (p. 1). [But he also says that many philosophers have in fact concluded that mental events are never causal, that is, that they are merely epiphenomenal (p. 2). I think Tse is implying that there is something so wildly counter-intuitive about a claim of "no mental control"—a denial of that sense of responsibility which is our chief ethical characteristic, usually called conscience (bad conscience being the penalty exacted by a weak will)—that it can be set aside, professional philosophers notwithstanding.]

Although his own neural solution is compatible with either determinism or indeterminism (2.1) [so that a sort of compatibilism sneaks in after all], Tse says that it is the core argument of reductionists against mental causation, a logical argument resting on the impossibility of self-causation, that must be challenged. [If I follow here, Tse is conceding that his "criterial causation" solution of the possibility of free will is not really a *final* neural solution, since it would work even under determinism, that is, the denial of the will; it is a *possible* physicalist realization of free will, if a certain kind of indeterminism is adopted *and* if the possibility of a separable, effective mentality is *presupposed*. It seems that the main question, the causal effect of will on brain, is being begged, though in a very suggestive way.]

The kind of indeterminism that will preclude the *causa sui* argument is "ontological indeterminism." [Before getting to Tse's indeterminism, in itself a fascinating exposition, I should say that the *causa sui* argument, that mental causation of motor events is self-causation, doesn't make much sense to me to begin with.

First, an event is called *self*-causation because an actor is acting on itself. But isn't that the case only under the prior assumption that mental will and physical brain are identical—albeit masked by metaphors like "realizing" and "supervening"—the very assumption denied by those who think there might be mental agency? If the mental action and the neural event are distinct, isn't it other- rather than self-causation? Second, this self-causation is proscribed because it implies that the effect is simultaneous with the cause: the mental will acts on the physical brain instantaneously. Physicalists do tend to interpret causation temporally: first cause, then effect; a mover moves, a mobile responds. But could there be non-temporal causes, so-called formal causes, forms atemporally present, which might direct the actions of organisms or objects either as external or internal blueprints? Or to cite a modern example, is a massive body moving in a force field in a temporal causal relation to it? Does the issue of simultaneity of cause and effect arise there?]

Ontological indeterminism is as unbalancing, and consequently as interesting, a notion about the nature of nature as I know of. It claims that when a particle's future is not uniquely but only probabilistically determinable, because certain measurements necessary to full determination are inaccessible to us, we are *not* entitled to assume a "hidden variable" that nevertheless determines it fully. If such a variable existed, the indeterminacy would be *epistemological*, that is, attributable to limits inherent in human cognition; nature would still be deterministic at its deepest, inaccessible level. But if, as seems plausible, the arguments for "counterfactual definiteness" fail (A1.5), then we must assume that indeterminateness is *ontological*, characteristic of a new kind of being, a thing that lacks some of the usual properties of thinghood such as full descriptive determinacy. [Such an object is about as strangely wonderful, I would say, as that bugbear of *causa sui* critics, a self-created and self-moving deity—which, incidentally, is *not* what Aristotle's "unmoved mover," sometimes cited in this debate, is: it is *un*-created and *un*-movable (*Physics* VIII 6).]

Tse subscribes to this doctrine not just because it is the only one left standing when compatibilism is excluded for being an equivocation on the term "will," determinism is excluded for being counter-intuitive, and epistemological indeterminism is excluded for being a crypto-determinism—but more substantially, because under it, basic nature offers a degree of indeterminacy that leaves an opening for top-down, mental-on-physical causation and therewith disposes of the *causa sui* problem (7.18–19).

This is evident from the self-causation claim as questioned by Tse: "How can mental events realized in or supervening on neuronal and, ultimately, particle-level events change the very physical events that give rise to them or on which they supervene?" (A 2.2). This action would seem to be bootstrapping, that is, self-causation [setting aside my argument that if the mental and physical events are not assumed to be identical, then there's no bootstrapping, and if the causation is formal, then there's no simultaneity issue]. But with a commitment to ontological indeterminism, there is now an open future—the particle-level does not determine consciousness completely, and a mental cause can have a future effect. Here Tse turns back from appendices to the main text for "a plausible physicalist account of mental causation," his original contribution.

The aim is to show that "patterns in [mental] input can be genuinely causal if there are physical detectors, such as neurons, that respond to patterns in input and then change the physical system in which they reside if the criteria for the presence of a pattern in inputs have been met" (1.16). The crucial feature of this proposal is *criterial causation*: effects or "realizations" that avoid what is proscribed—they do occur *not* instantaneously, that is, simultaneously with input, because these inputs preset, not individual neurons, but neurons in circuits and networks, that is, patterns (3.14, whose technical explanation, which is beyond my competence, is in Chapters 4 and 5) that respond if and when certain criteria are met. Criteria are not strictly proscriptive rules like natural laws, but conditions that can be satisfied in various ways, so that "the same mental state can be realized on the basis of numerous inputs" (2.8, 8.14).

Thus the three stages of criterial causation are (2.7): 1. new physical/informational criteria are set in a neuronal circuit on the basis of preceding physical/mental processing (t_1); 2. inherently variable inputs arrive at the post-synaptic, now pre-set neurons (t_2); 3. the pre-set criteria are met or not, leading to neurons firing or not (t_3).

"Such criterial causation is important because it allows neurons to alter the physical realization of *future* mental events in a way that escapes the problem of self-causation of the mental upon the physical" (2.7). [Aspects of this crucial conclusion baffle me. The burden of intelligibility seems to be on "physical realization." Do we already non-presumptively know that a mental event *can* be physically "realized"? Is "realized" a weasel word, a begged question, or a lucid event? Can a mental event even become real, "thinglike" (Latin: *realis*), that is, a sensorily observable particular? To be sure, we decide and then we—sometimes—execute, but is the thought-gap, the intellectual hiatus, between the one and the other *really* bridged by the term "realize"? Moreover, what is a "*future* mental event"? One might argue (as Augustine does in his *Confessions* X18, and as I believe) that we exist only in our—multilayered—present, the now of consciousness backed by memory of the past and occupied by projects for the future, both of these being trace-*presences* of what *is not*, the former of what is no longer, the latter of what is not yet. Only what is hard-determined has a fixed, that is, a predictable *real* future; what is free, though conscience-bound by what ought to happen, being capable at any instant of re-directing—often per-verting—the expectable course, has no fixed future. Does the physical real-ization preserve this radical freedom of mental action, or does it in fact jig future mentation and so make it effectively deterministic?]

Now for the application to free will: Suppose the *chief argument* against free will really is self-causation [as I would doubt, thinking—as this book is devoted to claiming—that the chief difficulty is not whether will is "merely epiphenomenal" or "really free," but whether "strong" will *per se*, the "clenched fist" notion of agency, is a necessary element of our nature—whether deeply thought-out conviction won't do much better]. Then the tripartite process of criterial causation overcomes self-causation thus: "*Self-causation does not apply to changing the physical basis of making a future decision.* There can obviously never be a self-caused event, but criteria can be set up in advance, such that when they are met, an action automati-cally follows; this is an action we will have willed to take place by virtue of having set up those particular criteria in advance." The criteria cannot be changed at the moment of action, that is, when they are satisfied at "some unknown point in the future;" the limits of these actions are *determined* for "the near future" by the physicalistically set criteria, but because they "can be changed in advance, *we are free* [my italics] to determine how we will behave within certain limits in the near future. Criterial causation there-fore offers a path toward free will where the brain can determine how it will behave given particular types of future input. This input can be milli-seconds in the future or, in some cases, even years away" (7.5). Because the criteria can be met "by many types of input" and because of other variabil-ities, "the outcome is *neither random nor determined*" (7.6). [My italics; the phrase is practically a (negative) description of the willing-mode. Queries: First, the willed behavior is originally said to occur very soon after the neu-ral patterning, but then, rightly recognizing that a version of willing which is something deeper than small-gauge deciding may take years to come to

fruition, it is said sometimes to eventuate years after. Are the neural patterns permanent? Can no later pre-setting override them completely? Has
Tse construed a true "*future* mental event?" Second, who is the "we" in the
description above? In the criterial causation theory, does "we" mean ourselves as mental agents, as it must if free will is to appear in it? Hence *we*
(mentally) set the *brain* (physically) for future will-like (that is, neither random nor determinist) action. But then it is the brain that is willing and not
we; we (mentally) have kicked the will-can down the road by pre-setting
the brain to potential decision-making. In a way, this is very persuasive:
Not for nothing is the word "will" futuristically connected to the verb "to
be." Willing is for the not-yet future; moreover, observers of the will have
claimed that particular willing must be preceded by a "will to will," a general disposition to engage, a readiness: "the readiness is all." Furthermore,
the criterial causation condition certainly mimics the experience of willing—that many experiential "inputs" can have the same behavioral "out-
put," and that this fact could be attributed to what I might call, after Tse,
the "ontological indecision" of the mind: we often really don't know what
to do and suddenly find ourselves with a mind made up, probabilities having been preconsciously—but not necessarily physicalistically—weighed
so that a conscious decision might supervene. (My assumption here is that
"pre-, sub-, or un-conscious" does not provably mean "neuronal." My question then is: Can a neuronal parallelism with conscious phenomena decide
causal priority?) Tse himself says that the theory does not seem so far to
speak to *the* great question of how mental events can be physically causative (7.33). That transition seems to me to be bundled into "we."]

Consequently, Tse undergirds the theory of criterial causation with a
discussion of the role of consciousness in mental representation (Chapter
8) and attention (Chapter 10). "Neuroscientists do not yet understand how
a propositional conclusion in working memory, such as 'I need to buy cranberry sauce' [not to speak of ethical willing: "Will I steal the jar?"] can be
translated into a motor plan to carry it out" (8.19). So *the* question, the possibility of interaction between mind and brain, *the* mind-body problem,
is so far unanswered. But Tse infers that, because of the speed with which
thought turns into action, the respective encodings of mental representations (together with the operations on them) and of motor plans must be
readily transformable into each other; hence he inquires into the most adequate theory of linguistic reference, that is, into the "encoding" of conscious
thought. The presupposition is that thought and its speech are "symbolic
and syntactic information processing" (8.26). [Here is a query: Will the linguistic theory be as "adequate" to human speech as it to physicalistic use?
In particular, is the "encoding" formulation an independently reached view
of mentation and language based on plausible evidence—it differs widely
from that reached by introspection, for example in Phenomenology, the

analytic description of consciousness—or is it a doctrine devised to analo-gize consciousness to a physical system? It seems full of difficulties, for ex-ample, how does a symbol re-present? Take a stop sign, surely the bearer of symbols. It may display a forfending palm, pictorially; or a canceling cross, conventionally; or an onomatopoetic word STOP, sensorily; or a ver-bal command, linguistically. Do any of these features belong to the essence of a word? Do words, most characteristically, function like pictures, signs, sounds, vocables? Or are they perhaps not symbols at all? I mention one alternative view: "intentionality," a "reaching" notion of word to object.]

Tse calls the experience of experience [my phrase] undeniable (10.5). Experience is identical with consciousness; it is the domain where endog-enous (internally generated) attentional tracking takes place. What is tracked are qualia-associated representations. [Qualia are defined as the objects of attention, circularly, because endogenous attention is defined as what focuses on a primary type of qualia—quite rightly, since there seems to be no way to articulate the qualitative states of inwardness that does not derail or circumvent the very nonverbal nature of a "feel."] Attentional tracking is closely related to volition. [In fact, I think that attention-focus-ing, that is, desire-invested consciousness, is one of the will's few accept-able objects.] And these elements of consciousness have evolved to our evolutionary advantage, the subject of Tse's next book.

"*Consciousness is thus required for endogenous attentional alloca-tion, . . . volitional executive control, . . . and manipulation of representa-tions* (10.37). The chief argument is logical: Unconscious objects cannot, *ipso facto*, be consciously tracked (10.33). It does not follow, however, that "consciousness per se is causal of motor acts"—Tse adds "or thoughts" (10.39). Indeed, the fact that consciousness must operate over conscious ele-ments might suggest that operations on physical items must also take place within their own domain. Mind-body interaction remains unexplained. [Moreover, it is not obvious that the operator/operand model of conscious-ness, like the symbolically encoded information-processing model, is true of experienced consciousness, which must be, it seems, the final arbiter of its own workings. Thus there are, to me evident, phenomena of a very high kind of consciousness not well caught by notions of encoding and process-ing: hints of actual spontaneity; aboutness as in thinking about thoughts as well as in thinking about thinking; desire-directed searching for the way things are—for example, whether consciousness, when studied *within a physicalist framework* can really ever turn up as unequivocally *other* than physical, that is, natural-law-governed, be it deterministically or probabi-listically; whether deeply-ingrained mental models *of* the world—world-structuring schemata—are separable *from* the world; whether the decision to buy a jar of cranberry sauce is sufficiently homogeneous with the reso-lution to change one's life to be "realized" in similar physical processes.]

If it is, as I think, the measure of a book's quality how hard it makes us think, this book ranks very high. Moreover, it is comprehensive in its problem-scope. Besides the topics touched on (which are treated in far more detail than my discussion does justice to), there are many pertinent accounts: of the framework within which mere inputs turn into "information;" of the Libet experiments and their arguable misdirection in respect to the will; of a feature of the will usually neglected in recent treatments, its time-extendedness; of criteria as a philosophical notion; of mental representation in general, of memory, and of attention. Of most interest to me is the above-mentioned attempted account of endogenous, that is, internally generated, experience or consciousness in terms of "qualia," the conscious "operands" on which attention, volitional tracking, operates. Unless I misread Tse's account of experience as attending, doing, planning (Chapter 10), it leaves untreated that kind of consciousness which has been most rousingly enigmatic, namely *self*-consciousness, where operator and operand are somehow identical and yet somehow separable, where attention is directed not to what is abstracted (that is, symbolic and content-remote) but concrete (present and fulfilled). A physicalist account of such metaphysical "activity" (Greek *energeia*) would be of ultimate interest. One last appreciative comment: His confident beginning notwithstanding, Tse is singularly candid about his science being in philosophically important respects still *in medias res*.

This chapter presented a small sampling of empirical investigations of the will, which are not, it seems, either as startling in themselves or even as incrementally additive as are discoveries in other departments of consciousness. So far, they do not any more settle deep questions than did the compatibilist debate in my previous chapter. They do, however, pose concrete questions about the correct location of the will in the human and natural economy—whether this relation is to be seated in consciousness or brain. And they do refine arguments concerning the consequences for the will arising from the relation between the free soul and the bound body—whether this relation can be subject to experiment or is in principle elusive.

In the next chapter, these findings and their unresolved perplexities will appear in attempts to say what the will *is* within a modern, empirical frame of mind—but also within a less time-determined frame-work.

chapter XI

Will Overwhelmed

Into the Twenty-first Century

In Satan's Hell, the fallen angels sing of

Their own heroic deeds and hapless fall
By doom of battle; and complain that fate
Free virtue should enthrall to force or chance.
Their song was partial, but the harmony
(What could it less when Spirits immortal sing?)
Suspended hell, and took with ravishment
The thronging audience. In discourse more sweet
(For eloquence the soul, song charms the sense)
Others sat apart on a hill retired,
In thoughts more elevate, and reasoned high
Of providence, foreknowledge, will, and fate,
Fixed fate, free will, foreknowledge absolute,
And found no end, in wand'ring mazes lost.
Of good and evil much they argued then,
Of happiness and final misery,
Passion and apathy, and glory and shame,
Vain wisdom all, and false philosophy:
Yet with a pleasing sorcery could charm
Pain for a while or anguish, and excite
Fallacious hope, or arm th'obdurèd breast
With stubborn patience as with triple steel. (My italics)

In this chapter, I will speak of lamentations (and jubilations) that chance might excuse vice, of the partial (both self-serving and many-voiced) enchantment of the cognitive tribe, of discourse both dry and flippant, of thinking reduced to fine-grained rationality, of the ceaseless back-and-forth about foresight, pre-cognition, will, and necessity: determinism, free will and certain prediction—inconclusive sophistication all and latter-day philosophy, yet exciting fallacious hope.[1]

I can't resist a brief amateur meditation on history, since my chapter heading needed to refer to an epoch. We, none of us, know whether history, as the sum of human actions and effects, does indeed add up, is in fact summable—whether the consequences of human actions produce on balance more intended or unintended effects, and whether these support ways of staying human or not. Put briefly: No one I have heard of *knows* whether history has a *qualitative* development, is a Progress or a Decline of humanity. That it has a *quantitative* drift is, on the other hand, patent: the one undeniable *Law of More*. I have a suspicion—nothing stronger— that quality and quantity in human affairs are in *some* respects inversely proportional.

I would offer as *one* cause of this loss-through-gain the simple lack of time inherent in current knowledge conditions—the overwhelming mass of material that the ethics of research and scholarship require *referencing* and the increasing complexities of the science involved that the interest of the subject require *citing*. The tsunami of this obligatory business can drown out the long reflection that is grounded in the textual tradition and its various humanly immediate and, yes, often naïve, but often complexly deep, accounts. The reputational profit to be gained from novelty, although soon picked apart and superseded, is a goad to incessant analytical concept-formation, a way of using reason that is distinct from the slow thinking-out of the way things are—which is rarely congruent with the institutionalized demand for "original contributions."[2]

The recent work on will, more precisely on free will, has been, since the later part of the last century, thus overwhelming; the will is "perhaps the most voluminously debated of all philosophical problems," and the volume of work has not abated in the twenty-first. (And here am I, adding to it.) One way, apparently the most academically engaging one for framing the debate, was in terms of "compatibilism" as reported in Chapter IX. In the course of becoming ever more tightly reasoned and finely honed, the discussion has—to my mind, spectacularly—lost its gravity, the will its scope, the human being its presence. The putative gain has been in a type of thinking that is ever more analytically fine-grained, in a reconceiving of a will that makes it laboratory-ready, and in a fairly sanguine acceptance of the loss of human autonomy.[3]

The last item particularly puts the community (nicely referred to, in social networking terms, as a "tribe") of professionals concerned with cognitive processes and their neurological underpinnings, their causal conditions, into a mode of perennial—private—perplexity. For *almost* all of them deny free will *sans phrase*, the unqualified human ability to origi-nate action, uncompromised by the counter-intuitive phraseology of com-patibilism. Yet in their concern for individual decency and social order, they do not want to forego attribution of responsibility entirely. True lib-ertarians, believers in our counter-natural origination of natural conse-quences, are out of fashion with the members of the cognitive community, who cannot bring themselves to believe in unmoved movers and spiritual interveners in nature, since they define nature as a law-necessitated system closed to spontaneity. To me it seems sensible to regard this as one of those terminally undecidable and *therefore* perpetually preoccupying questions that constitute philosophy. The compatibilists appear to me to have sought salvation in an essentially mealy-mouthed formulation, which depends on the hope that we'll generally want to do as we must. For my part, I would rather go, at least on crucial occasions, with Kant's wisdom, that in morally really difficult situations everything depends on our thinking selves lacerating our desiring nature. The hard-liners, who think that we are essentially automata, imagine—naively, it appears to me—that the gen-eral knowledge of their scientific conclusions will lead to greater humanity in the treatment of the transgressors. I think the opposite is more likely: perfect eliminative bloody-mindedness toward "bad seeds" as inaccessi-ble to social suasion, and thus to be eradicated precisely because they can't help it.[4]

I want to begin with a solution offered by the believers in a total absence of real free will: the profit in cherishing it as an *illusion*. The present-day rubrics I shall call on to delineate will, be it as a hard fact or a mere epiphe-nomenon, as an active faculty or a passive affect, as a unitary power or a "distributed" network, are, in order, Illusion, Intention, Agency, Self, and Freedom. These separate headings betoken that there are no grandly global contemporary theories, no postmodern ontologies of the will—that indeed it would be to mistake the de-systematizing postmodern mode to expect interest in such groundings. I do recognize that the claim that philosophic grandeur is in eclipse may be a premature judgment—but such judging is what each of us was put on this earth, at least its Western half, occasionally to attempt. One last comment: Notice how many contemporary concerns have their forerunner in Nietzsche's prescient writing—the will as illusion, as affect, as "distributed" (the cognitive way of denominating Nietzsche's many-souls-in-one theory). He is *the critical observer* of historical move-ments *par excellence*, and I refer to him here to express an ever-fascinating puzzlement concerning the balance of herd-mentality and personal enter-prise within what seems rightly named the "neurophilosophical move-ment." At the same time I recognize the arrogation of legitimacy involved in my personal attempt to grapple thoughtfully as an outsider with a pro-fessionally respectable establishment.

A. Illusion: Wegner

So then to will as a—wisely maintained—illusion. As often happens (giving rise to the mystical thought of historically, that is, supra-personally, occasioned movements), two notions of illusion came on the scene contemporaneously but independently.[5]

Saul Smilansky, in an article ranged under the heading "Nonstandard Views," considers these problems: His—and most investigators'—concern, he claims, is to preserve respect for "moral innocence." So the "worst thing" would be to point out to the public that under "hard determinism" neither the appreciation of innocence nor the attribution of objective guilt makes any sense, nor does the attempt to instill a subjective sense of guilt and of moral responsibility—and so remorse and compunction become "conceptually dubious."

Enter illusionism. Since there is no moral grounding once libertarian will is discredited (Smilansky thinks there is no "deep will" of any other sort), and since *we can't live* with the moral dissonance of needing the belief in this discredited free will (which, if needed, "ought not to be abandoned"), we require the relief of a "motivated mediation": a defense of illusion. We must bring ourselves not to "*see people from the ultimate perspective.*" "Motivated obscurity" will do it. This is, to be sure, an "elitist solution"; some limited part of the population, the scientists, will live with a practically disenabling knowledge, using it mainly to ameliorate the treatment of transgressors. The populace will maintain its ignorant morality. "The falseness of beliefs does not negate the fact that they exist for the believer." "[I]llusion serves a crucial *creative* function, which is a basis for social morality and personal self-appreciation . . ."

I find this faith in the terminal occultation of the cognitive version of hard determinism touching—this firm faith that its findings will nowise trickle down to the folk. Or that if they do, we can live with that proverbial white elephant, the one of whom we must avoid thinking for a day to win a treasure. Put otherwise: I think I understand living with ambiguity, when two perspectives yield contrary truths, but I cannot accept living with a deliberate equivocation, in which a desirable falsehood and its known contradiction are consciously and concurrently maintained. But this postulated illusionism spotlights the cognitive-ethical dilemma with real candor, while making the best of it with some creative morality.

The second approach, by Daniel Wegner, does not *recommend* self-delusion because it goes about *proving* it. The topic and thesis of his book is the illusion of *conscious* will, which implies that experienced consciousness as illusory is to be pitted against out-of-sight mechanism as real. He too, however, finds a way to ameliorate the fact of delusion. To put the conclusion ahead of the account, "Although the experience of conscious will is not evidence of mental causation" of action, it *is* a signal of "personal authorship." Thus it functions to induce both a "sense of achievement and the acceptance of moral responsibility." Wegner uses the example of a compass: It does not steer the ship. It can be said to be an "epiphenomenon," an a-causal appearance piggy-backed on the real action. Yet the pilot refers to it in making adjustments to the ship's course.[6]

So also is conscious will the mind's compass, (including, I imagine, our moral compass). When our actions correspond to our thoughts, then, just as a ship's compass (were it conscious) might think "I've kept her on course," so we think "I willed this." (The difficulty here is that in the cockpit it's the human helmsman who consults the compass to keep on course; this slippage in the metaphor corresponds to an indeterminacy in the book: Is or isn't will *finally* epiphenomenal? On the one hand, "Free will is not an effective theory of psychology;" on the other, "Will is a kind of authorship emotion"—shades of Nietzsche—and as such it "authenticates the action's owner as the self." The helmsman who sees by the compass that he's off course makes a course correction. Presumably the willing owner of an action, the self, sometimes does similarly. But then isn't the corrective will the source of doing, not a mere indicator of having done?)

Here is an abstract of the actual argument: "This theory of apparent mental causation depends on the idea that consciousness doesn't know how conscious mental processes work." However an apparently tacit fundamental postulate of cognitive science hypothecates that "unconsciousness and inscrutable mechanisms create both conscious thought about the action and the action, and also produce the sense of will we experience by perceiving the thought as cause of the action." ("Inscrutable" rings true for the inside-subject, but presumably it yields eventually to the methodical scrutiny of the external observer—thus nullifying the theory of "doesn't know.")[7]

Thus the illusory *experience* of volitional's cause can be analyzed as promoted by three principles that people perceive as telling features of external causation: *Causal* volitional events, intentions, are *prior* to their effects and yield a greater sense of will the closer to the effect they occur. (Two observations: First, Wegner defines *intention* as "normally understood as an idea of what one is going to do that appears in consciousness just before one does it. This is the thought that people usually associate most strongly with causing the action." It seems inaccurate and inadequate (see this chapter, Sec. B). Second, the principle itself is sharply contrary to *my* sense of volition: I form—serious—intentions long before their execution, and the longer my will is at work before action the more effect-like the action.)[8]

Next is the consistency principle. "Causes should *relate* to effects." An example is intending to eat a salad and then finding oneself eating it—the short-term will. Oddly, the chief examples Wegner gives are of *inconsistency* between intention and action, as when "a great idea pops into the mind;" we are said not to experience that as voluntary. (Not my experience: such immediately interesting ideas as suddenly come to me, come as a result of a long-dwelling and willing receptivity; they are hoped for, *invoked*.)

The third principle of the experience of causal volition is that of exclusivity. Multiple causes *should not compete* with each other. (This principle is directly contrary to the causal thinking I find most compelling—the "all roads lead to Rome" situation and its cross-inferences.)

Perhaps I have derailed the argument a little by expressing my doubts about these "key sources" of the common experience of causality. For Wegner's real point is that people transfer their notions of natural causation to mental phenomena, and in the absence of hard evidence one way or another, develop an illusion that will is temporally *prior* to, is really *related* to, and is the *one-and-only* source of, action-effects—in sum, is their cause.

The bulk of Wegner's book collects fascinating experiments with special conditions such as alienation of identity in ventriloquism, serious pathologies such as dissociative identity-disorder, and willing submission of the will to outside control in possession and hypnosis. (Here are my misgivings: In brain science, the relation of lesions to abnormalities of behavior is a principal diagnostic method. But do those persuasive connections carry over into psychology? Do the various illusions of voluntariness in *abnormal* situations carry over into normality so as to prove ordinary will illusory? Or are they to be regarded, *ipso facto*, precisely as abnormal and so revelatory only of what relatively sound willing is *not*?)

To conclude: An illuminating anecdote made the rounds among my friends who'd lived in the vicinity of the Freud family-in-exile in England. A niece was heard saying: "Oh, Uncle Sigi—he doesn't know much about people." A fancy way to put this is that a lifelike phenomenology of intention is sometimes forestalled by life-abstracted psychological theory. The illusion theory of volition seems to me, for all its experimental hedging, to be experientially inadequate because it works with somewhat gross psychological terms, for example, "intention," which is surely crucial to the problem of undeluded human agency and surely more subtly than the definition quoted above conveys.

The last encompassing, if negative, philosophical views of the will as a conceptual non-starter—Ryle's and Wittgenstein's (set out in Ch. VIII, Note 100)—didn't seem plausible. The first, more restricted, psychological account of the will as an adaptive illusion isn't persuasive either. As in the earlier accounts, some terms, particularly "disposition" were up in the air, so too in this later one not only the account of the will-experience but particularly the analysis of will-terms need, as I said, filling-in. So let the first of these be "Intention."

B. Intention: Anscombe

Whatever willing is, if it has any scope, it includes intentions understood as plan-invested desires, that is, wants which—as opposed to mere wishes—seem fulfillable and have therefore been clothed in practical designs. Or maybe the other way around: because ways to fulfillment have come to mind, mere wishes have been invested with intentionality. Recall that intention is already a will-term in Augustine, and is treated extendedly by Thomas Aquinas. Collecting his attributes, we get this straightforward delineation: *Intention* signifies the act of the will tending to objects according to a *rational plan* (that is, intention is not a function of the intellect but employs it); the object may be the *one final end, happiness,* or *some intermediate end; intending an end and willing what forwards it is one and the same act or motion,* though it can be thought of in parts. One might say that intention is here a descriptive word for will as *practical reason.*[9]

But recent treatments speak to contemporary will-concepts in more concrete terms.

G. E. M. Anscombe's *Intention* is a twentieth-century classic, devoted to a fine-grained analysis of intention. Intentionality is a notion with a long history and a wide application beyond directedness to objects of desiring, wanting, willing. But I shall focus on the pages bearing on the latter cluster of terms. (For Searle on intention see Note 10 to this chapter.)[10]

Here I wish to enter a grief with analytic non-language. She says: "It is a familiar doctrine that people can want anything; that is, that in 'A wants X,' 'X' ranges over all describable objects or states of affairs. This is untenable; for example, the range is restricted to present or future objects and future states of affairs; for we are not here concerned with idle wishing." Examples of idle wishing are that $\sqrt{2}$ were commensurable or that Troy had not fallen or that I might be a millionaire.

Now I think that an algebraic placeholder A with a wish-domain of X will indeed be at the tight-reckoning mercy of the analytic philosopher, but a real human being, with a world of desire-possibilities, including apparently unreal ones, jumps the bounds of tenable wanting; "idle wishes" are sometimes effective pre-intentions. It is from wishing something intensely, in the imagination, without regard to practicality—including altering the past—that some grandeur of being and an action-format to suit arises. Put otherwise: The modalities of flesh-and-blood humanity are gone—indeed deliberately stripped away—in these skeletal formulations. For what?

Think of all the fruitful mathematical activity consequent on the Pythagoreans' discovery of the incommensurability and their ardent desire not to have it so, of a possibly splendid counter-Iliad, of some young (if mis-guided) dreams of one day being even a billionaire!

However, in fairness to Anscombe's careful thinking, the relevant mark distinguishing idle wishing from wanting is not its (detachable) restriction to present and future objects. Rather the primitive sign of wanting is *try-ing to get*—not a mere stretching out (tending) to something, but doing it both with the knowledge that the thing exists and moving towards it: "the ascription of sensible knowledge and of volition go together." She shows that this holds even if the object of wanting is a general one or is as yet a mere idea.

So here, as it had through the ages, will *as* intention effects object-directed motion. (Here's my question: It's hard to imagine a human being who lives in the world, or out of it, without such intending; is will, under-stood as a—somehow piggy-backed—*tension* in the tending, a necessary concomitant? Does intention *imply* will? I hope not.)

To thicken the meaning, here are some contemporary ways of think-ing about intention. For example, here is a current psychological scheme for situating intending in the volitional process. It is interesting because in broad outline it is not in its elements so divergent from Thomas Aqui-nas's philosophical description of willing, though hugely less subtle; the elements, like Thomas, are partly tendencies that are at once initial and extended through the process (desire/goal), partly conditions that are in the background (means/ability), partly steps that are sequential (intention/enactment); the contemporary component-terms are usefully accompanied by corresponding legal *mens rea* concepts; *mens rea* means "agent mind," in law the responsible, chargeable aspect of a human being.[11]

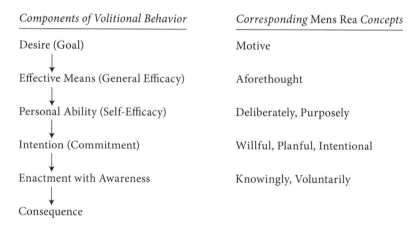

Components of Volitional Behavior	Corresponding Mens Rea Concepts
Desire (Goal)	Motive
↓	
Effective Means (General Efficacy)	Aforethought
↓	
Personal Ability (Self-Efficacy)	Deliberately, Purposely
↓	
Intention (Commitment)	Willful, Planful, Intentional
↓	
Enactment with Awareness	Knowingly, Voluntarily
↓	
Consequence	

The volitional rubrics speak for themselves; the *mens rea* side lists (though not in order) nouns, adjectives, adverbs, terms active in crucial decisions determining criminal liability, for example the gradations in killing from (unintentional) third-degree manslaughter through intentional up to (premeditated) first-degree murder. Intention is a major issue in the attribution of guilt as long as some sort of libertarianism prevails in the justice system, but it is here beyond my project. However, the understanding of volition expressed in this psychological analysis has another implication, one regarding collective will, that contrasts it with the hyper-personal will I discussed, not unappalled, in Chapter VII: The collective will that fits this analysis is literally a collection and not an amalgamation, hence basically *individual*; it arises from the individual intention to cooperate with a group in pursuit of a goal that becomes common *by virtue* of belonging to every individual, but remains individual *by reason* of each person's intentional self-identification with a community.[12]

There are alternative schemata for placing intention using a different vocabulary and having slightly, at least atmospherically, different meanings. For example "goal" might be called "motivation" and "consequence," "behavior." But in its volitional context intention seems always to be a *middle term* between two "ends": the desire for a fulfillment, which is the beginning of willing and the other end, the execution of a plan, which is the completion of the will-event. What thereupon eventuates is know-how plus pluck plus luck plus stamina—call it "after-will."[13]

A next question that can be raised about intentions concerns their consciousness—so far taken mostly for granted, at least by psychologists. In scientific settings (and I think in lay contexts too), the external index of consciousness is "operational," that is, defined by a procedure; the operation here is the subject's giving a report of intending. (The internal evidence, which is simply our thinking that we are intending, that we are self-consciously in the intentional mode, is, it seems, self-proving; it is a condition of terminal, unsurpassable self-evidence. Thus intending is, depending on one's frame of mind, either doubly convincing—since who's to say me nay when I'm so immediately involved and so sure—or it is twice condemned—when I'm unwarrantedly claiming privileged access and indubitableness to boot.)[14]

There is, however, good reason also to consider unconscious intentions, for they seem to exist. In fact, they're probably in the majority, being the sort of things we bring about habitually without giving them much attention: "[C]onsciousness deserts all processes where it can no longer be of use." This unconscious intention can be short term (proximal), either "by the way," such as unlocking your house door or an "expert performance," such as a practiced tennis serve. Long-range (distal) intentions tend to go in and out of consciousness in a peculiar way. If you're writing a book, for example, you do a thousand other things quite focusedly every day, but it *feels as if* you were, and perhaps somehow really are, intent on nothing else; everything turns into the grist for this mill. Of course, the problem of unconscious intention may be one of those "merely semantic" matters that depend on how the word is used and by whom—what the philosophers and what the so-called layfolk mean by it. To me, intention that is unconscious-in-stretches is a mark of classical willing—done by a soul simultaneously focused on its goal and carrying on with life.[15]

Yet another approach to intentionality is by types of intention. Examples are given in Note 16 of this chapter.[16]

So what, in sum are the elements of intention as collated from various sources? Intention is "a feature" of the mind that begins in a focused desire, which, borne by a "predictive belief," meaning a faith in one's volitional stamina, tends toward action. Another similar but longer formulation is that the initial desire elicits an idea, a mental representation of the required practical means; for intentions, unlike wishes, are "causally self-referential," meaning that to intend *is* to intend to be a cause; thus this idea, this cognitive aspect of intentionality, is both supported by and, in turn, supports a "volative desire," the fairly undeflectable determination to act, as distinguished from a mere "appetitive desire," a volatile wish. The whole process, from its inception as a desire to its fulfillment in a deed, is supported by a "sense of agency"—of an intention being indeed the cause of the action. These factors occur partly serially, partly simultaneously, forming a complex that often issues in a conscious beginning only long after many semi-conscious foreshadowings have flitted in and out of awareness, and it debouches in action that has not only the intended but also unintended consequences.[17]

Being a collation, the paragraph above lacks elegance, but it confirms, by its volitional language, that intention is an element of the will. As a "feature" of the mind it is not a potently independent power, but rather that phase of willing (here analyzed into its own sub-elements), in which desire has elicited a plan from cognition and therewith acquired a sense of agency.

C. Agency: Causality

A feature just touched on is, in the contemporary context, the most preoccupying, the most problematic of all: Is goal-intentionality causal? More specifically, do intentions cause "mental acts" (a dubious phrase) such as practical plans and designs? (Here arises the problem whether mentations are "caused" by mentations, ideas by ideas). Further, do they cause overt external acts, such as conduct and deeds? (Here arises the problem whether deeds are "caused" by thoughts, acts by willing.) In short, can humans be free agents—if by free agency we mean thinking out a plan on one's own and then enacting it? (For more on Agency, see Note 18 of this chapter.)[18]

The age-old inquiry into human action comes to a head in opposite views about a yet deeper question: Are agents necessary to begin with?

Thomas Aquinas says, *Actiones sunt individuorum*, "actions belong to individual [agents]" Nietzsche will ascribe this notion—that "all effects are due to an agent"—to the "rudimentary psychology of religious man," who, unable to credit himself with being the originator of his great feelings of power or accesses of passion, and supposing that he himself can be their cause only when he knows he willed them, invents a superhuman agent for his passions and his deeds. Thus Nietzsche, prescient as so often, puts the notion of agency itself in question, though in a roundabout way: the feelings of vitality, the springs of action in men of power do indeed lie within them—yet they are nonetheless not their causal agents, that is, the thinking wielders of an agent-will.[19]

So a great modern problematic develops about agency—the human capacity for deliberate, free, causal actions. Put very widely: First, what causes mentation itself? (In the older version, it was: What is the relation of human willing to God's omniscience? In the newer one: How does mind emerge from brain?) Put more narrowly: What starts willing? (In the older version: How does will move itself? In the newer one, similarly: "Are we prime movers unmoved" of our wants or desires?) Second, turning to the outside: How does consciousness cause the body to act? (In the older version: How does will command body? In the newer one: How does consciousness activate the somatic, mostly motor, systems, that are or seem to be volitionally controlled?) And third, going still further out into the world, if conscious will is a mere epiphenomenon, can we be held responsible for our external, or for any, actions? If we are indeed substantively causal, are we not derailing the law-ruled course of nature? (Here the problem really becomes predominantly modern.) And finally, fourth, if we are ultimately run by the law-bound interactions of the least and lowest natural entities, does agency become a vacuous term?[20]

There is a near-infinity of large-meshed concepts and finely-wrought specifications of "agent-causalism," but they wouldn't advance this exposition. (For a case in point see Note 21 of this chapter.) [21]

Therefore, back to human agency in larger strokes. Is a human being the agent, the true *doer*, of his actions? That question can be general: Am I (you can't think this out, it seems to me, without looking to the first person—so, *am I*, the conscious self writing this book) when all is said and done, the claimant *cause* of my actions? I can't let the noun "action" bear the brunt of decision here, as it would if it already *meant* "*my* doing," so that then "doing" already *meant* conduct (self-controlled comportment) as opposed to behavior (reactive response to stimulus). That would be begging the question. So it would be better to ask, *tout court*: Can I act?

More narrowly: Am I responsible, that is, answerable—summoned to defend myself—before a court whose sitting judge is myself (and perhaps a higher one) and a jury whose members are my fellow humans, the usual charge being either stupidity or badness, leaving it open which is the more serious? In short, when I act, are my actions imputable?[22]

Immediately another problem arises. (I should say that dealing with this problematic is like being in Hades with Odysseus, who can hardly hold off the shades crowding in to be heard first.) For, setting aside for the moment the currently most urgent problem that arises between freedom and *natural* determinism (since it is not yet decided even whether it *is* decidable), there remains *spiritual* determinism. Here is a way to see the perplexity. On the one hand, as noted before, a well-received understanding of free agency is "the ability to do otherwise." Yet, on the other, a paradigm case of conscientiously free dissent is Luther's previously quoted: "I can no other." Behind that assertion of a conscience determined by faith is a long pre-Protestant tradition that *goodness compels the will just as logic compels the reason.* It appears uncircumventably at odds with the notion of free agency as choice undetermined by any extraneous cause.[23]

It seems to me that the "could have done otherwise" criterion of free agency is often an outsider's view, and in several ways. In real life, it is mostly to the onlooker that there are obviously viable alternatives and that the perpetrator could, hence should, have done otherwise—thence the outsiders sense that blame might be imputed, whereas the doer feels compulsion, albeit not *external* compulsion. Thus, "could have done otherwise" is probably in many cases the language of a stranger not privy to the faith or despair, the principles or passions, that underlie the agent's decision. Moreover, in the many cases where really complex judgment calls are involved, those concerning the truest view of an opaque circumstance and the best resolution of a murky situation, the spectator can only guess at the psychic oscillations between "could" and "couldn't" that may have hopelessly fragmented the decision.

The insider's view, on the other hand, regards the necessities of the choice once made, be it by an instantaneous insight (though perhaps resisted for a while) or after lengthy deliberation (where the pondering scale perhaps never dips quite completely). There is a lot of "Should I have . . . ?" and "Why didn't I . . . ?" to be sure, but just as much "Because at the time . . ." The "because" suggests that yet another theory of free choice, that of *indifference* cannot capture the internal experience of such agonizing agency. For "indifference" here refers to a mind perfectly balanced on the cusp of equally motivated actions; it does not mean that the human being does not care. "Indifference" is a thin, perhaps even paradoxical notion of freedom briefly to be taken up again later on (see the Conclusion, C2 and Note 26). It seems to me to describe a rare but real condition of which the external theory does not quite jibe with the internal experience.

Let me, for a moment, just go on considering the "could have done otherwise" kind of agency, and since we're in Never-Never Land, stipulate that nothing compels me even slightly to action either way—no irresistible natural forces (including biological needs), no necessitating inner power (be it of passion or reason). For my part, in that situation I would indeed be like Buridan's Ass which starved to death between two precisely equidistant and equi-tempting piles of hay—unless Lucretian chance, a slight swerve one way or the other, saved me. But chance and agency don't go well together, as show the cogent arguments against hoping to save human freedom by an appeal to a probabilistic physics (one that admits small-scale indeterminacies). One might say that chance is irrational necessitation, the worst of both the human and the natural worlds: random unreason and meaningless compulsion.[24]

But when we transcend the understanding of human agency as *constricted by choice-terminology* such as "I can do otherwise" or even "I can no other," when we take it to be the capacity for acting, doing deeds pure and simple, it comes to this claim: I am an originator, a *causa suae* (being female, or otherwise *causa sui*), a self-cause, a sort of prime mover, who moves myself, myself selecting the motivation; in the end it's (within circumstantial limits) "up to me" what I do—not only *which option I finally choose* but—and this under-regarded item comes first—*what options I in fact propose to myself.* This conception is, of course, a scandal to naturalistic thinking. Nonetheless, because we can't live without it, we may just have to live *with* it—most people, the "folk," in fact do. One consequence is that, strictly speaking, there can be no complete science of man, since a true agent conforms to no universal law of action, and yet—here's the paradox—adheres to the paths of thought. The human lords of the universe are subject to its laws as bodies, perhaps also as souls, but not as intellects.[25]

And yet that which *motivates* an agent both from ahead of the action, as its fulfilling and final end, and from behind, as its initiating and maintaining motor, is generally agreed to be desire, an object-generated want. One might imagine desire by an analogy from physics. Life de-linked from desire is like inertial motion, going on indefinitely in a straight line with no causal push behind or pull before, while wanting is like accelerating motion, increasing in velocity-intensity as it approaches its center of attraction, its goal, or veering in direction as distracting force vectors intervene. (The analogy may also serve to remind us that ultimately nature herself labors under an agency problem: What's behind it all?)

But desire, an affect, is basically subject, for all its waywardness, to biological mechanisms. Doesn't that tie human agents immediately, non-metaphorically, to the laws of physical nature? One way of partially slithering out from under this bind is the notion of a second-order or master-desire (to be taken up below). A second-order desire (or volition) is piggy-backed on the primary one, the one that is directly related to the action; it is, as it were, the stamp of approval on the immediately activating "natural" desire. The same higher-level desire can also work to back up a want of lesser standing by giving it the larger framework of more expansively *felt reasons*. With this ratcheting-up into the realm of reason—desire by desire; volition by volition—passion and action begin to meld as desire develops its thoughtful aspect. Aristotle felicitously calls affects, including desire, "immattered reasons" (*enyloi logoi*). And so psycho-physical law becomes wishy-washily amenable to human agency. It isn't strictly logical, but it seems pretty reasonable as an account of the co-option of human nature by human freedom.[26]

As a conclusion to this inconclusive section, I will simply list a sampling of the problems currently raised. An article entitled "What Kind of Agents Are We," begins reasonably: "What kind of agent are we? . . . First, we do not know," but continues, "At this point in the history of inquiry, traditional notions of agency are dead and dying, and their replacements have yet to be born or yet to reach maturity." That confidence arises from the author's "naturalistic orientation" toward the human condition: Not only will scientific investigation discover the basis of human agency but its replicable findings will, *ipso facto*, transit from the researchers' personal opinion to accepted theory, held as expert communities hold mature notions—impersonally. Although the new theories are as yet unevolved and the future is open, the book on the past is closed. More particularly (and somewhat precipitously): "[W]e are not the ideal causal agents of our mostly theological ancestral world view." Here, in two lines of poetry is a summary of this antiquated theological view:

But God left free the will, for what obeys
Reason, is free, and reason he made right, . . .

Milton makes it clear that these free agents of theology are, in fact, compelled by right reason. (Happily why reason is right is not a problem within the purview of this book, or it would never end.)[27]

Some people, however, still think that agent-causality, taken ideally, as simply causative, is not as dead as all that—indeed that the salvation of their self-respect depends on such agency. To them the question is whether such originating agency is *compatible* with natural mechanisms, with physiological, neurological, and psychological lawfulness, it being understood that phenomena don't "obey" ordained law as people do for the most part, but that processes "express" immanent laws without thinkable exception—partial human obedience being an empirical observation and complete natural compliance a rational hypothesis. "Compatible" here should not mean "by some convenient redescription of the volitions that cause agents to act." Rather, what this realistic compatibilism probably has to be content with is a somewhat opaque but perhaps uncircumventable parallelism such as Kant proposes: purposive action and mechanistic processes run side by side. But immediately this problem arises: These parallels must cross or coincide somewhere short of infinity, else how is human action actually to change the natural world? Implicit is the question of dualism: How distinct is the realm of agents (souls and selves) from the realm of mechanisms (matter and force or whatever physical causality replaces mechanism)? Are non-naturalistic agents not only free but efficaciously free? As I said above, the selves of interest are of course natural, embodied; the question is: Do they have a salient aspect, freedom, that escapes a naturalistic understanding and is yet able both to direct our physical bodies and to intervene in nature at large? Is such freedom to be understood as arising in, evinced by complete objectivity, radical non-commitment, that is, as the above-mentioned indifference, or is it rather found in rational self-conscious necessitation? And, of course, the most immediate problem is the preservation of practical action: Is there individual responsibility, unbeclouded by ifs and buts? One, more urgent, way to put it is: Without "ideal" agency is there even a thinkable self? (For the fate of agency under the naturalistic theory of consciousness, see Note 28 to this chapter.)[28]

D. Self: Subject

I/soul and subject/self are two pairs it is more interesting to distinguish than to throw together. At the risk of being scandalously sweeping, I would say that I/soul *faces* the world and self/subject *is* the world. The ancients, by and large, think of the Soul that says "I" as being confronted with a world, an "It" (meaning every kind of otherness taken as one whole, be it material, ideal, even, somehow, ensouled). How this I apprehends the world is a problem variously solved: by the body's sensing of appearances and the soul's non-sensory intuitions of being (Plato); by the imagination's bringing the forms of sensory objects without their matter before the receptive intellect (Aristotle); by the soul-pneuma's ability to form re-presentations of the world in and before it (Stoics). In modern times, a Subject comes forth, one that confronts a world as its radical antithesis (Descartes' "thinking/ extended thing") or constructs it out of a formless influx (Kant's sensory manifold) or creates it *ex nihilo* or generates it *ab ovo* (the German Idealists' Absolute) or construes it in its own image (the Romantics' willed creation). The subject does not look to or into the world; it abuts, underlies, or bears it. As it imports subjectivity to its world, so it evinces subjectivity within itself. In other words, it becomes self-conscious in a more radically, objectlessly reflexive way than was ever meant by the "Know Thyself" of Apollo's Temple or the "examined life" of Socrates' practice. But such a self-regarding self is a Self *par excellence*.[29]

It is, to my mind, this Self, a self that has become a problem to itself, which secures—or fails to secure—"agency." For one thing, that's the language used in the contemporary literature—the problem (to the inquiring selves) being whether they themselves or others have—what Hume denied them—a "personal identity." Such identity seems to require some kind of subject-self, a unified, lifelong substrate to "synthesize" (as Kant would say) experience and to preserve its memory. Without such an underlying continuity, be it of soul or subject, it is hard to imagine how a "life," the subject of a biography, can even come about, not to speak of its entering into a comparison with others (a life such as Plutarch, the biographer of biographers, produced in his *Parallel Lives*: *hoi bioi hoi paralleloi*. I cite the Greek title because it displays the special word for a life-span, a whole: *bios*, as opposed to *zoe*, day-to-day living).[30]

I want to reinforce a rough, large-grained claim I am making here (well aware that generalizations rarely withstand close-up inspection, though believing that they need not therefore forfeit their office of marshalling thought): The ancients had, by and large, not a shallower though a simpler view of what later becomes our selfhood. Whether the soul with its parts, laid itself, as it were, alongside being with its gradations and tried to apprehend it (Plato), or whether it activated an organic body so as to receive from its senses forms of objects for the intellect (Aristotle), or any subsequent elaborations or reductions—the soul primarily faced its other, its object, be it real or ideal. And its ability to communicate with fellow-souls and to intervene in the world was a gift taken for granted.[31]

Here is a way to see what I am trying to express: Self-consciousness had not become a fixed problem, not because it was not the very path of philosophy to go to and "reflect" on the realm within, but because the soul was unabashedly conceived in metaphorical terms, as a territory which its possessor could perambulate from its front into its most intimate recesses—which were also its highest reaches, those wherein the commonalities of thought were located. Sense perception, imagination, discursive thinking, and insight or at-sight (intuition) were the ascending or increasingly inward locations in these figurative topologies. The most beautiful of these that I know of is Augustine's figure for our memory, its "fields and spacious palaces."[32]

In the shift from soul to self, problems emerge that are hidden by figurative soul-schemes, be they overt or implicit. How does the self, a subject, become an object to itself?—being a world unto itself it must somehow find its other within, or be psychically inert, uneventful. And even if it conceives of itself as not entirely self-sufficient, as living in an environment of influxes, this self cannot think of these as just given but, as I said, will regard them as material to be constructed, formed, or at least construed, interpreted. And so agency will not be, as it was in philosophical antiquity, a direct, naive consequence of a soul confronting a given world, enabled to apprehend it by the cooperative work of its psychic powers with which to receive, engage, and know it, a soul, moreover, *itself* open to *outside examination*. The self begins rather with an inner *cross-examination*: con-science and purity of will, where the internal other is another self, a *my-self*. I will want to propose that freedom is located in this conversation between a subject- and an object-self.[33]

But first to the fate of the self in current considerations. Here, as so often, the firm believers are to be found among practitioners. Psychiatrists, concerned with identity-pathologies, take selfhood as the baseline condition, a vulnerable one. "Schizophrenia appears to involve alteration in the sense of self"—especially in the conception of agency, be it by overextension of agency to others (delusions of influence) or by attenuation of agency over oneself (delusions of alien control). Yet the self is also "durable . . . in the face of major insult." Evidently when push comes to shove, it must be the self that is called on to serve.[34]

However, among the conceptualizers, that is, among the philosophers as opposed to the working psychiatrists, the self is problematized to extinction. Hume is the originating extremist here. To him, the "idea of self," of personal identity, is a mistake of the imagination. One current Hume-inspired direction is to distribute it over multitudes of psychic, brain-based mechanisms—without a supervening organ of unification—a "de-cerebralized, distributed, heterogeneous vision of the machinery of the mind." Another is to expand this machinery beyond the boundaries of an individual to include the inciting and guiding environment, for if so much of our self is already unconscious, why not distribute it to an external, non-biological cognitive economy? Or why not go for "ownerless streams of consciousness"? Yet another breakdown of the self is accomplished temporally; the traditional soul was figuratively spatial, that is, simultaneously present as an atemporal structure. The structurally temporal self is constituted from temporal segments, held together, as it seems, somewhat as are the fibers of a rope by being twisted up into each other; allied to this notion is the post-modern self as a narrative, as a story that people (apparently pre-selves) tell of and to themselves over time (though such a narrative may also at some point record a completed whole).[35]

I think Hume's radical denial of self is not so hard to deal with. His theory of the perceptions of the human mind as consisting of impressions of various degrees of vividness plus a small number of operations is, in its mechanicality, just not up to the task of capturing reflective and reflexive selfhood—perhaps even actually designed to evade it. The other more technical proposals, floated within the current cognitive climate, have specialized motivations, from a desire to forestall the hunting of this long-exposed snark to inciting a research program or at least contributing an analytic terminology. Interesting as they are, they run up against an apparently indefeasible experience of our identity, that is our self-sameness with ourselves, at moments and over time.

Yet it may well be that people's sense of self really does individually differ, that it is indeed (non-pathologically) episodic for some, a work-in-perpetual-progress for others, for some a search with or without direction, for others a self-told narrative under continual or continuous revision—or even a now-this-now-that, depending on the temperament we were born with or on the conditions we found ourselves in when we were children and the influences we chose to admit as we grew up. One way to put it is that, whatever is the real date of our *floruit* (as handbooks used to say), we may experience ourselves, now and then, as antique or medieval souls or modern or post-modern selves—discovering or constructing in ourselves a soul-shape that fits a found or chosen life-shape.

I think that beyond these modes there is a root experience, even a flawed description of which makes it difficult to be persuaded of reductionism, of the flat-out identity of brain and mind. To be entitled to say that one thing *is* another, it seems to me, you have to produce some sort of isomorphism, some sameness of form, under which two ways of speaking refer to the same thing. But a brain scan just doesn't seem to be transformable into the soul's "spacious fields and palaces." I think it is entirely plausible that the thinking efforts and the sensory experiences of the self "emerge" from underlying physicalistic entities, but I haven't yet read an exposition of emergence in which the words didn't claim more than the understanding could follow. In the respect here relevant, emergence is a "coming-forth from," a supervenience of conscious experience upon non-conscious matter and force. Such experience is not observable from the outside, objectively by any known instrument, but is accessible and reportable from the inside, subjectively and without instrumental intevention. How these twin miracles of transition from "the brain functions" to "I feel" or of "I experience" to "you observe" eventuate not a soul can tell. What good is it to call consciousness an "*epi*-phenomenon"? It may be that in a laboratory—to me it's the *basic* phenomenon.[36]

Here is my description of the sense of self (shading into soul): It feels as if it had a "far-back" and a "deep-down." "Far-back" is the feel of accumulated time-laminations (as it were), of temporally ordered episodes, recoverable directly or reached by steps. Thus arises my temporally *continual* self, whose *continuous* seamlessness is a spontaneous inference from my ownership of each event and from the transforming or confirming relation most events bear to the others. "Deep down" describes a sense of hierarchy, confirmed by time, of what belongs to the foundations of my being and to its own work together with my attachment to it, through deeply-based permanent interests up to merely passing frontal enthusiasms. This psychic hierarchy is anti-symmetric with the worldly one I also live with—its delvings descend back down from the sensory and emotional interface with the world into a deep inwardness, while my worldly explorations begin with before-the-eyes exteriority and go forth to penetrate its surface. Occasional seismic disturbances intimate to me that this inner structure is vulnerable to reality-earthquakes and psychic breakups. There is also a sort of huge treasurehouse; its contents are almost hyper-accessible; they are quite intrusive in some moods though they deny themselves to me in others; they consist of portraits of friends, figures from fiction, cherished insights and favorite facts—all with their verbal formulations. There is as well an atmospheric element, those moods that rise like local exhalations, and there is real weather boiling up over the whole territory, the affects: feelings, emotions, passions. There is also a lumber room where old misdeeds and embarrassments are piled up, out of sight, emitting occasional rumbles and once in a while an importunate escapee.[37]

But what most comes up front over time and is most pervasive in life is *thinking*. Not, God forbid, rationality, the disposition sometimes to rationalize (to recruit reasons for what has none), sometimes to formalize (to say in symbols what might be said in words), sometimes to resort to argumentation (when intimation and conjecture would be more in order). Of course there must be stretches of logical reasoning—though by its very nature, such formal sequences enter thinking in limited spans, since their beginnings require prior insight and their conclusions subsequent interpretation. However, when such inferential passages are called for, of course they must be valid; this is the demand of thought's bony armature, logic. By and large, the thinking I mean cannot be figured (to switch metaphors) as rule-linked straight chains but rather as self-crossing loops (even that unbounded one which symbolizes infinity), helical ascents (that are always at the same place of the cycle as viewed from above, though at a higher elevation), grounding circularities (since grounds are *ipso facto* self-grounded), and above all, the zig-zag of interior conversation (the reciprocity of pro and con by which *logos* lives).

Socrates says that thinking is the "voiceless dialogue within of the soul with itself." He means, I think, a somewhat more objectively dialectical pursuit than I do by the conversation between me and my self. I want to describe its way as precisely as I can, because, as I said, I think that it is the *condition of internal freedom*, my last element of willing as set out in this chapter. As I've said, such freedom is an issue to us far more than it was to the ancients. Thus it is a *modern* self-sensibility I am in pursuit of—not that human nature has changed, but that human interests have, though by no means irreversibly: We're still up to us.[38]

E. Freedom: Thinking

I think that "free will" and "will" are not the same, the sign being that one may think about the will as a capacity for choiceless self-subjugation; I'll continue to set that out in the Conclusion. Meanwhile, in current discussions the free-will problem dominates, so in collecting the ingredients of will freedom is crucial. It is also daunting. For one thing, there are at least two realms of freedom: first, inner freedom, often regarded, not quite rightly, I think, as primarily dedicated to free will, and second, external freedom, civil liberty, devoted to the politico-socio-economic condition. This latter has to do with the many ways of being able to do as one intends and chooses, from having the right freely to express oneself without fear of persecution to having the opportunity to make a living that supports a life of one's own with a decent chance of success. Happily this liberty is not the issue here, at least by my working fiat; in actual practice, inner and outer freedom seem to be—almost—inextricably related.

I have persuaded myself that freedom, as it pertains to the self, is not adequately captured by the different notions of free will: not by "having been able to do otherwise," that is, by the *ex post facto* judgment of having had alternatives; nor by terminal contingency, the last moment, unconditioned, out-of-nowhere decision; nor by indifference, be it the minutely balanced equality of motives that stymies choice or the complete absence of subjective preference that appears as perfect objectivity; nor illimitableness, the simple, gaping openness of mere possibility. Choice-freedom is just too narrow, contingency too causeless, indifference too disengaged; and illimitableness too vacuous for delineating freedom.[39]

What, then, *is* inner freedom? A great writer says, "The happiness of a writer is the thought that can become all feeling, the feeling that can become all thought . . . a pulsing thought, an exact feeling"—but you don't have to be a writer and happiness isn't its only name. Freedom seems to me to be such a sense-enkindled thought and a thought-elucidating feeling—for anyone. It is an *accompaniment* of inner life, not an *aim* as in political life. To be sure, it has external conditions, gifts of luck gratefully received (and perhaps more a gratuitous advantage than a strict necessity): anchorage in a just and prosperous country, absence of ill health and of acute trouble, availability of leisure and of steady sources of pleasure, fruition of well-placed love and steady effort. But the feel of freedom seems to me to arise *within*, not always but often, as an accompaniment to feeling-suffused internal dialogue, a bloom on self-communing.[40]

Now to particularize the way the sense of freedom supervenes on self-conversation (I write supposing that it's for me just as it is for my fellow-humans): At first, I'm often neither here nor there, disengaged and wandering in mind (perhaps this *is* a kind of liberty of indifference, though

the indecision is not between two fixed choices but among illimitable possibilities and awaits the pure contingency of a Lucretian swerve to start coag-
ulated mentation). Then I focus, I concentrate (and here I guess I *could* do
otherwise, circumvent myself, escape engagement—but not forever). And
thereupon I find myself dividing into two—questioner and responder—
but strangely enough without being able to distinguish them except by
function, distinct as personae but not as persons. I question and step forth
as asker. Step forth out of what? A sort of coruscating fog, an expectantly
unsettled mood, an intimation of depths to be drawn on. Then I listen
for an answer and come out with a response. Whence comes the answer?
From the same abyss, for which "Unconscious" is a hopelessly evasive term,
enmeshed in theory and unhelpfully negative.[41]

Where and what is freedom here? As I said, I think it is a thought-
infused feeling or feeling-steeped thought in the space opened up between
me and myself, where eventuates the interplay between my finite thinking
ability and the assertive demands of the being of things. In particular, it is
my power to coagulate, to shape out of the dormancy of my consciousness
that negative form of an answer which constitutes a question and which
will, on occasion, fit itself about the matter sought and haul it in. It is the
exhilarating sense that between the self that asks and the me that answers
we are sometimes adequate to ourselves and the world, that the joint effort
is now and then rewarded. And finally, to be honest (as politicians tend
to say, unmindful of the suspicion the phrase must cast on their previous
speech), there is the—temporary—exhilaration of finding a cleverly conclusive formulation of the inquiry that provides the passing relief of a premature finality—a freedom to call for temporary closure. I am encouraged
in these musings by an etymological fact: an early meaning of "to free"
is "to love." This inner freedom is, then, once again, a supervenient gift,
like—perhaps even identical with—the pleasure that Aristotle says is the
bloom upon rightly directed activity. Outer freedom, liberty, on the other
hand, is not a gift but a goal, and a high-maintenance one.[42]

This view of freedom, plus the claim that it delineates the primordial
freedom, is not novel, but it is, as they say, "nonstandard." The conception
I have bypassed here is the very one most agitated in the literature on will
and considered above, that of free agency. This more hard-edged freedom
mediates between the inner and outer kind; it is on the threshold between
willing and executing, where choosing launches into doing, decisions are
realized in action, and the will is ratified in the world. Of this freedom,
whose existence I only doubt occasionally but whose salubrity, quite often
(as set out in the Conclusion), there are scores of definitions.[43]

Here is a concise summary. A first distinction, broadly corresponding
to inner and outer freedom, is that between positive freedom and negative liberty. The first tends to be defined as *autonomy* (self-lawgiving) and

self-determination (self-control), the latter, in terms of the *absence of outside coercion* preventing one from doing what one wants—hence "negative" liberty. Ways of describing positive freedom include: a close enough identification with one's own goals and values so as not to be deflected by alien interferences; the ability to give higher order approval to one's first order desires; intentions and desires that effectively cause action, that is, a capability of mental acts to effect physical actions non-mechanistically. Extreme approaches to negative liberty include: the denial that there is external coercion when it happens to coincide with wishes and intentions, as in compatibilism; and, ultimately, the abolition of internality in favor of a naturalistic self which is of a piece with external nature and its laws, and so neither at liberty to act nor responsible. In between radical autonomy and complete heteronomy (subjection to other-imposed law, whether by nature or an alien will), there are any number of schemes for saving a semblance of liberty or rescuing responsibility without it. And, of course, there are many takes on freedom and liberty entangled: as the power of preference, of rational deliberation, of independence of mind, of worldly efficacy. Finally there is the last, relativistic, resort: freedom as radically context-dependent, defined by circumstances.[44]

F. Will Collected

> WE SCHOLARS: "Get rid of all masters"—here too this is what the vulgarian instinct wants; and after science has, with this happiest success, escaped from theology, whose "handmaid" she was for too long, she is now bent, in full presumption and non-comprehension, on making laws for philosophy, and on herself playing—what am I saying!—the *philosopher.*

As so often with Nietzsche's prognostications, he foresees wonderfully the terms of what will happen—only the event inverts the terms. Thus it is not the scientists who have arrogated philosophy to themselves, but the philosophical professionals who have been captivated by a possible science "of" human consciousness. The proposition is everything here: There *is* a flourishing science of what *underlies* embodied consciousness, but no commonly accepted conclusion that it is indeed a science *of* consciousness.

Is contemporary scholarship about the will coherent, can one collect it into a mainstream opinion? I think the answer is yes but no. That is because in current debate "will" means mostly "free will," and free will is precisely what disappears under determinism—which either in its aggressive or in its pusillanimous mode has nearly won the professional field. Thus thinking about the will is propagated more through the intricacies of its problematic than through its relevance to human conduct.

To save and reconstruct the remnants, one first thing is needful: to bring consciousness, and with it the will as a discernible human capacity, back from its reduction to a condition of the material brain or an illusion of the epiphenomenal mind. It seems that in the end this might be *done* in the same way as it was *known* in the beginning: If Descartes, by a pseudo-inference, could get from "I think" to "I am," then I might, by a tautological inference (so to speak) go from "I am conscious" (as I once *thoughtlessly* supposed) to "I *am* conscious" (as I now *thoughtfully* affirm). The explanation is that consciousness is a condition *more* than just self-evident; it is self-corroborating. The impossibility of proving this sense of being conscious to be false helps:

> We could discover all kinds of startling things about ourselves and our behavior; but we cannot discover that we do not have minds, that they do not contain conscious, subjective, intentionalistic states; nor could we discover that we do not at least try to engage in voluntary, free, intentionalistic mental states.

For we would be intending to do it with our consciousness, and neither could our intention be an illusion without some sort of conscious collusion from us, nor could a display of brain scans to our conscious comprehension do the trick.[45]

Supposing, then, that there is volition, and it has features, and these are collectible into a something termed "will." What are the salient features, what contours remain uneroded through the sandstorm of fine-grained and hard-edged debate?

First is a *very* salient non-feature that has remained fixed from the middle ages into the most present post-modernity: *fear*—fear faced with faith by our medieval theological forbears, with the fierce joy in humbug finally exposed by our modern philosophical progenitors, and with much virtuoso whistling in the dark by the contemporary scientific fraternity. The object of this will-connected fear changes: first fear of a vitiated will and consequent sin, then fear of being impeded by old inhibitions in the great project of re-forming the world, now fear, on one side of *folk* morality nullifying research and on the other of morality being undone by *insider* science.

These fears—or their inverse, that fierce satisfaction—seems to me to drive the most agitated framing of the will-debate, namely the contemporary versions of the compatibilism question, and its occasional recourse to a contorted, not to say sophistical argumentation: It *may* be the false impression of a layperson, but it looks to me as if a very local professional philosophical preoccupation had entered into a partnership with a heartfelt urgency of concern about the extinction of personal will—concern for its discrediting by neuroscience, but also its evaporation in the social media, where millions of miniscule expressions of willfulness issue in a hyper-personal simulacrum of human will. This is my point: Though it may be moderated into mere uneasiness by scholarly decorum, fear for human agency, whose inner motor is the will, infects current thinking about the latter; it is, willy-nilly, a constituent of the way will is conceived by those who want to save it.

One telling feature of this endangered will is that it is hosted by a self that has itself become doubtful. Is it as much a center of control, primarily of self-control, as is ordinarily supposed—by those many, at least, who have not given up on themselves? Introspection, it is argued, does not conduct us to a putative "Central Headquarters," since the sources of our decisions lie beneath consciousness: "[O]ur decision bubbles up to consciousness . . . We do not witness its being *made*, we witness its *arrival*." That is indeed a frequent volition-experience of the will narrowly conceived in the modern mode: Our willing is not in control because our self's self-*consciousness* does not go, by its very concept, far enough back into the latent hinterland of the *unconscious*, which instead sends forward directives: "*You* can no other." Long ago, at its first Augustinian formulation, the will was a proudly powerful capacity for sin, a potent desire for self-sufficiency and independence; the current will is a cowed creature, subject not to a revealed divinity but to an occulted subconscious—"an ill-favored thing, sir, but mine own."[46]

A second feature almost always ascribed to the will is rationality. In older versions of the will such as Thomas's, the intellect, both in its theoretical and practical aspect, dominates willing from way back in the process—indeed will *is* practical intellect. The closer we come to our time the more writers shorten the will-event, in the spirit of Hobbes, who reduces it to "the last appetite, or aversion immediately adhering to the action"; the preceding flip-flops together make up deliberation. Currently, willing is most often thought of as episodes of decision- or choice-making (decision and choice being considered to be pretty much the same), while the process of deliberation is more or less suppressed; indeed in laboratory experiments on willing, it is so curtailed as to be pretty much cut out altogether. The emphasis is more on forming intentions, and desires, beliefs, and reasons, pushing as motivations or pulling as goals, are all folded into this activity, be it long or short in duration. However ratiocination is conceived—mentally and freely, mentally but mechanistically, materially and reductively—the will is in fact rarely delineated without some rationality. But by and large it is an operational type of thinking, a figuring, a calculating of pros and cons, not some version of receptive insight. So the thoughtfulness of willing is curtailed, yet the feeling-tone of willing doesn't generally take its place, although one might expect it to.[47]

A third and last feature of willing turns up in passing in earlier works, but is laid out clearly and variously in contemporary treatments, first by Harry Frankfurt. It is will to the second power, W^2, and it might be thought of in general and in particular. It is the particular sort that has spread through the Anglo-American literature. The general W^2 stayed pretty much on the Continent. This first, general will to will an unspecified object is what Nietzsche says he means by the Will to Power: vitality seeking its own, mere expression, with an obscure practical object. The second, particular version, referred to above, is expressed thus: "Someone has a desire of the second order either when he wants simply to have a certain desire or when he wants a certain desire to be his will." To understand this key sentence, we must realize that "wants to have a certain desire" is a second order expression—"wants to want" ("wants" means "desires")—and one must know that a will is an "*effective* desire, one that moves . . . a person all the way to action." It is essential to being a person to have second order volitions. A creature that has only first order desires—simply wants something—or has only second order desires but no volitions—simply flabbily wishes to want something—is a mere "wanton." "When a *person* acts, the desire by which he is moved is either the will he wants or a will he wants to be without. When a wanton acts, it is neither." This description precisely matches the way a two-and-a-half-year-old whom I was babysitting, the very paradigm of nascent will, of terrible-twoness, once began a sentence: "I want not to want . . ."[48]

In other words, a person is a being who clinches its desires by willing them. That action at least intimates the feel of willing—that of gathering oneself to oneself, of self-clutching (one might say), which is generally missing in a literature so fixed either on the "could have done otherwise" or the "indifference" aspect of free will. However, this notion of a second order will, in offering a secondary solution to the problem of free will, almost eclipses it as a primary temperamental capacity.

One more word here about the "why" of this reductionist contemporary direction. I think the basic answer lies in the very way the problem is now framed, namely as an *opposition*, the opposition to physicalistic "determinism," (as it has been called since the second half of the eighteenth century) and as a defensive response to the accumulating findings of brain science beginning two centuries later. So while I'm at it, here is an *obiter dictum* on such nagging oppositions as an argument-type: I suspect—no, have learned from books and life—that solutions to perennial problems, short of the perfectly respectable one of declaring a mystery, often lie in showing age-old antitheses to be not mutually exclusive but complementary—not merely compatible, living alongside each other by tricky equivocations, but necessary to each other in the nature of things. So I shall try to frame my Conclusion in that inclusionary mode.[49]

Back to second order volitions and their relation to free will: Frankfurt refreshingly says that his conception "appears to be neutral with regard to the problem of determinism." However, there are other factors that are similarly but less acceptably not involved in his notion: an analysis of wanting or of evaluating a desire; an interest in morality or other values; a concern for the practical freedom to do what one wants (since he sanguinely thinks that the deprivation of the freedom to act does not necessarily undermine freedom of will); a somewhat more telling argument against the stymieing regress to yet higher order wanting (since he confidently—and surely rightly—claims that one may end the regress by a decisive commitment which then "resounds" through the potential regress of higher order). So second order volition, an effectively confirmed will, is not necessarily moral, or effective, or particularly reflective. It is instead the all-purpose, internal, limited activity of having evaluated desires, *preferences*—a desiccated but just recognizable delineation of a human capacity. But above all, the following factor is in this theory explicitly not necessary to acting "of one's free will," of "wanting ones will": that one's will should be *free*.[50]

This last condition appears to cast the theory into the class of paradox, as well it might, since it is in fact an early contemporary version of compatibilism. There is, to be sure, an explanation given for saying that it is not necessary for acting of one's own free will that one's will should be free and, moreover, that one has responsibility for actions done even if one's will was not thus free. It is this: To have a will that is free is taken to mean that "one could have done otherwise," here construed as that one was "in a position to have whatever will he wanted," hence that one was responsible. (But the difficulty is that one's "free" will is often not free in that way. The most famous example of a will being no longer free to want, or to want to want any but one thing, is the example from Luther that I have cited several times: "Here I stand, I can no other." This *seems* to be an announcement of a W^2, a secondary will—the W^1 would be "wanting indulgences to be abolished." But it is, in fact, a claim to have been compelled by conscience. So I see this inconsequence in the Frankfurt sophism: The Luther case, and cases of lesser moral standing, even down to yielding willingly to desire on occasion, are cases of *self-determination*, of conscience having been consulted and heard and obeyed. Be it conscientious necessity, romantic necessity, or any sort of more mundane inner necessitation—the experience is one of freedom *because* we feel compelled. And here there is no paradox. For the crucial moment in willing used to be called "the determining of the will." Willing is therefore *internally* deterministic in its final phases, necessitated by its very character as will. One reason the "could do otherwise" criterion of free will seems defective is that a will determined is precisely a free will confirmed. The external "you must" is oppression and in principle always resistible: Nathan the Wise says, *Kein Mensch muss müssen*, "No human being is compelled to be compelled." But self-*determination*, internal compulsion, self-compulsion, not being overcome by alien passion but acceding to one's own deepest thought-desire—that *is* the traditional understanding of freedom. If, however, "compulsion," even self-compulsion, appears to be too forcible a term here, perhaps "conviction," concurring in the victory of persuasive good, is better.)[51]

Thus it seems to me that this second order volition is a rank-ordered abstraction from that communing of my evaluating self with my desiring self in which the "con-science," the common knowledge to which we, myself and I, are together privy has been assigned to a higher-level self. Evidently speech about the will (as all speech of the soul) is often either *figurative*, and therefore in earnest contexts proscribed as soupy poetry, or *schematic*, and therefore rejected in serious inquiry as thin abstraction. The left-over will here collected, conceived in the latter, schematic, mode, is indeed a diminished capacity. It has lost its host-soul, its motivations are small desires, its *modus operandi* is narrow decision-making, and its freedom just iterated wanting.

It isn't much: Can we do with even less of it?

Conclusion

Un-willing

A. Will-Summaries

I've been working up to my conclusion by way of scores of other's opinions. Of the preceding eleven chapters, ten were given to human beings' expositions, but the middle one, Chapter VI, was devoted to our language, which also has, so to speak, something to whisper to us about the will.

Here are three of its intimations: An account of the will-root reveals (to my mind) a decline from *well*-fare to *will*-fulness, from good to be had to power to be asserted—and power asserted is incompetence confessed. Second, no Indo-European language appears originally to have had a pure simple future, meaning one built into the verb, not even the verb "to be" that provides the auxiliary form; I can say "I think, therefore I am," but not "therefore I will." For "I will" does not mean "I will *be* in the future"; it means "I *am* using my will." (Descartes would certainly have agreed to this new proposition, but it is not the famous one.) Indeed there is no such thing as "being in the future" since the future is a non-being, inarticulable—except as an intentional redirection of the present, a vectoral inflection of the now-point. Third, in the more meticulous usage of bygone times, the verb for "willing" (as distinct from "being") was conjugated thus: "I will, you and he shall." Why? Because "shall" (past: "should") means "ought," and I can tell you and him what ought to be done, but I can't direct your will; a commanded will is a cancelled will; will is inalienably *mine*, *yours*, and *his*. So language itself alerts us to the decline of the word will from objective good to *subjective* intensity, to the *intentional* nature of futurity, and the *inalienable* first-person nature of willing.

Now I will give brief summary reviews of a score or so out of the half-hundred plus versions of will reported in this book, those that seem to me most humanly poignant and/or most pregnant with modernity. I mean them to be both reminders for faithful readers and as a quick catch-up for those who skipped through the preceding three-hundred plus pages. I shall follow the not-always-chronological order of the chapters.

1. *Socrates* is (retrospectively speaking) pre-volitional. I say "Socrates" because we have black-on-white what the Socrates of the dialogues said but only speculatively what Plato, his author, thought. This Socrates simply lacks a notion of the will, because his "psychology" forestalls willings; his notion of good needs no intending will, and his maxim that "excellence is knowledge" implies that goodness needs no psychic enforcer, that between the deep-seated, whole-hearted, pan-psychic apprehension of the ways things are and the concordant action no volitional moment needs to intervene. For Socrates, "truly desirable" and "good" are coincident, and human virtue (*arete*) is competent knowledge. This dual hypothesis, that the good is lovable so that its study is attractive and that virtue is effective knowledge such as passes directly into action, is my twinned lodestar.

2. Nor is will to be found in *Aristotle's* works. Taking its notional place is intellectual appetite or appetitive intellect, desire informed by reason, which is simultaneously reason moved by desire. Choice, the deliberated counsel-taking, the plan-making selection of a means to a predetermined good, is a kind of proto-will that comes eventually to be identified with will. Though there is no faculty of will, there may be a will-analogue, a disposition which is, however, not even a virtue: *egkrateia*, "being in power [over oneself], self-control."[1]

3. The *Stoics*, the moderns of antiquity, are the runners-up in the emergence of full-blown will. Their formula "up to us" presages the contemporary will-definition "can do otherwise," indicating a choice among options, conceived as "this or not-this." Moreover, the element of something laboriously forcible is present in the renunciatory aspect of foregoing any option not within our power, of excluding imaginative aspiration—though just here the difference between "up to us" and will shows up as well: will is not self-renouncing. Furthermore, Stoic physicalism is the antecedent of modern materialism and thus of neurological volition.

The Epicurean *Lucretius*, less philosophically sophisticated but equally future-fraught, introduces the swerve of primordial particles, randomness, as the factor of free will, a forerunner notion, arguably, of Nominalist contingency, surely, of quantum-physical explanations of free choice and, most basically, of the idea that the "nature of *things*" is mirrored in human nature.

4. *Augustine* is *the* discoverer or inventor of will—it is the question of questions whether it is *found* as an element of human nature or *constructed* as a type of human conduct—of will (*voluntas*), that is, as a dangerously pervertible power. The will is given to us by God so that our creaturely faith in him shall be the more evident, and *ipso facto* as a capacity for prideful, rebellious self-assertion, for falling away, sinning, evil. This is the personal

autobiographical negative will; there is also its complementary antithesis, the positive, theological will; it appears in the human psychic economy as a binding, bridging power between polar mental powers, and as an analogue to the Holy Spirit of the Trinity it is, finally, Love itself.

5. *Descartes* will accord the will primacy in the mind, and the mind exclusivity in producing knowledge. His exposition contains, crucially, Stoic and Augustinian elements, though with a novel intention: certainty of knowledge for the sake of the mastery of Nature.[2]

The two modes of Cartesian mind are perceptions of the intellect and operations of the will. But the will is wider in scope than the intellect, indeed infinite, even as is God's will. We err by our own free will when we assent to those perceptions of the intellect that are not inerrant, namely neither clear nor distinct. As a self-affection of the soul, the will is the most self-sufficient of our capacities. This huge freedom of the will is, quite insouciantly, declared to be compatible with divine predetermination.

It might be said that Descartes brings together ancient premonitions, pagan as well as Christian, and melds them into a dominating complex that philosophically launches the modern will: Stoic freedom of choice as "up to us"—in current terms, "could have done otherwise"; their physicalist treatment of that willing soul; Augustinian volition as a self-willed capacity for errancy; the psychic primacy of will; the compatibilism of free will and theological determinism.

Now I reverse direction to turn to a philosophical theologian—or theological philosopher—it is a matter of contention—who combines pagan and Christian elements into a delineation of the will that is quite literally medieval, between the ages, and by the same token perhaps timeless.

6. *Thomas Aquinas* takes from Aristotle the distinction-moderating circular conception of an intellectual appetite that is as well (perhaps more definitively) an appetitive intellect. Such is the will taken as a whole, as the faculty of faculties; the circularity obviates the temptation to subordinate rationality to volition—the more future-fraught enticement. Thomas, also sees the operation of this faculty as temporally extended; willing has a number of sequential elements. Among these choice is only one, and it is indeed the locus of free will. For Thomas, as for Aristotle, choice is only one of the (pre-deliberated) *means* for achieving pre-set goods (or for deciding among equally permissible lesser goods). The will as a whole, however, is predetermined: Its first mover and its final end is God, in whom is happiness, the goal of all willing. Thus the will is our affective inclination toward, our desire for, God. Its apparent subjectivity is mitigated by the pull of an objective Good, apprehended by the receptive intellect, whose turn it is to be primary as it exercises that cognitive function. But then, again, the will is *self*-moving, self-assenting, self-controlling as well

as action-initiating, and in those potent operations, it is primary in its turn. This potency can, however, be depleted by passion.

7. As Thomasian will is altogether reasonable, so *Nominalist will* is terminally rational—and extremistically contingent. That event is said to be (logically) contingent which has no rational connections to any preceding event and which is unrelated to any necessity. It is a highly rationalistic conceptualization of terminal anti-intellectualism. Within it, Nominalist freedom is defined as moment-bound self-determination. This contingent human free will is conceived in analogy to God's will, an absolute will unconstrained by any limitation except the law of (non-)contradiction; such a God is *ipso facto* not directly knowable by us. Faith is all. So also is our will not intelligible to us, and its freedom is indemonstrable. Will is then only a useful hypothesis. So as to erase unnecessary entities, the will's freedom is declared to be not a separable quality of will but simply identical with it: Our will *is* our freedom, an absolute freedom, and our virtue resides not in our actions but entirely in the quality of the will's intention. Being contingent, wrenched loose from bonds of logical or physical causation, this will determines itself at the last moment; herein, as in much else, the Nominalists are future-fraught. While Thomas's phenomenology of time-extended will seems to have largely dropped out of contemporary considerations of willing, two Nominalistic notions resonate in modern will-philosophy: willing as a last-moment contingency and will as the sole locus of morality.

8. With *Hobbes* we are in modern times. The definition of will is brusque: It "is the last appetite in deliberation"; it puts a stop to doubt, that is, to the spontaneous succession of contrary appetites. Here Hobbes appeals to an invented etymology of "de-liberation," namely, "putting an end to the *liberty* we had of doing . . . according to our own appetite." Thus will is not so much a decision as just a last fixating moment. It is not, as the Scholastics argued, a power over its own initiatory power, a will to will—an absurdity for Hobbes—but just a stopping impulse when waffling goes over into sudden decision. The human mind is a material mechanism, and its will is compatibilistic, meaning that it is at once determined by, or rather, *is* a mechanistically mental moment and yet also a realization of one's desire. All that Hobbesian will lacks to be the will of neuroscience is the claim of discoverable, lawful, causal connections to previous conditions, for there is a touch of randomness, of a Lucretian swerve, in the final abrogation of deliberation. Hobbes's argument why imputation of blame and consequent punishment are nonetheless just is precisely that given by contemporary determinists: Punitive reactions direct the will-desire to socially useful behavior. A thoroughgoing physicalism, an ungrounded compatibilism, and will-mitigation as a means of social control—these are the avatars of our will-world.

9. *Hume* resists the will's traditional features: It is not a faculty; it has no inherent connection with its effect; it is not moved by reason; it has no liberty. Instead will is an indefinable impression, a mere epiphenomenon, an a-rational necessity, a concealed conjunction. In sum, it is an illusion; the illusory will is going to be a contemporary topic.

10. In *Kant's* Critiques, the will is refounded as a faculty in a revolution expressed terminologically thus: The denomination of will goes from "rational desire" into "practical reason"—desire drops out or at least back; freedom comes to the fore, since "practical" for Kant means at once what *ought to be* and what *is possible* through freedom.[3]

Freedom, in turn, is defined against law-determined Nature—a deeper refounding of the Cartesian dualism that comprehends all there is in an extended substance (nature) and a thinking substance (consciousness). Freedom is self-determination; thus it is surely a determinism, but a reflexive one, not other-imposed. In fact, desire is proscribed precisely for obeying a natural psycho-mechanism, for being other-directed. Thus the will, as free, stands not under universal laws as does nature, but under absolute commands—the categorical imperatives. They require simply that the will be true to its own being as practical and rational—practical in choosing what it ought to do and therefore can do (for the possibility of realizing the "ought" constitutes the realm of the practical), rational in choosing so that the choice is universalizable (for universality defines the realm of the rational).

Law-necessitated nature is at once the primal pre-conscious product of the underlying subject, the "I," and the external object of its experience, which yields an empirically fulfillable *theory*. But spontaneous freedom, which is always uncompromisingly non-empirical and sometimes counterintuitive, has for its arena of *practice* the subject's innermost conscious self and yields morality. (As an official morality, it had harsh consequences in the last century.) Kant has delineated a subjectivity that is, though ultimately volitional, will-centered, so self-disciplined as not to be willful. One might call it an antidote before the fact to Romanticism.

11. For *Fichte*, as a follower of Kant, the unbridgeable parallelism of nature and freedom poses a problem; Kant cannot explain *how* the will can be, so to speak, executively practical, can actually intervene in nature, how reason can become freely practical within a nature that is its own deterministically theoretical construct.

What is needed is a primary principle, one that is both intuitable (unlike the Kantian ego, the "I think" that accompanies all consciousness but is in itself beyond our knowledge) and involved in the generation of nature in such a way as to be capable of acting within it (unlike Kant's theoretical reason). This unitary primeval principle is self-positing intellect—self-derived and self-affirming. Thus it is a subject, an "I," but one that, unlike Kant's transcendental subject, soon develops marks of individual personhood, as well as marks of self-effecting will-hood. It "posits itself in space as a practical striving being," meaning that it generates nature as its own will-imbued and will-amenable domain; therewith the Kantian dualism is resolved. The will devolves by dialectical stages into recognizably human deliberative willing, though it is, from its origin, a primordial power really identical with the original self-producing I. "Willing . . . cannot be derived from anything higher." It is not clear whether this ego-will, although it descends into personhood, is originally individual—probably not. Early on, Fichte had proposed, as an object of faith, an infinite, suprahuman creator-will, a will-divinity—the first appearance known to me of a notion that in its personalized version enabled Romantic excess and in its politicized form sponsored tyrannical regimes.

I switch now to what presents itself to me, worlds apart though the detail of its various realizations may be, as a separable, generic way of regarding the will—as a supra-individual will, on a political or cosmic scale.

12. So *Rousseau* invents the notion of a "general will," which may be the will of no actual particular citizen. The Social Compact produces "a moral and collective body," whose Sovereign discerns what its general will is and makes the aberrant individual wills "conformable to reason," teaching each citizen what his true will is; he, "in fact, forces him to be free."

13. This blueprint for political totalitarianism is succeeded half a century later by a prescription for personal pessimism, when *Schopenhauer* conceives a noumenal, transcendent will that is the very internality of the world. It represents itself in the appearing world, which it "individuates"; it "objectifies" itself into embodied human wills. This will, the ground of the world and of human being, is a terrifying force imposing incessant, unforgiving, brutal striving, a chasing goad inducing fear and suffering, from which temporary relief is to be found only in esthetic contemplation and final escape only in renunciation of selfhood.

14. *Nietzsche* converts this cosmic pessimism into individual triumphalism—that of volitionally endowed superior human beings, aristocrats made to command obedience. This will is both an "affect-form" in chosen humans and a power beyond humanity; as trans-human, it is a potent ultimacy, the world's enlivening power. It is another will-notion fraught with potential political misapplication.

Next comes a quartet of authors whom I think of as the last ontologists of the will, the last thinkers (for the time being) to inquire into the will as seated within Being—human, cosmic, or world-transcending—before interest in willing and particularly in its freedom passes to the anti-ontological philosophers of mind and then to research-oriented cognitive and neuroscientists.

15. *Hegel* sites the will in his System in four main ways:

a. In "Logic" the will appears as a pure concept, at the last moment before the dialectical development of the logical notions' intrinsic meaning culminates in the complete Idea. While intelligence had so far taken the world as it is, will means to make the world as it ought to be, thereby acknowledging that the world is objective but that its own end, the Good, is merely subjective. The will learns of its inadequacy through the stubborn resistance of existence to its own projects, which are thus ever incomplete—indeed must be so, or willing as such would cease. But when the will is willing to become cognitive, it recognizes that the opposing world is "always already" implicitly what it, the will, wills it to be—rational in its reality. Thus it is reconciled with cognition in a union of identity-in-difference, as the theoretical and practical Idea become one and complete.

b. In "Mind" the will becomes specifically human. Again intelligence goes first, but now it turns into will when it recognizes that its thoughts, its content, are its own, freely determined by itself—that theoretical mind is in fact practical, active on its own. This will is at first selfishly focused on its particular ownness, while true freedom would lie in finding a universal content. The development of such willing is traced through its stages: an initial feeling of what ought to be, the development of individual inclinations, the response through choices that bring about a conscious personal interest in ends, and the final recognition that the free will must be free of particularity; this path culminates in the will's universal satisfaction, happiness. It is now a will whose very content is the will to will, infinite because not particularized to any external object; this is the happy, self-contented "actually free will." Hegel thus solves the problem of free will: freedom is not an attribute of choice but a way of being—"freedom *is* the will."

c. In "Right" the will unfolds itself into existence in the world. This is the objective phase of hitherto subjective mind: law (right and wrong), morality (good and evil), and ethics (social institutions). My exposition, however, stops with the subjective will.

d. In the "phenomenon" of the Terror, will enters history, which is the actualization in temporal figures of the logic that is history's plan set out in atemporal concepts. In "Right," the will in its claim to ultimate universality went into the world imperially. Now, as the Idea achieves reality in Spirit, the will as absolute freedom is incarnated in social human beings as a Rousseauian general will. Each subject in this generality thinks of its will as simply universal—abstractly, emptily willful, and thus easily perverted into ultimate singularity. Civil chaos ensues in this "self-willed punctuality," as generality falls apart into the discrete oppositionality of pointlike, atomic individuals. Now all are guilty, guilty of lacking generality, so each must perish. Ultimately the will as Absolute Freedom has one unmeaning, banal work: annihilating death. The intensity and precision of Hegel's analyisis of terror as will unleashed is unrivaled by any of my reading. Hegel's account of willing in general almost matches that of Thomas in acuteness of psychological observation, but he exceeds it in its awareness of one additional thing—a nightmare realization of the will Thomas had no occasion to dream of: the banal efficiency of modern willful totalitarianism.

16. *Bergson*'s understanding of the will is framed as an attack on a scientific mode in general and the geometricization of psychology in particular, on the notion that the soul's time can be symbolized as an extension. Extension, typically represented by a straight line, is quintessential externality: In its generation, the line extends away from itself; its elements lie outside each other; as measurable, it is additively quantitative. In mathematical representations of spatio-temporal nature, time perforce appears in just this way, as a homogeneous rectilinear extension. But that, Bergson says, cannot be the time of the soul, which is *intensive.* Successive psychic states are not outside each other and are not qualitatively homogeneous. Instead, each moment of sensed life has absorbed, has been qualified by, the previous one. Thus the now-moment has a qualitative degree of intensity that is the summation of a life lived; Bergson calls this intensive temporality "duration." It is a present that is, so to speak, pregnant with the past, as the past comes bearing the present.

Consequently, free willing is not decision, made at a last moment and free to have "gone otherwise." Instead, it is a self-determination issuing from a deep, cumulatively interpenetrating, past-in-present/present-in-past condition. Action is thus an expression of a temporally intensive self, and free will is the name for this spontaneous action based on a cumulative temporality, on a time-charged memory.

17. *Heidegger*'s view of the will takes many twists and turns, and this fact is not circumstantial but inherent to his—sometimes opportunistically—evolving thought.

One might expect the will to play a role in his early founding of existentialism, a philosophy centered on humans as existing in, cast into, a world in which they must deploy their possibilities. But not so; on the contrary, its ontological significance is subverted in favor of an original analytic of existence in whose terms the will and its quondam moral functions are very barely and problematically recognized.

In a next, brief period, the individual finds his freedom in yielding up his will to the *Führer.* As in the first phase individual will was occluded by being ratcheted up into objectless "resolve," so now it is degraded by deferral to a superior will.

After this miserable episode, Heidegger comes to grips with Schelling's version of will as the ultimate human essence, a subject-ground that strives to be and to know all the world, and that must be recalcitrantly evil so that the divine Truth, the Absolute, may reveal and exert the superior power of its Will to love. For Heidegger this inquiry exposes the ultimate impossibility of bringing together Absolute Truth and rebellious subjectivity. He takes the step Schelling shies away from and so aims to overturn the rigidified tradition of Western thought that adheres to boundless transcendents: There are only finite beings, and only they experience the truth of beings. But he retains Schelling's intimation that the will itself is evil in its self-assertion.

The last phase, then, applies this insight topically to current preoccupations. The evil will is identified with the technological framing of the world, the willful treatment of nature as a resource. This critique of modernity is complemented by a prescription for salvation: "letting-be." It begins in a *deliberate* rejection of the willful thinking characteristic of Western modernity, and so far it retains a touch of willing. But the issue is not so much *how* we think as *where* we look—in a direction, a wide expanse, that lets each thing emerge "in its own resting." Here finite human existence finds its function: to help in letting *things* be. But letting-be is also a *human* way of being. Since it is beyond the will, it is neither activity nor passivity. It is a waiting, a sort of expectant quietism, a "resolute openness." For what? Once again, individual decision—in Heidegger's etymology "non-scission from being"—is withdrawn from down-to-earth responsibility.

18. *Sartre* begins with the intentionality, the motivatedness of all true action, as distinct from mere behavior. But such motivation implies desires, wants, hence lacks or absences of the desired. Such absence is *our* doing; factual being can never exhibit these nothings. It is the "nihilating" power of consciousness that confers meaning on merely given, meaning-impervious Being and construes it as receptive to human intentions. And that is human freedom: our insertion of lack into the world. Freedom, although primal, is not the human *essence*, but rather our ever self-defining *existence*—a terminally non-generic, individual existence. Freedom is a way of existing: "I *am* it." Thus Sartre has obviated the free will vs. determinism debate, because his analysis sidelines the will. We are compelled to be free if we are to be human, and we are determined only insofar as we surrender our human existence by making ourselves into a piece of nature. The will as voluntary deliberation "is always a deception" because the existential choice has been made on the more primal ground of a prior freedom. Here the will is but freedom's loud-speaker of a deep intention.

19. I switch here from the synopses of authors to the summation of a widely held thesis, *compatibilism*. When choice becomes the defining

volition-issue in modern times, displacing ends and their fulfillment, the antithesis of freedom and determinism becomes, though the mode of modern inquiry be muted, an anxiety, not to say an agony.

Compatibilism offers relief, since it proposes that we may hold onto free will while accepting deterministic natural law. Since few accredited thinkers wish to go public as anti-scientific, while quite a few feel that they do make choices, compatibilism might attract some human—as its complex versions certainly do much academic—interest.

In one approach, compatibilism is made to work by a reinterpretation of the meaning of "willing." Its initiatory, originating *causa sui* sense is suppressed in favor of "willingness": If I get to do as I choose, what I wish, if, in a word, I act willingly, the question "could I have done otherwise?" is obviated, doesn't arise. In other words: When nature's determinism and my desire coincide, I *feel* free—and that is good enough. (Kant had thought that I can never be sure of my moral will's proper operation except when it hurts; this test is reversed by compatibilism; it's free will when it feels good.)

The above is a simple way of formulating the foremost current version; there are, however, many wrinkles to compatibilism and its relation to its on-the-face-of-it antithesis, determinism—which latter can in turn be articulated in versions that are not so hopelessly incompatibilist. I have persuaded myself that compatibilism is basically semantic subterfuge, made plausible by sophisticatedly, even sophistically, constructed examples.

20. In the later twentieth century, the relation of acts of volition to electrical brain activity was tested in the laboratory by *Libet*. He discovered that such activity began during a short observable interval before the volunteer-subject became conscious of having made certain simple decisions, such as whether to flick a wrist. This result was interpreted as showing that choosing began as an unconscious process preceding awareness, where "unconscious" was, in turn, equated with "physicalistic," that is, with brain-induced. A strange discovery was that there was a brief interval when the brain-dictated intention could be vetoed—in line with the intuition that will power is primarily interdictive: "Thou shalt not . . ." The Libet experiments have undergone searching critiques with respect to interpretation, but experiments in this century have not only corroborated the fact of brain activity antecedent to conscious mentation but have also shown that the brainwave patterns of subjects could predict who would succeed in solving simple brainteasers, that is, that brain activiy is very closely correlated to mentation.[4]

To me the conceptual problem in interpreting these results lies in identifying willing with choosing and in the precipitous identification of sub- or un-conscious volition or thought with the subserving physical event.

Finally, as investigations of volition become more diffused among competences, I forego authors in favor of current—though by no means ephemeral—issues, which I list in outline.

21. a. If, as it may for natural scientists, the will proves a mere *epiphenomenon*, an illusion-affect piggy-backed on a physical, law-determined event, then the question arises, what evolutionary function this delusory sense of agency serves (say, as an energizer of performance), and whether it is a social necessity (say, as an inhibitor of transgression) or whether we are better off dis-illusioning ourselves (say, to turn from retribution to therapy).

b. But for psychologists, the will remains an experiential fact, and the question is, what distinguishes it from mere wishing? One answer is intention—a commitment to action underwritten by a practical plan; as opposed to wish, will is intent on execution.

c. Then agency comes to the fore, and here the question is whether volition can be causal, whether intentions cause overt actions—more generally, whether consciousness causes bodily behavior and more simply, whether human beings are truly agents. Philosophical analysts and psychological therapists tend to separate here; what the former impugn on conceptual grounds, the latter assume as a therapeutic hypothesis.

d. If agency is admitted, an agency-self is involved. The modern notion of self replaces the older idea of soul. "Self" is inward-turned, reflexive, and its principal relation, that to "myself," is different from the "thyself" of antiquity's "Know Thyself;" it is more anxious about personal identity, more concerned with its self-determination, its freedom.

e. Thus freedom, subjective, personal freedom, becomes the central human issue that now—in the liberal West—begins to rival liberty, that is, objective political freedom. In the face of a vastly successful natural science, will becomes problematic in terms of physical-law-governed determinism as against free choice.

The complex perplexity that attends freedom-as-choice seems to me to fall apart into three connected queries: Is choice-freedom to be construed as pure contingency, absolute causelessness? That would be more freedom than I can support, a freedom without contours. Or is it a will-clinched decision, terminating some sort of causal chain? That would be less freedom than I can accept, a mere moment of abrogated dithering. Or is it a brief passage of choice regarding means in a goal-directed, temporally extended willing-process? That would be a better description of choice as part of benign willing, of will as rational desire, than goes with the first two choice-problems. But it would not yet be adequate to my sense of a freedom "worth wanting."

For what connects all three versions of choice-freedom is that, when it is pinpointed as choice, as decision, or as the terminus of deliberation, freedom is a mere episode. But to me it feels like the bloom of pleasure that graces right action (as Aristotle says) and also real thinking (as it seems to me), an affect that supervenes when I have been in "the sessions of sweet silent thought," when, in the course of long inner converse, meditating and inquiring in turn, I finally come to fix an insight in my inner vision and to formulate a plan in my internal scriptorium. It's during this span of time that I become aware of that supervenient affect of freedom. Thereafter it's outward bound, to join my colleagues in the deliberations of liberty.

B. Will Undelineated

Does it add up? Not on your life—and that very miscarriage emboldens me to launch myself with some élan into the conclusion of my project of "un-willing," of revoking the will's license.

The human capacities that I had set myself to study heretofore, enjoy—countermanding critical agendas notwithstanding—pretty fair agreement on their respective descriptions. Thus our feelings, principally the *passions* and *emotions*, are agreed to be *internal motions*, be it of soul or brain, often (not always) excited by an object thrusting from the outside in and often (perhaps too often) expressed by the subject emoting from the inside out. Thinking, particularly in its signature-activity of discriminating and distinguishing, is generally agreed to be characteristically evidenced in *naysaying* and *negation*, that is, in judgmental discernment and in logical operations; the intentional objects of reality-ranking and existence-denial, *inferior beings and nonbeings*, are accepted as central problems and sometimes acknowledged as mysteries. *Time*, the psychic elongation that is paired in human beings with somatic extension, is recognized as being both *triple-phasic*, a multiplicity, falling apart into past, present, and future, and also *continuous*, a uni-directional passage, be it conceived as an external reality or an internal experience. Finally, all these aspects of human internality—feeling, negation, time—come together in *imagination*, the storehouse of *feeling-fraught semi-beings* held in the preserved past of time-laminated, recollectable memory and the workspace for designing plans to be projected onto an expected future. Be it explicated as an experimentally observable internal quasi-space or as an emergent epiphenomenon of non-spatial operations or, most adequately, a feeling-fraught, magical show, of which we are at once producer, director, and viewer—the mental-image experience is a human commonality.

Not so the will. As the foregoing twenty selections culled from a multitude of conceptions begin to show, the will can be conceived as having the *nature* of a passion, a power, a capacity, a faculty, an agency, a decision—or an illusion. It can be conceived as an *operation* that is an extended process, a final impulse, a long deliberation, or a momentary choice. It can be conceived as having its *termination* in seamless execution or in aborted realization. It can be conceived in terms of its *causality*, as rationally connected or radically contingent. It can be conceived as having its *finality* in an external end or in itself. It can be conceived with respect to its *standing* as the highest human good in its obedience to duty or as a nugatory epiphenomenon in its subjugation to nature. It can be conceived in *scope* as a hyper-human force causing universal suffering, as bestowing individual potency, as a general determination overriding individual choice, or as the very principle of individuality. It can be conceived, looking to the soul's *salvation*, as vulnerable to perversion and sin or as analogous to binding love. But above all, it can be conceived with regard to *human selfhood* as being to some degree free from nature's determinism, as self-activating and deliberately deciding—or as altogether determined by natural law working on conditions fixed from way back. It's a notional miscellany.

This very roiled multifariousness does, however, point to a likely conclusion: The will is not an unimpeachably obvious, manifestly discernible capacity. Yet the way the roughly fifty writers on the will treated in the foregoing chapters and endnotes do not add up does not imply that they do add up to a big Nonsense. Each writer is illuminating for some aspect of the term "will," taken as probably *not* having reference to one fixed constituent of the human soul (meaning by soul our affective and our thoughtful aspects in their togetherness), but as having many, perhaps linked, perhaps disparate senses. For something that has attracted so much investment of ingeniousness from so many people cannot simply be evaporated into a nothing—though, by the same token, it may not be possible to coagulate it into a reality. Speaking in traditional terms, the will may not be readily established as a *faculty*. More about this in Note 5 of this chapter.[5]

At the risk of overkill, I shall now try to comprehend the will and willing in one more (not even the last) contraction, taking into account both the recurrent and aberrant features collected in the preceding chapters and summarized above, though I already know them to be pervasively antithetical: Will and willing don't, as they say, compute—or, won't, as I say, accept delineation. I ask the reader's indulgence for thus grinding in a crucial point: Will is an aggregate not an organism—a heap, not a whole. It remains undelineated.

Will, then, one last time, is to some a modular faculty, to others, a global capacity, a supervenient affect, an epiphenomenon, even a deceptive illusion, though *ipso facto* acknowledged as the denotation of a term. The will's activity is willing, understood as an extended, phased process, or as a concluding moment of decision that is either the mere linear last in a continual flip-flop of desires and decisions or the cumulative outcome of preserved previous psychic states, either a well-deliberated outcome or a moment's choice among options—a grave or a trifling effort. Willing is considered as largely submerged, though this unconscious activity is regarded as subject to psychological and neuroscientific observations and to phenomenological and logical analyses and to ethical and theological explanations. Willing is understood as agency-causal, capable of intervening in the physical world, or as a mere side-effect of deterministic behavior. The failure of will power, the capacity of willing to terminate in execution, is thought of as a character issue or as a pathology, namely the inability to convert wishing into plan-directed intention. Will evaluated is, when good, esteemed as the most limitless of human goods, but when seen as pervertible, it is the most dangerous human endowment, most prone to the sin of pride, most corruptible into self-will. It is the very interiority of ourselves as individuals and it is a hyper-human, a transcendent, a primeval force. Will is the seat of freedom, or conversely, freedom is the source of will. As practical reason, will issues universalizable commands encoding duty and suppressing natural desire, but as rational appetite it pursues what the intellect constrains it to love. I could add dozens of particularizations of the type Bacon calls "vermiculate," but with very marginal profit.

C. Will Un-willed

In beginning my final reflections on the will, I want to enter this re-inversion of Marx's proposed inversion of Hegel's philosophizing. Marx says:

> The philosophers have *interpreted* the world in various ways; the point, however, is to *change* it.[6]

That may be true of Hegel, but it seems false of "the philosophers." A good many of them, especially in modern times, have reasoned about natural, human and divine beings precisely in order to master the natural universe, reform the human world, and even discipline the divine realm. To save philosophy from ideology, let's, then, invert the inversion:

> Quite a few philosophers have tried to *change* the world to various specifications; their true business, however—true, that is, to the meaning of their assumed title as "lovers of wisdom"—is to try to *interpret* the world, to search out its meaning.

Change—the real kind, individual, small-scale, local—might indeed subsequently, even consequently come—not unhoped for and not unintended, but not the primary aim either. To my mind, the most trustworthy practical change is *incidental* to the discovery of meaning.

Here, in this postlude, I want to reaffirm what I said in the Preface. While I would be glad to see the will demoted, I wouldn't want to rectify either readers' volitional language or, God forbid, to manage of their moral intentions. I *would* like to elicit some meanings and evolve some formulations. Inquiring thought would sooner illuminate and ground our preconceptions than confound and dismantle them. Hence I hope to have transformed the prejudice with which I began (where else can an inquiry start, if it is to be movingly interesting to the inquirer?—surely not in gaping curiosity) into a "post-judice," a thought-out prejudice.[7]

Accordingly, I will try listing just by name authors who frame volition grandly but do not quite achieve what I have in mind, although some do eschew the will I decry as a faculty for imposing one's intentions with noisy or silent insistence, for executing one's dug-in desires come what may, for bestowing moral cachet on a mood of righteous self-assertion, for turning the open mind into a clenched grasp.

Then Descartes, Rousseau, Schopenhauer, Kant, and Nietzsche are the major protagonists of this last, the willfully imperial will.

In a class by himself is Heidegger, who means to overcome the will in "letting-be." He wants to usher in the end of Western willfulness, and not surprisingly approaches a version of Buddhist wisdom in this attempt. This slide toward the East too seems unhelpful for us, as I'll explain in Note 8 of this chapter.[8]

The kinder, gentler will is put forth by Thomas, who understands it as rational appetite; by Hegel who identifies will and freedom; by Bergson who conceives it as past-fraught present.

These are the pick of the pick of authors representing a spectrum of the most forcible to the most relaxed volitional modes, modes figuratively representable as the tuning of a string instrument, from the tensest, most high-strung note to the most mellow, lowest note, or a clenched fist and an open hand.

There is, however, a way to perform in the world that is an alternative to putting the soul under tension or sending it eastward or involving it in quandaries of freedom.

1. Socrates

I have called the two twinned teachings of Socrates my lodestar in this inquiry (A1), but actually it is Socrates himself to whom I look. So this is the moment to engage in a concluding exercise, the delineation of an imagined life, *the un-willed life*, and of my chief model for it, *Socrates*.

First, then, the model, who is actually not *the* but *a* good model, for Socrates was surely not all a human being has ever been known to be: not the last word in either acuity or comprehensiveness of intellect—matching in these neither his intellectual biographer Plato and certainly not Plato's pupil, Aristotle. Nor an instance of the greatest poetic sensibility—though depicted in Plato's dialogues as making (or at least telling) philosophical

myths of great grandeur, he is also presented as a late, minor and derivative poetaster who turns Aesop's prose fables into evidently forgettable
poetry and who, on his death-day, claims to be co-servant to Apollo with
the swans who, in dying, sing to the god their "most beautiful" swan-song.
—In fact, swans honk.[9]

For all that, which precludes worship, the figure of Socrates (who knows
or much cares about the once living, now dead "real" man?) is the most
trustworthy philosophical guide I know of—for this one thing: his *immediacy*: He is the patron of perpetual beginners. I'll explain below.

I turn to his trial for help with a pending problem on the way to a delineation of un-willing, understood in the dictionary meaning I discovered:
un-doing the will (see the Preface). My sense is that a certain notion of
divinity is deeply germane (though not, for all that, necessary) to a specific
conception of the will I wish to bracket and to its widespread entry into
human consciousness. This divinity, the one that demands faith, requires
belief—not only belief *that*, but belief *in*, that is, faithful, trusting love. It is
the Christian God of persons, who is as Father at once unapparent, invisible, known only from Scripture and externally evident only through the
testimony of his visible creation, but also directly visible, tangible, humanly
approachable as incarnate in his Son. The word for this kind of belief in the
Greek New Testament is *pisteuein*, "trusting faith."[10]

Socrates' trial is a test case for the claim that Greek gods, on the other
hand, are not required to be, and indeed are not, "believed in." He had been
accused over a long time of being what we call a physicalist, an associate of
meteorologists who studied and worshipped the heavens. Aristophanes, in
a riskily hilarious comedy, *The Clouds*, that resonated into the trial, cari-
catures Socrates as such a scientist who inspects the heavens butt up, and
he lampoons the Socratic forms as a chorus of vaporous, wordy Clouds
invoked and worshipped by Socrates. The current charge against him, as
Socrates himself reports it, is that he corrupts the young and "does not
believe in the gods in which the city believes . . ."—as the translations go.
But that is not what he says. His verb is *nomizein*, from *nomos*, law or custom, and it means "acknowledges, recognizes, cultivates as is the custom."
He conceives himself to be accused of disrespecting the civic customs and
setting aside the gods that figure in them, but not, as I read him, of a spiritual lack of faith. The charge is political, not doxological.[11]

Faith was not an issue for the Athenians who prosecuted Socrates,
because their gods *appear*, if no longer directly, then in poetry, paintings,
and statues. But where there is imaginative receptivity, that is enough:
Mind's-eye-manifestations, especially when underwritten by glowing artifacts, easily pass into all-but-realities, and along with this transit comes the
pious desire to receive friendly notice and help from these figures. And that
is all that is wanted; agonies of doubt-ridden longing to believe, fraught

feelings of sin for failure, are for these Athenians, in our favorite term of blame-avoidance, inappropriate.[12]

The situation so described, then, calls for no forcible suppression of self-willed recalcitrance, since no angrily willful divinity, anxious for creaturely love, is expecting such resistance. And since this pressure is off, or rather hasn't come on the scene yet in pagan cities, the perverse will, the will to do evil for evil's sake, is all but inconceivable—certainly to Socrates. Not that people are not full of vice, or that the way from good intentions to their execution isn't often blocked—but not, he thinks, by reason of the pervertible power of a fierce but failed faculty.[13]

Far be it from me to imply that Socrates' opinions come to him because he was a pagan—they could be anyone's thoughts, anytime. But his prosecution for impiety might have—would surely have—come much sooner, before he had completed, as he did, a full life-span, had he lived in a community of *faith*.

I shall now turn to Socrates' way of un-willing the will before its time. Meanwhile, I must say in all candor that I am uncertain whether the foregoing little meditation on the relation of paganism to will-lessness is really of the essence or is an extraneous circumstance, whether it helps or hinders my election of Socrates as an, no, *the*, exemplary incarnation of a life not entailing will—or perhaps rather entailing non-will. For as standards of public reference, the pagan gods, the Olympians, will be thought by sober contemporaries to be well past their time. So in deference to this opinion (which I don't completely share), my depiction of his way will do without them—as indeed his fellow-Athenians accused him of doing.

He did in fact have a godlet of his own, his *daimonion*, a remarkably un-pagan divinity: an inner voice, shapeless, invisible, neuter—and negative. Our students tend to call it a conscience, though it never says "you must," but only "you shouldn't"; it is a nay-saying divinity (and in that, strangely akin to the divine utterances engraved on Moses's Tablets).[14]

I understand this aversive "godlike thing" within Socrates to be the negative complement of his *ontological optimism*, his trust in the goodness, the desirability, of those beings, the "forms," that stand above and beyond the appearances and make them intelligible, and his consequent eagerness to behold them. Badness presents itself to him only as what is to be avoided and what all of us, did we but recognize it, would in fact avoid. It is a way of saying that, while he acknowledges badness, he cannot conceive evil, that is, *desired badness*, the avid plunge into formlessness, badness as unholy joy in transgression—willfulness.

Here is a vacancy in Socrates' temperament that seems to me to harmonize with his aversive divinity: A young companion, Phaedo, ends his account of Socrates' last day with a summary of his excellences: "The best, and yes, the most thoughtful and the most just" of the men we've come up against. It is a sort of compendium of the set of four virtues Socrates spent his life investigating. But why is one of these—why is courage missing in this account of serene death? Well, precisely because it is an unwilled blithe-ness, not a self-controlled restraint that Socrates has so naturally evinced in this final example he makes of himself for the sake of his young friends. For him this dying day is no different from any living day. Here and now, on any day, he transits to the pagan Beyond, to Hades (*Aides*), the realm of the Invisible (*aides*)—of his forms. For facing a recalcitrantly oppositional eternity in the Christian Below, in Hell—for that, courage is needed: "the unconquerable will,/And study of revenge, immortal hate,/And courage never to submit . . ." But that is Satan speaking. Socrates needs no courage to go in death where his inquiries have taken him in life.[15]

So far it's been Socrates as the imagined figure of a *man*, but the aspect of his nature that makes him what he is to me, to us, is his *thought*, or rather his *thinking*. For his thought is, for the most part, *in statu nascendi*; "in the state of being born." His maxims are few, his working terms hypo-thetical, his conclusions tentative, but all are steadfastly and persistently, through and through thoughtful. His desirous thinking saturates his soul.

Of course, I don't mean by thoughtful thinking rationality, that is, rigorously formal progress from explicit assumptions to not-unexpected conclusions by means of rule-governed inferences, nor warranted general-izations from sufficient cases, nor even compromise-ready reasonableness. None of these methods can deal with Socrates' perpetual beginnings, the ever-renewed immediacy of his thinking: questions about what we really mean by the words we use to tell our adherences, and what we must really be thinking to validate our allegiances. Such question-pursuing thought-fulness often overleaps itself into strictly speaking inaccessible realms, attends to barely audible resonances, has recourse to (suggestively false) etymologies, summons penetrating insight and comprehensive super-vision, avails itself of piercing gimlet-probes and fixating grasps—and occasionally even regards itself as having found a deep truth because it makes the being of things seem witty. I can expend myself here in meta-phors, but the workings of the inquiring, as distinct from the logic-bound or researching intellect, are a mysterious, though cultivatable, gift—which Socrates has in overplus. Of course, he often engages in stretches of tightly-argued dialectic, but these seem to me, in Hume's memorable phrase, to "admit of no answer and produce no conviction." (In effect, though, any bright-enough interlocutor, including the reader, *could* answer back, and is, I think, expected to do so.) So to begin with, strictly rational mentation is not Socrates' way.[16]

Next, Socrates as a *psychologist*. He has a vision of the human soul that excludes the will. It is tripartite, because he discerns a hierarchy of three major activities in us, often at odds: thought, temperament, desire. Temperament (*thymos*) would be, I think, the location of will and will power, were they already in existence. It is the place of courage, pride, shame, of all the assertive passions, and their cowed complements. But *thymos* is expansive in itself and readily obedient to thought—neither clenched negation nor recalcitrant forcibleness. Desire, however, is the crucial part of my argument.[17]

As so often in Socratic hierarchies, the bottom level is the most pervasive, the driving power. Desire is at the bottom of the psychic tri-archy, required to submit both to shame and to reason. And yet, to each of the three soul-kinds, Socrates says, belong, as its own principles (*archai*), its own pleasures and *desires*. In fact, the soul as a whole is a "loving" soul, which has a desire-satisfaction-loving, an honor-loving, and a wisdom-loving (*philosophon*) aspect. Thus Socrates views human beings as through and through desirous—desirous of, loving, good, as I claimed above. Thus in the grand tradition, of which Socrates is the originating pivot-point, the proto-will comes down from the ancients as *rational desire* and, at its highest, as *intellectual appetite*, while the will I am inveighing against is the more (achronologically) original will, a self-assertive, self-intending power rather than a lovingly desirous passion. To come right out with it: All the millennial fuss is about the compatibility of free will with determinism, but the truly grave incompatibility is between will and love, for will's way is uptight, while love opens up. It couldn't be clearer where in this debate Socrates belongs, who claims to know nothing but love-matters (*erotika*).[18]

So much for Socrates the psychologist, but now to the Socrates of (very few) *maxims*, above all to his most pervasive and ever-present adherence and the belief most pertinent to this book: Virtue is knowledge.[19]

Arete, human excellence, virtue, is the collective name for specifiable, publicly admired qualities. Wisdom, courage, soundmindedness, and justice are the four on which Socrates most often focuses, but for him these are not merely qualities or character traits. They are ways of being, of being *effectively* human, of being up to functioning so as to fulfill the human purpose for being. *Arete* is not a *good will* enclosed in its subjective self-sufficiency nor a *morality* expressible in a set of rules to be obeyed—not even a personal character evinced as an *ethics*. It is an on-the-brink power, a readiness to pass to thoughtful doing without intermediate exertion of an executive will—the paradox of a habit-on-the-alert. It expresses itself as the very sanguine simplicity, the smooth serenity that Socrates displays in his dying deed when, having refused to become a scoff-law to his own city just to postpone his death, he spends his last day in the flesh as any other by inviting his young friends to reflection.[20]

This self-certainty about *what to do* in a man not given to claiming to know many truths for certain comes, I think, from the fact that in matters of human purpose he does—sufficiently—know what's what, having thought it out over time. And this unhesitating passage to action, *that he does it*, comes from the very same fact, from doing deep, affirmative thinking. By "knowing what's what," by "deep thinking," I mean not local know-how, but global wisdom: Knowing whence, whither, wherefore. But thinking, the pursuit of knowledge, is for Socrates a movement of desire, of love, whose salient object is human excellence, virtue. And although virtue as an object of desirous thought is, by his own testimony, engrossingly beautiful to mental sight—it is a form, one of his hypotheses—yet as incarnate in humans it draws thinking directly into the sometimes ugly external world, into the human community. That is what I mean by Socratic immediacy: he simply coopts the body as his soul's external agent—there is no daylight between thinking well and being good.[21]

2. Free Will and Will

Perhaps the delineation of what I might as well, candidly, call the malady of the will should have come before Socrates and his *pharmakon*, his antidote. However, I did not want to paint a defensive Socrates but an unburdened one. So let me now try to cast the sum of willful will's qualities. I'll begin—truly one last time—with a quick, curtailed, and unattributed collection of opinions about the will recorded in the preceding pages.

a. *The action of the will*: a faculty now of recalcitrance and now of love; a rational desire, progressing extendedly by the reciprocal interaction of intellect and will; a last moment succeeding deliberation, either causelessly contingent and chance-like or mechanistically determined and necessitated; a metaphysical ground of both nature and consciousness; a hyper-personal principle of cosmic vitality; a self-determining faculty for commanding in accordance with universal law; an outcome of inner activity cumulatively preserved in intensive time; a rationalizing self-deception posterior to existential freedom; a momentary choice between alternatives; an illusory epiphenomenon.

b. *The organ of will*: a faculty, a power, an affect, a disposition.

c. *The motives of will*: uncaused, self-caused, self-determined, intellect-commanded, passion-driven, neurologically determined, evolutionarily advantageous.

d. *The scope of will*: from world-spawning-and-animating to flicking a wrist.

e. *The theories denying or affirming free will: Determinism*, which comes in variations and gradations, denies free will in behalf of necessitating theological, psychological, or physical causation, the latter two being causally related (if a mind not identical with the brain is admitted) or identical. Determinism is a postulate of neuroscience and thus not expected to be demonstrable. (The determinism-dominated sciences feel oddly free to set their own limits). It is a bedeviling proposition for moral life, since doing away with the will by reducing it to an epiphenomenon also cancels responsibility. As a principle for public policy, determinism is a dangerously idle wisdom since, even if its theoretical postulate were better grounded, there would never be enough information to determine definitively what causes have really necessitated any particular actual behavior. Moreover, "folk psychologists" find it inadequate to general human experience, and so do I.

Its opposite is *libertarianism*, the view that we have a will and it is free, *tout court*. This position tends to be defined simply in opposition to determinism, with the, probably intentional, effect of circumventing inquiries into the ontology of freedom. As a formal position it is, as of now, a losing proposition; as a popular faith, it's probably ineradicable.

The intermediate, or better, the linking theory is *compatibilism*. It claims that the first two positions can be held simultaneously—that we may have free will although the universe be deterministic. There are several versions and subtle defenses of compatibilism; the one that has currency in this country seems to proceed by redefining free volition as voluntariness, that is, free-willing as willingness, since one may well act willingly even if one "could not have done otherwise"; this following of one's inclination is then termed an act of free will. There is some sophistry in this.[22]

The point of these repeated recapitulations is to show one last time how hopelessly disparate opinions about the will's nature are and how unsatisfactory the theories of its freedom must be even to those who have faith in it. So far, the will is simply a confusingly polymorphic subject. Now I want to collect the evidence that it is a fascinatingly perverse one. The poets are the experts here, for they are "of the Devil's party."[23]

The Romantic poets, at least those belonging to its "unbridled" faction, were the most overt worshippers of the "free, untrammeled will," sometimes with catastrophic results, first of all to themselves personally, though by a possible construal, eventually also in politics—but Will-in-the-World is beyond my present scope.[24]

So here's a potpourri of testimony to the repulsive attraction exercised by various facets of Augustinian will. On *willfully recalcitrant difficulty*—this could be Augustine himself speaking, though it is Valery: "*Moi*—my essence—is difficulty, will, refusal." And on *willful suffering*, Shakespeare, over and over—Charmien: "Be comforted, dear madam." / Cleopatra: "No. I will not."; the same on *blind self-affection*—Hector: "And the will dotes that is inclinable / To what infectiously itself affects, / Without some image of the affected merit . . ." Again on w*illful self-cultivation*—Iago: "Our bodies are our gardens, to which our wills are gardeners, . . . so that if we will plant nettles or sow lettuce . . . , why, the power and corrigible authority of this lies in our wills." On *willful submission to passion*—Robert Bridges' poem of blank-visaged Eros, that "tyrant of the human heart," whose face shows nothing "But shameless will and power immense," but for whose embrace we long with eyes averted from his loveless look. Finally, W. B. Yeats on *poetry as consequent on un-willing*—". . . the mind liberated from the pressure of the will is unfolded in symbols."[25]

I add, on my own, the shared venial sins of *willful self-protection* to which we are all subject—the obtrusive recessiveness of self-centered (adult) shyness, of exoneration-seeking perfectionism, of fake-pathological procrastination, and of all the similarly masked cramps and seizures of the will.

Sometimes, when you've worked out a claim from several angles, you suddenly wonder if you've ever stated it straight and simple. So here's my claim: Will and free will differ as a process of the soul does from a moment of decision, as a way of being does from an episode of choice-making. This free will, commonly compressed into the *ex post facto* phrase "could have done otherwise," poses an insoluble problem. The extended will, however, in its involvement with reason, is an undeniable human possibility, and the invocation of its power is at crucial moments an uncircumventable necessity. But for life by and large there is an even better mode.

Between here and the end of the book I want to frame this better way and, incidentally, to dispose of free will—by relocating freedom away from the will. Meanwhile, free will looms as *the* renitent problem, remaindered from the magnificent stock of medieval treatments. As a stand-alone issue, denuded of its extended temporal context, it seems to be, as I said, hopeless. It was once a fairly minor moment in willing, the moment of choice among equally-desirable goods and the means to get them; the ends of all willing were already given by the appetitive human intellect: the happiness of obtaining the good. Alternatively and more originally, that is, not as a tweaking of tradition, the will came on the scene as a capacity for perverted desire, the desire for evil, of being bad for badness's sake. And here, too, the aim of desire, God, was given—though willfully rejected. In yet a third, its hyper-personal image, the will is aboriginal impersonal domination, of which, inevitably, a human tyrant becomes the administrator who arrogates its force. Now freedom means, at best, vitality, at worst, mere asserted power.

In this pervertible will, construed as a capacity for evil, freedom did indeed become crucial, but it was more located in the agony of defeating one's own recalcitrance to good than in unforced choice. In the will that was conceived as rational desire, on the other hand, the moment of freedom was understood as an episode of "equivalence": the choice among equally desirable goods plus the selection of means.

Here is a short insertion on "liberty of indifference," an extreme version of this equivalence elevated to an explanation of free will. I have so far neglected it, because its defining phrase is hopelessly multi-semantic.

It might signify any of these: flaccidly free from a lack of decisive interest, appetitively neutral, but ratcheted up into the sphere of will by nothing more than a theoretical impulse. Or it might mean "motivational equilibrium," such as (you will recall) caused Buridan's ass, placed equidistant between equi-enticing bales of hay, to starve to death. Or it might signify whatever brings a human being, placed mid-point between two dinners, to self-incline toward one of them, thus exercising a sort of choice, thinly "free" precisely because it was not determined by the least inner preference or external stimulus. But the last case immediately falls into several equi-potent possibilities: Either this free will is simply causelessly swerving randomness or it is self-caused spontaneity. Or it is even rationally irrational decision-making driven by the over-arching need to eat—a very viable human mode: "Never mind rational, or any, preferences—I want my dinner"; and before you know it, one dinner is appropriated (and maybe the other one as well). This essentially choiceless decision is the free will analogue of cutting the Gordian knot; when Alexander hacked apart the knot, which he couldn't untie, was he descending to mere violence or ascending to resolute rationality? Was this dinner-seizing the trumping of locked choice by the compulsion of hunger or by the operation of a more reasonable rationality? Anyway, "indifference" only compounds the puzzles of free will.[26]

Indeed, all these puzzles have something about them which, for all its murkiness, seems to me dispositive: an underworld air, as of the above-referenced inquiries carried on in hell, where fallen angels go forever round and round and round

> In thoughts more elevate, and reasoned high
> Of Providence, foreknowledge, will and fate,
> Fixed fate, free will, foreknowledge absolute,
> And found no end, in wand'ring mazes lost.[27]

I hope in the next and last section to present a freedom extricated from will and a remaining will we can live with, the life-spanning rational desire delivered from nugatory momentary choices. For I know this and have already said it: I have intentions for this afternoon but not the *faintest notion* what niggling thing I'll do within the next moment of my "specious present." No one, least myself, knows what little motion I'll make in the *immediate* future, but that's *not* a proof—anything but a proof—that I can be seriously free in a Now. To make knife's-edge decision the locus of freedom is to confuse the explosion of impulse with free action.[28]

3. Un-willed Life

I'm moved to end this book (well, sort of "end"—there *are* the endnotes) with a sketch of the effect a will relaxed might have on a life well lived.

I know perfectly well that the passage of years is far more helpful to the project of un-willing than the pages of any book, but the imparting of premature wisdom is the pedagogue's unsuppressible part—and I've been a teacher all my life. Moreover, I'm ultimately undecided about the way to go about un-doing or decommissioning the will without falling into the paradox of doing it willfully. Certainly the philosopher of the West who, in my reading, wrote most extensively about "Letting-be, Letting-go," has not solved that problem of the willful abrogation of the will. Nonetheless, I call one last time on a wiser philosopher, Socrates, who showed that whenever a conclusive argument against the possibility of a life-grounding activity is given, one may nullify the logic by just doing the thing. For what is unexceptionally valid is often terminally false.[29]

Now to it. A poet says:

> Every eye must weep alone,
> Till "I will" be overthrown.

And elsewhere he speaks of the "fright and fidget" of the will. This is the very will, a self-segregating tyrant-ego, tear- and fear-ful, waiting for release by auto-rebellion, that I have had in mind—if a little weepily expressed, as is proper to poetry.[30]

So it is not, once more, freedom *of* the will but *from* the will that is to be attempted. And this somewhat disheveled overthrow, this messy self-release, has modes quite different from respectably upright self-determination (understood as fixing one's choices by calling on the will's very own imperatives), both in feel and act. In its meditative mode, this irenic revolt relies on our experiential sense of the expedients that keep the world coherent as a whole, combined with our sympathies for fellow-humans one by one. In its executive mode, it concedes that good outcomes are largely dumb luck and that unintended consequences are the most reliable predictions. Thus this volitional apostasy renounces reliance on the bully-mode of will power both for itself or in others, for it is open to other empowerments. The Germans have a revealing word for the will's self-control, *sich zusammennehmen*, "to take [pull] oneself together." Well, collectedness is achievable by other means than by strenuous inward-drawing. Here they are.[31]

We can *find* ourselves irresistibly moved by the attraction of a lovable being (of any sort), moved at once inwardly into our center and externally toward the beckoning object; we can *keep* ourselves stabilized by faithfully maintaining the attachment, mostly by disposing ourselves to find what was at first so moving later very interesting—for *interest*, though it is surely less passive and so less a passion than love (which isn't all that passive either), is *ipso facto* a more persistent engagement, whose appetite increases with its nourishment, so that it comes to be love-like. Hence the un-willed life is, in its active surrender to love or interest, simply more engaging than life in the master-mood of strenuous will power or even the duty mode of the very good will.

Where is the energy in such a way of life? The Stoics express it in the phrase "up to us" but make its meaning severely restrictive. What is "up to us" is mostly what is within us, what we want. Thus Stoic wisdom talks down our desires and tries to keep us serenely self-contained by arduous abrogations. But there is so much more up to us than is descried, or dreamed of, in their philosophy—in fact Stoics are constitutionally dream-deprived. There is so much that is outside us but subject to our mastery, a mastery beyond their imagination, though they themselves, as staunch physicalists, laid the basis of modern science. Yet these same Stoics do seem to have a point. Be it by way of theory or practice, thinking or doing, much of our construing and constructing in the world is not conducive to insight or contentment.[32]

The un-willed way is not to shut down desire but to vitalize it as receptivity. Along this path it is necessary and even urgent to construct roofs that don't leak and to construe laws that apply fairly to cases, to observe phenomena according to public protocols and to form explanatory theories obeying agreed-upon criteria. But though it may seem to countermand our current urgencies, it might be even more necessary sometimes to leave things unmade and rights unlitigated, to decline to see all our world's contents through the regulatory screen of established concepts and to nullify the latest experiment on the human psyche by letting it self-degrade, unreplicated. That is the first, the negative phase of receptivity; I mean it as a moderately realized withdrawal from business as usual—a gently fostered pushback to the creeping complexity advanced by one more convenience and the paralyzing overload induced by one more piece of information.[32]

The positive activity along this way is now and then to contemplate beings and to do it untrammeled by the interventionist techniques of knowledge-producing research, to view things in their individual substantiality—which is not the same as their individualistic idiosyncrasy. The former focuses interest on what beings have in common as *particular* instances of a kind, while the latter lavishes curiosity on what makes them different as *peculiar* items on their own. Not that the fun of people-watching isn't largely in simply savoring peculiarities, but that's just fixing on the comic costume issued to the *humani dramatis personae*; it's a recreation.[33]

The demand for solid factuality, the aversion to vaporous fancies, is a special province of the hard-bitten will to reality. (In the U.S. of A. a whole state is dedicated to no-nonsense: Missouri, the "Show-Me State.") It has its cob-web-clearing virtues, especially in respect to practical planning, but it doesn't do much for imaginative living. Here some fudging of the hard-edged boundary prescribed by the will in its fear of indeterminacy is in order. I have in mind, for example, that melding of the realms of fact and fiction which allows the figures of the imagination to function as the illuminating penumbras, or even more paradoxically as the life-enhancing non-beings they are meant to be. It's when the willful fact-shield is penetrated that poetry can become fully operative—without ceasing to be philosophically problematic. I am thinking of that famous "willing [not willful] suspension of disbelief" necessary for doing justice to artful fiction. Isn't it an invitation to un-willing?[34]

So far I have depicted the de-volitioned life as more pulled by love than pushed by duty and more open to the beings, be they facts or fictions, that we find in the world than bent on its reformation, be it a mere (though expensive) tweaking or a radical (and dislocating) reconstruction.

That brings me to the more particular positive action implied in this un-willed mode of life. To begin with, when the will is in abeyance, what becomes of change? Change might well be termed the defining issue of the present era, our entrenched mantra. Our world is commonly—nearly universally—presented as a "fast-changing world"; the world—it is, by now, a mere courtesy to call it "our world," electronic interconnectivity not withstanding—is changing with or without us, on its own, faster and faster. This change is said to come on us *volens nolens*, "willy-nilly"; the human will appears to be set aside by an unstoppable secular destiny, perhaps even an awesome terrestrial miracle. It makes one almost wish to rehabilitate recalcitrant will.

In fact, however, this sort of uncoupling of the will from human action can be construed as the last word in willfulness, a perversion of our blessed human finitude that turns it into an excuse for self-subordination to— what? An unanswerable question, for the greater the rate of change, the less definable becomes its end, purpose, or aim.

But surely it makes no sense to give up one's own will to be swamped by anonymous tides of willful submission to the cloudy agendas of everyone and no one, to surrender the pace of one's life to crowd-sourced sentiment. The supply-generated demand for yet faster increasing speed—since acceleration provides the one vital sign for the type of change that is indeterminate in its object—is, I think, both cause and consequence of people's willfully will-less withdrawal from the investment in the slow, quiet time needed to figure out what is humanly good. Yet this is certain: the faster the change, the more every purpose, aim, and end becomes merely quantitative in its diagnostic description and correspondingly elusive as a culminating fulfillment.

Thinking about the nature of change is a crucial element in the life I am working out. Could one not argue that the confirming complement of a thoughtful participation in change is the well-considered decision occasionally to opt out? A human being unafraid of change is, *ipso facto*, it seems to me, unafraid not to change, for such stoppage is indeed quite a change—of change. Might there not be a reasonable (if perhaps a-rational) argument for going on doing something because we've always done it— and, oddly enough, *especially* if it's a tradition whose origins have disappeared into the mists of time and are therefore irrecoverable? Or couldn't one even offer a thoroughly rational argument against unnecessary change in economic terms: the high "opportunity costs" to the human psyche in terms of the value foregone, namely the cost in peaceful concentration on human essentials in the distracting business of redoing circumstantials?

Locke says that it is not the will that is free but the man. On first reading, that seemed to me to be a distinction without a difference, but I am beginning to see the point, if not of his argument, at least of his claim. He says, "Liberty, which is but a power, belongs only to agents and cannot be an attribute or modification of the will, which is also but a power." (Though how, I wonder, could there be diverse powers if they were not differently qualified?) Then liberty, here understood as the freedom to guide inner intention into executed action, seems also to belong, in Locke's spirit, to human beings primarily—as agents of deeds, and to wills only derivatively—as to the faculty of choice. For not every sensible deed is preceded by a choice. Some actions, among which are those most expressive of our moral being, are, colloquially speaking, "no-brainers"; they are already decided, without case-by-case deliberation. Such actions are undeliberated not because they are thoughtless reactions, but precisely because we have anticipated the critical moment by previously sequestering some quiet time to the sessions of sweet silent thought, to the unbusy soul-searching that explores the whole psychic territory in a mode both thoughtful and passionate. It is from this preparation, I've wanted to claim, that the moment of action issues in smooth, undeliberated continuity with life so far.[35]

(This mode of action is not the willingness of compatibilism, that is, our willing collusion in our predetermined behavior, for it is not willingness that makes the way smooth but preparedness. Even less is it determinism (that secular stand-in for predestination) for it is not fixed natural law that lays out the path but long-breathed human spontaneity. It seems to me that this from-way-back sort of agency is forever beyond the reach of natural explanation, in part because simply too much of unobservable, unrecordable life goes into it, too many moments, memories, moods. Thus, incidentally, the will-foregoing life escapes deterministic necessity, though it is not determinism as a postulate that is nullified but the human agent as a subject that is withdrawn from it, by reason of the length, diffuseness, and immensity of the physical events subserving the soul.—Not to speak of the fact that the laboratory protocols often require attaching reported mental activities to observed neural events, and here candor may stop at confession; reserve may vitiate the match-up between the private experience and the scientific observation, if the former has some complexity. Plainly put, are there people so shameless that they *would* come clean about themselves in an experiment, and if they would, *could* they, in a finite time?)[36]

Yet, there's a proviso to my prescription of the de-volitioned life. It is: *if* conditions are reasonably favorable, *if* there is atmosphere enough to bear up the slow free gyres of considering thought. For the genial air that floats the thought-and-desire-borne life can be suddenly sucked away, and we crash uncushioned into the earth's hard contrarian unbiddableness. Then will shows up in its residual, indeed ultimate, function. Those are times when what we want and what we approve have become incomposably antithetical, when all we desire points one way, and all we think right another. Then there is some remote, forbidding quarter in our soul, blindingly white, where are flooded out all the images and melodies that wreathe about harmoniously emerging action; here is the depository of pure moral principle and the seat of its enforcer, the uncompromising will. It is a region at once sacred and terrible. A happy life is rarely summoned there, and a good country does not often send its citizens into it. Once there, I whimper, "I don't want to," and the will says, "You must"—and behold, the will turns out to be my final self—not much good for the lifespan of many days, but all-important for that one moment of true choice. For if the will's blind power of obedience to principle fails—though "being principled" may merely be the submission to some insensible abstraction of arid rightness that's somehow gotten into most of us—if our will is not now forcibly self-compelled to decide as it ought, then there is infirmity at the center of the self and shame, and the less strenuous "un-willing" delineated in this book is devalued. Have I let the will back, way back, in? Well, in my metaphor it has its personality and its place, but in reality this is a strictly occasional power, rarely activated in most of us. It seems to me to be a coagulation, a compaction, so to speak, of our right opinion into what might be called a hyper-desire, a tense desire which, by reason of its moral force, can sometimes trump our aversions and appetites—for desire best modifies desires.[37]

With the will thus relegated to special occasions, what takes the place of will-associated rationality? As Plato builds a tripartite polity to show the soul's functions writ large, so Alexander Hamilton reads our Constitution as representing three functions of the mind: force (the executive President), will (the legislating Congress), and judgment (the decision-issuing Supreme Court). Of these, the Supreme Court is said by him to be "the least dangerous branch," because it has "neither FORCE NOR WILL, but merely judgment." The Court's main decisions concern whether certain particular intentions (laws) are in harmony with the fundamental intention (the Constitution) and should remain in effect. In the terms of this inquiry: Which Congressional desires, having been expressed as intentions, should the Court allow to go forth as the will of the people? I cite Hamilton here because his "faculty" view of governance, a magnification of the human psychology (where faculty means, recall, a separable mental power), models the possibility of a deliberate judging that is divorced from willing. However, Hamilton, for once, was wrong, I think, in one aspect: in the innocuousness he ascribes to the seat of judgment, in what he calls its "natural feebleness." In fact the Court has proved to be the mover of social transformation, and that too is to my point: judgment not immediately willful can be as effective within the psychic constitution as in the political Constitution.[38]

The actual individual analogue to making juridical decisions seems to be the "judgment call." We survey the situation and judge which desires in the given situation should become intentions, because they harmonize with our or our communities' fundamental ends, because they are prudent, feasible now and apt to work out in the long run,—and because they are our will.

Such individual judgment calls are, indeed, anything but innocuous or feeble. As I said, a conveniently pertinent feature of the Hamiltonian figure is that it delinks judgment from will on the principle that an "independent judiciary . . . is essential" to the preservation of rights. To be sure, traditionally the phase of the will called "deliberation," which seems analogous to the judgment call, is, in fact, confined to the choice of means (and the preference among indifferently desirable options), and is thus far more restricted than judgment. Nonetheless the Hamiltonian metaphor is pertinent to what seems to me a fact of experience: judgment needs to be divorced from the will if it is to accord the situation its rights. Once more, thoughtfully decisive judgment can do without the will.[39]

Just above, the word "options" slipped in. If I have occasionally suspected that I'm fighting windmills it is because in the consuming part of our lives (which needs curtailing) the fierceness of original will has been damped by dispersion over the market, by a wild hypertrophy of options that has driven out the old salubrious scarcity of choices. But even in its asthmatic gasps the will needs critiquing.

I can think of just one great figure—great by reason of his hugely minimalistic self-assertion—in whom preferences really are life choices: For Bartleby, the Scrivener, "I would prefer not to," terminal self-withdrawing willfulness, leads to inanition; he dies of his mild, insipid, indefeasible negative preferences. "Ah, Bartleby! Ah, humanity!" is Melville's adieu to this extreme exemplar of desiccatedly tenacious anti-vital volition. For normally, who of us would really wish to call their life's devotions "preferences" or its forking paths "options"?[40]

Yet preferences, slackly differential desires, and options, marginally diverse possibilities, dominate the remains of the will in this "era of choice." Variety being the spice of—a *stable*—life, there is a mild pleasure in exercising preferences, and good management being the requirement of an independent one, there is some convenience in being offered options.[41]

But surely the mode of an option-ridden life with its endless small investments of time—if fairly deliberate, expending itself in screen-bound research, if indiscriminate, in joyless glut—is the very incarnation of Pascal's "diversion," that failure of simplicity which lets life leach away into diversionary complexity. (See Note 42 of this chapter.) Willing is at work here in its most diminished form; it almost makes one long for the grand will of Thomasian rational desire or the terrific will of Satan's self-assertion. Indeed, Bartleby had hold of the right term to be employed so negatingly.[42]

To locate human freedom in these last gasps of the will is ludicrous. (When I say "last gasps," I mean the individual will; the pernicious faith in hyper-human will, the special bugbear of this book, is ever-alive.) Thus arises the penultimate question of this work: Wherein lies the freedom of our life if it cannot lie, as I have claimed above, in the choice-will (*liberum arbitrium*), be it grand or niggling in scope?[43]

Public freedom, civic liberty, has not been my subject here, partly because it begins where inner freedom finds external expression and enters into a new relation with the will that now switches from an executive to a sustaining mode and becomes a staying power. But partly it has not been my preoccupation because I live in a country that has found a way to check the millennial tendencies of rulers to push their subjects' wills to the wall, exceeding even the extremities that normal nature, human and non-human, contrives on its own. For this land is so constituted as to offer material opportunities for those who know their way around and civil rights for all—these together being the conditions for a civic liberty, which, even though imperfectly realized, is the miracle of the ages. So I have attended just to the unregenerate human soul.

What, then, is freedom beyond the kind so problematically attributed to willed decisions? I think that an answer is terminally elusive—and that this very unavailability directs us to a sort of existence proof, which we need more urgently than a definition of essence. Augustine said, "What, then, is time? If nobody asks me, I know; if I want to explain it to him who asks, I don't know," because time is peculiarly a non-entity: extinct as past, vanishing as present, unborn as future. Freedom is similarly peculiar—not a nothing but also not a something. For one thing, it is, as I said, mortifyingly unamenable to definitive comprehension, but what is worse, dangerously incapable of displaying existence. Every attempt to prove oneself free is vitiated by the very attempt, which is, perforce, forcibly willful. Try proving just to yourself that you can raise your finger at will, and you are caught in a driven intention to intend freely. Or try demonstrating your larger freedom, and you are enmeshed with yourself in a mutual calculus of self-defeating second-guessing. Perhaps the ultimate failure to prove the grandest freedom—that of "to be or not to be"—is exemplified by Dostoevsky's Kirillov, who means to die freely as a God and perishes abjectly as a beast.[44]

Though freedom will not let itself be caught either in essence or existence by an argument, it will allow itself to be lived in simple fact by a human being. I know this unquestionably, though, as it were, only that way: when I'm not asked. What we can do is to transfigure negative definitions, such as *the absence of constraint*, and incomprehensible concepts, such as *causeless swerves* into one or another metaphor of an experience: for instance, to figure freedom as a weightless, odorless, fine-grade lubricant that keeps us from grating on ourselves, limbers us up so that we can freely talk to ourselves, lets us glide over our antic, impulsive motions as occasional intrusions from a Lucretian world, and smooths the path to self-forgiveness. For such suppleness marks the mind's readiness for real thinking, such as is, I think, the most humanly human activity—and our ability to do it, to do what is most ours to do, *is* freedom.[45]

Thus coming into one's own feels as free as fenceless familiarity. But it only feels globally free because it is locally bound—fenced in by my flagging attention and my finite ability, bound by the pull of the problem, constrained by the adequacy of the proceeding, but above all, determined by *the truth of the object*. It is *mine* to attend, focus, seek, but *its* to be attractive, to be an entity, to be found. That *it* is the occasion and the termination of freedom; it occasions self-originated activity and sets a term to construct-making originality. All this is describing, not explaining a mystery. One way to put it is this: I am trying to levigate the dried up problem of free will into a more fluid inquiry.

Fluidity, flexibility of thought and ensuing action, surely increase when the will's dominance is diminished. Such fluidity turns up particularly in respect to time. To the forcing will, the present (in fact the moment of our *existence* here and now as distinct from our *being* in timeless thought) is a lacerating knife's edge of decision, and the future (in truth a vacancy to be filled by the imagination) is an amorphous plasma to be fixed, determined, coaxed into existence. But the past (in actuality quite alive in memory) is condemned in part to impotent fixity and in part to unredeemable oblivion by this will, bent as it is on power, which is image- and memory-less; the will-captured past is either propaganda or crematorium. And that allusion to the violated past raises just about the most interesting question concerning our freedom: Does it cease with the done deed? Is the past really mere victim, closed to freedom? Is there no Schengen passport for the territory of time? Is it impossible to amend a graceless act, revoke a false word, recover a missed moment, reform a bad deed—or even to relive past grandeur? My surmise is that with some fluidity of imaginative thought it is not impossible to recall and reopen, to re-do, re-institute the past. On a grand scale, that is called "renaissance"—but that promising topic extends this inquiry beyond its plan.[46]

After having once more described the receptivity of the un-willed life, I return to its activity: its moderate skepticism about participating in interminably accelerating change and its appreciation of the slow preparation for smooth action; its acknowledgment of residual will-moments; its inclination to answer calls for broadly human judgments applied to indefeasibly individual cases rather than to engage in decision-driven deliberation; its readiness to escape the time-consuming oppression of weakly passionate options and preferences; and finally, its freedom for being at home within, thinking at once freely and responsively while out from under the assertive static of self-will. Now, at the end, I want to go back to that first feature of the un-willed life, receptivity, to delineate a way of thinking that complements it.[47]

That way seems to me to be *reflection*. The word comes from the Latin *reflectere*, "to bend back." I think thinking bends back in three ways: First, it goes toward, tends to, *intends* its object and returns, bringing it back in the mode of thought. (The logic of intentionality fills volumes, but the term's inbuilt metaphor is that of the reflection from a mirror.) When I reflect, I do not as *I will* but as the *object or subject wants*, and it, in turn, more often nudges than necessitates my thinking. Second, reflection *attends* to itself, it thinks, or better, I think about my thinking itself and the being, myself, that does the reflecting, this is the "Know Thyself" of Apollo's temple and Socrates' teaching.

Third, and above all, reflection as I understand it, *intensifies* life. In doubling back, it turns awareness into self-awareness, brings life to life, so to speak, and so renders it twice-lived—once in experience and again in feeling-fraught thought: only the twice-lived life is actually lived— as Socrates said and I think. Here is an amended version, in latter-day language, of Socrates' notion that life requires reflection to have really happened: If thought, as our most human capacity, is drawn by—intermittent—impulses, *longings*, toward its this- or other-worldly objects, the soul, as our personal whole, is at home in its sustaining element, *interest*, "being attentively with and among" beings (for that is what Latin *interesse* means). Loving interest is, I think, our best long-term prospect.

In such reflection, born of interest, as distinct from concept-mongering produced by will, thought is open rather than scrunched up, delighted to come on a new notion, its own or another's, but entirely unashamed to dwell over and over on the multitude of interesting semi-solutions to the

perennially insoluble, the real, problems. These are the humanly significant questions, the ones proscribed by positivists, the questions that, considering our finitude, are not likely to produce progress but only clarifying
formulations and life-supporting hypotheses:

> We must not follow those who counsel us to think human thoughts, being
> human, or mortal thoughts, being mortal. But as far as may be, we must
> practice being immortal (*athanatizein*) and do everything toward living in
> accord with what is most excellent in us.[48]

Notes

Preface

1. *Oxford English Dictionary*, p. 3556. For the verb "to unwill" Mrs. Browning is cited: "Now, your will is all unwilled—now, your pulses are all stilled" ("Duchess May," 1844).

2. At St. John's College in Annapolis and Santa Fe.

3. Gelassenheit: this is a term derived from the German mystics. Thus Meister Eckhart (born c. 1260) entitled one of his talks of instruction "Of the people who have not let go (*ungelassene Leute*) and are full of self-will," and in it he says, "Therefore begin first with yourself, and *let go.*" *Meister Eckhart: Deutsche Predigten und Traktate*, ed. and trans. Josef Quint (Munich: Carl Hanser Verlag, 1978), 55. By a not infrequent etymological development of a meaning into its opposite, the modern noun *Gelassenheit* ordinarily means "self-composure." Heidegger plays on this double meaning and implicitly on yet a third, submissive "resignation," in a discussion written a decade before and then appended to his essay *Gelassenheit* (1955). The "teacher" in this conversation agrees that "being awake" for *Gelassenheit* involves weaning ourselves from willing: "We should not do but wait." (For Heidegger on *Gelassenheit*, see Ch. VIII, Sec. D, herein.) That sort of withholding from life is not what I hope for. (See Conclusion, Sec. 3, herein.)

Nirvana: in one Buddhist understanding is the evacuation of all desire. My point here is that these are not the routes I mean to take.

4. Eva Brann, *The World of the Imagination: Sum and Substance* (1991); *What, Then, Is Time?* (1999); *The Ways of Naysaying: No, Not, Nothing, and Nonbeing* (2001). All: Lanham, Md.: Rowman & Littlefield Publishers. A fourth book on the soul treats of affectivity in general: *Feeling our Feelings: What Philosophers Think and People Know* (Philadelphia: Paul Dry Books, 2008).

5. This figure goes back to the Roman scholar Varro, quoted in Cassiodorus, *De Artibus ac Disciplinis Liberalium Litterarum*, chap. III, "On Dialectic." Varro is comparing concise terse dialectic to copious relaxed rhetoric.

6. Desire, though sometimes irrational, is in itself non-rational rather than *un*-rational, i.e., basically inimical to reason. The reflexivity of the self, its constitutional self-referentiality, its being bent back on itself, as in "self-consciousness," both in its cognitive and emotive senses, will be a topic in this book (Ch. XI, Sec. D). The word "self" itself announces this reflexivity, since it began as an adjective that became a suffix, as in "myself," giving the pronoun a self-embracing sense; used in apposition with a pronoun, here "I," it yields an even more intense ingathering sense (George O. Curme, *A Grammar of the English Language*, vol. 2, *Syntax* [Essex, Conn.: Verbatim, 1977], under 56D).

Chapter I. Before Will

1. Sir Arthur Conan Doyle, "Silver Blaze," *The Memoirs of Sherlock Holmes* (1894).

2. Hamartia: Aristotle, *Poetics* 1453 a 10—the dictionaries list "sin" among the synonyms for *hamartia*, though at least at first it means making a mistake. The mistake made is a *hamartema*; Aristotle cites a poet's depiction of a horse throwing both right legs forward (1460 b 18), a simple, sinless error of observation; spear-throwing: *Iliad* V 287—*embrotes* is the second person singular of the verb *hamartano*, from which *hamartia* is derived.

3. Chaste fondling: *Odyssey* XIII 287 ff.

4. Examples of "will" for *boule* in *Iliad* I 5: George Chapman (1598, celebrated in Keats' poem "On First Looking into Chapman's Homer"), Johann Heinrich Voss (1793, the great German translator of Goethe's day), Richard Lattimore (1951), Robert Fitzgerald (1974), Robert Fagles (1990). But many others, including the latest, Anthony Verity (2011), accurately say "plan."

5. The most potently Socratic Socrates: I mean, as compared to Aristophanes' comic meteorologist in the *Clouds* but also to Xenophon's dispenser of what the Germans call *Lebensweisheit* in the *Memorabilia*; **methodos**: for example, *Republic* 531 c, 533 b, c. The point is that Socrates has no method in our sense, namely, a rule-directed procedure; **the beautiful and young Socrates**: he occurs in Plato's *Second Letter* (314 c), where Plato disclaims any "writings of Plato." That the dialogues are not his *writings* is in a wonderfully cunning way true: no doctrines are announced in the author's behalf and no first person appearance is made—only two third-person references, *Apology* 38 b and *Phaedo* 59 b; **Alcibiades**: he is himself the most beautiful of men but only in his visible looks; on a memorable night he opens up ugly Socrates to display his inner divinities, his beauty of soul (*Symposium* 215 b).

6. Perhaps Socrates does say it outright, but conditionally and negatively: "Thus, if there were anything else good, separable from knowledge, perhaps virtue would not be a kind of knowledge" (*Meno* 87 d).

7. Lie in the soul: *Republic* II 382 b; **choice in a cosmic framework**: X 617 e ff.; **choice of life**: X 617 e ff., which bristles with forms of the verb "to choose" (*hairesthai*).

8. Examples of choice of life in other dialogues: *Philebus* 21 d, *Laws* V 734-c (*boulesis tes haireseos ton bion*, "intention in the choice of lives").

9. Life-choice: for example, Socrates seems to demand such a choice of Callicles in the *Gorgias*.

10. Turning on a dime: This "sudden" (515 c) turn, achieved, to be sure, with help, is called *periagoge* (518 d), a "bringing round"; a contemporary way to put this is: Socrates carries on his life "ethically" that is, imbued by virtue: he does not perform acts "morally," that is, governed by willed decisions.

11. Meno, a thoroughly bad man (Xenophon, *Anabasis* II 6), mounts a superficially clever argument against inquiry along these lines: We can't engage in a search for what we're ignorant of because how will we know that we've found what we didn't/don't know (*Meno* 80 d)? In other words, as ignorance seems to him incapable of knowing itself for ignorance, so it can't recognize its remedy.

12. Recollection (*anamnesis*): *Meno* 81 d. If one must speak of consciousness with respect to Socratic cognition, I think it would be better to say that recollection recalls knowledge from the subconscious rather than the Unconscious, which is a technical term fraught with Freudian meaning. To put it concisely: Socrates thinks that deep truths now unavailable are by no means forever inaccessible to us, but can be reached through a soul cure based not on a psychological theory of therapy but on an ontological hypothesis of cognition.

13. No one knowingly desires bad: *Meno* 77 c ff. Put positively: We desire [only] good things: *Symposium* 204 e. "Desire" and "love" (or their verbal forms) are more frequent than the occasional "wish."

14. Companion: The dialogues named after Alcibiades and Charmides foreshadow these pedagogical disasters; history books tell the rest: treachery and tyranny.

15. Ontological innocence: The tradition of badness as non-being assumes ontological shape in the Platonic dialogue *The Sophist*, which Socrates instigates but then listens to in silence. Here the being of Non-being and its diversifying as well as its deteriorating effects are established, to be fully worked out by Plotinus and in some Christian theologies; particularly relevant for my book is Augustine; **the *daimonion***: for example, *Apology* 31 d, *Phaedrus* 242 b, *Theaetetus* 151 a.

Contrary to the more sophisticated current view, some people of great talent and acute insight actually find the tranquility of goodness more desirable than the *frisson* of vice. Witness Jane Austen at the end of *Mansfield Park*:

Let other pens dwell on guilt and misery. I quit such odious subjects as soon as I can, impatient to restore everybody not greatly at fault themselves to tolerable comfort, and to have done with the rest.

16. Middle ground excluded: In fact, Socrates *does* introduce—his very own thought—such a middle ground between knowledge and ignorance and attaches to it a qualified cognition and its efficacy. Its name is *doxa*, "opinion, seeming, deeming." It is deficiently grounded and untethered knowledge accompanied by the laudable effort to make it *right* or even *true* (*orthe or alethes doxa*, for example, *Meno* 97 b ff.; *Republic* V 476 d ff., VI 509 d ff.; *Theaetetus* 200 d ff.).

17. I have never read a formal logical version of a philosophical thought process that did not present it as hopelessly inspissated (so to speak) with insufficiency in its progress and affected with dubieties at the beginning and doubt at the end.

18. Meno the rogue: See Note 11 above. The dialogue ends with a completely disgusted Socrates taking up Meno's "some other way." It suggests with the most cutting sarcasm that virtue is ours by a "divine portion." The dialogue *Ion* (533 d) confirms that this suggestion is indeed meant as sarcasm.

19. In the *Meno*, where the question is whether virtue is teachable, Socrates shifts to *phronesis* (98 d).

20. Courageous exertion, self-government ("rule over oneself"): *Meno* 86 c–d; *askesis*: for example, in *Republic* 536 b, the learning involved in philosophy is called an *askesis*.

21. Xenophon: *The Defense of Socrates Before The Jury* 1–9; in Plato's *Phaedo*, Socrates condemns suicide as being cowardice, like that of a soldier stationed in a garrison running away (62 b). See also Eva Brann, "The Offense of Socrates: A Rereading of Plato's *Apology*," in *The Past-Present*, ed. Pamela Kraus (Annapolis, Md.: St. John's College Press, 1997), 81–98.

22. Civil disobedience: Martin Luther King in his "Letter from Birmingham City Jail" (1963), evidently referring to Plato's *Crito*, cites Socrates' civil disobedience (defying unjust law but facing the legal consequences) as partly responsible for our academic freedom.
Weeping: *Phaedo* 117 d; **banter**: throughout the dialogue; **features**: 118; **program of perplexities**: Eva Brann, "Socrates' Legacy: Plato's *Phaedo*," in *The Music of the Republic* (Philadelphia: Paul Dry Books, 2004), 36 ff.

23. Well-doing and knowledge: *Euthydemus* 281 d; *eidos* means "looks, aspect"; as beings they belong to "the realm of the invisible" (*aeides*) to which the soul also belongs: *Phaedo*, passim, especially 79 b ff.; **forms brought in as hypotheses**: *Phaedo* 100 b, *Republic* 511 a–b. In the *Republic*, a Socratic *hypothesis* seems to be, from its very etymology, ambivalent—insofar as it is "something put," a *thesis*, it is a mere *hypothesis* in our sense, a conjecture or assumption; insofar as it is put "under," *hypo*, taken as a ground, it is a first "beginning," an *arche*, and a firm belief; **goodness** of world: *Phaedo* 99.

24. No one's teacher: *Apology* 33 a; **no deliberation on his defense**: Xenophon, *Defense* 5.

25. Aristotle, *Metaphysics*: I 1, 980 a; XIII 7, 1072 a.

In contrast, the God of the last canto of Dante's *Divine Comedy* moves "the sun and the other stars" by a love emanating *from*, not terminating *in* him; and by this love Dante's "desire and will (*il mio desiro e il velle*) were rolled / as if by a wheel that moves equably." Note, for future use, that desire and will roll in tandem.

Students at my college mount two well-attended extracurricular seminar series (reading-discussion groups), Plato-in-Springtime and Shakespeare-in-Fall; I was asked to lead the last of the latter in the very month of this writing (December 2011). I chose three sonnets, including the famously enigmatic no. 94:

> They that have pow'r to hurt and will do none,
> That do not do the thing they most do show,
> Who, moving others, are themselves as stone,
> Unmoved, cold, and to temptation slow;

ending,

> Lillies that fester smell far worse than weeds.

Several students, being well-read in the love literature of the West, in which Aristotle's *Metaphysics* stands high, got at once what, it seems to me, the most reputable commentators missed: Here is a post-pagan lover's rebellion against a beloved who appears as an inhumanly human facsimile (notice the use, early on, of the ungendered relative pronoun "that" where "who" would have been possible) of Aristotle's divine *Nous*, the philosopher's god, who moves the heavenly and, ultimately, earthly bodies as an unmoved mover by the attraction—*unreciprocated*—of his perfectly actual being (XII 7); he is the object of love, but being without deficiency, feels none. The sonnet's lover, mindful of the Christian God, who is Love, both as its object and its responsive subject, demands some—any—attention. Thus the sonnet first expresses hurt at the fact that the beloved mortal god does not act out of the Love—even if angrily and injuriously—of which he appears to be the incarnation, does not respond at all as the real, the temperamental God would. And then, in the last six lines it assuages this hurt by a vengeance fantasy: the going to rot of the stone-cold, the internal infection of the externally insusceptible. There is an intimation that a human non-lover's impassivity is *willful*.

   26. Aristotle, *Metaphysics* XII 7, 1072 a. In my translation I have expanded by a few words Aristotle's (or his note-taker's) all-too-compressed diction.

   27. Aristotle: *Nicomachean Ethics* III 2, 1111 b ff., 1113 a; *On the Soul* III 9–10, 432 b–433 a.

   28. Immattered reasons: *On the Soul* I 403 a.

   29. The word *boulesis*: Hjalmar Fisk, *Griechisches Etymologisches Wörterbuch* (Heidelberg: Carl Winter, 1960), under "boulomai;" **rational desire**: Sarah Broadie, *Ethics with Aristotle* (Oxford: Oxford Univ. Press, 1991), 106; **boulesis within the rational part**: *On the Soul* III 9, 432 b (*en toi logistikoi*). An attempt to work out Aristotle's realm of appetite schematically: Eva Brann, *Feeling Our Feelings*, 68 ff.

   30. Merely self-controlled: Aristotle, *Nicomachean Ethics* VII 9, 1152 a.

   31. Unwilling action: III 1, 1109 b ff.

   32. Prohairesis: Aristotle is not for suddenness but for the long run—long writings, demanding extended working through, so also long habituation and daily application. For Plato, who also believes in lifelong devotion, the *exaiphnes*, the "sudden" turning, the sudden insight, are nonetheless an element of philosophizing, perhaps a Socratic inheritance (*Republic* 515 c, *Symposium* 210 e, *Seventh Letter* 341 c); Socrates is, after all, somewhat suspicious of ethical habit, the very condition Aristotle values.

   33. Human being as origin of deeds: Aristotle, *Nicomachean Ethics* III 3, 1112 b.

   34. As an antidote to my understanding of the ancients on will, the reader is directed to Michael Frede's *A Free Will: Origins of the Notion in Ancient Thought*, Sather Classical Lectures 1997–98 (Berkeley: Univ. of California Press, 2011). Our conclusions don't differ grossly, but the why's and wherefore's do; it is a consequence of different ways of reading.

   For Frede, too, the notion of a will does not appear in Aristotle; it is, so to speak, preempted by "willing," Frede's term for "rational desire" (24). But it seems to me that cannot be the real reason, for Frede is working from a schematized definition of free will as the possibility of choosing (7). And for Aristotle, choice is *of means* only; ends are the objects of rational appetite. *That* ought to be, for Frede, the reason why will does not appear: because in the grand tradition ends are *not* chosen.

   Again, Frede sees the notion of the will emerging among the Stoics (31). I would argue that it *is* there, but precisely *submerged*, an unacknowledged spook.

   Finally, Augustine—where we do really differ. Frede thinks that Augustine is "very much an ancient figure," whose notion of the will is largely borrowed from Plato and is "just a more complex version of the Stoics" (153, 159). The latter attribution seems to me way overstated in view of Augustine's intense self-inquisition and the explicit prominence of the will; the former is simply unpersuasive in one great point: Augustine's radical newness lies not only in the *cognitive* primacy of the will, but in the vivid announcement of a novel, a *very un-Platonic* human capability: the will to do evil, the perverse will. But these are debatable cavils.

   Frede regards his "inquiry as purely historical" (6), and that is where perplexities particularly fascinating to me arise. I cannot attach a clear meaning to "purely historical." He faults his predecessor Albrecht Dihle (*The Theory of the Will in Classical Antiquity* [Berkeley: Univ. of California Press, 1982]) for conducting his inquiry on the basis of a *specific* modern notion of will as being, *ipso facto*, free will: "sheer volition." That is, to be sure, controversial. So to begin with, "purely historical" must mean inquiring without some specific notion of a free will, "but simply trying to find out when and why a notion of free will arose . . . and what notion this was." It seems to me that intention passes too easily over the devilishly subtle boot-strapping required when one attempts to recognize a concept without bringing to it some identifying template. (This is *the* problem of Plato's *Meno*, introduced with an obstructionist intention by that rogue Meno at 80 d, but nonetheless taken very seriously by Socrates.) In fact, it can't be done, and Frede acknowledges that by having recourse to the *general* schema of the will referred to above (7). This general idea is obtained by "benefit of historical hindsight." Here historical in- or hindsight seems to mean abstracting from the particularities of authored texts as if they were idiosyncrasies—when, as I think, they *are* the writer's "own-most" thought (to call to aid a Teutonism). I think such thought is—this is a mystery of our humanity—the very aspect of mentation that makes it interesting to all of us in common. Then "purely historic" means "denaturedly general"—and hopelessly melded into an environment, encouragingly called the "context."

But that's not the real trouble, which is rather, it would seem, that you really can't conduct such a schematizing abstraction without in fact possessing—as Frede acknowledges—a guiding interpretative procedure. In this case, what is at hand is a word that is recognized as meaning "will" according to some preconceived notion—and the same for "freedom." But that has pitfalls. For example, Frede says that the "standard [early] Greek term for will is *prohairesis*, literally choice . . ." (8). *Prohairesis*, however, is Aristotle's crucial term, and he is said by Frede not to have a notion of the will. What's worse, Frede's sentence implies that will *is* choice, which is indeed a most contestable notion, both because in Thomas, for instance, choice is only one element in the process of willing, and also because, as Frede points out, not all will is free will, although choice seems to imply freedom—"free choice" is surely in most circumstances redundant.

The basic prejudgment that makes Frede's inquiry historical seems to be that there is a concept of "ancient thought" within which notions such as will "arise. It seems true to me that "antiquity" is indeed a discernible conceptual complex, but not that it applies to all ancients; thus the Stoics are moderns *par excellence*, discernibly so by their representationalism, their physicalism, and their privileging of subjectivity.

Can I do better? Well, it is better, I think, to allow individual expression (descended to us as texts) to remain the initial and the terminal points of reference, to observe the hermeneutic principle of charity, which says that texts of a great quality are to be approached as potentially interesting and to be read as making—often novel—sense. It is better to be ever mindful of the bootstrapping aspect (meaning the logically indefensible conjunction of self-intrusion and self-denial required by conceptual inquiries into texts) and then to proceed by alert muddling through. It is better to regard temporal sequence as humanly rather than intellectually significant, namely as the constraining condition of one human being learning from another (which is the principal way of being influenced, be it absorbently or recalcitrantly) rather than as the necessitating cause of an abstracted conceptual development.

Does the above anti-pragmatic pragmatism add up to a "hermeneutic," a theory of interpretation? No—more to an injunction to myself to carry on under certain guiding convictions—though those, in turn, are underwritten by two faiths: Whatever a writing human being has thought out, I, a reading fellow-human, can recover and rethink, and whatever my convictions are, I can both bring them to awareness and hold them in abeyance while I enter upon another's.

Chapter II. Pivot Points

1. 270 years: Aristotle died in 322, Lucretius c. 52 B.C.E.; both the *Nicomachean Ethics* and *On the Nature of Things* are thought to be late compositions, so this number seems a fair guess.

Free will: *On the Nature of Things* II 256–60; **Venus**: I 28; **human swerve**: II 259; **bitter cup honeyed at rim**: IV 12.

Major edition: Cyril Bailey, *Titi Lucreti Cari, De Rerum Natura Libra Sex*, with commentary (Oxford: Clarendon Press, 1947). The claim that "free will" is first mentioned by Lucretius is made by Richard Sorabji, *Emotion and Peace of Mind: From Stoic Agitation to Christian Temptation* (Oxford: Oxford Univ. Press, 2000), 333. This reference is in the very knowledgeable chapter "The Concept of Will." Equally helpful in comparing Epictetus and Aristotle on the will is the chapter "Self as practical reason: Epictetus' inviolable self and Aristotle's deliberate choice" in

Sorabji's *Self: Ancient and Modern Insights about Individuality, Life, and Death* (Chicago: Univ. of Chicago Press, 2006). For the term "free will" itself, see my Preface.

2. Snippets: *Stoicorum Veterum Fragmenta*, 4 vols., ed. Hans von Arnim (1903–5) (New York: Irvington Publishers, 1986); **Stoic modernity**: Eva Brann, *Feeling Our Feelings*, 109–12, 140–44.

3. Epictetus's deviations: Sorabji, *Self*, 91 ff.

4. Tusculans: This edition is very helpful: *Cicero on the Emotions: Tusculan Disputations 3 and 4* (45 B.C.E.), trans. and comm. Margaret Graver (Chicago: Univ. of Chicago Press, 2002). Cicero had lost his daughter early in the year 45 and had withdrawn from public life; he was writing, as he says in a letter and in the work itself, to console himself, p. xiv, *Tusculan Disputations* III 76 and IV 63.

5. The ablative *voluntate*, "by intention": in legal contexts, Graver, *Cicero on the Emotions*, 113; **Stoic *boulesis***: *Tusculan Disputations* IV 12; **intrusions on original doctrine**: I shouldn't really claim that well-passions (*eupatheia*) and most non-rational affects were all *later* modifications of early Stoicism, since I don't know that; what I mean is that there is a coherent Stoic gist; nonetheless, I note that *eupatheia* is not attributed to the founders in the *Stoicorum Veterum Fragmenta*. On the difficulty of good Stoic passions, see Julia E. Annas, *Hellenistic Philosophy of Mind* (Berkeley: Univ. of California Press, 1992), 144, n. 27; **passions as judgments and opinions**: *Tusculan Disputations* IV 14–15.

6. *Voluntate*: Graver, *Cicero on the Emotions*, 113.

7. *Tusculan Disputations* III 61.

8. Empty mind (*vacuus animus*): *Tusculan Disputations* IV 38; **object of desire (*quod libidinem moveat*)**: IV 62.

9. Perturbation of mind: *Tusculan Disputations* III 7–8; **arguments and consolations**: most of *Tusculan* III is devoted to this. Here is a somewhat unfair example: Homeric hero tears his hair out in grief, Stoic wiseacre—"Is baldness, then, a cure for sorrow?" (III 62).

10. Distress: *Tusculan Disputations* III 25; **mortality of child**: III 30, actually quoted in the section on Epicureans, but clearly also Stoic; **letters**: Graver, *Cicero on the Emotions*, xiv; **quotations from end**: *Tusculan Disputations* IV 84. Cicero had said early on in a similar context *sanabimur si volemus*, "we will be healed if we wish," III 13. He never quite gets round to calling the mastery of the passions by the Greek Stoic term *apatheia* or the Latin *indolenta*, in English "impassivity," meaning "passionlessness."

11. English text: Epictetus, *The Discourses, the Handbook, Fragments*, ed. Christopher Gill, trans. Robin Hard (London: Everyman, 1995). I've made occasional changes in the translation, using the Teubner Greek edition. Book and paragraph references are standard.

12. These following references are only examples, since the notions are scattered throughout the *Discourses*. **Epictetus's reading**: e.g., Chrysippus, I 4, 12; **philosophy**: I 15, II 9–10.

13. "In our power" is really an augmenting gloss. Epictetus does sometimes use the verb *dynasthai*, e.g., II 1 (14), from the noun *dynamis*, "ability, power," but when he is on point, it's *eph'hemin*; the phrase has a sort of elegant boldness with a soupçon of complexity; *epi*, "upon," with the dative *hemin* betokens the responsible condition upon which something happens, namely we ourselves, and "up to us" catches that felicitously. *Ta eph' hemin*, "things up to us" occurs in Aristotle, *Nicomachean Ethics*, e.g., 1111 b 30, 33.

John Buchan in *Prester John* (1910), chap. VIII: "I was all alone and it was 'up to me,' as Americans say . . ." Evidently the Stoic locution sounded transcontinental to Scotsmen.

14. Processed appearance: *phantasia* derives from a verb *phantazein*: the *azein* ending denotes a making-function; **impression-type**: I 27 (1).

15. Extirpate, expel: II 6 (45); this Stoic loves to expel and purify—a very untranquil extremism; **logic**: I 17; **criterion**: I 11 (10 ff.).

16. Choice: II 16 (1).

17. Freedom: IV 1 (1 ff.); **indifference**: II 6, 19 (13); **for there is nothing**: *Hamlet* 2.2.244.

18. Preoccupation with slavery: IV 1 (128 ff.).

19. Miserable *hegemonikon*: I 20 (11).

20. Factual Stoic helpfulness: see the Gill edition of the *Discourses*, 347 ff., for a reprint of U.S. Vice-Admiral James Stockdale's account of how Epictetus's principles helped him to survive with honor in a Vietnamese prison camp.

21. **Initiatory education**: *Republic* VIII, *Seventh Letter* 340 b ff.

22. **Stoic training**: *Discourses* II 9 (13 ff.), III 2.

23. *Credo quia absurdum est*: Tertullian, whose doctrines resemble that of the Stoics in that he combines a thorough-going materialism with a contempt for sensuousness; **habituation**: Aristotle, *Nicomachean Ethics* II 1103 a 30 ff.; *boulesis*: *Discourses* I 12 (15), 1 27 (11), II 14 (7)—this candidate-term for will occurs only three times in the *Discourses* (the first time in the plural) and clearly means "wish."

24. **Struggle**: I 24, II 18; **affects and reason different**: Brann, *Feeling Our Feelings*, 457 ff.

25. A candidate for proto-will might be Socrates' formulation of spirited pride, *thymos*, a part and function of the soul mediating between reason and desire. *Thymos* is willing to listen to reason more than desire is, *Republic* IV 439 d–440 e.

26. References to Marcus Aurelius's *Meditations* are only examples, since, again, ideas are scattered throughout the individual meditations. References to book and paragraph are standard. **Stoic actions**: VIII 5; **citizenship**: IV 4, VII 55, IX 23. With the emperor's civic sense contrast Epictetus's quietism, for example, in his management of a tyrant: regard him, Epictetus advises, as powerless to do anything to his subjects that matters, *Discourses* I 19.

27. **Present**: *Meditations* VI 32, VIII 98; **imagination**: VI 17, 29, VIII 29.

28. **Facts**: I mean by "fact" a hard bit of datum, devoid of any judgmental envelope, which is what Marcus is after, I think. But the term is, in one respect, anachronistic: A "modern" fact is precisely recordable evidence and projectible into and out of the present. On the other hand, the hard bit where the character of "modern" fact is prefigured (once again the Stoics are out ahead) is in Marcus's concentrations on the bare, present presentation as yet un-enveloped in judgment—for the sake of right judgment, to be sure, but based on the pretheorized given. Yet there again, it can be argued that no fact can arise without a theoretical environment. See Mary Poovey, *A History of the Modern Fact: Problems of Knowledge in the Science of Wealth and Society* (Chicago: Univ. of Chicago Press, 1998). She emphasizes the role of writing, especially accounting, in the genesis of "modern" fact (chap. 2) and distinguishes it from ancient (Aristotelian) particulars, which do not in themselves count as knowables (p. 10). But my point is that there is, so to speak, an original modernity that might be attributed to this imperial Stoic's version of factuality.

Doing and dreaming: Wittgenstein will claim (*Zettel* 621)—wrongly, I think—that we cannot see and imagine the same thing simultaneously. Shakespeare asks: "What is your substance, whereof are you made / That millions of strange shadows on you tend?" (Sonnet 53), which *is*, it seems to me, seeing the being and its imaginative projection simultaneously.

29. **Ruling principle**: IV 1, 8, VII 16, VIII 48; **free will**: I 8, XI 36.

30. **Opinion**: XII 22.

31. **The rationalistic West**: e.g. Robert C. Solomon, *The Passions* (1976); **Augustine on memory and time**: *Confessions*, Books 10–11, and Husserl: Edmund Husserl, *The Phenomenology of Internal Time-Consciousness* (1905–10), ed. Martin Heidegger (Bloomington: Indiana Univ. Press, 1964), 21; **Augustine's anticipation of Husserl's theory**: Brann, *What, Then, Is Time?*, 116 ff., 126 ff.

32. In order—Andean Aymara: Rafael E. Nuñez and Eve Sweetser, "With the Future Behind Them," *Cognitive Science* 30 (2006): 401 ff.; Aztecs of Tenochtitlan: Inga Clendinnen, *Aztecs: An Interpretation* (New York: Cambridge Univ. Press, 1991), 89; Kallatiai of India: Herodotus, *Persian Wars*, III 38; Inca of Peru: William H. Prescott, *History of the Conquest of Mexico, and History of the Conquest of Peru* (1847) (New York: The Modern Library, 1936), 749; Cameroonian Dowayo: Nigel Barley, *The Innocent Anthropologist: Notes from a Mud Hut* (1983; reprint, Long Grove, Ill.: Waveland Press, 2000), 168; Amazonian Yanomamö: Napoleon A. Chagnon, *Yanomamö*, 4th ed. (Fort Worth: Harcourt Brace, 1992), 53 ff.

33. Augustine, *On Free Choice of the Will* (395 C.E.), trans. Thomas Williams (Indianapolis: Hackett Publishing, 1993); *The Confessions of Saint Augustine* (401 C.E.), trans. John K. Ryan (New York: Doubleday, 1960); Saint Augustine, *The Trinity* (419 C.E.), trans. Edmund Hill, O.P. (Hyde Park: New City Press, 1991); Augustine, *The City of God*, trans. Marcus Dods (New York: Modern Library, 1950). I also used other translations, in particular the beautiful Elizabethan *Confessions* by William Watts in the Latin Loeb series. There are numerous editions of these works.

The book that first made me aware of Augustine's originating role with respect to the will is Hannah Arendt's *The Life of the Mind: Two/Willing* (1971); **arbiter**: A. Walde and J. B. Hofman, *Lateinisches Etymologisches Wörterbuch* (Heidelberg: Carl Winter, 1938).

34. Socrates: see Ch. I, Sec. B, herein.

35. Stoic vacancy: This paraphrase is of *On Free Choice* I 12. The discussion up to here is based on I 1–12; **self-will**: If a natural and common propensity (i.e., not just an individual character flaw) for willfulness, for self-will, ever shows itself, it must be in the "terrible twos." A little terror I was baby-sitting told me, repeatedly and unforgettably: "I *want* not to want," whatever I offered him; it made that ordeal worthwhile.

36. Happiness: *On Free Choice* I 14; **law**: I 15.

37. *On Free Choice* II 20.

38. Unless you believe: Isaiah 7:9; **common and private**: *On Free Choice* II 7; **numbers**: II 8–9; **unchangeable truth**: II 12; **superior and inferior**: II 10; **inner rules**: II 12; **God as craftsman**: II 16; **Descartes**: *Rules for the Direction of Mind* (1628).

39. A perverse will, truth held in common: *On Free Choice* II 14; **free will a good from God**: II 18; **powers of the soul, reflexivity of the will, sin**: II 19.

40. The reader of *On Free Choice* might be startled to see that by the beginning and end of Book III the conversation is in fact a "book" (III 1 and 25). In Augustine's "Reconsiderations" (printed in the Williams translation), we learn that the conversation was real and took place in Rome, and that it became a composition only when Augustine returned to Africa. Its development is marked by the evolution of Evodius's perplexities that head the three books: 1. Is evil from God? 2. Even if it not from God but from us, because we have the free will that allows sin, isn't it really from God who gave us a free will to sin? 3. Even if free will is a good as coming from God, who is thus not responsible for our misuse of it, how is its turn to evil to be explained?

It follows that the nature and operation of free choice is only an ancillary, almost incidental, purpose of this, *the* founding work on the will. That is not accidental but indicative of an overbearing enigma, the unintelligibility of the will's misuse—a more unsettling problem than even its freedom.

41. Sophism: I will make bold to offer a better argument: It is not *fore*knowledge that an omniscient God has but *a*temporal, panoramic, all-at-once oversight. His knowledge therefore has no futurity; it is not anticipatory. (It's my own, but bound to be old hat to theologians—in fact, I found it later in Boethius; see Ch. IX, Note 21, herein.)

A sinner better than a stone: *On Free Choice* III 5.

42. This note covers the three preceding paragraphs. **Two sources of sin**: III 10; **perhaps a third source**: I say "perhaps" because, although Augustine has introduced derivative sin (III 20), he doesn't call it a third source.

43. Sin as neglect, pride, his own God: III 24; **pride, the beginning of all sin and apostasy from God**: Ecclesiastes 10:13 and 10:12, *On Free Choice* III 25.

44. Theft: *Confessions* II 4.

45. Perversity: VII 3, 16.

46. Two wills: VIII 9.

47. Will not a faculty: *Confessions*, trans. John K. Ryan, 396, chap. 9, n.1; *The Trinity*, trans. Edmund Hill, 24–25; *facultas*: VIII 8.

48. Plethora of terms: VIII 8–10.

49. What I would: Romans 7:15.

50. Freer sin: *Confessions* VIII 10.

51. Derailment: VIII 5 and 9.

52. Images: Genesis 1:27, Corinthians 11:7; **complexity**: one example is his treatment of internal time-consciousness: temporal beings live in the present, albeit a present of things past, a present of things present, a present of things future, subserved respectively by memory, perception, expectation; all are in our present (*Confessions* XI 22).

53. Early mention of will: IV, sec. 30. The Trinity is the subject of the first seven of the fifteen books of *On the Trinity*; the application to the mind starts with the eighth book. These are the chief passages I will use (references are to book and sections): IX 7, 9; X 11, 13, 17–19; XI 6–12, 14–15, 18; XII 25; XIII 26; XIV 11; XV 41–43.

54. **Augustine's anticipation of Cartesian willed doubt in** *Meditations* **I 22**: *Trinity* X 13–14; **If I doubt**: *City of God* XI 2.

55. *Cogitatio*: *Trinity* XI 6; **Cartesian** *Cogito*: *Meditations* II 25 ff.

56. **Utterly indivisible**: *Meditations* VI 86; **anti-representationalism**: A central work is Richard Rorty's *Philosophy and the Mirror of Nature* (1979); **Augustine's direct cognition**: *Meditations* X 5 (mind) and XI 3 (body); **nothing is easier**: II 34.

57. **Direct knowledge of mind**: *Trinity* X 5–6; **Know Thyself**: X 7; **mental defect**: X 7; **Pascal's diversion**: *Pensées* VIII, "Diversion."

58. **The great Trinity**: *Trinity* XI 6 ff.—there are many other trinities: Trinitarian triplicity is the cognition-constituting principle. There is the sensory trinity of object and sensation, mediated by the attention-directing will; there is the psychic trinity of a memory image joined to the mind's vision, again by the will. In fact there are as many trinities as there are cognitive acts.

Wills: X 10, XV 38; **undivided unity**: XII 4.

59. **Mental functions**: XI 6–8; **quasi-parents**: XI 9–12; **will as spirit**: this is an especially serendipitous identification in English, where "spirit," as a translation for Greek *thymos*, is close to the force of will; **will as weight**: IX 18; **number**: *On Free Choice* II 11 ff.

60. **Wisdom vs. knowledge**: *Trinity* XII 25; **will as love**: XIII 26, XIV 5, 10; **Spirit as love**: XIV 32.

61. **Self-love**: IX 2, XIV 11; **will of will**: XV 38; **God as being his own greatness**: V 11—here is foreshadowed Anselm's great argument for God's existence: He is a being so inclusively maximal both in conception and in reality that he must necessarily encompass his own existence as a quality he could not be lacking (Anselm, *Proslogium* II; for an analysis of Anselm's "ontological argument," see Brann, *The Ways of Naysaying*, 103–107); **God as ultimate cause**: III 8.

62. **Image and panel**: XV 43—this analysis of an image becomes a topic in Phenomenology (Brann, *World of the Imagination*, 649); **will moved by passion**: XV 41.

63. **Theme of** *City of God*: I Preface; **will**: V 10, XII 3, 6–9, XIV 6–7, XXII 1–2, 30; **the will is them all**: XIV 6; **Aristotle**: see Ch. I, Sec. C, herein; **passions volitional**: in Descartes.

64. I have been writing as if Descartes took ideas from Augustine. He says in a letter to Colvius that he borrowed a book by Augustine, but that letter is dated 1640, after his first formulation of the *cogito* (passage quoted in the Matthews edition of *On the Trinity*, p. xxviii). Even if he had had Augustinian texts at hand earlier, he might only have peeked at them, and priority alone does not establish influence. In any case, the Preacher says that there is nothing new under the sun, and that is mostly borne out for philosophical writing. Nonetheless, two notions do seem to me to matter: 1. that the Preacher is wrong in one case: It was a long time before the will as a basic human capacity was acknowledged in books, and this recognition *was* indeed something new, and 2. that priority issues aside, it is interesting to follow out the consequences for humanity from different versions of willing—particularly the will's will to take over.

Moreover, when it comes to priority with respect to the *cogito*, Aristotle trumps both Augustine and Descartes: ". . . to be aware that we are perceiving or thinking is to be aware that we *are*" (*Nicomachean Ethics* IX 1170 a 33).

65. The texts by Descartes I mainly used are, in order: *The Passions of the Soul* (1649), *Principles of Philosophy* (1644), *Meditations on First Philosophy* (1641).

The edition used for the first is René Descartes, *The Passions of the Soul*, ed. Stephen Voss (Indianapolis: Hackett Publishing, 1989); references are given by Part and Article. The second two are found in *The Philosophical Writings of Descartes*, trans. John Cottingham, Robert Stoothoff, and Dugald Murdoch, vol. I, *Principles of Philosophy* and vol. II, *Meditations* (Cambridge: Cambridge Univ. Press, 1999); references are given in standard terms.

66. **Pineal gland**: *Passions* I 31 ff., Brann, *Feeling our Feelings*, 193, 202 ff.; **action and passion**: *Passions* I 1–2; **volitions**: I 17 ff.; **objects of perception**: *Principles* I 48; **psychic perceptions willed**: *Passions* I 41.

67. **Willing, memory, imagination, etc.**: I 41 ff.; **proto-Kantian**: Kant will insist that the will must act purely, that is, for the sake of its own integrity, and that morality cannot be based on the satisfaction even of better desires but must be achieved by their subjugation to the will's command. (See Ch. V, Sec. A, herein.)

68. **First occurrence of free will**: *Passions* II 144; **up to us, error**: ibid.

69. Like God: *Passions* III 152.

70. Meaning of "meditation": Dennis L. Sepper, *Descartes' Imagination: Proportion, Images, and the Activity of Thinking* (Berkeley: Univ. of California Press, 1996), 255 ff.; **sixth day**: beginnings of Second and Fourth Meditations. There is a long church history of *Hexamera*, "Six Days' Homilies" (see Chaninah Maschler, "What Tree Is This? In Praise of Europe's Renaissance Printers, Publishers, and Philologists," *The St. John's Review* XLVII [2003]: 57–58). But the *Meditations* don't feel like a pious preachment.

71. All five items come from Part One of the *Principles*. One: 32; Two: 34; Three: 35; Four: 43, 35, 42; Five: 39–41. Descartes deals with the compatibilism by simply admitting that, though we know clearly and distinctly that God's power is infinite and so is his preordaining will, our finite intellects can't grasp how this leaves us free to act, although we know this too, innately and clearly—and experientially. For this freedom is so great as to enable us to abstain from believing what is not yet certain; and this very matter that we could not doubt even while abstaining from belief "is as self-evident and as transparently clear as anything can be." In other words, it is this experienced freedom of the will that gains us certainty of knowledge.

Here is Shakespeare, in a much more down-to-earth mode:

> This is the monstruosity in love, lady, that the will is infinite, and the execution confined; that the desire is boundless, and the act a slave to limit. (*Troilus and Cressida* 3.2.85)

72. Selfhood: *Meditations* II 28; **wills not**: there is an archaic verb that would fit here: "nills," meaning "does not will."

73. Sometimes, *mind*: myself insofar as I am merely a thinking thing, *Meditations* VI 86; **willing more than a perception**: this roused an objection by Hobbes (dismissed by Descartes, see Cottingham et al., vol. II, 128). Hobbes on his part dismisses will by reducing it to "the last appetite in deliberation," a mere final moment before something happens (*Leviathan*, 1651, I 7).

74. Let there be light: Genesis I:14, 16; **God's will**: Thomas Aquinas says that His creatures are in some way like God, but God is not like them (*Summa Theologiae*, Pt. I, Q. 4, a. 3). I think Descartes disagreed.

75. Essential will: in the *Passions* I 17 and in the *Meditations* IV 57–58; **indifference**: IV 58 (see Conclusion, Note 26, herein); **Stoic indifference**: e.g. Epictetus, *Discourses* I 20, II 9, 19; **voluntariness same as freedom**: Cottingham et al., vol. II, 134.

76. Error: *Meditations* IV 56 ff.; **not using will correctly**: IV 59; **privation in operation of will**: IV 60.

77. Objections and Descartes' replies are all in Cottingham et al., vol. II, **First**: 218, 259; **Second**: 220, 260.

78. Propositional attitudes and assertion: A. C. Grayling, *An Introduction to Philosophical Logic* (Totowa, N.J.: Barnes & Noble Books, 1982), 27 ff.; L. S. Stebbing, *A Modern Introduction to Logic* (New York: Harper and Brothers, 1950).

79. "Intensive" in the somewhat out-of-use sense of "not piecemeal" but "all-in-all." Thus an intensive magnitude, for example, a feeling, such as of power, is one that is experienced all at once; though it might have successively different degrees of intensity each moment is a whole. Contrasted to intension is "extension," such as characterizes spatial being, which has its parts outside each other and can be measured piecemeal part by part. Cartesian extension is identical with body, for it is what is apprehensible about body, and that is what makes corporeal things "the subject matter of mathematics," both geometry and algebra.

There is an allied logical meaning: The intension of a class is the concept that defines it is a whole; its extension is its members one by one.

Imagination not of the ego's essence: *Meditations* VI 73; **corporeal things subject of mathematics**: VI 74; **man's dominion**: Genesis 1:26.

80. Discourse: Descartes, *Discourse on the Method of Rightly Conducting One's Reason and Seeking the Truth in the Sciences* (1637), VI 77–78.

Chapter III. Mainliners and Extremists

1. Besides mainliners and extremists, there are also outliers, remarkable writers who seem to have neither the grand tradition behind them nor a wide effect before them. Among these is the earliest of the authors here called on out of those usually ranged among the medievals, John Scotus Eriugena, whose work, *On the Division of Nature* (c. 866 C.E.) deals with the Will of God in Neoplatonic terms. This will of wills is too—unattributedly—resonant in modernity, though in transmogrified ways, for me to omit, so here is a brief review.

Such a review wouldn't be well grounded, however, without some account of ancient Neoplatonism. Eriugena (the epithet means "the Irishman," man of Erin; in those days the Irish were also called Scots) used as his Neoplatonic source the writings of Pseudo-Dionysius (end of fifth century C.E.), whom he translated; I will, however, cite in comparison what is one of the grandest treatises of the arch-Neoplatonist Plotinus, the eighth treatise of the sixth *Ennead* (VI 8), "On Voluntariness (*hekousion*) and the Will (*thelema*) of the One." (Plotinus founded his school in Rome in the mid-third century C.E.; Augustine both absorbed and resisted his systematized Platonism sometime in the late fourth century [*Confessions* VII 9].)

One reason why the Plotinian treatise is pertinent to the study of the will is its large will-and-power vocabulary: "the 'up to him'" (*to ep'autoi*, the Stoic phrase turned into a substantive, used of the Intellect's power); "will" (*boulesis*, the usual ancient term, the plural seems to be used for "wishing"), "wishing, wanting, willing" (*to thelein, thelesis, thelema*, various nominal forms of the verb *thelein*, used increasingly along with *boulesis* of the activity of the One); *hekousion* (the Aristotelian term for what is voluntary); *autexousia* (self-authority), *kyrios* (empowered), *archon heautou* (self-ruling).

Thus Plotinus's inquiry concerns freedom and power. It begins with will in human being and then "dares" to ascend to first beings (VI 8, 1; hereafter I give only the last, the section number). What is "up to us" as human beings? Various perplexities are raised: We might be enslaved to our wish-will, or our passions might actually be raised by our calculating thought. The solution is that voluntariness and self-authority must be granted to him who, freed from bodily passions, depends on the activities of the Intellect (*nous*), the noblest principle. That raises the inquiry into the divine realm. In the Plotinian scheme, *nous*, whose activity depends on an object, if only itself, is below the Good, also called the One, which is self-sufficiently complete *and* completely unified. The Good is not what it is by necessity but because it is the best. Nor did this One, which is itself the necessity and law of others, bring itself into existence, for that would betoken duality. It is itself the substantial ground (*hypostasis*) of all grounds and therefore has no ground (10). The rest is silence (11)—or the way of negation.

Here begins Eriugena's parallelism, because now the problem arises: How does the One, the Good, which rests in itself, go out to its world—in Christian terms, its Creation? Plotinus has a simile in which all the terms of the image are negated: The One, which has no place, is like a point from which radiates a circle delineated by emanating radii (11, 18). In this circle, the One that is nowhere is everywhere; like a father, it gives to others their being. Although it is "borne to its own inside" and does not look out, "loving [only] himself, so to speak," yet everything happens about it and looks to it; it is lovable, somehow, and is also love as well as self-love (15–16). So again, speaking contradictorily, it also makes itself not by chance but as it *wills*; its *willing* is not random but of the best. It is an actuality, self-made by its will, but not as its own ground. It is prior to the self-divided Intellect, which in the circle image, "runs round" the center as a kind of come-apart god. The One is altogether self-related and self-willed, yet it is everywhere with the others. In another simile, it is like the rational root of a huge tree, the pervasive "ruling source and basis" (*arche kai basis*) of a huge plant (15). Thus it itself is "everywhere" and "everything" (16), and all things are held together by "a certain participation" (*metousia*, 21) in it.

The One's holding itself together, collecting all that it (speaking analogously) is, is *its* will, for it could not be the will of a "god not-yet in being" (*boulesei theou mepo ontos*, 21); this *will is nothing other than its being*, and though it is primarily the being of the One, it is also a generative will: It is its freedom to be before all existence and also to allow existence to be (21).

Here, I think, humanity divides around the opinion that "whereof one cannot speak, thereof one must keep silent" (Wittgenstein, *Tractatus*, end) and the opinion that, where logical speech fails, alternatives must be attempted—Plotinus's version of "going away in silence," namely in self-contradiction and the *via negativa* (9, 11).

Eriugena chooses the latter path. Here, in order, are some of the Neoplatonic notions found in Plotinus that turn up in Eriugena's dialogue between a master and his student in *On the Division of Nature*, Book I 11–14 (found in *Philosophy in the Middle Ages: The Christian, Islamic, and*

Jewish Traditions, eds. Arthur Hyman and James J. Walsh [New York: Harper and Row, 1967], 138 ff.): God is *anarchos*, "unbegun": He is beginning, middle, and end of all things—their beginning because all things participate in his essence, their end because all things seek him as seeking quiet and perfection. He is uncreated: The name of God (*theos*) may be—falsely—related to *theo* "I run," because somewhat like Plotinus's Intellect, he courses about everything. He is moved not outside himself but within, by the appetite of his will—though he is actually unchangeable, for he contains no oppositions; speech of motion is a creature's metaphor for the Creator. Divine nature is nothing else but divine will, so that the internal "motion" of the divine will, the unchangeably proposed plan of his will, is the founding of all things.

Since, moreover, God's being and his will are the same as God's proposed creation, he is created in his creation—he *is* his creation. For everything good is so by participation in his good, and everything that exists does so by participation in his nature: "Divine nature, which is nothing else than divine will, therefore is said to be *made* [my italics] in all things." This is heterodox. The mainline position is, on the contrary, that God exists in things not as their essence "but as an agent is present in that upon which it acts" (Thomas Aquinas, *Summa Theologiae*, Part I, Question 8, 1).

What can be predicated of God? About that, one should either be silent and rely on faith or, once in an argument, resort both to affirmative and negative theology; the former speaks metaphorically, creaturely talk; the latter is a straight expression of God's incomprehensibility to human beings. Plotinus chooses mostly this latter mode; is it then inapprehensible? Not if we regard it as the preparation of an experience intended to convey the susceptible student to the edge of an illumination—as rational mysticism.

However, negative expression failed in the following respect: Plotinus was unable to express the *will*, the assertion of effective power, on the part of an impersonal, self-sufficient and self-enclosed One except in piles of paradoxes and figurative coruscations. Here Eriugena too becomes positively implausible in explaining the being-will of a personal Creator who, himself uncreated, brings creation into existence out of nothing as an other self—a self-theophany. The difficulty is that in this divine manifestation there is an undeniable duality; the will's proposal, once realized, stares back at its Creator. This division between Creator and creation might, it seems, be overcome either by downgrading creation, making it somehow unreal (which is the pagan, Plotinian way but which would take Eriugena far from Scripture) or by upgrading the inaccessibility, the negativity, the nothingness of God into something convertible into a created manifestation (III 19). It is no wonder that *On the Division of Nature* was condemned and Eriugena turned into an outlier, for his work demonstrates at once the inviting similarities and the uneasy fit of Neoplatonism and Christianity. We should not ignore him, because he presages in two related ways (without his influence being acknowledged) what is to come: 1. in being, by one interpretation, a proto-pantheist, and pantheism has a special propensity to privilege the will, as in Spinoza's *Ethics* (see Ch. VII, Note 1, herein), and 2. in emphasizing that in God essential being and creative will are one—an identification that will have terrific consequences both for God's role in religion as a willful despotism unmediated by natural law between him and mankind (Ockham Ch. III, Sec. C, herein), and for mankind's position in the world as a godlike creator, untrammeled in creating a second nature on earth (Romantics Ch. V, end, herein).

   2. The oppression that can attend being the beneficiary of a well-curated tradition is caught with colorful exactitude by Walker Percy in *The Last Gentleman* (1966). The scene is the Metropolitan Museum of Art:

> In here the air is thick as mustard gas with ravenous particles which were stealing the substance from painting and viewer alike . . . The particles were turning the air blue with their singing and ravening . . . Now here comes a citizen who has the good fortune to be able to enjoy a cultural facility . . . There is the painting that has been brought at great expense and exhibited in the museum so that millions can see it. What is wrong with that? Something . . . For the paintings were encrusted with a public secretion.

Of course, you can cut through the cultural mustard gas by some deliberate directness.
   3. Thomas's main texts on will: *Summa Theologiae* (1265–70 C.E.), Part I, Questions 80, 82, 83 (Man), Part I of II, Qq. 6–17, 19 (Human Acts); Qq. 74, 77 (Sin). The main edition I used: St.

Thomas Aquinas, *Summa Theologiae*, vol. 17: Psychology of Human Acts, trans. Thomas Gilby (Cambridge: Blackfriars, 1970), also vols. 11, 25; *On Truth* (1256–59 C.E.), Qq. 21–29. Also: St. Thomas Aquinas, *Truth*, vol. 3, trans. Robert W. Schmidt, S.J. (Chicago: Henry Regnery, 1954). Compendious collection: *Basic Writings of Thomas Aquinas*, 2 vols., ed. Anton C. Pegis (New York: Random House, 1945).

All the texts give parallel works of Thomas himself and references to his sources in the footnotes.

Since truth is the object of the intellect and goodness that of the will, the presence of the nine long questions on the will in *Truth* is something of a problem (see Schmidt's preface to *Truth*, vol. 3, p. v). However that may be, the treatment of the will in this work is the forerunner of that in the *Summa*, which however seems to me to be, by and large, more definitive.

4. The references, all from Part I of the *Summa*, are for the items enumerated in the preceding paragraph of my text (Question, article): Q. 5, a. 1; Q. 16, a. 4; Q. 19, a. 12.

5. Q. 19, a. 4; Q. 59, a. 1; Q. 59, a. 3; Q. 63, a. 2; Q. 63, a. 3; Q. 64, a. 2.

6. The intellect is in turn divided into speculative and practical, Q. 79, a. 11. The practical intellect is *not* the will (as later in Kant), but falls under the truth-pursuing intellect insofar as it is directed to operating in life (as in Aristotle). (Q. 79, a. 11; also *Truth* Q. 22, a. 11, Answer no. 4.)

Since we are on classification: In the *Summa*, will and intellect are co-ordinate, or rather mutually inclusive, but insofar as will is *intellectual* appetite, the intellect is in one schematization taken to include the will (*Truth* Q. 22, a. 11, Answer no. 3). Thus the Intellect has two subdivisions, appetitive and apprehending; the former is the will, the latter includes the speculative and the practical intellect. In the *Summa* the Intellect is said to be the higher power insofar as its object is "the very notion of appetible good," and it is this good that is the will's object. Since the notion is higher than the actual object, according to Thomas, the Intellect is "in itself and absolutely" higher and nobler than the will; relatively, however, the will can be higher, if it goes out to a good object that is better than the knowledge of it in the soul; for example, the love of God is better than the knowledge of God (Q. 82, a. 3). These mutual embracings and reciprocal trumpings make one's head spin—as the subject requires. Fr. James Lehrberger reminds me that this mutuality is an instance of the very exemplar of such self-embracing, the Trinity: One is three and three is One.

Power: In Shakespeare's *Troilus and Cressida* 1.3.109 ff.), Ulysses models the political defender of an earthly hierarchy of "authentic place," of "degree." It alone defends the world from universal strife:

> Take but degree away, untune that string,
> And, hark! What discord follows; each thing meets
> In mere oppugnancy . . .

Then follows an order of subordination of human faculties which is both the inverse of Thomas's and a negative version of Aristotle's, for both of whom appetite as love is ultimate (see Ch. I, Sec. C, herein):

> Then everything includes itself in power,
> Power into will, will into appetite
> And appetite, a universal wolf
> So doubly seconded with will and power,
> Must make perform a universal prey,
> And last eat up himself.

So power subsumes "everything" in the world, but will subsumes power, and appetite in turn subsumes and consumes all the world and itself—the self-embracing self-cannibalism of an un-subordinated, un-ruled humanity. This chaos-wreaking, unholy hierarchy, appetite → will→ power, emerges in the absence of goodness, when appetite becomes ultimate lust, undiscriminating will its mere mediating agent, and power without "authentic place" its enabler.

7. This note refers to the two preceding paragraphs. **Intellect**: *Summa* Pt. 1, Q. 79 ff.; **appetitive power in general**: Q. 80; **will**: Q. 82, cf. *Truth* Q. 21, which helps in unscrambling the mutual involvement of True and Good; **free choice**: *Summa* Q. 83.

8. Aristotle calls choice "deliberative appetite" (*bouleutike orexis; Nicomachean Ethics*, 1113 a)—*nota bene: not* "intellectual appetite." **Will as a psychic activity:** *Summa* Pt. I of Pt. II; **rational appetite:** Foreword to Qq. 6–7; **passivity of intellect:** Pt. 1, Q. 79, a. 2.

9. Will as specifically human: Q. 6, a. 1; **lust and fear:** Q. 6, a. 7; **will can resist passion:** Q. 10, a. 3.

10. Circumstances of action: Q. 7, a. 1; **objects of willing:** Q. 8; **why will wants good:** Q. 8, a. 1; **Aristotle on the good as final object:** *Nicomachean Ethics* I 1.

11. In the Platonic–Neoplatonic tradition, Good is above and beyond Being (*Republic* VI 509 b); in the Aristotelian–Thomist tradition, it is convertible with being, and Thomas puts this claim nearly at the beginning of the *Summa*: "Goodness and being are really the same" (Pt. 1, Q. 5, a. 1). I have coined to myself the term "ontological optimism" for the quondam-mainline view. I cannot tell whether I believe it because it is true or because it is desirable. This is to me the ultimate human uncertainty; it will either remain unresolved or be resolved when I am past telling.

12. Rationality of appetite: *Summa* Pt. 1 of Pt. II, Q. 8, a. 1; **end and means:** a. 3.

I am leaving Thomas's order here to take up choice (Q. 13) and deliberation (Q. 14) in connection with end and means. Thomas's *electio* is significantly different from Augustine's [*liberum*] *arbitrium* though both are translated as "choice." The former is a specific part of the will, the latter really is the will itself as a power of arbitration between good and bad acts (*On Free Choice* II 18).

Discursive reason as part of practical intellect: *Summa* Pt. I, Q. 79, a. 8; **choice as melding reason and desire:** Pt. I of Pt. II, Q. 13, a. 1.

13. The devil's fixed will: Pt. I, Q. 64, a. 2. What could it mean to have one's desire fixed absolutely on evil except to mean to be unhappy, perhaps lustfully unhappy?

14. Self-motivation: Pt. I of Pt. II, Q. 9, a. 3.

15. Subjective-objective: a. 1; **sensory desire:** a. 2; **sensory object:** a. 4; **first mover, God:** a. 6.

Objective, subjective: In scholastic terms "objective" is what is in the intellect, "subjective" is what underlies or confronts it; we have reversed the meanings.

Thomas, treating the will's motivation analogously to a natural being's self-motion, follows Aristotle, who, at the end of the *Physics* says plainly that, strictly speaking, there are no ultimately self-moving beings; ultimately an external (unmoved) prime-mover and more immediately a causative environment is needed (VIII 6, 259 b). Happily this is not the place to get to the bottom of this ultimate countermanding of his definition of a "nature," a natural being as having the principle of motion within, or for that matter, of how self-motion works within any one substance. For the will, as I said, it seems well observed.

16. Way: *Summa* Q. 12, a. 1; **intention:** Q. 12; **enjoyment:** Q. 11.

17. "Pursuit" as meaning the following of a profession in the eighteenth century: Arthur M. Schlesinger, "The Lost Meaning of 'The Pursuit of Happiness,'" in *A Casebook on the Declaration of Independence*, ed. Robert Ginsberg (New York: Thomas Y. Crowell Company, 1967), 216–18; **leaky jar:** *Gorgias* 493 b; **pleasure as unfulfilling:** *Philebus* 34 d ff.

18. Consent, found in *Summa* Pt. 1 of Pt. II, Q. 15, doesn't seem to be in *Truth* yet, though its germ is in Q. 22, a. 13 on Intention.

19. Will as moving the intellect: Q. 15, a. 1.

20. The process of willing: Q. 15, a. 3; **use of the will:** Q. 16, a. 4. The account I give is somewhat reconstructed. As I said, the current treatments tend to telescope the time-consuming process of willing. Shakespeare knows better: Macbeth says, "Being unprepar'd/Our will became the servant to defect" (2.1.17–18).

21. Consent in the higher power: Q. 15, a. 7; **sin in the will:** Q. 74, a. 1; **moral actions stay within the will:** ibid.; **acts for good in the world:** for example, *Summa Contra Gentiles*, chap. III; **consent in the lower power:** *Summa* Pt. II of Pt. I, Q. 15, a. 4.

22. Higher power: Q. 15, a. 4; **lower appetite:** Q. 77, a. 1 and 2; **libido in Freud:** *New Introductory Lectures on Psychoanalysis* (1932), especially Lecture XXXII.

23. Use: Q. 16; **use as last stage:** Q. 16, a. 4; **God not a means:** a. 3.

24. Hobbes: *Leviathan* I 6. In the "Treatise on Will," Thomas asks for almost every stage of willing whether animals are capable of it and, in effect, denies it. Hobbes defines deliberation as an alternation of appetite and aversion and says explicitly that beasts deliberate and therefore they also will. For Thomas, willing is a *human* act.

25. **Free will**: *Truth* Q. 24; **free judgment**: *Summa* Pt. 1, Q. 83, a. 3; *electio*: Pt. I of Pt. II, Q. 13.

26. **Command**: Q. 17; this is the longest of all the questions, because the most involved; **bidding motion**: Q. 17, a. 2; **root of freedom**: a. 1; **mutually reflexive**: a. 3; **commanding the will**: a. 5; **commanding the reason**: a. 6; **commanding sensory desire and the body's functions**: as. 7, 8, 9.

27. **Love seated in will**: "Treatise on the Passions," *Summa* Pt. I of Pt. II, Q. 27, a. 1.

28. Also *Summa* Pt. I, Q. 82, a. 5.

29. Ontology of will: *Summa Contra Gentiles*, Pt. II, chaps. 47–48, in Thomas Aquinas, *Selected Philosophical Writings*, ed. Timothy McDermott (Oxford: Oxford Univ. Press, 1993), 169–71.

30. Christian Wolff, *Johann Sebastian Bach: The Learned Musician* (New York: W.W. Norton, 2000), 308–9.

31. **Thomas on free decision**: *Truth* (1256–59 C.E.), trans. Schmidt, Q. 22, a. 5; Q. 24, as. 1–6, also *Summa* (1265–67), trans. Gilby, Pt. I, Q. 83, and *Quaestiones Disputatae de Malo* (1269–72), Q. 6, in Aquinas, *Selected Philosophical Writings*, 171–83; **non-necessary turning from good**: *De Malo* Q. 3, as. 1–2, p. 292; **non-necessary ends**: *Summa* Pt. I, Q. 82, a. 2.

32. **Free decision**: *Truth* III, Q. 24, is the source of the narrower perplexities and resolutions, those concerning that particular moment in the will's process when deliberate choices are made among options; **freedom**: *De Malo* Q. 6, is the source for the will's activity as a whole and the ends that move it.

33. **I think because I want to**: *De Malo*, Q. 6, p. 177. This sentence is revealingly opposed to Descartes' "I think, therefore I am," because it implies that affectivity is at least coeval with thinking; I say "at least," because Thomas might conceivably have claimed "I desire, therefore I think," but he didn't. In any case, his human being is no thinking thing and, having relations of creaturely desire to its Creator, has no need to establish its existence.

34. Aristotle's God (*Nous*, "Intellect") is, however, neither the Creator of the world nor a personal triad, nor person of persons. Nor is happiness (*beatitudo*) Aristotle's *activity* of the soul, since it is, as an object of will, an *attainment*, a state of bliss rather than a "being-at-work" (*Nicomachean Ethics* I 9).

35. **Intention of ends close to choice of means**: *Truth* II, Q. 22, a. 14 and *Summa* Pt. I of Pt. II, Q. 12, a. 4.

Choice (Latin: *electio*, Greek: *prohairesis*) is *not* identical with willing but is only one element of it in Thomas's subtle and extended phenomenology of the will. (For Thomas, the will as a power is called *thelesis* in Greek as distinct from *boulesis*, the act of choice.) This fact of choice being but a link in the chain of willing is of the greatest consequences in thinking about prevailing contemporary views of the will, which by and large exactly collapse Thomas's distinction and identify choice (in turn equated with decision) as will. Since will desires ends, choice so understood is: 1. the primary place of—now petty—ends, and 2. the locus of freedom, if any. The form of its decision is binary, between "this and that," or even more simply, between "this and not-this." Then, the formula for this freedom of choice—in hindsight, for purposes of imputing blame—is "could have done otherwise," the contemporary will-mantra.

Augustinian judgment-decision (*arbitrium*) and Kantian choice-will (*Willkür*) are, to be sure, conceivable antecedents of this version of will as an act seizing on formulated choices in a moment of decision, though these earlier versions were respectively conceived within more complex theological and moral settings than are the contemporary research protocols (see Chs. X–XI, herein).

For Thomas, however, following Aristotle, choice pertains essentially to the means for realizing a pre-given end. (In my exposition, I follow the more thoughtful *Summa* rather than the earlier *On Truth*, which still suggests that choice chooses ends, Art. 1, 6.)

For Thomas, then, choice follows judgment or verdict (*judicium, sententia*, *Summa* Q. 13, a. 3, Reply), and that, in turn, follows deliberation (Q. 14, a. 4, Reply to 1). So choice is a *consequence* of thinking things out, with the end already willed. In fact the act of willing that engages with the *given* end is called "intention" and naturally precedes the phases of willing mentioned above.

Thomas, ever reasonable, allows that choice is indeed sometimes of ends, namely insofar as these ends are also means. For example, bodily health is a medical end, though it could be a means in the cure of souls. But by and large, choice is only a passing moment in willing, though for him, too, it is the locus of freedom (Q. 13, a. 6, Reply), albeit in two very particular respects: 1. insofar as the power of reason "is disposed towards opposites," and 2. insofar as a man may choose to will or not to will. But all in all, will is much more than free choice, for as desire it is primarily about contents, ends, and those are not ultimately free to be chosen.

Yves R. Simon, in *Freedom of Choice* (1951; ed. and trans. Peter Wolff [New York: Fordham Univ. Press, 1969]), gives a largely Thomistic account of willing, though he differs from Thomas in thinking of choice as being of ends. (He has some warrant, to be sure, in an earlier question of the *Summa*—I, Q. 83—on Free Choice, which *seems* to credit choice with election of goods.) But in the course of this possible deviation, he explains most illuminatingly just *how* the will makes choices and how subsidiary goods come to be objects of judgments. Here is how I understand his explanation.

Human goods in their plurality are "subsidiary" because the one fixed, necessary end of human will is the "comprehensive good" (Thomas: *bonum in communi*). That is the overarching object of desire. Now Simon says: *The indifference of the practical judgment does not originate in any indetermination of intellect or will, it originates in the natural superdetermination of the rational appetite* (106). This requires explanation.

The "indifference" of the judging will is the bugbear of people trying to understand what it means to decide. If there is not an equi-valence of reasons, no deliberate decision is needed; the preponderance makes decision instantaneous—and that is not deciding. On the other hand, if there is indifference of reasons, how can will ever be moved off center? Buridan's infamous ass is starved between two equally tempting bales of hay. (See Ch. XI, Note 24 and Conclusion, Sec. C2, herein.)

However, if this indifference does not originate in the *indeterminacy* of the two human powers but in an *excessive determination* of their combination, then the case is not hopeless. Now rational appetite (the will understood as reason and desire in mutual embrace) is superdetermined in being altogether devoted to the all-encompassing good (actually, God) as its object. For this good is "too great and too strong" ever to be satisfied by any particular good—no lesser end can impose itself on the mind and meet its determination. The power of decision is, so to speak, stunned by this disproportion. This analysis, however, informs the will of its problem: It is "to achieve the perception of the discrepancy between the particular and the comprehensive good" (116). That done, the indifference that, after all, originated in the emotive dismissal of a discrepancy, is removed and an "active indifference" (118) asserts itself—an openness to possibilities, an effective responsiveness, that is readily attracted to the better of two or the best of several goods (or feels repelled by the detestableness of evils). Thus effective freedom of choice and equipoise of decision are reconciled.

36. Will's going out and reflection: *Truth* II, Q. 22, a. 12.

37. Loving God: *De Malo*, Q. 2, a. 2.

38. Love: *Summa* Pt. I of Pt. II, Q. 26; **love as passion and its circular motion**: Q. 26, a. 2.

39. Imperative power: *Summa* Pt. I of Pt. II, Q. 17, a. 2; **the demon's true obstinacy and false sorrow**: Pt. I, Q. 64, a. 3; **evil cannot be intended**: Pt. I of Pt. II, Q. 78, a. 1.

40. I have used *Duns Scotus on the Will and Morality*, sel. and trans. with an intro. by Allan B. Wolter (Washington: Catholic Univ. of America Press, 1986). These texts are pulled together from various, not very accessible sources, so I shall simply refer to page numbers in this book. Also: Duns Scotus, *The Oxford Commentary on the Four Books of the Sentences*, Bk. I, Distinction III (pp. 560–63), Dist. XXXIX (pp. 590–97); Bk. II, Dist. XXV (pp. 597–601), in *Philosophy in the Middle Ages*, eds. Arthur Hyman and James J. Walsh (New York: Harper and Row, 1967). It would be ungrateful not to mention the succinct and reliable accounts in volume 2 of Frederick Copleston's *History of Philosophy* (Garden City, N.Y.: Image Books, 1962–74). Duns Scotus (1265–1308) lived a short generation after Thomas Aquinas.

41. One of my favorite footnotes appears in an author who himself is, to me, more readable than persuasive. In *Enquiry Concerning Human Understanding* (Sec. XII, Pt. II, n. 1) Hume says of fellow philosopher's arguments "that they admit of no answer and produce no conviction." To forestall this effect, Scotus, trying to enforce belief in contingency as a first principle, cites as a predecessor of his own violence the great Persian Aristotelian, Avicenna: "Those who deny the first principle [of non-contradiction] should be flogged or burned until they admit that it is not the same thing to be burned and not burned, or whipped and not whipped" (Scotus, *Sentences*, 592). The practical refutation of this repulsive thought is surely that if you get people to where they'll say anything, anything they say is void.

It seems to me that people of a highly logicistic turn of mind have a different relation to first principles from those who regard rationality as having a certain obligation to be reasonable: The latter propose them through an appeal to consensual self-evidence, the former (sometimes) go into an enforcer mode.

Some being is contingent: Scotus himself says that one should not only say that something is contingent but that it is "caused contingently." See Duns Scotus, *Philosophical Writings*, trans. Allan Wolter (Indianapolis: Hackett, 1987), 55. But he does do it himself.

42. God has Will and Intellect: Scotus, *Sentences*, 563; **contingency not in his intellect**: 593.

The naturalness, that is, the object-bound character of God's intellect results from its ideas being somehow at least logically prior to his will. God is said to produce, by a knowledge of his own essence and of his creatures, a reflection of that essence in a system of divine ideas that are objects for his intellect. By these, as preceding the free action of his will, that is, his free causality, he is bound in the way of nature.

Considering that Scotus's aim is to elevate God's will, it seems somewhat desperately circular to achieve the secondariness of the intellect by raising its products to logical antecedence. Helpful: Copleston, *History of Philosophy*, vol. 2, pt. II, 253 and the same in Wolter, *Duns Scotus on Will and Morality, op. cit.*, p. 24.

43. God's single volition and extent of contingency: Scotus, *Sentences*, 596; **positive contingency**: 597. Scotus's arguments are more numerous and far more logically formal. Some of them I can't figure out.

44. Mover and moved, free proximate attribute, deliberation pointless, contingency and indeterminacy: Scotus, *Sentences*, 599.

45. Decoupling of intellect and will: The will does have a "natural inclination" to act in accord with right reason, *Will and Morality*, 34, 183. See my Note 46; **will alone commands**: *Will and Morality*, 31.

46. References for three preceding paragraphs: **inclinations of the will**: *Will and Morality, op. cit.*, pp. 179–81 (Commentary, pp. 39–42); **natural will**: pp. 180–83 (Comm., pp. 41–42); **happiness**: p. 182 ff. (Comm., pp. 42–45); **elicited act**: an act accomplished by the faculty itself as opposed to commanded by it.

47. Since Ockham's treatment of the will is at once concise and scattered, my account is largely derived from secondary sources and their quotations.

First, texts: Ockham, *Philosophical Writings*, trans. Philotheus Boehner (Indianapolis: Library of Liberal Arts, 1964); *Philosophy in the Middle Ages*, eds. Hyman and Walsh, 1967; William Ockham, *Predestination, God's Foreknowledge, and Future Contingents*, trans. Marilyn McCord Adams and Norman Kretzmann (New York: Meredith Corporation, 1969); *Ockham's Theory of Terms: Part I of the Summa Logicae*, trans. Michael J. Loux (Notre Dame: Univ. of Notre Dame Press, 1974).

Then, secondary books: Gordon Leff, *William of Ockham: The Metamorphosis of Scholastic Discourse* (Oxford: Manchester Univ. Press, 1975; Leff quotes copiously in Latin and English); Marilyn McCord Adams, *William Ockham*, 2 vols. (Notre Dame: Univ. of Notre Dame Press, 1987); Armand Maurer, *The Philosophy of William of Ockham in the Light of Its Principles* (Toronto: Pontifical Institute of Medieval Studies, 1999).

Surveys: Copleston, *History of Philosophy*, vol. 3, pt. I, "Ockham (5)," 113 ff.; Ernest A. Moody, "William of Ockham," in vol. 9 of *Encyclopedia of Philosophy*, 2nd ed., ed. Donald Borchert (Detroit: Thomson-Gale, 2006).

Ockham (c. 1285–1306) wrote a very short generation after Scotus, whom he regarded as his most distinguished opponent (Adams, *William Ockham*, p. xii).

48. Influential: Influence is a word to which it is easier to give utterance than meaning. I have the sense that Ockham started "will" onto a world-changing path on which he is still operative, but I can't really figure out how. One may think of originating texts as beads strung on a (probably branching) string that transmits "influence." But just how that influx runs down time on that conduit is mystifying. There is a learnedly fantastical exposition of how it works with romantic poets—how anxious and avid successors subdue and appropriate their predecessors by misreading them and are the stronger for it: Harold Bloom, *The Anxiety of Influence* (1973). Some sober version of that intensely personal battle may also fit less temperamental latter-day philosophers—but a late thirteenth-century ontological logician? Moreover, while Ockham had studied Scotus and both absorbed and refuted him, certainly on the will, there is twentieth-century Ockhamism in writers for whom I have seen no evidence that they read his work. Thus Wittgenstein's solution of the "problem of universals" in terms of a generalization on the basis of "family resemblance," that is, a sort of serial family likeness that brings similar objects under a common term, is the spitting image of Ockham's replacement of real species (the descendents of the ancient forms, mental entities with real being) by a generalizing abstraction educed from the experience of real individuals in the world that are similar. Is that influence?

There is another rather remarkable case of special interest to me. Ockham's "nominalism"—the view that universals such as species are names, not real entities—could be put in these terms: "First intentions" are thoughts expressed as terms that are predicable of single realities, as "man" refers to this, that, and the other real man. "Second intentions" signify linguistic signs such as "man" and the abstracted concept they express (*Ockham's Theory of Terms*, 73–75). Now Ockham thinks that his "realistic" predecessors made the logical mistake of taking second for first intentions, that is to say, abstractions for realities. In response, he ushered in an inclination to forget about ideal being and attend to hard-edged real individuals, the kind amenable to sensory observation and construable into facts.

Now here is what is remarkable: One twentieth-century understanding of the origin of a most powerful aspect of modernity is that it is thoroughgoingly *symbolic* in the way concepts are formed, given to thinking in abstract formalisms. Especially its mathematics, the kind most instrumental to the conquest of nature, is *symbolic* mathematics, algebra. Here is the point: What makes modern mathematics symbolic is precisely that the mathematicians of the late sixteenth and earlier seventeenth century, Descartes among them, take—*not* mistake—second for first intentions. They operate with symbols *as if* they were things, with huge practical consequences (Burt Hopkins, *The Origin of the Logic of Symbolic Mathematics: Edmund Husserl and Jacob Klein* [Bloomington: Indiana Univ. Press, 2011]. This work is, in large part, a paragraph by paragraph exposition of Jacob Klein, *Greek Mathematical Thought and the Origin of Algebra* [1936], trans. Eva Brann [New York: Dover Publications, 1992]). So they did on the one hand—the more effectively for not altogether consciously—just what Ockham had so explicitly censored. On the other hand, he himself had, indeed, prepared this very second intention for just the use to which the mathematicians put it. He had accomplished that by emphasizing the abstractive origin of its concepts. These were now nothing but acts of re-conceiving the names of real things as cognitively useful general terms two levels removed from real things, but for that very reason these terms were convenient to the mind in manipulating its concepts. They satisfied one basic meaning of a *symbol*: a sign, the product of an abstraction, intending no real thing immediately, but itself treated like a thing and related to other symbol-things by the mind's logic. That symbol (most often appearing as x) became the basic term of the new mathematics, liberating it to become the miraculously efficient language of science. In time the abstracting propensity itself went popular in a kind of thinking characteristically modern—unimmediate, hovering above concrete things, flying among cloudy abstractions without even sporadic touch-downs: read committee-produced position papers. Should one say that is Ockham's influence showing up?

A last way of putting the perplexity: The beads-on-a-string figure assumes a documentable continuous tradition: Ockham certainly read Scotus's works, though that guarantees nothing in general. Take a successor B, in time. He could have *thought* of A's idea *before he read* him and if, in addition, he was younger at the time than A had been when he wrote his books, one might even say that B was A's precursor in thought. Was there "influence"? Yet again, there is a second source of "influence," even more undeterminable than the effect of direct mental contact: atmospheric influxes. Thoughts are "in the air." Are they unborn of man but engendered by vagrant opinion, upon receptive circumstance? And a third source: the sheer oppositionality, the driving force of the Western dialectic tradition, by which a predecessor is sacrificed for the "next" phase, an early case being the parricide committed on Parmenides by his ontologically advanced son in Plato's *Sophist* (241 d). Is the incitement to negation a form of influence as well?

Let me remind the put-upon reader what prompted this aporetic disquisition: I am about to leap from the late thirteenth-century logician to two polemicists of the sixteenth, several philosophers of the seventeenth, more of the eighteenth century, and so onward. Some of these successors in volitional concerns seem to me the heirs of Ockham's extremism (which I am about to work out). Yet I cannot quite tell how, and I am convinced that if my knowledge of the string as it connects the smaller beads were less incomplete, the perplexity (as I see it) of the gathering triumph of the will would still not be resolved—in fact, would be complexified.

I end by referring to a book that puts Ockham's philosophy at the very beginning of another terrific strain of modernity: nihilism—in particular, Ockham's understanding of God's Will as radically willful, a notion I shall consider below. The book, Michael Allen Gillespie's *Nihilism before Nietzsche* (Chicago: Univ. of Chicago Press, 1995) traces the transformation, really a slow flip, of God's omnipotent Will into a human absolute will and the nihilistic consequences.

For Augustine's "influence" on Descartes see Conclusion, Note 2.

49. Maurer, *Philosophy*, 4–5, discusses Ockham as a *modernus*.

50. Aristotle's distinction: *Physics* 184 a. The Aristotelian distinction isn't really quite appropriate, since Ockham devises, for his totally patent world of individuals, a mode of cognition, the "intuitive," by which the intellect apprehends whatever object is before it directly and evidently, yielding a judgment of its factual, contingent existence. If the object is an outer, a sensory one, the senses will be affected, if it is internal, such as a feeling, then introspection will be at work. But the point is that the cognition is an immediate awareness yielding an evidential judgment that a fact exists—where all facts are, as we will see, contingent. The abstractive cognition referred to in Note 48 is directed at the *same objects* in situations where their *existence* is not evident; that is, where the object is no longer the direct evidential cause of a cognition, which is now rather of its abstracted concept (Leff, *William of Ockham*, 6 ff.; Maurer, *Philosophy*, 470 ff.).

Knowledge of God not analogical: Both on the basis of a detailed logical critique of "analogy" (Leff, *William of Ockham*, 159 ff.) and because God cannot, for Ockham, be known by the sort of correspondence analogy implies but only by a composite abstraction culled from his creatures, a cognition that is not real knowledge (366 ff.); also Maurer, *Philosophy*, 281 ff.

51. The absolutely omnipotent God of the Nominalists, who causes directly a world of individuals, might be thought of as the Christian patron of what is often called Baconian science, the fact-gathering empiricism of Bacon and Hume, whereas the God of the "realists," who binds himself to "secondary causes," and works by his "ordained power" (see Note 62 below) to uphold the laws of nature, stands behind the hypothesis-verifying mathematical science that is the other—and more potent—aspect of modern science. (The northern Christian Nominalists were preceded by an analogous, long-lived, and yet more extreme school of Islam, the Asharites. That they exercised an inhibiting effect on the development of an Islamic modernity is the—perhaps somewhat single-minded but very plausible—thesis of Robert R. Reilly, *The Closing of the Muslim Mind: How Intellectual Suicide Created the Modern Islamic Crisis* [Wilmington: ISI Books, 2010].)

Connection of God's will to contingency: This is an unprovable theological truth, though naturally persuasive (Leff, *William of Ockham*, 460). For if contingency is the possibility at any moment to do otherwise, without causative constraint, then that is what a radically free will does. Ockham's argument against extra-mental universals (such as Platonic forms) is very succinctly set out in *Ockham's Theory of Terms*, 79–82, from the *Summa Logicae*, 15.

52. Ideal notions: Ockham too attributes ideas to God, but merely as mental objects without reality; they are not universals but individuals and are infinite in number. In other words, these are God's intentions for a possible act of creating (Leff, *William of Ockham*, 460); **God's self-willing**: Maurer, *Philosophy*, 244; **will to be a will**: God *is* his will—and all his other attributes are mere names for our conceptions. Anything real, as God is, is all one, *this one-and-whole particular*. That is what Ockham means by something being real—not to be a bundle of attributes. Maurer, 184 ff.; Leff, 363 ff., 404 ff.

53. God's annihilation: *Sentences* Bk. I, Dist. I in *Philosophy in the Middle Ages*, 619; **cry of leaves**: Wallace Stevens, "The Course of a Particular."

54. Principle of parsimony (sometimes called "Ockham's razor"): Leff, *William of Ockham*, 35.

55. God's free (undetermined) will and human freedom, how conceived, how connected, how beyond understanding: Ockham, *Predestination*, 23–26, 50; **God's foreknowledge**: Ockham, *Philosophical Writings*, 148–50, quotation on p. 148. It must be said that Ockham stoops to analogy in conjecturing about the divine will.

56. Parts of the soul: Ockham, *Philosophical Writings*, p. xlix; Leff, *William of Ockham*, 528 ff., esp. 531.

57. My summary account of Ockham's ethics is mostly taken from Moody, "William of Ockham," 315–16. The more extended discussion refers mainly to Leff, *William of Ockham*, 476 ff.; also Adams, *William Ockham*, vol. 2, 1115 ff. and Maurer, *Philosophy*, 451 ff.

58. Ockham's sparseness on psychology is generally remarked by scholars.

59. No act of the will: Ockham, *Philosophical Writings*, 161 (*Quodlibeta* III, Q. 3).

60. God's grace: Leff, *William of Ockham*, 476; **second paradox**: 491 ff.

61. Good object of will: 501 ff.

62. Notorious example: Maurer, *Philosophy*, 529; **God's absolutely free will**: Ockham distinguishes between two aspects of God's power—his "ordained power" (*potentia ordinata*), by which he acts in accordance with his own desires, and his "absolute power" (*potentia absoluta*), which is simply his freedom to do anything (Leff, *William of Ockham*, 16).

63. The possibility that God might be conceived to wait—anxiously—to be disobeyed brings to mind Abraham's willingness to sacrifice Isaac, his son (Gen. 22; verse 1 says that God "tempted" Abraham: in what sense?). I have a colleague who once argued that the fate of the Jews might have been less hard had Abraham disobeyed, as God expected. Looking backward from the Christian Bible, it might even seem as if God's own parental sacrifice had been diminished by the Hebrew's prior willingness.

64. Desperate opposite: I am purposely overemphasizing the dire outcome. Shades of Ockham turn up everywhere in perfectly positive, even cheerful places; thus in Descartes, who read the Scholastics early and late. See Roger Ariew, "Descartes and Scholasticism: The Intellectual Background to Descartes' Thought," in *The Cambridge Companion to Descartes*, ed. John Cottingham (New York: Cambridge Univ. Press, 1992), 74. And Hume—catch him giving credit to a scholastic!—might nevertheless have heard of one who denied that we can apprehend the soul as a substance or that the existences are connected by essences or that effects are inherent in causes—the prototype opinions for Hume's denial in the *Treatise* of "personal identity," or of a "real connection" between existences, or of any connection between cause and effect beyond our observation of a "constant conjunction."

Denial that there is a nature of things: Isaiah Berlin, *The Roots of Romanticism* (Princeton: Princeton Univ. Press, 1999), 117.

65. Erasmus (1467–1536) and his younger contemporary Luther (1483–1546) were an unevenly matched pair of antagonists concerning free will—a self-denigrating compromiser (who described his battle with Luther as that of "a fly with an elephant") and a dominating bully (who asks Erasmus "to suffer my lack of eloquence as I . . . will bear with your ignorance"). Gone are the patient subtlety and responsive civility of the medieval philosophical theologicians; the rebirth that theology underwent in these Renaissance reformers was attended by nasty squabbling. The two polemecists went at each other in these two works: Desiderius Erasmus of Rotterdam, *A Diatribe or Sermon Concerning Free Will* (De Libero arbitrio, 1524), and Martin Luther, *On the Bondage of the Will* (De servo arbitrio, 1525). The texts are in *Erasmus and Luther, Discourse on Free Will*, trans. and ed. Ernest F. Winter (London: Continuum, 2006), where Luther's long book is heavily excerpted. Erasmus replied in 1527 with a longer *Diatribe*, of which I have only read reports. Much of it was *ad hominem* rhetoric, Scriptural appeal, and protestations of self-protective meekness against assertions of confident intolerance. The duel between these two is examined as "the first and foremost dualism of the modern world" (meaning the "cross-rivalries" that are formative for the issues of our world) in Ricardo J. Quinones, *Dualism: The Agonies of the Modern World* (Toronto: Univ. of Toronto Press, 2007), 23–97.

These seem to me to be the points of substance:

Erasmus: Not every truth needs announcing; even if it were true that there was no free will and only sheer necessity, it would be better not to say so, since it would have deleterious consequences, "pouring oil upon the fire" of human wickedness. Thus it matters more than the disputation itself not to enter the labyrinth of argument and refutation (7).

The definition of free will is, in this connection, "the power of the human will whereby man can apply to or turn away from that which leads to eternal salvation" (13). Erasmus reviews Scriptural passages supporting this free will and other passages apparently against it, especially Luther's use of them. Since Scripture cannot contradict itself, it is apparent that the two sides read the same Scripture with different eyes.

Thus a *middle way* is necessary, avoiding, on the one hand, the dangerous opinions of those who have "either diminished the freedom of the will so that it would contribute absolutely nothing to good works or . . . have eliminated it altogether by introducing an absolute necessity in all happenings," and on the other, of those who, despairing of salvation by reason of religious indifference, have attributed too much to free will (51).

Erasmus's approach to free will is learned, irenic, and tolerant, but it is also commitment- and thought-avoiding. In that, it is exemplary for an aspect of Renaissance Humanism and the academic humanities descended from it—a kind of self-imposed insipidness. Luther has no such inhibition.

Luther: He calls Erasmus a Proteus and accuses him of flaccid skepticism: But "the Holy Spirit is no skeptic" (605). "I shall harry you" until "you define for me the power of free will . . . [and] heartily repent ever having published your Diatribe" (615).

Let me take out a moment here for a note within a note on "Proteus," used as a derogatory epithet by Luther. He means by it a skeptic, someone who has unfixed, changeable opinions. Just the opposite view is held of this Proteus, "the old man of the sea," first found in Homer (*Odyssey* iv 417), who "will try to become everything," by Pico della Mirandola in his "Oration on the Dignity of Man" (1486). There Proteus is *celebrated* for being infinitely transformable—not blamed for suspending his opinions but praised for reveling in possibilities. Thus Pico's manifesto of the Italian Renaissance breathes a spirit antithetical to the German Reformation: It exalts human self-will. In it God says to man:

> The nature of all other creatures is defined and restricted within laws which We have laid down; you by contrast, impeded by no such restrictions, may, by your own free will, to whose custody we have assigned you, trace for yourself the lineaments of your own nature.

This, "our chameleon," God says, inspires awe and greater admiration than any other being by reason of its mutability. That is the nature, capable of transforming *itself*, of self-creation, which is symbolized by Proteus. Pico quotes Asaph (King David's choir director) who sings, "You are gods, and sons of the Most High" (Psalms 82:6), and he urges that a high ambition should invade our souls—that of human divinity, sponsored by God Himself.

In this remarkable—and long—harangue, man has more free will than God, who is bound by secondary causes, namely the laws of nature. Man is admired by God himself for having an even less substantial soul than Ockham accords him—for being godlike, self-made, but having the edge over an immutable God in being perpetually transmutable, having a will free not only to *do* anything but to *be* anything—as if contingency had gone hyperactive. And all this cluelessly hopeful, inexhaustibly exuberant celebration of the divinely human will (while still acknowledging—no, co-opting—God) comes forty years before Luther's dour reinterpretation of the *liberum arbitrium* tradition. To which I now return, stopping just to recall to myself that I am not dealing with a linear development but with a rough beast slouching—devastatingly— towards somewhere.

There is no circumventing the fact that, for all his self-pleasing rudeness and self-righteous assurance, Luther is by far the weightier, by far the more interesting, of the contestants. First I must say that I do not—cannot—know what he is talking about except literally, that is in mere words, when he speaks of grace. A nonbeliever might understand what Pindar means when he sings of moments, in which all things coming right, there is a divine grace upon things, but not what is meant by God's grace so operating that it has "put my salvation out of the control of my own will and into the control of His" (783). Yet this is the belief-gist, the sum-total, of his argument, an assertion whose temperamental motor is unforgiving, uncompromising extremism: "I will not accept or tolerate that moderate middle way which Erasmus would, with good intention,

I think, recommend to me: to allow a certain little to free will . . . [W]e must go to extremes, deny free will altogether and ascribe everything to God" (755).

Luther trained in part under Nominalists, though he abjures their subtle distinctions (663), some of which have been, appreciatively, reported above. Again I ask myself, is it to be counted as influence to turn Ockham's argument for near-absolute human free will inside out? Probably so, since, side by side with this reversal, he accepts Ockham's position that God's will (his *potentia ordinata*, 719) is not bound by right, but right is what God wills (712).

What so infuriates Luther in Erasmus's desire for peace and tranquility (625)? It endangers Christian liberty. Luther had already written a tract, the most concise statement of his position, *The Freedom of a Christian* (1520), to which *The Bondage of the Will* (which he regarded as his best book) is, so to speak, the negative complement. In *Freedom*, the will plays no role, because, I imagine, for Luther Christian freedom is not *of* the will but *from* the will.

That is "the very hinge" of the dispute (613). Erasmus gives human will a role in salvation; Luther thinks that not to know better is not to be a Christian: Liberty is release *from* laws and traditions (627). Necessity does not mean, as Erasmus claims, the compulsion that is the opposite of free will. It is this very free will that has the "necessity of immutability," for we, immutably, willingly, crave to do evil, and it is beyond the power of the will to change itself. Only God working in us can free us from our "free will." The will is like a beast of burden that only goes as God wills when God rides it. So understood, the will is powerless—an ineffective power, a contradiction in terms. If there is a use for the term "free will" it is at the most for things below, for works in the world (634–38). Thus the contention is "for the grace of God against free will" (661).

That is the precise refutation of Erasmus's definition of free will, given above, as the ability of conversion to—or from—God, a "vertable-" or "mutable-will" (661). Luther critiques this understanding of willing as a self-turning, for it implies that *between* will and action there is a power of turning (663). And that is Luther's most crucial argument against free will in terms of an analysis of will itself: He rejects the radical reflexivity necessary for a righting of the will; it is a power that human will simply does not have. Citing Augustine, Luther says that human will left to itself is a *slave* will, *servum arbitrium*; men need to be driven by the Spirit of God (Romans 8:14); they need special grace.

To conclude, the implication of this limitation of free will to man's temporal works means that even good works cannot save (though they may be the consequence of faith: "works neither can nor ought to be wanting," 767). Luther finds it personally comforting that his salvation is out of the control of his will but lies instead in God's will and the favor of his grace and mercy (783).

Thus for Luther, responsibility for virtuous external action has but an incidental, secondary connection to faith. Faith is the totally *inward* relation of a *helplessly* evil human being to a *solely* free God beyond, a deity who cares less for good conduct than true faith. The psychic consequences can be dismal and the political implications dire. Would that Erasmus had had more vitality!

Chapter IV. Will Reduced

1. Besides, or by means of, its beauty, Hobbes's speech is also irrepressibly witty. Its enlivening principle is an Ockhamite animus against "insignificant" speech, meaning universal and transcendent terms, and such impatience makes for mordant concision. But concision is the soul of poetry and causticity is the heart of critique; together they yield beauty with bite.

2. Definition of deliberation and will: *Leviathan*, Pt. I, Ch. 6; **doubt:** Ch. 7; **motion:** Ch. 6; **imagination:** Ch. 2; **endeavor:** Ch. 6, see also my Ch. VII, on *conatus*, "endeavor"; **end of liberty:** Ch. 6; **last appetite and most desirable:** Mortimer Adler, *The Idea of Freedom*, vol. 2, *A Dialectical Explanation of Controversies About Freedom* (Garden City, N.Y.: Doubleday and Company, 1961), 395.

3. War: *Leviathan*, Pt. I, Ch. 13; **accidents:** *Concerning Bodies* (1656), Ch. 8, 2–3.

4. His opponent was the Anglican Bishop John Bramhall, who argues well in the great tradition for free will; he is particularly good at lucid distinctions. But this exchange is similar to the Erasmus-Luther debate in this: The man who makes life more livable is not the more forceful thinker (though both these Englishmen maintain civility).

The text I used was *Hobbes and Bramhall on Liberty and Necessity*, ed. Vere Chappell (Cambridge: Cambridge Univ. Press, 1999). Hobbes's treatise is called *Of Liberty and Necessity*; Bramhall's discourse is called *The Defense of True Liberty*. The discussion of which these works are the fruit took place in 1645. There were antecedent and subsequent tracts from both sides.

5. *Hobbes and Bramhall*, 15–16: Bramhall responded, but weakly, I think (44–45). I'll cite him when he seems to nail Hobbes. I omit the battle waged by means of Scripture.

Perhaps Bramhall's trouble is that finally his defense of free will rests on a strong intuition. I have read that Dr. Johnson, irritated by the endless back-and-forth, said: "Why, sir, we *know* the will is free and there's an end of it!" It's perhaps too nonchalant, but it may be true.

6. Intention of law: *Hobbes and Bramhall*, 25; **voluntary**: *Leviathan*, Pt. I, Ch. 6.

7. Compulsion: *Hobbes and Bramhall*, 30 (Hobbes) and 54 (Bramhall).

8. Will as last feather: *Hobbes and Bramhall*, 34 (Hobbes) and 12 (Bramhall); **reasoning**: *Leviathan*, Pt. I, Ch. 5.

9. Summary: *Hobbes and Bramhall*, 36–39. Bramhall's paragraph-by-paragraph refutations mainly address Hobbes's loose use of terms (58–64). In a scholastic context, his variable wording would matter because there the devil really is in the detail. But Hobbes's whole attitude is to be done with the notion of freedom, and so perhaps the bishop, though right, is nit-picking.

10. My reasons: *Hobbes and Bramhall*, 39–41; **imagination**: 81 and *Leviathan*, Pt. I, Ch. 2.

11. Bramhall on Hobbes's reasons: *Hobbes and Bramhall*, 64–65.

12. My texts are: John Locke, *An Essay Concerning Human Understanding* (1690), ed. and abr. by A. S. Pringle-Patterson (Oxford: The Clarendon Press, 1960), Bk. II, Ch. 21, "Of Power," 135–47, and Gottfried Wilhelm Leibniz, *New Essays Concerning Human Understanding* (c. 1709, completed after Locke's death), trans. Alfred Gideon Langley (La Salle: Open Court, 1949), 174–221. Leibniz's Ch. XXI corresponds to Locke's Ch. XXI, and Leibniz quotes a large section of Locke's paragraphs nearly verbatim, putting it in the mouth of his own Philalethes ("Truth-lover"); he himself responds under the name of Theophilus ("God-lover"); so the *Essays* are a dialogue held with a book.

13. Knowledge of the knower: Socrates, whose inquiry into knowledge in the dialogue *Theaetetus* ends in perplexity, had, in the *Charmides*, actually thrown doubt *both* on the possibility and the wholesomeness of a knowledge of knowledge (167 b ff.), and Hegel, in the Introduction to the *Phenomenology of Spirit* (para. 76), will show the self-stymieing consequences of inspecting the instrument of knowledge before getting to work on knowing.

Copernican revolution: Kant, *Critique of Pure Reason* (B XVI).

14. Locke on God: He was interested in existence proofs (*Essay*, Bk. IV, Ch. 10), but he wrote to Molineux that because of the weakness of his understanding he couldn't make human reason consistent with divine omnipotence (*Essay*, p. 319, note 2).

Molina: He introduced a solution to the ever-lasting quandary of God's foreknowledge and human free will that bespeaks a new humanistic approach (1558, Copleston, *History of Philosophy*, vol. 1, pt. II, 161). He applies epistemology to God's knowledge from a human perspective, dividing it into visionary foresight, logical understanding, and a third "middle knowledge" (*scientia media*). The first is knowledge of what did and will happen, and the second of what is possible and could happen. Molina's new third kind, of particular importance to human acts, is God's infallible knowledge of what, though logically possible, *will not happen* because he has not provided the necessary conditions for actualization. Thus God knows all possible conditions and the human will's decision under each of them, in abstraction from their realization or non-realization. Therefore, he has knowledge, impossible to humans, of *futurabilia*, conditioned future events, even counterfactuals. Hence, he can, if he wills it, decree those conditions which he knows will gain a human being's consent, the new circumstance now making the choice possible. This helpful decree, *although it preceded the human decision, does not have any intrinsic efficacy*; it has no causal effect, and does not preempt human choice, whose freedom is preserved. But so, as well, is God's foreknowledge preserved, for the *scientia media* is, in fact, a vast extension of it. The middle science, to be sure, is the subject of controversy; for one thing, if God intervenes temporally in the conditions for human action, omniscience becomes subject to adjustment. (Later I report Boethius's early solution to Molina's late problem in terms of saving the compatibility of Providence and free will, Ch. IX, note 21.)

15. The chapter "On Power" is in Book II, XIV. Since Leibniz's commentary is keyed to Locke's Arabic-numbered paragraphs, only one number needs to be given, here para. 1.

Aristotle on motion and *dynamis*: *Physics* III 201 a, *Metaphysics* IX 1050 a; **Leibniz on dynamics:** "Specimen dynamicum" (1695), in Gottfried Wilhelm Leibniz, *Philosophical Papers and Letters*, ed. Leroy E. Loemker (Chicago: Univ. of Chicago Press, 1956), 711–36; **Leibniz on Locke's physics:** *New Essays*, on para. 4; here also on Descartes' error (whence Locke derived his idea) that unsigned, i.e., directionless, momentum (mv) is conserved rather than "living force" (mv² or kinetic energy); directed mv is actually conserved. For Leibniz's reinterpretation of Aristotle's *energeia* see *Philosophical Papers*, 455–63.

16. Thinking not from bodies: Locke, paras. 4–5.

17. Ancient: Aristotle, *Nicomachean Ethics* X 1177 a (later fourth century B.C.E.); **modern:** Lessing, in Leibniz, *Philosophical Papers, op. cit.*, p. 104, n. 1, from *Theologische Streitschriften* (1778).

18. My Ch. VII will be devoted to the will as world principle and Ch. X to the contemporary turn toward determinism.

19. My previous two paragraphs: Locke, paras. 1–7, 14, 21.

20. My previous four paragraphs: Locke, paras. 21, 23, 25, 26, 30.

21. My previous two paragraphs: Locke, paras. 31, 35, 36, 40, 41; **Locke's self-contradiction:** first separating will from desire, then readmitting it, occurs in paragraphs rewritten for the second edition of the *Essay*. Locke had earlier taken for granted the common opinion that the greatest good determines the will. On "stricter inquiry" he came on the substitute notion of "uneasiness" and evidently decided that desire was a possible name for it, because, I imagine, somewhere in the mind's background lurks that absent object of desire.

22. One paragraph: Locke, paras. 47, 48, 52. The nearly exact original of the phrase of the Declaration, "pursuit of our happiness," and a variant, "our endeavors after happiness," occur in para. 47. Jefferson was an avid reader of Locke's *Essay*; see Carl L. Becker, *The Declaration of Independence: A Study in the History of Political Ideas* (1942; reprint, New York: Vintage Books, 1962), 27.

In *Liberty Worth the Name: Locke on Free Agency* (Princeton: Princeton Univ. Press, 2000), a closely reasoned exposition of Locke's theory of free will, Gideon Yaffe denominates one of its elements as "the Elusive Something," a something required for a full-fledged freedom of the will as often informally understood (20). He defines it as present when someone's volitions are "causally determined by . . . correct judgments as to what is good . . ." (38), in other words, when the good (in fact, the greatest good) determines the will. He finds that Locke at first reluctantly, but later more readily, agrees to this element (54). I cite this "Elusive Something" here because I think I might have discerned its locus in Locke's mental economy: the time of "suspension of desire," when thought is at work.

23. Besides trenchantly deep criticisms, Leibniz—a much more widely learned man than Locke (in the Ancients and Scholastics and in logic and physics, see my Note 15)—adds distinctions and corrects Locke's often loose terms. For example, necessity is not properly opposed to liberty but to contingency (paras. 9, 13); freedom has an external meaning, that is, civil rights, such as slaves lack, and several internal meanings, among which is freedom of the will, considered in my text below (para. 8).

Some of Leibniz's commentary is given over to attempts to assimilate Locke's treatment to Leibniz's system.

I review Leibniz's responses up to paras. 1–38, after which the discussions tend toward detail and morality.

On power and faculty: paras. 3–6; **conatus:** para. 5 (See Spinoza's introduction of the term, Ch. VII, Note 1, herein.)

24. My previous three paragraphs: **Freedom of the will:** para. 8; **controlling will:** paras. 12, 22, and 17; **people's usage and questions:** paras. 15, 22, 35; **what we really ask about:** para. 21; **willing to oppose reason:** para. 25. Leibniz thinks that willing to will would lead to infinite regress, but that seems to me to rest on a possibly misleading assumption, namely that the meta-will is the same sort of will as the primary will. It might be that, as we ascend in and transcend our primary mentation, iteration ceases and the reflexive act is final. I can't pretend that this is a completed defense of the will's—or any mental activity's—reflexive finality, but it's a beginning.

Leibniz also thinks that where the will appears to oppose reason just to display its own power, it is the pleasure of that display that moves it, rather than bare willing (para. 25). On the other hand, he admits that previous choices do determine later ones, and so the will does act on itself (paras. 23, 25).

25. Velleity: para. 30.

26. Leibniz cites a large part of Locke's paras. 31–35 uninterruptedly and replies at length.

Unconscious impulses: para. 36, note that Leibniz has thought about unconscious desire well before Freud; **bare unactive speculation**: Locke, para. 38; **imagination absent in *Essay***: Bk. I, Ch. II, 2; the mind is stored with the products of sensation or reflection only, and "the dominion of man in this little world of understanding" cannot add or subtract one atom from what these two provide, beyond repeating, comparing, or uniting them.

After para. 36, these topics come forward in detail: the questionable power of images of absent good, the causes of human moral failure, the admission that desire is inevitably present in voluntary acts, the complexity of volition as a resultant of many forces, the asymmetry of desire and the larger notion of uneasiness, the infinity or finitude of pleasure understood as happiness, happiness as the only aim of desire, the suspension of desire falsely called free will, and the formulation of judgments of good and evil. With its ample quotations from Locke's *Essay* and its even ampler responses, the chapter "Of Power" in the *New Essays* is pretty nearly three times as long as its inciting original in the *Essay*.

27. My text is David Hume, *A Treatise of Human Nature: Being an Attempt to Introduce the Experimental Method of Reasoning into Moral Subjects* (1739), ed. L. A. Selby-Bigge (Oxford: Clarendon Press, 1960). (This edition has a very convenient analytic index.) The main treatment comes in the significantly entitled Book II, "Of the Passions," Part III, "Of the will and direct passions," Sections i–iii. I shall cite passages by Book, Part, Section.

By "experimental method" Hume doesn't mean laboratory experiments (though he might have welcomed those) but close introspective and external observations of apparent "facts." The *Treatise* contains a multitude of these, few of which are, however, at least for me, reduplicable (Brann, *Feeling Our Feelings*, Ch. VIII). Thus this method raises a continual perplexity: Are the inner landscapes of our introspective selves (to which, thus complicating the matter, Hume denies any substance [*Treatise*, Appendix, pp. 633–36]), together with the external scenes before our observant eyes, sufficiently the same for all of us for this method to yield convincing results? Are some individual's "experiments" more authoritative than others? Hume's favorite phrase is "Tis evident"—why so often not to me?

28. True skeptic: *Treatise* Bk. I, Pt. IV, Sec. vii. Here Hume says that those who do not find in themselves this easy-tempered skepticism should go away and await the return of good humor; **complexity of Hume**: Brann, *Feeling Our Feelings*, chap. VIII, 297–99, an attempt to diagram the whole of Hume's horrendously complex account of the perceptions of the mind.

29. The previous three paragraphs refer to *Treatise* Bk. II, Pt. III, Sec. i.

Condition for will's effect: *Treatise* Bk. I, Pt. I, Sec. iv; **cause and effect**: Bk. II, Pt. II, Sec. I, also Bk. I, Pt. III, Sec. xiv–xv and *An Enquiry Concerning Human Understanding*, Secs. VII–VIII.

Young savages: leaving aside the questionable felicitousness of comparing sexual congress to the adhesion of two smooth marble slabs, any amateur reader of anthropology knows that these two young "savages" will not so inevitably copulate. In Peter Matthiessen's classic, *Under the Mountain Wall: A Chronicle of Two Seasons in Stone Age New Guinea* (1962), a people as close to being "savage" as any surviving, is sympathetically delineated. Dogged by shyness and prudence, tribal taboos and damping child marriage, personal aversions, and survival preoccupations, Stone Age sex seems to be anything but uniformly regular. My point is that Hume's examples, when not false, are not probative.

Chance as concealed cause: *Treatise* Bk. I, Pt. III, Sec. xii.

30. The previous three paragraphs refer to *Treatise* Bk. II, Pt. III, Sec. ii.

Liberty of indifference: recall that for the scholastics not indifference but contingency was the opposite of necessity; indifference is lack of determining preference; contingency is the radical origination of willing itself and of its choices. **Freedom from violence**: Hume says little about this liberty, the only one "which it concerns me to preserve"; it is disentangled by George Botterill, "Hume on Liberty and Necessity," in *Reading Hume on Human Understanding: Essays on the*

First Enquiry, ed. Peter Millican (Oxford: Clarendon Press, 2002), 291 ff. For more on liberty of indifference, see my Conclusion, Sec. C2 and its Note 26, herein.

31. My four previous paragraphs refer to *Treatise* Bk. II, Pt. III, Sec. iii.

Definition of impression, idea, reason: Bk. I, Pt. III, Sec. iv–vii—to distinguish reason from understanding is happily not within my self-assigned brief here, for the relation is terminally obscure; **atomic beings**: Bk. III, Pt. I, Sec. i; **mathematics**: Plato, Leibniz, and Newton are among Hume's predecessors who care more about the "moral" efficacy than the worldly applications of the study of mathematics, cosmology, and mechanics—"moral" herein in the large sense of human good and bad.

32. Reason inactive: Bk. III, Pt. I, Sec. i; **acorn's parricide**: ibid.; **promises**: ibid., n. 3.

33. Morality, gentle passion: Bk. II, Pt. III, Sec. iii; **moral qualities like natural abilities**: Bk. III, Pt. III, Sec. iv; **emperor of the will**: *Treatise* (Selby-Bigge), Appendix, p. 632—just before the quotation, Hume is attacking those who believe that the idea of power is projected from the obedience of our body and mind to the will outward as a quality onto matter—he is referring to Locke, *Treatise*, Bk. II, Ch. 21, para. 4.

34. Just in case: the Cheshire cat appears (and disappears) in Lewis Carroll's *Alice's Adventures in Wonderland*, chaps. VI, VIII; **direct passions**: the Part-title is "Of the Will and direct Passions"; **passions of reflexion**: Bk. I, Pt. I, Sec. ii; **power and exertion of the will**: Bk. I, Pt. I, Sec. iv; **definition of will**: Bk. II, Pt. III, Sec. i.

Some clarification is provided in the later, shorter *Enquiry Concerning Human Understanding* (1748, second ed. 1751). Hume disowned the *Treatise* in the "Author's Advertisement" prefacing the *Enquiry*, which latter preface damps, even obliterates, his earlier sharp rejection of the doctrine of liberty. Nevertheless, since it doesn't so much matter what Hume came to think as what is thinkable given his premises, the radical version was more interesting.

What the *Enquiry* provides in Sec. VIII, Pt. I is precision and reduced complexity (my comments are in parentheses): We cannot think anything we have not sensed externally or internally. To be acquainted with the "idea" of "power or necessary connexion," we must examine its "impression." But looking to external bodies, we have no inward impression whatsoever, that is, no experience, which suggests power understood as necessary connection. (Therefore the idea of *power* must be a *reflective* impression, only internally experienced.) Here we first notice that our body obeys "the command of our will . . . [But] the energy by which the will performs so extraordinary an operation" must forever escape our inquiry. To understand it, we would have to understand the secret of the union of soul and body. (In other words, we commonly *experience* what we can never *understand*.) This holds true even when "by an act or command" of the will we raise up and consider a new idea. (Now the commanding is definitely an *act*.) This command "of the mind over itself" and over bodies is limited, weaker even over passions than over ideas, though we neither know the reasons for, nor boundaries of, this limitation. (Here our *minds*—we—command.) Thus there is in spiritual and material substance a secret mechanism or "structure of parts" on which the effect depends, wherefore the "power or energy" of the will is incomprehensible. In particular, there is nothing to be found in volition, which is an act of mind with which we are very familiar, that explains how it comes to be a "creative power" such as raises "from nothing a new idea and with a kind of Fiat, imitates the Omnipotence of its Maker . . ." (Here the cat is out of the bag: It is the modern fixation—*omnipotence*); Hume attacks those who ascribe novel internal conceptions to God the Creator rather than to the human creator-will. (Pt. II proceeds to a much plainer statement of the gravest consequence of Hume's inability to find a source for the idea of "power or necessary" connection: the denial of inherent causality. The will, in this aspect, is a *casualty of Humean causality*.)

Sec. VIII, Pt. I, ends with the attempt to reconcile liberty and necessity by what is nowadays called semantics: the age-old dispute was "merely verbal." "By liberty then, we can only mean *a power of acting or not acting, according to the determinations of the will*";—then comes the *subversive* exegesis: "that is, if we choose to remain at rest, we may; if we choose to move we also may. Now this hypothetical liberty is universally allowed to belong to every one who is not a prisoner in chains." ("Hypothetical liberty" means, I think, freedom of action, action understood as a doing *not conditioned* by external constraint; it is what, since Aristotle, has been thought of as a willing going-along or voluntariness. "Universally" is the usual skeptical totalitarianism; it is to be opposed, I think, not by a counterclaim about what *everyone* does think, but by surmising that *some* might say that that isn't what they mean by a free *will*.) This kind of liberty is compatible with the sense of necessity arising from the observation that there is a certain uniformity conjoining actions with motives, inclinations, and circumstances. When "by necessity" is taken to mean an inherent connection, this hard determinism is beyond our ability to establish. And when, working from the other side, liberty is taken as simply opposed to necessity, it morphs into chance, "which is universally allowed to have no existence." (That necessity has chance as its opposite is simply a presumption; in the tradition, the proper opposite could be *contingency*, that is, radical but not irrational originality. See Note 30 above.) Hume's reconciliation of the dispute is to opt for a necessity that is merely the impression of constant conjunction and whose complementary, and not opposed, freedom is willingness—lack of internal objection, which is voluntariness, as well as lack of external obstruction, which is practical freedom. (Hume considers neither Thomas's free choice nor Ockham's contingency, so this is not a reconciliation with the keenest opponents. Liberty of the will as the simple, perhaps mystifying, origination not so much of novel action as of un-prognosticable intention is, consequently, as proscribed in the *Enquiry* as it was in the *Treatise*. Why, I ask myself, was a writer so willing to consign items to unintelligibility, so unwilling to accept the mystery of free will? Could it be that skeptics, *ipso facto*, can't tell the difference between an epistemological problem and an ontological mystery?)

35. Dogmatic slumber: Kant, *Prolegomena to Any Future Metaphysics*, "Introduction"; **mark of freedom**: *Critique of Pure Reason* B 718.

Chapter V. The Will as Ego Founder

1. The main text for the next paragraphs is Immanuel Kant, *Critique of Pure Reason* (A edition, 1781; B edition, 1787). This is the first of three *Critiques*. There will be occasional references to the *Prolegomena to Any Future Metaphysics* (1783).

Connection: B 232.

Copernican Revolution: B XVI. I mean that up until the first *Critique* all the philosophies I know of saw into or looked behind an external world such as we normally experience, no matter how earth-bound their researches into the factual world or how adventurous their forays into transcending realms might have been. Kant shakes loose this essentially world-centered position, in which the human being is located within a cosmic or noumenal environment. He makes the human subject, so to speak, the environment within which the natural and ideal universes are structured. It is remarkable how quickly we learn to live past these and all the subsequent revolutions, be they mathematical, physical or psychological, and continue to carry on as if we were *in* an independently existing finite world in which time is yet independent of space, souls are still separable from bodies, and right or wrong are, for practical purposes, even now ascertainable. I think that this conservatism of ordinary life under the continual intellectual assault of counterintuitive advances is due less to the half-blessed, half-regrettable fact that many more people don't read philosophy or study physics than do—for there *is* a trickle-down effect—than it is the result of a kind of self-neutralization that these intellectual overthrows often seem to bring with them, meaning that they are susceptible to opposite interpretations for application to life. (For example: Is the Theory of Relativity not really a Theory of the Absolute World? Is a thoroughgoing physicalism not ultimately indistinguishable from a complete idealism? Composing an inventory of such re-inversions would be wicked fun.) Kant himself thinks of his epistemological inversion as analogous to the Copernican cosmological revolution, because when Copernicus was making no progress neatly rationalizing celestial motions as long as the stars were thought to turn about a fixed observer, he tried letting the observer revolve and leaving the stars to their rest. Thus Kant, seeing that he could get no *a priori* knowledge of things when our intuition has to conform itself to them, tries to see whether it won't work better to let the things adjust themselves to our cognitive faculty (B XVI–XVII). However, the analogy isn't very close, since the Copernican observer, now on an earth spinning about its own axis and carrying out yearly revolutions about the sun, is a traveller still *out* in space, not a Kantian subject constituting the space *within*. My point is that the Copernican Revolution was relatively easy to absorb, since mariners still (well, until recently) navigated by the heavens that *revolve* about the earth, and jobholders expect the sun to *rise* in a timely manner. The Kantian inversion, moreover, is much more radical than the Copernican Revolution, since it is not about motions within the universe but about the very universe, the place of the world itself. Yet it too will be re-inverted by interpretation: Kantian subjectivity instead of *constituting* the world critically will again *inhabit* it psychologically. The will is going to partake in this migration, sometimes spectacularly: It will come to haunt, even *be* the world (see my Ch. VII, Secs. B and C, herein).

Ursache: *Prolegomena*, para. 53.

2. Imagination: B 233–34; **hidden power**: B 180–81; **central function**: B 150–56—the treatment of the imagination in the A edition has psychological elements that were erased by Kant in the more strictly transcendental B edition; since, however, this more logical version, more closely tied to the understanding, is surely abstracted from the psychological experience of imagining, this latter need not be set aside if the critical intention is kept in mind; for more on this see Brann, *World of Imagination*, 89–99; **synthetic product**: B 233–34; **critical-transcendental**: *Prolegomena*, Pt. I, end; **newly discovered**: A 120, note; **world construction**: B XVI ff., *Prolegomena*, para. 17, end; *a priori* **manifold**: A 100.

3. Human freedom: freedom has turned up in the first *Critique* from the beginning as the backgrounding antithesis to nature, but the decisive introduction is in the "Transcendental Doctrine of Method" (B 785 ff.), which is indeed a sort of annex to the critical edifice in which the architectural blue prints (B 680) of the *Critique* are stored.

New departures: e.g. B 479; **only negative**: B 823—this assertion of the main profit of the great philosophical grounding of Newtonian dynamics takes me aback, and I doubt whether Kant meant more than that he was now well set up to return to an early preoccupation, the metaphysics of morals. (See Lewis White Beck, *A Commentary on Kant's* Critique of Practical Reason [Chicago: Univ. of Chicago Press, 1963], 6, n. 9; 7, 17.) The reason for my doubt is that the *Opus Postumum*, the huge unpublished labor of his old age, was largely devoted to—one might say fixated on—bringing even the particular, empirically discoverable, elements of physics under the transcendental principles of the first *Critique*. (See Eva Brann, "Kant's Afterlife," *The St. John's Review* XLVII, no. 3 [2004]: 59–86.)

4. The following references are for the preceding two paragraphs. **A faculty for beginning**: B 561; **idea of reason**: B XXVIII–XXIX; **pathological**: B 830; **freedom in the practical sense**: B 561–62.

5. Aristotle includes a third kind of thinking, "productive" (*poetike*) besides "practical" (*praktike*) and "theoretical" (*theoretike*). Of course, the last is primarily concerned with being, not cognition: *Metaphysics* VI 1025 b; **political-practical life**: *Politics* VII 1024 a; **reason and understanding**: these are the terminological ghosts of the *nous* and *dianoia*, intellect and reasoning, thought and thinking, distinguished by Plato, *Republic* 511 d (but not so unequivocally by Aristotle).

6. The unified use of practical and pure reason: in the first *Critique*, particularly B 832 ff., where the absolute need to bring the two uses together is sketched out. Notice that the question whether or not our soul harbors two separable root-faculties, of thought and of affect, that I, for one, find preoccupying (Brann, *Feeling Our Feelings*, 449–69), is by Kant already tacitly settled when he speaks of the "final and of the pure use of our reason" (B 825): the pure reason is the one, the *cognitive* root-faculty. The *Critique of Practical Reason* was written in part to work out more precisely the ultimate coordination of reason's two functions.

7. *Arbitrium liberum*: B 562—*Willkür* is the larger term including both animal desire and the human will insofar it allows itself to be sensually affected. *Will* proper is not so affected. *Arbitrium* does, in fact, mean "choice," but more exactly "judgment, decision." (See Ch. III, Note 36, herein.) *Willkür*, the faculty exercised in the actual world, is indeed closer to decision-making than *Wille*.

8. Sensorium of space and time: space and time are presented in the first part of the first *Critique* (B 33–73) as the transcendental, that is, cognitive receptacles (so to speak) into which we as subjects receive the sensory material, the manifold, that is given to us, and within which we bestow spatiality and temporality on it. The pure space, again so to speak, contained in the informing form is imaginable as a potentially mathematicizable matter in which sensation, mere appearance, receives a three-dimensional Euclidean structure and so begins to become *a priori*, pre-empirically, amenable to Newtonian mathematical physics. Being three-dimensional, the spatial sense is the "outer" sense, more accurately, the sense of *outerness* realized in the measurable extension of mutually external parts.

Time, the "inner" sense, is the form of self-apprehension; in it we sense ourselves, our internal condition, as an ongoing succession of conscious moments. Time, however, is one-dimensional (B 47) and, again so to speak, a flux rather than a territory. That is one reason that Kant thinks that psychology cannot be a proper natural science—not because there is something hyper-physical in it, but because a continuous, one-dimensional flow can't yield much mathematics (proper natural science being mathematical)—not to mention the fact that other human subjects won't "submit to our investigations" and that would-be researchers distort the state of the subject when they treat it as object (*Metaphysical Foundations of Natural Science*, Preface, para. 471).

9. Absence of pure psychology: since time is the inner sense, not only as a sense of myself as a conscious subject, but also of myself as the theatre of nature, it is the origin-sense "to which all modifications of the soul are subject" (A 98); just so, space is not only the outer sense as extended externality but also the sense on which influences from outside the subject impinge. Therefore one of the most startling passages in the *Critique* is the concession in B 77–78 that inner sense can yield no experience of itself without being determined by outer sense: External objects, things appearing in outer sense, are demanded for the subject (oneself) to be determined, that is, for becoming the subject of definite predication. So our self-knowledge is mediated by nature; we could not experience ourselves as living through time (except as empty countable pulses), if the extended world did not display changes and motions lawfully modifying underlying stabilities (substances). Note that while there is only a meager apriori psychology, there is a rich practical anthropology: humanity as shaped by nature (*Anthropology*, 1798).

10. *Groundwork*: *Grundlegung zur Metaphysik der Sitten* (1785) is the more accessible foundational work bearing on the will. (I shall draw on the later, more comprehensive, and more difficult second Critique, the *Critique of Practical Reason*, to supplement the exposition.) My English text is Immanuel Kant, *Groundwork of the Metaphysics of Morals*, trans. Mary Gregor (Cambridge: Cambridge Univ. Press, 1998). Sometimes I emend from the German text. I here cite by Kant's sections and by page numbers in Gregor's translation.

11. Good will: *Groundwork*, right after Preface, sec. I.

12. Morals: the German word is *Sitten*, cognate with Greek *ethos*, so that "Ethics" might be the better rendering of the word in the title of the *Groundwork*. However, it has become standard to speak of "ethics" when the emphasis is on individual virtue (for which view Aristotle's work called *Ethics* is the model) and of "morality" when rules of conduct define human rectitude (for which approach Kant's works are paradigms). A contemporary writer who makes use of the distinction is Alasdair MacIntyre, for example in *After Virtue* (Notre Dame: Univ. of Notre Dame Press, 1981), chap. 9. Kant himself defines "ethics" as a doctrine of virtue, where virtue (*Tugend*) is not a personal endowment or a rational habit but rather a disposition to act in accordance with the concept of duty.

The Metaphysics of Morals: Trans. Mary Gregor (Cambridge: Cambridge Univ. Press, 1996) (cited pages numbers are for this translation); "metaphysics" for Kant means "a system of *a priori* cognitions from concepts alone" (Doctrine of Right I, p. 10), where *a priori*, literally, "from the very first," means, as elsewhere, "antecedent to all experience," that is, arising from our cognitive constitution alone. Here (Doctrine of Right III, p. 18) *Willkür* is redefined from its wide scope in the first *Critique* to be in tune with the *Groundwork*: it means a subordinate but also the sole freedom, not, indeed, to act for or against the moral law but to be the source of maxims. Will itself is neither free nor unfree. This, so far opaque, definition will be cited again and elucidated below.

Lying: *Metaphysics of Morals*, Doctrine of Value, pt. I, ch. II, p. 182; **murderer example**: "On a Supposed Right to Lie for Philanthropic Reasons" (1799)—recall that the French Terror of 1793–94 had come and gone!

13. Will good without further purpose: *Groundwork* sec. I, p. 10.

14. Second, third propositions: p. 13.

15. Categorical imperative: p. 15; **"categorical"**: sec. II, pp. 25–26—the categorical command formula is contrasted with a hypothetical one, where the injunction is based on a conditioning purpose: "If you want x, do y"; **reason as a capacity for universals**: *Critique of Pure Reason* B 378–79; **universalizable**: in Beck, *Commentary*, 160; **one reason**: this problem concerning the unity of pure and practical reason is ever interesting and with it the question of primacy, that is, whether we are ultimately thought- or will-centered beings; see Note 6 above.

Evidence for Kant's underlying assignment of primacy keeps going this way and that; see also Note 7 above. For example, evidence for the primacy of practical reason: Reason, the intellect of old, has been by Kant decisively deprived of its object, the *noumenon*, the object of intellectual insight, whose evaporation is the aim of that half of the *Critique* which is critical in the ordinary sense. It contains the "Transcendental Dialectic," which exposes the logic of the illusions that transcend possible knowledge. Practical reason, on the other hand, which is not a speculative faculty to begin with, has massive control. And generally there is no question of Kant's explicit opinion: without subjection of one mode of reason to the other, there would occur a contradiction of reason with itself, and it is speculative reason that is subordinate to practical reason: *Critique of Practical Reason* Bk. II, Ch. II, Sec. iii, "Of the Primacy of the Pure Practical Reason in its connection to the Speculative Reason." Yet in the very Preface of the *Groundwork* itself Kant makes the point that a critique of pure reason is *more urgent* than that of practical reason, since in "moral matters human reason can easily be brought to a high degree of correctness and accomplishment, even in the most common understanding" quite *without* the practical critique. And when he first works out what freedom of the will positively is, he derives it not from reason's practicality, but from its rationality (*Groundwork* sec. II, pp. 53–54). See text, below.

What it seems to come to is that Kant, although finding the dialectic of pure reason and the analytic of understanding (its necessary antecedent) more intellectually preoccupying, thought that the moral critique was more humanly dignifying.

16. **Moral law inexplicitly before everyone's eyes**: *Groundwork* sec. I, p. 16.

17. **Popular morality**: sec. II, p. 19 ff.; **metaphysics**: Preface, p. 1; **below observation**: sec. II, p. 19.

18. **Categorical imperative** (first and second version): sec. II, p. 31; **third version**: p. 38; **kingdom of ends**: pp. 41–42.

Kant's description of the kingdom of ends has a crucial feature reminiscent of Rousseau's "general will" (Ch. VII, Sec. A, herein): Kant's "systematic union" lives under common, universal laws. Now "if *we abstract from personal differences of rational beings as well as from all content of their private ends*" (my italics), we get a systematic connection of members who *are* ends and *have* ends but no private object of interest. What is comparable in Kant's "kingdom of ends" to Rousseau's "moral body" is that they both arise by abstraction from embodied human beings.

19. **Rational vs. natural beings**: *Groundwork* sec. II, pp. 44–45.

20. Previous two paragraphs. **Ought**: p. 24; **duty**: p. 10; **objective necessity**: p. 46; **will as pure practical reason**: on Kant's confusing usages, see Beck, *Commentary*, 39; **footnote on faculty of desire**: *Critique of Practical Reason*, Preface [16] note; **desire**: Kant's *Anthropology from a Pragmatic Point of View* (1798) contains a long treatment of "pathological" desire (Pt. I, Bk. II, "The Feeling of Pleasure and Aversion," Bk. III, "The Faculty of Desire")—Kant also, somewhat aversively, refers to the will in traditional terms, as a faculty of higher desire, but this desire is not a feeling, not pathological (*Critique of Practical Reason* Pt. I, Bk. I, Ch. I, para. 5, Remark 1)— it is, in fact, "interest." See Note 21 below; **Socrates on philosophical dying**: Plato, *Phaedo* 67 e.

21. **Interest**: *Groundwork* sec. I, note, p. 25 and sec. III, p. 54 ff.; **pure ideas arouse interest**: pp. 63–64.

22. Previous three paragraphs. **Supreme principle**: *Groundwork* sec. II, p. 47; *Groundwork* **to Practical Reason**: sec. III, title—"Transition from metaphysics of morals to the critique of pure practical reason"—the book by this title, i.e., *Critique of Practical Reason*, didn't exist yet; **rational beings *ipso facto* free**: see Note 15 above.

23. **How we can have an interest in morality**: *Groundwork* sec. III, pp. 63–64; **something left over**: p. 65; **reason would overstep all bounds**: p. 62; **how the categorical imperative is possible**: p. 64.

24. *Critique of Practical Reason*: this second *Critique* (1788) is more than twice as long as the concise *Groundwork* and therefore, although more circumstantial, sometimes easier to read.

How does the will go to work? Kant calls this inquiry "moral anthropology" and treats the subjective conditions that hinder people from doing their duty. This "anthropology" (experiential study of human beings) is broached in the *Metaphysics of Morals, Doctrine of Virtue*, where he is still working with the concepts of the *Groundwork*. It goes completely experiential in the charming, sometimes even intentionally humorous *Anthropology*; see Note 20 above. This work is termed "pragmatic" meaning conducive to worldly wisdom, useful for life, just as is Aristotle's *Nicomachean Ethics* (I 1095 a): "for the end of this kind of study is not knowledge but action."

25. Fact of pure reason: Beck, *Commentary*, 166 ff., works out the meanings of "fact" and the argument behind freedom's factuality—this commentary is *really* helpful; **ordinary folks**: *Critique of Practical Reason* Pt. I, Bk. I, Ch. I, para. 7 (Remark), para. 8 (Remark II); **how is the categorical imperative possible?**: *Groundwork* sec. III, pp. 58–59; **world of reason**: Kant actually says "understanding" but this is a broad use.

26. Will and will: Beck, *Commentary*, 177.

27. Law as expression of freedom: 179; **full of affects**: 90–99—Beck reviews the affective faculties; **interest as that through which will becomes practical**: *Critique of Practical Reason* Pt. I, Bk. I, Ch. III, also *Groundwork* sec. III, note, p. 63; **interest inexplicable**: *Groundwork*, p. 63; **authentic self**: ibid., p. 62.

Ex post facto: There may be an argument for the moral feeling being an anterior incentive: Janelle De Witt, "Respect for the Moral Law: The Emotional Side of Reason," *Philosophy*, October 2013, 1–33.

28. On what common ground: In the first *Critique*, this is laid out in the "Schematism of the Pure Concepts of the Understanding" (B 176 ff.), to my mind, the heart of its theoretical part; **model and type**: *Critique of Practical Reason* Pt. I, Bk. I, Ch. II, "Of the Typic of Pure Practical Judgment." The brilliantly ingenuous solutions, presented in two thorny texts, are highly satisfying, if only one can find one's own formulation, as does the "beautiful soul" of Hegel's *Phenomenolgy* (VI Cc).

29. Dual will: Beck, *Commentary*, 198–202—a review of the "dual will" controversy.

30. As if: H. Vaihinger, *The Philosophy of "As if"* (1911), trans. C. K. Ogden (New York: Barnes and Noble, 1966), 289–95.

31. Assigning blame for public disasters to philosophers is fraught with dilemmas. If you argue that philosophers are never responsible, because they are like the poets of whom Auden not completely ironically said that their "poetry makes nothing happen" ("In Memory of W. B. Yeats"), then philosophy has been neutered. If, on the other hand, you do assign blame, then defenders will say that the philosopher's philosophy has been bowdlerized and abused. This point might be well taken, but then the question arises whether philosophers aren't responsible for the bowdlerization of their thoughts; they could think more soberly—for example it is hard to imagine that Aristotle's doctrine of the virtuous mean could be very badly abused, badly enough to induce evil.

Although talk about Kant's "Prussian philosophy"—Kant as the proponent of unconditional obedience—is fairly called absurd (Beck, *Commentary*, 202 and n. 78), yet there is something very deliberate in the metaphysics of morals that seems practically (in Kant's sense) dangerous: Being rational does—sometimes systematically—forestall being reasonable. Thus a colleague, a German historian, Beate von Oppen, told me long ago of her conviction that the German officer corps, trained in a code of honor thought to be derivative from Kantian morality, was in fact stymied in its incipient resistance to Hitler by his cunning device of making them take an oath not to the nation but to himself personally. (For the oath, see William Shirer, *The Rise and Fall of the Third Reich* [New York: Simon and Schuster, 1963], 227.) Oath-breaking, as included under the severely proscribed evil of lying (see text above), was simply the greatest breach of duty under a soldier's version of the categorical imperative. But to trace the actual lineage of this conduct back to Kant, in other words to trace influence, takes, at least in the absence of explicit documentation, more insight than I would attribute to even the most acute historian; see Ch. III, Note 48, herein.

32. Plato's intentions: the Good beyond Being, *Republic* 509 b; **Doctrine of Science**: the text I am using is Fichte's late revision of the early, famous *Groundwork of the Entire Doctrine of Science* (1795), published from his students' lecture notes after his death; it was even then a work in progress: *Fichte: Foundations of Transcendental Philosophy (Wissenschaftslehre) Nova Methodo* (1796–99), trans. and ed. Daniel Breazeale (Ithaca: Cornell Univ. Press, 1992). Breazeale's book employs several sets of paginations; my references will be to the ordinary pages of the book itself. The "new method" consists: 1. in the interweaving of the previously separate theoretical and practical parts, and 2. in starting with *Tatsachen* ("facts") rather than *Tathandlungen* ("deed-actions," see my text below), that is, with human experience rather than with the absolute I. For 1, see first Introduction to the *Doctrine of Science by a New Method* (Breazeale, 85); for 2, see para. I (Breazeale, 110).

Schlechthin: usually translated "absolutely," but it really means that this event is an immediate, sole, and uninferrable act of the I; see Breazeale, 113 n. 16; **willing original**: Breazeale, 113.

33. Personal will: This is a modern ego-version of an old problem: Is the intellect individual and many or one and universal? (Thomas Aquinas, *Summa Theologica* I, Q. 76, art. 2; the Doctor Angelicus, down-to-earth as ever, is absolutely for individually embodied plural intellects).

The attempt to deduce everything from one absolute principle that is itself ungrounded, a principle that is a version of the Kantian I but is now deemed accessible to some sort of direct insight, is characteristic of what in histories of philosophy is called "German idealism," a school that builds a bridge from Kant to Hegel. Both of these decline, to be sure, the description of idealist, since they hope to have treated the world in its concrete existence. Fichte, and Schelling, his correcting follower, are the chief proponents of this idealism. Both put the will at the beginning and both supply, in later works, a faith-based beginning in a divine Will, a beginning that, although the analogy with the human I is patent, jibes uneasily with the transcendental deduction of the latter. I'll begin with the theological Will in my brief account of Schelling's theory (as I shall for Fichte), since it is more comprehensive in its grounding brief.

It is set out in Friedrich Wilhelm Joseph Schelling, *Philosophical Researches on the Essence of Human Freedom and the Objects Connected with It* (1809) in *Schelling's Werke*, Hauptband IV (Munich: C. H. Beck und R. Oldenbourg, 1927), 223–308.

God within time has two principles which are, however, to begin with, undifferentiated in him. One is real, unconscious, unformed material. "Now the *Beingness* (*das Seyn*, "beyng," see Ch. VIII, Note 71, herein) of God is not *one and the same* with God himself," but effectively different, "*as in the human being*" (327, the latter italics mine). God in the strict sense is the other principle, God as *Being*, as existing. This is the ideal, the conscious God. The unconscious aspect of God is only for the sake of the conscious, to give it a source-ground (my term). The differentiation of true being from mere beingness is in God, as in man the highest *moral* act. The human being that can't depart from, become independent of, mere beingness is deformed, sunk in selfhood (egoism), incapable of elevating itself.

A second expression of the relation between the two principles is that they are as Being to Not-being. The "proper gravity, the crux of all philosophy" is to inquire into Not-being (308). One consequence of misunderstanding the latter is the mistaken notion that creation arose out of nothing. Finite beings are created not from Nothing but out of Not-being, which, as a non-subject and thus no bearer of predicates, is always merely relatively antecedent to Being. In certain relations it is evil, a condition that could not-be and yet is—not in its ground real, yet possessing a terrible reality. An example is sickness, a condition contrary to nature. (So far this reads like a moralized version of Plato's *Sophist*.)

Now the application to will. The first principle, the "material-out-of-which" (my term) is a first "primordial power" (*Urkraft*) through which God is *individual*; it could be called the egoism of God. If that was his only power, God would be cut off, alone; there would be no creation. It is a state analogous to the psychic power of a self-enclosed, reserved human being, a dark soul. But from eternity there is an opposing principle, that of love, through which God is the essence of all essences. This conscious principle would, however, become diffuse did it not find a delimiting opposition in its unconscious. Again, a human being would dissolve if it only loved, were it not opposed by a prior principle of—anger.

The divorce that is the first—atemporal—step in creation brings forth nature, elevates the ideal over the material principle. Nature is matter which is overpowered by love: God's egoism is its material principle, the power of materiality. Thus nature's material root is in God's egoism, its ideal root in his love. Schelling has deduced a knowable Nature from God's dual being, and he has done it by rooting God in potential evil. (It is a highly anthropologized working out of the Platonic and Neoplatonic perplexities with source-principles of materiality and formlessness and, finally, evil; a primal example is the "indeterminate dyad" attributed by Aristotle to the Platonic Academy. See *Metaphysics* XIII 1081 a and also Plotinus's essay "On Matter," *Ennead* II 4.)

Are we closer to will? Yes, because both principles are wills (Schelling, 251 ff.). Humanly speaking, the first principle is will without understanding, an unarticulable longing to give birth to itself. It is, in a way, the Will of understanding but as an unconscious, presentiment-will. This dark yearning leaves a pall of melancholy over Nature, once generated. The second principle is, so to speak, the Word of God (253), the word of longing mirrored in God's spirit, in consciousness. Spirit and longing together are a second, a freely creating and omnipotent Will that uses the originally unruly Nature as its tool. And so arises conceptual particularity, so arise the distinctions of thought.

The duality descends to mankind. Every being arising in nature has it within itself. In accord with the first principle, which is dark self-will (*Eigenwille*), the creature is divided from God; it opposes the universal Will of its Creator. It is sheer rage or passion, this particular will. But the process of creation is a kind of transformation of the originally dark principle. When this transmutation in God and man is accomplished, and dark transfigured into light by the progressive distinctions of understanding, the will of man is still individual but also one with the primeval Will, now turned into understanding. Thus man, because he too arises from God's dark, egoistic ground, preserves a principle of relative independence from God. But insofar as he has been transfigured into light, this same man is spirit (*Geist*). The human will is to be seen as a band of living powers. As long as man lives in unity with the divine universal Will, his soul is in balance. If he separates, the band becomes a rebellious army of lusts, and the individual will must devise an eccentric life of ruination and evil (257).

Schelling summarizes oracularly: "The will of man is the shoot hidden in the eternal longing for a God now present only in the ground, the divine look of life which God espied when he conceived the Will to Nature. In him, in man alone, God has loved the world" (255). For a summation, I shall cite Schelling approvingly paraphrasing Spinoza: "In the final and highest instance there is no other Being but Willing (*Wollen*). Willing is primordial being." To it belong all ultimate predicates and "all philosophy strives to find this highest expression" (242).

In private lectures given the next year (1810, *Schelling's Werke*, 309 ff.), Schelling details the development of the human will in somewhat eccentric terms: 1. Temperament (*Gemüth*): what is real in man, the dark principle; 2. Spirit (*Geist*): what is personal in man, the seat of "conscious desire," will; it, again, has two sides, first a real one that refers to human individuality—self-will, and second a side without which the first would be blind—understanding; 3. Self (*Selbst*): what is truly divine, thus impersonal, that is, not particular in man, without the spirit's potentiality for evil or its possible participation in goodness, but goodness itself.

This remarkable onto-mythological creation story, in which God is made in the image of man, is also the most positive piece of theology imaginable. Less extravagant, but possibly more faithful theologians walk the *via negativa*, the way of negation, which cautiously delineates God by what he is not; they certainly don't transcend him to posit his dark ground.

This story has been an ascent from Schelling's much earlier deduction of the whole system of reason from one principle, the I. Since I am presenting in the text itself a brief review of Fichte's deduction, I shall here do the same for Schelling's deduction even more concisely and confine myself, except for the briefest prelude, to Schelling's treatment of the will in his earlier work. My text is F. W. J. Schelling, *System of Transcendental Idealism* (1800), trans. Peter Heath (Charlottesville: Univ. Press of Virginia, 1978).

The system, Schelling announces, "completely alters and even overthrows the whole view of things" in life and in most sciences (Foreword, first sentence). What is new is an early form, a proto-version of Schelling's most original thought, which came to be called the "system of absolute identity." In it, that which is absolutely first and certain, the (Cartesian) proposition, "I exist," is established as being identical with "There are things outside me"—the self as identical with nature, the ideal as identical with the real (Introduction, Corollary 2, p. 7, Pt. II, p. 40; a later version, on the divine level, appears in the work on human freedom considered above). Thus the I, by an activity that is something like an intellectual insight (the kind proscribed by Kant) and belongs to it as yet pre-consciously, elicits its non-I from itself. Now Schelling, following Kant, develops first a system of theoretical philosophy, which is largely a deduction of the science of nature (Pt. III), and then a system of practical philosophy, which is a deduction of the "thinkability" of morality (Pt. IV). The will is introduced at the end of Pt. III and further prepared for in Pt. IV. The productive self-knowledge of the self eventually advances (not temporally but conceptually, of course) to self-consciousness. It engages in an act of "absolute abstraction," which is Schelling's term for a completely original, unconditioned act whereby the I's insight, its intuiting intelligence, "raises itself absolutely above the object." Insofar as this act is explicable at all, it can be so only from the I itself, which, as intelligence, has an ultimate principle of action within it.

"*This self-determining of the intelligence is called willing*" (Pt. IV, Cor. 1, p. 156, my italics). It is only through the medium of willing that intelligence becomes an object to itself, that is to say, becomes self-conscious. While the I was producing its other, it could not see itself as a whole, as I and its own object. This new self-consciousness is actually of a higher degree than the mere consciousness of having an object. Now the whole complex of knower and known becomes an object to the self. So the hopeless parallelism of theoretical and practical reason is overcome in transcendental idealism: The willing of the self is *at once* self-understanding and active autonomy; it is both an "idealizing" knowing and a "realizing" acting. The aim to deflect the parallelism so as to result in a meeting of its lines is clear enough, although the deduction is somewhat obscure. Willing could be said to be both the I's delimiting *definition* of itself to itself, and its autonomous doing of deeds. (I might comment here that *almost* always in this line of thought the problems discerned are more permanently engaging than the solutions produced.)

One more phase needs to be noticed because it grapples so directly with the deepest problem of Kantian moral will: It can't *appear* in the world (for what appears is Nature and necessary), and thus, remarkably, the subject, the I, as a will can't meet other personal wills *in the world*, at least not directly. Schelling means to solve this problem by arguing from the requirements of free-willing. Since it *is* a drive for knowledge, the intelligence goes out to an object of cognition, and if it is to be a determinate cognition, it must meet resistance in, and delimitation by, the object to be known; it must meet with a negation. This resistance, this restriction, if it is active, must be an external intelligence. (If it were passive, it would be, because it is determined by law, Nature.) So to gain a self-insight as actor in the world, the I must run into other intelligences. (I have a suspicion that in this setting-out, the existence of other individual intelligent wills and their "preestablished harmony" with each other—a Leibnizian adaptation—is really a postulate, a demand; in any case I can't find a deduction here). Thus, the following conclusion is an answer, if not a solution, to Kantian subjectivity: "*Only by the fact there are intelligences outside me, does the world as such become objective to me.*" So the I needs other intelligent wills in the world, for if "*willing . . . is the action whereby intuiting is fully posited in consciousness,*" then that can't happen in the absence of an external resistant will. That is to say, for each individual not only are "these other individuals . . . the external bearers of so many mirrors of the objective world," but (as has been explained above) since knowing and acting are identical, will *is in the world*. And its going into the world is enabled by other wills (Pt. IV, E I B, pp. 173–85).

How, in what form, does the will appear in the world? As it needed other wills to reveal itself to itself, so to act it demands an external object, one to which it is blindly directed by *natural inclination*. This drive is not willing at all; it is the self-interest by which the I becomes conscious to itself as an individual. Obtaining its object is called happiness. It is by this drivenness that the I becomes conscious of itself, as self-determining will. But many drives may come into play, some opposed to each other. Here the absolute will again becomes an object to itself, for it makes a *choice*. Only this act persuades the will that it is free: It turns out that freedom is not found in the Kantian pure law-giving will but in the "choice-will," the selector of preferences. In sum, "the alien factor on which the absolute will is dependent for purposes of appearance, is the natural inclination in contrast to which alone the law of the pure will is transformed into an imperative" (Pt. IV, E II, p. 185 ff.). In choice, our freedom becomes "objectified" and thus, having an object to become conscious of, we in fact arrive at consciousness.

So Schelling has projected the action of the will into the external world. But the price has been the loss of Kant's astounding thought that freedom is self-given law, for it is now choice—self-interest.

34. Johann Gottlieb Fichte, *The Vocation of Man* (1800), trans. Peter Preuss (Indianapolis: Hackett Publishing, 1987); **the will, not the intellect**: Bk. III, "Faith," p. 72; **I must do as I ought**: Sec. iii, p. 96; **raise itself to the One**: Sec. iv, p. 107; **creator of the world**: Sec. iv, p. 110.

35. For the full title of both works and a full reference to the revision see Note 32 above.

Fichte's postulate: "Major points of the *Wissenschaftslehre* of 1798–99," para. 1, Breazeale, 65; **thoughts without content**: *Critique of Pure Reason* B 75; **one posits oneself**: Breazeale, 65; **I (or self)**: in English translations "the I" is often rendered as "the Self" which not only reads more easily but also includes an aptly reflexive, self-referential sense; ***Tathandlung***: *Doctrine of Sci-*

ence, Pt. I, para. 1; **coming apart of an identity**: para. 1, which renders this self-confronting identity as "A=A," but the logical formula is derived from the transcendental insight.

36. Being as Not (-I): para. 2, Breazeale, 66–67. In the earlier *Doctrine of Science*, Pt. I, para. 2, the formula (substituting I for Fichte's A) that renders this self-opposition of I to Not (-I) is: Not (-I) = I. It expresses greater complexity in the terms of the identity than does A = A. Here -I stands for the cancelled being or activity of the I, and Not (-I), the double negation, stands for the I's activity of going negative, that is, of going into opposition to its negative self so as to reclaim its positivity. The whole formula expresses this inner activity of the I as opposed to the original simple I. This is opposition in sameness, or the I as its own *object*—itself *and* outside itself.

37. Real and ideal: para. 3, Breazeale, 66–67; **abstracting from facts**: first *Doctrine of Science*, para. 1; **ultimate ground**: Breazeale, 67.

38. Theoretical and practical: para. 4, Breazeale, 68.

39. Drive: para. 6, Breazeale, 68–69; **representation and space**: paras. 9–10, Breazeale, 70–71.

40. Rational being: title of para. 11, Breazeale, 71. At this paragraph of the "Major Points" (see Note 35 above), I turn to the full presentation, numbered in parallel with the former; the will is treated in paras. 12–18, Breazeale, 258–445.

Striving: in his youth, Fichte was a Spinozist but recanted; it is tempting to read his understanding of striving as a displacement of Spinoza's *conatus*, the endeavor wherewith each thing strives to persevere in its own being; thus *conatus* is any thing's essence (*Ethics* III, Props. VI–VII, see Ch. VII, Note 1, herein). Fichte's striving is, on the contrary, outreach, an urge to cross over to another being, even to exert force on it.

41. The rest of my exposition follows paras. 12 and 13 of the *Doctrine of Science by a New Method*, and I shall cite Breazeale's pages.

Causal power: para. 12, Breazeale, 258; **willing as an original**: 259.

42. Nothing exists: 260; ***noumena***: distinguished from *aistheta*, "sensibles" in Plato, *Republic* 508 c, though Plato uses "visibles" to stand for sensibles—*noumena* is the neuter plural passive participle of the verb *noein* from *nous*, "intellect"; **all representations originate**: 261 and editor's note G.

43. Self-affectation: 264–65.

44. Definition: 264—the starting definition does seem to be a "fact" of appearance, as the New Method promised, see Note 32 above; **factors involved**: this tracing out begins in para. 12 and takes up para. 13. I will stick with para. 12.

45. Temporal succession: 269—Fichte here reverts to Kant's schematism, which brings together concepts and intuitions. See Note 28 above.

46. In fits and starts: 270.

47. The whole paragraph: 268, 270, 271, 275—Fichte has many ways of making the point, of which I have chosen a few; **New Method**: See Note 32 above.

48. Circle of young Romantics: My chief reference here is Ricarda Huch, *Die Romantik: Ausbreitung, Blütezeit und Verfall* (Tübingen: Rainer Wunderlich Verlag, 1951). See the chapters on "Novalis" and "Romantische Philosophie." Besides the chief exponent, Novalis, the circle included the brothers Schlegel, and Schleiermacher. Outside Germany, Coleridge studied both Fichte and Schelling; see *Idealism and the Endgame of Theory: Three Essays by F. W. J. Schelling*, trans. Thomas Pfau (New York: State Univ. of New York Press, 1994), Appendix on Coleridge.

Ludwig Tieck: the drama is called *William Lovell*, after its anti-hero who utters the lines quoted; see Huch, *Die Romantik*, 148; **Novalis's notes**: 141, 149.

49. Responsibility: see also Note 31 above; **idealism as emanation of Romanticism**: Copleston, *History of Philosophy*, vol. 7, pt. I, 29–30.

There are many ways to describe the continuous revolution that is modernity and numerous moments to cite as its crux-revealing junctures. Tzvetan Todorov suggests a neat confrontation of old and new. Fleshed out, it runs like this: The devil tempts Jesus after forty days' fast in the wilderness with "all the kingdoms of the world . . . if thou wilt fall down and worship me" (Matthew 4:5–6), and Mephistopheles offers Faust the heights and depths of experience against a penalty of post-mortem servitude (Goethe, *Faust* I 1531 ff.). Jesus refuses to change masters, but Faust accepts, setting aside the devil's fair warning with the words: "But I will it." Therein we may discern a chief characteristic of modernity: The center of gravity shifts from God and his created Nature to Man, "from the objective world to the subjective will; the human being no longer bows to an order that is external to him, but wishes to be himself a creator, to establish this order himself." But in agreeing to the Satanic proposition, the heedless humanists, though gaining worldly mastery and secular excitement, sanguinely commit crimes on earth and light-mindedly indenture themselves to infernal powers. (Tzvetan Todorov, *Imperfect Garden: The Legacy of Humanism*, trans. Carol Cosman [Princeton: Princeton Univ. Press, 2002], 1, 9–10; Todorov delineates a modern humanism, an anthropocentrism, that hopes to escape the Satanic bargain. Goethe, to be sure, lets his Faust get away with it in any case. Sponsored by his victim, Gretchen, he gains entrance to heaven after all, and with this moral trivialization the "tragedy" ends.)

Chapter VI. A Linguistic Interlude

1. The pursuit of original meanings: it is given a philosophical basis by Husserl through his Phenomenological notion of "sedimentation," an obscuring of original significations through familiarity, conceptual development, or formulaic transmission; this covering-over requires reactivation, if we are to understand what underlies our progress—what losses its gains have involved (Edmund Husserl, *The Crisis of European Sciences and Transcendental Phenomenology* [1936], trans. David Carr [Evanston: Northwestern Univ. Press, 1970], 52, 361). True or false, etymologies (the Greek writers reveled in the latter) often have the ancillary power of poetry, but to make revelations of truth depend on them is, I think, disingenuous. It *might* have some bearing on the absence of will proper in Greek texts that the words most nearly approaching "will" and "willing," in meaning, *boule, boulesis*, have no etymological connection to "will." There seems to have been a connection of meaning of *boulesthai*, the verb, to *ballesthai*, "to throw," as in *ballesthai toi thymoi*, "to throw oneself in one's heart [upon something]" (Frisk, *Griechisches Etymologisches Wörterbuch*, see under *boulomai*, I 259); **my first love**: I published the late Geometric and Protoattic pottery holdings (late eighth–seventh century B.C.E.) of the Athenian Agora Excavations (1962).

2. Whereas in logic, "modal" does not seem to apply to propositions in what might be called the zero mode—the ones simply relating a predicate to the subject—in grammar, all the ways of qualifying that relation are called moods.

3. *Will*: Calvert Watkins, "Indo-European Roots," in *The American Heritage Dictionary of the English Language*, 3rd ed. (Boston: Houghton Mifflin, 1992), 2133; **voluptas**: Eric Partridge, *Origins: A Short Etymological Dictionary of Modern English* (New York: Macmillan, 1963), 788, "volition," n. 4; **Wahl**: Friedrich Kluge, *Etymologisches Wörterbuch der Deutschen Sprache*, 19th ed. (Berlin: Walter de Gruyter, 1963), 861, "Wille"; **willful**: Ernest Weekley, *An Etymological Dictionary of Modern English*, vol. 2 (New York: Dover, 1967), 1636, "Will." The *OED* has upwards of 38 columns on *will* and associated words; **degeneration of meanings**: this downhill tendency seems to be more common than upgrading. Connotations can become condemnatory or tenderized, for example our word *discriminating*, which used to mean "using refined judgment" and now more often means "making prejudiced distinctions," or ancient Greek *kalos k'agathos*, which in classical antiquity signified "noble, gentlemanly" and in modern Greek, as *kalokagathos*, means "kind"; I don't know if it's current.

4. John Lyons, *Semantics*, vol. 2 (1977; reprint, Cambridge: Cambridge Univ. Press, 1994), 815–20; the future tense in non-Indo-European languages seems also to have been originally modal (817). Lyons interweaves his linguistic observations with reflection on futurity and its relation to willing.

The present of "to will" is also odd and suggestive. The progressive or "durative" present must be very rare; who has ever heard anyone say "I am willing," meaning "I am in the process of developing my will?" Yet it is one of the chief theses of this book that if willing is to be intelligible at all, it must have duration, be a progressive activity, as Thomas Aquinas takes it to be.

Usually "I am willing" is construed as a copula and an adjective, "willing," and then it means "I am (flabbily) agreeable." As a reply to a marriage proposal it would be a let-down—except in one famous case. In Chapter V of Dickens's *David Copperfield*, Barkis the carter sends word to Peggotty the cook: "Barkis is willin'." But this is in fact a proposal of marriage, an admission of readiness that Barkis repeats as his last words on his deathbed in Chapter XXX. So "willing," in accordance with its etymology, has several tonalities. Dickens's novel is full of them. (See Charles Dickens, *David Copperfield*, intro. and notes by Jeremy Tamblin [London: Penguin Books, 2004], 962, n. 3 to Ch. XXX. I might add here that on recently rereading Cervantes' *Don Quixote*, I discovered in this Knight of the Sad Countenance the very model of a modern mode of willfulness.)

One more item concerning the use of the auxiliary "will" for the future: Some languages can use the present to convey the future, e.g. German: "*Kommt er? Er kommt*"—"Will he come? He will." There is a study claiming that languages like German, which don't require distinguishing present from future as does English (mostly), induce in their speakers a propensity for saving their money now, while languages with strong future time references, e.g. those that use "will," make their speakers less disposed to present parsimony, the future being farther off. (*Yale Alumni Magazine* [January–February 2012]: 32; this finding illuminates the imposition of austerity by Germans on their improvident fellow-Europeans). English, however, can in fact also use a present or a continuative for the future: "Does he come? Is he coming?" can be said even before he has started.

5. My examples come from Charlotte Yonge, *The Clever Woman of the Family* (1865), a hilariously stuffy and curiously engaging tome from England's most popular novelist of her time.

6. There are, of course, other ways of speaking futurally. Some express intention: "He's going to . . . ," "He plans to . . ." One, cited in Note 4 above, uses the present projectively: "He comes tomorrow." All circumvent a hopelessly missing direct locution. In German the future indicative is formed with the auxiliary *werden*, (which seems to mean something like "turn toward, become"), the future infinitive with *wollen*, cognate with *will*.

7. Etymology of *shall*: C. T. Onions, *The Oxford Dictionary of English Etymology* (Oxford: Clarenden Press, 1966), 8155, "shall"; **I will arise now**: William Butler Yeats, "The Lake of Innisfree"; **loss of distinction between *shall* and *will***: C. T. Onions's *Usage and Abusage: A Guide to Good English* prints a typical letter of complaint about the solecisms of the colonials. (This book bears the brave epigraph *Abusus non tollit usum*, "Abuse does not make away with [correct] usage.") An illustration of the will-solecism which works just fine is the poem "Wine Bowl" by H. D. Doolittle (American) which has 93 lines and 20 first and third persons of the auxiliary "will"—very melodiously obliterating the distinction.

8. George O. Curme, *A Grammar of the English Language*, vol. 2, *Syntax* (Essex, Conn.: Verbatim, 1977), chap. XVIII 5, "Future Tense," 362–71. Both Partridge and Curme set out the correct use of *shall* and *will*. Curme, however, goes widely into the modal issue. The shall/will rules are subject to qualification. There is, for example a modal first person *shall* as in questions: "What shall I do" or after deliberation: "I shall [have decided to] write a book" (Curme, 364).

9. Opinion: in the sense here used it is a Socratic notion, whose nature is clearly delineated in Plato, *Republic* V 477 ff.; the people Socrates talks to usually have opinions to begin with, which are then tested; **deontic**: Lyons, *Semantics*, 817.

10. The verb *to be*, besides having multiple roots (to be found in the "Indo-European Roots" Appendix of the *American Heritage Dictionary*) has two separate but problematically involved uses: as signifying being or existence: "I think, therefore I *am*," and as coupling subject and predicate: "I *am* a thinking thing."

Being has a future: See Ch. VIII, Note 73, herein, on Heidegger.

11. Specious present: Charles Sherover, *The Human Experience of Time: The Development of Its Philosophical Meaning* (Evanston: Northwestern Univ. Press, 1975), passim; **future**: Brann, *What, Then, Is Time?*, 172–75, 183–85; **the free will that is to fashion it**: add "and the chance that correlates with its ignorance."

12. Will as faculty of new beginnings: Arendt, *The Life of the Mind*, vol. 2, *Willing*, 28 ff., 108–10 and Stephen Campowski, *Arendt, Augustine, and the New Beginning* (Grand Rapids: William B. Eerdmans Publishing, 2008), 146 ff.; **spontaneous**: a Kantian use, not a very helpful attribute of will, since *sponte* is synonymous with "freely, willingly." It makes a curious kind of sense that Hannah Arendt is at once the proponent of the will as a datable novelty in history and as a faculty of newness whose paradigm is creation (*Life of the Mind*, 2: 5, 29). Putting two and two together here yields: the will is self-created.

13. "Let there . . . and it was good": Genesis 1:14–18

Chapter VII. Un-possessed Will: *Communal and Cosmic*

1. Spinoza's version of will is set out in his *Ethics: Demonstrated in Geometric Sequence*, which was completed by 1675, but for prudential reasons not published until after his death. Here is what will is not: "There is in no mind an absolute free will, but the mind is determined for willing this or that by a cause which is determined in turn by another . . . and so on to infinity."

The will is, moreover, not a faculty of desire or aversion but of affirming and denying ideas, that is, of judgment—not, however, a faculty different from intellect, but the same. Hence Spinoza opposes Descartes' notion that the will extends further than the intellect, and that error lies in that differential zone. Rather, just to have an idea is to have it affirmatively or negatively. Spinoza goes further: There is in fact no faculty of willing at all, but only this or that particular idea affirmed or denied. Volitions are thus integral to conceptions not as a whole but one by one (*Ethics* II Props. 48–49). The faculties are assimilated to each other and in turn distributed over the ideas, which are not the objects of mental powers but just the mind's actions themselves (*Ethics* II Def. III).

That, volition and conceiving being identical, the will should be understood as judgment, and regarded as no freer than the intellect—that is, bound to the nature of particular beings— is intelligible on its own. But what motivated this identification, and why Spinoza says that this doctrine benefits our life, namely by teaching us that knowledge of God is our happiness, that we should learn how to face affairs of fortune "not in our power" and how to live as social beings and as free citizens—that would require an exposition of Spinoza's whole system. For he is a philosopher who most freely adapts terms—sometimes out of recognition—to his own purposes so that these propositions attain their specific sense only within the whole. But that exposition is not within my aim here (see, however, Brann, *Feeling Our Feelings*, 231–287), especially not since his heterodox view of ordinary human will is not, I think, Spinoza's most significant thought, that is, his most positive, deepest, and most future-fraught notion—that is his thorough-going, impulse-driven physicalism based on modern natural science.

Here, then, is what the Spinozist will is: endeavor, *conatus*, a striving, urging impulse. In this most fundamental sense, desire has been returned to its elemental function. It is nothing like that rational desire of the main tradition, which follows the good:

> This endeavor, when it has reference to the mind alone is called *voluntas*, but when it refers simultaneously to the mind and body, is called *appetitus*, which is therefore nothing else than the *essence of man* [my italics] . . . and therefore man is determined for acting in this way . . . It may be gathered from this that we endeavor, seek, will, or desire nothing because we deem it good, but on the contrary, we deem a thing good because we endeavor, will, seek, or desire it. (*Ethics* III Prop. IX, Note; when appetite is conscious it is called *cupiditas*, "desire.")

This not the relativism it sounds to be, because we act as "modes" of "God or Nature," and Will is simply God's motion (as intellect is his rest, *Ethics* I Prop. XXXII, Cor. II), while the striving endeavor (*conatus*) "wherewith a thing endeavors to persist in its being is nothing else than the actual essence of the thing" (III Prop. VII). *Conatus*, or "power" (III Prop. III), is a term used in the physics of Spinoza's time; for instance, by Leibniz ("The Theory of Abstract Motion," 1671), where it is a precursor of the notion of an instantaneous action of force to change momentum; when integrated over time, it will be called "impulse" in classical physics. It seems to be Spinoza's signaling of God as Nature—which makes him a pantheist or an atheist, depending on one's apprehension of his god-affirmation in the fifth book of the *Ethics*. This, at least, is clear to me: His awe before and reverence for this "God or Nature" are those of a man of faith.

In any case, since *conatus* is will in its mental mode, both in man and in the God of whom man is a modal "affection," this power becomes the world-driving, endeavoring strife. As such it will have a huge effect, direct or indirect. For example Goethe, who admired Spinoza as one of his teachers—into whose writings he occasionally dipped—lets the Lord say, approvingly, that man will err as long as he strives (317) and that

> *Ein guter Mensch in seinem dunklen Drange*
> *Ist sich des rechten Weges wohl bewusst.*

> A good man in his dark endeavor
> Is of the right way well aware.

Faust, I "Prologue in Heaven" (329–30)

"Striving" was a topic in Fichte's idealism, and it was also a Romantic preoccupation; no doubt Spinoza was a source.

As I began with an undecidable question about this truly original author—Is he an atheist or a pantheist?—so I want to end with one: Is Spinoza a determinist or what will come to be called a "compatibilist"? It is a question to grapple with (perhaps inconclusively) on the basis of my Chapter IX on Compatibilism.

2. Jefferson in France: Dumas Malone, *Jefferson and the Rights of Man* (Boston: Little, Brown and Co., 1951), 15–16; **Jefferson a Rousseauist**: Merrill D. Peterson, *The Jefferson Image in the American Mind* (New York: Oxford Univ. Press, 1970), 117. This charge continued past the Civil War, which some Southerners blamed on Jefferson's radical democratism (214); **Madison on Rousseau**: *The Mind of the Founder: Sources of the Political Thought of James Madison*, ed. Marvin Meyers, rev. ed. (Hanover: Brandeis Univ. Press, 1982), xxiv ff., 190–194—Rousseau's plan of 1761 was for a league of sovereigns to prevent war; Madison thought this was perpetuating arbitrary power wherever it existed. (Here, incidentally but irresistibly, in view of our present financial crisis, is Madison's prescient opinion on war-debts: He thought "that each generation should be made to bear the burden of its own wars, instead of carrying them on at the expense of other generations" and "that the taxes . . . should include a due proportion of such [war expense] as . . . being wrapped up in other payments may leave [the people] asleep to misapplication of their money," 193); **general will**: thinking out the implications of this notion might cast doubt on Rousseau's heart as well.

3. The general will appears first in Jean-Jacques Rousseau, *Discourse on Political Economy* (1758, first printed as an article in Diderot's *Encyclopedia* in 1755). The motion pervades *The Social Contract* (*Du contract social*, 1762).

4. Four wills: *Social Contract*, Bk. III, Ch. II; **private will**: Bk. I, Ch. VII; **the will of all**: Bk. II, Ch. III; **sum of differences**: ibid.

5. Wills made conformable: Bk. II, Ch. VI.

6. People kept from communicating with each other: Bk. II, Ch. III; **no partial association**: this proscription of private association is at odds with the long footnote to Bk. III, Ch. IX, that praises the glory of faction-ridden times. **Politic to multiply**: this *sounds* like Madison's *Federalist* 10, but isn't; see Note 14 below.

7. Social compact: Bk. I, Ch. VII; **forced to be free**: Bk. I, Ch. VII.

8. Sovereign: Bk. I, Ch. VIII; **everything it ought to be**: ibid.; **division of powers**: Bk. II, Ch. II.

9. Inversion: Bk. II, Ch. IV.

10. Enacted will is law: Bk. II, Ch. VI; **will made conformable to reason**: ibid.; **censorship**: Bk. IV, Ch. VIII.

11. Free vote: Bk. II, Ch. VIII; **general will by counting votes**: Bk. IV, Ch. II; **not in a state of freedom**: ibid.

12. Nation of gods: Bk. III, Ch. IV. Compare Madison in *Federalist* 51: "If men were angels, no government would be necessary." Rousseau concludes against democracy, Madison for controls on government.

13. Half-century old text: Jean-Jacques Rousseau, *The Social Contract*, ed. Charles Frankel (New York: Hafner Publishing Co., 1948); **seductive Rousseau**: there is something in his shameless self-contradictions and deliberate incompleteness that appeals to the perennial postmodern in some of us; even Madison accorded Rousseau an honorable heart, and the latter was surely a man of sentiment.

My critique is not isolated: see *Rousseau's Political Writings*, ed. Alan Ritter and Julia Conway Bondanella (New York: W.W. Norton, 1988)—"Reactions to Rousseau," 191–218 and "Commentaries," 219–306—both pro and con. Here is an example of what puzzles me in a number of appreciators of Rousseau: One commentator quotes the paragraph from Bk. II, Ch. VII, in which Rousseau declares his intention of altering the human constitution (with which I shall end my review) and prefaces his quotation with what reads like words of genuine admiration: "And what a welcome relief it is from the somewhat evasive language we tend to get in our own time on this vital matter!" After the quotation he concludes: "Precisely. So declared Robespierre and Saint-Just" (Robert Nisbet in *Rousseau's Political Writings*, 258–59). These two are, of course, the instigators of the first modern ideological mass murder, the French Terror, in which c. 17,000 souls were executed. Both were great admirers of the *Social Contract*, which was indeed a hugely popular reading during the French Revolution (255). It is an example of the intellectuals' disconnect between talkative mentation and concrete imagination, just what Jefferson's opponents meant by calling him—not altogether justly—a "Rousseauist doctrinaire."

14. James Madison, *Federalist* 10 (on factions and their control). Madison is not in favor of factions but thinks that, since where there is liberty and individuality there will be interest-groups, it is better to control their effects than to destroy their causes, a remedy "worse than the disease." The effects are controlled by letting them play against each other within a representative, constitutional republic. This is his genius: getting something bad to work its good.

15. Manipulativeness: the same spirit is evident in Rousseau's educational classic, *Émile* (1760), which subjects the boy to sub rosa stratagems rather than to candid punishments; **guardian of our spiritual life**: Eva Brann, "Madison: Memorial and Remonstrance," in *Homage to Americans* (Philadelphia: Paul Dry Books, 2010), 85–134.

16. Virtue and general will: *Discourse on Political Economy* II (*Rousseau's Political Writings*, 67); **Kant's indebtedness**: Ch. VI, Note 18, herein.

17. *Social Contract*: Bk. II, Ch. VII.

18. Thomas Aquinas: *Summa Theologiae*, Pt. I, Q. 1, art. 8, reply to obj. 2; **Schopenhauer**: *The World as Will and Idea*, Bk. II, para. 28.

19. Arthur Schopenhauer: *The World as Will and Idea* (1819, with 50 supplementary paragraphs, 1844); **contents**: Bk. I—Idea; Bk. II—Will; Bk. III—Art, Bk. IV—Affirmation and Denial of the Will to Life; **my idea**: Bk. I, para. 1; **esse is percipi**: George Berkeley, *A Treatise Concerning the Principles of Human Knowledge* (1710), Pt. I, 3. Berkeley argues that an Author's Will (God's) imprints ideas on our senses directly. These *perceptions* are what there *is* for us: ideas we actually perceive without their being dependent on our own will (such as imagined objects). So will is the direct agent for either origin of perception, divine or human. No external object, no internal things are needed; "real things" are perceptions not in our power (paras. 27–33); their reality is of the order of abstract ideas, whose erroneousness Berkeley criticizes in his Introduction. His theory, looking back to Ockham, appears to me as a simplified nominalism—simplified in erasing the intervention of factual reality between God and man. **Spinoza**: see Note 1 above.

20. Subject: *World as Will*, Bk. I, para. 2.

21. Noumenon: Kant, *Critique of Pure Reason*, B 294 ff.

22. Enigma: *World as Will*, Bk. II, para. 18; **object coincides with subject**: ibid.

23. Ground as relations: Bk. I, para. 2; **forms of sensibility**: ibid.; **as content**: *Critique of Pure Reason* VB 39 ff.—see Brann, *What, Then, Is Time?*, 62 ff., on "pure intuitions," i.e., a pure *content* of the sensibility.

24. Object is for subject: *World as Will*: Bk. I, para. 6; **falling apart**: Bk. I, para. 7.

Schopenhauer vehemently distinguishes himself from the "identity philosophers" of my previous chapter (Bk. I, para. 7), but from a distance there is a similarity: the determination to get behind appearance to one ultimate root.

25. Different side: Bk. II, para. 24; **our body**: Bk. II, paras. 18–19; **appearance of the will**: Bk. II, para. 20; **fourth ground**: Bk. II, para. 24.

26. Nihilism: Bk. IV, para. 71 (final).

27. Wheel of Ixion: Bk. III, para. 38; **Eastern wisdom**: see my Conclusion, Note 8.

28. Effect of a work of art: Bk. III, para. 34; **adequate objectification**: Book III, para. 33.

Platonic Ideas imitated by artist: Schelling's system culminates in a theory of art as the final unconscious self-production of the I. So does Schopenhauer's.

In Plato's *Republic*, the arts are proscribed as being doubly removed from genuine being: They produce images of images, copies, that is, of the appearances that are themselves images of the forms, the Ideas. This most radical, because ontological, attack on the arts raises two related problems not faced directly in the *Republic*. Plato's Socrates is himself presented as a maker of grand myths, verbal images of great poetic force, and moreover, Socrates himself hints that there might be arguments for readmitting artists into his *kallipolis*, his "beautiful city" (607 c–d).

Schopenhauer's theory of art (already found in Plotinus, *Ennead* V 8, 1, "On Intelligible Beauty"), in which the poet copies the Ideas directly, is, to my mind, a solution to both problems together: The permissible artist, the Socratic word-painter, looks to the Ideas directly for his images (Eva Brann, "Imitative Poetry: Book X of the *Republic*," in *The Music of the Republic*, 256–71). Schopenhauer, understandably, became the artist's philosopher, notably Thomas Mann's, who presents the reading of the chapter on "Death and its Relation to the Indestructibility of our Essence in Itself" (*World as Will*, Supplement to Bk. IV, Ch. 41) as a redeeming moment in the decline of Thomas Buddenbrooks, the hero of *Buddenbrooks* (1901), Mann's earliest masterpiece. He later wrote an essay on Schopenhauer (1938) in which he admitted—"thus the artists treat a philosophy"—that the Buddenbrooks chapter was written in the intoxication that a "metaphysical magical potion" had induced in the twenty-year-old author. Schopenhauer's actual death chapter is, however, a coolly sober, yet intense assessment of the annihilation of the individual but the survival of the will. Thus not: I disappear and the world survives; rather: the world disappears and the will survives, albeit without memory and individuality, and just for that reason ready to enter a new life. Out of this cold comfort Thomas Buddenbrooks extracts: "I will live," and is restored—until the next morning.

29. Metaphysics of music: Supp. to Bk. III, Ch. 39; most of my paragraph refers to this chapter; **auditory appearance of the will**: Bk. III, para. 52; Schopenhauer says about the imitative relation, the "point of comparison" of music to world, that it lies "deeply hidden"; this is similar to what Kant says of the merging of sensibility and understanding (*Critique of Pure Reason* B 180–81). These junctures, where the analytically heterogeneous parts of world and soul have to be synthesized, are to me always the focal points of interest—where the mysteries emerge.

30. Shadow not essence: Bk. III, para. 52; **numerical formalism**: Supp. to Bk. III, Ch. 39; **gratification of the will**: ibid.

31. The inquiry: Bk. II, para. 17; **life-mood**: as before with Hobbes, Schopenhauer's style, ever clear and often witty, larded with apt quotations and spiced with epigrammatic formulations, honeys, as Lucretius says, the rim of the bitter cup. Schopenhauer somewhere (I can't find the place) calls himself an "oligograph," a "little-writer," because he spent his life essentially on one book; actually his style is as expansive as Hobbes's is concise; the pleasure given is opposite in kind but almost of the same degree.

32. The human body: Bk. II, para. 20; **name of will**: Bk. II, para. 22; **will guided by rational motives**: ibid.; **low-grade expressions of the will**: Bk. II, para. 27.

33. Most of paragraph: Bk. II, paras. 27–28; **primacy of will**: Supp. to Bk. I, Ch. 15; **character**: Bk. II, para. 26; **individual not Will itself**: Bk. II, para. 23.

34. Hungry will: Bk. II, para. 28; **aimless will**: Bk. II, para. 29.

35. Whole paragraph: Bk. IV, but particularly para. 59.

36. Free will: Supp. to Bk. II, Ch. 25.

37. Knowledge of will: Supp. to Bk. II, Ch. 23.

38. Creative will: Supp. to Bk. II, Ch. 25; **will to life**: Ch. 28; **objectification**: Ch. 19.

39. Friedrich Nietzsche, *Der Wille zur Macht* (Notes written from 1883 to 1888), English edition: *The Will to Power*, ed. Walter Kaufman, trans. Walter Kaufman and R. J. Hollingdale (New York: Vintage Books, 1968). The background of the publication's history is clearly set out in the Editor's Introduction.

The other books I shall refer to are *Beyond Good and Evil* (*Jenseits von Gut und Böse*, 1886) and *Genealogy of Morals* (*Zur Genealogie der Moral*, 1887). Quotations are translated from the text directly.

40. German dance: I know only two German authors who, in stark contrast to Luther's oddly gripping bully-German, have this elegance: the novelist Theodor Fontane (b. 1819), who writes in the mockingly plainspoken dialect of my own birth-region, Mark Brandenburg, and the poet Christian Morgenstern (b. 1871), whose mordantly witty surreal verses are simply acrobatic.

System: For Kant, philosophy is all or nothing—systematically complete or else defective, because reason, being itself a systemic *unity*, is consequently an "architectonic," that is, a *system- or edifice-building* faculty (*Critique of Pure Reason*, e.g. B 502–3).

41. All the citations are only examples. **My precursors**: *Will to Power* II 463; **pessimism**: II 379 and passim; *not being over being*: III 685; **freedom from effects and will**: III 612; **art is denial of life**: III 812; **access to thing-in-itself**: *Beyond Good and Evil* I 16; **old wives morality**:

V 186; **deification of will**: *Will to Power* IV 1005. In the early essay "Schopenhauer as Educator" (1874), Nietzsche was still a follower; he only found "a little error here or there."

42. Title announced: *Genealogy* III 27.

43. Will and way: *Genealogy* II 12; **life as will**: *Will to Power* III 689.

44. Schopenhauer's misunderstanding: I 84; **I assess**: II 382.

45. Away and towards: *Beyond Good and Evil* I 19.

46. Will as affect: ibid. **Second derivative**: the symbolization of a change of change, like the speeding up of speed (acceleration) or the willing of willing (if willing is an intensity of the soul, see Ch. VIII, Note 30, herein).

47. Will is not desire: *Will to Power* III 668; **no such thing as willing**: ibid.

48. Revaluation: *Genealogy* III 27; **life is will to power**: *Beyond Good and Evil* IX 259; **leave them to their devices**:—and emigrate to democratic America (my prescription).

49. Ground-affect: *Will to Power* III 693–703; **salvific function**: Eric Salem points out to me that without Nietzsche's insight into the profundity of suffering he is just a metaphysical Machiavelli.

50. First quotation: *Beyond Good and Evil* II 36; **second quotation**: *Will to Power* IV 1067.

51. Will not an effect: in *Will to Power* III 689, Nietzsche says that, psychologically reckoned, the concept "cause" is just our feeling of power from so-called willing, and our concept of "effect" is the superstition that this feeling of power is the power itself that moves; **summary**: Martin Heidegger, *Nietzsche* (Pfullingen: Verlag Günther Neske, 1961), 48, 70, 76.

An exposition of the Will to Power as the "being of beings" (that which makes individual beings be, their "basic character") is to be found in Heidegger, *Nietzsche*, particularly the first eighty pages of volume I. Heidegger regards the notes for *Will to Power*, although a work in progress, as sufficiently definitive. He claims that the Will to Power is for Nietzsche the basic character of beings (*Seiendes*), and further, that their being (*Sein*) is the Eternal Return (26–33). "For Will to Power is *becoming*" and "*that everything returns* is the most extreme *approach of a world of becoming to that of being*:—the summit of the reflection" (*Will to Power* III 617). Heidegger's identification of the two great Nietzschean constructs, the Will to Power and the Eternal Return, seems to me textually unexceptionable, but it does not answer what I want to call the more intimate question: What is the Will's personal—or rather, impersonal—description: How am I to feature it? Heidegger admits that Nietzsche leaves these features undeveloped (47). He then attempts an answer, as summarized in my text.

By the way, he also answers the question raised above, why non-human forces need the aid of pioneering philosophers: because truth has its effective origin in strong contention. It is in a serious attack on traditional illusion (37) that a new basic position asserts itself. But that is as much as to say that human delusion, left to itself, is more potent than the Will to Power—and so to bring it back among human beings, to make it humanly defeasible. Yet that, in turn, goes counter to Heidegger's claim that "If life itself is Will to Power, then it is itself the ground and the principle of valuation. Then a Should does not determine being but being the Should" (41). Being, however, is not (human) beings. An answer, if there is one, must lie in the nature of the Eternal Return. (See this Chapter, Note 57.)

52. Willing not individual: Heidegger, *Nietzsche*, 73.

53. Affect-form: *Will to Power* III 688; **voluptuousness**: ibid.

54. Unity of Will to Power and Eternal Return: Heidegger, *Nietzsche*, 26.

55. Nietzsche on metaphysics: *Will to Power* III 574.

56. Christian Morgenstern, *Galgenlieder* (Gallows-Songs, 1905), "Das Knie" (first stanza):

> *Ein Knie geht einsam durch die Welt.*
> *Es ist ein Knie, sonst nichts!*
> *Es ist kein Baum, es its kein Zelt!*
> *Es ist ein Knie, sonst nichts.*

57. Here it is, again and again: the question of responsibility, here Nietzsche's responsibility for one of the several catastrophes of the twentieth century. Is it permissible to write so arcanely, so oracularly, that misconstrual—caricature—is inevitable? I say "inevitable" because I come from reading Peter Gast's "Introduction to the Train of Thought of *Thus Spake Zarathustra*." Gast was acknowledged by Nietzsche as his true and trusted friend. The essay, which identifies the author of *Zarathustra* with its hero and almost deifies Nietzsche, is an ecstatically affirmative extraction from Nietzsche's works of all that is, denuded of its intended subtlety, to become terrible in the Germany of the twentieth century: worship of barbarism, militarism, and war and world-conquest as the only salvation now available from mere comfort-seeking; furthermore, master race, genetic improvement of the human race, "extermination of all the sick and decadent, and parasitic," and finally, the great blessing, unconsciously desired by the rabble, "of again having a lord, a *Führer* . . . above oneself," together with the contempt for democratic institutions—helped linguistically by Luther's conversion of the word "people" into *Pöbel*, "rabble." (It is not to the point, it is no defense at all that the principal targets of extermination for the Nazis, the Jews, are emphatically *not* the objects of contempt for Nietzsche, when there was so much other human trash to contemn. We Jews have an apt saying: "With friends like these, who needs enemies?") A serious question: To what degree is Nietzsche to be held responsible for this spokesman?

Gast is strangely silent on the will, but to my sense, the terrific overestimation of the will as first in the scale of affects is *the* most dangerous aspect of Nietzsche's teaching. As I said, Schopenhauer's will-based system is saved by its pessimism, which induces the ultimate renunciation of willing—and so has no direct political implications. But Nietzsche is—in his way literally—an eternal optimist. He says "My philosophy brings the victorious idea of which all other modes of thought will ultimately perish" (*Will to Power* IV 1053; why do the alternatives have to perish?). If the victorious idea is the Eternal Return, that is endurable only by means of the invigorating thought of the Will to Power (IV 1059); there is no sign of its renunciation.

In this context arises the question, what really is the power of the will to power? In itself it is eminently non-physical, sub- or hyper-physical (IV 1063–64), for it is feeling, affect (III 688); its power is not the kind of force that has a quantum. In fact, for science there is no willing (III 667); this turns out to be prescient, for determinism, the denial of free will, is almost universal in contemporary, science-based will-studies (set out in my Chapters X–XI).

In the notion of the Eternal Return, however, non-quantifiable power enters into an—unspecified—alliance with physical force and energy: If the infinite recurrence of events is made bearable to us by the present joy in a sense of power to be infinitely, reiteratedly, evinced, its actual eventuation requires a physical law of the conservation of energy and the conservative force behind it. Nietzsche, however, gives no evidence of thinking of mathematically formulable force laws (IV 1061–63). The Eternal Return is, to be sure, saved from an objection that might come from a future thermodynamics, namely, that organizations in open systems degrade over time: Nietzsche stipulates a finite, closed world. The fact that this world is uncreated, temporally infinite, does save the notion from the side of psychology. For if a human being remembers previous cycles, then the cycles are thereby not strictly repetitive, since living a life with the memory that makes it a repetition prevents it from being really a repetition, while reliving a life without such a memory makes of the recurrence an idle speculation. But happily that is not, after all, quite true. If I have lived an infinity of times through the same occurrence, what is nullified are the separate remembrances, which all collapse into one, thick "once again." And that seems to be exactly what Nietzsche's teaching is intended to effect: to subject present experience to a huge, impending sense of "forever before and forever again," to supply our life with a sense, an acquired memory, of *returning* eternality.

It is the *nunc stans*, the "standing now," of *celestial eternality* pulled apart into *terrestrial passage*. Its intention is to regain stability by making it inherent in flux: "Recapitulation: to *impress* on Becoming the character of being—that is the true *Will to Power*" (III 617). Nietzsche himself calls this attitude toward the theory of the Eternal Return its "incorporation" (*Einverleibung*); see Heidegger, *Nietzsche*, 330 (Note 51 above) for a reprinting of a sketch by Nietzsche dealing with the teaching of the "Return of the Same" as it affects his own life.

As for the dangerous political repercussions of the will triumphant, how is it possible not to think of Leni Riefenstahl's filming of the Nazi *Parteitag*, the Party Convention, of 1934 in Nuremberg—without rival the grandest piece of cinematic propaganda ever produced—which is called *Triumph of the Will*? The producer was really the National Socialist Party, since this is not a documentary in the sense of documenting of an independent event. This celebration was staged for the director, Riefenstahl, who was suited to the enterprise by being both a superb filmmaker and apolitical to the point of consciencelessness. I remember the sense of unholy shock at the movie's opening: Hitler is flying into the medieval city in his private plane, which casts the shadow of a cross over the cityscape as it descends. (Oddly, I read of the same, this time unintended, effect among the Christianized Amazonian tribe of the Kamsá who, when the first airplane overflew them, thought it was a great crucifix [Wade Davis, *One River*, 1996, p. 268].) Then and there arise the questions: Whose will? The movie manages to meld the Führer's will (he is always shot cutting off tumultuous salutes with curt, dismissive gestures and a basilisk-expression of dangerous willfulness) with the people's devotion. It is an incarnation of Heidegger's "deferred will" (see Ch. VIII, Sec. D, herein), here the deference of the nation, of Germany—there are none but type-representing human figures, mostly uniformed—to its Leader, Hitler. And what is the object of the will? Resurgence, power, but no particulars of the ensuing human life—sheer willful willing. This is the Will to Power gone forth from a philosophical phantasy into a submissive world.

It is as crudely absurd, so it seems to me, just to blame this artistic monster with its apt and reminiscent title on Nietzsche as it is evasively pusillanimous not to wonder—to expect so little providence from a great writer and hence to deny philosophy its insidious potency, that of capturing souls *especially* in its crudified version. Besides, an awful suspicion arises: that Nietzsche, who would most certainly have found the Nazis an abomination, would have done so more because of their vulgarity than their crimes—and so would have made a matter of taste what should, in plain decency, be a matter of humanity. But of course, I don't know that.

A historical footnote to *Triumph of the Will*: In 1945 a racially integrated service team with Jews in its line-up played an exhibition baseball game in the stadium where much of the Riefenstahl film was shot—a poignant moment of triumph, American style.

One more sub-note: Nietzschean resonances come in various tonalities, none of which are, to be sure, precisely imputable to Nietzsche. One of these has been termed "Heroic Vitalism." It is to be heard, for instance, in D. H. Lawrence's proto-fascist spasm, *The Plumed Serpent*, a novelistic intervention into Mexican life—the attempt to reanimate Quetzalcoatl (an artist-god who deserves better), with amazingly prescient proto-Nazi pageantry. In this weird second coming of the Plumed Serpent, there is no commanding will at work but rather a squishier quasi-Nietzschean blood-aristocracy and gendered (male) self-assertion. (See, e.g., Witter Bynner, *Journey with Genius: Recollections and Reflections Concerning the D. H. Lawrences* [New York: The John Day Company, 1951], 209, 227.) So once again: the conundrum of influence.

Chapter VIII. Will's Last Ontologies

1. 1830 is actually the date of the third, definitive edition of the *Encyclopedia of the Philosophical Sciences in Outline* (ed. Friedhelm Nicolin and Otto Pöggeler [Hamburg: Verlag von Felix Meiner, 1959]). Heidegger's *Of the Essence of Human Freedom: An Introduction to Philosophy* was a lecture course delivered at the University of Freiburg in 1930. (See Note 74 below.) This pre-post-ontological century should be extended by a little over a decade to include Sartre's *Being and Nothingness* (1943).

2. My particular sources are: the *Encyclopedia* in various English versions cited below, paras. 473–82; also Hegel's *Philosophy of Right* (1821), trans. Alan White (Newburyport, Mass.: Focus Press, 2002), with Additions (*Zusätze*, in this edition called "Elaborations") based on Hegel's students' lecture notes and "Supplements" from student transcripts more recently published (see xi–xii), paras. 4–28.

Dialectically unfolding: dialectic is the self-movement of concepts whose "moments" logical thinking unfolds: *Encyclopedia* I, para. 14; **circle of circles**: para. 15; **logic as thinking of thinking**: Michael Inwood, *A Hegel Dictionary* (Oxford: Blackwell Publishers, 1992), 271. This dictionary, as well as W. T. Stace, *The Philosophy of Hegel: A Systematic Exposition* (New York: Dover Publications, 1955), a paragraph by paragraph explanation of the System, are really helpful in grasping a sometimes hellishly difficult text.

The will treated preliminarily: *Encyclopedia* I, paras. 232–35. The will also appears in the general introductory chapters to the *Logic* (paras. 53–54), as a part of a brisk critique of Kant's "practical reason"; its gist is that his self-consistent will is empty of content, for it leaves unanswered the question of what in particular it is good to do; **Spirit**: *Encyclopedia* III, paras. 473–

82; **Spirit issues from Nature**: II, para. 376—the dialectical transitions between triads are often so obscure as to be unintelligible, to me *the* warning signal throwing in doubt the tight coherence of the System.

3. **Cognition**: *Encyclopedia* I, para. 226; **demonstration**: para. 231; **it must be apprehended**; para. 232; **it has passed over**: para. 232.

4. **While Intelligence merely proposes**: *Encyclopedia I*, para. 233, note; **the simple uniform content**: para. 233; **it imagines the actualizing of the good**: para. 234; **finitude of will**: para. 234, note.

5. This whole paragraph follows *Encyclopedia* I, para. 234 and its note.

6. **Good is really achieved**: para. 235.

7. **Absolute idea**: para. 244. The main paragraphs for my consideration of the Will in the third part of the *Encyclopedia*, called *The Philosophy of Mind*, are paras. 468–82 (Subjective Mind) and para. 483 (Objective Mind). For an earlier, more dialectically precise exposition I shall call on *The Philosophy of Right*. (See Note 2 above.) A political manifestation, taken from the *Phenomenology of Spirit*, is given in Note 28 below.

8. The "Phenomenology" phase of the *Encyclopedia* is fleshed out in the first part of the *Phenomenology of Spirit*, or more accurately, the experienced types of the latter are schematized, that is, systematized, in the former.

9. **Psychology**: *Encyclopedia* III, para. 440.

10. **Last negation of immediacy**: para. 468.

11. **Representative modes**: these are preceded by a direct mode, Intuition or Intelligent Perception, an immediate feeling of knowing. Hegel blasts the—still current—sense that *my* self-feeling of assurance is good enough "knowledge" (para. 447).

One element of intuition is Attention, "an active self-collection" (para. 448), which will define willing for William James. (See Note 47 below.)

12. Whole paragraph: *Encyclopedia* III, paras. 452–67.

13. **Thinking is determinate intelligence**: para. 445; **thinking**: paras. 465–67.

14. Whole paragraph: *Encyclopedia* III, paras. 168–469.

15. **Selfish will**: para. 469; **conservative**: it seems to me that in philosophy two polarized relations to the past are distinguishable: inclusiveness, in which preceding thought is to be absorbed, and rejectionism, in which it is to be defeated; the first yields newness, the second novelty; my leanings are hereby confessed.

16. **Practical Mind as feeling**: *Encyclopedia* III, paras. 469–72; **feelings**: para. 472, Addition. Hegel, however, thinks that a person of "character" can find something in harmony or disharmony with his will without giving way to feelings of joy or pain.

17. **The Ought**: III, para. 472.

18. **Impulses and Choices**: II, para. 473.

19. **Passions**: III, paras. 473–74.

20. **Interest**: III, para. 475. William James will use "interest," in his theory of will; however, he attaches the term to the idea of an object as attention-catching and will-concentrating, rather than to the volitional subject as having an interest in his own willing. (See Note 47 below.)

21. **Choice**: III, paras. 476–77.

22. **Happiness**: III, paras. 478–80; **universal satisfaction**: Kant, *Critique of Pure Reason* B 834; Aristotle, *Nicomachean Ethics* 1098 a.

23. **Volitional intelligence**: *Encyclopedia* III, para. 469, Addition; **reason**: III, para. 438.

24. **Desire**: III, paras. 426–29—desire is much earlier (lower) in the System than will and so at this stage no longer nakedly available; **Aristotle, appetite as ultimate**: Brann, *Feeling Our Feelings*, 70–72.

25. **Free mind**: *Encyclopedia* III, paras. 481–82.

26. **Stations of Objective Mind**: III, para. 483 ff.; **Right**: III, para. 487 ff.; **conscience**: para. 511; **Ethics**: para. 503 ff.; **Mind as self-conscious substance**: para. 517.

27. **Property**: III, paras. 88–92; **English influence**: e.g. Locke, who in his *Second Treatise on Civil Government* (1690) institutes property *before* any original civil compact; property is either in one's own person or in whatever a person has mixed his labor with (chaps. V and VIII). On the other hand, the notions of property and possession have already turned up in Subjective Mind

(*Encyclopedia* III, para. 468), where thinking, foreshadowing will's way of appropriating property by putting itself into it, gains possession of its thought contents by determining them and so making them its "property," meaning its own qualifications.

28. Below are brief accounts of: (1) Hegelian will acting in the world and (2) an alternate development of a world-ready will.

(1) A case of the external will comes from Hegel's *Phenomenology of Spirit*. I include it here not only because it shows how the System appears when cast into time but particularly because in it Rousseau comes on the scene (albeit namelessly, as do all the figures in this dialectical drama). It happens in a subsection within that part of the *Phenomenology* which is devoted to "Spirit" and is called "Absolute Freedom and the Terror" (paras. 582–95 of the A. V. Miller translation [Oxford: Clarendon Press, 1977], and BB, B, III in the *Phenomenology*'s own Table of Contents; I use my own translation). The case comes from a chapter on "Culture," set between "Ethics" and "Morality." Note that this temporal order inverts that of the System, where morality precedes ethics; thus the System is not, as I said above, a conceptual chronology, that is, a history of ideas.

For a clear assignment of the dialectical position of the "Absolute Freedom and the Terror" and for a lucid explanation of the section itself, see Peter Kalkavage, *The Logic of Desire: An Introduction to Hegel's* Phenomenology of Spirit (Philadelphia: Paul Dry Books, 2007), 315 and 308–14 respectively. For the inversion of Ethics and Morality, see 503, n. 2; the reasons are beyond my scope here.

Why is culture interposed between Ethics and Morality? Culture (*Bildung*, literally, "shaping, forming," ordinarily the word for "education," is related by the German Mystics to *Bild*, "picture") marks a revolutionary passage, an episode in which Man, now enmeshed in a social world and a free citizen of a State (hence within the Objective Mind phase of the System) educates himself out of his communal loyalties into a recalcitrant individuality, an ego. Within this setting arises Absolute Freedom (where "absolute" does not mean "completely determined and self-determined," but just the opposite: completely simple and indeterminate—for Hegel's usage here, see Inwood, *A Hegel Dictionary*, 29).

This Absolute Freedom belongs to a human being who thinks that "essence and actuality is the knowing of *itself*.—It is conscious of its pure personality and therewith of all mental (*geistigen*) reality, and all reality is only something mental (*Geistiges*); the *world is simply its will*, and *this is a general will*" (para. 384, my italics). This is not the empty thought of a will that consents silently or allows itself to be represented. (So much for a representative democracy—its citizens, Hegel implies, have abrogated wills.) It is a *real* general will in which every single individual participates; every *single* person's will as such counts; everyone always does it all. Therefore, what comes on the scene as the doing of the whole is also the immediate conscious deed of each one. Then Hegel says: "This undivided substance of absolute freedom elevates itself to throne of the world."

What is the outcome? It is the Terrible incarnate, the Terror, the model of all the ideological doings-away-with, the engineered disappearances of whole human kinds: "the Fury of Vanishing" (i.e., Making-to-Vanish, *die Furie des Verschwindens*, para. 589).

(This is remarkable: Hegel, the keenest analyst of the phenomenology of this historical event, cannot bring himself to condemn what he deems a dialectically necessary event, here the purging of institutions the Spirit had outgrown. See Kalkavage, *The Logic of Desire*, 502 n. 35. They say the devil is in details—I think he might rather be in Systems. Another observation: It is not until the twentieth century that the small-scale model, the French Terror—17,000 guillotined, as I mentioned,—has its full-blown realization in German, Russian, and Cambodian mass murders and in Chilean "disappearances." Thus if one seeks the phases of the System in time as real history they do not appear as just linearly progressive; the system repeats its states beyond "their" time; I am in doubt whether that fact corroborates or undermines it; Hegel, in fact notes such repetitions himself, for instance, in religious fanaticism (see this note, under 2. below).)

How—roughly—does the Terror fall out dialectically from Absolute Freedom? The latter, as the simple union of consciousness with itself, of an ego with its confronting object, is abstract, empty. Consequently the ego becomes simply, abstractly oppositional—each subject opposes every other. For each personal, particular will thinks of itself as universal, since the general will is its arena of functioning. And since it has no concrete object in its volitional intelligence, mere chaos ensues. All the civil institutions of the State are confounded. Now really nothing is left but the freedom and singularity of the individual. The generality of the general will, now unrealized in organizations, falls apart into "the discrete, hard brittleness" of a sapless generality, an object without content or existence on the one hand and "the self-willed punctuality" of the actual individual self-consciousness, on the other. This opposition is pure, unmediated negation—the negation of the individual when understood as existing in the general.

The only deed left to Absolute Freedom in this phase is thus death, banal, as meaningless as the "decapitations of a head of cabbage." Whoever gains power governs, but the government is only one, the victorious, *faction*. Yet because it is a mere faction it must perish, for it is guilty—guilty of lack of generality. The ruling faction has nothing real and external to put forward that might plausibly place the guilt on the inactual losing generality. Instead it assigns the meaning of "being guilty" to "intention" (a will-term in the *Encyclopedia*, para. 505, there meaning deep, responsible purpose, the essence of having an aim), and to "becoming suspect" of harboring intentions. There follows the "dry extermination" of the suspect element, from whom the current government can take nothing but its existence. Here is the high-point of the Terror: fatal suspicion of deviation. (Later incarnations will supply a propagandist ghost of an excuse to give the "guilt" content: racial contamination or ideological corruption.) Here I stop; expect a flip to the better from Hegelian dialectic: Morality (596 ff.)—one of the most stunning inversions in the *Phenomenology* (Kalkavage, 315), beyond my brief here.

But one more item: the connection to Rousseau. Readers will have recognized him in the general will: Hegel clearly ascribes to him much responsibility for the Terror, as seemed necessary to me in my foregoing treatment (Ch. VIII, Sec. A). To me the danger in the general will appeared to lie in its cloudy supra-human character that is an invitation to human abuse because it suffers from a risky ambiguity of status: Is it the will of every single citizen somehow amalgamated into one? Or is it the will of an in-the-know faction or leader which should prevail? Or is it a notional abstraction to be approximated by the willing citizens?

Hegel, however, admires the notion as a principle that is rational in form and content, and he criticizes it only for leaving the individual, private will intact in the collection of wills: The general will is not genuinely universal, which means that it is constituted as a collection of individual caprices and so lacks the rational element essential to a genuine will (*Philosophy of Right*, para. 258, Addition; I feel compelled to say that a real regime built on a universal—ideological—rather than a general—idea-void—will would seem to me to transit from terrible to ultimately terrible, because it would, as did the Soviet Union, have a certain ideological plausibility and with it a meretricious stability).

(2) Hegel's *Philosophy of Right* parallels the "Objective Mind" section of *Encyclopedia* III (whose first edition, 1817, precedes the *Philosophy of Right*, 1821 in which Hegel refers to it). This fleshing-out of the *Encyclopedia* outline proves to me how important for Hegel is Will in the World, will existent (present in space and time), real (objectively present within or without), and actual (thought-determined). Again I shall stop just at the point where, I suspect, Hegel cared the most, where the will actually forms civic institutions, mental and material; I shall address—and do so briefly—only the *Introduction* (paras. 4–29, including both Text Additions and Supplements in the White edition; translation independent). Here the concept of the will as subjective mind is developed, preliminary to its objective phases: "The basis of Right (*Recht*) is, in general, Mind; its precise place and point of origin is the Will, which is free" (para. 4). Since this account diverges from that of the *Encyclopedia* in being not psychological, that is, concerned with mental modes, but rather speculative, that is, closer to the basic Logic of concepts, my point will be to pick up illuminating differences. Of these the first one is that Hegel himself now explicitly calls on our introspection to exemplify his specific characteristics of the will—which, I have claimed in the text, indeed produces corroboration of Hegel's observations.

The watchwords of the *Introduction* are "Freedom *is* the will" and "the theoretical is essentially contained within the practical" (para. 4).The latter is qualified: Spirit as thinking develops into will through feeling (as in *Encyclopedia* II, para. 471 ff.); thus Thomas's mutual embrace of Intellect and Will is now distinguished into a final, logical, and a genetic, temporal, aspect). So freedom is the issue both as an end and as a project. (Sartre is going to disrupt this still somewhat equivocal priority relation of freedom and will: freedom is absolutely first. See this chapter, Sec. E.)

In willing I can turn in on my self; this is the "pure reflection of the I into itself" (para. 5). It dissolves every determinate content, need, desire, impulse—a bad infinitude of universality as absolute abstraction, freedom as a negating voiding of all passion—"the fury of destruction" or "making-to-vanish." (This phrase is, as was noted, used in the *Phenomenology*, para. 589, of the same fanaticism of pure willing, a form of freedom that "comes forth often," for example, in Indian Brahmanism and again, in its European repetition, as the French Terror.)

This mere object-devoid willing transits by a negation of negativity to a more thought-out, determinate content. (Here Hegel criticizes Fichte for taking these two moments as abruptly opposed rather than as related through a dialectical development; see Ch. V, Sec. B, herein.) Now, by including both moments, will proper arises and with a more concrete freedom. The will was, therefore, not an underlying something (*substratum*) receiving qualities, but, viewed speculatively, that is, through the logic that is the ultimate wellspring of all activity and life, it comes about in the course of its own "self-mediating activity."—In its going out to its objects and returning to itself, it becomes the more self-possessed (one might say) and the more self-aware. That Logic is life is demonstrated in Hegel's examples here, which, oddly, are more human than those of the *Encyclopedia*'s psychology. The example for this stage of freedom is friendship, in which I restrict myself gladly in relating to another and thereby know myself *as* myself. This freedom is determinacy and indeterminacy at once: selfhood felt through otherness. But there is yet bondage in it (paras. 7–8).

The bondage comes from a residue of immediacy, meaning that the will is not yet fully cognizant of itself. In Hegel's terms it is free *in itself*, in its concept as we see it, but not *for itself*: It is not yet fully its own object. Its freedom is a mere capacity, possibility: It is a natural will, for its impulses ("drives" in the White translation), its desires and inclinations, are given, given by nature. This content is, being mental, ultimately rational, but not yet explicitly so; as given, it is a multiple mass of impulses: at once universal and indeterminate. Now is the moment for the will to "resolve on" (*beschliessen*), "to be resolute in" (*sich entschliessen*) something particular (terms used by Heidegger, see this chapter, Sec. D). Hegel calls this the will that "posits itself as a determinate individual." Without coming to such a restrictive conclusion, the will was not actual or fully free: particular individuality, a human being of character, arises together with determinate choice. Such choice (*Willkür*) is possible precisely because the will was really indeterminate but not really infinite ("infinite" meaning: "not hemmed in by its object"); it had many objects which it cared about *en masse* but not in particular. Choice has fixed that (paras. 9–14). These paragraphs are parallel to *Encyclopedia* III, para. 473 ff.; but they are, as I have said, more speculative, that is, logically dialectic, rather than psychological, that is, concerned with mental modes.

Choice ("Willfulness" in the White translation) is "contingency manifesting itself as will"; one might say: arbitrary preferences held fast in mind. That is what most people regard as freedom. (Hegel has it right—that is the currently circulating notion.) But it is not true freedom, which is dialectically but not fixedly rational, individual but not idiosyncratic. For what was willfully chosen can be similarly renounced, as choice indeed does, always electing one impulse for satisfaction and so nullifying the others. Nor does establishing a hierarchy of desires help, because that too is willful.

In fact, the judgment of inclinations flip-flops, because as naturally immanent, made of my own will, they are all good, as, in our estimation, are we. However, the Christian doctrine of *original* sin (drawn in here by Hegel) knows better: being determined by irrational impulses is bad *because* they are natural. Impulses should be purified, freed both of the immediacy, the naturalism of their form, and the irrationality, the contingency of their context: They ought to constitute the *rational* system of the Will's determinations. (The System as a whole is rational as being the product of Reason, which is the intrinsic motor or moving principle driving the moments in dialectic, especially by producing and dissolving particularizations of the universal, para. 31.)

In sum, the will's inner distinctions, which were, earlier in their dialectical becoming, impulses, must now become its rational determinations. To grasp them thus is what the Science of Right does (as was shown for "Possession" in the text of this chapter).

When reflection first "relates itself to impulses," it compares their relative satisfactions to a totality of satisfaction, called Happiness (*Encyclopedia* III, paras. 479–80). And Happiness, too, contradicts the highest concept of freedom, self-determination (or, otherwise put, self-sufficiency), since Happiness depends on the outside, on natural means, for its satisfactions. Hence the human being is in a condition of dependency and subject to contingent change. So happiness is supposed to be, on the one hand, universal (as total satisfaction) for me—and so it is. But it is also, on the other, for all its universality, supposed to be determined through and through (not empty and abstract) in itself—and that it isn't. For this determinate content is just the satisfaction of those dependency-inducing impulses which are highly particular and so for Hegel evanescent. However, when once my universality finds "a determining that corresponds" to it, when it achieves a universality that determines *itself*, then indeed it "is the will, it is itself freedom."

So self-determining universality is demanded to supplant the merely "formulaic" universality set out above. We must transit "from the goal of happiness to the goal of the will." Then we have abandoned natural impulses and all externality, whatsoever. This true will has one object: the Will itself. This is "thinking imposing-and-infusing itself (*sich durchsetzende*) in will . . . only as thinking intelligence is will a true and free will." Free will is the identity of will and its willing, when "freedom wills freedom" (paras. 15–21; *durchsetzen* with the reflexive pronoun means "to prevail," without, "to permeate"—Hegel is a linguistic virtuoso.

This is the will completely "at home with itself." For it is: 1. related only to itself and relieved of all external and internal dependency, because 2. its content, its objects, are completely appropriated, so that 3. all its particularities are abrogated in universality, and thus 4. its concept is completely realized in its existence, so that "pure concept has the intuition of itself in its reality" (paras. 22–24).

(When freedom is understood as perfect independence and radical self-determination, then will is, so to speak, its unique mental embodiment. For what conceivable other concept could include the above four determinations—except one of an infinite, a-rational omnipotence, such as the Nominalists' God? But that concept would contravene Hegel's postulate of the rationality essentially contained within the will. Nonetheless a question must arise for any reader: Is Hegelian freedom not sheer infinite self-sufficiency, sheer godlike solipsism?)

Recall that all these developments take place within Subjective Mind in the terms of the *Encyclopedia*. How to get out of this apparently water-tight sphere of subjectivity? Hegel says, "The will's activity consists in suspending the contradiction between subjectivity and objectivity," thus translating its internal into external goals, while remaining at home with itself. But how?

"Subjective," in respect to the will, betokens the side of individuality and self-consciousness; it is "abstract reliance on self" but also willful particularity—and thus tied to a merely subjective, an unaccomplished aim. "Objective," on the other hand, has so far meant that the will is itself before itself, and though adequately thought out, is still submerged in circumstance and opposed to its own subject. The will can become truly objective only through the actual accomplishment of its aim—through casting itself into the world.

Here an Addition explains why subjectivity and objectivity have just been set out in general terms as "opposed determinations of reflection." It was to underscore that they pass—their significance changing with the context—into each other, that they are, not rigidly, but fluidly related (paras. 25–26). (I think this dialectical digression is a sort of apology, motivated by the fact that the transition from inner to outer will, from solipsistic freedom to real freedom expressed in social institutions, has just been accomplished somewhat surreptitiously. As so often in Hegelian dialectic, the transitions are elusively brief. In respect to the will, his system is no worse than the frameworks of others. Even Thomas—to me the gold-standard on will—has no better way to explain the leap from intention to execution. Nor does anyone else, professional thinker or mere human—or even neuroscientist: *realizing one's intention must be declared a human mystery.*)

This, then, is it: "The absolute . . . impulse" of free Spirit (the term perhaps henceforth more appropriate than "mind") is to make freedom its object—that is, freedom makes freedom its object. It does so in two ways: as Idea in the completion of its own system and as immediate actuality in the world: "The abstract concept of the Idea of the will is, after all, 'the free will that wills the free will,'" and "Spirit makes freedom its object in order to be itself as Idea what will is in itself" (paras. 27–28), and famously and finally, "What is rational is actual, and what is actual is rational" (Preface). (I infer from this formidable concatenation of quotations that Will as the will to freedom is going to inform the conceptual system. As developed rationality, as Idea, it goes over, when cast into natural and human time, into intelligibly existent reality.)

Will is now in the world, first as Right. For "Right is any existence at all that is an existence of free will . . . In right, freedom has its actualization." The *natural* condition of human beings is not Right (*Recht*) but Wrong (*Unrecht*, which means both "injustice inflicted" and "being in the wrong"). For, as they make the transition to consciousness, that is, as they separate their I from its thinking, they "are no longer naively *unschuldig*, innocent, but have become *schuldig*," meaning both "guilty" and "owing something," that is, "indebtedly responsible." (This is the worldly version of Hegel's doctrine of original sin; see para. 18.) In Right, then, freedom "has its actualization," and it "gives itself existence." But "Existence is a universal expression, and this entire treatise is intended to introduce the particular modes of existence." And the first such mode is the possession of property—where I ended in the text on *Encyclopedia* III, para. 488 ff.

(I want to say here that whether or not the systematicity of the system is in every detail persuasive, I come away enriched with so many notions, relations, and distinctions as to believe that Hegel is right about dialectical logic—which is thought developing—as opposed to formal logic—which is thought fixed: Life in general is a mere happening until re-viewed dialectically. And the will in particular is an undeveloping conundrum until worked through in this logical mode; then it acquires a new interest as essentially *freedom*, while the latter, in turn, gains substantial intelligibility as identical with *self-determination*: Thus freedom is, so to speak, self-definition, so that consequently the will is our work of self-contouring—an intriguing thought, whether welcome or not.

29. Henri Bergson, *Time and Free Will: An Essay on the Immediate Data of Consciousness* (1889), trans. F. L. Pogson (Mineola, N.Y.: Dover Publications, 2001). The French title did not include *Time and Free Will*, for Bergson's concept of will falls out from his phenomenology of consciousness, which is thus the main concern of the *Essay*. The pertinent chapter is III, "The Organization of Conscious States: Free Will."

30. Intensity: Bergson, *Time and Free Will*, 1 ff. Qualitative intensity was a preoccupation of the Scholastics, who found ways to represent it mathematically, that is, extensively, by lines. Anneliese Maier's *An der Grenze von Scholastik und Naturwissenschaft* (Rome: Edizioni di Storia e Letteratura, 1952) is devoted to this topic. Thus Nicolas Oresme, who invented figures that are forerunners of coordinate systems, line graphs, and areas under them (integrals), says in his *On the Configuration of Qualities* (c. 1360): "Therefore, every intensity which can be acquired successively ought to be imagined by a straight line perpendicularly erected on some point or points of the [extensible] space or subject of the intensible thing," that is, whatever supports qualification by an intensity, be it a spatial distance or a temporal span (I 1); the summing of those perpendiculars yields a sort of proto-integral.

One fascinating result derivable from the *Configurations of Qualities* (I 8, I 3) is the foreshadowing of a way to geometricize laws of motion. Let the "extensible subject" be *time*, depicted as a base line, and on it uprights expressing the uniformly increasing speed-intension of a mobile proceeding through time, the subject of a quantified quality. The resulting configuration will be a triangle, for (by a not yet justified method) the uniformly increasing upright infinitesimals are, as I said, summed into a plane figure. This picture could be interpreted as showing the coverage of distance achieved by the expenditure of a uniformly increasing intensity of speed over a span of time, expressed as a plane area, a continuous quantity. Note that "velocity," *velocitas*, is here not yet a vectorial but a scalar quantity: not really a velocity but speed or perhaps the intensity of effort producing it.

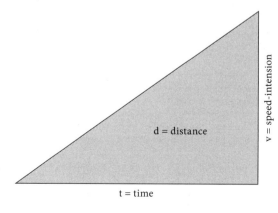

d = distance

v = speed-intension

t = time

If the speed-intensity is interpreted as a velocity, d/t, then the triangular area, expressed in (anachronistic) algebraic symbolism, actually equals $v \cdot t/2$, i.e., d/2. The geometric imagination thus represents the distance run through by a mobile as a sort of proto-integral of velocity-intensions over time; for each time the distance is generated as a triangular area. In terms of proportions, one would say that the distance transversed is compounded of the velocity-length and the time-length; in terms of variations, the expression would be that the distance varies as time and velocity, or $d \sim vt$. When $v \sim t$, meaning that velocity increases as the time of the motion, then $d \sim t^2$, a version of the law of free fall, as in the diagram. And indeed Galileo proves the law geometrically in his *Two New Sciences* (1638), using an Oresme-like diagram upended (Third Day, Prop. 1). One fairly arresting result is that distance, which is linear, is now unabashedly represented as planar: Representation has cast loose from intuition.

The notion of intensity is not (or no longer) used in modern physics, where, as Bergson says, every quality is turned into a quantitative dimension, geometrically or numerically representable: Thus the sensed experience of warmth is transmuted into a degree-number read off a mercury column in a thermometer. If it's 92°, you're expected to feel hot, but 92° isn't itself hot.

A forerunner of Bergson's notion, that intensity is a characteristic peculiar to *experience*, is to be found in Kant's *Critique of Pure Reason* B 207 ff.

31. Interpretation of the ways things are: here is the occasion to argue that there is, after all, a connection, though by no means a coincidence, between Hegel and Bergson, namely with respect to two major concerns of the latter: time and symbols. Hegel says in *the Philosophy of Nature* (*Encyclopedia* II, para. 257, Addition) that time is "perpetual self-sublation," meaning that each of its moments *supersedes* and abrogates the one preceding; this will be precisely what Bergson denies, since he thinks that each new moment *preserves* and holds within all those in the past. As for symbols, Hegel thinks they are an inadequate to conceptual life, because they are static and it is fluid (para. 259); Bergson will agree, but because symbols are extended in space and psychic life is intensive through duration.

Time reversible: besides friction, Bergson is here overlooking time-irreversible processes in nature, the so-called "arrows of time," such as take place most characteristically in thermodynamics but also in other kinds of physics.

In 1908, well after *Time and Free Will*, J. Ellis McTaggart published his famous distinction between the A and B series of time. The B series, of which mere "earlier and later" are characteristic, is analogous to Bergson's reversible, deterministic, mechanistic, extensive time. The A series is time that has the phases of past, present, and future and thus depends on an observer's *now* and his memory and expectation. A-time, as tied to human experience, is at least analogous to Bergson's irreversible, free, dynamic intensive time. (See Richard Morris, "The Five Arrows of Time," chap. 8 of *Time's Arrows: Scientific Attitudes Toward Time* [New York: Simon and Schuster, 1986], 131 ff.; also Eva Brann, *What Then is Time?*, 160–61.)

32. Example of curved line: Bergson, *Time and Free Will*, 11 ff. There follows an analysis of beauty: Is art not in a certain sense prior to nature in respect to beauty? For nature *expresses*, while art *suggests* feeling; thus art elicits responsiveness, and this receptivity, coming to a soul already imbued with a thousand sensations, in time completely engrosses it (14 ff.).

33. Duration: Bergson, *Time and Free Will*, chap. II, 75 ff.—Bergson begins with a critique of Kant's conception of time as a homogeneous medium. And indeed, Kant's inner sense, a psychic kind of counting, is curiously inhospitable to the investments of memory and is, moreover, only open to inspection when projected into space—a fact at once evident and startling (*Critique of Pure Reason* B 274 ff.; Brann, *What, Then, Is Time?*, 78–79); **eliminate mobility:** Bergson, 111.

34. Organization of conscious states: Bergson, chap. III, 140 ff.; **law-governed mechanism:** see Note 31 above; **inertia:** Bergson, 141—"Every body continues in its state of rest or of uniform motion in a right line, unless it is compelled to change that state by forces impressed on it" (Newton, *Principia*, Law I).

35. Epiphenomenon: Bergson, 152; **irreversibility:** 153–54; **geometric depiction:** 163.

36. Line drawing: 176; **symbolical diagram:** 190; **contrary action equally possible:** 177.

37. Stereotyped memory: 187; **aggregate of psychic points:** 165.

38. Whole of self: 166.

39. Predictability: 189, 198.

40. Charles Sanders Peirce, *The Essential Peirce: Selected Philosophical Writings*, vol. 1 (1867–93), ed. Nathan Houser and Christian Kloesel (Bloomington: Indiana Univ. Press, 1992), principally chap. 20, "A Guess at the Riddle" (1887–88), 245–79.

41. Non-Trinitarian: In fact Peirce planned, but never wrote, a chapter on the triad in theology (246) expounding the thesis that "Faith requires us to be materialists without flinching." This seems to me to be the frame of mind of these early American Pragmatists (as distinct from their contemporary heirs)—their natural vitality of spirit has so much grace that their earth-bound philosophy is (I want to say) as good as transcendent.

42. Ideas so broad: Pierce, chap. 1, "Trichotomy," 247–49; **potential variety:** 259.

43. Prime example of thirdness: 250. Peirce recognizes a lacuna in ancient physics that must strike any student of Aristotle's *Physics* as crucial: the absence, indeed the denial, of the possibility of *acceleration*, understood as change of change. He is right: "There is no . . . change of change" (*metaboles metabole*, 225 b 15). Acceleration, however, is just that, the secondary rate of change piggy-backed upon a primary rate of change, namely velocity. Peirce points out that missing this concept prevented ancient qualitative physics from becoming a real dynamics. For cause and effect are qualitative poles; between them as a mediating third is acceleration, which, when seated in bodies, is force (ma). It is, thus, not a mere "kinematic" relation between two successive positions, as is velocity, but a "dynamic" relation.

44. Cognition: Peirce, 260.

45. Will: 259–60; **strongest desire:** this reference might be to Hobbes, who, however, he says not "strongest" but "last"; **"In Dreams Begin Responsibilities":** title of a Delmore Schwartz short story (1937)—the story leaves undetermined whether the title's proposition will be affirmed.

46. Psychological triad: Peirce, 262–63.

47. I include William James on the will in a note since, although he is in his treatment a psychologist rather than a grand theorist of the will, it would be a loss to omit him (*Principles of Psychology*, 1890, Ch. VI, "Will," and James's own abridgment, *Psychology*, 1892, Ch. VI, "Will"). The reasons are that 1. he is a most observant psychologist, which is to say, a fine phenomenologist of the will, 2. his description of willing is, after all, satisfyingly consistent with his pragmatic orientation, thus, in that respect, veracious, and 3. he writes such pleasantly personal and agreeably plain American, that for someone—me—embroiled in the volition-literature, James's tone itself brings, if not conviction, at least refreshment.

James has observed that *"Effort of attention is . . . the essential phenomenon of will."* He appeals to his readers' experience for corroboration.

What I might call the "objective correlative" of mental effort is the impulsive or inhibitive quality of ideas, their capacity to compel attention, what James calls their *Interest*. "Interesting" is a title covering a variety of objects, or rather their ideas. (James understands ideas or thoughts to be "of objects"; thus an idea is the mental representation of the object and imparts to consciousness the interest inherent in the object.) When pleasure and pain are the impelling or repelling qualities of ideas, so that they urgently compel us, the ideas have "volitional effects."

So the exposition of will as attentional effort begins by observing that some objects arouse—as ideas in the mind—desire or aversion, feelings that form a subset of their general interest. (Recall the traditional understanding of will as "rational desire.") Attention, then, is the mental response. If that response is, so to speak, whole-minded, if an idea steadily prevails, then the volitional process is complete. That *is* willing. In considering "the more intimate nature of the volitional process," we see that "with the prevalence, once there as a fact, of the motive idea the *psychology* of volition properly stops."

The next step is the more persuasive for being radically agnostic. As will become evident in my next three chapters (IX–XI), will-students and volition-researchers divide around the answer to this question: Does the executive aspect of willing involve a sharp discontinuity having the status of an uncircumventable mystery, or is the agency part of volition a protocol-amenable continuum of naturalistic processes? James says: "The *willing* terminates with the prevalence of the idea: and whether the act then follows or not is a matter quite immaterial; . . . volition is a psychic fact pure and simple, and it is absolutely completed when the stable state of the idea is there. The supervention of motion is a supernumerary phenomenon depending on executive ganglia whose function lies outside the mind"—which is to say that mind and body are mysteriously discontinuous though normally connected. James indeed recognizes that connection: "The movements that ensue are exclusively physiological phenomena, following according to physiological laws upon the neural events *to which the idea corresponds*" (my italics). In other words, James is what might be called an "incitement dualist" in the description, but an agnostic in the explanation, of the will's actual execution.

This psychological theory appeals to me because it corresponds to an introspective sense I have, as, I imagine, do other people: When the mind is sufficiently replete with an object of thoughtfully appropriated desire, action comes about without further mental ado, directedly, energetically, even blithely. It is a mode I mean to discuss in my Conclusion: a fact of our nature and a mystery as well.

For James as psychologist, "the heart of our inquiry into volition" is reached when we ask "by what process it is that the thought of any given object comes to prevail stably in the mind." For, as was said, this holding fast of an object before the mind, this resolve, "is the *fiat*; and it is a mere physiological incident that . . . motor consequences should ensue," now or later.

Here, without explicit reference, is where James's philosophical pragmatism seems to me to come in. Will is altogether *effort* of attention and *consent* to the idea's demand for undivided attention: "For Nature here 'backs' us instantaneously and follows up our inward willingness by outward changes on our part"—certainly if the volition is a "motor volition." (That *is* a way of obviating the millennial mystery of execution.) As far as the mind is concerned, our will can experience only one resistance, that which "*an idea offers to being attended to at all.*" Thus James amends the notion of mere attention—there must be "*express consent to the reality of what is attended.*" We say "Let it be reality"—and this imperative mood is, just as it is in grammar, an ultimately inexplicable but practically effective category: We "make it so," as captains used to command.

Pragmatism "is a method only"; it stands for no special results. It looks to theories as "instruments, not answers to enigmas . . ." and so it looks "*away from first things, principles . . . toward last things, fruits, consequences, facts.*" In a wider sense it is a theory of truth and, as such, a *genetic* theory: "*Ideas (which themselves are but parts of our experience), become true just in so far as they help us to get into satisfactory relation with other parts of our experience.*" To attain perfect clearness in our ideas "we need only consider what conceivable effects of a practical kind the object may involve—what sensations we are to expect from it, and what reactions we must prepare." The above is the principle of pragmatism as formulated by Peirce: William James, *Selected Papers on Philosophy*, "What Pragmatism Means," from *Pragmatism* (1907) (New York: E. P. Dutton, 1947), 198–217. James's exposition of the will is in accord with this principle. "Reasonable decisions" are made under this method of establishing truth by the criterion of a practically acceptable relation to some stable part of life, some "right conception" of the case which fits in with a recognized class and which flows so naturally from things as to give us a sense of freedom from coercion. There are, however, other modes of deciding, in particular a type that is *sui generis*—when nothing tilts the balance, and the "slow dead heave of the will" alone turns the scales; it is the occasion for feeling ourselves effortfully volitional. James gives a beautiful phenomenology of this deliberate thorn in the flesh, this possible moment for naked dutifulness. In introducing this deadweight "liberty of indifference" (cf. Conclusion C.3.), he outdoes later philosophers in making vivid the phrase (to be much bandied about) "could have done otherwise."

How the decision, this last act of will, should fall out, pragmatism does not tell. James concentrates on the interest of the object, the attention to its idea, the integrity of the effort. *What* should interest us in an object, *why* its idea should capture our attention, *whether* the effort is good or evil—that is not in the pragmatist's scope. Thomas, the prime example of the bad old philosophizing, seeks first principles, and so will in general has a motive in general, the good—and he can specify it: God. James cannot say, or so it seems to me, why an object could and *should* incite interest, why the mind *should* hold fast before itself a particular idea—even in the face of strong opposition. This is motivation without motive, method without principle. Perhaps "rational desire" can still be a description of this will, but this reason has gone merely instrumental and this desire merely prehensile. Its beauty is its consistency with pragmatism and its defect the same—and that is future-fraught: In my next three chapters, will is to be largely a mechanism and free will a tricky problem.

James solves it as a practical problem. He regards the question of free will as psychologically insoluble, but he does point out that determinism is a *scientific* postulate, while it is a *moral* postulate that bad acts cannot be fated—and good ones must be possible. (I would add: by whatever criterion either is established.) When two possibilities are at war and objective proof is unobtainable, then there must be a choice of belief—a choice here to be made precisely by an undetermined will. So, "Freedom's first deed should be to affirm itself." Hence a pragmatist opts for free will, not as a truth but as a method—and for method as a source of pragmatism's good, its morality: The first criterion for choosing is that the object *be chosen*—not that it be choice-worthy.

Thus the heart of the psychological inquiry, once again, concerns the process by which the thought of an object "comes to prevail stably in the mind." Here James's eloquence makes vivid the phenomena of ideas filling or failing to fill our consciousness. It follows that success or failure in "the intimate nature of the volitional process" is humanly all-important, for *"To sustain a representation, to think,* is, in short, the only moral act, for the impulsive and the obstructed, for sane and lunatics alike." (I detect here a very Protestant reminiscence of Kant's Will as the only absolute good there is, except that James offers a lived *psychology,* the veritable *feel* of the collectedness that gets work done—a revised, more humane, an American version of the forcible willing that constitutes one side of the will-tradition. (Yet it is a question to me whether, in the long run of human life, objects can be interesting and command attention merely because practical life demands that minds be made up—whether effort can be incited by the bare choice to choose, without "first principles," without transcendence. Another way to put it: When will is rational desire, theoretical and practical intellect are in mutual embrace; when practical reason triumphs over metaphysical theory, can attention be sustained? Is it humanly feasible to love utility, to be engrossed for long by means—even if the utility is a finer practicality, a way of making life work, of integrating our experience?)

48. I append here a reference to John Dewey's Pragmatistic development (as it seems to me) of James's theory of will as attention-effort. (John Dewey, *Human Nature and Conduct,* 1922: *The Middle Works of John Dewey,* 1899–1924, vol. 14, ed. Jo Ann Bydston [Carbondale: Southern Illinois Univ. Press, 1988], chap. 2, "Habits and Will.") He reduces will-effort to disposition-tendency long before Gilbert Ryle put the word *disposition* into general circulation; Dewey calls it "*habit*": "The word habit may seem twisted somewhat from its customary use . . . [B]ut we need a word to express the kind of human activity which is influenced by prior activity and in that sense acquired . . ." (31). "Habits are demands for certain kinds of activity; and they constitute the self. In any intelligible sense of the word will, they *are* the will." (I want to say here that where James's description meets exactly my introspective experience when I'm in the practical mode, Dewey's theory makes me say: That's not my essential self—constituted of habits, be they actionable or supine. Habits are my serviceable self, but when I'm most myself, I'm not so serviceable.) To make will a habit, a "projectile power," permits Dewey to liquefy morality; there is, he says, a "relative and pragmatic" distinction between moral and non-moral activity which has been, by a fatal error, solidified into an absolute distinction. Character, then, is "the name given to a working interaction of habits." (Thus character is, one might say, hydraulic, an interaction of habit-pressures resulting in a directional tendency of action-flow. "The word 'principle' is a eulogistic cover for the fact of a tendency.")

Nonetheless, it seems to me, there is a lot of common sense in this fluid view of human nature and action, but it is common sense taken to uncommon extremes. Indeed in Dewey's "Classification of Instincts" (chap. 11, 98–99), will as habit takes a distinctly Nietzschean turn: "Each impulse or habit is thus a will to its own power"—the will to will. An affect "is successful when it effects some change outside the organism . . . Activity is creative insofar as it moves to its own enrichment as activity, that is, bringing along with itself a release of further activities." (It seems to me rampageous optimism to suppose that this willful bustling-about must necessarily come to some good; in such contexts a long-dead colleague used to quote a Russian-Jewish proverb: "Your word in God's ear.")

49. Bret W. Davis, *Heidegger and the Will: On the Way to* Gelassenheit (Evanston: Northwestern Univ. Press, 2007).

50. Martin Heidegger, "Profession of Loyalty to Adolf Hitler of the Professors at the German Universities and High Schools," Address of 1933. To my mind, beyond evincing a fixation on the will, this passage withdraws itself from sense. Indeed it induces a sort of mental retching.

51. Political misadventure: Davis, *Heidegger,* xxiv; **blunder**: 61.

52. Turns and turnings: ibid.

The willingness to change one's mind, the condition for learning more and anew, is surely the thinker's virtue. Yet I have misgivings about Heidegger's radical rethinkings, said to bear "signs of inner continuity," a continuity very obscure to the common understanding, one that leaves devotees in the lurch, and that for several reasons: Each thought epoch is in turn magisterially set forth. Should deference to one's own finitude not have called for a more provisional tone? And, more questionably, is it not a sign of what might be called philosophical character to stay the course, to end as one began, with adumbrations, digressions, honings, revisions, tweakings, reformulations, recenterings, elaborations, emphasis-shiftings, to be sure, but always advancing, now crabwise, now arrow-like, on one and the same way? And thus the question of questions in this context: Does not philosophy require character, here meaning the pursuit—without abandoning open receptivity—of some final, lifelong intellectual adherence? Should there not be some moral self-limitation that restricts the urge to self-outdoing?

53. I have related misgivings about philosophical "originality." I think of the word in two significations: 1. going to the origins, the roots, the ground of things and souls or, at least trying, and 2. being hell-bent on novelty, on saying something other than the others—or as I've put it before, wanting to be last-and-first. This is originality as willfulness; it is a character issue. To me it appears deeply implicated in the will-ambivalences set out in the text below. I regard the notion that common decency is not the *basic* philosophical virtue as sophistry.

54. In this chapter, all the references are to Davis, *Heidegger on the Will*, including quotations from Heidegger's works, which are, however, given in terms of the standard editions, together with the Davis page number.

Unsaid: this "unsaid" is not an esoteric teaching withheld but an implicit problematic left unarticulated (Davis, 25); **second-order phenomena**: Davis, 35.

55. Willing ontologically: Davis, 35, Heidegger, *Being and Time*, 194; **disclosedness**: ibid., 220–21; **care**: ibid., 193 ff.

56. For-the-sake-of: Davis, 32 ff.

57. Existential voluntarism: Davis, 38.

58. Four interpretations: Davis, 40 ff. Davis's distinctions are highly detailed—I give a mere summary.

59. Will embraced as human freedom: Davis, 64. The wrought-iron gate to Auschwitz I, the slave-labor division of the concentration camp complex, bore the legend *Arbeit macht frei* ("work makes free") as a logical fall-out from the national-socialist we-will that *is* freedom, meaning that it determines its own character within its sphere of power.

60. Failed venture into politics: Davis, 78 ff. He omits to make clear that, as Heidegger became disenchanted with the vulgar mass-meeting mentality of the Nazis, so they rejected him for pursuing his "private National Socialism"; two books dealing with the odd situation of Heidegger's falling out with the Nazi party after 1934, because he had a purer version of National Socialism than its officials, are Robert Denoon Cumming, *Phenomenology and Deconstruction*, vol. 4, *Solitude* (Chicago: Univ. of Chicago Press, 2001), 107 ff., and Herman Philipse, *Heidegger's Philosophy of Being: A Critical Interpretation* (Princeton: Princeton Univ. Press, 1998), 246 ff.

Jeffrey Sonheim, an alumnus of my college, in which all seniors read Tolstoy's *War and Peace* (1869), reminded me that it ends, in the "Second Epilogue," with a meditation on the topics broached in my text: the national will, the great man's will, the small individual's will.

Tolstoy rejects the theory that chosen men bring about historical events by their will, their *fiat* (chaps. I–III). Indeed, the Napoleon of his novel is the incarnate absurdity of an imperial will, who thinks that his imperatives are actually executed: "The more directly [men] participate in performing the actions the less they command," and the inverse: the man at the top may issue commands but that's not what determines the event (chap. VI). Again, the novel fleshes out this truth: Doers don't issue the orders under which they act, and commanders don't execute their own will. On the other hand, individuals regard themselves as individually free. And once more there's a hitch: if each human particle really were free, "history would be a series of disconnected incidents," though it seems that, regarded from a historical point of view, there *are* inevitabilities: "Man in connection with the general life of humanity appears subject to laws which determine that life" (chap. VIII). Here too the novel has fleshed out the contradiction: All the characters live as if exercising their own will, yet all the marriages of the First Epilogue seem to enact a destiny. (One might argue that it is those very last-chapter fate-fullfilments that make novels more interpretable than life.)

Tolstoy solves the quandary of history in the terms in which he has formulated it—individual freedom vs. collective law-boundness—and he does it with a mathematical metaphor adapted from an old version of the calculus: the *integration of infinitesimals* (chap. X), the formation of a two-dimensional whole, an integral (history), from a summation of one-dimensional minimals or even infinitesimals (individuals); see Note 30 above for such integrals.

So Tolstoy's solution to the free-will vs. historical necessity problem is by means of perspective and scale. Looking back from the perspective of a half-century's distance—from the 1860s back to 1812—the war has assumed some features of inevitability, intimated in the novel and incarnated in old General Kutuzov, whose strategy is to wait for that to happen which must happen. Tolstoy is very fond of him, for to Kutuzov by instinct then and there, as for Tolstoy by research fifty years on, the war has become an integral, intelligible event. However, looking into it up close, Tolstoy sees the summable atoms, the infinitesimals of history, as finite, fleshed out, free human beings, unaware and little touched by the rational geometry into which they will merge as time passes. They think of themselves as independent within their situation, and what bondage they experience is of their own making. I know no novel that contains more human verity than *War and Peace*, but it comes forth when Tolstoy writes not as a philosopher of history but as a novelist, when he is up close and personal, so that his people are multidimensional and blessedly finite.

Is this perspectival solution persuasive? In fact, it's not a solution but a description of that historian's faith which makes intelligible history possible. Long views yield normative law; very long views yield inevitability. What Tolstoy hasn't explained is how this enigmatic transmutation of freedom into necessity, accomplished by remotion in time and space, comes about—and for that matter, whether it even takes place. Surely Tolstoy's truth lies more in his fictional beings than in his historical theory—as Aristotle presciently intimates in his *Poetics* (1451 b), before there were either novels or historiography: poetry is more serious than history. Indeed, the absorption into a mathematical metaphor of such living presences as Natasha and Petya Rostov seems to me like authorial manslaughter.

Twisting free: Davis, 60; **critique of Schelling**: an intervening work on the will is Heidegger's *Nietzsche* (see Ch. VII, Note 51, herein); **system of subjectivity**: Davis, 113; **leap to finitude**: Davis, 101.

61. Evil: Davis, 114 and 289–301. The latter set of pages deals with the consequences of rejecting, as Heidegger does, the notion of evil as a falling-off from, as a privation of, good, and settling this—now positive—negativity in the very heart of being. (The rejected falling-off view has, I think, more immediate, delineable practical consequences: Badness is a void to be fought by filling it with good; decency consists of the felt obligation to discern even an incipient falling-away and of filling the lacuna left with some good.)

When evil is thought of as having its place deep in the ground of things, and expressed, as it is for Heidegger, in one notion, that of the *Gestell*, technology, which turns everything into a resource on which the will may wreak its will, then, first, all evil in the world has the same standing. Thus the "motorized food industry" is "the same thing in its essence as the production of corpses in the gas chambers" (quoted by Davis, 297 from vol. 79, p. 27 of the *Gesamtausgabe*). And second, all evil is, as it were, justified as coming from beyond human origination.

In my account of the will, its relation to good and evil, to human practice, that is, to ethics, has been somewhat slighted—as opening too vast a field, namely the will's application in theory and practice. One beginning for thinking this out is Max Scheler's Phenomenological treatise *Formalism in Ethics and Non-Formal Ethics of Values: A New Attempt Toward the Foundation of Ethical Personalism (Der Formalismus in der Ethik und die materiale Wertethik*, 1913–16), trans. Mansfred S. Frings and Roger L. Funk (Evanston: Northwestern Univ. Press, 1973). This huge work (620 pages) is contemporary with Heidegger's early writings (1912–16). The tiny section here considered is Pt. I, Ch. I, Sec. 3, editor's subtitle: "Purposes of Willing, Goals of Conation, and Values," 38–44, chosen because it analyzes the act itself of willing and its relation to good and evil. Two later sections specific to the will are "Volition Directions . . . Arise from Positive Feeling-States as Sources" and "The Foundations of . . . Positive Willing in Happiness." The first of these sections observes that willing cannot produce deep emotional states, but, inversely, just these can be and *are* "the *emotional source and origin* of willing and acting" (349). The second says that since "all feelings of happiness and unhappiness have their foundations in *feelings of values*," it follows that "morally good willing streams forth" from happiness (359). These later sections in fact illuminate the section on the purposes of willing about to be set out.

"Conation" (*Streben*, striving, 30–38) is a more primitive feeling-state than willing, be it an impulse toward or away from a goal, what Kant calls, more mildly, an "inclination." The goals of conation lie in its very process; they are immanent to striving, not posited by us, as they will be in wishing.

What is a goal? Two possible components of a goal can be distinguished: the value (*Wert*) and the picture. Value is the *quality of a content, including good and evil*, an objective, feelable aspect of a value-bearing object that possesses a determinate rank in a scale of higher and lower (17). Value *precedes* pleasure: If pleasure is the goal of a conation, it is so by virtue of its value. The pictures are the representational aspect of a goal; they are secondary in conation, selected from possible contents as carriers of value-content. In other words, for Scheler value selects the objects pursued in our impulses: first the impulse toward a good, then the intellectual activity of representation. (The significance of this view seems to come out best as a total inversion of Aristotle's notion of desire: first the image, then the passion, *On the Soul* 433 b. The great question here is whether we humans are fundamentally first receptive to intelligible being in general or to its rank order of worth; I think of these alternatives as mirroring our relation to the two divinities: pagan Intellect-divinity vs. Christian personal God; see xxiv, Scheler on God).

"In contrast to this, the *purposes of willing* are, first of all, *the represented contents* (of a somewhat variable kind) *of goals* of conation" (39); thus in the willing that follows striving, the image is first, as for Aristotle). The goal-content already given in primitive striving is now represented by a special act that betokens a withdrawal from the immediacy of impulse to a consciousness of purpose. However, nothing can become a purpose that was not first a goal. We cannot just "posit" a purpose without a previous conation toward something. (That is to say, all willing has immediate impulse behind it; this seems to me phenomenologically accurate in general—except for the pure extreme of willing, *willfulness*, the will to will, in which willing is itself ratcheted up into a goal.)

The picture content, to become a purpose, must have an additional aspect: It must be given as "*to-be-realized*," as something that "concretely ought to be." This is willing proper, not mere wishing, which lacks just this aspect. "Every willing of purpose is thus grounded in an act of representation," but in a particular kind of representation, that of "*a goal of conation*" (40). In other words, there is no willing without having an object-representation in mind and with it a value, for goals of conation are founded on values. (I think, as I said above, that this is not quite accurately observed. There *is*, it seems to me, blind willing, a pure, blind volitional cramp of the mind, whose intentional object, if any, is willing itself.)

The purpose in willing originates in an act of choosing, "since it is an act of preference among the value-goals of conation" (41). Thus the choices of will have their ground, their primal *apriori*, in the preferences of conation, and those preferences are pre-representational. Both, conations and choices, are intentional, that is, they have the structure of "aboutness." The conation, a feeling, "has the same relation to its value-correlate as 'representing' has to its 'object,' namely an intentional relation" (258). The difference is between a pre-cognitive and cognitive intention—in willing something, the purpose is consciously known.

Scheler therefore calls his whole ethics (into which the will is integrated) an "emotional intuitionism and non-formal apriorism" (xxiii). He explicates it throughout in distinction from Kant's "ethical formalism," in which formal lawfulness stands ethically above felt value and goodness arises with right willing. He is, in other words, rehabilitating human *nature* in its affective aspect. A theology lies behind this non-formal ethics, one that understands good and evil as not first issuing from a divine, law-giving *Will*, but believes good to lie in something prior: God's *Essence* (212).

Actuality of evil: Davis, 115; **other quotations**: 114–15.

62. Essence of being is finite: 116.

63. Blake: 21. For perverse will, see Ch. II, Sec. C, herein.

64. Representational, *Gestell, Bestand*: Davis, 174–78.

65. Coopted into the *Gestell*: 180–81. **Meister Eckhart:** Davis devotes a whole chapter (chap. 5) to the meaning of the word *Gelassenheit* in Eckhart (127 ff.) and to a critique of Michael Gillespie's critique of Heidegger's skewed relation to theology; Gillespie argues that his inattention to the Christian tradition results in Heidegger's inadvertently proposing a notion of the "will of Being" that is really akin to the Nominalist willful God (Gillespie, *Nihilism*, see Ch. III, Note 48, herein; Nominalist will, Ch. III, Secs. B–C, herein). Davis replies that it is reductive to impute to Heidegger's rejection of willful subjectivity a turnabout to will-being. He explains that the turn from subjectivity is really to a form of non-willing, *Gelassenheit*. (Here is my question: At what point may one call halt to one's pursuit of the turns and turnings of an unfixed soul and claim, as Gillespie has done: This is it?)

66. Translation of *Gelassenheit*: Davis, xxiv–xxvii reviews the general meaning, history and translations of this theologically grave word. Among the theologians it means the emptying of a creature to be filled with God, the giving up of self-will to receive the will of God. Of course, there must be a different filling for Heidegger.

67. Will undisrupted: Davis, 195–97. Heidegger's chief works on *Gelassenheit* here considered is in *Feldweg-Gespräche*, vol. 77 of the *Gesamtausgabe* (Frankfurt am Main: Vittorio Klostermann, 1975–). Also: *Discourse on Thinking*, trans. John M. Anderson and E. Hans Freund (New York: Harper and Row, 1966).

68. *Gegend*: Davis, 97–98—on its intimated meanings I've gone off somewhat on my own; **place of forms:** Aristotle, *On the Soul* 429 a.

69. Return to *Gelassenheit*: Davis, 198–99; **waiting:** 199; **release oneself:** 201 and Heidegger, *Gelassenheit*, 1944–45 (Pfullingen: Neske, 1992); **trace of will:** Davis, 201–3.

70. Ascetic abrogation and paradoxical willing: 203, Davis's summary.

71. Decision: 204–7.

In his later thinking Heidegger began to distinguish the non-metaphysical notion of "beyng" (*Seyn*, found in Schelling, see my Ch. V, Note 33, herein) as an event that takes place in a region and brings about time for humans, from the traditional transcendent *being*, a substance that is hyper-local and a-temporal (Davis, 231).

Here, reporting the last element of Heidegger's rejection of the will as discerned with the help of Davis's book, I should mention that Davis has an agenda complementary to a close reading of Heidegger's texts, namely to connect Heidegger's abnegation of the will to the East Asian Buddhist background familiar to Heidegger himself and obviously germane even to a reader like myself who has only a cursory acquaintance with that tradition. Were I to embark on this dual study, I think my guiding questions would be, first, impersonally: Which tradition is better equipped to solve, assuage, obviate, the paradox of non-willing? And then, personally: Is that the same rejection of the will which I think of as salubrious? In response, I have these proto-suspicions: First, the Eastern sage does better at paradoxes than the Western philosopher, being more sanguine about them. And second, no, these ways of relinquishing the will are, I will say, too far beyond the individual human soul, too deeply embedded in an alien vision, to speak to my more limited intention; see my Conclusion, Note 8.

72. Responsibility: see Davis, 258, 298 ff.

73. Jean-Paul Sartre, *Being and Nothingness* (*L'être et le néant*, 1913), trans. Hazel E. Barnes (New York: Simon and Schuster, 1956); **on the will:** part 4, chap. 1; **limitedly helpful:** Joseph S. Catalano, *A Commentary on Jean-Paul Sartre's* Being and Nothingness (Chicago: Univ. of Chicago Press, 1980).

The question of derivation: Existentialism was anticipated by the Nominalists. (See Ch. III, Secs. B–C, herein.) However, questions of priority seem to me mostly moot in philosophy, since whoever thinks, "thinks for himself" as the surely redundant phrase goes. These questions do arise—and bring out one's moralistic streak—when a writer is plainly suppressing a borrowing and reneging on a debt (see Note 87 below). However, besides the triviality of assigning kudos for priority, there is involved here a deep, perhaps the most deeply vexing question of philosophy: Philosophy has a beginning in Heraclitus and Parmenides. Does it therefore have an end—and a directional development withal? Its questions are, over time, rigidified into set problems and given terms—a process, as far as I know, begun by Socrates in the *Phaedo* where he bequeaths to his young followers on his dying day the terms of the inquiries he leaves behind barely begun (see Brann, "Socrates' Legacy: Plato's *Phaedo*," *Music of the Republic*, 36), and taken up very explicitly by Aristotle when he formulates the "problems" of philosophy in his *Metaphysics* (995 a ff.). Are these the same questions, continually elaborated, therewith brought nearer solution—or dissolution? Or does each aspirant pour truly new wine into old bottles, or even break them and blow his own? Heidegger is, as the section on his version of the will has shown, the most radical defender of an intelligible history of philosophy, albeit a downhill one, with a subverted beginning and a contemporary end—in his own anti-metaphysical metaphysics. The radicality consists in the claim that not only do the—unwitting—historians of Being, the metaphysicians of the West, in effect write out such a history, but that Being itself in fact traces out a development—that Being is time-bound. Thus he, who, as I have said, aspires to be last and first, was not pleased by Sartre's "misappropriation" of *Being and Time* in his *Being and Nothingness*. This very rejection seems to confirm that there was indeed something underivative, something original, in Sartre's appropriation (Robert Denoon Cummings, *Phenomenology and Deconstruction* [Chicago: Univ. of Chicago Press, 2001], passim). For Heidegger, however, it seems the rub in this "misappropriation" was not so much in its deviation as precisely in the fact that Sartre presents his "voluntaristic existentialism" as directly derived from him; Heidegger denies this kinship. (See Note 57 above; Davis, 42–43.) It makes sense that he should be averse to any attempt to develop further his own thinking, for that would make him but a stop in an open progress. For the work by Heidegger that may in fact, in spite of his own rejection, support Sartre's claim of derivation, see my text and its Note 74, below. Anyhow, to forfend discipleship seems to me soundminded, but to reject the acknowledgment even of a deviationist debt seems to me graceless.

74. Martin Heidegger, *The Essence of Human Freedom: An Introduction to Philosophy* (1930), trans. Ted Sadler (London: Continuum Press, 2002). The text is based on a lecture course delivered by Heidegger in 1930 and published as *Vom Wesen der menschlichen Freiheit: Einleitung in die Philosophie* in 1982; 2nd ed., 1994, as vol. 31 of Heidegger's *Gesamtausgabe*. Although the fundamental theme is human freedom, or better, freedom as the ground of human being, the bulk of the work, as I said in the text, is devoted to an explication of Kant's practical reason in Heidegger's terms.

I am very much aware that the huge topic of freedom, so germane to the will, has been treated skimpily in this book, but see Ch. XI, Sec. E. Its study can call to aid an encyclopedic treatment by Mortimer Adler in *The Idea of Freedom* (1961).

75. Philosophy in general: Heidegger, *Essence*, para. 2, p. 14, also para. 1, p. 10; philosophy as a whole is revealed "*in properly grasped particular problems.*"

76. Diagram: Heidegger, *Essence*, para. 3, p. 19.

77. Spontaneity: p. 16—there is a possible precursor that is much later and more specifically Heideggerian, the notion of *Gelassenheit* set out in the Heidegger section above. But *Gelassenheit* is not only beset with ambivalences; it is, in any case, a "comportment 'toward'" rather than a root of existence. Sartre probably has to be credited, willy nilly, with being original.

78. Consciousness unaffected by real existence: a very old issue is whether existence is a quality or a property, or in a different category altogether. (See Brann, *The Ways of Naysaying*, 103 ff.) If it is a quality like any other, its presence or absence will clearly qualify its subject: A hundred dollars existent in your bank account will be in some inherent way different from that amount of money which just isn't there—particularly in your consciousness. Or is it? The Phenomenologists, able to discount (bracket) existence as necessarily qualifying the phenomena of consciousness, are clearly set up to investigate very subtly the efficacy of the imagination, the capacity for having present in mind non-existent beings (see Brann, *The World of Imagination*, 120 ff.).

79. This abbreviated account of Sartre's difficult introduction, though couched in my own language, owes a lot to Catalano's *Commentary* (see Note 73 above), 4–13.

80. The discussion will be based on *Being and Nothingness*, starting from part 4, "Having, Doing, and Being," chap. 1, "Being and Doing: Freedom," sec. I, "Freedom: the First Condition of Action," to the concluding paragraph on the will, 559–83 in the Barnes translation.

Human nothingness: On the face of it, Aristotle's Intellect (*nous*), which is potentially all things (*On the Soul* 430 a), bears some resemblance to Sartre's aboriginal nothingness. But the differences are as heaven is to hell, starting with the fact that *Nous* does not make itself and ending with the fact that it is a divinity.

81. Action on principle intentional: *Being and Nothingness*, 559.

82. No factual state: 562.

83. Cause and motives: 564.

84. Heidegger: 656. **The why's and wherefore's of the priority of existence:** is Existentialism, I ask myself, simply an ontological preference, a consequence of a deeply lodged bent in our temperament—as, of course, would also be what in this context I must, reluctantly, call "Essentialism"? Is the latter perhaps a tad better suited to philosophy—if the love of wisdom works precisely to break the spell of mere existents by inducing wonder for their whatness? And above all, which makes for better judgment concerning life's engagements, public or private?

Two root-values: The temperamental propensity for existence calls, as experiential, for beginning not with a philosophical but with a novelistic exposition, and that is just what is accomplished in Sartre's novel *Nausea* (1937), trans. Lloyd Alexander (New York: New Directions Publishing, 2007), especially 127–35. The epiphany of existence converts it from "simply an empty form which was added to external things without changing anything" to "the very paste of things" (see Note 78 above). And the absolute absurdity of this sheer, piercing, unaccountable contingent facticity, the brute, revolting bodiliness of things, infuses Roquetin, this first existentialist hero (actually first only in Western Europe—there is Dostoevsky's *Underground Man*) with nauseas (in the plural) of various sorts, among them a sense of being *de trop*—superfluous. What isn't fully worked out but foreshadowed is the exhilarating existential freedom specific to *human beings* as a salvational counterweight to the nauseating contingency-freedom of *things* that is (so to speak) celebrated in *Nausea* (131).

85. How then are we to describe: *Being and Nothingness*, 565.

86. Learns his freedom: 566.

87. Hegel: 567.

Unlike Heidegger, Sartre gives Hegel his due, even in disagreement: "But if Hegel has forgotten himself, we cannot forget Hegel" (329). From reading Heidegger, one would never know that Hegel anticipated (and provided?) Heidegger's chief term *Dasein*; consider also *entschliessen* in the double sense of "resolving" and "self-disclosing," said of the logical Idea as it culminates by "freely releasing itself (*entlassen*) as Nature (*Encyclopedia*, para. 244, *Science of Logic*, end; see Note 28 above, part 2).

88. Determinism: *Being and Nothingness*, 567; **hiding:** 568.

89. The crucial distinction: 568; **discovery:** 569.

90. Negative observations: 571.

91. Nihilation: 571.

92. Courses, motives, ends: 577; **experience itself as a project:** 578–79.

93. Made-past: 578–79; **given myself an essence:** 580.

94. Deliberation always deception: 581.

95. Voluntary act: 582; **goal:** 581.

96. When chips are down: 581.

A full phenomenology, such as Sartre calls for, was in fact offered seven years later, though not in his spirit: Paul Ricoeur, *Freedom and Nature: The Voluntary and the Involuntary* (*Le Volontaire et L'involuntaire*, 1950), trans. Erazim V. Kohák (Northwestern Univ. Press, 1966). This is the first volume of a trilogy, *The Philosophy of the Will*.

The English title makes explicit the very modern Kant-derived, science-inspired assumption of the book, that there are two realms, one of human freedom and one of natural necessity. In renaming them as the voluntary and its negative, Ricoeur signals the hypothesis of a reciprocity and a project of reconciliation: The involuntary, consisting of natural needs, emotions, habits, has no meaning of its own but acquires a complete significance only in relation to the voluntary, that is, the will, which these elements of human nature solicit, dispose, and generally affect. The will, in turn, bestows on them their significance, determining them by its choice, moving them by its effort, and adapting them by its consent (4–5). Thus the will "comes first"; falsely to reverse this priority is the effect of the scientific revolution.

The voluntary seen in terms of a freedom/nature dichotomy is just what it will be in the chapters to come on the will in neuroscience: It is the will reduced to decision-making. Its phenomenological description is an expansion of the terms in the following summary: Decision is an intention aiming at a project, that is, a future action, which depends on me and which is within my power (43). Moreover there are no decisions without motives, though motives are not causes, for causes are understandable without their effects, while the final meaning of a motive "is tied in a basic way to the action of the self on the self which is decision" (67).

The phenomenological description is accompanied by a Husserlian "bracketing," that is, by a parenthesizing suspension of existence, or aspects thereof. Ricoeur's pure phenomenology of the will brackets "Transcendence," here meaning experience of a spiritual realm (29), and "the Fault" (*La Faute*), a sort of fall, a disruption in existence (xxxiv). It turns out to be attributable to the passions, by which the soul imposes a bondage on itself, a bondage to vanity, to Nothing. The genesis of passion is in the imagination, which, with its myths, makes "the soul succumb to the charm of Nothing" (23). Emotion, normally "the physical stirring of passion" (277), is later somewhat rehabilitated as a participant in willing. It contributes no ends, but appearing "as the province of involuntary action," it gives those ends that are already present before conscious-ness "a certain physical prestige whose efficacy is partly of the order of nascent movement" (251). However, the full removal of the brackets around the passions and spiritual life will occur only gradually over later volumes of the *Philosophy of the Will*.

This first volume of 500 pages is hard going—wordy and woolly, abounding in idiosyncratic uses of borrowed terminology and in recherché complexities of conscious life not evident to the ordinary sensibility. I did not read more than was necessary for the above précis.

97. Could have done otherwise: *Being and Nothingness*, 584 ff.; **our very being is origi-nal choice**: 595.

G. E. Moore, in the chapter "Free Will" of his *Ethics* (1912; New York: Oxford Univ. Press, 1965), analyzes the meaning of "could have done otherwise." His hypothesis is that "the mere fact (if it is a fact) that we sometime *can*, in *some* sense do what we don't do, does not necessarily enti-tle us to say that we *have* Free Will. We certainly *haven't* got it, unless we can; but it doesn't fol-low that we *have* it just because we *can*. Whether we have or not will depend on the precise sense in which it is true that we can" (87). Warning to American readers: In Moore's analysis, "can" drags in, besides its past and conditional "could," also "should" and "would." The latter two are used quite rulelessly in perfectly good American speech, in subjunctive (conditional), optative (desiderative), or imperative (enjoining) moods—not to speak of the fact that pages upon pages in grammars contain such (actually relevant) information as "[W]e employ as future subjunctive forms, to indicate a future result, the past potential . . . *should* in the first person and *would* in the second and third." Consequently, if "shall" and "will" was a challenge (my Ch. VI), "should" and "would" is an exasperation to the American ear—and Moore uses them copiously in crucial settings. I'll report what I can make out of his analysis of "can."

Moore's inquiry is ethical; it concerns attribution of right and wrong—not *what* is right and wrong but *whether* one can impute these judgments to actions. His theory does *not* say that the right or wrong of an action depends on what the agent "absolutely *can* do," but only what he can do *if* he chooses. And this makes an immense difference (85)". Moore considers that the "abso-lutely *can* do" view is directly involved in the free-will controversy.

I must point out here that the foregoing puts the controversy on a level below the heights of denial of free will reached in those contemporary treatments that *refuse the very protasis*, the "if he chooses" clause—by claiming that our sense of choice is an epiphenomenon, an idle accompa-niment, or an illusion, a self-protective delusion. Moore does not ignore this possibility but con-siders it unjustifiable, since we quite ordinarily make distinctions between what 1. *did* happen, and 2. what *didn't*, either 2a. although it *could* have, *or* 2b. because it *couldn't* have. And in the category 2a, what could have happened but didn't, belong the "if the agent had chosen" actions, which we all in practice believe in. In other words, there are possible and impossible actions, and choice is among the former. (Reading the analytical philosophers produces the contrarian con-viction that precision can be the enemy of intelligibility.)

What then does "can" or "could" mean? In one sense, if everything is indeed causally deter-mined, as Moore concedes, nothing ever could happen other than it does. This is the first, hard meaning of "can." But if "can" and "could" are ambiguous, then "universal causality" and "could happen otherwise" might not be "inconsistent" (p. 90). Since "not inconsistent" connotes "com-patible," Moore appears to be proposing his version of compatibilism, the school that becomes dominant later in the twentieth century (my Ch. IX).

The relevant second meaning of "could" is: "He would have if he had so chosen," that is, "If I had performed a certain act of will, I should have done something which I did not do" (91; I think "would" and "should" are here used as the past potentials with future results, mentioned above, of the future volitional forms "he will, I shall.") Now people who think that "can" *must* be used in the sense of "able, causally sufficient," people who therefore fail to supply mentally the clause "if he had so chosen," that is, the hypothetical protasis, will conclude that a disease and a crime are equally misfortunes: He could not help committing the crime or catching the disease. But "*if* he had so chosen" makes all the difference, and, supposing that the action is physically possible, as avoiding the disease may not be, this choice-making, this element of acting *voluntarily* may be "*all* that we usually understand by the assertion that we have Free Will" (93).

Moore says that this may not be sufficient. For, as a reader will have seen, it throws the whole burden on choice, and (this is my, not Moore's observation) that begs the question, if the whole question is *whether we* can *choose*. Moore simply claims that "it is absolutely certain that, in two different senses, at least, we could have chosen" (93). One sense of "can choose" is that we *can choose to choose*, make an effort to choose. Another is that it is quite certain that 1. we often should have acted differently if we had chosen to, and 2. so also if we had chosen to choose, and 3. it is always *possible* that we should have chosen other than we did in the sense that no one, including ourselves, can know now that we shall not make a given choice, for example that we shall not choose as we ought to—though our belief that we *shall* not so chose tends to prevent that choice. Moore thinks that senses 2 and 3 *are* what we mean by Free Will (94; sense 1 is, I suppose what we mean by free agency; see Ch. XI, Sec. C, herein). Then Moore disposes of the main modern point: People will argue that the above is still insufficient; they think we must show that "we were *able* to choose, in some quite other sense," sense 4.

But no one has so far been "able to tell us what that sense is" (94). (Sense 4 will be that mental activity is governed by brain activity and "able to choose" means having sound brain circuitry. It seems to me that Moore-style conceptual and linguistic analysis cannot reach the modern mind-brain perplexity raised by sense 4—nor any older determinism, such as that possibly inherent in God's omniscience. So Moore's compatibilism sidesteps or indeed begs the hard question: Is "can do otherwise" compatible with natural causality? For it gives "can" the *meaning* of "could if I would," that is, it makes its meaning conditional on real choice, when the true spontaneity of choice is the problem. This problem is not soluble by claims of fact or distinctions of meaning which tend toward question-begging trivialities.)

98. Last chapter: "Doing and Having," 724; **impermeability and density**: 723; **man as a useless passion**: 784; **not-so-exhilarating note**: Sartre's Conclusion ends with anguished questions.

99. Fyodor Dostoevsky, *Demons* (1872), trans. Richard Pevear and Larissa Volokhonsky (New York: Vintage Books, 1994), pt. III, chap. 6, 619.

100. My texts are: Ludwig Wittgenstein, *Philosophical Investigations*, Part I (1945), nos. 611–29; and Gilbert Ryle, *The Concept of Mind* (1949), chap. III, "The Will."

(1) *Wittgenstein*'s eighteen observations on the will, though written in the plainest German, exceed in difficulty those of the most abstruse ontologist. The reasons are: 1. He offers accounts of what we feel, think, or say that make me wonder (what I least want to believe) whether different people, even those belonging to the same civilization, perhaps experience and express their lives in hopelessly different ways; 2. It is an iffy enterprise to decide whether or not his needling questions and his insistent pointings to ordinary phenomena imply answers, and when the replies people might make, proffered by him with question marks, are intended as suggested or as rejected answers; 3. It is not readily discernible whether he is attacking a particular philosopher's position or just making general allusions.

The first number is an example:

> 611. "Willing too is only an experience," one might wish to say (the 'will' too is only a 'representation' [*Vorstellung*]). It comes when it comes, and I cannot bring it about.
>
> Not bring it about?—Like *what*? What then can I bring about? With what am I comparing willing when I say this?

(Could Wittgenstein be attacking Schopenhauer? No, because then a *Vorstellung* is just what I do bring about; see Ch. VII, Sec. B, herein. Probably he is setting up an answer: Willing is not a doing to be brought about or an instrument to be summoned, separable from and antecedent to an overt action.) The sense in which willing can be made to occur is by just doing the deed:

613. . . . In this sense I bring about the willing to swim by jumping into the water. I surely wanted to say: I couldn't will the willing, that is, it makes no sense to speak of willing-willing. "Willing" is not the name for an action, and thus also not for a willful one. And my false expression came from this, that one wants to consider willing as an immediate, non-causal bringing about.

The mistake here, Wittgenstein continues, is a false analogy to a mechanical connection that may fail.

(This significance-laden number is full of radically destabilizing but dubious assertions. First, Wittgenstein collapses internal intention with overt execution, thus in fact overriding the former; the sense of *prior* willing—or the prior sense of willing—is discounted. Then he simply denies the "second power" of willing, the pure will to assert the will with respect to an object, though his is the very intensity of volition repeatedly cited in the tradition, the sense of the will-fulness of will. And third, he simply asserts that the originating motion of the will is generally understood as *non-causal* rather than *self-causing*, and that it is then erroneously regarded as analogous to a mechanical disconnection; the former claim requires an argument why *causa sui* is unacceptable, and the latter needs to attend to the way freedom feels to at least some of us: not like a failure of linkage.

No. 627 deals with the proper description of voluntary action: Wittgenstein claims that this is the wrong way—and what no one in fact says: "I decide to raise my arm at a certain signal, and behold, my arm raises itself on the signal." This is the right way: "On the signal I raise my arm." Thus (No. 628) one could say that voluntary movement is characterized by the absence of won-der [*Staunen*], and Wittgenstein adds, he wants to prevent the question "*Why* is one not seized by wonder here?" (It's true that the "behold" description is inappropriate to daily doing and no one gives it—but it's perfectly natural once we stop to think, and then it *is* what someone will say. Moreover, I have the deepest misgivings about the explicit proscription of wonder, which I first ran across in Descartes' *Passions of the Soul*, Art. 76; it is an aspect of the conversion of philoso-phy from inquiring into attractive beings to exposing disabling errors.)

In No. 629 Wittgenstein asserts that "when people talk about the possibility of a foreknowl-edge of the future, they always forget the fact of the foretelling of [one's own] willful movements." (On the contrary, by and large, futurologists, be they private or professional, seem normally to include human intentions in their predictions, though not forgetting that the actual execution even of an announced intention is only partly foreknown by the agent himself and even less prognosticable by an outsider. When a canny predictor meets a willful actor bent on stymieing the attempt at being second-guessed, one strategy is to apply the will to its own relaxation and to let it go terminally random—one kind of "willing-willing," namely un-willing willing—a curi-ous capacity we just happen to have: going deliberately antic.

Wittgenstein's handful of observations is surely consequence-fraught; the will in effect dis-appears as a motive force. This desirable outcome seems to me, however, to be an ill-gotten gain; it simply declares certain experiences as vacant because they are not quite clearly observ-able or lucidly communicable. Couldn't one argue that such residual recalcitrance is a *proof* of their reality?)

(2) *Ryle* mounts an attack on the will as part of "the dogma—or myth—of the Ghost in the Machine." This is his figure for Cartesian mind-body dualism, the (no-longer) "official doctrine": Our spatial bodies are subject to mechanical laws and their states are publicly observable. But we also have non-spatial minds with private careers only known to ourselves. Thus we live two col-lateral lives, one external (as a machine), the other internal (as the ghost). The latter mind, my very own, is said to be open to a special kind of inspection, introspection, self-viewing, but there is no direct access to other minds. "Only our bodies can meet" (Ch. I). There is, however, a spe-cial mental-conduct language that signifies to others particular episodes in our secret history. Willing-language belongs to this language. (Note that this "ghost-in-the-machine" description matches Wittgenstein's account of people's false view of willing as a failed mechanical linkage.)

Ryle means to explode the myth of the ghost by showing that it involves a category-mistake, that is, a way of speaking of two logically different things as if they belonged to the same cat-egory. We think that, since mental-conduct words are not construed as signifying mechanical processes with physical causation, they must be intending non-mechanical processes with non-physical causation, for both events pertain to the category of "thing" (*res extensa, res cogitans*). Things, however, are thought of as existing in a framework of stuff, attribute, cause, effect, etc.

Ryle corrects this category-mistake specifically insofar as it affects the will in his chap. III. (Ryle's account of the inevitably category-transgressing, otherwise put, metaphorical, language used of the soul, treating it as a disembodied body, seems to me exactly right; the question is whether such trans-logical approaches *are* subject to logical rectification or whether that's throwing the baby out with the bathwater—the soul with its metaphor. But, of course, that may be the very intention of the "philosophy of the mind.")

Most mental-conduct language is well known to us in its application. Not so, Ryle says, volitional language, which we do *not* know how to apply in daily life. For like "phlogiston," it has no utility. (Phlogiston-flogging is the philosopher's obeisance to science.) Volition is a myth.

Volition is falsely postulated as a special act "in the mind," one by which it "gets its ideas translated into facts," ". . . [A]s my thinking and wishing alone are unexecutive, they require the mediation of a further executive process. So I perform a volition, which somehow puts my muscles into action." Ryle rejects this story as an extension of the ghost in the machine; the language of volition as causal assumes a para-mechanical theory of the mind. Here are Ryle's objections (ch. III 2):

1. No one actually talks of volition in terms of operations that are hidden counterparts of overt actions, except to endorse the theory—not even novelists. (Read Dostoevsky! See this Chapter, end.)

2. "It is admitted that one person can never witness the volitions of another . . ." One can only infer them from external indices. Moreover, the agent himself can't know whether his will was the actual cause, say, of pulling the trigger. (That's the human condition: We infer from indices and guess by intimations—why proscribe what little we've been given?)

3. Admittedly, the causal connection between will and motion is a mystery. But Ryle thinks it belongs to the class of soluble mysteries, that is, those that can be shown to rest on a theory that is in conflict with itself, because it both asserts and denies that mental and bodily transactions are linked. (Is the experience of a self-contradiction the explosion of a mystery or its corroboration? Is the noting of a paradox the end or the beginning of an illumination?)

4. If volitions are postulated to originate bodily movements, the question arises: What originates volitions? Are they themselves voluntary or involuntary acts? Is there an infinite regress? No, volitions cannot accept those predicates—nor others, like "good" or "bad." (This objection brings out the crucial importance of the traditional insistence that there is indeed a will to will, a second-order volitional state and that it can be good or evil; "willing-willing" is a way of speaking about volitional self-origination and responsibly. As ever, the question is how much—fully explicit—para-logical language is permissible in human matters.)

What, then, is willing, if it is rejected as a causal hypothesis? First, Ryle is far from regarding Nature as exhaustively describable in terms of mechanisms; moreover, he does not think that all questions have a physical answer (ch. III 5). The real problem is that philosophers have stretched willing beyond its meaning in actual use. They apply "voluntary" and "involuntary" to reprehensible and to meritorious actions, and this expansion is partly responsible for the specious problem of free will. The undistorted ordinary use of this pair does not usually include reference to moral imputability of actions, and it does not concern itself with occult episodes of willing. Instead, people judge whether a deed could have been done or omitted, whether the agent was or should have been competent, resolute, etc., and they assign blame only if they see failure. The will, free or otherwise, is simply under their radar in practical life. (I don't think this claim is quite right—as often happens in professional philosophers' observations of "ordinary" behavior. The law, for example, grades killing by premeditated intention, that is, by willing, ranging from manslaughter to first-degree murder, and ordinary readily people buy into those gradations.)

What of will power? Again it is for Ryle a matter of overt behavior. Strength of will is a propensity to stick to tasks; it is evinced in performances and not attributable to a special internal operation.

(Ryle's evaporation of will as a psychic force seems to me to rest on two transliterations, as it were: the Cartesian mind-body dualism transitions into a nature-logic duality and the traditional self-inspector passes into an other-observer. However, in the end it's a question of one's avidity to eradicate category "mistakes" because they might be logical confusions though perhaps also philosophical illuminations, and one's willingness to be talked into a curtailed solipsistic scope for one's internal self-knowledge, a locked-room privatism of the soul, thereupon to be invalidated. Ryle's descriptions of the will, however, as a concept more dubious than other mental activities seems to me plain true. Only there must be other ways to supplant it than by going completely external.)

Chapter IX. Compatibilism: *An Academic Question*

Sources

The following is a tiny fraction of the scholarship on compatibilism and its opposing positions; these are the works I have consulted, with brief abstracts.

Arpaly, Nomy. *Merit, Meaning, and Human Bondage: An Essay on Free Will.* Princeton: Princeton Univ. Press, 2006. [Especially chaps. 1–3. A question often overlooked in the compatibilism debate is whether we choose our mental states, like motives and desires, i.e., whether we choose our "second-order volitions" (see Harry G. Frankfurt, *The Importance of What We Care About*, chap. 2), such as our desires. These, as distinct from determinist reactions, are "*reason responsive*," and therein lies a "new compatibilism."]

Balaguer, Mark. *Free Will as an Open Scientific Problem*, chap. 2. Cambridge: MIT Press, 2010. [Argues that in the assumed absence of a precise definition of free will, the truth of compatibilism is undecidable.]

Banks, William P. "Does Consciousness Cause Misbehavior?" In *Does Consciousness Cause Behavior?* Edited by Susan Pockett, William P. Banks, and Shaun Gallagher. Cambridge: MIT Press, 2009. [Nuanced review and critique of versions of incompatibilism, particularly libertarianism; defense of a moderated compatibilism that supposes a continuum among neural systems, unconscious, conscious ideas, and feedback loops that result in a "product," namely our sense of self and feeling of selfhood, a sense of ownership.]

Dennett, Daniel C. *Elbow Room: The Varieties of Free Will Worth Wanting.* Cambridge: MIT Press, 1984. [A spirited realization of Ryle's abandoned plan "to exhibit a sustained piece of analytical hatchet-work being directed upon some notorious and large-sized Gordian Knot," namely, the freedom of the will—Ryle, quoted on p.IX.]

Fischer, John Martin, Robert Kane, Derk Pereboom, and Manuel Vargas. *Four Views on Free Will.* Oxford: Blackwell Publishing, 2007. [Closely argued articles on the spectrum of the compatibilist-incompatibilist debate, frequently used in my text.]

Frankfurt, Harry G. *The Importance of What We Care About: Philosophical Essays.* 1988. Reprint: Cambridge: Cambridge Univ. Press, 2005. [Contains restatements of his two main contributions to the debate: "second order" desires and the Frankfurt example (set out in my text, this Chapter).]

Grim, Patrick. *Philosophy of Mind: Brains, Consciousness, and Thinking Machines.* Chantilly, Va.: The Teaching Company, 2008. [Lecture 18, "Do We Have Free Will," concisely outlines various compatibilist arguments.]

Guyer, Paul. "Indeterminacy and Freedom of the Will." In *Indeterminacy: The Mapped, the Navigable, and the Uncharted.* Edited by Jose V. Ciprut. Cambridge: MIT Press, 2008. [Critiques the indeterminism (of physics) as a ground for ascriptions of responsibility but accepts that "probability (incomplete knowledge) remains the guide to life."]

Haji, Ishtiyaque. "Compatibilist Views of Freedom and Responsibility." In *The Oxford Handbook of Free Will.* Edited by Robert Kane. Oxford: Oxford Univ. Press, 2002. [Surveys five compatibilist views, dividing them into two classes. One range of attitudes, like resentment and guilt, ascribe responsibility to others, and these "reactive attitudes," these ascriptions of responsibility, said to be immune to determinist exoneration, constitute responsibility—our attitudes toward one another *are* what is meant by responsibility. In the other class, a "mesh" between the agent's choice and his desires (voluntariness) constitutes the freedom necessary for responsibility.]

Honderich, Ted. *How Free Are You? The Determinism Problem* (chap. 9). 2nd Ed. Oxford: Oxford Univ. Press, 2002. [Traces the history of compatibilism back to Hobbes; dismisses the debate between compatibilists and incompatibilists as one of talking past each other because they have different conceptions of the freedom they want, the former meaning voluntariness, the latter also origination of action; he thinks that it is a mistake to attempt to settle a question of attitudes by logico-intellectual-philosophico-linguistic means.]

Mele, Alfred R. *Effective Intentions: The Power of Conscious Will.* Oxford: Oxford Univ. Press, 2009. [A clear review of the terms and positions of the debate, and a sample of the sort of empirical discovery that would prove that there is no free will on either the libertarian or the compatibilist view. No such negative discovery has been made; on the other hand, free will is to be looked for in the natural order.]

———. "Psychology and Free Will: A Commentary." In *Are We Free? Psychology and Free Will.* Edited by John Baer, James C. Kaufman, and Roy F. Baumeister. Oxford: Oxford Univ. Press, 2008. [Brief, clear review of compatibilism debate.]

Perry, John. "Compatibilist Options." In *Freedom and Determinism.* Edited by Joseph Keim Campbell, Michael O'Rourke, and David Shier. Cambridge: MIT Press, 2004. [Perry prefers a "strong" theory of laws (that the laws of nature are true even before the last instance is in) and a "weak" theory of ability (that it doesn't follow from the fact that someone won't do a thing that they can't) for underwriting compatibilism, i.e., "hard determinism" plus "could have done otherwise."]

Pink, Thomas. *Free Will: A Very Short Introduction* (chaps. 3–5). Oxford: Oxford Univ. Press, 2004. [A long view of compatibilism as having two sources, a rationalist or a naturalistic conception of freedom. The former projects compatibilism way back into ancient and medieval times; what is compatible here is freedom of choice with the necessities of reason. This compatibilism is thought to be unsustainable because it denies the very character of freedom. The naturalistic compatibilism—Hobbes is its initiator—is simply unobstructed attainment of desire, the familiar voluntariness.]

Russell, Paul. "Selective Hard Compatibilism." In *Action, Ethics, and Responsibility.* Edited by Joseph Keim Campbell, Michael O'Rourke, and Harry S. Silverstein. Cambridge: MIT Press, 2010. [Suggests a "selective hard compatibilism" under which the question about the attribution of responsibility shifts to the controller, who is not entitled to assign blame to the controlled, though others may.]

Shariff, Azim F., Jonathan Schooler, and Kathleen D. Vohs. "The Hazards of Claiming to Have Solved the Hard Problem of Free Will." In *Are We Free? Psychology and Free Will.* Edited by John Baer, James C. Kaufman, and Roy F. Baumeister. Oxford: Oxford Univ. Press, 2008. [Exposition of "dual-aspect" compatibilism resting on "identity dualism," the theory that third-person neurons (brain) and first-person experiences (consciousness), though *materially* identical, are *ontologically* different.]

Walter, Henrik. *Neurophilosophy of Free Will: From Libertarian Illusions to a Concept of Natural Autonomy* (pp. 262–67). Translated by Cynthia Klohr. Cambridge: MIT Press, 2009. [Characterizes compatibilism as being on the lookout for a theory of agency not involving initiation, i.e., being able to do otherwise. Review of the core of "hierarchical theories of will," among which is Frankfurt's theory of first and second order desires and volitions (i.e., wanting to want and willing to will). It is here interpreted as a theory of agency: One has freedom of will if one *wants to want,* i.e., when one owns one's desire, and freedom of action when one acts according to this authenticated will—which freedom does not require being able to do otherwise.]

1. For complete citations, see the Bibliography above. For compatibilism before the invention of the term, see Index.

Though some writers comment on the peculiarly professional character of the compatibilist debate, in the sense that compatibilism is not something "naturally believed" (Pink, *Free Will,*

43) the outcome of the controversy is in some sense not "strictly academic." For example, a huge research project, announced in 2010, entitled "Big Questions in Free Will" offers generous funds for an inquiry into the ontological and conceptual foundations of free will; it states in its guiding document that "proposals for projects that assume compatibilism is true probably would not be competitive," though, to be sure, the consideration of compatibilist critiques of incompatibilist models would receive serious consideration. The proposals are expected to employ terms in accordance with a "Lexicon of Key Terms" provided. Such restrictions seem to me to betoken a sense that something crucial is at stake—that ducks must be gotten in a row toward marshalling a non-casuistic defense of free will and personal responsibility, for compatibilist arguments do often have a whiff of equivocation about them. But when opinion is restricted and vocabulary is preset, the activity may be called "research," meaning a protocol-guided study of a set problem, but not an "inquiry," meaning the open pursuit of a developing question.

By nonetheless calling this controversy academic I do mean to attribute certain specific features to it:

a. That it *is* a controversy in the sense that it can lose its freshness by losing itself in evermore complex technical arguments—as never could the same issue, treated as a living philosophical problem. (It has become the custom to denominate all the opposing positions by their authors. That, I think, ought not be the way of thoughtfulness; recall Heraclitus: "Listen not to me but to what I am saying.")

b. That it tends to trade in thought-packets: first of all, the "isms," then "the W-principle," "the X-argument," "the Y-type example," the "Z-objection"—a mode of investigation in which thinking is from its beginnings terminologically encapsulated. Put positively: precision gained, progress achieved, problems settled—these profits are meant to be enshrined in these formulations. (It is, however, possible that when philosophy is thought of as progressing in truth, settling problems, and achieving results, it has already met its end.)

c. That the language is deliberately forbidding, bristling with neologic phraseology, devised by professionals, and so, intentionally or not, excluding general humanity. (Thus productivity of concept-construction makes philosophy a specialty inaccessible to lay persons.)

d. That the intendedly tight logic is often very dubious for the innocent listener-in. For example, propositions at which one might balk are presented as "non-controversial," or inferences which seem unpersuasive without a lot more conversation (not argument) are confidently announced. For example: "No person would change the past or the laws of nature, *even if* they wanted or tried to, because no one has the power to do it" (Fischer et al., *Four Views*, 12: a statement of the determinist argument).

This seems clear until you think it out: The past that is unchangeable is purely notional; the past we have comes from our external (documentary) or internal (personal) memory and is thus pliable: Archaeological finds and documents are subject to contestable interpretation; personal recollections are often unfalsifiably false. There *is* no unalterable past, and we *have* no producible past. Moreover, such past as is real for us we can sometimes relive. My favorite line in one of my best-loved novels, Scott Fitzgerald's *The Great Gatsby*, is spoken by Jay Gatsby himself: "'Can't repeat the past?' he cried incredulously. 'Why of course you can!'" (ch. VI). And if you can repeat the past, you surely have also changed it—changed it from a first event into a second coming, and repetition reflects back on the event repeated. Jay thinks he has the power of repetition, and *he* all but achieves it; it's Daisy who isn't up to it.

So also for the "laws of nature," only known to us in their human formulations, which are not now entirely what they were, say, in 1686 when Newton published his Laws of Motion, or in 1905 when Einstein announced his theory of Special Relativity. When I say that both past and laws of nature are "notional"—at least as far as we human beings are concerned—I mean nothing antically imaginative, but only that the past is not factually available to us and that the laws of nature have been—so far—always in a state of revision. Therefore no hard and fast inferences from our powerlessness concerning the past seem warranted: You have to make some pretty daring assumptions about time and knowledge to speak so unqualifiedly—though frequently such position-occupying is qualified out of all distinct shape by weasel-language.

e. That the academic style favors formalisms which cannot be regarded as either embellishments or clarifications. Here is a fine example:

SI. S has, throughout a span of time t, a standing intention to A, if (1) throughout t, S has a nondeviantly produced standing true belief that he acquired (or had) an intention to A and (2) he has nondeviantly come to be so constituted that the activation of this belief at any time during t will quickly generate an occurrent intention to A.

Figure SI [Standing Intention] out, and you will learn that we sometimes have a normally conceived intention [standing intention] to do a certain thing, though not to do it right now; however this [somewhat dormant] intention predisposes us, when the occasion arises, to be ready to act [occurrent intention]. (Why make the obvious obscure? Why translate ordinary language into formalistic lingo?)

f. That the imagination is reduced, be it from abnegation or atrophy. The examples are *all* banal, taken from our smallest common humanity. For free decision, it tends to be the raising of an (all too well-exercised) finger; for free will, it tends to be the eating of (nutritionally toxic) cookies. Could it really be that our freedom is expended in little stirrings and minor sins? I would think that an early concern would be whether instances have to attain a certain gravity, draw in a certain larger humanity that we all do have, to be cases of human freedom. (Perhaps this is caviling, but the mistreatment of imaginative evidence seems to the point: Borges' story, "The Garden of Forking Paths," is cited and accepted as an example of a future preceded by a linear past, leading to a present, a point of decision, whence branch several future possibilities [Fischer et al., *Four Views*, 5 ff.].) Such alternatives are thought to be the, or at least, a condition of free will (of which more in the text). And yet the "branching paths" of Borges's actual story are worked into a spytale of, for him, rare straightforwardness. They depict a recluse's fantasy, which is just the opposite of a unique line leading up to a point-present of branching possibilities: In his imagination "he chooses—instantaneously—all of them." Thus *all the possible worlds* are realized at once; it is a universe of parallel real worlds and does not foreclose all but one outcome—as choice normally does. In this fiction within a fiction, Borges reverts to his characteristic mode: He treats the logic of things as Escher does their geometry: as the latter draws geometrically harmless-looking pictures that confound our orientation in space, so Borges articulates events that ensnare the imagination but perplex our sense of existence (which, however, some physicists now take quite seriously: in their theories of existing alternative worlds).

Before ending this long note, I want to return to the point I made above about certain unrelievable ignorances to which we are condemned (or by which we are blessed). It will serve as an argument of my text. On December 2, 2005, Freeman Dyson lectured at my college about possible experiments to discover the graviton, a gravity-particle analogous to the photon, the light-particle. It turns out that to capture as few as four of these hypothetical particles it would be necessary to have an instrument with the mass of the earth to hold its position within permissible limits. It amounts, he said, to a "conspiracy of nature telling you this can't be done." The impossibility is not, however, that of a "no-go" experiment, an impossibility *in principle*, such as arises from the uncertainty principle, which says that measuring the position and momentum of an electron simultaneously with absolute accuracy is, by the very theory of instrumental observation, impossible. It is rather an impossibility *in practice*, imposed by our, the observer's, limitations of space and time. Dyson said that he finds this fact very satisfying. To me his talk was eye-opening, as if Gödel's incompleteness theorem—which states that in a logico-mathematical system there will be found propositions of arithmetic whose truth cannot be decided within the system—had been rewritten for *empirical science*. To repeat a point made above: Since modern (non-theological) arguments about free will depend on having fixed notions of the "past" and the "laws of nature," the thought of our *perhaps merely practical but certainly ineradicable ignorance* of at least the first, but probably both of these factors, should become part of the debate. (For Dyson's further development of the consequences of *practical* impossibilities in physics, see "How Incompatible Worldviews Can Coexist," in *The Institute Letter*, Institute for Advanced Study, Princeton [Spring 2013]: 7.)

2. Compatibilism defined: by John Perry ("Compatibilist Options," 231); **positions of the debate**: Fischer et al., *Four Views*, passim; **determinism that makes free will impossible**: there are, of course, alternative understandings of determinism, see Mele, *Effective Intentions*, 150 ff. Especially tricky is the relationship of determinism to "psychological causalism," the scientist's axiom that all psychological events are *caused*—but perhaps strictly deterministically, perhaps probabilistically.

3. History's explanatory value: it is odd that for Hobbes, the hardest of deterministic hard-liners, personal history is not much of a determining factor, since the last moment alone determines the will, and there is no reason to think that the chain is cumulatively causal (though it might be). As for history, I am not implying that it has explanatory value even in a non-deterministic world. That would involve knowing whether History (capital H, the happening, not the report) is something real, that is, a discernibly independent unitary force and if there were such a substance, how it interacted with individual human thinking and choosing, or alternatively, whether these latter micro-events are summable into a coherent; meaningful whole. (See Ch. VIII, Note 60, herein.)

4. I've chosen for a wider-carrying critique an article that is both acute and sweeping, therefore a fair sample of the hard-determinist, anti-free-will argument and its practical consequences. (I might say here that I find myself unconvinced by the arguments *against*, yet by no means persuaded by the case *for* free will. This is clearly not a case to be resolved by setting aside the argument of the excluded middle that says: *tertium non datur*, "a third is not available," if, as I believe, the terms themselves are somehow falsely opposed.)

The article: Joshua Greene and Jonathan Cohen, "For the Law, Neuroscience Changes Nothing and Everything" in the *Philosophical Transactions of the Royal Society*, London B, 359 (2004): 1775–85. Joshua Greene, a former colleague, lectured on these issues on November 11, 2011, at my college. I am, of course, curtailing the exposition. My comments, as usual, are in parentheses.

The thesis is that the "net effect of this [the neuroscientific] influx of scientific information will be a rejection of free will as it is ordinarily conceived, with important ramifications for the law . . . [O]ur criminal justice system is largely retributivist" (1776a).

"Retributivism" (one of those thought-packets I am leery of) is the doctrine that punishment is intended to give perpetrators what they "deserve," to pay them back, vengefully, as it were. The authors say that, given the understanding of (hard) determinism as the complete determination of events and actions by the past plus the laws of nature, and of free will as the ability to do otherwise, retributivism requires the rejection of determinism. Positively stated, it requires that human beings be in control of their actions and could thus "have done otherwise" than they did. This is the condition under which blame can be assigned and retribution exacted. As is usual, choice in this article is nugatory, such as "soup over salad" (1777b). The authors point out, as is also common, that, should nature be shown to be subatomically probabilistic and your behavior "determined by the laws of physics, so that your actions depended on the state of the universe 10,000 years ago *and* the outcome of myriads of subatomic coin flips," the libertarian, i.e., the believers in free will simply, would nonetheless not be helped. For then our choices would be random, in the sense of indeterminable, and that also betokens: not controlled by us. They reject libertarianism because "there is not a shred of scientific evidence to support the existence of *causally effective* processes in the mind or brain that violate the laws of physics" (1777b; but ask yourself: What could be meant by scientific evidence for an event *defined* as para-scientific? Is scientific instrumentation designed to detect deviations from the laws of nature? Isn't that a conceptual—though perhaps not a practical—impossibility? As my first reader put in the margin: "What my net can't catch, ain't fish." For would a discovery of such a violation not be regarded as an invitation to develop explanations, perhaps modifications in the known laws? Take the case, for example, of the Michelson/Morley experiment (1887), which showed that the ether, a hitherto indispensable notion for the propagation of light, was undetectable; the consequence was a new relativistic physics. In sum: Natural law is inviolable as a postulate, not as a finding; though designs for experiments to detect the reverse influence of consciousness on neural activity have been proposed [see Ch. X, herein] but had, by 2008, not been realized. Could they be?)

With free will gone, then, retributionism is plain untenable, for you should not be punished for what you could not control—and so rewards are also out of the picture—no bonus for just being a bright boy. (There is a much older and deeper argument for exacting retribution than intuitions of individual deserving. It is the grander vision that the cosmos is out of kilter, the world out of balance, if payment is not exacted. Anaximander [frag. 112], one of the Presocratic so-called physicists, says that the things that come and cease to be so "according to a 'must'—

they pay the penalty and give retribution for their injustice . . ." I think this sense of things having to be set right quite impersonally, cosmically, is ineradicable in human beings—and in the long run much more powerful than a meaner sense that people should get what's individually due to them.)

The preferred doctrine of punishment (or reward) under hard determinism is, therefore, "consequentialism," a forward-looking view that sets aside questions of free will and cares only "for promoting future social welfare" (1775b). (The authors acknowledge several dangers and difficulties, but not the obvious one: Who gets to decide *future* social welfare and what *present* impacts it? They also underrate the dangers which seem to me an inevitability: Public opinion, far from opting for a mild consequentialism because transgressors can't help themselves, will turn to thoughts of extermination of defective classes of people; the science-backed notion of an "evil seed" will induce systematic bloody-mindedness.)

Free will, as a common human experience, is now given a place: "If we like, we can say that the actions of rational people, operating free from duress, etc., are free actions, and such people are exercising their free will" (1783): This appears to me as some kind of compatibilism, one that throws the load of free will onto rationality. (Now, "being rational" can mean anything, from thinking philosophically to thinking rationalistically, from thinking reasonably to thinking formalistically. The pertinent question for any and all ways is: Is thinking in *my* control (construction) or *under constraint by its object* (adequation), and wherein does *its* freedom consist? Before that's clarified, to base free will in reason may be—indeed seems to me to be—the answer, but its justification is as yet out of sight. So this, the rationalistic version of free will, is not here well grounded.)

The authors think that the influx of neuroscientific information that must wean us away from old style free will and retributive justice will be pretty precise. They imagine a high resolution scanner generating a film on which we will be able to watch images of the brain deciding between soup and salad. (It is not, however, clear that it is *in practice* possible to track completely the huge numbers of interactions contributing to a specific emerging decision—which would be required to confirm convincingly the hypothesis that brain activity is not only a necessary but also the absolutely *sufficient* condition for a choice. But set that aside, and—since we are in the futuristic mode—imagine yourself watching this process of decision in real time. On the screen, you identify a tendency in yourself to choose soup over salad—on the anti-Hobbesian hypothesis that it is not just the very last moment before the decision-impulse kicks in that determines the outcome. You say to yourself—and at this moment willing has cast loose from an object other than itself, that is, it has become willfulness, the will to will—"Who is the brain, to decide my life?" if life is indeed soup and salad. You intervene, your own Frankfurt intervener. The screen changes. Now is that because of your spontaneous intervention, or was that action foretold in the brain's cards, too, so to speak? Later on I will discuss a series of laboratory experiments, the Libet experiments, purporting to establish that the initiatory free will is a psychological illusion and that brain activity detectably precedes the sense of choice. If, as the deterministic formula goes, the mind *is* the brain, it is now acting in what I imagine as a frantic real-time dual mode: watching itself externally on the screen while driving itself internally as—illusionistic—will, matter in mentation observing its image: That way madness lies—madness or what the medievals called *acedia*, the despair of anything being itself or making a difference. (For a discussion of the logical possibilities of this willing-and-watching: Alfred Mele, "Recent Work on Free Will and Science," *American Philosophical Quarterly* 45 [April 2008]: 117.)

And that brings me to my fundamental difficulty. What are the authors "doing" in writing a piece clearly intended to ease the labor pains of a new thought being born? One problem is the everlasting one of assisting prognostications of inevitability—why bother? But here the more serious one is a new version of the old Cretan liar paradox: A Cretan says: "All Cretans always lie." Here a neuroscientist opines: "All our opinions are predetermined." That is to say, he's not a *scientist* telling *truth* but a bit of *nature* being *natural*. Then my quandary is: Do I believe or resist his thesis because *I* think he's onto something or because I'm a bit of *nature* predetermined to receive or resist? If the latter, isn't all his speech really what is rightly called rhetoric, which is persuasive by reason of setting off a law-governed effect in the passions rather a free judgment of reason? That way lethargy lies—or would lie, if it were mine to choose—but then, again, even here: perhaps it *was* I myself who chose to supervene on nature with choice of quietism.

There are ways out. One might assert that some kinds of speech are exempt from determinism—scientific speech. But these authors would never agree to such exceptions, precisely because they are *responsible* scientists.

5. Much of my libertarian account comes from Robert Kane's "Libertarianism" in Fischer et al., *Four Views*, 5 ff. **Frankfurt examples**: almost all the items listed in the above Bibliography give an account of this—apparently—fascinating construction, with the journal references.

Himself: readers will notice that I often use the masculine pronoun, namely whenever it seems that males are apt to be the perpetrators of what I'm talking about. It has become a—mildly irritating—habit for men to write "she," often where they mean themselves, in an—I think, misguided—urge (enforced, I am told, by some editors) to transgender themselves in the cause of marrying scholarly exposition with social reconstruction. In the interest of full disclosure, I am, first and last, a First Amendment freak (as my students would say)—that is, a Madisonian adherent to the protection of religions from each other and from the government, and of speech from everyone whatsoever (excepting only the restrictions that protect children against predators and prevent incitements to violence or panic). So I attribute gender according to life's facts rather than my agenda—in the spirit of one connotation of this book's title: Un-willing.

6. Luther: there is some doubt whether the words were actually said. Nobody doubts that he thought it. The excommunication was the consequence of the "Ninety-five Theses" Luther had fastened to the church door in Wittenberg, in which he attacked the common practice of "indulgences," that is, the commutation of penalties and the absolution from sin, for money paid to accredited papal agents. The "Diet of Worms," which often elicits grins, refers to "diet," meaning an assembly of dignitaries and "Worms," a German city on the Rhine; for Luther's view of freedom, see Ch. III, Note 65, herein; Luther is mentioned in this context by Dennett in *Elbow Room*, 133 n. 14; **agenbite**: James Joyce, *Ulysses*, e.g. Episode I, 481 (Telemachus), in Don Gifford with Robert V. Seidman, *"Ulysses" Annotated*, rev. ed. (Berkeley: Univ. of California Press, 1988), Index.

7. Critique of Frankfurt examples: Robert Kane in Fischer et al., *Four Views*, 167–72, especially 169. Many other critiques are found in the books listed in the above Bibliography.

8. In-principle vs. in-practice experiments: See Note 1 above.

9. Aristotle on nature: *Physics* II, 198 b 36.

10. Pre-Nazi movies: see Ch. VII, Note 57, herein; **evil scientists in movies**: *The Cabinet of Dr. Caligari* (1920) and *Dr. Mabuse* (1922), in Siegfried Kracauer, *From Caligari to Hitler* (1947), chaps. 5–6. Literary forerunners are, of course, the monster-maker of Mary Shelley's *Dr. Frankenstein* (1818) and Captain Nemo ("No-man") of Jules Verne's *Twenty Thousand Leagues under the Sea* (1869); **Joseph Mengele**: Nazi doctor at Auschwitz who conducted criminal, scientifically valueless experiments on prisoners; **phone-implants**: I read this in the Technology Insert of a January 2012 issue of *The Economist*.

11. Will and willingness are distinguished in antiquity as *boulesis* and *hekousion*; **willing as lengthy process**: under Thomas Aquinas, Ch. III, Sec. A, herein.

12. Chapter Bibliography: precedes the notes to this chapter; **semicompatibilism**: John Martin Fischer, "Compatibilism," chap. 2 of *Four Views*; **Kant as compatibilist**: this too has been proposed; see *Four Views*, 81; **not a difference but *a* statement**: 82.

13. Hot, wet brain: David Hodgson in *The Oxford Handbook of Free Will*, 86; **quantum physics**: *Brain and Being*, ed. Gordon G. Globus et al. (Amsterdam: John Benjamins Publishing Co., 2004)—articles on non-classical physics as a possible explanation for the way consciousness emerges from the brain, but, significantly, *not* as an account of free will, i.e., non-deterministic consciousness.

14. Panicky metaphysics: Strawson's term, applied to Libertarianism, quoted, for example in Dennett, *Elbow Room*, 76. Dennett himself applies it to "agent causation," a "mysterious doctrine" analogizing the free human to an unmoved mover, thus making him a *causa sui*, a self-causer. He also delineates the "self-induced panic, the false pretext for much otherwise unmotivated system building and metaphysical tinkering" of those who are seized by a self-created "free will problem" (6). For *causa sui*, see Chs. X D and XI, Notes 20, 25.

15. Two understandings of will: Honderich (*How Free Are You?*, 119) makes a similar argument; **free will worth wanting**: from the subtitle of Dennett's *Elbow Room* ("The Varieties of Free Will Worth Wanting").

16. Industry: not my derogatory term—Honderich refers to "industrious philosophers . . . [who] say more than anyone is likely to have the fortitude to consider" (*How Free Are You?*, 4); **If you want to be a scientist**: George Howard in *Are We Free?*, ed. Baer et al., 261; **indeterminist libertarianism**: Robert Kane in *Four Views*, chap. 1; **extra factors**: ibid., 25; **information-responsive complex dynamics**: as so often in these studies, I can't quite comprehend whether this a formulation of the problem (how does decision-making work?) or its solution (by a complicated teleological system). In any case, it turns out that the concept of emergence is called on; it is a mystery located on the interface of science and philosophy: How do simple elements allow a qualitatively distinct whole to emerge, e.g., how do two molecules of hydrogen and one of oxygen aggregate into sensible water?

17. "Hovering happily": Dennett, quoted in Mele, *Effective Intentions*, 160; **soul in body**: alternative examples appear in Plato's *Timaeus* (36 d), where the cosmic body is *in* the soul; in Aristotle's *On the Soul* (412 a), where the soul is the *form* or *energeia* of a body, its "being-at-work"; in Leibniz's *Monadology* (19), where it is a simple *substance* having perception; and in Descartes' *Meditations* (II), where it is parallel to the body, a *res cogitans*, a thinking, willing, imagining *thing*.

18. Unmoved mover, *causa sui*: see Note 14 above; **if we are responsible**: Roderick M. Chisholm in *Agency and Responsibility*, ed. Laura Waddell Ekstrom (Boulder: Westview Press, 2001), 134. See Chapter XI, Note 20, herein.

19. Endorse: that is the language of the profession, as if my agreement made the position negotiable, ready to be "cashed out"; **responsibility under hard determinism**: see Note 4 above.

20. Consequence Argument: Robert Kane, *Four Views*, 10; the formulation there given by Peter van Inwagen; **they that make them**: Psalms 135:15; **not nature itself**: For Kant, to be sure, nature and its science are nearly identical, since we recognize in nature what we precognitively determined her to be; **idolatry**: Brann, *World of the Imagination*, 696.

21. The earliest solution that I know of to the problem that invokes what I call "theological compatibilism" occurs in Anicius Manlius Severinus Boethius, *The Consolation of Philosophy* (523 C.E.), Book V, chaps. II–VI, especially in chap. VI. Boethius's problem is: How can we exercise our will freely when God has foresight (*providentia*)? We cannot think that God's Providence merely predicts what is to come insofar as it necessarily must happen; this would make God's knowledge like human knowledge, bound by the way things are. Nor can the converse be the case, that Providence precedes events; this would make human free will (*arbitrii libertas, volendi nolendi libertas, voluntatis libertas*) impossible, since human choice can never contravene God's foreknowledge (ch. III). So far, then, Divine Providence and human free will seem incompatible.

But when Providence is rightly considered, they *are* compatible. Philosophy herself is the teacher; she says: Eternity is "the perfect and *altogether-at-once* (*tota simul*, my italics) possession of unending life" (ch. VI). Such is God's life; his time does not progress from past to future as does ours. Our life has not yet, and never can have, achieved and comprehended the future, and therefore can never be there all at once. In a word, God is eternal (*aeternus*), the world merely perpetual (*perpetuus*). And so God's foreknowledge (*praescientia*) is "of an instant that never runs short" (*numquam deficientis instantiae*); it is not of a thing to come, that is, of the future. Consequently, it is rightly not called *praevidentia*, "foresight," but—so Boethius—*providentia*, "oversight," meaning a comprehensive overview. God sees *all* things in his eternal present as we see *some* in our present, and of these, some as necessary, some as voluntary. "Therefore the divine anticipation (*praenotio*) does not change the nature of things and their property . . ." Thus Providence does not cancel free will; they are compatible, since God *knows* atemporally and we *act* temporally.

I'll let Chaucer's Nun's Priest have the last word: He cites, among others, Boethius on whether God's "worthy forwiting" constrains "nedely for to doon a thing. / ('Nedely' I call simple necessity). / Or else, if free choice be granted me / To do a thing or do it not / Though God foreknew it ere it was wrought; / . . . I want nothing to do with such matters; / My tale is of a cock . . ." (l. 474 ff.)—I'm all for hearing about Chauntecleer.

Let that suffice on compatibilism, except for a remarkable fiction, to which my colleague, Peter Kalkavage, alerted me: L. P. Hartley's *Facial Justice*, a dystopic depiction of a compatibilist society (1959).

But first, its hyper-egalitarian "New State" is also an incarnation of Rousseau's general will (see Ch. VII, Sec. A, herein): The "all-embracing order" of this society causes all to be on the same "level of littleness and equal in insignificance." The Voice of the faceless dictator ("Darling Dictator") insists that this order is "not imposed, it is, in the good sense, voluntary, the expression, through my Edicts, of your own Free Will." (The Voice's irruptions into daily life are announced by a debased jingle, a derisory quotation of Isaiah 40:4: "Every valley shall be exalted and every mountain . . . shall be made low" as set in Handel's *Messiah*.)

The exposition of the nature of free will in this state shows it to be a Frankfurt-style compatibilism as set out in my present chapter. Recall that this compatibilism is a construct (but then, so is Hartley's dystopia), in which a controlling intervener fixes the subject's brain so that any incipient deviation of the latter from the former's intention is immediately detected and rectified; consequently the subject always acts willingly, in accordance with its own wish, though never freely in the sense of non-deterministically, of having had the chance to wish and do otherwise. Accordingly, in *Facial Justice* the dictator's Voice says "[I]t was to me that you owed the power to express your individual longings. Did you realize that my provisions for you are the form your free-will takes?" This free will is the subject taken up in Hartley's chapter 20, at the literal center of his book.

The book is called *Facial Justice* because its chief leveling device is a reverse-cosmetic "betafication" of pretty female alpha-faces into inexpressively standard beta-faces. It is this obliteration of physical individualism that contributes most to the extirpation of active freedom in the betafied bearer of the mask and of all discriminating feeling in the pursuing male. So the novel acknowledges that human freedom belongs to the incarnate soul.

Chapter X. The Science of Will: *Neuroscience and Psychiatry*

Sources

Ainslie, George. *Breakdown of the Will*. Cambridge: Cambridge Univ. Press, 2001.

——. "Précis of *Breakdown of the Will*." *Behavioral and Brain Sciences* 28 (2005): 635–73.

Baars, Bernard J. "Contrastive Phenomenology: A Thoroughly Empirical Approach to Consciousness." In *The Nature of Consciousness: Philosophical Debates*. Edited by Ned Block, Owen Flanagan, and Güven Güzeldere. Cambridge: MIT Press, 1998.

Banks, William P. "Does Consciousness Cause Misbehavior?" In *Does Consciousness Cause Behavior?* Edited by Susan Pockett, William P. Banks, and Shaun Gallagher. Cambridge: MIT Press, 2009.

Baumeister, Roy F., Matthew T. Gailliot, and Dianne M. Tice, "Free Willpower: A Limited Resource Theory of Volition, Choice, and Self-Regulation." In Ezequiel Morsella, John A. Bargh, Peter M. Gollwitzer, eds. *Oxford Handbook of Human Action*. Oxford: Oxford Univ. Press, 2009.

Gazzaniga, Michael S. *The Ethical Brain*. New York: Dana Press, 2005.

Georgopoulos, Apostolos R. and Elissaios Karageorgiou. "Representations of Voluntary Arm Movements in the Motor Cortex and their Transformations." In *Understanding Events: From Perception to Action*. Edited by Thomas F. Shipley and Jeffrey M. Zachs. Oxford: Oxford Univ. Press, 2008.

Güzeldere, Güzen, "The Many Faces of Consciousness: A Field Guide," Introduction to *The Nature of Consciousness*. Edited by Ned Block, Owen Flanagan, and Güven Güzeldere. Cambridge: MIT Press, 1998.

Libet, Benjamin. "Do We Have Free Will?" In *The Oxford Handbook of Free Will*. Edited by Robert Kane. Oxford: Oxford Univ. Press, 2002.

Mele, Alfred R. "Autonomy, Self-Control, and Weakness of Will." In *The Oxford Handbook of Free Will*. Edited by Robert Kane. Oxford: Oxford Univ. Press, 2002.

——. *Effective Intentions*. Oxford: Oxford Univ. Press, 2009.

——. "Free Will: Theories, Analysis, Data." In *Does Consciousness Cause Behavior?* Edited by Susan Pockett, William P. Banks, and Shaun Gallagher. Cambridge: MIT Press, 2009.

——. *Motivation and Agency*. Oxford: Oxford Univ. Press, 2003.

——. "Persisting Intentions." *Noûs* 41, no. 4 (2007): 735–57.

———. "Recent Work on Free Will and Science." *American Philosophical Quarterly* 45 (April 2008): 107–30.

Passingham, Richard E. and Hakwan C. Lau. "Free Choice and the Human Brain." In *Does Consciousness Cause Behavior?* Edited by Susan Pockett, William P. Banks, and Shaun Gallagher. Cambridge: MIT Press, 2009.

Sebanz, Natalie and Wolfgang Prinz, eds. *Disorders of Volition.* Cambridge: MIT Press, 2006.

Tse, Peter Ulric. *The Neural Basis of Free Will: Criterial Causation.* Cambridge: MIT Press, 2013.

Walter, Henrik. *Neurophilosophy of Free Will: From Libertarian Illusions to a Concept of Natural Autonomy.* Translated by Cynthia Klohr. Cambridge: MIT Press, 2009.

Wegner, Daniel M. *The Illusion of Conscious Will.* Cambridge: MIT Press, 2002.

1. The term phenomenology first appears in 1764 in J. H. Lambert's *New Organon*, a work setting out how Appearance is related to Truth. It has system-specific meanings in Kant and Hegel; my use is adapted from Husserl, who appropriated the word for a primarily descriptive discipline that reflects on the appearances (phenomena) of *subjective experience*, particularly on the way consciousness *intends* its objects.

2. The brain study of the emotions has become accessible to lay people particularly through the books of a pioneer in the field, Antonio Damasio, for example, *The Feeling of What Happens* (New York: Harcourt, Inc., 1999) and *Looking for Spinoza: Joy, Sorrow, and the Feeling Brain* (New York: Harcourt, Inc., 2003).

3. For example, the first five articles of Sebanz and Prinz, *Disorders of Volition*, 1–85.

4. An accessible review by Benjamin Libet himself of his experiment, its design and results, with a bibliography, is given in Libet, "Do We Have Free Will?" 551–64, 599.

5. Occluded consciousness: perhaps what I am thinking of should be called sub-conscious rather than "unconscious," which invites reference to Freud's "Ucs System," a distinct part of the psychic topography (e.g., "The Unconscious," 1915). To be sure, Freud regarded this atemporal, alogical, amoral, psychic underground, and indeed the whole psyche, as ultimately materially based; **knowledge no more present**: Aristotle distinguishes a first condition of the state of fulfillment (or "actuality," *entelecheia*), which is the possession of knowledge even in sleep, and another, which is its present exercise (*On the Soul* II 412 a).

6. Libet experiment itself: see Note 4 above; **fine-grained critique**: Mele, "Recent Work"; Mele, "Free Will"; Mele, *Motivation and Agency*, 180–94; Mele's is the primary critique. Also: Banks, "Misbehavior," 237–40 and Walter, *Neurophilosophy*, 245–52.

7. Quotation: Libet, "Do We Have Free Will?" 551.

8. Earlier experiments: in Wegner, *Illusion*, 50–52, summary of Kornhuber and Deecke (1965) on readiness potential; in Walter, *Neurophilosophy*, 245–48, summary of Libet (1979) on backward referral.

9. Window of opportunity: Libet, "Do We Have Free Will?" 556–57; **veto possibility**: 557; **free won't**: Gazzaniga, *The Ethical Brain*, 93, quoting Vilayanur Ramachandran.

Here is a fascinating hypothetical question: If it could be demonstrated that some conscious mentation was precisely simultaneous with its brain activity, what would that show? Would it nullify the "which causes which" problem? Would contemporality indicate a causal mutuality, i.e. *causa sui*? Is a Libet-type experiment resultless unless the reaction times to a stimulus are askew?

10. Ten Commandments: Exodus 20:17; "Honor thy father and mother" (no. 5) is the only positive one; the injunction to "Remember to keep the holy Sabbath" is then repeated as a prohibition (no. 4).

11. Monkey experiment: Georgopoulos and Karageorgiou, "Representation of Voluntary Arm Movements," 229–44.

12. Critical scrutiny: see Note 6 above; also Tse's chief criticism in Ch. 9 of *The Neural Basis of Free Will* is that Libet's willing paradigms are too nugatory to generate genuine conscious feelings of willing to begin with. (See Section D herein.)

13. Distal and proximal intentions: Mele, *Effective Intentions*, passim; **acquired intentions**: Mele, *Motivation and Agency*, 185; **forming intentions**: Mele, in "Persisting Intentions," an article devoted to intentions in the sense germane to willing, says hardly anything about the background of intention-formation; **willingness to cooperate**: Mele, "Recent Work," 166.

14. **Wants not volitions**: ibid., 117–18; **urge rather than intention**: Mele, "Free Will," 192–97; **ethical implications, "original sin"**: Libet, "Do We Have Free Will?" 561—Libet actually says this!

15. **"Unconscious mental causation"**: Banks, "Misbehavior"—a thoughtful introduction to a critique of Libet's experiments and the philosophical implications of will-study. (Banks is a graduate of my college.)

There seem to be two main approaches beside the neuroscientific postulate: the Freudian "topographical" Ucs (Note 5 above) and the cognitive Unconscious of cognitive science, which appears in terms of many dichotomies: Güven Güzeldere, "Many Faces of Consciousness," 20–21 and Bernard J. Baars, "Contrastive Phenomenology," 187 ff. The latter gives this apt example of the cognitive unconscious (190): The word "will" is "locally ambiguous" [in a given sentence], but readers won't realize that because "normally only a single one of multivalent events will become conscious at a time." I like this example because this particular multivalence plays so large a role in Will Shakespeare's Sonnets—which count on the multivalent meanings of [W]ill oscillating equivalently beneath or above the cognitive surface:

> Whoever hath her wish, thou hast thy will
> And will to boot, and will in overplus (Sonnet 135)

Stephen Booth thinks it is idle to try to decide which "Will" should be capitalized (*Shakespeare's Sonnets* [New Haven: Yale Univ. Press, 1977], 466).

16. **Philosophical basis**: Walter, *Neurophilosophy*, 249–52—here D. C. Dennett and R.G. Millikan are cited as critics; **actual willing**: Passingham and Lau ("Free Choice," 67–68) make this point too, but in terms of different brain areas involved in the goals people actually set themselves and in laboratory tasks; in particular, they point to the prefrontal cortex as a "global workspace" where relevant information for real-life decision is integrated. Intentions are taken up in Chapter XI, Sec. B, herein.

17. **Imaginary experiment**: Mele, *Effective Intentions*, chap. 7, 131; **in principle not possible**: Banks raises an issue preliminary to mine—the lack of evidence that readiness potential is a necessary and sufficient condition of unconscious activity. However, he goes along with the assumption, on the expectation that tests will confirm or disconfirm the assumption ("Misbehavior," 240).

18. Théodule Ribot (1839–1916) was a French experimental psychologist most famous for his work on memory. His *Diseases of the Will* (1883, Chicago: Open Court, 1915) anticipates contemporary will research. He was a *practical* compatibilist: "We take the volitions as facts . . . without investigating whether these causes suppose other causes *ad infinitum* or whether there is added to them some degree of spontaneity. The question is thus placed in a form acceptable to the determinists and their adversaries, and reconcilable to either hypothesis" (2). But he was, as a scientist, a *theoretical* determinist: "[I]n every voluntary act there are two entirely distinct elements: The state of consciousness, the 'I will' which indicates the situation but which has in itself no efficacy; and a very complex psycho-physiological mechanism, in which alone resides the power to act or restrain" (2). Or again, the volition observed by "subjective psychologists . . . is for us only a simple state of consciousness. It is merely an effect of that psycho-physiological activity . . . only a part of which enters into consciousness under the form of a deliberation. Furthermore *it is not the cause of anything*" (133). Volition is—recall Hobbes—simply the last in a series of states, but here understood as a causal chain, a coordination of anterior states, "a legacy from numberless generations enregistered in the organism" (113). The above is the most elegant evaporation of will into an epiphenomenon I have come across.

Ribot thinks that abnormalities of will, its morbid states, throw light on its nature. Thus he has case studies of Thomas De Quincey (*Confessions of an English Opium Eater*, 1822) for *aboulia*, or incapacity for willing, that is, "defect of impulse," and of Coleridge for "impairment of voluntary attention," and consequent "unbridled automatism," of which his composition of the poem "Kubla Khan" (1797) is to be regarded as an example (30, 73). This pre-professionalized psychology has the charm of recognizing a case while yet describing a man.

19. *Akrasia*: Conclusion, Note 1; **reductionistic approach**: Ainslie, *Breakdown*, 11–12.

20. Explanation of feeling of freedom: 129.

21. Therapeutic consequences: Ainslie is writing as a practicing psychiatrist; addictions, which are the clearest examples of short-sighted alternatives to the rational behavior of weighing costs and benefits and thus true "breakdowns of the will," are his special interest: Ainslie, *Breakdown*, chap. 4.

22. Economic Man: 16; **parabolic and hyperbolic discount curves**: 28 ff.; Ainslie, "Précis," 636.

23. Hyperbolic curve: Ainslie (*Breakdown*, 31 ff.) thinks that the hyperbolic curve is actual people's natural discount curve, and a sign is that the two curves, parabolic and hyperbolic, cross in choice-experiments where the subject is offered a choice between a small reward on short delay and a large one at a longer delay. If he chooses according to the rational curve, the curves for both choices are parabolas bowed so as not to cross; however, if he rationally chooses the larger reward at a longer delay but switches to the smaller one as it comes close, the resulting steeper hyperbolic curve will cross the parabolic one—and that is a representation of what actually tends to happen. I should say here that both the evidence for and the consequences of these people-experiments are much richer than my account—and more convincing than were the neural ones described above. Ainslie thinks neurophysiology so far can't explain conflicted and contravened decisions concerning intense propensities (10).

24. Quotation on will power: Ainslie, *Breakdown*, 116. Will power is a notion whose reality I have little faith in, because those credited with it usually reveal themselves, on closer acquaintance, as in fact being in the grip of some sort of passion—sometimes a cold implacable fixation, sometimes a hot, dominating desire, sometimes a sweetly reasonable attachment—but more of that in the Conclusion.

The point of this note is that, nonetheless, under scientific investigation, will power evinces a quantitative side—it becomes a "depletable resource": Baumeister et al., "Free Willpower," 487–508. Will power was tested in a laboratory setting for two aspects that proved to be related: self-regulation and choice. For example, to study the first, hungry participants were instructed to resist sweets and eat radishes instead. Afterwards they gave up much faster on frustrating tasks set for them; this betokened "depletion" of will power. For choice-making, participants were induced to choose between small options, such as consumer items; a control group rated these without being required to choose. The choosers showed greater decrements in self-regulation than the control group—ate more cookies, solved fewer math problems. These results were interpreted as some sort of energy depletion, and the question became: what energy aside from highly metaphorical kinds, such as Freud's "ego depletion"? The experimenters cite studies to show that willingness of the volunteers to continue to exert themselves was not the issue. They concluded that the depletion is in fact non-metaphorical: low glucose levels: "Glucose provides the power in willpower" (497). Their practical conclusions are modest: In the short term a shot of glucose can boost the stamina necessary to will-power. The long-term empowerment of self-control is much more complex.

25. *Egkrateia*: Conclusion, Note 1; **intertemporal bargaining**: Ainslie, *Breakdown*, part II; **willpower**: chap. 5; **Sirens' Song**: *Odyssey* ii 178—for the temptation in their song, namely nostalgia for the bad old times at Troy, see also Brann, *Homeric Moments* (Philadelphia: Paul Dry Books, 2002), 208–10; *akrasia*: Aristotle, *Nicomachean Ethics* VII, 1147 a and Ainslie, *Breakdown*, 80; **categorical choosing**: Ainslie, *Breakdown*, 80.

26. Intertemporal cooperation: 104; **imagination**: on its powers see Brann, *The World of the Imagination*, passion.

27. Alternative view of the will: Ainslie, *Breakdown*, 188; **experimental evidence**: ibid., 120; **additive calculus**: ibid., 84–85; **experience of free will**: ibid., 129.

Chapter XI. Will Overwhelmed: *Into the Twenty-first Century*

Sources

Anscombe, G. E. M. *Intention*. Oxford: Basil Blackwell, 1957.

Arpaly, Nomy. *Merit, Meaning, and Human Bondage: An Essay on Free Will*. Princeton: Princeton Univ. Press, 2006.

Baer, John, James C. Kaufman, and Roy F. Baumeister, eds. *Are We Free?: Psychology and Free Will*. Oxford: Oxford Univ. Press, 2008.

Balaguer, Mark. *Free Will as an Open Scientific Problem*. Cambridge: MIT Press, 2010.

Block, Ned, Owen Flanagan, and Güven Güzeldere, eds. *The Nature of Consciousness: Philosophical Debates*. Cambridge: MIT Press, 1998.

Brown, Warren S., Nancy Murphy, and H. Newton Malony, eds. *Whatever Happened to the Soul?: Scientific and Theological Portraits of Human Nature*. Minneapolis: Fortress Press, 1998.

Campbell, Joseph Keim, Michael O'Rourke, and Harry S. Silverstein, eds. *Action, Ethics, and Responsibility*. Cambridge: MIT Press, 2004.

Ciprut, Jose V., ed. *Freedom: Reassessments and Rephrasings*. Cambridge: MIT Press, 2004.

Dennett, Daniel C. *Elbow Room: The Varieties of Free Will Worth Wanting*. Cambridge: MIT Press, 1984.

Edelman, Gerald M. *Second Nature: Brain Science and Human Knowledge*. New Haven: Yale Univ. Press, 2006.

Ekstrom, Laura Waddell, ed. *Agency and Responsibility: Essay on the Metaphysics of Freedom*. Boulder: Westview Press, 2001.

Feinberg, Todd E. and Julian Paul Keenan, eds. *The Lost Self: Pathologies of the Brain and Identity*. Oxford: Oxford Univ. Press, 2005.

Fischer, John Martin, Robert Kane, Derk Pereboom, and Manuel Vargas. *Four Views on Free Will*. Oxford: Blackwell Publishing, 2007.

Ford, Anton, Jennifer Hornsby, and Frederick Stoutland, eds. *Essays on Anscombe's* Intention. Cambridge: Harvard Univ. Press, 2011.

Frankfurt, Harry G. *The Importance of What We Care About: Philosophical Essays*. Cambridge: Cambridge Univ. Press, 1988.

Gazzaniga, Michael S. *The Ethical Brain*. New York: Dana Press, 2005.

Honderich, Ted. *How Free Are You? The Determinism Problem*. 2nd ed. Oxford: Oxford Univ. Press, 2002.

Horst, Steven. *Laws, Mind, and Free Will*. Cambridge: MIT Press, 2011.

Kane, Robert, ed. *The Oxford Handbook of Free Will*. Oxford: Oxford Univ. Press, 2002.

Kelso, J. A. Scott, and David A. Engstrøm. *The Complementary Nature*. Cambridge: MIT Press, 2006.

Larmore, Charles. *The Practices of the Self* (2004). Translated by Sharon Bowman. Chicago: Univ. of Chicago Press, 2010.

Mele, Alfred R. *Motivation and Agency*. Oxford: Oxford Univ. Press, 2003.

Morsella, Ezequiel, John A. Bargh, and Peter M. Gollwitzer, eds. *Oxford Handbook of Human Action*. Oxford: Oxford Univ. Press, 2009.

Murphy, Nancy. *Bodies and Souls, or Spirited Bodies?* Cambridge: Cambridge Univ. Press, 2006.

Ross, Don, David Spurrett, Harold Kincaid, and G. Lynn Stephens, eds. *Distributed Cognition and the Will: Individual Volition and Social Context*. Cambridge: MIT Press, 2007.

Searle, John R. *Intentionality: An Essay in the Philosophy of Mind*. Cambridge: Cambridge Univ. Press, 1983.

———. *Minds, Brains and Science*. Cambridge: Harvard Univ. Press, 1984.

Sorabji, Richard. *Self: Ancient and Modern Insights into Individuality, Life, and Death*. Chicago: Univ. of Chicago Press, 2006.

Thagard, Paul. *The Brain and the Meaning of Life*. Princeton: Princeton Univ. Press, 2010.

Walter, Henrik. *Neurophilosophy of Free Will: From Libertarian Illusions to a Concept of Natural Autonomy*. Translated by Cynthia Klohr. Cambridge: MIT Press, 2009.

Wegner, Daniel M. *The Illusion of Conscious Will*. Cambridge: MIT Press, 2002.

———."Précis of *The Illusion of Conscious Will*," *Behavior and Brain Sciences* 27 (2004).

1. John Milton, *Paradise Lost* (1674), 2nd ed., ed. Scott Elledge (New York: W.W. Norton, 1993), II 549 ff. (my italics in the quotation). "Partial" here means *both* self-serving *and* polyphonic. These hellish activities sound much like the Great Books conversations of my college.

2. **Loss of tradition**: one not so good consequence of having no direct relation to works whose citation carries cachet is ludicrous misquotation and misapprehension. For example, some

of the lines just cited from *Paradise Lost* are alluded to in a lead article on free will; it was lost on the author that his predecessors, these debating angels, were in fact citizens of Pandemonium (see also Ch. IX, Note 1[f], herein). It will happen to us all, but perhaps it shouldn't so much.

3. Most voluminously debated: Kane in *The Oxford Handbook of Free Will* (p. 3) quoting a 1987 history of philosophy; it's been exponential since then.

4. Distributed self: for example, Andy Clark, "Soft Selves and Ecological Control," in Ross et al., *Distributed Cognition*—"[A]ll kinds of human activities turn out to be partly supported by quasi-independent non-conscious subsystems" (110)—not exactly Nietzschean diction, however.

5. Two notions of illusion: Saul Smilansky, "Free Will, Fundamental Dualism, and the Centrality of Illusion" in Kane, *Oxford Handbook of Free Will*; and Daniel M. Wegner, *The Illusion of Conscious Will* and "Précis of *The Illusion of Conscious Will*."

6. Compass example: Wegner, *Illusion*, 317.

7. Epiphenomenal will: ibid., ix, 318, and "Précis," 29 ("Open Peer Commentary"); **authorship emotion**, i.e., the will as affect: Wegner, *Illusion*, 325 ff.; **consciousness doesn't know unconscious processes**: 67—this is, of course, true only before the cognitive scientist clues out these processes; **inscrutable mechanisms**: 98.

8. Three principles: 70–95; **intention normally understood**: Wegner, p. 18.

9. Thomas Aquinas on intention: *Summa Theologia*, First Part of the Second Part, Q. 12, "On Intention." (Recall that there is a broader meaning of intention as the mental reach for and comprehending of its object; see Ch. III, Note 48, herein.)

10. Intention: Anscombe, *Intention*, 67–70; also Anton Ford et al., *Essays*; **intentionality**: John R. Searle, *Intentionality*. Searle deliberately omits reference to older inquiries to get to his own theory. (For the revival of the medieval topic of intention see, for example, *The Cambridge Companion to Brentano*, ed. Dale Jacquette [Cambridge: Cambridge Univ. Press, 2004].) This analysis of all sorts of intentional phenomena contributes the following clarifying distinction: "Belief and desire are what is left over if you subtract the causal self-referentiality from the Intentional contents of cognitive and volitive representational Intentional states" (*Intentionality*, 103–5). In other words, having something in mind and wanting it are something over and above mere belief plus desire. This extra feature, "causal self-referentiality," is Searle's term for the very intending force: Intention "figures its own conditions of satisfaction," meaning that intending itself causes its own fulfillment; if I know something I want, I'll go after it—when I'm in the intending mode. I'll put it this way: Willing is to wishing as cognition-plus-volition is to belief-plus-desire.

A discussion of "Belief-Desire Psychologies" by Steven Horst (*Laws, Mind, and Free Will*, chap. 12), dealing with "attempts to craft scientifically rigorous psychological theories that make use of intentional notions" (228), introduces another helpful distinction for thinking about will, somewhat different from Mele's "distal" and "proximal" intentions: "dispositional and occurrent states." "Disposition" is the mystery word of Ryle's will-analysis, but it is one recognizable way to speak of what I have been urging as a deep characteristic of genuine willing—a "from-way-back" feature, a having something in mind without necessarily thinking of it explicitly now or ever. Very strictly speaking, a dispositional intention is for Horst a belief and desire we might deeply hold but have never really articulated, yet recognize upon hearing it made explicit for us, e.g., "This is a bad situation," and also "Peace at any price." Occurrent situations are in the mind here and now.

11. Volitional process: William R. Miller and David J. Atencio, "Free Will as a Proportion of Variance," in John Baer et al., *Are We Free?*, 280.

12. Collective will: 286–89.

13. Alternative schemata: for example, motivation → practical reason/motivational machinery → behavior, in Mariam Thalos, "The Sources of Behavior: Toward a Naturalistic, Control Account of Agency" in Ross et al., *Distributed Cognition*, 130. It should be said that human nature, being terminally wayward when its schematic capture is attempted, there are endless construable cases where the proposal simply fails (since rigorously analytic intellects refuse Aristotle's sensible rule that nature is what happens always *or for the most part*). The resolution of the paradox in the above title, namely "Naturalistic Control" (that is, deterministic vs. "agential") comes from the divorce of cause from control such that control is compatible with non-causal intention. "Control is a global affair," a matter of rank, authority of top-down directives that kick in when there is conflict, while causation is local, "as all causal matters are" (138). I can't tell whether this analysis does not beg the question: In a military command structure (the paradigm given), at some point a directive seems to me to have to trickle down causally.

14. Operational definition of consciousness: Alfred R. Mele, "Conscious Intention," in Campbell et al., *Action, Ethics, and Responsibility*, 85; **internal evidence for consciousness**: this introspective evidence, which seems not just to me, but generally, to be assumed as the necessary antecedent to "reporting consciousness" (though terminal reductionists might not go along), provoked this question for me: What is the relation of "I experience consciousness, therefore I *am* conscious" to the Cartesian "I think, therefore I *am*"? It is, so it seems, that Descartes is thinking so as to *conclude* from thinking to existing, while I am *reflecting*, doubling back, from a secondary self-consciousness so as to *confirm* a primary fact of experience. That's not an inference so much as a direct internal report, inner speech about an internal state. Such articulation, however, in fact *corroborates* us to ourselves.

15. Consciousness deserts: William James, quoted in Alfred R. Mele, "Conscious Intentions," 100—that's, of course, not always so: there are highly useless persistent states of consciousness, such as the inability to get a worn-out thought out of one's mind. **layfolk**: 102.

16. Subtypes of intending: there are quite a few, three of which are described here:

1. Trying-intending: an agent might have a volition to *try* to do rather than to do something, betokening an uncertainty of expectation concerning execution; so he might, for example, begin by intending to find out whether or not he could do it (Carl Ginet, "Trying to Act," in *Freedom and Determinism*, eds. Joseph Keim Campbell et al. [Cambridge: MIT Press, 2004], 93–94). Aristotle makes determination of doableness part of every deliberation.
2. Biological-intending: Here intentionality is divorced from consciousness and attributed to the development of structure, from organs to mental states, by evolutionary causes, that is, selection; our knowledge structures are intentional, "meant for something" or "about something," because they have become suited to the world, adjusted to it, in the course of evolution (Walter, *Neurophilosophy*, 196–98; he warns that the chasm between a "biology of knowledge" and human knowing is as yet deep).
3. Collective-intending: the question is whether groups can have intended states (shades of Rousseau's general will!). If what makes creatures possess an "intentional system," is the development of goals, along with internal dispositions to guide them in reaching these goals in their environment, can a group be such a creature? Evolutionarily developed organisms are models of a unified intentional system with sub-goals and sub-dispositions. So might, on a human level, be a squad of soldiers; the individual soldiers might have different intentions in participating in the mission: solidarity with buddies, safety in numbers, joy in warfare, fear of court-martial—while the unit's mission and its tactical plan is not even known to anyone but the lieutenant. This unit is an intentional group. (Todd Jones, "The Metaphysics of Collective Agency," in Campbell et al., *Action, Ethics, and Responsibility*). This analysis, here much simplified, concludes that it is unclear whether such intentional groups can be moral agents (232). I have doubts about the group-intentional argument; couldn't one say that moving from intentionality (a personal feature) to an intentional system (a group feature) is begging the question by generalizing the intentional subject before showing that intentionality may be so impersonalized?

17. Intention in sum: Ted Honderich, *How Free Are You?*, 57–62; **unintended consequences**: I find myself using the notion without recalling its exact source; it comes from the sphere of anti-dirigiste economists opposed to central planning, even (or especially) by experts, who intend one outcome and eventually get another (because "the best laid schemes o' mice an' men gang aft agley"). Last-minute discovery: The first analyst of the notion is Robert Merton in an article "The Unanticipated Consequences of Purposive Social Action" (1936). The paradigm is Adam Smith's "Invisible Hand."

18. Mental acts: Searle (*Intentionality*, 3) critiques the phrase with respect to "dispositional" terms such as desiring and intending (a usage featured in Ryle's *Concept of Mind*), because if you ask people, "What are you doing now?" they don't answer, "I am now desiring to read a really good book on Intentionality." (To be sure, I can imagine a wit saying just that; most speech held impossible in linguistic analysis is quite possible in quirky life; it also seems to me that someone cogitating can answer the question "What are you doing?" by saying "I'm thinking," and upon being offered a penny for the done thought-deed can deliver a thought. I should say that Thomas Aquinas treats mental agency in the mode of Aristotelian *activity*, in Latin: *operatio*, by distinguishing between that which issues in an external *act* and that which, like desire, "remains within the agent itself, perfecting it"—*Disputed Questions on Truth*, 1257 c.e., Qq. 8, 6.)

A word on act, action, and activity, agent, and agency: In writing on agency, the first three are used interchangeably, though the dictionary says that an "act" is a single deed, and an "action" is often the process of acting. "Activity" is often used of energetic action, also of the state of acting and the nature of acts. (It is also a standard translation for Aristotle's term *energeia*, "being at work," in the sense of being all there.) "Agency," the chief term of this section, means the condition of being an agent; one who *causes action* represents "agent-causation (AC)."

19. Thomas on agent and action: e.g., *Disputed Questions on Evil* (1272 c.e.), Q. 6, Reply; **Nietzsche on invention of agency**: *The Will to Power* (begun c. 1887), no. 136.

20. Thomas on self-moving will: *Disputed Questions on Evil*, Q. 6, Reply: will "clearly . . . moves itself just as it moves our other powers" and "will . . . is not itself moved by any other power than itself "; **will** (somewhat ironically) **as "prime mover unmoved"**: Roderick M. Chisholm, "Human Freedom and Self," in Ekstrom, *Agency and Responsibility*, 134 nn. 11, 12.

21. Near-infinity of agency questions: here are two polar-opposite approaches, early and later: Maurice Blondel, in his *Action* of 1893 (trans. Olivia Blanchette [Notre Dame: Univ. of Notre Dame Press, 2007]) revived the long lapsed reflection on the title theme. His book is a philosophical theology of action, taken to mean all human responses to reality, including willing. Human beings have a deliberated "desire will" (*volonté voulue*), which operates in the phenomenal world and whose achievements are never adequate to the seeking engaged in by a second, primordial "willing will" (*volonté voulante*) which acts in the superepiphenomenal realm. The gap is filled only by a supraphenomenal action, that of God immanent in humans who are supported from beyond by divine Grace. (The book is huge and obscure, and I had recourse to encyclopedic summaries.)

The *Oxford Handbook of Human Action* (ed. Morsella et al.), on the other hand, offers thirty scientific articles devoted to the "reverse engineering" of human action, that is, to taking apart the evolved biological mechanism so as to discover the basic elements from which emerge actions as unregarded as carrying a spoon to the mouth or as significant as recruiting will power, as general as mind moving body and as focused as the voluntariness of skeletal muscles. The lay reader's residue-question will be a more informed version of the perennial problem: *Given* that all human agency is—probably—subserved by biological-neural mechanisms, do these *fully account* for voluntary conduct?

22. Responsible agent: Chisholm, "Human Freedom," 126 ff.

23. Do otherwise: ibid.; **goodness compels**: e.g. Thomas, *Disputed Questions on Evil*, Q. 6.

24. Buridan: Jean Buridan (born c. 1300 c.e.) introduced the notion of impetus to the West; **probabilistic physics**: for a review of opinions on its bearings on free will, see David Hodgson, "Quantum Physics, Indeterminism, and Free Will," in Kane, *Oxford Handbook of Free Will*, 99 ff. Of course, the nature of probabilistic physics is not one of "meaningless compulsion" but of perfectly rational mathematics. In its application to human action, however, it appears that way.

25. Prime mover: Chisholm ("Human Freedom," 134) makes this point (without exactly endorsing it), going so far as to say that some attribute unmoved mover capacity only to God (not exactly Aristotle—both the human soul and the planets are *sorts* of unmoved mover, unmoved from the outside, self-movers (*Physics* 192 b ff., *Metaphysics* 1073 a ff.); **no science of man**: Chisholm says this, p. 134.

This ancient phrase, "up to us" or "in our power," which became a Stoic formula (though it already occurs in Aristotle; for example, forming a mental image is "up to us," *On the Soul* 427 b), might be a candidate for a basic definition of agency, except that the Stoics meant it more as an action-preventative, or as a restriction to "immanent action," that is, to action that stays within the soul. For they thought that the agency practiced upon ourselves is the one agency the efficacy of which we control (my Ch. II, Sec. B, herein).

26. **Immattered reason**: Aristotle, *On the Soul* I 403 a; **second order desire**: Frankfurt, "Freedom of the Will and the Concept of a Person," in *Importance*, 13 ff.; **felt reasons**: Mele (*Motivation and Agency*, 222 ff.) identifies such a higher-order desire as "a desire to act for superior reasons." In my version, such a desire is indeed infused with reason but reciprocally, such superior reasons are also elevated desires.

Of course, "second order" mentation seems to pose the problem of an infinite regression for self-consciousness, thinking of thinking and wilfull willing—"turtles all the way up," so to speak. But, as I said, I think the regression might be stopped by imputing—occasional—reasonableness to reason: that's enough!

27. **Traditional views are dead**: Paul Sheldon Davies, "What Kind of Agent Are We? A Naturalistic Framework for the Study of Human Agency," in Ross et al., *Distributed Cognition*, 3, 58. This article consists of four "directions for naturalistic exploration," said to be uncontroversial; here recounted in my, somewhat simplified, terms: 1. Expect high-level notions to be eliminated by, reduced to, low-level mechanisms, 2. do not hang on to, "save," concepts respected by virtue of tradition or culture, 3. the same for psychological ideas, 4. include evolutionary explanations. These pretty imperious directives, more precisely specified in the article, prevent "conceptual imperialism" in favor of progressing exploration. Naturalism-as-exploration is said *not* to be a metaphysical thesis. To expect to discover truth by predetermining what it is not and to tell others where to look for it seems to me metaphysical as hell; thus the (uncredited) forerunner of this undertaking, Descartes' *Rules for the Direction of the Mind* (1628), needed to be underwritten by *Meditations on First Philosophy* (1641).You no sooner read the above directives than you see why I am excusing myself here from attempting the relevant metaphysics; it would have to be a huge grounding work entitled *On the Things of Nature*. The latter part of this rousing article is occupied with showing that late in his *Illusion of Conscious Will* (see this chapter, Sec. A), Wegner, in admitting control and responsibility, muddies the pure naturalism of the illusion thesis.

quotation: Milton, *Paradise Lost* IX 351–352.

28. *The Oxford Handbook of Free Will* (ed. Kane) was my source book for problem formulation. Three recent books present naturalist theses of consciousness that would do away with the ideal agent. They are by Michael S. Gazzaniga, Gerald M. Edelman, and Paul Thagard (Bibliography above).

In each of these there is a crucial argument or formulation that I simply cannot make out. It appears to me like the fallacy of transiting into another genus. Writing on free will, Gazzaniga says: If the human brain carries out its work before one becomes consciously aware of a thought, it would appear that "the brain enables the mind" (*Ethical Brain*, 92). (He is referring to Libet's experiments, for the critique of which, see Ch. X, Sec. B, herein; in fact brain lesions, which affect mental functions, show the same negatively.) My problem is how to get from "enable" to "determine." Moreover, although he says that neuroscience will never find the brain correlate of responsibility because responsibility is a social construct (101), this argument seems to leap over the phenomenon of conscience. He *might* argue that conscience is only social judgment internalized, but that takes a lot of psychological hypothesizing. In any case, why is a social construct *ipso facto* without a neurophysiology?

Edelman clarifies the logic: There is an error in "the failure to distinguish physical causation from logical entailment . . . [N]eural action in the core *entails* consciousness, just as the spectrum of hemoglobin in your blood is entailed by the quantum mechanical structure of that molecule" (40). Now "entails" in logic means if A is true B must follow; I can see that consciousness must follow from neural action, but once again, "follow from" is not the same as "determined by" (i.e., fixed in respect to all the qualia); moreover, how do I know whether the emergence of blood-constituents from quantum mechanics is even remotely analogous to the emergence of consciousness from neural activity?

Thagard, in his section "Decisions of the Brain," asks us to "consider how the brain represents actions and goals" (*Brain and the Meaning of Life*, 123 ff.) and uses representational or encoding language throughout. He concludes that decision making is not the serial inference of arguments or the mathematical calculation of decision theory (which, of course, isn't what I think, to begin with) "but rather a process of parallel constraint satisfaction performed throughout the coordination of multiple brain areas" (125). My general difficulty here is that the language of representation and encoding awards implies the priority of representable goals non-neurally conceived. In the quotation above, the particular problem is: What are the criteria of satisfaction; how are they known, and who is the beneficiary to be satisfied? It is simply unclear to me which really comes—perhaps unconsciously—first for the writer: conscious agent or neural mechanism.

29. Soul and self: Sorabji's *Self* is a mine of thoughtful analysis and of references to ancient, modern, and contemporary treatments of the self. He makes a careful case for an ancient notion of the self (interpretable as contradicting the view in my text) and argues specifically against "Apparent Denials of an Early Philosophy of Self" (48 ff.). It turns out, however, that his understanding of the early self is very wide. It includes *individuality*, 'I'-thoughts, not as an "extra entity besides the embodied human being," but as having *reflexivity*, that is, the I-sayer means himself; it has *thickness*, that is, the I-sayer means much more than a thin "subject of awareness" and intends references to personal history; moreover the self is a "person," here meaning it takes complete *ownership* of thoughts and psychological states. All these features do *not*, Sorabji thinks, add up to an essence, but the "thick" self does give us a sense of *identity*, though this same self would cease to exist if its autobiography were modified ("What is the Self?" 20 ff.). This description will, indeed, hold both of soul and self; it simply does not concentrate so much as I would on the reflexivity of *my*-Self. That self-intention, however, seems to me crucial as being a way to speak of self-consciousness, self-objectification—the source, as I think, of consciously responsible agency.

30. Self: the reflexive pronoun "myself" precedes in time the substantive [my] Self, which is developed from it (*Oxford English Dictionary*, p. 2715). Of course there are *reflexive*, self-referring pronouns in Greek and Latin (acc., *heauton, se*), but they: 1. are gendered, and 2. have no nominative, so they are not so easily understood as analogous to "I, my-self." There is, however, an *intensive* Greek *autos* and Latin *ipse*. I think the English Self includes both the reflexive and the intensive sense: self that has become a problem to itself; actually this is Augustine speaking: *quaestio mihi factus sum*, "I am made a question to myself." That only goes to show that there are ancient moderns: Augustine, the inventor of the will and some of its problems, and the Stoics, the inventors of naturalistic representationalism, the prevailing modern cognitive theory.

31. Plato: *Republic* 511 d–e; **Aristotle**: *On the Soul* III 8—I think that Aristotle's notion of mind thinking itself is *not* self-consciousness, for thought of thought (*noesis noesos: Metaphysics* XII 1072 b, *On the Soul* II 430 a), be it God's or ours, leaves no reason for an extra self to be conscious; the whole mind so activated is its thought without remainder. Put another way, this is not doubling-back, self-reflection: "I *on* myself"; but identification, self-absorption: "thought *with* itself."

32. "The field and spacious palaces": Augustine, *Confessions* X viii—for all his pathbreaking, Augustine is here an ancient.

33. Subject becomes object: I wonder whether the reversal of the meaning that subject and object undergo at the beginning of modernity is related to the shift from soul to self: "subject," which used to mean what subjects itself to the soul's scrutiny, now means the underlying I that scrutinizes itself (see Ch. II, Sec. D, herein).

34. Believers among practitioners: this holds over a large number of terms practically proscribed by the present philosophical profession, but still current not only among the "folk" but also among the intellect's working stiffs. For example, *Representation*, impugned in philosophy, is a working term in cognitive science; *Soul* is totally out of fashion in philosophy and science but not among, for example, my students who tend to think they have one, not to speak of believers, a large segment of Americans. (An account of the soul's disappearance is given in Murphy *et al.* and in Brown (Chapter Bibliography). These books defend a non-reductionist physicalism, in which the higher spiritual functions "emerge" from lower physical ones.)

There is, furthermore, *beauty*, more or less proscribed in contemporary esthetics but alive and well in ordinary conversation; above all, there is *will power* (hence, by implication, will), thrown in doubt by neurophilosophy, but alive in parental and pedagogical exhortations, and numerous moral ascriptions; **identity pathologies**: the brain anatomy underlying healthy agency has been mapped by the scanning of subjects who used either an engaged joystick to control a visually presented cursor or a disconnected joystick while watching a cursor moving under the experimenter's control. When the joystick is disengaged and there is a mismatch between the subject's action and the observed effect, different brain locations are activated than when there is a sense of control because the joystick is effective (Seth J. Gillihan and Martha J. Farah, "The Cognitive Neuroscience of the Self: Insights from the Functional Neuroimaging of the Normal Brain," in Feinberg and Keenan, *The Lost Self*, 23–24). Also see "The Enduring Self" by J. Allan Hobson in the same volume.

35. Hume, self: Daniel C. Dennett, "My Body Has a Mind of Its Own" and Andy Clark, "Soft Selves and Ecological Control" in Ross et al, *Distributed Cognition*; **ownerless streams of consciousness**: Sorabji, *Self*, 265 ff.; **narrative**: 172 ff.

36. Emergence: in the mind-brain debate, there are three dramatically distinct claims: flat-out identity (reductionism), emergence (supervenience), and dualism (two-substances). Of these, emergence seems to me the most promising. Its proponents wrestle with the problem of converting a seeming miracle into a scientific explanation: to show how a higher-level state, displaying new characteristics, *results* from lower-level elements, in particular how introspectively reported psychic phenomena arise from externally observable somatic events; see Eva Brann, *Feeling Our Feelings*, 507–8 n. 5.

37. Description of self: an anthropological distinction is applicable to this endeavor— that between "experience-near" and "experience-distant" (or "phenomenological"/"objectivist," etc.). "Love" is an experience-near concept, "object cathexis" is an experience-distant one. The distinction comes from Clifford Geertz, "'From the Native's Point of View': On the Nature of Anthropological Understanding," in *Local Knowledge* (New York: Basic Books, 1983), 56–57. It is from the native's point of view that I wish to think about myself; much of academic writing about the will is so experience-distant that natives in the throes of experience can't relate its concepts to their own will.

Even a great anthropologist can get himself into discipline-derived difficulties, though. Geertz says (committed observer of cultural uniqueness that he is) that empathy of the fieldworker for his subjects is not possible and that an anthropologist gets at the most intimate notion of what a Javanese, Balinese, or Moroccan self is, not by imagining himself as someone else, but by searching out and analyzing the symbolistic forms—words, images, institutions, behaviors— in terms of which people represent themselves to each other: "The concept of person is, in fact, an excellent vehicle by means of which to examine this whole question of how to go about poking into another people's turn of mind" (58–59). The trouble is that the resulting description reads very much like *being* in an other's mind; in any case, it seems not unlike the way we go about looking for or into our own selves: "In the country of the blind, who are not as unobservant as they look, the one-eyed is not king, he is spectator" (58). So, I say, is this intro-spector to her own responding self; she is *both* one-eyed observer and blind inhabitant. In Mischa Berlinski's wonderful novel *Fieldwork* (2007), such a watcher-dweller is poignantly delineated.

38. Voiceless dialogue: Plato, *Sophist* 263 e.

39. What freedom of will is not: see Note 46 below.

40. Great writer: Thomas Mann, *Death in Venice*, the Phaedrus passage; **accompaniment**: Aristotle speaks of pleasure as a supervening feeling in somewhat this way, *On the Soul* 413 b and Brann, *Feeling Our Feelings*, 51; **self-communing**: it is, naturally, possible to think the opposite; Charles Larmore devotes his thoughtful book *The Practices of Self* to an analysis and a critique of self-reflection, the more appealing for eschewing philosophical methodology. Larmore devalues the "cognitive" reflection by which we try to *know* ourselves better in favor of "practical" reflection in the course of which we *espouse a belief* and with it a resolve to care—a commitment to a practice. I shall want to urge that a really good antecedent to action, sliding fairly smoothly into doing, is the—impractical, meaning non-utilitarian—inquiry into self and being. But Larmore's approach has attractions, to me the chief one being his opposition to a programmed life, a life-plan that makes a lifetime an object of control, often based on chosen conformity to given models. In my terms, this would be a willed life, one not open to the not-yet-imagined (177 ff.).

41. For my fellow humans: Geertz ("Native's Point of View," 60) says of his Javanese that, for all the shabbiness of their lives, "perhaps most importantly, the problem of the self—its nature, function and mode of operation—was pursued with a sort of reflective intensity one could find among ourselves in only the most recherché settings indeed." Why recherché? You'll find it wherever people have the courage to open up—for example, among our students, and sometimes our campus security, and housekeeping people—our whole community.

42. Negative shape: Eva Brann, "The Second Power of Questions," in *Critical Reasoning in Contemporary Culture*," ed. Richard A. Talaska (New York: State Univ. of New York Press, 1992), 317; **exhilarating sense**: Nietzsche, who, most of all thinkers I've read, incessantly calls attention to the lonely suffering of the true philosophers of the future, "the heroic burden bearers" (*Will to Power*, no. 971), is not the most reliable witness for the feel of thinking, because: 1. he is, after all, engaged in willful subversion and radical origination of thought, rather than in the deliberately submissive tradition that seeks the "adequation of intellect and thing," and for that rogue mode there is and ought to be a price paid, and 2. he expresses himself in a German in which eloquence and wit enter an alliance of perfection and spice, and the very exploit of embodying non-conforming views in such canonical diction cannot help but be a consolatory exhilaration; **free means love**: "Indo-European Roots" Appendix of the *American Heritage Dictionary* (1992) under "pri," p. 2121; **Aristotle**: *On the Soul* 413 b.

43. Not novel: I imagine—although I have not found any references attesting to this, my sense—that many people must have the experience described in the text. Yet, for example, in a book specifically on the term, *Freedom* (ed. Jose V. Ciprut), all the articles, even those dealing with salvation, are framed in terms of externally experienced or bestowed liberation.

44. Negative Liberty: Bentham's phrase, also Isaiah Berlin, "Two Concepts of Liberty" in *Four Essays on Liberty* (Oxford: Oxford Univ. Press, 1971); **ways of formulating**: *Oxford Handbook of Free Will*, 211, 339, 357, and 457; **responsibility without freedom**: Ch. IX, Note 4, herein; **takes on the meaning**: see Campbell et al., *Action, Ethics, and Responsibility*, 47, 105, 175, and 254, the argument against contextualism.

45. Quotation: Searle, *Minds*, chap. 6, p. 99. Not being able to prove the claim of existence for consciousness false isn't, I think, the same as the admittedly disabling inability to make it falsifiable, that is, to frame it so as to admit arguments against it; **I am conscious that I am conscious that I am . . .** : this turtles-all-the-way-down argument, this infinite regress, or better, iteration, seems to me to thicken and bring about the very conviction that I can't get rid of the thought that I *am* conscious, all the way down. But that sense is like mathematical induction: You don't have to think the steps to get the whole.

46. Our decision bubbles up: Dennett, *Elbow Room*, 78; **central headquarters**: this is a Stoic formulation, the *hegenomikon* (Ch. II, Sec. B, herein). Dennett thinks that "faced with inability to 'see' (by 'introspection') where the center or *source* of our free action is" (79), we fill the cognitive vacuum with a magical entity, the active self, an "unmoved mover." (See Ch. I, Sec. C, herein.) To undercut this theory of a mysterious inner sanctum for a free central agent, Dennett develops the notion of the self as a locus of self-control through a process of social interaction and personal self-improvement and meta-level-control reasoning (87)—a process of self-creation. (You might call it a "be-as-you-go" plan.) The problem Dennett acknowledges is that, in a determinist setting, it seems to be the case that whom we make ourselves into, able decider or "patzer," is a matter of luck (91 ff.). So the question becomes what *can* this self achieve? Of this, below.

But meanwhile I want to say that often I simply can't follow Dennett's further argument in the sense that I stall at the propositions set out. Example I: "It seems that we can conclude that *if* determinism is true, then any belief we ever have about there being more than one possible future for us is false" (102). That doesn't seem right: Such a belief would not be false but *senseless*, since "possible future" would be meaningless, just as much human talk would be evolutionarily determined, somehow advantageous, babble. Example II: Determined deliberation is *real* because "Wouldn't a determined thunderstorm be a real thunderstorm?" (103). That doesn't seem right: A determined deliberation is a contradiction in terms; a determined thunderstorm is a redundancy (at least on the hypothesis of natural-law determinism, and neglecting weather-science probabilism). Example III: The deterministic world produces creatures who will "pass, in a final self-annihilating spasm of ratiocination, into complete stolidity" (104). Though I am fascinated by imagined quandaries of deterministic agency, that doesn't seem quite right: In real life, even committed determinists blithely make decisions—the victory of living wisdom over academic theory. After all, the perplexity is that chosen apathy and illusionist action are *exactly* equally pointless—and equally appropriate—under determinism.

What Dennett's argument for naturalistic freedom seems to evade is this stubborn perplexity: How can we purposefully intervene in nature's law-determined state of affairs at any moment—unless: 1. we ourself step out of our natural being, and 2. nature proves amenable to redirection from outside itself? Here is the bold, duplex truth collected from a lot of books: Nobody knows how; no one *in effect* believes it doesn't happen. Otherwise put: No one knows whether human beings have extranatural powers of interference or whether nature offers remissions from her determinism or both. But Dennett tries.

So back to "can"—what *can* the self do? "Can" has to do with possibility; there is logical possibility (consistently describable), physical possibility (compatible with the laws of nature), and *epistemic* possibility (consistent with my knowledge). This last kind is clearly subjective and relative, and in it, Dennett thinks, lies our "I can." For it, nature's cooperation is required and happily available. Nature is divided into a stable (law-determined) part and a chaotic, probabilistic part. It is the latter that offers epistemic possibilities, action consistent with what we already know, action applied to natural situations that are independent enough of strict law to be amenable to intervention. An example is this: Each of two people "on purpose" go to the marketplace, where they meet "by accident." A is owed money by B. A makes the most of the coincidence to dun B. (I've substituted a modified example from Aristotle, *Physics* II 196 b f., because I think it's more illuminating than the one cited by Dennett.) Observe that on Dennett's own "naturalistic" model, what happens between pouncing bird and hopeless insect in the meadow (an example he actually gives) is not essentially different from what happens between lender and borrower in the market place. In each case a fortuitous meeting issues in a fortunate outcome for a party evolutionarily endowed with the machinery of "can do," of affecting a favorable outcome.

I have recounted this argument (offered, to be sure, as a mere gesture toward a self in control, an agent) because it is a very rare attempt to tell how nature does in fact admit purposeful human intervention. But there seem to be difficulties, both on our, the epistemic, side and on nature's, the random, side. On our side, why are we, who are to proceed consistent with our limited knowledge and enabled by evolutionary machinery—to take practical advantage of an opportunity—why are we thought to have been freed from the opportunity-seizing *mechanism* by which the bird snaps up the insect? What would prove that we are so freed? Moreover, how does the incompleteness of our knowledge, which does indeed allow for accidents—renamed "opportunities"—profit us, except insofar as it encourages us to do what seems consistent with our knowledge so far? But Dennett has already pointed out that by and large the theory of determinism damps nobody's activism.

It is actually, so it seems, not our but nature's epistemic possibility that does the work here. Some of nature's systems are not only (epistemically) unpredictable *for us in the limit*, but are (ontologically) loose in *themselves right now*. But why should that "'practical' . . . independence of things" be receptive to our willing? We don't know how the will breaks into mechanisms, but wouldn't its insertion into a probabilistic situation be far harder, since it might well derive subjective indecision from objective undecidability? I don't see how the problem of problems has been solved.

An ill-favored thing: *As You Like It* 5.4.60

47. Choice and decision the same: The Index of *The Oxford Handbook of Free Will* refers "decisions" to "choice." Choice, however, means both the act of choosing (decision) and each of the framed options (choices). Establishing choices takes wisdom, making choices takes prudence, realizing choices takes will power; **will rarely without rationality**: flagrant counterexample—Nietzsche (Ch. VII, Sec. C, herein).

A citation for references to rationality in willing would read simply "passim."

48. Harry G. Frankfurt: "Freedom of the Will" (1971) in *The Importance of What We Care About*; **Nietzsche**: see Ch. VII, Sec. C, herein; **second-order volitions**: Frankfurt, *Importance*, 16, 19; **to want means to desire**: 13 n. 2.

49. Determinism: first named by Ch. W. Snell in *Determinism* (1789), cited by Walter, *Neurophilosophy*, 14. Walter quotes ten pretty compatible definitions; I quote the most succinct, by van Inwagen: "The thesis that there is at any instant exactly one physically possible future" (15); **oppositions complementary**: the arguments for complementary contraries in nature are given in Kelso and Engstrøm, *The Complementary Nature*. The book ends with a complementary-pair dictionary, well over 2000 entries! For a heartfelt argument in favor of the mutual necessity of opposites, even true and false, see also Brann, "Mile-high Meditations," in *Homage to Americans.*

50. Second order volitions and free will: Frankfurt, *Importance*, 19 ff.; **actions of one's free will**: 24.

51. Preferences: 19 n. 6; **responsibility**: 24; **romantic necessity**: Arpaly, *Merit*, 124 ff.; **Nathan the Wise**: Gotthold Ephraim Lessing, *Nathan the Wise*, l. 385.

Conclusion: *Un-willing*

1. The Aristotelian analogue to will power would be *egkrateia*, "[the disposition] to be in power [over one's self]," self-control or continence. It is *not* a virtue, since it signifies struggling against and containing one's bad impulses, while a virtuous human being is free of these by nature and habituation. See Sarah Broadie, *Ethics with Aristotle* (Oxford: Oxford Univ. Press, 1991), 267 and Joe Sachs, *Aristotle's Nicomachean Ethics* (Newburyport, Mass.: Focus Publishing, 2002), 211.

2. Augustinian elements: for references, present or missing, to Augustine in Descartes' writings, see the Index to Volumes II (*Meditations*: Objections and Replies) and III (*Correspondence*) of *The Philosophical Writings of Descartes*, vols. II–III, trans. John Cottingham et al. (Cambridge: Cambridge Univ. Press, 1984–91); there is, of course, more scholarship on this, I think subsidiary, issue. The most revealing mentions occurs in Descartes' letters. Thus Arnauld, through Mersenne as intermediary, cautions Descartes to attend to Augustine's explicit objection to admitting only what is "clearly perceived" in all respects, that is, including matters of faith. The point here is that Augustine seems to criticize Descartes explicitly before the fact, which means that they are thinking along the same lines, though in opposite directions (Vol. II, p. 152). But passages bearing directly on parallel thinking leave it unclear whether or when Descartes knew of his avatar. To be sure, the acknowledgment of indebtedness is an issue of interest only insofar as it bears on the question: How radically new are the thoughts that went into the founding of modernity? How much is all the proud innovativeness promoted by difficult access to, how much motivated by self-serving depreciation of predecessors? Descartes says that he has not been able "to obtain the works of the Saint" (1638, Vol. III, p. 129). But a little later he reports to Mersenne without comment that "my *I am thinking therefore I exist*" is to be found "in Book Eleven, chapter 26 of *De Civitate Dei*" (1640, Vol. III, p. 161). Similarly, when Arnauld reminds him that in *De Libero Arbitrio* Augustine argues that it is impossible to make a mistake about one's own existence, Descartes sanguinely accepts this as supporting—not anticipating— his own argument in the *Meditations* (Vol. III, pp. 139, 154); see Peter Markie, "The Cogito and its Importance," in *The Cambridge Companion to Descartes*, ed. John Cottingham (Cambridge: Cambridge Univ. Press, 1991), 167 n. 1. I would add that in Augustine's *On the Trinity* (X 10) there is a complete presentation of what we think of as the Cartesian device of "radical doubt," beginning with "Let us remove from consideration all knowledge which is received from without," and ending with "Whosoever therefore doubts about anything else, ought not to doubt of all these things," that is, his own mental life. I should say here that Arnauld, as a Jansenist, was a student of Augustine and would have known this passage, but apparently he did not make a point of alerting Descartes. No more does he appear to have commented on Descartes' use of the word *cogito* for "I think," a word on which Augustine had focused in the *Confessions* (X 11).

And as so often, here again vexatious "influence" is at issue: Had Descartes somehow absorbed Jansenist interests, or was this a case of two intellects, nearly one-and-a-quarter millennia apart, thinking in parallel?

3. The distinction between theoretical and practical reason comes from Aristotle, who, however, means by "practical" something closer to our usage—nothing particularly to do with freedom: "For what appetite pursues [namely the object of desire], that is the starting point of practical intellect" (*On the Soul* III 433 a 16); thus the end of practical reason is to obtain something desired.

The gist of my Conclusion could be put in Aristotelian terms, thus: Let practical judgment (*phronesis*) be now and then interleaved with philosophical thought (*sophia*).

4. Later experiments: reported in *The Economist*, 18 April 2009; research by Joydeep Bhattacharya and Bhavin Sheth.

5. It is a bonus of my claim that the will is not an original, unitary, mental function that I can evade the everlasting debate regarding its seat in the mental architecture, a debate that ranges from denial that there are any specialized structures to a highly specified faculty-psychology. A rigorously argued introduction to this problem from the point of view of cognitive science is found in Jerry A. Fodor, *The Modularity of Mind* (Cambridge: MIT Press, 1984). Fodor claims that, although there may be "global systems" (really, non-systems, absence of mental architecture) that are responsible for "belief fixation," the works of "input analysis" must be done in localized "modules" of the mind (formerly, "faculties"), especially if there is to be a science of cognition. Of course, this theory demands neuroscientific underpinnings, and so the thesis remains a topic in brain science (e.g. Steven Horst, "Modularity and Cognitive Pluralism," chap 1.4 in *Laws, Mind, and Free Will* [Cambridge: MIT Press, 2011]).

6. Karl Marx, "Theses on Feuerbach" (1845).

7. Rectify volitional language: Speaking of the misuse of will-words, Locke felicitously says: "Nor do I deny that those words . . . are to have their place in the common use of languages that have made them current. It looks like too much affectation wholly to lay them by: and philosophy itself, though it likes not a gaudy dress, yet when it appears in public, must have so much complacency to be clothed in the ordinary fashion and language of the country" (*Essay Concerning Human Understanding*, Bk. I, Ch. 21, Sec. 14); **post-judice**: listed in *Oxford English Dictionary* (p. 2253) as a nonce word, one made up for a specific purpose; both Ruskin and Chesterton did so.

There is, to shift the topic only a little, a strong relation between linguistic invention and willfulness, the prime example being invented languages, from Esperanto to Klingon (Michael Adams, "Do-It-Yourself Language," *Humanities* 34, no. 1 [January/February 2013]: 17). They might be regarded as reversing God's intention expressed in the babble of the Tower of Babel: language dispersion for the sake of suppressing united mankind's unrestrained ambition (Genesis 11:4–9). The invented languages are meant to abolish post-Babel language-diversity so as to reunify humanity and make mankind more potent. But such rectifications of ethnic, idiomatic speech tends toward administrative domination. The deadly serious case is set out in George Orwell's *1984* (1949); it is "Newspeak," the fictional type of all totalitarian language constructions, be they Nazi, Soviet, or universal Bureaucratese. Such linguistic reformism is quite different from the occasional and perkily charming neologisms devised for new notions or items, such as "glitch" or "quark," etc.

This is the place to refer to Aristotle (*Nicomachean Ethics* 145 b), who, ever-reasonable, says that in ethical inquiries the best course is to deal with the difficulties in the various established opinions so as to save the latter as far as possible.

8. Heidegger's *Gelassenheit* seems to me far too quietist. To be sure, in this giving up of will to waiting, Heidegger is far from the Buddhist school favored in this country, which combines serenity with activity.

Nonetheless I hope I won't be construed to be advocating some sort of American-Eastern wisdom. My reading and the reports of our students tell me that, when the West goes east, it takes over, but when the East comes west, it is itself taken over and alienated. For one thing, even when presented primarily as a practice, it becomes wordy—wordy with a Western vocabulary that, as even a non-adept can tell, skews the wisdom with false resonances. I am thinking here of the American adaptation, for example, of Zazen practice, enthusiastically supported by Japanese teachers who were enchanted—to me most understandably—by the intelligently eager freshness of their young American disciples. One of our students, as it happens, the typist of this book, lent me the most popular introduction to a favored school of Zen, from which, together with some other readings, I made up for myself this Pythagorean-like Table of Oppositions between Western philosophy as I know it and Eastern wisdom as represented, evidently not aberrantly, by one master, Shunryu Suzuki in *Zen Mind, Beginner's Mind* (Boston: Shambhala, 2006).

Before I try my hand at this differentiation, I should recall to the reader that consanguinities between both Meister Eckhart's mystic and Heidegger's neo-mystic *Gelassenheit* (Ch. VIII, Sec. D, herein) and East Asian thought have in fact been seriously considered; see Bret W. Davis,

Heidegger and the Will, xiv–xv, 58–59, 261–65. In any case, this *Gelassenheit* is different from the "un-willing" that I have in mind and am trying to delineate in this Conclusion.

The differentiating themes I can discern, broadly characteristic of *Western philosophy* versus *Eastern sages*, are these:

1. *Self-consciousness vs. Immediacy:* The philosophers of the West value arduous self-awareness and effortful reflexivity, be it as soul or as subject; the Zen master preaches getting past self and consciousness to absolute directness. (Something not dissimilar, however, can be found in Marcus Aurelius's Stoic devotion to pure factuality; see Ch. III, Sec. B, herein.)

2. *Dualism vs. Oneness:* The West favors oppositional dialectic, be it for purposes of preference or reconciliation; the Zen master directly discerns unity in opposites. (A distinguishing feature of dialectical opposition is its temporal extension—opinions appear apart in time.)

3. *Study vs. Practice:* The philosophers esteem an intellectual ascent over somatic effort; the Zen master puts bodily disposition first—as really undistinguishable from "mind." (Therefore intellectualized excellence, the ascent's ethics, counts for much in Western texts.)

4. *Articulation vs. Mental Condition:* The philosophers aim at clarity and distinctness even in approaching paradox or mystic insight; the Zen master uses language as self-canceling. (Even Plotinus attempts philosophically communicative articulation; see Ch. II, Note 1, herein.)

5. *Dialectic vs. Discipleship:* The philosophers argue and transform; the Zen master guides and relinquishes. (Dialectic is the idea-motor of the West and rebellion is its human face.)

6. *Attachment vs. Non-Attachment:* The West values passionate particularity as a way to the universal; the Zen master preaches a calm, non-attached entering of emptiness. (Socrates thinks philosophy begins in singular erotic love; Aristotle starts with particular substances; see Ch. I, Secs. B and C, herein.)

7. *Heights vs. Plane:* The philosophers of the tradition distinguish the ordinary business of daily ongoing existence from the high holy days, the heights, of revealed being; the Zen master melds meditation and life, enlightenment and familiarity, putting all on one plane of extraordinary ordinariness. (No matter how leveling the impulse of our latter-day philosophers, their tone is often hieratic.)

I have picked out those differences that together might bear on distinguishing a Western sort of de-volition from an Eastern one; here is my summary of the West's ways: (1) Self-reflection, (2) Dualistic distinctions, (3) Book learning, (4) Verbal expression, (5) Dialectical energy, (6) Passionate devotion, (7) Sought elevation. "Un-willing," far from obviating any of these, engages all of them.

9. Poetaster: Plato, *Phaedo* 61 a–b; **swansong:** 85 a–b.

10. Pisteuein: this verb is not used in earlier Greek with the preposition "in," as it will be in the New Testament, nor as far as I can tell, is it used of the gods. A chief meaning is "to trust" (with the dative), thus, "to trust [in] the oracles of the gods" (*pisteusai theon thesphatoisin*, in Aeschylus, *Persians* 1.800).

I have to omit consideration both of will with respect to the God of the Jews and of faith in this God as required by Judaism because of my insufficient learnedness in this (my own) tradition; I know neither Hebrew nor the biblical commentaries. This, however, is clear: The Pauline point of view (he was, after all, a Jew himself) is that those who "denominate" themselves Jews "*rest in the law*" (*nomoi*, my italics) and think that suffices (Romans 2:17 ff.). Therefore I cannot tell if belief in the Christian sense of an exigently love-requiring faith is a great issue in the Hebrew Bible, where *obeying* God's Law is paramount, or whether there too God's will demands *loving* faith.

The term for will in the New Testament is *thelema*, a word rare in classical Greek (only once in Aristotle: *On Plants* 815 b 21). It is gotten from the verb *ethelein*, to wish, to desire. (I think classical Greek speakers were resistant to developing an unambiguous will-word like Latin *vol-*

untas.) God certainly has wrath (*orge*) in both Bibles and that is, to be sure, often the passionate evidence of the tone-setting willfulness of the deity.

11. Clouds: Aristophanes, *The Clouds* (423 B.C.E.), l. 269 ff.; **accusations**: early slanders, *Apology* 19 b, and current charges, 24 b–c.

12. Mind's-eye-manifestation: Brann, *Homeric Moments*, chap. I, "The Gods."

13. Evil will inconceivable: perhaps not so much simply inconceivable as untenable on close inspection, e.g. *Meno* 77 c ff. I understand the "bad things" (*kaka*)—which, Meno believes, people actually desire, but which, Socrates shows, they can want only insofar as they ignorantly consider them good—to include vice itself. For when Socrates has settled that people actually want only "good things" (*agatha*), and Meno has reiterated his notion of virtue as the power to procure such good things as gold and silver, Socrates asks whether "these things," if acquired unjustly, are "*virtue . . . just the same*." The answer is: no, they are *vice* (*kakia*, 18 d, my italics). I conclude that for Socrates vitiated goods *embody* vice and that he simply cannot believe that anyone would knowingly *want* to acquire such concrete badness. In the *Symposium*, Socrates' teacher Diotima says: "Then we must say simply that human beings love the good" (206 a).

In the *Republic*, Socrates describes the typical tyrant as himself internally tyrannized, as self-enslaved (577 f.). This is, I think, as close as Socrates comes to a perverse will, but it is a bad passivity rather than an evil activity.

14. Daimonion: e.g., *Apology* 31 c–d.

15. Missing courage: *Phaedo*, trans. Eva Brann, Peter Kalkavage, and Eric Salem (Newburyport, Mass.: Focus Publishing, 1998), 24; **dying day**: Socrates has said that philosophers practice death and dying in life; he means that they try to live in the realm of invisible being *right now* (*Phaedo* 80 e); **Hades, the Invisible**: 81 c; **Satan**: Milton, *Paradise Lost* I 106–8.

16. Hume: *An Enquiry Concerning Human Understanding*, Sec. XII, Pt. II, note against Berkeley.

17. Tri-partite soul: *Republic* 436 a; **thymos**: 439 e ff. I translate *thymos* as "temperament" because the word suggests irritability, anger, intensity, as well as pride—all renderings of *thymos*.

18. Socratic hierarchies: The power of recognizing images, for example, is at the bottom of human capacities (*Republic* 513 e), but it proves to be the power of philosophy itself, that of recognizing appearances *as* images; **pleasures and desires in every part**: *Republic* 580 d–581 c; **Socrates knows nothing but love-matters**: *Symposium* 177 d–e.

19. Pervasive: I haven't conducted a count, but I think that dialogic references to the maxim that virtue is knowledge or to one of its several versions or cognate notions (among which is the above claim that no one chooses evil except through ignorance) are as frequent and widespread as to any of Socrates' thoughts: e.g., *Laches* 194, *Meno* 87–88, *Phaedo* 69, *Phaedrus* 277, *Protagoras* 357, *Theaetetus* 176.

20. Four virtues: e.g., *Republic* 427 c–434 d; **excellence as effectiveness**: 353 b; **good will**: the reference is to Kant; **morality or ethics**: the distinction between a morality of universal laws and an ethics of personal virtue comes from Alasdair MacIntyre, *After Virtue*, 2nd ed. (Notre Dame: Univ. of Notre Dame Press, 1984), 150 ff.; **Socrates' refusal**: *Crito* passim.

21. Virtue as beautiful to mental and somatic sight: e.g., *Phaedrus* 247 ff.

22. Theories of free will: chief general references are to *The Oxford Handbook of Free Will* (2002) and to Fischer et al., *Four Views on Free Will* (2007); **redefining will**: the suggestive ambiguity starts right in the Latin *voluntas*, which means both will and wish; thus *benevolentia*, though translated as "good will," really means "well-wishing."

23. Poets: of course free will figures favorably as well—"'Of all the gifts God in His bounty extreme / Made when creating, most conformable / To His own goodness, and in His esteem / Most precious, was the liberty of the will, / With which creatures that are intelligent / Were all endowed, they only, and are so still . . .'" It is Beatrice speaking in Paradise (Dante, *Divine Comedy*, "Paradiso," Canto V, l. 19 ff., trans. Lawrence Binyon); **Devil's party**: In *The Marriage of Heaven and Hell*, William Blake says of Milton that "he was a true poet and of the Devil's party without knowing it."

24. Romantic poets: Ch. V, Sec. B, herein; **untrammeled will**: In *The Roots of Romanticism*, Isaiah Berlin presents the elements of romantic irony, a root notion of Romanticism, as the "free untrammeled will and the denial of the fact that there is a nature of things" (p. 117)—in other words, as a willful, limitless subjectivity.

Harold Bloom, in *The Western Canon: The Books and School of the Ages* (New York: Riverhead Books, 1994), writing about Shelley, mentions the Protestant will, which "turned upon the individual soul's self-esteem and on the allied right of private judgment in spiritual realms" (p. 230)—an implicit referral of the Romantic will to its Protestant avatar; **politics**: the effect of romanticism on politics is a tricky and perspective-dependent subject. To me, death-glorifying, grandiosely sentimental, and above all, will-worshipping, tyrannical regimes seem the very incarnation of the romantic complex. On the other hand, Carl Schmitt, in *Political Romanticism* (1919, trans. Guy Oakes, Cambridge: MIT Press, 1986), proposes that "romanticism is a product of bourgeois society" (p. 99)—that bourgeois liberalism (rather than *déclassé* reaction) is the romantic's necessary home, since his untethered subjectivity and his self-divinization require a rule-governed order that permits self-isolation to thrive—in other words, that romanticism is a- or even anti-political in its politics.

25. Valéry: from *Cahiers* I, quoted in Hugh P. McGrath and Michael Comenetz, *Valéry's Graveyard* (New York: Peter Lang Publishing, 2011), 53; *Anthony and Cleopatra* 4.15.2; *Troilus and Cressida* 2.2.59; *Othello* 1.3.322; Robert Bridges, "Eros"—as it happens, "volition" and "voluptuousness" are cognate; **Unfolded in Symbols**: W. B. Yeats, "The Symbolism of Poetry," quoted in Reuben A. Brower, *The Fields of Light*, Philadelphia: Paul Dry Books (2013), p. 58.

26. Chooser weakly free: Descartes calls liberty of indifference "the lowest grade of freedom" (*Meditations* IV, para. 58); **Buridan's ass**: Spinoza is pretty irritated by this ass, and his response is that only an ass would get into this fatal bind (*Ethics* II, Prop. XLIX, note); **self-caused spontaneity**: Hume, in *A Treatise of Human Nature* (Bk. III, pt. II, sec. ii), says that "spontaneity" is distinguished from "indifference" as that which is opposed to violence is distinct from that which negates necessity and causes. He also describes yet another notion of a liberty of indifference, namely that which arises from a false sense of looseness, when we are performing actions with "a want of determination." Upon reflection, that looseness disappears (I will urge below that that's just when the sensation of "liberty" turns up); **indifference compounds puzzles**: hence the indifference explanation was a minority position, see James A. Harris, *Of Liberty and Necessity: The Free Will Debate in Eighteenth-Century British Philosophy* (Oxford: Clarendon Press, 2005), 6 and passim. Here's my own prescription for relieving the will of niggling indecision: Toss a penny; however it turns up, do the opposite—don't let a penny run your life.

27. Quotation: Milton, *Paradise Lost* II 558.

28. Specious present: the tiny time-span needed for perceptions to register, the now of lived awareness (Brann, *What, Then, Is Time?*, 142, 177, 203).

29. The philosopher: Heidegger; **Socrates**: in the *Meno* 80 d, 82 ff.—recall that for Socrates the absence of inquiry, the activity at issue, is what makes life not so much "not worth living" as "unlived, unlivable" (*Apology* 38 a).

30. Every eye: W. H. Auden, *Another Time* (1940), excluded from *Collected Works* edited by Edward Mendelson; **fright and fidget**: *New Year's Letter* (January 1, 1940). In the same part, Auden speaks of a Buxtehude *passacaglia* as making "Our mind a *civitas* of sound / Where nothing but assent was found." That's one description of the decommissioned will; **ego tyrant**: in Plato's *Republic* (571 ff.), Socrates depicts the self-tyrannized soul, the inward personal portrait of the external political tyrant, in just this way. It is a description that exactly matches reports of twentieth-century tyrants in their bastions and bunkers; see Note 13 above.

31. Will's own imperative: according to Kant.

32. Among the matters more "up to us" than the ancient Stoics could know is the management of the political and material world: democracy and technology. But there are less concrete realms more "up to us" than some latter-day realists suppose, for example, the past. The past is nowhere in the world, for old surviving artifacts and dead writers' texts are *here and now* and become past only by imaginative memory, more or less candidly exercised on the evidence. So it is up to us both that *there be* a past and *what it is to be*. (See Brann, "Past and Memory," in *What, Then, Is Time?*) Moreover, the past can be undone: reversed, redeemed, recovered, repeated. Young, single-minded passions, such as (once more) Jay Gatsby's, can do it: "Can't repeat the past?" he cried incredulously. "Why of course you can!" And he would have, had his love not been misplaced (F. Scott Fitzgerald, *The Great Gatsby*, 1925, chap. VI); see Ch. IX, Note 1 [d], herein.

33. Individual substantiality: the reference is to Aristotle, e.g., *Metaphysics* 1017 b 10 ff.; **people-watching**: Jane Austen is the mistress of such fun: "For what do we live, but to make sport for our neighbors, and laugh at them in our turn?" says the good-naturedly cynical Mr. Bennett in *Pride and Prejudice* (vol. II, chap. XV), but Jane Austen herself, in a much more affectionate mode, refers on the penultimate page of *Mansfield Park* to changes that time is forever producing in "the plans and decisions of mortals [and, I suppose, in their surface affectations] for their own instruction and *their neighbors' enjoyment*" (my italics).

34. Willing suspension: Coleridge, *Biographia Literaria* (1817), chap. 14.

35. Locke: *An Essay Concerning Human Understanding*, Bk. II, Ch. 21, para. 14. Just below his quotation follows this declaration (quoted in Note 7 above) against proscribing terms in common use; **action smoothly continuous**: this formulation is close to Bergson's notion of intensive time (Ch. VIII, Sec. B, herein). A beautifully pertinent novel about the sure immediacy of action that may go with a slowed-down nature is Sten Nadolny's *The Discovery of Slowness*, trans. Ralph Freedman (1983; reprint, Philadelphia: Paul Dry Books, 2005). The slow man fictionalized is the explorer Sir John Franklin. The book was the founding text for a "Slow Movement"; see Sarah Bakewell, *How to Live: Or a Life of Montaigne in One Question and Twenty Attempts at an Answer* (New York: Other Press, 2010), 72–73. The slowness Montaigne advocates and Franklin displays is, however, pondering slow-wittedness; I'm thinking more: active intellect / slowed-down life.

Nor is my own notion of slowness, of taking time, like the "slow thinking" set out in Daniel Kahneman's *Thinking, Fast and Slow* (New York: Farrar, Straus and Giroux, 2011). There, two metaphorical cognitive constructs are set out: System 1, intuitive, automatic, and immediate, and System 2, rational, effortful, and deliberate. The latter queries, corrects, and controls the rich but mistake-prone former—all for the sake of more efficient, secure decision-making. Thoughtfulness, as I think of it, is not a system: It is time out from decision-making and going to ground for reflection.

36. Compatibilism: Ch. IX, herein; **length, diffuseness, immensity**: on science overwhelmed by data, see Ch. IX, Note 1, end, herein.

37. Desire modifies desire: Spinoza, *Ethics* (Bk. IV, Prop. VII), says that an emotion can only be hindered or removed by a stronger contrary emotion.

38. Tripartite polity and three mental functions: Plato, *Republic*, mainly Bk. IV; **Constitution**: Alexander Hamilton, *Federalist* 78, "The Supreme Court." Aristotle says: Practical wisdom (*phronesis*) issues commands, understanding (*synesis*) makes judgments (*Nicomachean Ethics* 1143 a).

39. Traditional deliberation: originally *Nicomachean Ethics* III 1112 b.

40. Bartleby: Herman Melville, "Bartleby, The Scrivener: A Story of Wall Street" from *The Piazza Tales* (1856); **"Ah, Bartleby"**: last line of the story.

41. Era of choice: Edward C. Rosenthal, *The Era of Choice: The Ability to Choose and Its Transformation of Contemporary Life* (Cambridge: MIT Press, 2006).

42. Screen-bound research: here's a meow about these time-investments. If people valued the time of their life properly, would online comparison-shopping post a profit? **Pascal's diversion**: Blaise Pascal, *Pensées*, trans. A. J. Krailsheimer (London: Penguin Books, 1987), VIII, "Diversion."—Diversion is a way not to think about the human condition (no. 133); the sole cause of man's unhappiness is the inability to stay quietly in his room; even a King's "limp felicity" will not keep him going without diversion by some novel passion; diversion prefers hunt to capture (all in no. 136); diversion is a way to keep men occupied and distracted lest they have time to think of who they are (no. 137). It would take a Pascal to go properly to town on our preferences, options, and "likes."

43. Hyper-human will: Ch. VII, herein; *liberum arbitrium*: Ch. II, Sec. C, herein.

44. Time: Augustine, *Confessions* XI 14; see Brann, *What, Then, Is Time?* Pt. II, Ch. II; **Kirillov**: see Ch. VIII, Sec. E, herein. Suicide is a crux in musings on free will. In Thessaly, at Meteora, there is a forest of high pinnacles carved out by erosion from the surrounding rock. This or that one has a monastery perched on top. Here it is possible to walk to the very edge of the abyss. Then one is seized by a sudden, terrible insouciance, a vacant temptation: Why not? This is the heady aroma of "liberty of indifference" at its extreme. You step back and understand forever that (except for the insane who are *ipso facto* out of it) freedom cannot lie on the knife's edge of a moment of choice: The downward pull of nothingness (and a saving miracle—its scriptural exemplar is Satan's temptation of Jesus by setting him on a "pinnacle of a temple" and bidding him leap, Matthew 4:5–6) was simply marginally less than the tether of life—or *seemed* so in a moment of existential light-headedness; in truth it was overwhelmingly weaker, as the next moment revealed: I was never going to leap.

45. I have tried my hand at "Self" and "Freedom." See Ch. XI, Secs. D–E, herein.

46. **Schengen passport, just in case**: eliminated border controls between European countries that are signators to the Schengen agreement; **the past**: Brann, *What, Then, Is Time?*, 166 ff.; **renaissance**: Brann, *The World of the Imagination*, 727.

47. **Assertive static of self-will**: the most blatant assertion of willful philosophizing I know is in Nietzsche's *Ecce Homo* (no. 2): "Out of my will to health, to life, I make my philosophy."

48. **Openness**: my prime example of will-constrained, boxed-in, action-stymieing argumentation: "Only if x [usually a widespread, deep-rooted, solution-recalcitrant social condition] is reformed, can y [usually some local, restricted, remedy-ready trouble] be remedied"; **perennially insoluble problems**: I desire to be absolved from having committed any creative originality in this book; **quotation**: Aristotle, *Nicomachean Ethics* X 1177 b 32–36; *athanatizein* is a wonderful coinage, a "denominative" verb, from the adjective *athanatos*, "un-dying, immortal," and a suffix *izein*, often signifying "to do something in the manner of," literally "to immortalize."

Readers are welcome to construe this final meditation as a wish-autobiography.

Index

H

hamartia (mistake), 1–2, 265–266n. 2
Hamilton, Alexander, 259–260
happiness: Aristotle on, 143, 279n. 34;
  Augustine on, 26; Hegel on, 143; Leibniz on, 81; Locke on, 79; Scotus on, 63;
  Socrates on, 17; Thomas on, 45, 48, 49
Hartley, L. P., 336–337n. 21
Hegel, Georg Wilhelm Friedrich, 137–147,
  238–239, 308–309n. 2; on Absolute Freedom, 310–314n. 28; on appetite, 142; on
  choice, 142–143; on cognition, 138–139;
  on Consciousness, 139; on desire, 143–
  144, 309n. 24; on Ethics, 145; on feelings,
  141, 309n. 16; on free mind, 144, 238; on
  free will, 143, 144, 145, 146; on French
  Terror, 310–314n. 28; on the Good,
  138–139; on happiness, 143; on imagination, 140; on impulses, 142; on inclination, 143–144; on interest, 142–143; on
  inwardizing (*Erinnerung*), 140; on Kant,
  308–309n. 2; on knowledge, 287n. 13;
  on law, 145; on logic, 137, 138–139, 140,
  238; on memory, 140; on morality, 145;
  on nature, 137, 139; on Objective Mind,
  144–145; on ought, 141; on passion, 142;
  on possession, 145; on Practical Mind,
  141, 309n. 16; on property, 145, 309–
  310n. 27; on psychology, 139; on representative modes, 140, 309n. 11; on Right,
  145, 238, 309–310n. 27, 311–314n. 28; Sartre on, 324n. 87; on selfish will, 141; on
  Spirit, 137–138, 139–141, 309n. 7; on Subjective Mind, 139; System of, 137–138,
  146, 308–309n. 2; on Theoretical Mind,
  140–141; on thinking, 140–141, 144; on
  time, 315n. 31; on volition, 138; on volitional intelligence, 143–144; on will in
  the world, 138–139, 310–314n. 28
hegemonikon (ruling center), 20, 23
Heidegger, Martin, 155–163, 308n. 1; *Being
  and Time*, 156–158; on cognition, 159,
  160, 320–321n. 61; on *Dasein* (therebeing), 156, 157, 168; on decision, 163;
  on environment of beings, 157; *Essence
  of Human Freedom*, 164–165, 323n. 74;
  on "Eternal Return," 135, 306n. 57; on
  evil, 159, 160, 320–321n. 61; on existential voluntarism, 157–158; on freedom, 158, 164–166, 323n. 74; on *Gegend*
  (region), 162, 322n. 68; on *Gelassenheit* (non-willing), 161–163, 246, 265n. 3,
  322n. 66, 322n. 67, 323n. 77, 351–352n. 8;
  on *Gestell* (re-framing), 160–161, 320–
  321n. 61; on history of philosophy, 322–

323n. 73; Nazism and, 155–156, 318n. 50,
  319–320n. 60; *Nietzsche*, 134, 306n. 51; on
  Schelling, 158–159, 240; on *Seyn* (*Beyng*),
  162–163, 322n. 77; on *Sorge* (care), 157; on
  transcendental freedom, 165–166; turns/
  turnings of, 156, 319n. 52; on the Unsaid,
  156–157; on we-will (relinquished will),
  158
historical inquiry, 268–269n. 34
history, 206, 341–342n. 2
Hobbes, Thomas, 51, 70–74, 235, 286n. 1,
  286–287n. 4; on appetite, 70–71; compatibilism and, 72, 176, 181, 333n. 3; on compulsion, 73; on deliberation, 51, 70, 71,
  73, 278–279n. 24; on freedom, 71, 73–74,
  287n. 9; on free will, 71–72, 73–74, 181,
  287n. 5; on God, 74; on imagination, 74;
  on law, 72; on passion, 70–71, 73; theory
  of motion, 70–71
Homer: *Iliad*, 3, 11, 266n. 4
Hopkins, Burt, 281–283n. 48
Horst, Steven, 342n. 10
Hume, David, 81–87, 236, 280–281n. 41,
  289n. 27; on cause and effect, 82–83,
  88–89; on command, 290–291n. 34;
  Enquiry Concerning Human Understanding, 280–281n. 41; on experiment,
  289n. 27; on freedom, 83–84, 289–
  290n. 30, 290–291n. 34; on indifference,
  354n. 26; on intellect, 84–85; on morality,
  85–86, 290n. 33; Ockham and, 284n. 64;
  on reason, 18, 84–85, 290n. 31; on self,
  221; skepticism of, 81–82, 289n. 28; *Treatise of Human Nature*, 81–87, 289n. 27
hybris (overreaching), 1
hypothesis, 267n. 23

I

identity, 219; self and, 346n. 29
ignorance: Meno on, 266n. 11; Socrates on,
  4, 5
illusionism, 208–211
imagination, xii–xiii, 257; in academic style,
  332n. 1; Hobbes on, 74; Kant on, 89,
  292n. 2; Leibniz on, 81, 289n. 26; Marcus
  Aurelius on, 23
impressions, 19, 84, 86–87, 270n. 14
indeterminism: compatibilism and, 183, 185;
  in Lucretius, 15; ontological, 199–200;
  Scotus on, 63; Tse on, 199–201
indifference, 83, 216, 253–254, 289–290n. 30,
  354n. 26, 355–356n. 44
influence, 64, 281–283n. 48
intellect: Aristotle on, 279n. 34, 323n. 80;
  Fichte on, 108; Hegel on, 140–141;